Vietnam:
A Dragon Embattled

Vietnam: A Dragon Embattled

by JOSEPH BUTTINGER

Volume II
Vietnam at War

 FREDERICK A. PRAEGER, *Publishers*
New York · Washington · London

FREDERICK A. PRAEGER, PUBLISHERS
111 Fourth Avenue, New York, N.Y. 10003, U.S.A.
77-79 Charlotte Street, London W.1, England

Published in the United States of America in 1967
by Frederick A. Praeger, Inc., Publishers

Second printing, 1967

Library of Congress Catalog Card Number: 66-13682

Printed in the United States of America

Contents

Volume II:
Vietnam at War

VIII

The "Bao Dai Solution"

1

O F THE MANY ARMED CONFLICTS that make this century so distressingly rich in human misery, none has lasted as long as the struggle for Vietnam; and although other conflicts have had deeper effects upon mankind, none compares with it in political complexity and unresolved consequences.

The first phase of the struggle for Vietnam culminated in what history now calls the Indochina War, a war that is commonly said to have lasted eight years. This, however, like almost everything else about the Indochina War, is a matter of dispute, for the good reason that the parties that fought each other differ widely as to when the conflict can be described as having turned into war. Yet this question must be settled because it is fundamental for determining not merely the duration but the very nature of this war. What was it fought for? By whom was it brought about? What made it last so long? And why did it end without also ending the struggle for Vietnam? Satisfactory answers to these questions can be found only if the controversy over the beginning of the Indochina War can be settled.

If war is the use, by two or more nations, of military means for political ends, the Indochina War started in September, 1945, when the French with British help ousted the Vietnamese administration installed by the Provisional Committee of the South in Saigon. According to the almost unanimous opinion of the Vietnamese, the war therefore resulted from French aggression. The official French version, however, is that the war did not start until December 19, 1946, and that its outbreak was the result of a Vietminh attack on the French in Hanoi. Vietminh aggression, the French say, destroyed the Franco-

Vietnamese agreement of March and the *modus vivendi* of September, 1946, both of which testified to the fact that the two countries were officially at peace. But if peace was an official fact, war was a fact of life. Peace, of a most precarious sort, existed only in the northern half of Vietnam (not, however, until December 19, but only until November 23, when the French staged their brutal attack on the Vietnamese of Haiphong). War, on the other hand, had been raging almost without interruption all over the southern half of Vietnam since September, 1945. Even from a French point of view it would, therefore, be more correct to admit that a state of partial war existed in Vietnam after September, 1945, and that December, 1946, marks not the beginning of the war but merely the collapse of the efforts to prevent its spread over the entire country.

If the fact of peace in the North makes the question when the Indochina War started one about which disagreement seems not too absurd, the fact of war in the South nevertheless proves rather conclusively who was responsible for its outbreak and also determines its political nature. A Vietnamese administration, established in Saigon after a national government had proclaimed the country's independence, was ousted by the French through military action, which led to a state of war. War in Indochina, therefore, was brought about by the refusal of the French to settle their conflict with the Vietnamese national movement peacefully; the French, after World War II, were determined to re-establish themselves in Vietnam by force. In the words of General Navarre, spoken long after the event, the action France took aimed at "re-establishing if not the colonial regime, at least something close to it." [1] This from the start made the Indochina War an attempt to re-impose colonial rule, a colonial war which to its very end was primarily a clash between the forces of Vietnamese nationalism and the political factions of French imperialism whose interests and convictions imposed upon France a policy of colonial reconquest.

In their efforts to deny this, the French not only clung to the theory that the war started in December, 1946, and that it was unleashed by the Vietminh; they also claimed that far from waging a colonial war, they fought in Indochina solely to prevent Vietnam from falling under a Communist dictatorship. This was a war directed not against the Vietnamese people and their national freedom, but rather against the Communist leadership that had provoked the armed conflict and had to be defeated if Vietnam were to be free. In their most preposterous proclamations, the French claimed that there really was no war, that the fighting was merely a necessary action of pacification against an aggressive minority, and that France was sacrificing her wealth and manpower to preserve Vietnam for the "free world." The conflict was described as one between Democracy and Communism. This war, said General Jean de Lattre de Tassigny in July, 1951, "no longer concerns France except to the extent of her promises to Vietnam and the part she has to play in the defense of the free world. Not since the Crusades has France undertaken such disinterested action. This war is the war of Vietnam for Vietnam." [2]

It is because these claims stand and fall together that the French hold so tenaciously to their contention about the date the war began. If the war had really started only in December, 1946, it would have been much easier to show that it was not unleashed by the French; and if the Vietminh could have been unmasked as the aggressor, it would have been less obvious that the French were conducting a colonial war. They could not deny that the fighting had started in September, 1945, but because the struggle remained confined to the South, it was really not a war but a temporary state of public disorder caused by local rebels; and if the French furthermore showed that only the Communist-led minority behind the Vietminh put up armed resistance, the fighting could not be termed a war even after it had spread to the North. The claim, however, that France was conducting nothing but a police action against a minority faction of the Vietnamese was an extreme version of French propaganda that had to be dropped after the hopes for a quick military solution of the conflict evaporated.

Once the whole country was engulfed in war, the evidence that the French had brought it about, and that it was a war of colonial reconquest, became overwhelming. It no longer depended merely on an admission of the historical facts of French aggression in September, 1945, in Saigon and in November, 1946, in Haiphong, nor was it henceforth necessary to accept the view that it was French provocation in Hanoi that led to Vietminh aggression on December 19, 1946. What mattered from now on was the attitude of the two parties engaged in war toward the question of under what conditions peace could be re-established. For the French to prove that they had not sought the war, that they were innocent of aggression, that they were defending themselves after having been attacked by the Vietminh, merely required evidence that they were interested in working out terms for a return to peace, whereas the Hanoi Government was not. To prove that they were not conducting a war of colonial reconquest, they had to relinquish their wish to rule Vietnam and hold forth to their former colony the prospect of early and full independence.

In both respects, the French acted contrary to the claims of their international and local propaganda. After December 19, the men who decided French policy in Indochina firmly rejected the idea of seeking peace through negotiations with the Vietminh, just as they had done for more than a year in regard to the fighting in the South, although there they had lacked the excuse that France had been attacked. The military, with few exceptions, gleefully welcomed the outbreak of hostilities in the North, and the political leadership in Paris hypocritically deplored the extension of the war, but both were united in their firm refusal to negotiate the conditions for an end to the fighting with the government France had recognized in March, 1946. They knew from their previous negotiations that this required the recognition of independence for Vietnam, and this the French were unwilling to grant to Ho Chi Minh or to anyone else. As there was for the time being no one else to negotiate with, the refusal to seek peace through talks with the Vietminh meant that the French only were interested in peace through victory. France, declared High Commissioner d'Argenlieu on December 27, 1946, would not relinquish her hold on Indochina; she insists "on the maintenance and development of her present influence." [3] The French military, having learned nothing from the failure to suppress the rebellion in the South, believed that now that they at last had a free hand throughout the country they could quickly bring about a decision through military action. Indeed, the short-sighted realists, not only in Saigon but also in Paris, who insisted on the maintenance of French influence in Indochina, had long known that their objective required the use of force. Unwilling to forgo their aims, they had always accepted the means required to achieve them, including the necessity of making war. Even the extremists among the French now no longer objected to promises of concessions to the Vietnamese, but such concessions could be talked about only after "order" had been re-established. This, of course, meant that the French were willing to talk peace with the Hanoi regime only after the Vietminh was defeated.

2

In speaking of the French, however, it is important to stress that in 1945, the nation, although fairly united behind a policy of "French presence" in Indochina, was not at all of one mind in regard to the purposes of this presence, and even less as to the methods with which, in the face of native resistance, France should try to maintain herself in Vietnam. Without a clear view of these differences among Frenchmen, French policy toward Vietnam, which has been described as one of in-decision, vacillation, and duplicity, remains an unsolved puzzle.

Of these divisions in French opinion, the one most talked about after World War II was that between the French in Indochina and the men in France itself actively engaged in colonial affairs. A study of the French press in Saigon after September, 1945, might easily lead to the conclusion that this was indeed how the French were divided. This press reflected, stronger than ever and with greater intemperance, the old convictions of the colonialists, the military, and the administrators that only they knew what French policy in Indochina ought to be. After 1945, they were convinced that they, not Paris, were the ones best qualified to deal with the native demand for political freedom. These seasoned colonialists failed to see that Vietnam was going through a genuine national revolution. There was unrest, admittedly more than there had ever been before, and Paris, consequently, had to supply more troops to pacify Indochina; but the new government of France was not to interfere in the affairs of the colony, which the French in Indochina still considered theirs alone. The radical leaders of colonial society, who had always been able to make French opinion in Saigon and Hanoi, failed to see that the cause of the new crisis, and the reason for its depth and duration, was their outmoded native policy; they put the blame for it on metropolitan interference. These people had only one explanation for the growing strength of the Vietminh and French inability to defeat the rebels in the South: the "soft" policy toward the nationalist movement, as exemplified by Cédile's negotia-tions with the rebels in Saigon, by the recognition of the Hanoi regime in the March agreement, and by the subsequent attempts to reach a compromise with the Ho Chi Minh government at the Dalat and Fon-tainebleau conferences. The older planters, prewar colonial officials, landowners, and heads of banks and of once-prosperous commercial firms regarded the Vietminh as a group of criminals and bandits. For a long time, these former collaborators with the Japanese denounced the revolution as a Japanese scheme to get France out of Indochina. Colonial society also knew who was directly responsible for the soft policy toward the rebels: If France, instead of using her army to crush the rebels, had entered into negotiations with them, the fault lay with the "new men" sent by Paris, the so-called "Gaullists," who had replaced some of the worst Vichyites as well as Admiral Decoux—about half a dozen new men for every old one dismissed.[4] Some of the old colonialists went so far as to accuse even Admiral d'Argenlieu of following a policy that encouraged rebellion. In the pursuit of their selfish goals, which had never been of benefit to France, and out of fear over the threatened loss of their privileges, the leading members of colonial society suffered a new, though by no means the last, collapse of their ability for sound political judgment and rational action.[5]

But their shrill denunciations of the "Gaullists" failed to convince the Vietnamese nationalists that Frenchmen like d'Argenlieu, Leclerc, or Sainteny were less determined than the old colonialists themselves to maintain the French position in Indochina. Indeed, the new men, far from wanting to relinquish Indochina, were merely less obtuse than their critics in pursuing the same aim, and motivated more by what they held to be the interests of France than by considerations of personal position or gain. Although divided among themselves, they recognized that France, in a world that was witnessing a vast movement of emancipation from colonial rule, could maintain her position in Asia only if she was willing to pay a price. This price, they believed, consisted of substantial political concessions, short of independence, to the peoples of Indochina. The difference between these men and the colonial diehards concerned not ends but means. As to French aims in Indochina, there never existed a sharp division between Frenchmen in Saigon and metropolitan France, and only an apparent conflict of opinion between the members of the older colonial society and the newer administrators appointed by the Fourth Republic after 1945. Had not these new men entered Indochina with the declaration of March, 1945 —"as carriers of this totally outmoded text"[6] with which the de Gaulle government thought it could meet the urgent needs for political realignment in postwar Indochina, a text which could just as well have been drafted by the most obfuscated member of colonial society?

And had not the most prominent of all Gaullists in Indochina, Admiral d'Argenlieu, in criticizing the March agreement, openly sided with "colonial society" and its militant extremists against Leclerc, Sainteny, and Paris?

The astonishing truth is that after the war, the French, regardless of political parties and opinions, including the Communists, agreed that Indochina should remain within the French colonial empire. The differences of opinion that existed among Frenchmen were between the Left and the Right, and for a long time concerned not aims but methods. The Left, in particular the Socialists and Communists, but also sizable factions of the Radicals, wanted, at least up to December, 1946, bona fide negotiations with the Hanoi Government, and agreements that would make the promise of a free state within the French Union a reality; they therefore opposed the use of force in the South and the tactics of d'Argenlieu and General Valluy, which aimed at applying force also in the North. In this quarrel over methods for maintaining the position of France in Indochina, these two men were more often at odds with Paris than with colonial society, which had the full support, in Parliament and press, of the Right. There is no doubt that the fundamental division among Frenchmen in regard to Vietnam, from August, 1945, to December, 1946, was clearly between the Left and Right. The split between the French at home and in Indochina was not only temporary but also had little effect on the course of events.

After December, 1946, as these events unfolded, the quarrel, which for a long time still did not concern aims but methods, revealed a number of deeper and more lasting divisions of French opinion. However, these divisions, which produced one of the bitterest disputes of recent French history, were again not between Frenchmen in Indochina and at home, but ran, now even more distinctly, along the traditional lines of political division in France. The Left (apart from the Communists, who wanted negotiations with Ho Chi Minh and no one else) began to recognize the advisability of negotiations with nationalists other than the Vietminh, and even to accept the necessity of promising independence to a non-Communist Vietnam. The Right, including the Rassemblement Populaire Français (the new formation behind de Gaulle), opposed not only negotiations with Ho Chi Minh but the granting of independence to any Vietnamese regime that might emerge. In this alignment of forces, which lasted to the end of the Indochina War, the Frenchmen in Indochina acted merely as the radical wing of the parties of the Right and Center, both of which continued to demand a military solution. Colonial society in Indochina was again able to play a separate and significant role only after France, haltingly and much too late, began to make concessions toward eventual independence, concessions that colonial officialdom was in a position to sabotage. It was this systematic undoing, in Saigon and Hanoi, of concessions made by Paris that gave French policy its aura of duplicity. But in this respect too, colonial society, although acting under its own egotistic impulses, acted politically as a faction of the colonial party of France. Its sabotage could have been broken by Paris only if the French Left, by advocating a consistent anticolonial policy for Indochina, had succeeded in defeating the imperialist position of the Right.

The quarrel over Vietnam that tore France apart politically, although soon reduced to the question of when and how to grant independence, consisted, between 1945 and 1954, of a number of subdisputes not all of which have been resolved. These disputes not only divided the Left and Right, but they also split the Left itself. Furthermore, there existed a parliamentary "Center," represented in all postwar French governments, which on the problem of Indochina always threw its weight to the Right. The main group of this Center was the Catholic Mouvement Republicain Populaire, which on domestic policy frequently sided with the Left.[7] This, and the fact that France during this period had fifteen governments, only a few of which lasted even a year, accounts for the indecision and vacillation of French policy in Indochina on which every writer on the subject has dwelled.[8]

During the early months of 1947, the chief dispute in regard to Vietnam was whether the conflict should be settled through further political negotiations or with purely military means. These were the months when the Left, except the Communists, temporarily adopted the position of the Right, which was that there could be no negotiations before "order" had been restored. When the expectation of a quick military decision had to be given up, Right and Left again moved apart. The new split, which opened up in the spring of 1947 and widened as the war continued and hope for victory diminished, at first concerned only the question of whether France should again negotiate with the government of Ho Chi Minh, which after all was France's opponent in this war. The Right unanimously said no, while the Left, which headed the government, was badly split: The Communists, who stayed in the government until May, 1947, and most Socialists, advocated such negotiations; the Catholic MRP, without whose participation no leftist government could stay in office, and most Radicals, firmly opposed them. Therefore, no negotiations took place, although the idea was no longer officially denounced. This was one of the many periods when, largely for domestic political reasons, nothing was decided and nothing was done, a period when critics, both of the Left and Right, claimed that France had no policy in Indochina, obviously discounting the fact that the war, vigorously pursued, proved that French policy still was an unavowed attempt to solve the entire problem by military means.

It was during this period that the question of whether or not to resume negotiations with Ho Chi Minh intensified a debate that had started immediately after the appearance of the Vietminh on the Vietnamese scene. Although this debate was to last beyond the end of the Indochina War, it produced a governmental decision in May, 1947, that basically determined French policy toward Vietnam until spring, 1954. The subject of this debate concerned the nature of the Vietminh. How great was its popularity? Was it a national coalition truly representative of the Vietnamese people aiming only at independence, or was it an instrument forged by the Communists for the realization of their specific partisan aims? Or more perplexing still: Was the Vietminh both? Between the Left and Right, this question took on a particular aspect: Do we refuse to negotiate with the Hanoi regime because a military decision must precede all further talks about Franco-Vietnamese relations, as the Right maintained, or merely because the Vietminh government, dominated by Communist extremists, is not sufficiently representative of the Vietnamese national movement? This was, by and large, the position of the non-Communist Left. In this instance, the Center, and in particular the MRP, sided with the parties of the non-Communist Left. What they said had already been preached and practiced by Admiral d'Argenlieu: There must be negotiations, we must be ready to make concessions to the Vietnamese, but negotiations can no longer be conducted only with the government of Ho Chi Minh, and in making concessions we cannot go so far as to grant full independence.

Out of the refusal to negotiate with the Hanoi regime therefore arose the question with whom to negotiate, and out of the rather arbitrary decision that the Vietminh government was not really representative of the Vietnamese people arose the further question whether, for the purpose of negotiations, any other Vietnamese government could be created. Could such a government be made representative enough to become politically effective against the Vietminh? And in order to become a national force capable of taking the wind out of the sails that had carried the Vietminh to power, would it not have to obtain in negotiations with the French what the Vietminh now, after the failure of negotiations, tried to achieve through armed resistance, namely full independence? But what was the point of pursuing this war, some Frenchmen began to ask themselves, if for political reasons France can win it only by renouncing what she is fighting for—her continued presence in Indochina?

Thus would the French, and in particular the Left, during seven more years of political dissension and continuous war in Vietnam, debate the Indochinese question, and not until all means of self-deception had been exhausted was the country forced to make the decision that, had there been men of greater political foresight, would have been made in 1945: to grant independence to the three Indochinese states.

3

The Indochina War was, no doubt, one of the great errors of French policy in this century. That is why the question of responsibility for this costly and futile venture will agitate all students of contemporary history for a long time to come. Why did the French lack the insight, possessed by the British and acquired slowly also by the Dutch, that the age of Western domination of Asia was coming to an end?

Although none of the major political parties, including the Communists,[9] is free from blame for the failure to prevent the Indochina War, the forces chiefly responsible for its outbreak, and even more for its duration, are the parties of the non-Communist Left. It was they who ruled France during the first crucial postwar years; it was under their leadership that the fateful decisions that made this war inevitable were taken. The parties of the Left, with all the power they needed to oppose the imperialist aspirations of the Right, embraced these aspirations and turned the government of the Fourth Republic into a tool of France's reactionary colonial party. They adopted the interpretation, advanced by the parties of the Right and by colonial society, of the Vietminh as a solidly Communist movement; they tolerated d'Argenlieu's sabotage of the March agreement, condoned General Valluy's provocative actions, and with their pettiness at the conference table destroyed the chance for a more lasting agreement at Fontainebleau. Nothing was done by the leftist governments of France to strengthen the forces of non-Communist nationalism in Vietnam; on the contrary, it was with French help that the Vietminh succeeded in almost wiping out these forces. And with arguments entirely borrowed from the Right, the leftist governments of France rejected all Vietminh offers for re-establishing peace after the war had spread over the entire country. It has been said again and again that during the period when a solution without war was still possible, France had no Indochinese policy at all. The truth is that there was a definite policy, the rightist policy of colonial reconquest, and that the Left, in control of the government but lacking a policy of its own, adopted the catastrophic course advocated by the Right.

Most significant for the failure of the Left to impose the liberal intentions it frequently voiced toward Vietnam was the role played during these years by the Socialist Party of France. A study of the statements made by men like Léon Blum and Guy Mollet, and of congress resolutions adopted by the party between 1945 and 1953, proves that, from 1945 on, of the major political groups, the Socialists alone had an adequate answer to the problems created for France by the Vietnamese national revolution. During 1946, the Socialists consistently opposed d'Argenlieu's policy of sabotage of the March agreement. After the war had become general, Léon Blum, as temporary Premier, recognized the right of the Vietnamese to national freedom, and openly proclaimed the old colonial system as finished.[10] All during the years 1947 and 1948, when the government declined to enter into peace negotiations with Ho Chi Minh, Socialist Party congresses kept demanding such negotiations. Gradually, the party began to embrace the concept of total independence for Vietnam, and its press became more and more outspoken in its criticism of the policy France was pursuing. Yet the Socialist Cabinet members, as long as they codetermined, and even directed, French policy toward Indochina, consistently acted contrary to these enlightened views. Well-disposed critics, therefore, called the Socialists prisoners of the colonial party; angry Vietnamese accused them of being accomplices.

One argument has always been offered to explain why the Socialists, in principle opposed to French policy in Vietnam, cooperated effectively in its execution: For compelling innerpolitical reasons, the Socialists clung to the strong position they had gained in the governments of liberated France; as long as their coalition partners preferred them to cooperation with parties of the Right, the Socialists looked at participation in the government as an obligation toward their electorate which they could not disregard. If they had made independence for Vietnam a condition for maintaining the coalition with the Radicals and the MRP, these parties would have formed governments supported by rightist parties two years before they actually did.

This holds true for most leading Socialists—men like Felix Gouin, Paul Ramadier, and Jules Moch—for the simple reason that France was closer to them than was Vietnam. Theirs was a position of painful compromise; they themselves regarded their attitude as a necessary sacrifice but did not feel that it was a betrayal of Vietnam.

This defense cannot be made of the Socialist Marius Moutet, who, during the most critical period before and after the outbreak of the war, was Minister of Overseas Affairs. Moutet's prominence derived entirely from the role he played as one of the personalities who shaped and defended French colonial policy after World War II. There is, of course, no need to question Moutet's motivation. It was obviously political, and although the role he played was hardly creditable, nothing is to be gained by doubting his integrity. But Moutet's thinking, like that of many of his colleagues, suffered from the main defect of all moderately successful Socialist leaders of our time: their belief that the cause of their parties can be served through participation in governments even if this obliges them to act contrary to their professed principles and specific programs. It is a fallacy to believe that the evils of a policy one knows to be wrong can be reduced by taking its execution into one's own hands, a fallacy based on the assumption that motives in politics are in the end more important than behavior. Moutet no doubt believed that French policy in Indochina, although steadily evolving toward the necessity of conducting a colonial war, would be a less disastrous and less reprehensible policy if presided over by a known friend of the colonial peoples instead of by an aggressive colonialist.

Thus Moutet became a prisoner of the colonial party. And once he had allowed this to happen, he could act, and defend his actions, only as an accomplice of this party. Throughout his career as Minister of Overseas Affairs, he did so with diminishing restraint. There is only one alternative to the assumption that he consciously betrayed the cause for which he had earlier, often effectively, fought: He had entered a trap which, after it had closed on him, he could not help but regard as a freely chosen place. However, he thought that he was free to do what he liked only because he had come to accept as right what his position as spokesman of France's colonial policy forced him to say and do. He ended by believing that the aims of France in Vietnam could be achieved only by making war.

Most of Moutet's colleagues supported his policy with grave misgivings—like a woman who accepts an unwelcome pregnancy hoping for a miscarriage. Many felt that if the Socialists in the government could not persuade their coalition partners to abandon the policy of colonial reconquest, they could at least slow down the ongoing campaign of aggression and, if an opportunity arose, seize it and impose their own solution. But this was an illusion, and the most outstanding leader of French socialism, Léon Blum, a true proponent of freedom for Vietnam, also fell victim to it. Blum had the misfortune of heading the French Government when hostilities broke out in Hanoi—an all-Socialist caretaker government that, as intended, lasted only a few weeks.[11] Obliged to speak as Premier of France, which, according to all reports from Saigon and Hanoi, had been attacked, Blum in a speech on December 23, 1946, based his justification of the policy of force on the dubious assertion that responsibility for the outbreak of the war lay entirely with the Vietminh. When he spoke thus, he did not know that Saigon was withholding from the Premier of France the peace proposals that Ho Chi Minh had addressed to him on December 15. Blum spoke movingly and no doubt with a heavy heart, reiterating that in the end Vietnam must be given her freedom. He expressed his view that only negotiations could produce lasting and friendly relations between France and Vietnam. But he failed to see what had produced the war: not primarily the unfortunate methods practiced by the exponents of reconquest in Saigon and Paris, but the official aims of France as proclaimed in 1945, and firmly pursued during 1946. His failure to see that these aims called for the methods that were applied made him, too, a prisoner of the forces that determined French policy in Indochina after World War II.

The particular issue that trapped Blum and his party in December, 1946, was the seemingly plausible demand that the necessary condition for peace negotiations was the return of public order; only after order was re-established could the good intentions of France, which Blum undoubtedly nourished, become effective. But the Vietnamese knew that France had given no evidence of such intentions before the outbreak of the war. The demand for order could mean for them only that they must surrender or be militarily defeated before negotiations could be resumed. With his request for order Blum, therefore, stood in the forefront of the forces of aggression which he had so often denounced. Not only as a Socialist, but as a French statesman of integrity and foresight, he should have denounced these forces again, and furthermore have rejected the aims of France, whose pursuit was the chief cause of the existing disorder. Had he done so, his government would probably have lasted only four days instead of four weeks, but his party would not have become an accomplice of the many hypocrites in France who insisted that Vietnam could be given freedom only after French armies had again deprived her of it. It is even conceivable that Blum might have alerted his country and shortened the senseless Indochina War.[12]

4

The Socialists, as well as all other opponents of aggressive colonialism, committed their fundamental error immediately after World War II. This consisted in their failure to recognize that the Indochinese states had in fact become independent and that the leaders of at least one of these states, Vietnam, were determined to mobilize their people against the reimposition of colonial rule. A policy of continuous "French presence," therefore, would ultimately face France with the necessity of imposing this presence by force, a necessity which the anticolonial forces of France refused to admit. There existed only two ways of solving the Franco-Vietnamese conflict created by the triumph of the anticolonial revolution: the peaceful solution consisting in the gradual granting, over a period of years, of full independence, with good prospects that Vietnam would remain in a French union that was a commonwealth of truly free states. The alternative to this, pursued while a peaceful solution was seemingly still being sought in negotiations, was the attempt at military reconquest. What made the position of the proponents of force so unassailable was that if France, as everyone agreed, had to maintain her position in Indochina, she ultimately had no choice but to fight.

By rejecting the establishment of national independence in 1945 as the premise of their Vietnamese policy, the French Left adopted in fact the position of the Right—i.e., that Vietnam had never been lost; the revolution was a rather unusual state of disorder, and the fighting not a real war but the sum of military and police actions to pacify the country. As long as the Left, and in particular the Socialists, subscribed to a policy of continued French presence in Indochina—an aim that could be achieved only by force—their criticism of the rightist position, and their attempts to subdue the proponents of aggression on the Indochinese scene, remained ineffective. The advocates of force proved right, and in fact determined French policy in Indochina—up to the point when the failure of force and intrigue proved that France was no longer able to hold on to Indochina. It was the pressure of circumstances rather than true insight that brought the non-Communist Left in 1954 to the realization that France must relinquish her injudiciously chosen aims. Only then was the Left able to curb the aggressiveness of the Right.

It is therefore wrong to say, as the Left in France still does, that the war broke out because the nobler intentions of France were continuously thwarted by the advocates of force who held strategic positions both at home and in Indochina.[13] If d'Argenlieu and Valluy acted contrary to the wishes of Paris, why was it that later French governments declined to accept the suggestion that these men, and others who acted in their spirit, be replaced? Marius Moutet himself, courageously standing by his conviction, in a speech in the Chamber of Deputies on March 18, 1946, destroyed the legend that d'Argenlieu was out of step with Paris. Replying to critics who blamed the admiral for the failure of the negotiations between March and December, 1947, Moutet stated: "What I reproach Admiral d'Argenlieu for is not that he did not follow the directives of the government. I reproach him for having anticipated them." [14] This is indeed convincing testimony that the High Commissioner's aims were those of the French governments that had sent him to Indochina and kept him at his post until spring, 1947. D'Argenlieu pursued these aims more openly and with great energy, in contrast to his superiors in Paris, whose policy suffered from "indecision and vacillation," and who defended their aims with a touch of hypocrisy that was not to the liking of d'Argenlieu. The differences between Paris and Saigon during 1946 were only of temperament and tactics.

But even these differences were wiped out by the events of December, 1946. Marius Moutet, sent by Léon Blum to Indochina on a mission which the Hanoi Government hoped was one of seeking peace, arrived in Saigon on December 25. Two days later he made declarations that differed only in tone from the belligerent ones d'Argenlieu was making in Paris before his return to Saigon. The statement made by d'Argenlieu on December 27 that France would not relinquish her hold on Indochina but "was determined to maintain and develop her present influence" was echoed that same day by Moutet, who spoke in Saigon of "the necessity of maintaining the presence of France [in Indochina]." France has been attacked, France has to fight back—that was how Moutet, in complete harmony with the most militant local colonialists, reacted to the outbreak of fighting in the North. At a dinner given by the Cao Dai leader Le Van Hoach, who had served the Japanese as a high police official and now served the French as head of the separatist government of Indochina, Moutet warmed the hearts of all the men who had so successfully sabotaged the March agreement by putting the blame for the outbreak of the war entirely on the Vietminh. Instead of rushing to Hanoi to see what had really happened and whether there was still a chance of stopping the fighting, Moutet paid a leisurely visit to Cambodia and Laos, both firmly in French hands. He praised these nations, holding them up as examples to the Vietnamese; he was obviously convinced that their love for France, not their weakness, was the reason that they offered little armed resistance to the French. With words normally used only by the most narrow-minded of chauvinists, the Socialist Moutet asserted that there was peace and order wherever the French flag flew. He seems not to have recognized that peace and order would still have reigned in the rest of Indochina had the French not insisted that their flag fly again over Vietnam.

When Moutet, on January 3, 1947, finally went to Hanoi (where the French had proclaimed martial law on December 23), his chief concern was that no member of his mission seek contacts with representatives of the Vietminh government. He firmly declined negotiations with any representative of Ho Chi Minh, negotiations for which the radio station of the Vietminh continuously appealed during his brief stay in Hanoi. Later, when Moutet came under attack for his failure to explore the chances of a cease-fire while in Hanoi, he defended himself by denying, despite the testimony of others, that any member of his mission had received any peace proposal from representatives of the Vietminh.[15] But on leaving the still-embattled city, he made it clear that such proposals were unwelcome to the French Government, in whose name apparently he personally decided that negotiations with the Vietminh were out. "Before any negotiations," he told *Le Monde* of January 5, "it is necessary to have a military decision. I regret," he added, "but one cannot commit the sort of acts of madness the Vietnamese have done with impunity."

The men of war had won a total victory: Official France, under an all-Socialist government, now openly accepted the demand that the Franco-Vietnamese conflict be resolved through a "military decision." The new attitude of the men who had advocated a "peaceful solution" and who, after December 19, 1946, also demanded a "military decision," confirmed that they had negotiated in the hope that war would be unnecessary because the Vietnamese could be persuaded to surrender what they had gained. When this proved a vain hope, the so-called men of peace became men of war.

A deeply disturbed Léon Blum, in his efforts to find a way out of his predicament as leader of France, turned to the man whose role in 1946 had been decisive in getting France to accept the March agreement with Ho Chi Minh—General Leclerc. Blum wanted him not only to give the government a valid appraisal of the military prospects but also to be on the spot in case a chance for a peaceful solution should develop. He asked Leclerc to return to Indochina, against the open opposition of d'Argenlieu, who, since the March agreement, regarded Leclerc as an appeaser of the Vietminh. Apparently sharing d'Argenlieu's fears, General de Gaulle, too, strongly opposed Blum's proposal that Leclerc again become Commander in Chief of the French armies in Indochina.

But Leclerc, who went to Indochina on a brief inspection tour, refused both the post of Commander in Chief and that of High Commissioner offered him a few weeks later. He refused not because d'Argenlieu disapproved of him or de Gaulle advised him against accepting either position;[16] nor was his reluctance to return to Indochina based on his knowledge that no government would grant him what he considered the minimum required for military success against the Vietminh: a well-equipped army of 500,000 men. His reasons were deeper, and they underline the scope of his political intelligence. Leclerc had more than merely a premonition that the war could not be won at all. "In 1947," he said, "France will no longer put down by force a grouping of 24 million inhabitants which is assuming unity and in which there exists a xenophobic and perhaps a national ideal." Furthermore, in sharp contrast to d'Argenlieu and General Valluy, who now concentrated all their efforts on a quick military solution, Leclerc stated: "The major problem from now on is political." [17] Unlike the Socialist minister, the conservative general said nothing that gave comfort to the *colons*, administrators, and military men in Indochina. On the contrary, he pleaded for a peaceful solution through negotiations "with all political factions of the Vietnamese people," in other words, negotiations also with the Vietminh.

Among the military in Indochina and the colonial extremists there and in France, Leclerc's warning fell on deaf ears; it merely confirmed them in their suspicions that the respected general was, if not an "appeaser" of the Vietminh, at least a confirmed "defeatist"; not so in Paris, however, where since January 21, the government was again based on a coalition of the MRP, Socialists, Radicals, and Communists, headed by the Socialist Paul Ramadier, with Marius Moutet once more Minister for Overseas Affairs. The new government was greatly disturbed by Leclerc's warnings, whose validity many Cabinet members were inclined to accept. But with the exception of the Communists, they had all tied their hands with their dogmatic refusal (based on their claim of Vietminh aggression) of any further negotiations with the Hanoi regime. Recognizing to some extent the accuracy of Leclerc's analysis, and embarrassed by his appeal for negotiations "with all factions of the Vietnamese people," the spokesmen of the French Government tried to convince public opinion, in a manner that can only be called puerile, that not the French but the Vietminh refused to seek peace through negotiations. The Vietminh broadcasts asking for peace talks, it was said, could not be regarded as official proposals. The attempt to reach Moutet in Hanoi through members of his mission were brazenly denied. When the government finally had to admit that it had received written peace proposals, Premier Ramadier resorted to the shoddy device of claiming that according to expert testimony, Ho Chi Minh's signature on the document was not his own. But there was one proof that the French denial of Vietminh peace proposals was patently untrue: Even if Ho Chi Minh had never really wanted to have his proposals accepted, the attitude of the French would certainly have induced him to repeat them as often as possible, if only to embarrass opponents who, through their own dogmatism, had deprived themselves of all latitude for political maneuvering. Government policy remained rigid: no negotiations with the Hanoi regime. Even the Communist Cabinet members, who kept demanding talks with Ho Chi Minh, did not make their demand a condition for maintaining their coalition with the non-Communist Left, and when they did resign in May, they did so over a question of internal policy, not over Indochina.

However, when, after two months of fighting, it became evident that in the military sphere prospects for a quick solution were anything but good, Leclerc's belief that the main problem was political rapidly gained ground in the more enlightened circles of the Left and Center. The military leaders in Indochina remained ludicrously optimistic, claiming that victory was around the corner. But the government began to concern itself with the political steps that could be taken to improve the position of France in Vietnam. Ramadier spoke of the necessity to enter into a new "constructive phase" of policy for Vietnam. To determine what this was to be was not easy, since both Assembly and Cabinet were deeply split over the central issue of negotiations. Negotiations yes, but with whom? With Ho Chi Minh, said the Communists; the majority of the Socialists and some Radicals favored Leclerc's formula—"with all factions of the Vietnamese people," which meant with the as yet undeveloped and unorganized forces of anti-Communist nationalism, but also with the Vietminh; the majority of the Radicals and some Socialists, but above all the influential MRP, said "with all factions of the Vietnamese people except the Vietminh." Who these factions were also was hard to say. It would have been too absurd to seek them among the discredited individuals whom d'Argenlieu had persuaded, in most cases by offering them lucrative positions, to collaborate with the French against the Vietminh. Could they be found among the followers of the VNQDD and the Dong Minh Hoi? They were anti-Vietminh, but apparently no less anti-French than the Vietminh itself, which was the reason the French, in the summer of 1946, cooperated with the Vietminh in their political destruction. Who else was there with whom an anti-Vietminh movement could be created for the purpose of Franco-Vietnamese negotiations, since according to a vital French premise the Vietminh was not sufficiently representative of the Vietnamese people, of which it was at best one faction?

There was as yet nobody, at least nobody who counted. The problem, therefore, was not only with whom to negotiate, but rather how to create, in negotiations with the right people, a popular movement and, based on such a movement, a Vietnamese government willing to cooperate with the French against the Vietminh.

Gradually, a plan emerged whose outlines had existed in d'Argenlieu's mind for some time. The basic feature was to unite, behind the former Emperor Bao Dai, all anti-Communist forces of Vietnamese nationalism, to create a government headed by Bao Dai, and to negotiate with this government a settlement acceptable to France.[18] The expectation was that this would reduce the Vietminh from its position as leading force of nationalism to one of its "factions." After thus being decisively weakened, the Vietminh would either come to terms with the French, on a basis short of full independence, or be defeated by the combined forces of the French and the new government of Vietnam. If the Vietminh refused to submit, the war would continue but would change its character. It would become a war between two Vietnamese governments, that of Bao Dai and Ho Chi Minh, a civil war, no longer a colonial war, and, moreover, a war between "Communism" and "anti-Communism," in which the role of the French would merely be to support the "anti-Communist" regime against that of the Vietminh.[19]

After this course was decided upon, the French line of conduct was set for the entire duration of the Indochina War. The policy of force was now combined with political intrigue. Vietnamese nationalism was to be used to defeat Vietnamese Communism, under the false assumption that Communism, not nationalism, was the force that strove to prevent the "presence" of France in Vietnam.

But the fundamental problem of the French in Vietnam could not be solved by political intrigue. The success of the scheme to use Bao Dai against Ho Chi Minh depended on conditions which, if fulfilled, would make the entire scheme useless for the French. An anti-Communist Vietnamese government could serve the French only if it weakened the Vietminh, which in turn required that it gain a broad popular base. If it failed in that, the Vietminh would continue to command the allegiance of the people. But how could an anti-Vietminh government gain popular support? Only if it were as truly nationalist as was the Vietminh, since nationalism, not Communism, was what made the Vietminh strong. In order to gain any popular support, therefore, an anti-Vietminh government would have to obtain from the French concessions close to those for which the Vietminh fought, concessions that opened the way toward full independence. Without satisfying Vietnam's basic national aspiration, which demanded independence, no nationalist regime could ever become an anti-Communist force. Again it was Leclerc who, looking further ahead than most of his compatriots, succinctly formulated the problem as early as January, 1947: "Anti-Communism," he said, "will remain a useless tool as long as the problem of nationalism is not solved." [20] His warning was not heeded: Anti-Communism became official French policy in Vietnam for the next seven years.

5

Prevented by its own illusions and by rightist pressure from making the necessary political decisions, the leftist government of France proceeded to make a gesture meant to indicate that a new course was about to start. In March, 1947, it did what it should have done in March, 1946: It recalled High Commissioner d'Argenlieu. This was a gesture designed chiefly to impress the Vietnamese.

There is no doubt that the recall of d'Argenlieu would have been necessary if France had really decided upon a new course in Vietnam. But it was equally necessary for the purpose of executing merely a new tactical scheme. The admiral had denounced the March agreement, worked against all concessions at the Fontainebleau conference, aroused the Vietnamese with his separatist policy for Cochinchina, and unabashedly made himself known as a proponent of force and an enemy not only of the Vietminh but also of all Vietnamese with national aspirations. The Vietnamese could not be expected to believe in new and better French intentions as long as d'Argenlieu held his post.

But the recall of d'Argenlieu was necessary also for other reasons. His mission, whether planned as such or not, had been to undo the March agreement, with tactics that allowed the French to put the conflict on a military plane. Together with the head of the French forces in Indochina, General Valluy, d'Argenlieu had achieved his mission. As the policy of force was not to be abandoned, there was no need to replace General Valluy. His efforts to bring about a military decision had to be continued. But precisely because the state of general war had made the maneuverings of 1946 against the Vietminh obsolete, a new game had to be played on the political level, one for which d'Argenlieu by temperament, but even more because of his past, was unfit. He was replaced by Emile Bollaert, a civilian and member of the Radicals, a party that had long insisted on a larger role in shaping French policy in Indochina.

Both the tragic turn that Franco-Vietnamese relations took on December 19, 1946, and the political impasse that had resulted from the refusal to talk to Ho Chi Minh were challenges that Bollaert was eager to meet. He was at first given no more than six months to accomplish his mission, for which he had requested a free hand in all negotiations, including a secret permission to negotiate with the Vietminh if for tactical reasons this should become advisable. Bollaert, in return, promised to take no decisive step without prior consultation with Paris.

What Premier Ramadier had called the "constructive phase" of French policy toward Vietnam began with the arrival of Bollaert in Saigon early in April, 1947. He lifted the censorship in Saigon and the state of siege in Hanoi and Haiphong. He also removed d'Argenlieu's political adviser, Léon Pignon, from his staff, replacing him with Paul Mus, a man known for his sympathies with Vietnamese national aspirations. Nothing else that was striking was either said or done, except that Bollaert, in explaining why there could be no negotiations with the Hanoi regime, introduced a change of reasoning, in preparation for the plans the French had for Bao Dai. Instead of insisting, as Moutet had in January, that the aggressors had to be defeated before the French would talk with them, he now emphasized that the Hanoi regime was insufficiently representative of the Vietnamese people: The Vietminh was controlled by the Communists, who were obviously only a small faction of the nationalist movement. France was willing to negotiate and make concessions, but only to a truly representative government, and one willing to agree that the free state of Vietnam remain a member of the French Union. Bollaert advised the leaders of Vietnamese nationalism to cooperate with him in preparing such a government.

As soon as Bollaert established his first contacts, he hit upon the main obstacle for the creation of a national government with which effectively to oppose the Vietminh regime: the refusal by the best known anti-Communist leaders to cooperate in this scheme. Every respected nationalist recognized the attempt to form an anti-Vietminh government as a maneuver to avoid making the concessions for which the Vietminh fought and the population yearned. If his mission had allowed him to learn, Bollaert would have realized that the moment to solve "the problem of nationalism" was now, and that if it was not solved now, anti-Communism would never become "a useful tool." "Make the concessions to us that you say you cannot make to the 'Communist' Vietminh," he was told by nationalists who stayed aloof from the Hanoi regime. "Give us independence! If we cooperate with you on any other basis, the rest of our small following will go over to the Vietminh." The new High Commissioner may have been impressed by these truths, but as long as France wanted to hang on to Vietnam, he and his successors could not allow them to determine their actions.

Among the more prominent men Bollaert approached were the Catholics Ngo Dinh Diem and Nguyen Manh Ha. Ngo Dinh Diem had once publicly broken with the colonial administration over the issue of modest reforms; in 1945, he had been considered as a possible head of a Japanese-sponsored government of "free" Vietnam. The Japanese found out in time that he was too independent for such a role. Later, he rejected an invitation by Ho Chi Minh to join the Hanoi Government. Nguyen Manh Ha, on the other hand, although certainly not a Communist, had accepted such an invitation and had served as Ho Chi Minh's Economics Minister until December 19, 1946; when Ho's Cabinet fled from Hanoi, Nguyen Manh Ha stayed behind. Both he and Ngo Dinh Diem now refused to join a French-sponsored anti-Vietminh government. But their refusal was not only an act of personal political integrity. It was also an expression of the national mood. Immediately after the war spread to the North and Ho Chi Minh had called the nation to arms,[21] even the exiled anti-Vietminh leaders of the VNQDD and Dong Minh Hoi appealed to the people to join the fight against the French. Their hatred for the Vietminh was undiminished, but, like the anti-Communist leaders at home, they knew that to condemn the Vietminh at the moment when it proclaimed a war of national liberation would have been regarded by the people as siding with the French. For the time being, and indeed for a long time to come, the Hanoi Government was the incarnation of the people's will never again to submit to any form of foreign domination. The Vietminh over the years had succeeded in creating an image of itself as an anti-French, anti-Japanese, anti-Chinese force. Nobody liked the war, but it never occurred to the people to put the blame for it on the leader of the Vietminh. Ho Chi Minh had negotiated with the enemy, the Chinese as well as the French, and although always faithfully observing the interests of his party, had never betrayed the aims of militant nationalism. By choosing armed resistance rather than any further retreat, he had proved himself the most determined patriot in the nationalist camp. Other nationalist leaders could stand up against Ho Chi Minh only if they could offer the people what he was fighting for.

In seeking to enlist men of a solid political reputation, however, Bollaert was merely preparing the ground for the role the French wanted former Emperor Bao Dai to play in the political campaign they were about to mount against the Vietminh. As Bao Dai was the key figure in the French plan, Bollaert's failure to enlist prominent nationalists was not considered critical.

Bao Dai had been residing in Hong Kong since disengaging himself from the Vietminh in March, 1946. There he was seriously hampered in his quest for pleasure by a lack of funds and a host of scruples. His urge to serve his country was far from dead, and he was apparently still able to suffer pangs of conscience. That the French thought of using him against the Vietminh, Bao Dai had already learned in January, 1947, from an emissary d'Argenlieu had sent to feel him out. Ever since then, and particularly after Bollaert's arrival in Saigon, messengers and old collaborators of the French had been going to Hong Kong, only to confirm to Bollaert what d'Argenlieu had learned in January: that Bao Dai, his will strengthened by cautious advisers, remained aloof. He was apparently not tempted once more to become the head of his nation under French auspices. The first official contact, however, was made by Paul Mus, formerly political adviser to Leclerc and now to Bollaert, who came to Hong Kong in May. Bao Dai told him that if the French wished to win his cooperation, they would have to offer him at least as much as Ho Chi Minh demanded. The Cochinchinese Government had to be dissolved and Vietnam reunited under one government; and, of course, Vietnam had to be given independence. Thus did the French learn that "on the fundamental themes, unity and independence of the country, Bao Dai presented exactly the same demands as Ho Chi Minh." [22]

To many Frenchmen, in Saigon as well as in Paris, this came as a surprise. Misled by the Emperor's behavior soon after his assumption of the throne, they looked at him as a playboy. They did not realize that his escape into dissipation was in part due to despair over the undignified role the French expected him to play. Bao Dai's seemingly "natural diffidence and indolence" in regard to public affairs resulted largely from his unwillingness to be an active tool of the French. The man behind this mask possessed "an intelligence of a high order" and a "shrewd ability to divine the intentions of others." [23] In approaching him in the spring of 1947, the French were quite ignorant of Bao Dai's dormant political abilities and greatly astonished to see that the "play-boy," if he cared, could himself turn into a master schemer, a man determined to outwit his opponents.

Indeed, in the spring of 1947, Bao Dai not only cared but was fully aware of the game the French intended to play. They were trying to circumvent the necessity of granting Vietnam independence by reducing the problem of nationalism to a simpler question, namely how the former Emperor and a few of the less discredited national leaders could be induced, through appeals to their anti-Communism, but also through the lure of high positions, to cooperate with the French. But that was not all. Bao Dai conjectured, even before the French themselves fully realized it, that in this game, talks between the French and the Vietminh might very well become necessary at some point, if only as a means of putting pressure on him. He also anticipated another possibility: The French might use the threat of forming a "legal" government for Vietnam under Bao Dai, and the even greater threat of granting this government independence, merely as a means of pressuring Ho Chi Minh into a new compromise, in which case Bao Dai's role would once more have been that of a French pawn.

Such were indeed the intentions of some of the people in Paris who made policy for Indochina. Bollaert, however, was not one of them. His idea was to use talks with Ho Chi Minh only as a means of putting pressure on Bao Dai. At the time Bollaert was ready to leave for Saigon, French policy toward Vietnam, always a shaky compromise between the parties needed to keep a cabinet in office, had in fact become less dogmatic on the question of negotiations with Ho Chi Minh. A secret agreement to allow such talks, if Bollaert considered them useful, had been concluded before Bollaert's departure. In part, this was the price for the support the Communists gave to the Ramadier Cabinet and its Indochina policy. The Communist Cabinet members voted for the credits needed to conduct the Indochina War; in the Chamber vote, the Communist deputies merely abstained.[24] But a more important reason for secret talks with Ho Chi Minh was the recognition, at least on the part of Bollaert, that in his dealings with Bao Dai his hands would be tied if talks with Ho Chi Minh were ruled out entirely. The Communists and Socialists were satisfied because such talks were at last being considered; the Radical and MRP Cabinet members agreed because they regarded them only as a necessary requirement for the success of the scheme to use Bao Dai against Ho Chi Minh.

That these people really believed this scheme could succeed underlines their distressing mediocrity. Its promoters were, of course, otherwise motivated, since talks with Ho Chi Minh and Bao Dai could mean so many different things. Even the proponents of force could agree to sit down with Ho Chi Minh, if only to offer proposals tantamount to unconditional surrender. Bollaert and his supporters who really believed that Bao Dai was the key to the solution of the Franco-Vietnamese conflict conceived of talks with Ho Chi Minh essentially as a maneuver, while another faction, consisting mostly of Socialists and Radicals skeptical about Bao Dai's usefulness as an anti-Vietminh force, nursed the illusion that a new compromise acceptable to France could be worked out in negotiations with Ho Chi Minh. They interpreted the peace proposals Ho Chi Minh continued to make as proof of fear and as a sign that he was ready for such a compromise. They, too, approved talks with Bao Dai, but merely as a means of frightening Ho Chi Minh. There was nothing to be lost in such a maneuver. Military action against the Vietminh would have to be relentlessly pursued while political negotiations with other than Vietminh forces were being conducted. If the French brought in another 100,000 troops, and at the same time offered substantial concessions to Ho's nationalist opponents, the Vietminh leader would recognize the folly of continued resistance. With no prospect of winning the war, and knowing that substantial French concessions to his nationalist opponents would weaken him considerably, Ho Chi Minh would be forced to accept a peace that would allow the French to maintain their position in Vietnam.

How plausible this reasoning would have been had it not overlooked the fact that the Vietnamese, whether pro- or anti-Vietminh, insisted on full independence! And how cleverly the French might have operated if the great historical forces of this century could have been fought with the shoddy weapon of political intrigue!

6

In the three-sided tug of war staged by the French, the Vietminh, and Bao Dai, the parties took up their positions with demonstrative firmness during the month of May, 1947. Bollaert, in a statement to *Le Monde* of May 17, said: "France will remain in Indochina, and Indochina will remain within the French Union." [25] But France was ready to negotiate, now obviously also with the Vietminh, for Bollaert added: "Let the representatives of all parties come to us." Bao Dai made his position clear to Paul Mus: He would negotiate only on the basis of unity and independence for Vietnam. That this was also Ho Chi Minh's position had, of course, been known for a long time. But how would Ho Chi Minh react if the French, agreeing to talk to him, proposed talks for a cease-fire, on condition, however, that the Vietminh accept being treated as only "one faction" of the Vietnamese people?

It would be naïve to assume that Bollaert could not have guessed how Ho Chi Minh would react to proposals for a cease-fire, since this depended entirely on the nature of such proposals, in whose formulation the High Commissioner had the last word. Bollaert even knew, from Ho Chi Minh's many previous declarations, the Vietminh's conditions for the acceptance of a cease-fire: the return of both parties to the positions they held before the outbreak of hostilities in Hanoi on December 19, 1946. Why, then, did Bollaert bother to send his political adviser, Paul Mus, on a perilous journey to Ho Chi Minh's headquarters, with proposals that amounted not only to a virtual ultimatum to surrender but also contained conditions which, according to Ho Chi Minh's own words, only a man without honor and a coward could have accepted? Mus himself, who knew Ho Chi Minh well, admitted that the French "requests for guarantees" were "equivalent to surrender," and he agreed that in Ho Chi Minh's place he, too, would reject the French demands.[26]

The so-called Mus Mission must be considered one of the most extraordinary episodes in Franco-Vietnamese relations, one that revealed not only the complexity of Bollaert's task but also the breadth of his desire for the support of all shades of French opinion. In conceiving the mission, Bollaert tried to satisfy the Socialists in the government (the Communists had left it early in May) by establishing contact with Ho Chi Minh without arousing his own party and the MRP by opening too wide the door for negotiations. Bao Dai had to be shown that his stubbornness might tempt the French to seek another "March agreement," yet he was not to be frightened into believing that the French wanted to deal with Ho Chi Minh rather than with him. But

more than anything else, the Mus Mission revealed the foolishness of
the men in power, civilian as well as military, whose wish to impose
their solution, strengthened by the expected arrival of massive reinforcements from France, beclouded their minds then and for seven
more years.[27] Not only General Valluy, who believed he could defeat
the Vietminh, insisted that Bollaert demand surrender; the Minister of
War, Paul Coste-Floret, a member of the MRP, was of the same opinion. After returning to Paris from an inspection tour in Indochina lasting from April 26 to May 3, Coste-Floret said that there was no longer
any military problem in Vietnam; the success of the French arms, he
asserted, was complete (even though, as he himself admitted, "the
greater part of the country remains in the hands of the Vietminh"[28]).

Bollaert did not share the unfounded optimism of Valluy and Coste-
Floret. Moreover, his later actions showed that he considered the conclusion of a cease-fire important for an agreement between the French
and "all factions of the Vietnamese people." Yet he, as so many proponents of a peaceful solution before and after him, gave in to the combined pressure of the military, colonial society, and the Right wing of
French political life, which, at every crucial turn in Franco-Vietnamese
relations, blocked the road of peace to keep open the road of war.
The men who favored a peaceful solution cannot all have been either
fools or cowards; their failure must have had a deeper, less personal
cause. In retrospect, it is not difficult to see what this was: a peaceful
solution was possible only if France agreed to withdraw from Vietnam; it was incompatible with a policy of continued "French presence" in Indochina. This aim, as long as its attainment was not recognized as an illusion, could be realistically pursued only through a
policy of force. An inner conviction, not admitted to themselves, that
this *might* be the case, broke the will of many honest "men of peace,"
while the fact that this actually *was* the case made their efforts to mitigate the policy of force ineffective. This alone can explain why the
Mus Mission came about, a mission that Bollaert should never have
ordered and Paul Mus should never have taken on.

This was the situation two months after the French had embarked
on their new "constructive phase" in Vietnam: General Valluy was
deep in preparations for a great offensive which he was sure would
crush the Vietminh; but on the political front, where the French had
expected a decisive breakthrough, nothing had changed. The attempts

to persuade Bao Dai into collaboration and to threaten Ho Chi Minh into surrender had failed.

Not willing to accept defeat, Bollaert now went himself to Hong Kong, trying to squeeze some benefit out of the failure of the Mus Mission by assuring Bao Dai that his fears of a new Franco-Vietminh deal were unfounded and warning him against the dangers of a course that looked as if he tried to make common cause with the Vietminh. But Bollaert's hopes that he might succeed where his emissaries had failed did not materialize. Bao Dai still refused to play the role the French had assigned to him unless they promised him unity and independence for Vietnam. He even refused to take a public stand against the Vietminh, to which he frequently referred as the "resistance," thus emphasizing that he did not regard all nationalists who had taken up arms against the French as Communists. In July, in an interview for a Saigon newspaper, Bao Dai went so far as to state that he was "neither for the Vietminh nor against them. I belong to no party." [29] However, on the advice of his counselors, he rejected an offer by Ho Chi Minh, submitted by a non-Communist emissary, to negotiate also on behalf of the Vietminh government, an offer which clearly indicated that the Vietminh, unafraid of negotiations to settle the conflict, no longer insisted on excluding other nationalist forces from a new Franco-Vietnamese deal.[30]

After his return from Hong Kong, Bollaert, a patriot not entirely devoid of a sense of reality, decided that the impasse into which he had maneuvered himself could be broken only by a bold political step. Always eager to have the support of his government, he went to Paris to obtain authority for a new plan with which he hoped to unhinge the unpromising *status quo* in Franco-Vietnamese relations by at least startling Bao Dai out of his rigid stand. How the Cabinet, which was as divided as ever, gave its authorization to Bollaert's new plan is still a secret. He himself felt that he had the backing he needed. Back at Saigon, he startled the Vietminh more than Bao Dai by saying that France wanted a truce without victors or vanquished; he was ready to talk to all Vietnamese parties and groups.

Bollaert's new plan was based on the assumption that the Vietminh was keenly interested in ending hostilities and beginning negotiations with anyone the French chose, as long as they did not exclude the Hanoi regime. Feeling sure of this, Bollaert ordered a cease-fire without prior agreement with the Vietminh. It was to become effective on August 15.[31] Sealed orders to this effect were transmitted to all commanders in the field. On the same day, Bollaert intended to make a speech in which a representative of France, speaking of the future status of Vietnam, was for the first time to utter the word "independence."

But now, during the next few weeks, occurred an instance of "vacillation" of French policy that, better than anything else before, showed that in spite of all temporary liberal deviations, the course of military reconquest remained the one steady line of French conduct in Vietnam. Colonial society staged an uproar, fully supported by General Valluy, who claimed that the offensive he had prepared for the dry season would once and for all destroy the Vietminh. Now it was his turn to rush to Paris in order to alert the country, the Assembly, and the government against Bollaert's untimely project for a cease-fire. War Minister Coste-Floret and former Premier Georges Bidault vigorously supported General Valluy, denouncing the idea of seeking peace when at last the long-expected "military solution" was at hand. They won over the majority of the Cabinet, and the Socialists, unwilling to risk the life of the government, concurred. Premier Ramadier called Bollaert to Paris. The projected cease-fire was called off, and the speech in which France was to hold out the prospect of independence for Vietnam within the French Union never delivered.[32]

After this sorry episode, French policy toward the Ho Chi Minh Government reverted to what it had been before Bollaert went to Indochina. The idea of negotiations with the Vietminh was buried. On the political level, all stakes were henceforth put on Bao Dai. To persuade him, if necessary buy him, or maneuver him into a position that would force him to play the game of the French—this became Bollaert's rather degrading and unpromising task. The military counterpart of this "policy" was the expected destruction of the Vietminh. There would be more disputes, more skirmishes over Vietnam between the Left and the Right, the military, and some civilians, and more "hesitations and vacillations"; but nothing could alter the fact that from now on the only means by which the French hoped to regain control of Vietnam were force and intrigue.

On September 10, Bollaert, in a speech at Ha Dong, submitted the "new" French policy to the Vietnamese "parties and groups" whose cooperation against the Vietminh he sought to enlist. The truce, which some weeks ago he had regarded as a necessary condition for successful negotiations, was never mentioned. Instead of independence, he offered "liberty within the French Union." [33] "Liberty" meant that the army, diplomacy, the so-called "federal services" (customs, public works, immigration, the issuance of currency, etc.), and the federal budget would remain in French hands. The ethnic minorities were to have a "special status," which meant that the regions they inhabited would remain under direct French rule. Bollaert made much of what he thought was one generous French concession: Vietnam would regain her unity if the people of Cochinchina desired to rejoin Annam and Tongking—a promise already made in the March agreement; but even this concession was robbed of its possible value by the stipulation that the French High Commissioner for Indochina would act as the "arbiter" between the local governments of the three "regions" of Vietnam. And with an arrogance that showed how totally ignorant the French still were of the real mood of the Vietnamese people, Bollaert proclaimed that negotiations could not modify the French position: Since his offer was final, the Vietnamese had only the choice of either taking it or leaving it.

Bollaert's speech was an unforgettable lesson for all Vietnamese, whether pro- or anti-Vietminh. Since the French so adamantly refused to grant independence to the anti-Communist nationalists behind Bao Dai, it was evident that not Ho Chi Minh's Communism, but the determination of the French to remain masters of Vietnam was the cause of the Indochina War.

7

The first ones to express their disappointment with Bollaert's Ha Dong speech were the Vietminh. Their discontent, moderately formulated, was aroused not only by the nature of Bollaert's proposals; although the High Commissioner had addressed his appeal to "all spiritual and social families of Vietnam," the contents of his offer, as well as the preparations of the French for the fall offensive, made it clear that the idea of talks with the Vietminh had been dropped. In respect to the Hanoi regime, the French had decided to stake everything on force; the objects of their attempt to advance their cause by political means were henceforth the anti-Vietminh nationalists who, the French expected, would rally behind Bao Dai.

For Ho Chi Minh and his followers to be excluded from all further Franco-Vietnamese negotiations was, however, just another of several disappointments. The year 1947 had so far been one of great personal hardship and many political setbacks for these men. It was the first of the seven and a half years of all-out war. Driven from the relative comfort of Hanoi, Ho Chi Minh and his colleagues had to house themselves primitively in rugged mountain territories and inhospitable jungles. In order to escape capture—once French parachutists almost succeeded in taking the government prisoners [34]—they were forced to change their headquarters frequently and obliged to make a great many of the sacrifices that the war imposed upon the men whose lot it was to carry arms, hide in swamps, fight, and die. Ho Chi Minh never tried to dodge these sacrifices. On the contrary, he welcomed them as a simple duty. Even the necessity of sharing physical discomfort with his people was turned into a political weapon by this truly popular leader. What made life hard for these dedicated revolutionaries was not the hardships they had to endure but the reverses suffered.

Ho Chi Minh's main disappointments of the year 1947 were not in the military field. He had known before the war broke out, and had often said, that the struggle would be long and difficult. At first, he had said, the Vietnamese would lose ground and remain on the defensive for a long time. They would not be able to prevent the French from taking all major cities. But almost everywhere resistance had been surprisingly strong, and if the Vietminh had not been able to hold or destroy the cities themselves (with some exceptions, Vinh for instance), they had in most cases at least destroyed all their vital installations. The fighting in Hanoi, to the surprise of the French military, lasted until mid-February. It was only a rear-guard action, conducted chiefly by the militia (Tu Ve), but it enabled the Vietminh to complete the evacuation of their cadres and the removal of all important official documents, as well as of machinery and other means of production. The government and its auxiliaries retired into the old rebel country between the delta and the Chinese border known as the Viet Bac. This region was for the time being as inaccessible to the French as were the large Vietminh-held territories in northern Annam and their mountainous retreat south of Hue.

The loss of the cities and their immediate surroundings did not dishearten Ho Chi Minh. "We shall temporarily lose terrain," he stated soon after the outbreak of the war, "but we are determined not to lose the heart of the people." And he added prophetically: "Keeping the heart of the people gives us the certitude of regaining temporarily lost terrain." [35]

But unlike the military situation, which turned out as Ho Chi Minh had expected, developments in the political field blighted a great many Vietminh hopes. The outbreak of the war, although largely the result of systematic French provocations not entirely approved by Paris, failed to arouse pro-Vietnamese sentiments in France. On the contrary, metropolitan France reacted with more antagonism toward Ho Chi Minh than he had known existed. Public opinion echoed the reports of the press, which at that time were fabricated almost exclusively by colonial officials in Hanoi and Saigon. Not only the Socialists, the Communists too abstained from making Vietnam a central issue of French politics.

Equally distressing for Ho Chi Minh was the total lack of international recognition and support for his regime. By the beginning of 1947, the Vietminh leaders had lost even the moral comfort they had derived from the anticolonial feelings of the American officers stationed in North Vietnam after August, 1945. The United States was then still far from actively siding with the French; the defense of Southeast Asia was as yet not a pressing U.S. concern. But Washington also abstained from criticizing French policy in Vietnam, or from supporting the nationalist cause, as it did in the case of Indonesia. Secretary of State Marshall confined himself to expressing a noncommittal wish for an early return to peace.[36] A number of American journalists tried to convey their misgivings over the French policy of reconquest in Vietnam,[37] but it seemed that no strong anticolonial feelings could be aroused against the French among the American people, nor any sympathy for a country of whose problems very few Americans had any knowledge.

Nor did the Vietminh, already widely suspected of being Communist, receive the slightest encouragement from Labourite Britain. On the contrary, Foreign Minister Ernest Bevin stated in the House of Commons on February 12, 1947, that the problem of Indochina concerned only the French. The British, although they themselves answered Asian nationalism by preparing to withdraw from Burma and India, continued to sell some of their equipment in the Far East to the

French, knowing well that it was being used to crush the Vietnamese national revolution.

Recognition by the Soviet Union might have been a doubtful blessing for the Hanoi regime in 1947, but the lack of any Soviet support, moral or material, was a bitter pill for the Communists of Vietnam. Are we being punished, they must have asked themselves, because we decided on war rather than on surrender, without asking Stalin's advice? Stalin, indeed, was then still more concerned not to antagonize the French than to curry favor with the nationalists of a remote and apparently unimportant country, and more interested in strengthening the French Communist Party than in supporting an anti-French Vietnamese revolution. Contrary to her attitude in the case of Indonesia, the Soviet Union even abstained from putting the war in Vietnam before the United Nations.

On the home front, too, Ho Chi Minh suffered several disappointments, all of them related to the one problem for which his resourcefulness was unable to find a solution: No matter how many concessions he made to the non-Communist elements of the Vietminh, he could not remove the stigma of Communism from his government. Not that the accusation of Communism diminished his popularity among the people, but it severely limited his chances of mobilizing the entire nationalist movement, including his opponents, against the French. During July, 1947, when it looked as if Bao Dai might be persuaded to cooperate with the Vietminh, Ho Chi Minh drastically altered the composition of his government in favor of its non-Communist component. The Socialist Hoang Minh Giam was promoted to Foreign Minister, the Oxford-educated "independent" Ta Quang Buu became Minister of National Defense. The two most prominent Communists next to Ho Chi Minh, Vo Nguyen Giap and Pham Van Dong, were dropped from the Cabinet. A non-Communist Catholic was made Minister of Veterans and Invalids, while the important Ministry of the Interior was given to the former Imperial Delegate for Tongking, Phan Ke Toai.[38] (The venerable Huynh Thuc Khang, the former Minister of the Interior, had died.) In Cochinchina, too, the Committee of the South gave important functions to "official" Catholics, Buddhists, "independents," and dissident sect leaders who claimed to represent substantial Hoa Hao and Cao Dai groups. Ho Chi Minh even had Bao Dai reconfirmed as Supreme Counselor of the government.[39]

It was all in vain, since both the French and Bao Dai, although they used the threat of negotiations with the Vietminh against each other, were quite determined not to make common cause with Ho Chi Minh even for purely tactical reasons. In his struggle with the French, Bao Dai's position was identical with that of the Vietminh. Both insisted on unity and independence. But in his struggle with the Vietminh, Bao Dai's position gradually became identical with that of the French. The Vietminh, he and his advisers kept saying, was dominated by the Communists, and they represented only a small faction of the national movement; consequently the Hanoi regime was no longer a true representation of this movement, and since the insurrection of December, 1946, in fact no longer the legal government of Vietnam. Ho Chi Minh, therefore, had ceased to be the authorized spokesman of the country.

By accepting this French view of the government of Ho Chi Minh, the anti-Communist nationalists made their most serious political mistake. Bao Dai and his followers knew quite well that total Communist control of the armed resistance movement, although a danger, was as yet far from being a fact. But since their aims—replacement of the Hanoi Government—excluded a real compromise with the Vietminh, they began to denounce armed resistance against the French, if led by the Vietminh, as a plot to make Vietnam a Communist state. Denouncing resistance as Communist, however, also implied a condemnation of all non-Communist nationalists who fought in the ranks of the Vietminh. These nationalists were thus made into what they themselves, in taking up arms, had not chosen to be. Placed before the alternatives of renouncing armed resistance or continuing the fight led by the Hanoi Government, these people were virtually forced, precisely because of their uncompromising nationalism, to move closer and closer to the Communist heads of the Vietminh, who in the end did indeed achieve complete control of the entire resistance movement. Bao Dai and the French could later say that they had correctly anticipated what would happen. What matters, however, is not that they had foreseen this future, but that they had helped shape it. Once again anti-Communist policy turned more nationalists into Communists than were made by Communist propaganda.

In 1947, there still existed a good chance of preventing this transformation of nationalists into Communists or Communist sympathizers from becoming the dominant trend of Vietnam's political evolution. This required the creation of a non-Communist movement as firmly nationalist, as consistently anticolonial, as the Vietminh—an anti-French movement of resistance capable of attracting all non-Communists who were fighting with the Vietminh. Contemporary history offers no clearer evidence for the political ineffectiveness of anti-Communism as such than the failure of Bao Dai and his advisers to be as convincingly nationalist as the Vietminh. The only effective way of fighting Communism in Vietnam was to fight the French. A non-Communist movement against colonialism need not necessarily have restricted itself to armed resistance. Passive resistance, absolute noncooperation with the colonial regime, uncompromising insistence on unity and true independence, open acceptance of all the demands for which the Vietminh Government fought—all nationalists could have agreed on that, and it might well have been a program for rallying all those who still preferred Communist leadership to giving up the struggle against the French. Only in its positive manifestation as militant nationalism could anti-Communism have become politically effective.

This is not to say that such a course could without fail have undone the progress Communism had made in Vietnam before and after 1945, nor that it would have been without danger for the non-Communist national leaders. Popular sentiment strongly favored the Vietminh; it would have forced any other truly nationalist movement to cooperate with the Hanoi regime, and only if led by men who were a match for the Vietminh could anti-Communist nationalism have survived such cooperation. The Communists, relying on past experience, were confident that any alliance with other nationalists would turn to their advantage. This is why Ho Chi Minh encouraged Bao Dai's temporary penchant for militant nationalism, expecting that this would force his antagonist to become an ally of the Vietminh and as such end up sharing the fate of all Vietminh allies. But it did not upset Ho Chi Minh that Bao Dai was careful not to respond to his wooing. What disturbed him was that it seemed that Bao Dai rejected the Vietminh as a true nationalist, and not because he was eager to cooperate with the French. During 1947, it looked for several months as if the former Emperor would on his own raise the banner of anticolonialism and initiate a movement of noncooperation with the French. If this had come about, the monopoly of militant anticolonialism enjoyed by the Vietminh would have been seriously threatened. The pity of it was that in the end Ho Chi Minh's fears of Bao Dai as a nationalist rival turned out to be unfounded. Bao Dai would very much have liked to force the

French into granting Vietnam independence, thus depriving Ho Chi Minh of the glory of fulfilling the country's manifest destiny; but he lacked the particular talents needed to achieve this end. Bao Dai was an adroit tactician and not without a measure of perseverance. As a spokesman of his nation, he was frequently eloquent and for a long time sincerely concerned. But he was by temperament neither a political leader nor a determined fighter and therefore quite unfit for the tough job of heading his people in their struggle for national liberation.

8

The weakness of Bao Dai's stand, which during the summer of 1947 had been well concealed by firm political declarations, became apparent soon after Bollaert's speech at Ha Dong on September 10.[40] The speech was of course a great disappointment for Bao Dai and his entourage, but although Bollaert had accepted none of the conditions made by Bao Dai for assuming the role the French wanted him to play against the Vietminh, cooperation on the terms of the French was rejected in surprisingly mild language.

The reason for this was more than merely Bao Dai's lack of firmness when faced with a real test. By the beginning of September, the disoriented and bitterly divided forces of anti-Vietminh nationalism had begun to regard Bao Dai as the bright star who might lead them out of the political desert into which they had been cast by the success of the Vietminh. Men as antagonistic to each other as were the collaborator Le Van Hoach and the stubborn dissident Ngo Dinh Diem traveled to Hong Kong in the hope of winning Bao Dai over to their views on how to deal with the French and effectively oppose the Vietminh. There existed as yet no organized movement in support of Bao Dai, and no agreement on the conditions of cooperation with the French beyond the demand, now raised by all who desired to play a role, that Vietnam be given independence. A few dozen ambitious men, many of whom claimed to represent "parties," offered to support Bao Dai, some urging him to stand firm, but the greater number pleading with him to grasp whatever opportunity might arise for action. Claiming, against massive evidence, that theirs was the voice of the people, they urged Bao Dai to drop his calculated reserve (which was a composite of tactical shrewdness and fear of action); they were convinced that in him

they had at last found the key to a life of dignified and promising political activity. They jumped on his bandwagon before it had started
rolling, giving conflicting advice to a man reluctant to command.

Bao Dai's defects as a nationalist leader were soon made obvious by
the doubtful caliber of the men who rallied to his support. After all, it
was he who selected his following by refusing to reject the many discredited and incompetent "leaders" who spoke for no one but themselves. The first ones to prepare themselves for a return into officialdom under Bao Dai were the spokesmen of the moribund VNQDD and
of the Dong Minh Hoi who had fled to China. At a conference in
Nanking in February, 1947, they founded a United National Front; at
another conference, held at Canton in March, they decided to withhold
all further support from the Vietminh Government and to place themselves under Bao Dai's direction.[41] Only three months after their call
to armed resistance they indicated their willingness to cooperate, behind Bao Dai, with the French, who, six months earlier, had assisted the
Vietminh in their political elimination. Cooperation with the French
was, of course, made dependent upon "equality and independence,"
which, however, was not to be had before armed resistance had defeated the French. This the few remaining adherents of these parties in
the country knew better than their leaders. They consequently continued to fight the French. There existed at that time many local nationalist authorities over which the Vietminh had no control and who,
without direction from any anti-Vietminh national leadership, defied
both the Vietminh and the French.[42]

The United National Front of these exiles was a poor beginning for
an organized popular movement behind Bao Dai, but at least it consisted of men who had so far refused to collaborate with the French.
Soon afterward, another United National Front arose in Cochinchina,
this one promoted chiefly by men who either were, or were preparing
to become, collaborators of the French. Its guiding spirits were
Nguyen Van Sam, head of a "Social Democratic" group supported
chiefly by members of the Hoa Hao sect, and Tran Van Tuyen,
former chief of cabinet for the VNQDD leader Nguyen Tuong Tam
while the latter was Foreign Minister under Ho Chi Minh. This United
National Front consisted of the Cao Dai and Hoa Hao, most of whose
factions had by that time completed their transition from resistance to
cooperation with the French; of the small remaining VNQDD groups
(the Dong Minh Hoi had virtually ceased to exist in the country); of

some Buddhist sects and the usual number of ephemeral national "parties" whose quarreling leaders always outnumbered their actual membership. (The Binh Xuyen sect had not yet made its peace with the French; it joined the Bao Dai camp only much later, but then gave the ex-Emperor, for a high price, his strongest organized support.)

On August 18, a conference of this United National Front held with French blessing sent a telegram to Bao Dai asking him to return to Vietnam. But as a "voice of the people," this organization, based mainly on the sects, carried little weight with Bao Dai, who knew that most sect leaders were questionable proponents of the national cause. Both the Hoa Hao and the Cao Dai were more interested in concluding their own special deals with the French than in using their influence to extract from them the national concessions demanded by Bao Dai. This became quite evident in January, 1948, when the sects signed agreements with the French giving them full administrative control of vast Cochinchinese regions in exchange for their promise to fight the Vietminh. Besides, the sects, dependent both on popular support and on arms and money from the French, were constantly torn by internal conflicts over policy. Their divisions and frequent changes of tactics made them devious collaborators with the French, erratic supporters of Bao Dai, and at times also unreliable opponents of the Vietminh.[43]

Bao Dai's most loyal supporters were the royalist mandarins of Annam and Tongking, whose chief weakness, however, was their lack of popular support. The most prominent among them had been led into collaboration with the French by their hatred for the Vietminh long before Bao Dai had proclaimed that collaboration was contingent on vital political concessions. Their spokesmen actually headed the so-called Administrative Committees of Annam and Tongking set up to camouflage direct French rule. In Tongking, this was Truong Dinh Tri, formerly a VNQDD member of Ho Chi Minh's Cabinet; in Annam it was the prominent Catholic Tran Van Ly. Outside of Cochinchina, these two men, who consistently opposed talks with the Vietminh, were the most active proponents of a national government headed by Bao Dai. Others in Annam and Tongking, less inclined toward collaboration, listened to the advice of the Catholic Ngo Dinh Diem, whose chief concern was to keep Bao Dai from abandoning his firm nationalist position. Diem spoke for the majority of Vietnam's Catholics, who had so far refused to be drawn into either collaboration with the French or an aggressive attitude toward the Vietminh. This position was unmistakably expressed by the cautious attitude which the bishops of the Catholic provinces Phat Diem and Bui Chu in Tongking adopted toward the government of Ho Chi Minh.[44] For a long time, these provinces, which the Catholics later defended with their own militia, remained unmolested by Vietminh guerrillas.

But against these restraining influences rose the mounting pressure of all active and would-be collaborators, including the discredited separatists who had cooperated with d'Argenlieu in creating the Republic of Cochinchina. Since these men knew what they wanted, and since their aim was to get Bao Dai moving, they were infinitely more active than those who warned Bao Dai against premature steps. Outstanding among these gravediggers of anti-Communist nationalism were the two leading separatists, Le Van Hoach, still head of the Republic of Cochinchina, representing politically the Cao Dai, and Nguyen Van Xuan, whom the French in the meantime had promoted from colonel to general—the first Vietnamese to achieve this rank. Since Xuan spent most of his time in Paris, he very likely still had not learned to speak Vietnamese, but since he owed his political weight entirely to the French, he did not feel that his language deficiency disqualified him as a spokesman for the Vietnamese people. As soon as it became clear that the French considered dropping Cochinchinese separatism in favor of a national anti-Vietminh regime, Xuan returned to Saigon, and in a repulsive show of opportunism transformed himself from separatist into nationalist. Then he rushed to Hong Kong, where he had been preceded by his rival Le Van Hoach, who was also trying to become a national leader without, however, entirely renouncing the cause of separatism of which he was still the official spokesman. Xuan was able to exploit Hoach's somewhat embarrassing position. He forced his rival to resign from the government, and after making himself President of the Republic of Cochinchina on October 1, offered Bao Dai to liquidate separatism in exchange for a leading role in a national government. He began by dropping the name "Government of the Autonomous Republic of Cochinchina" in favor of "Government of South Vietnam."

This slippery salesman of his own mercurial convictions nevertheless continued to serve the French; he created his new image as a spokesman for the entire nation with their open approval, and since the French preferred him to anyone else as the chief promoter of Bao Dai, they allowed him the widest possible latitude for political maneuvers.

Xuan even indicated, at a time when French tactics had not yet precluded talks with Ho Chi Minh, that he would be glad to serve as arbiter between Bao Dai, the Vietminh, and the French; but after the French dropped the idea, he quickly denounced talks with Ho Chi Minh as a surrender of "freedom" to Communism.

Le Van Hoach, after his ouster from the government of Cochinchina, devoted himself to a task which he considered vital both to the creation of a Bao Dai regime and to its political effectiveness against the Vietminh: the organization of a "popular basis" for a national government. As a leader of the Cao Dai movement to which the French had had to make concessions, Hoach knew that without organized popular support, Bao Dai could be no more than a puppet of the French. What Hoach did not know was that popular support for a national regime could crystallize only if its proponents, and above all Bao Dai, fought as adamantly for independence as did the Vietminh. Hoach thought it was enough to unite all existing anti-Vietminh groups, factions, and personalities under one roof, and to create strength not by overcoming, but simply by combining their manifest political inadequacies. The National Union which he founded at the end of 1947, and which absorbed the various national fronts that had preceded it, indeed exercised no greater attraction than had its constituent members before they united behind Bao Dai. They were the Hoa Hao and Cao Dai, the remnants of the VNQDD, the deeply divided Dai Viet, and some loosely organized Buddhist and Catholic groups. Even Ngo Dinh Diem, "for the first and only time, joined a party of which he was not the founder." [45]

But even before this fragile coalition of discredited collaborators, ambitious masters of intrigue, incompetent sectarians, and a smattering of honest leaders without a following had created this "popular base" for their crusade against the Vietminh, Bao Dai, in a moment of weakness he soon came to regret, took the first step on the slippery road of capitulation.

9

In order to understand the fixed resolve of the French, expressed by Bollaert at Ha Dong, to refuse Bao Dai even the prospect of eventual independence, one must remember that General Valluy's offensive to end Vietminh resistance was then in the last stages of preparation.[46] It was to begin in October, and even the least sanguine among the French expected it to produce, if not the collapse of the Vietminh, at least a marked improvement of the French position. Since Bao Dai's bargaining power depended entirely on the French need for his political support, a real defeat of the Vietminh meant that Bao Dai would indeed have either to take or to leave what Bollaert had proposed at Ha Dong.

In three interviews given to the Saigon press by Bao Dai's spokesman, Tran Van Tuyen, during the month of August,[47] the former Emperor had not retreated an inch from his earlier position: He would return to Vietnam to head an anti-Vietminh government only if the French agreed to his demands for unity and independence. But both he and his leading supporters, although fully aware of the danger of concessions on these issues, also knew that an absolute rejection of all French proposals short of full independence threatened to deprive them of any role whatsoever in the struggle between the French and the Vietminh. Their dilemma was caused not only by their wish to play a role but also by genuine political concern. Those driven by naked ambition saw only the dangers of inactivity and political isolation; those whose ambition was tempered by a desire to advance the national cause warned against totally separating anti-Communist nationalism from the men who fought the French. They all knew that they were the instrument of a French scheme, which, if they let it succeed, could only render them more helpless against Vietminh propaganda. But they were, and remained forever, divided on how this scheme could be turned to their own advantage, how to inject into the movement for Bao Dai the life it still lacked, and whether or not to compromise if the French should reject their basic demands of unity and independence. What divided them was not doctrine or the programs of established parties under collective leaderships. There were no such parties. Most of these men were responsible to no one; they fought only their personal battles, unrestrained by obligations toward organized groups holding democratically arrived at positions. Their differences were differences of temperament, of intellectual ability, of degrees of ambition, and of skill in promoting themselves. In competing for the places in a future government headed by Bao Dai, the anti-Communist nationalists displayed, as they would again and again, their tragic inability to subordinate these differences to the common purpose of serving the national cause.

When Bollaert made his well-advertised speech at Ha Dong, a great many of these anti-Communist nationalists were gathered at Hong Kong around Bao Dai. For one obvious reason, they were not all nationalists of the purest gold: Those who came from Vietnam had to have passports and Hong Kong dollars issued to them by the French. Yet among them were some well-known nationalists, such as the head of the then still existing National Front, Nguyen Van Sam, the Cao Dai leader Tran Quang Vinh, and the journalist Nguyen Van Long, all three from Saigon; there also were the heads of the Administrative Committees of Annam and Tongking, Tran Van Ly from Hue and Truong Dinh Tri from Hanoi, the former speaking for the Catholics, the other for the VNQDD. This party was represented also by its exiled leaders Nguyen Hai Than and Nguyen Tuong Tam, who had come from China. Present also were Bao Dai's counselors Dinh Xuan Quang and Phan Huy Dan, the latter a self-styled Social Democrat who had proposed a Bao Dai government against the Vietminh long before the French took up the idea. It was a gathering of nationalists who in spite of their shortcomings still had "the means of limiting the power of the Marxists, provided they were given a chance to prove that a policy of understanding with France was possible and worthwhile." [48]

Since they had sense enough to see that Bollaert's proposals denied them this chance, their immediate reaction to them was deep disappointment. The men in exile went back to China, their hopes gone that the French would let them return to Vietnam and give them the weapons they needed to fight the Vietminh. Nguyen Van Sam's National Front at Saigon quickly decided to reject Bollaert's ultimatum. Only the moderate nationalists around the former Emperor who were sworn and uncompromising enemies of the Vietminh were cold-blooded enough to reject Bollaert's conditions without entirely renouncing the idea of a political mission for Bao Dai. Upon their advice, Bao Dai, on September 18, issued a proclamation in which he stated (under the pretext of complying with a request of the Vietnamese people to arbitrate the conflict) his willingness to enter into contact with the French. True, he repeated his demands for unity and independence, calling them the ideals for which the resistance was fighting; nevertheless, his failure to slam the door in the face of the French who had so plainly rejected his demands was the first crack in the armor of his resistance. He widened this crack with gratuitous statements against the Vietminh, whose destruction the French kept predicting, but whose ruin, Bao Dai must have known, would have been also the end of his hopes for concessions by the French: With nothing to fear any longer from armed Vietminh resistance, the French would hardly have felt the need to continue to woo Bao Dai.

The leaders of the Bao Dai movement, whether men of principle or mere addicts of expediency, now found themselves in a serious predicament. Their difficulties increased when Valluy's offensive against the Vietminh led to some initial success in October, but by the end of November its only decisive results were to be found in the communiqués of the French: The anti-Communists wanted the Vietminh to be defeated, but realizing that the French had use for them only as long as the Vietminh remained strong, they also wanted the French offensive to fail. What they would have liked was both the French offensive to fail, yet the Vietminh to be defeated. The end of the Vietminh should come after its opponents had won independence from France, and as a result of it.

This predicament naturally paralyzed the honest nationalists more than the born opportunists, who now became the more active wing of the Bao Dai camp. Spearheaded by Le Van Hoach and Nguyen Van Xuan, the clique of hardened collaborators, urged and assisted by the French, battled in Hong Kong to win over Bao Dai, while the French fought in Tongking to get rid of Ho Chi Minh. Neither struggle was won, but the French, who soon learned that their military offensive against Ho Chi Minh had failed, were not entirely unsuccessful in their campaign to win Bao Dai. At a new conference held in Hong Kong on September 24, Bollaert's offer was again rejected, but at the request of the collaborators the door was left open with an invitation to Bao Dai to seek a political solution of the Franco-Vietnamese conflict. As a result, Bao Dai, after much hesitation, agreed to meet Bollaert to see whether the French had anything new to offer. The meeting took place aboard a French warship in the Bay of Along on December 7. Bao Dai had been told by his counselors only to listen and under no circumstances to sign any binding document without a firm French promise of independence. But signing a "protocol" specifying the conditions for collaboration was precisely what he did. The concessions France made and Bao Dai accepted on this day fell so far short of true independence that even the keenest advocates of a Bao Dai government told him that he had seriously jeopardized his cause. Since Bao Dai was

no fool, nobody quite understood why he signed a statement that was
denounced not only by Ngo Dinh Diem, but also by a shrewd collaborator like General Xuan, a man quite willing to sell out, but not for
nothing. It is not likely that Bao Dai was already "bought" at this early
stage, since he regretted his act and in fact did not live up to his commitment. Perhaps Bollaert really had, as Lacouture and Devillers suggest, "taken him by surprise." [49]

Ngo Dinh Diem and the head of the Administrative Committee of
Annam, Tran Van Ly, persuaded Bao Dai to extricate himself from
this embarrassing situation by raising new demands, such as the immediate dissolution of the Cochinchinese Government in favor of an Administrative Committee for the South, as a first step in reunifying the
country.

It seems unbelievable that the French lacked the sense to comply
with this simple request and thus hold Bao Dai in the net in which
Bollaert had caught him. Since no other concessions were made either,
Bao Dai, in order to avoid being held to his commitment, decided to
remove himself from the scene. At the end of December, 1947, he left
Hong Kong for Europe. Thus began his peregrinations, a combination
of both pleasure trips and flights. He went first to Geneva, with
Bollaert right on his heels, and soon afterward to Paris. There, the
difficulties the French, and in particular Bollaert, had in catching up
with him increased with the number of places of amusement he visited.
(It is still not known who was paying his expenses.) Bollaert arranged
for a new meeting on February 13 at the Bay of Along, but Bao Dai
simply did not show up. It was then that Bao Dai acquired the epithets
"unreachable mediator" [50] and "night club emperor," [51] the latter a
misnomer: Bao Dai had not only freely abdicated as emperor; one of
the reasons for amusing himself in Paris was his refusal to accept the
French conditions for again making him emperor.

Bao Dai's undeniably compulsive quest for pleasure was not the main
reason that he was in Paris and remained reluctant to negotiate with
the French. He had gone there chiefly to see for himself what forces
determined French policy in Indochina and what chances they offered
for cooperation under conditions he could accept. He did not at all like
what he saw. In November, 1947, France again got a new government,
in which a shift to the Right that affected Indochina became evident in
the leading positions held by the procolonial MRP. Both the new Premier (Schuman) and the Minister of Overseas Affairs (Coste-Floret)

were members of the MRP. It was this government that made the policy
of no negotiations with the Vietminh official, by publishing, on December 23, 1947, an order to High Commissioner Bollaert "to carry on,
outside the Ho Chi Minh Government, all activities and negotiations
necessary for the restoration of peace and freedom in the Vietnamese
countries." [52] "Peace," without negotiations with the Vietminh, could
of course mean only winning the war, and "freedom," Bao Dai had
known since December 7, meant his return as the head of an anti-
Vietminh government with Vietnam still under French control. There
was also talk of a further increase of rightist strength in new elections.
General de Gaulle's Rally of the French People was by many expected
to form the next government. Its ultracolonial position was to reject
any agreements of its predecessors that undermined the position of
France in Indochina. Although the Schuman Government was definitely
committed to what came to be known as the Bao Dai solution, the man
on whose consent its realization depended, when he left Paris for Hong
Kong in March, 1948, had little hope that this solution, if it ever
came about, would be a decisive step toward the liberation of Vietnam.

During Bao Dai's stay in Europe, between December and March, little could be done in Vietnam to break the impasse in Franco-Vietnamese
relations his flight from Hong Kong had created. But his followers, whose impatience kept growing, were by no means idle. Le Van
Hoach proceeded to put together the so-called National Union, composed of groups and people all of whom claimed to be better nationalists, better anti-Communists, and more loyal followers of Bao Dai than
any of their rivals, besides enjoying more popular support. It was a
sorry beginning for a movement created to supply a popular basis for a
national government, something needed both to resist the French and
to reduce the power of the Vietminh. But it constituted progress in
one direction: although primarily an anti-Vietminh formation, the National Union gave little comfort to the French. For fear of losing their
small following to the resistance, which had by the end of December,
1947, demonstrated that it could not easily be destroyed, the groups
inside the National Union competed both with one another and with
the Vietminh in verbal expressions of nationalist militancy. This was
true even of old collaborators. The more intelligent separatists like
Xuan and Hoach, for instance, now proclaimed that unity of Vietnam
was an absolutely indispensable condition for any kind of Franco-
Vietnamese collaboration.

Some of these people, however, expressed their new nationalist fervor out of fear not only of being entirely cut off from the people, but also out of fear for their lives. The Vietminh, faced with the efforts of the collaborators and other opponents to create a movement for independence directed against their government, reacted vigorously as soon as Bao Dai discarded the idea of a common front with Ho Chi Minh. Anyone who worked for a deal with the French to the exclusion of the country's legal government was branded a traitor to the nation and threatened with execution. To give credence to this threat, the Vietminh formally pronounced death sentences against two men actively engaged in promoting a Bao Dai–French deal. They were the founder of the first pro-Bao Dai National Front in Saigon, Nguyen Van Sam, and the head of the Administrative Committee for Tongking, Truong Dinh Tri. At the end of October, 1947, Vietminh agents in Saigon and Hanoi killed both within twenty-four hours.

In March, however, after Bao Dai returned to Hong Kong, the feeling that something had to be tried, that one could not just wait until the French were ready to grant full independence, began to dominate the political thinking of most followers of Bao Dai. On the French side, too, a desire to break the deadlock, if necessary with some sort of new concessions, was transmitted to Bao Dai by an increasingly impatient Bollaert. A full year had passed since the French had decided to use Bao Dai as their chief political weapon against Ho Chi Minh, but no visible progress had been made in the realization of this scheme.[53] The matter was now the more urgent, since the first great attempt to destroy the Vietminh militarily was known to have failed.

But the key to a solution was Bao Dai. Exposed again to pressures from the French and to appeals from his countrymen, he would hardly be able to defer a decision for long. The hour to prove himself, and to show that he was ready to fight against both colonialism and Communism, was now at hand.

10

Bao Dai unfortunately lacked the strength of his royal ancestors. The year 1948 brought the gradual erosion of his resistance; 1949, its collapse. It is possible that the task history required of this man was beyond the powers of any human being. It was not beyond Bao Dai's intelligence to realize that he was being used, yet to say no and thereby prevent the exploitation of his name required strength, a quality nature had denied him. During 1948 and up to the spring of 1949, Bao Dai continued to fight, sometimes bravely and skillfully, only to give up his struggle, in a mood of self-destructive resignation, by giving in to the French and the collaborators in his camp.

The taming of Bao Dai went through three stages. First, soon after his return to Hong Kong, he endorsed the formation of a national government without having obtained independence. Second, on June 5, 1948, he approved the so-called Bay of Along agreement of Franco-Vietnamese cooperation against the Vietminh concluded with High Commissioner Bollaert. And third, in spring, 1949, he consented to return to Vietnam as head of the state, although he recognized that the independence France had by then twice formally granted was a blatant deception.

The French obtained Bao Dai's endorsement of an anti-Vietminh government by a move that can be described only as shady. They sent an emissary, Louis Caput, a French Socialist known as an opponent of the Bao Dai solution, to Hong Kong and leaked the "information" that he was to establish official contacts with the Vietminh. No negotiations were intended, and Caput never even saw a representative of the Hanoi Government. The purpose of his trip, apparently unknown to Caput himself,[54] was merely to frighten Bao Dai and his supporters—a maneuver that was highly successful. The entire Bao Dai camp was gripped by fear of a new Franco-Vietminh deal that would put an end to its own political aspirations. Instead of fighting back by threatening to make common cause with the Vietminh,[55] most Bao Dai-nationalists, dissatisfied with their chief's procrastinations, began to look for a way out of the impasse created by their rejection of the "protocol" of December, 1947, which Bao Dai had signed but later disavowed.[56] Still unwilling to commit himself on this basis, Bao Dai tried to obtain better conditions for collaboration from the French, but Ngo Dinh Diem, whom he sent to Saigon on March 30 to negotiate with Bollaert, returned with empty hands.

Bao Dai's more impatient supporters decided on a strategy that would allow them to act without initially involving the ex-Emperor. They were ready to accept what the French were now willing to offer, hoping for more later, when it became evident that without Bao Dai the French scheme could never succeed. At a conference in Hong

Kong on April 29, it was decided, in the presence of the heads of the Administrative Committees of Tongking and Annam, and of the Government of Cochinchina, to form a provisional central government, which, once constituted, would begin to liquidate Cochinchinese separatism. Bollaert agreed to seek the consent of Paris for this project, but insisted that Bao Dai endorse this government and countersign any agreement between it and the French, who by then had decided to make the concession of using the word "independence" to describe the status of Vietnam vis-à-vis France. The real content of such an agreement, however, would still be the formerly rejected "protocol" of December, 1947, which the men who insisted on forming an anti-Vietminh government were now obliged to accept. They had thus maneuvered themselves into the ridiculous situation of having to obtain French permission for doing what Bollaert had urged Bao Dai for a full year to tell them to do.

The government to be formed under these conditions could not be in the hands of upright anticolonialists. Men like Ngo Dinh Diem refused not only to join it but even to endorse it. With Bao Dai's blessing, General Xuan, the most notorious of all collaborators in the anti-Vietminh camp, became its head. Xuan had known even when he first became head of the Cochinchinese Republic that separatism would be dropped once the French got a central Vietnamese government to their liking. Xuan obtained his "mandate" from a "congress" of about forty people he had managed to assemble in Saigon and to whom he was able to show a letter from Bao Dai asking him to form a provisional central government. On May 27, he was able to present his government to Bao Dai in Hong Kong.[57] Paris only "took notice" of its formation, and Bao Dai, without whose consent the Xuan Government could not have come into existence, had second thoughts. He issued a declaration in which he made it clear that this government could not act in his name. And he still refused to return to Vietnam.[58]

Bao Dai would also have liked to avoid being involved with the treaty on which the French and the Xuan Government based their collaboration. But this Paris and Bollaert would not permit. On June 5, 1948, the High Commissioner and General Xuan met in the Bay of Along to sign in Bao Dai's presence the agreement through which France, publicly and "solemnly," recognized the independence of Vietnam.[59] However, the solemnity of this promise in no way made up for its hollowness. The army and diplomacy were to remain in

French hands, while the transfer of governmental authority in other fields was envisaged only on the basis of separate accords to be concluded later. The protocol containing the stipulations that made this independence a gesture without practical significance remained secret.[60]

Bao Dai, loath to enter into any further commitments, again removed himself from the scene. On the evening of June 5, he hurriedly departed for Europe. In a letter to Bollaert on July 11, he dissociated himself openly from the Bay of Along agreement, saying that he had been present only as a "witness" at its signing. The agreement, he added, could not bring peace to Vietnam and could not serve as a basis for a lasting understanding between the French and the Vietnamese people. Bollaert's inability to enlist Bao Dai against Ho Chi Minh without meaningful French concessions became evident in a final interview between the two men at Saint-Germain on August 25. The ex-Emperor once more stated that he would return to Vietnam only after the liquidation of the separatist regime in Cochinchina and after receiving adequate guarantees of real independence for Vietnam.

The Bay of Along agreement briefly raised hopes among many anti-Vietminh nationalists for an improvement of their political fortunes, since it was they who had at last extracted the promise of independence from France. If this promise had been kept, the agreement might indeed have become a "turning point" for Vietnam, as some observers expected.[61] Some of the many non-Communists fighting under Vietminh leadership were said to have left the *maquis*, which they had joined not out of love of Ho Chi Minh but in order to force the French into granting independence. For a while it looked as if the Communists had reason to fear that their hold over all nationalists determined to fight the French would be broken. Thanks to French duplicity, this fear lasted only a few weeks. By the end of August, 1948, it could no longer be doubted that the creation of the Xuan Government and the Bay of Along agreement had not in the least advanced the project with which Bollaert, in spring, 1947, had hoped to mobilize Vietnamese nationalist energies against the Vietminh. The establishment of a central government, which was announced from Hanoi on June 6, brought no increase at all in anti-Vietminh sentiment. It was greeted with indifference by the people who recognized it as "nothing but a trick." [62] And it did not lead to more unity, but rather to increased dissension among the nationalists opposed to the Vietminh.

The government was headed by a discredited collaborator whom no one trusted and no one liked; it lacked not only popular support, but also Bao Dai's approval; it was prevented by French sabotage from exercising any important governmental functions and from realizing the promise of independence and of national unity contained in the Bay of Along agreement. It was government without moral authority, without finances, without an army, a government over which the French civil service retained full control.

For all these reasons the Xuan Government, although a tool of the French, was politically useless to them, and of no value whatsoever to the Vietnamese national cause. On the contrary, its formation was just another step toward the ruin of anti-Communist nationalism. As Devillers put it: "In those few weeks, the French pulled the rug from under the anti-Communist nationalists." [63] Ho Chi Minh had been on safe ground when, on June 7, he denounced the Xuan Government as a puppet of the French. He declared that the government and the people of the Democratic Republic of Vietnam considered "null and void any document signed by these puppets with any foreign country." [64] Xuan was tried by the Vietminh "in accordance with national laws" and sentenced to death. Because the discredit Xuan brought on anti-Communist nationalism could only benefit the Vietminh, no efforts were made to execute this sentence.

The main reason for the ineffectiveness of the Xuan Government was the French reaction, both in Indochina and France, to the Bay of Along agreement. On the part of the Schuman Government, this reaction was a case both of indecision and duplicity. In defending the agreement before the Assembly, Minister of Overseas Affairs Paul Coste-Floret stated on June 8 that France was not firmly committed either to independence or to unity. Cochinchina was still a French colony. Its status could be changed only by the French legislature. The agreement did not constitute automatic French recognition of Vietnamese unity. The government would wait and see before taking action on this issue. And it was, of course, decided to maintain French control of diplomacy and national defense. Not until August 19 did the High Commissioner obtain ratification of the agreement and open support of his action by the French Government, which was no longer headed by Schuman but by the Radical André Marie. The Radicals, although not much more eager than the MRP to comply with the agreement, did not want to repudiate their party colleague Bollaert.

This attitude of the French Government, and a campaign by the rightist parties and the colonialist press against "betraying the interests of France in Indochina" [65] greatly encouraged those Frenchmen in Vietnam who were both determined and in a position to sabotage both the transfer of authority to the Xuan Government and the liquidation of the separatist regime in Cochinchina. The heads of the French services were "in no hurry to abandon their administrative powers," [66] and the beneficiaries of separatism, whether French or Vietnamese, knew themselves more in harmony with Paris than with Bollaert in delaying the dissolution of the government of Cochinchina. Under the leadership of Tran Van Huu, the old rival and successor of Xuan as the head of the separatist government, they effectively opposed all attempts to extend the central government's authority over Cochinchina.[67] The cities of Hanoi, Haiphong, and Tourane (now Danang), which were French enclaves, were understood to remain outside of Vietnamese control. Directly administered by the French were also the "autonomous regions" of the South inhabited by the various tribes of *montagnards* created under d'Argenlieu. With the same end in mind, the French in March, 1948, had established an "autonomous" federation of the Thai peoples in the North over which the Xuan Government had no authority either. It was in fact a government that governed nowhere since, due to rivalries in the nationalist camp and French connivance, the Administrative Committees of Annam and Tongking also remained outside the control of the central government. No wonder that Xuan had trouble finding ministers, that many left his government after brief service, and that no firm and respected nationalist joined any of the governments created later in the name of Bao Dai.

A nationalist opposed to the Bao Dai solution, Dr. Phan Quang Dan, later described the role that the members of all "national" governments set up to combat the Vietminh were expected to play. Dan tells of a visit he paid to the then Minister of the National Budget, Dinh Xuan Quang, who was also Minister of Health. "The entire Ministry of Budget had only one room, and the personnel consisted of only one clerk. When I entered [the Minister] was reading newspapers. He said: 'I know nothing of Public Health. As they do not find anybody willing to be Minister of Health, they appointed me as interim Minister. As for the Vietnamese National Budget, the French take care of that. So I come to my office just to read newspapers!' " [68]

It is not surprising that a great many of those who agreed to enter these governments were motivated more by a desire to fill their pockets quickly than by an urge to serve their country.[69]

11

The Xuan Government, although useless to the French and damaging to anti-Vietminh nationalism, was allowed to survive a full year. It took this long until the stagnation in Franco-Vietnamese relations caused by the establishment of this "government" was overcome in favor of the ardently pursued genuine Bao Dai solution. This year was also the second one in which the French made no progress in the war against the Vietminh.

Behind the delay in bringing about the Bao Dai solution was a complex of diverse French and Vietnamese attitudes indicative of a widespread doubt about the political effectiveness of this "solution." The treatment accorded by the French to the government they desired to use against the Vietminh deeply discouraged all true anti-Vietminh nationalists and even some of the more intelligent collaborators: What hope was there of rallying the people behind Bao Dai if the French, instead of allowing him to return as a national hero, insisted on destroying "whatever prestige the man still had whom they wanted to oppose to the Vietminh?" [70] The ardor of these people for the Bao Dai solution diminished, and with it their pressure upon the ex-Emperor to reconsider his refusal to return to Vietnam. In Saigon the journalist Nguyen Phan Long, a future premier, vigorously attacked the Xuan Government in the *Echo du Viet Nam*, emphasizing that Xuan would fail in regard to the most urgent issue: bringing about peace in Vietnam. In Paris, Buu Hoi, claiming to speak for the entire royal family, warned the French early in 1949 against erecting and supporting "artificial governments"; it was idle to expect that they could attract popular support. It was at this time that Buu Hoi's father, Ung Uy, a great-grandson of Emperor Minh Mang, went to live in the Vietminh zone.

On the French side, doubts and reservations, and even open opposition against the Bao Dai solution could be heard from many directions —counting neither the Communists, who considered Ho Chi Minh the only man qualified to speak for the Vietnamese people, nor colonial society and its allies, who opposed making concessions to Bao Dai as vehemently as they had opposed making them to Ho Chi Minh. Also, within and close to the fragile coalition that governed France, there were people whose position, although based on opposite premises, had the combined effect of putting a brake on the men who still favored the Bao Dai solution. The Socialists began to reject it. "Negotiations with Bao Dai," wrote the party's secretary, Guy Mollet, in January, 1949, "cannot lead to an accord with the people of Vietnam. . . . The ex-Emperor does not enjoy any authority in the country." [71] The spokesmen of the Right, on the other hand, opposed Bao Dai because of his rigid insistence on unity and independence. Between these two fires, the government, no longer led by André Marie, but since September, 1948, by his party colleague Henri Queuille, chose the trodden path of indecision. It was the fourth French government since the hatching of the scheme to use Bao Dai against Ho Chi Minh under Premier Ramadier. The Cabinet's tendency to postpone decisions was unexpectedly endorsed by the still authoritative voice of General de Gaulle, who, asserting once more his role as a false prophet in regard to Indochina, stated at a press conference on November 17, 1948, that time was working for France. "The true rule to observe at this moment in Indochina," he said, "is not to rush anything. We must know how to take our time. . . . Sooner or later the French solution will have to be accepted." [72] In trying to force Bao Dai's hand and to justify their refusal to unify Vietnam and transfer authority to the Xuan Government, the French continued to use the formula that decisive steps could be taken only after Bao Dai himself had become the head of an anti-Vietminh government. There was hardly a day when officials and the press did not tell Bao Dai that he must go home and head the government of Vietnam. His answer was to spend more and more time on the Riviera.

One consequence of this new impasse was that Bollaert, the architect of the Xuan Government and of the Bay of Along agreement, whose objectives had evidently not been accomplished, was relieved of his position. He himself had announced on September 2, 1948, that he would not accept another extension of his mandate, which originally was to have lasted only six months. The new High Commissioner, appointed in October, 1948, was Léon Pignon, a man whom Bollaert, regarding him as an obstacle to Franco-Vietnamese cooperation, had removed from Indochina in April, 1947. [73] Pignon had been political adviser to Admiral d'Argenlieu; he was known as a promoter of Cochinchinese separatism and a saboteur of the agreement of March 6, 1946.

His appointment, however, did not portend a complete reversal of French policy in Vietnam (the resumption of the course pursued by d'Argenlieu was no longer possible); but the return of Pignon certainly presaged a hardening of the French position, due both to the political decline of the parties of the Left and the failure of their policy in Indochina. Two years after the war had spread over the entire country, the French had neither defeated the Vietminh nor succeeded in mobilizing nationalist forces that would enable them to present the conflict, which remained a war of colonial reconquest, as a war between Communism and anti-Communism, a war in which France, at great sacrifice to herself, merely supported the cause of an anti-Communist Vietnam.

But this was precisely why even Pignon, although resentful of Bao Dai for demanding what France had refused to Ho Chi Minh, realized that the efforts to generate a politically effective anti-Vietminh regime friendly to France could not be abandoned. In January, 1949, the Chinese Communists took Peking. For a Frenchman to predict the early collapse of the Chinese Nationalist armies, which occurred on October 1, 1949, and brought the Chinese Communists to the border of Vietnam in December, required nothing more than the courage to face unpleasant realities. With a Communist China in the rear of the Vietminh, the struggle for Indochina more and more began to assume the aspects of a local skirmish in the world-wide conflict between East and West. The United States could hardly remain indifferent if a Communist victory over the French in Vietnam opened the gate for the subjugation of Southeast Asia to Communist China. Sooner or later Washington would feel obliged to extend moral and material aid to a France engaged in containing Communism in Asia. But this "internationalization" of the conflict was possible only if the United States could be persuaded that support for the French in the Indochina War had ceased to be support of French colonialism and had instead become a vital interest of the "free world." This, however, required that the Vietnam which was to be denied to the Communists would be not a colonial but an independent Vietnam; that Bao Dai, if he should be her leader, must not be a puppet of France; and that anti-Communism, if it should ever become effective against the Vietminh, must serve the cause of national freedom and cease to be a device for maintaining French rule.

Since the people who decided French policy had, up to the spring of

1954, little intention of relinquishing France's hold on Indochina, and since their real aims could no longer be openly admitted, French conduct in Vietnam, and French propaganda at home and abroad, assumed more and more the character of systematic deception. An aura of intrigue therefore still surrounded everything the French said and did to bring about the Bao Dai solution. There is also no doubt that people like Pignon regarded the politically inexperienced Vietnamese elite as vastly inferior to themselves and confidently expected to manipulate, bully, and bribe the followers of Bao Dai into cooperation with France, on terms compatible with the maintenance of French rule.[74] After 1948, the French were no longer afraid of granting "independence," since this could be done without translating independence from solemn promise into political fact. After all, as long as the war was not over, France could not relinquish vital positions of command. "You cannot survive without our presence," the promoters of full independence under Bao Dai were constantly told. Had experience not already demonstrated that anti-Vietminh nationalism was doomed unless the French Army succeeded in destroying the power of the Vietminh?

There were many in Bao Dai's camp who believed this to be true, but the ex-Emperor himself saw no reason to admit it. "Make me the one who brings to Vietnam true independence," he kept saying, "and you will see how quickly the people will turn away from the Vietminh." Indeed, before French sabotage had dashed the hopes raised by the Bay of Along agreement, "some thousands of [Vietminh] combatants had left the Maquis." [75] Bao Dai had considerably weakened his own position by dropping the threat of making common cause with Ho Chi Minh, but his refusal to lend his authority to the anti-Vietminh government the French needed in view of the "internationalization" of the conflict was still an effective weapon. By the beginning of 1949, Bao Dai realized that international circumstances were likely to have a favorable effect upon his position vis-à-vis the French. As early as October, 1947, William C. Bullitt, former U.S. Ambassador to France, had visited Bao Dai in Hong Kong, and had hinted, in an article in *Life* magazine, at the possibility of American support for a government headed by Bao Dai.[76] If the United States should feel compelled to support the French, which was likely once the Communist powers openly assisted the Hanoi regime, the prospects of genuine French concessions to anti-Communist nationalism were bound to improve. American aid, Bao Dai reasoned, could not be obtained for the purpose of maintaining colonialism in Indochina. It had to be justified with reference to the defense of "freedom" against Communism. The French, therefore, could not forever prevent the emergence of a free Vietnam; an anti-Communist government under Bao Dai would make sense only if it was not to be merely "a screen for the French administration." [77]

These were the hopes and fears that led the two sides to reconsider their positions. After long negotiations in January, 1949—Pignon even went to Cannes to talk to Bao Dai—a new accord was concluded on March 8, 1949. It took the form of an exchange of letters between Bao Dai and French President Vincent Auriol and became known as the Elysée agreement. This new agreement reconfirmed the independence of Vietnam and her status as an associated state of the French Union, but it was notable chiefly for the progress in regard to the unity of Vietnam. For the first time, the French went beyond the mere promise of liquidating Cochinchinese separatism, spelling out the measures to bring it about. They also relinquished the administration of Hanoi, Haiphong, and Tourane, which had remained "French" territories in the Bay of Along agreement. But they still refused to return to the Vietnamese Government the two "autonomous regions" of the *montagnards* in the South and the Thai people in the North.

More important, however, than this imperfection in the country's unity were the limitations of Vietnamese sovereignty to which Bao Dai gave his consent. Defense and foreign relations remained in French hands. The national army to be created would not be under Vietnamese command; but since the French desired native help in beating down all forms of Vietminh-led resistance, the Vietnamese Government was soon to be allowed its own police force. It could also appoint a few ambassadors and delegates to the Assembly and High Council of the French Union, two bodies distinguished only for their total lack of influence upon French policy.[78] In matters of real importance, however, the Elysée agreement stipulated either permanent restrictions of Vietnamese sovereignty or made its transfer dependent on separate accords to be concluded later. Independence, in other words, would become a reality only when the French were ready, and to the extent they were willing, to relinquish the posts of control and command they held. French citizens, for instance, could not be tried by Vietnamese law; the currency of Vietnam remained tied to the French monetary zone and to that of the other Associated States of Indochina

(Cambodia and Laos), with which Vietnam would also maintain the existing customs union. This meant that even the Indochinese Federation, of which the French had long ceased to speak, would somehow continue. The Elysée agreement also forbade any measures that would have reduced French control over the economy of Vietnam. Not until a later conference concluded the many separate accords necessary for the transfer of sovereignty would the Vietnamese know what degree of control the French would permit them over their own treasury, the country's communications, its foreign trade, its customs, its postal and telegraph service, and its general economic policy.[79]

Only Bao Dai's belief that the need for American aid would induce the French to fulfill their new promises could explain the optimism he voiced over the Elysée agreement. He told the French press that "an era of reconstruction and renovation would open in Vietnam. The country will be given democratic institutions that will be called on primarily to approve the present agreement. . . . Profound economic and social reforms will be instituted to raise the general standard of living and to promote social justice, which is the condition and guarantee of order." This, of course, supposed "the union of all Vietnamese regardless of their political and religious tendencies, and the generous support of France on which I can count." [80]

Bao Dai was far too intelligent to act as if he really believed what he said. Holding on to his one remaining weapon, he delayed his return to Vietnam until the steps promised to bring about the unity of Vietnam were taken. It turned out that this was no simple matter, since the constitution of the French Union contained provisions for such a change that had to be observed. They demanded the creation of a territorial assembly for Cochinchina, which would then decide whether this old part of Vietnam should again be governed by a central Vietnamese government. But permission to create such an assembly had to be given by the French parliament, and after the Cochinchinese Assembly was constituted and had presumably voted to reattach Cochinchina to Vietnam, the French legislature had to give its approval.

The French Assembly authorized a Cochinchinese Assembly on March 12. It was to have sixty-four members, of whom sixteen were to be French. The idea of direct, popular elections advanced by the Socialists was rejected in favor of indirect elections by the various existing local bodies and provincial councils, and by the professional, syndical, and corporative organizations of the French, such as the Chambers of Commerce and Agriculture. The trouble was that many of the provincial councils had either ceased to exist or lost most of their members through death or desertion to the Vietminh. Councils and membership had to be renewed in so many instances, all through administrative appointment, that at least forty of the sixty-four Assembly members were elected by people picked by the administration. The "elections" were held on April 10, amid general popular indifference, including those allowed to vote, most of whom regarded the whole procedure as a farce. "Only some 5,000 Vietnamese in Cochinchina had the right to vote, and of these, little more than 700 actually did so." [81]

This was a poor beginning for a "new era" with its promise of "democratic institutions." But much worse was yet to come. Many of the sixty-four people thus elected regarded their vote, which they knew Bao Dai and the French Government wanted, as a commodity for which they could ask a high price. "Twenty million francs had been distributed at friendly meals presided over by General Xuan in person" before the Assembly met on April 19. Other votes needed for a majority to end Cochinchinese separatism were obtained by "diverse pressures," including "threats of death." [82] Even so, it took four days before the Assembly, on April 23, voted that Cochinchina would rejoin Vietnam.[83]

Bao Dai had promised to return to Vietnam as soon as the Cochinchinese Assembly had made the expected decision. He did so on April 25, 1949, after an absence of more than three years. However, he did not immediately take over the government. He went quietly to his mountain resort Dalat, where he waited until the French Assembly had also voted that Cochinchina should again become part of Vietnam. The bill to this effect became law on June 4. On June 13, Bao Dai went to Saigon under heavy French protection, displaying a lack of enthusiasm matched only by the total indifference of the population.[84] At the end of the month, he received the formal resignation of the Cochinchinese Government. Separatism had at last come to an end.

But the unity of the country, which Bao Dai had extracted from the French, was of little value to the Vietnamese without true independence. Realizing this, Bao Dai used both persuasion and pressure on the French to speed up the process that would make independence real, at least to the extent outlined in the Elysée agreement. The sad truth, still hard to believe, is that in this Bao Dai was totally unsuccessful. With exasperating slowness, the French yielded certain administrative positions, but kept them under their control; the Vietnamese were given offices but no authority, titles but no power, and a government allowed to govern only in the narrow spheres where its actions did not conflict with established colonial interests and did not clash with the continued exercise of French rule. About a dozen separate accords to implement independence were signed in the conventions of December 30, 1949, and at least on paper, much progress was made at the conference of Pau, at which, between June and November, 1950, the three Associated States of Indochina tried to settle their economic and financial problems with France.[85] In regard to the central question, which was who had the power to make vital military, economic, and financial decisions, the many agreements concluded between France and the Vietnamese had little or no restraining effect upon French behavior. One of the important decisions at the Pau conference was that the rate of exchange between the Indochinese piaster and the French franc could be altered only by mutual agreement. On May 11, 1953, the French Government, in open violation of this accord, reduced the exchange rate from 17 to 10 francs to the piaster. It did so not only without agreement, but even without prior consultation with the Associated States.[86]

Proving how French sabotage between 1949 and 1954 prevented self-government for the Vietnamese from becoming effective today requires only few illustrations.[87] In the fall of 1950, Prime Minister Tran Van Huu, although a confirmed collaborator, in desperation demanded a new treaty that would give Vietnam independence, something the Elysée agreement had apparently not done. "Many people are dying every day because Vietnam is not given independence. . . . We want the right to decide our own affairs for ourselves." [88] Three years later, the Vietnamese were obviously even farther away from their goal. In May, 1953, a French parliamentary mission of inquiry accused High Commissioner Letourneau (who also headed the new Ministry for the Associated States) of having instituted a "veritable dictatorship, without limit or control," over Indochina, and of playing a game of "power and intrigue." Of Bao Dai's ministers, the report of this mission said that they "appear, in the eyes of their compatriots, to be French officials." [89]

As if to admit that the promise of the Elysée agreement was still not fulfilled, the French Government, on July 3, 1953, felt obliged to say that it was now time "to perfect the independence and sovereignty of the Associated States of Indochina" by transferring to them competencies which France had so far withheld—"in the interest of these States, and because of the dangers due to the conditions of war." But not until March, 1954, did the new negotiations begin that produced, on April 28, a Franco-Vietnamese declaration recognizing what it called "total" independence for Vietnam, thus confirming that until then, independence had existed only on paper. It was, as some put it, only a "shabby independence," and the "Bao Dai solution" was a "bastard solution." Bao Dai himself knew this and admitted it as early as 1950: "What they call a Bao Dai solution turns out to be just a French solution." [90]

12

The political evolution of anti-Communist nationalism between 1949 and 1954 underlined the extent to which the denial of independence contributed to the final triumph of the Vietminh over the French. By collaborating with the French it discredited and corrupted the circles that tried to fight Communism; it forced those anti-Communists unwilling to compromise on the issue of independence to move closer to the Vietminh; and it created the nationalist camp described as *attentist*, consisting of a growing number of people who preferred to do nothing, to wait rather than to side with either the French or the Vietminh. Far from advancing the cause of anti-Communism or from helping the French, these three attitudes were, in different degrees, of help only to the Vietminh.

Most effective in this respect were the people who allowed themselves to be used to camouflage the fact that Vietnam was still ruled by the French—the heads and members of the several governments under Bao Dai, and Bao Dai himself. The ex-Emperor, it can be said to his credit, for a long time suffered from the conflict between his dubious comportment and his nobler convictions. But although he was largely a victim of circumstances likely to defeat the best of men, his sad political fate aroused no real pity, because Bao Dai chose to drown his sorrows in expensive distractions, for which he accepted "personal advantages and large subsidies" [91] from the French; in a role made for tragedy he never suffered the agonies of a totally frustrated good will. "The ex-Emperor," wrote Dabezies, the keenest analyst of the Vietnamese political mind, "seems to combine an astonishing lack of character, a real dislike for power, and a deep conservatism, which together condemn to failure his sharp political sense and his lively intelligence." [92] Many who knew him called him kind and a "man of good will," but nobody ever mistook him for a hero. His failure, therefore, lacked the dimension of the tragic.

Bao Dai himself headed the first cabinet after his return. He "retained" the title of Emperor but henceforth called himself only Chief of State. He said it was not for him to decide whether Vietnam should be a monarchy or a republic, and he solemnly proclaimed that the future constitution of Vietnam would be decided by the people who had fought heroically for the independence of their homeland.

This statement was one of the frequent gestures with which Bao Dai and some of his followers tried to lure the non-Communist resistance leaders into their own camp. They knew that their regime could gain popular support only if they succeeded in detaching substantial numbers of non-Communists from the Vietminh. They even kept several cabinet posts reserved for such people. When Bao Dai visited Hanoi in the summer of 1949, "he laid a palm branch on the monument to the Vietnamese who had been shot by the French after December 19, 1946. Members of Bao Dai's household talked of the guerrillas as 'our heroes.' " [93] But Ngo Dinh Diem, who for his own reasons carefully avoided public attacks on the Vietminh, told Bao Dai that as long as the French prevented the fulfillment of Vietnam's national aspirations, these wooings were pointless, since they could be regarded only as an invitation to resistance fighters to become collaborators. Ngo Dinh Diem himself, who had always refused to play such a role, declined an offer by Bao Dai to head his first cabinet. He would agree to head a government only after the national aspirations of the Vietnamese people were satisfied, which meant for him "the day when our nation obtains the same political status which India and Pakistan enjoy." And hinting that this day would put an end to the role of the collaborators, he added: "I believe it is only just to reserve the best posts in new Vietnam for those who have merited most of the country: I speak of the resistance elements." [94]

Ngo Dinh Diem did not expect the day when Vietnam would be as free as India to arrive soon. Since he could support neither the French nor the Vietminh, he became, for several years, the leading *attentiste* of the nationalist camp. He left Vietnam during 1950, and many other prominent nationalists followed his example. [95] Ngo Dinh Diem and the growing number of nationalists who adopted this stance decided that if there was nothing they could do to advance their cause, they could at least refrain from doing damage to it by collaborating with the French. As a result, the only people available for Bao Dai for his several governments between 1949 and 1954 were known collaborators, unprincipled demagogues, and aspirants for any position that promised personal gain.[96]

The first government Bao Dai formed consisted largely of men from the South, where the sects and a few other groups constituted at least a façade of popular support. An old enemy of the separatists, the journalist Nguyen Phan Long, held both the Ministries of Foreign Affairs and the Interior, but the notorious General Nguyen Van Xuan was made Vice-President. His rapid transformation from a pro-French separatist into a voluble spokesman for Vietnamese unity (under French auspices) had done nothing to enhance his reputation. Tired of Xuan's intrigues both in France and in Vietnam, Bao Dai dropped him when he reconstituted his government in February, 1950.

In what seemed a last attempt to assert himself against the French and to rid himself of the taint of all-out collaboration, Bao Dai handed the Premiership to Nguyen Phan Long, who was known not only for his insistence on greater concessions by the French, but also as the earliest advocate of a policy built on the expectation that U.S. pressure would sooner or later force France to drop her opposition to genuine Vietnamese independence. He asked that American military and economic aid be given to the Vietnamese without French intermediaries. The idea of strengthening his regime against the French with direct American aid, which some people regarded merely as "premature," was in fact quite erroneous; it was, furthermore, only one of many mistaken notions this man entertained. He also confused stubbornness with adherence to principle. His natural disappointment over being misunderstood convinced him that almost everybody lacked his unique and profound insights. He thought that he could extract concessions from the French by starting a noncommittal flirtation with the Vietminh; he even believed that direct and sufficient U.S. aid to his government would enable him to defeat the Vietminh in six months. When the French decided that they must get rid of him, no one stood up in his defense. Bao Dai dropped him after only three months in office.

Of Nguyen Phan Long it could be said that he made no substantial contribution to the ruin of anti-Communist nationalism. This was a

merit of which none of his successors before the appointment of Ngo
Dinh Diem in June, 1954, could boast. The next head of Bao Dai's
government, Tran Van Huu, was a rich landowner engaged in financial speculations, a French citizen, and a separatist who, as Governor of
Cochinchina, had obstructed the transfer of this administration to the
central government up to May 6, 1950, when he himself became Prime
Minister of Vietnam.[97] His usefulness for the French is beyond doubt,
since he was able to hold on to his position from May, 1950, to June,
1952. But he, too, was forced by the ever-growing nationalist sentiment to demand that the already twice solemnly granted independence
be given real meaning. Since the French had known Huu for many
years as a reliable collaborator, they helped him stay in office as long as
he served their purposes. To this end, they even made concessions to
him which improved at least upon the image if not upon the substance
of the country's so-called independence. The Huu Government was
allowed to appoint a greater number of ambassadors and to staff its
ministries and other governmental agencies with more high officials.
But the ambassadors had neither authority nor function, and the ministries and other agencies continued to be run by French secretaries.
These appointments, far from making independence more real, only
increased the number of places for people willing to let themselves be
corrupted. One instance of the general use of government positions for
personal enrichment (an art in which Huu himself displayed consum-
mate skill) was the case of Phan Van Giao, Governor of Central Vietnam, "who had acquired a legendary reputation for bold speculations,"
and who was said to have transferred to France, during the months of
January and April alone, the sum of 84 million francs.[98]

The Huu Government was also allowed to recruit more and more
Vietnamese troops, but its army remained under exclusive French
command. Only in one government department were the Vietnamese
given almost as much autonomy as they wanted. This was the Department of Public Security, which devoted itself, with eager French blessing and help, to the persecution of the nationalists who fought the
French and their Vietnamese tools. The head of this department was a
man who more than any other gave to the Huu Government its character as a French instrument to combat the resistance. This was
Nguyen Van Tam, who had acquired renown as a loyal servant of the
French and ferocious anti-Communist long before the war and the
Japanese occupation.[99] Tam had also been an outstanding separatist

and had already headed Public Security under the Cochinchinese governments of Dr. Trinh and Le Van Hoach, in preparation, as it were, for the job of arresting, "questioning," imprisoning, or killing—now on a national scale—persons known to be or merely suspected of being followers of the Vietminh.[100] Tran Van Huu once aptly described the man whom he himself had made the most important figure of his government: "Tam is not a Vietnamese patriot, he is a French patriot." [101] And this was the man who, thanks to his energy in fighting not only the Vietminh but also all other nationalist opposition to the French, was to become the next Prime Minister of "independent" Vietnam.

The political attrition of Tran Van Huu, like that of the Bao Dai's prime ministers before and after him, can be traced back to one basic cause. This was that the Bao Dai solution, no matter how skillfully applied, was doomed to failure by its inner contradictions.[102] All Bao Dai governments were politically ineffective, and therefore also useless for the French, because they failed to split the non-Communist resistance from the Vietminh. Since neither the collaborators nor the *attentists* succeeded in satisfying the people's national demands, the nationalists who opposed the Vietminh remained as weak as ever. Furthermore, in order to maintain a minimum of popular support, their reluctance to support Bao Dai's French-sponsored government turned more and more into open opposition and even into occasional rebellion. This was true of all groups, in particular of the politically capricious and divided armed Cao Dai and Hoa Hao sects. Mercenary as their leaders were, they, too, were subject to the nationalist mood of their followers. This obliged them to raise demands with which neither Huu nor his successor Tam was in a position to comply. Both antagonized the sects when they tried to extend the central government's authority over sect-held territories and to force the military units of the sects into the national army. The opposition of the sects and the parties forced Tran Van Huu to form his second cabinet, installed on February 21, 1951, with only "technicians" and political "independents."

Two of the men who refused to join Huu's second Cabinet were the Dai Viet leader Nguyen Huu Tri and Phan Huy Quat, the latter only a Dai Viet sympathizer. The Dai Viet, although as badly split over the issue of support or opposition to Bao Dai as all other nationalist groups opposed to the Vietminh, was at this time the strongest and best organized of all anti-Vietminh factions. It attracted many nationalists who had formerly supported the VNQDD and Dong Minh Hoi, but also many former mandarins and government officials in Annam and Tongking. It seemed to many that the firm anti-Communism and extreme nationalism of this party, combined with the ambition and vitality of its leaders, predestined the Dai Viet to play a decisive role in a government subject neither to Communist nor to French control. In pursuit of power the Dai Viet leadership tried to persuade the French and Bao Dai to create an "autonomous zone" administered by their party without French interference and defended against the Vietminh by a party militia that had been clandestinely built up, and for which the French were to supply the necessary arms and equipment. The plan, on the surface ingenious but politically naïve, was to make independence real, and at the same time defeat the Vietminh, by gradually extending this zone over the whole of Vietnam. French determination to control both the administration and the conduct of the war excluded acceptance of this plan. Nevertheless, the Dai Viet came out in support of Bao Dai, and at the risk of splitting its own ranks, entered the governments created after June, 1949, only to leave them after realizing that the lack of true independence barred collaboration as a road to power. The Southern party leader Nguyen Ton Hoan made brief "guest appearances" as Minister of Youth under Nguyen Phan Long and in Tran Van Huu's first cabinet, but soon found out that no degree of tactical elasticity could advance his party's untimely ambitions.[103]

To refurbish the soiled image of the Dai Viet as the only nationalist group consistently opposed to both the Vietminh and the French, the leaders now began to intensify their propaganda for genuine independence, attacking not only the Tran Van Huu Government but also Bao Dai and the French. The latter decided that the Dai Viet must not be pacified with concessions but had to be fought and removed from all positions of administrative control held by its members. Dai Viet members and sympathizers among the former mandarins had in fact successfully "infiltrated" the administration, particularly in the North, where the Governor of Tongking, Nguyen Huu Tri, the Mayors of Hanoi and Haiphong, and many provincial administrators were members of the party. The pretext for their removal, and for the suppression of the Dai Viet's legal activities, was a conflict that arose when Governor Tri attempted to do away with the administrative autonomy enjoyed by the two Catholic provinces of Phat Diem and Bui Chu, where, under Bishop Le Huu Tu, the Catholics not only ruled but also

defended their domains with their own troops. With his customary
ruthlessness, Security Minister Tam conducted the elimination of the
Dai Viet, on direct orders from General Jean de Lattre de Tassigny,
who, on December 10, 1950, had become both Commander in Chief of
the French armies and High Commissioner of Indochina, succeeding
Léon Pignon. (As Commander in Chief, de Lattre replaced General
Marcel Carpentier, who, in September, 1949, had succeeded General
Blaizot, interim Commander after Valluy.)

De Lattre, who had been called upon to repair the military reverses
the French had suffered in the fall of 1950 at the hands of the Vietminh, was known not only as an autocrat but also for his truly Napo-
leonic megalomania—a man who conceived of relationships in public
life only under the terms of command and obedience. To make this
born "proconsul" head of the civilian administration as well convinced
most anti-Communist nationalists that in regard to independence, the
French had no intention whatsoever of making concessions. The general, unable to tolerate opposition even from a Frenchman, was certainly not going to put up with opposition from a Vietnamese. Instead
of hitting the Vietminh politically by giving nationalists like Nguyen
Huu Tri a freer hand in running their country, de Lattre insisted that
the Huu Government remove them from office and silence the Dai
Viet, which was then the only party with a chance of gaining popular
support for the Bao Dai regime. As Dabezies puts it, "we preferred
once more the valet to the master"—the valet being Security Minister
Nguyen Van Tam. "By sacrificing the Dai Viet to his pride, General
de Lattre lost the last chance we had in Tongking, and perhaps in all of
Indochina, to erect a solid political barrier against the Vietminh." [104]

As a result of this policy, the Huu Government became a political
liability to the French as well as to Bao Dai. The sects disliked it, the
Dai Viet fought it, the Vietminh effectively denounced it as a puppet
of the French, and the population despised it. Sooner or later it had to
be dropped. In trying to save himself, Huu chose methods that could
only hasten his downfall. He attempted to increase his popularity by
posing as a more ardent patriot than Bao Dai, and by expressing, albeit
unconvincingly, nationalist sentiments abhorrent to the French, without whose approval his government would never have come into existence.

Although Huu's behavior antagonized Bao Dai, he hesitated a long
time before debasing himself again by giving in to the pressure of the

French, who demanded Huu's dismissal. Totally disillusioned and more and more dependent on the revenues he derived from his position, he finally consented to replace Tran Van Huu with Nguyen Van Tam, the only prominent Vietnamese who was known as being "entirely devoted to the French." [105]

When Tam was made Prime Minister in June, 1952, the nationalists of all shades, including most collaborators, knew that the Bao Dai solution was dead.

IX

Political Failure and Military Decline

1

THE APPOINTMENT, in June, 1952, of the "French patriot" Nguyen Van Tam as Prime Minister of Vietnam, although no turning point in the evolution of the Bao Dai regime, had one irrevocable effect. It removed the last doubts in the camp of anti-Vietminh nationalism about the nature, purpose, and role of Bao Dai's "state" in the struggle for control of Vietnam: Bao Dai and his government were tools of the French; the purpose of the Bao Dai "solution" was not to bring about independence but to help prevent it. To expect this regime ever to become politically effective against the Vietminh was a pitiable delusion. On the contrary: The existence of the Bao Dai regime was bound to strengthen Ho Chi Minh, since it gave credence to his claim that his government alone was fighting for national independence. There can be no doubt that the appointment of Tam was greeted with great satisfaction by the leadership of the Vietminh.

Deeply satisfied as well were the French, whose interests and passions continued to erode their ability for lucid political thinking. At last, they said, Bao Dai had chosen a true anti-Communist to head his government, a man of energy on whose devotion they could count. Tam would never flirt with the Vietminh, never indulge in extreme nationalism to gain popularity, never raise demands with which the French could not comply; he would accept the limitations of Vietnamese sovereignty, which the French now said were a condition for the successful conduct of the war. Moreover, Tam would "get things done."

Among the deeds expected of Tam was the rapid creation of a large Vietnamese national army, which the French had come to consider essential for the defeat of the Vietminh. Gone were the days when the French High Command predicted victory for every new campaign scheduled for the end of "the next rainy season." Not only did everyone of these campaigns fail; by the middle of 1952, with the war in its sixth year, the territory under French control was smaller than in 1947; the Vietminh had greatly increased their military strength and begun to conduct large-scale offensive actions; a stalemate had developed, which, since the French lacked the strength to strike decisive blows, would probably end with new Vietminh attacks on an ever-growing scale. It was evident that after five years of costly and arduous efforts to break Vietminh resistance, the French were farther from their goal than immediately after the outbreak of hostilities in the North.

The Indochina War, although an uninterrupted and merciless struggle costly in human lives and remarkable for destruction on a prodigious scale, had so far produced only a few engagements large enough to be called battles. In these battles, the defeat of one side was not necessarily a victory for the other. This was one of the many confusing peculiarities of this war, whose history has yet to be written, and whose true lesson has yet to be learned.[1] Moreover, another peculiarity must be added to the fact that most defeats suffered by either side in this war allowed no claims of victory—i.e., these defeats were largely inflicted on the side that in the end can be said to have won the war—the Vietminh.

At the very beginning, the war went badly for the Vietminh. They lost not only Hanoi, Haiphong, and Hue, but by the end of March, 1947, also almost all towns in Tongking and northern Annam, and many of the lines of communication between these towns. The poorly armed local militias and regional fighting units of the Vietminh charged with the defense of their home towns and provincial capitals were no match for the well-equipped, heavily armored, and at that time still fast-moving units of the French Army. When the first showdown was over, the Vietminh Army, most of which had not been engaged in any fighting, was largely intact. It had been moved, before the fighting broke out, into the so-called Viet Bac, the mountainous region north of Hanoi, where Vo Nguyen Giap, before the August revolution, had built up the nucleus of the Vietminh Army. Even small groups of Vietminh soldiers, mainly for geographical reasons, could hold off large and heavily armored units that tried to invade this region. The Viet Bac, for the duration of the war, remained the chief training ground, supply base, and command center of the armed forces, as well as the headquarters of the government, the organizations, and the press of the Vietminh.

The decision of the Vietminh leaders to save their army and to concentrate first on doubling and then tripling its original strength was followed by their refusal, maintained for over three years, to use their main forces in open and large-scale encounters with the French. This, of course, meant that the Vietminh leaders knew that it would take many years before they could hope to defeat the French; Ho Chi Minh was apparently not just warning the French when he said the war might last ten or fifteen years. But it also meant that Vo Nguyen Giap, when, in the fall of 1950, he decided to throw the French out of the positions they held between Hanoi and the Chinese border, disposed of a well-trained and well-equipped regular army of at least 60,000 men, conventionally grouped in five divisions of 12,000 each.[2] The effect of this cautious policy on the French was to mislead them into underestimating for years the strength and fighting ability of the regular Vietminh Army—an error for which they were to pay their first heavy price in October, 1950.

More immediately detrimental to the French, and an even worse omen for the future, was another imperfection of their initial victories over the forces of the Hanoi regime. This was the inability of the French Army to occupy the entire country and to exercise sufficient control over the thousands of villages where the vast majority of the Vietnamese people lived. This failure, particularly pronounced in the North, revealed at an early stage (though not to the closed French mind) why the struggle for Indochina was likely to end with the triumph of the Vietminh. The key to the failure of the French to bring the countryside under their control was the one great change that had taken place in Vietnam since the pre-World War II years: In 1940, the French had been able to control all of Vietnam with only a fraction of the troops at their disposal in 1947; if their vastly increased army and police force now failed to subdue and effectively control the entire country, this was because control of the countryside was actively denied them by the very people whom they believed they had just defeated—the armed Vietnamese, acting as guerrillas, and, in larger groups, as the so-called regional forces of the Vietminh. (In size, train-

ing, and equipment the regional forces ranked between the small guerrilla units and the regular army, but like the guerrillas, they were not
uniformed and were likely to be peasants or laborers when not fighting.) Guerrillas and regional troops were evidence that the broad
masses of the people, not only the army, were taking part in the war
against the French.

Behind the great change that had taken place in Vietnam between
1940 and 1945 was the rise of strong nationalist and anti-French feelings among almost the entire population. If this did not altogether
explain the existence of the guerrillas and regional fighters, it explained
at least their surprising effectiveness and ability to survive. Without
necessarily manifesting itself in popularity for the Vietminh, the anti-
French sentiments of the people explained the widespread and continuous popular support the local fighting units of the Vietminh enjoyed.
This support enabled them to assemble without being discovered, to
hide when the French appeared in force, to conceal their weapons, to
replenish their ranks, and to create an intelligence network that kept
them informed about the strength, the movements, and often even the
plans of the French.[3] Popular support alone prevented the destruction
of these local and regional forces and made it possible for the Vietminh
leaders to start and maintain a constant guerrilla war while preparing
their regular army for the day when it would be ready to give battle to
the French.

In the strategic scheme of the Vietminh, between 1947 and 1950, the
task of their guerrillas and regional units was twofold. They had to
keep the French out of regions important to the Hanoi Government as
sources of food, manpower, minerals, and other natural products,[4] and
they had to keep on harassing the French wherever they had established themselves, in order to reduce their ability to prepare and execute large military operations. The first task required regional forces
strong enough to block access routes into territories not yet or no
longer garrisoned by the French. If the French could not be stopped,
their supply routes had to be cut and their posts isolated and attacked
until the difficulties of reinforcing and supplying them led to their
evacuation. Hundreds of small positions with which the French tried
to extend and maintain their control over regions difficult of access became too costly to hold. The Vietminh fighters, as ubiquitous and persistent as the country's mosquitoes and leeches, never ceased their
attacks, and if they did not succeed in driving the French from their

positions, they at least succeeded in immobilizing the men needed to hold them. As a result, the French finally recognized that they had to limit their military occupation of Vietnam to select regions considered important for either strategic or economic reasons.

In these regions, from which the Vietminh could as yet not evict the French, the guerrillas and regional forces concentrated on the other half of their task. They blew up bridges, built road blocks, ambushed patrols and convoys, assassinated collaborators, and attacked and eliminated numerous watchtowers and small road posts set up by the French in hopes of keeping the enemy out and their own lines of communication open. The Vietminh fighters did their work chiefly by night; as a result, many regions controlled by the French during the day became Vietminh territory after darkness fell.

Both as regards keeping territory out of French hands and immobilizing French troops (of which more and more were needed to defend French-held territory), the Vietminh guerrillas and regional units were strikingly successful. Before General Valluy started his fall offensive designed to capture or destroy the main Vietminh forces concentrated in the Viet Bac, at least half the territory of Vietnam was fully controlled by the Vietminh; additional vast regions were theirs at night. This was quite obvious in Tongking and Annam, or, as the Vietnamese would henceforth say, in the North and Center. Even before the Vietminh started their offensives in 1950, they controlled more than half of Tongking fully and much of the other half partially. The French from the beginning were determined to hold on to the rich and thickly populated Red River Delta, from about 50 miles north of Hanoi down to the sea; they also spared no effort to save the coal mines of Moncay by keeping the Vietminh out of a narrow landstrip between Haiphong and the Chinese border. Until October, 1950, the French also maintained increasingly isolated outposts along the Chinese border in the northwest, including the towns of Caobang and Langson (along Colonial Route No. 4, which was destined to become the first road of disaster for the French); and they loosely controlled most of the northwestern highlands between the Red River and the Black River, populated chiefly by Thai minorities, and bordering on China in the north and on Laos in the west. With a number of strong garrisons, such as those at Nghia Lo, Son La, and Na Sam, they kept a tenuous hold on the south and center of this region; with posts at Lai Chau and Laokay, they maintained themselves precariously in the more distant

northwestern Thai provinces. All other Tongking provinces were held
by the Vietminh and administered by agents of the Hanoi Government, which was master not only of the entire country northeast and
east of the Red River and Hanoi, but also of the vast fertile provinces
south of the Red River Delta down to northern Annam, including the
towns of Thanh Hoa and Vinh.[5]

South of these important provinces, in northern and central Annam,
Vietminh domination of the countryside was even more extensive than
in Tongking. Between the towns of Vinh and Qui Nhon, approximately
450 miles to the south, the French held only a narrow coastal strip beginning somewhat north of Quang Tri and ending slightly south of
Tourane. This kept the former capital city Hue in French hands; but
the French did not succeed in wresting the woody and hilly land a few
miles west of Hue up to the border of Laos, as well as most of the hin-
terland of the central Annam coast, from the Vietminh.[6] Apart from
the vast but thinly populated highland held mostly by the French, it is
safe to say that close to 80 per cent of both the land and people of
northern and central Annam were under Vietminh control. They remained in Vietminh hands to the end of the war.

The situation was not at all the same in southern Annam and Cochinchina. There the reconquest by the French had begun back in
October, 1945, fifteen months before the start of the war in the North.
Because the Vietminh had always been relatively weak in the South,
French control, although far from either total or secure, had reached a
scope and stability entirely lacking in the Center and North. The
French held all cities, including the distant highland towns of Kontum
and Pleiku. Most routes between the cities, although never safe, could
be kept open at some sacrifice of men and equipment. The French, understandably, also spared no effort to prevent the Vietminh from controlling the rubber lands in Cochinchina and Cambodia, even if this
meant the stationing there of troops badly needed for action elsewhere.
But although the Vietminh in the South had to rely almost entirely on
guerrilla action—there were only a few larger groups of regional fighters and no units of the regular army—they had been successful in keeping a few regions completely out of French control, and also in making
this control in many other parts extremely fragile. The province of
Vac Lien, at the southernmost tip of Vietnam (the point of Camau),
had never fallen to the French. This was true also for most of the province of Rach Gia and for a large region around Hatien near the Cam-

bodian border—territories that fifteen years later would again be controlled by the armed forces of the so-called National Liberation Front of South Vietnam. In fact, all of Trans-Bassac—the entire region beyond the Bassac River, a western arm of the Mekong—was largely guerrilla-controlled, as was the Plain of Reeds to the west of Saigon, much of the provinces of Tay Ninh to the north, and Baria to the southeast. In addition, the Vietminh maintained bases of changing size and location all over the South—several in the Mekong Delta, one near the town of Phat Tiet, another one between the coast and the hilly approaches to Dalat, and even a large one near Saigon, in an area just west of Thu Mau Dot. This guerrilla base (Zone D) extended at times all the way up to the Cambodian border. The French could never spare enough troops to eliminate these enclaves from which the guerrillas staged their attacks on convoys and small outposts,[7] and dominated by night much of the adjoining country nominally under French control. Thus the guerrillas were able to levy taxes, recruit soldiers, collect rice, indoctrinate the population, extend their net of informers, and if necessary terrorize villages considered hostile to the Vietminh. The Vietminh succeeded in shipping rice from the surplus areas in the South not only to territories where they were short of food, but also to Singapore, where they sold it on the black market. Arms bought in Singapore were brought in by sampan to the guerrillas in the Trans-Bassac region.

The inability of the French to eliminate these Vietminh pockets, and to deal effectively with the guerrillas, was mainly why they never had a chance to win the war. It was bad enough to know that the enemy was everywhere and might attack at any moment, always having the element of surprise in his favor. Even more exasperating was the elusiveness of the guerrillas. Whenever the French, after long preparations, proceeded to move against them in force, they invariably disappeared. In such actions, the French as a rule conquered only empty space, of which there was enough in the marshes, jungles, and mountains to allow the Vietminh to become invisible. They dispersed, only to reassemble again at a base 5 or 10 miles away, and they would repeat this maneuver if the French continued their pursuit. Sooner or later, the French found themselves too far away from their own bases, out of supplies and ammunition, and had no choice but to return, usually followed closely and harassed continuously by the reappearing guerrillas. To occupy permanently sites from which they had driven the Vietminh fighters was beyond the means of the French and would have been utterly pointless. Wherever it was done, it merely pinned down another contingent of the French Army in a hard-to-supply, isolated position, doomed to inaction or to mere defensive action, and limited in its control and protection of the people to a small area around their post. The more such posts were established, the fewer troops were available to the unhappy general who was trying to assemble a mobile army strong enough to invade the main centers of Vietminh power and to destroy whatever force the enemy should dare to pit against the French in open battle. To immobilize as many as possible of the troops at the disposal of the French High Command was precisely the aim pursued by the Vietminh with their guerrillas and regional units.

Evidence of the success of this strategy soon became abundant in the region the French considered important enough to hold, against never-ending Vietminh attacks, at any cost in men and equipment: the Red River Delta. Its great fertility, its 6–7 million inhabitants, its centers of industry such as Nam Dinh, and its vital communication links, especially between the harbor city of Haiphong and the capital Hanoi, made the Red River Delta by far the most valuable prize in a war for control of Vietnam. The Franco-Vietminh duel for the delta, which ended only on the very last day of the war, consequently produced the longest, bloodiest, and most bitterly fought engagements before the battle of Dien Bien Phu. Had the Vietminh been wiped out in the delta, they would have found it hard to survive, since it would have meant not only the loss of a great source of manpower, rice, and taxes,[8] but also the freeing of a substantial part of the Expeditionary Corps for offensive action. For the French, the stakes were even higher. To be driven out of the delta would have meant losing to the Vietminh the entire North, from the Chinese border down to Quang Tri or Hue. It was the desperation they felt about control of the delta that made both the Vietminh and the French generals commit their biggest blunders of the war.

In the uninterrupted struggle for the delta, both parties made tremendous efforts even before they engaged in major battles—in troops employed, lives spent, equipment used up, and sacrifices imposed on the hapless population. The French tried to wipe out the Vietminh troops operating inside the delta and to close its borders against further infiltration; the Vietminh fought to make French control of the delta ineffective by limiting it, through incessant guerrilla activities, to towns, fortifications, and heavily patrolled waterways and roads. Since they were extremely successful, thousands of villages and their inhabitants remained subject to Vietminh rule.

Early in 1951, Giap, now in possession of a strong regular army well equipped with both light and heavy weapons from China, made a number of ill-advised attempts to drive the French out of Hanoi and Haiphong, and thus force them to give up the delta. The French defeated him in these first great battles of the Indochina War. Thereafter, the Vietminh, for the remaining years of the war, contented themselves with incessant minor operations inside the delta, conducted by their local guerrillas, their regional troops, and some battalions of their regular army which they had managed to get behind the French lines. They pursued these tactics with mounting success. French control was soon effective over only half of this important region, and by 1953, over no more than one-third. The famous "de Lattre line" of watchtowers and small fortifications built in 1951 to stop further infiltration was about as effective as a sieve. The process of subverting French control behind it was called the "rotting away" (*pourrissement*) of the delta.[9]

The immediate and direct achievements of the guerrilla warfare in the delta, and to a smaller degree in many other regions of Vietnam, were of immense help to the Hanoi regime, since they secured it manpower, taxes, food supplies, and vital information. But the extended territorial control exercised by local guerrillas and regional troops, even if such control was incomplete or temporary, accomplished something of much greater importance for the outcome of the war. It forced the French, in the South and Center, but above all in the Red River Delta, to use an ever-growing number of troops—more than half their entire Expeditionary Corps—for purely defensive and stationary duties.

This, rather than political insight, was the reason why the Generals de Lattre, Salan, and Navarre, who commanded the Expeditionary Corps between 1950 and 1954, insisted on the rapid creation of a Vietnamese national army. They needed this army, they said, to take on the task of defending and pacifying French-held territories exposed to infiltration and subversion by the Vietminh. Only if a Vietnamese army freed their troops now engaged in these duties, they held, would they be able to dispose of the manpower necessary for invading Vietminh-held territories, destroy Giap's army, and thus bring the war to an end.

2

When, in October, 1947, General Valluy launched the Expeditionary
Corps' first offensive to "wipe out" the Vietminh, the French were still
largely unaware of the advantages their opponents enjoyed in a military contest for control of Vietnam: the mountains in which to create
bases difficult of access; the jungles and marshes that always favored
the guerrillas and forever prevented their destruction; the seemingly
inexhaustible manpower reserves of the guerrillas and their skill and
constant aggressiveness; and above all, the extent of popular support
for the Hanoi regime, the main reason for the guerrillas' survival and
success. Only slowly did the French become aware of these Vietminh
assets, and of several others responsible for the lack of progress their
army made after the spring of 1947.[10]

Valluy started his offensive with an army of 30,000. His objectives
were to penetrate the Viet Bac, destroy Giap's regular army, and capture the Vietminh leaders. He hoped to achieve his objectives by first
encircling and then attacking the Viet Bac. He moved north along the
Clear River toward the Chinese border, and lavishly using paratroops
in his strategic moves, he dropped them as far north as Bac Kan.
French penetration of Vietminh territory led to the occupation of several provincial capitals, including Thai Nguyen and Tuyen Quang at
the eastern and western confines of the Vietminh retreat. In this offensive, the French also took the important city of Yen Bay on the Red
River almost 100 miles northwest of Hanoi. An armored column with
which Valluy intended to pounce on the Vietminh from the North
rolled via Langson up Colonial Route No. 4 as far as Caobang, and a
strong contingent with which to complete the encirclement tried to
move in boats up the Clear River along what was then the western
boundary of the Viet Bac. All that the French possessed in modern
arms and heavy equipment was being used in what was undoubtedly
the greatest military action in French colonial history.

This colossal effort bore only bitter fruit. With their vehicles, tanks,
and heavy artillery, the French were "prisoners of the roads," as they
themselves came to recognize. Roads were few and poor in the vast region that had to be invaded, and nowhere did they lead into the depths
of the Viet Bac mountains. Instead, they led through narrow, densely

wooded passes and jungles which were both difficult and senseless to penetrate in search of an invisible enemy. In their slow progress, the French columns, equipped with weapons considered capable of smashing all resistance, traveled for weeks without meeting a single Vietminh soldier; day after day passed, one more depressing than the next, without a shot being fired in that great first campaign to destroy the Vietminh. The people, too, had disappeared. Yet the French knew that the enemy, although invisible, was all around them, always close by, refusing to fight, but giving evidence of his presence much more distressing to the French than the expected and longed-for encounter in open battle. The villages the French passed were burning, the towns they reached were destroyed, the bridges over the many small rivers were blown up, and the roads they were forced to travel were made increasingly impassable by mines, ditches, and ingenious barricades built by men who watched their slow removal at a distance of no more than 50 yards, from the unstirring jungle, patiently biding their time.

Their time came soon after the French had reached the ruined and empty towns west, east, and north of the Viet Bac, which were their pointless first destination. They were now low in fuel, their rations were depleted, but even worse, the confidence with which they had started out was shattered. If now they ventured out from their main positions, they were ambushed by the Vietminh, who attacked from the jungle wherever their roadblocks forced the French to stop. A counterattack meant pushing into a void, and if pursued too far, going into a trap: The jungle was the ally of the Vietminh, allowing them to prepare their ambushes, and condemning pursuit by the French to failure.[11] A wave of guerrilla attacks rolled over the entire region immediately after its "conquest" by the French, exploiting the havoc wrought by the "scorched-earth" tactics that had greeted their arrival. Soon the chief concern of the French commander was not how to reach and destroy Giap's regular army in its many impenetrable hide-outs, but rather how to prevent the Vietminh from cutting the lines of communication to the distant bases from which his own army had to be supplied. A point was reached when the fighting strength of the French had to be devoted almost entirely to the protection of their supply convoys and to other purely defensive actions against increasingly frequent and massive Vietminh attacks. Lacking the courage to admit failure, Valluy kept postponing the inevitable decision to withdraw, thereby adding to his losses in men and equipment and rendering more difficult the task of extracting his army from a hopeless position. The French could do no more than defend themselves, and if they waited too long were in danger of being ground to pieces. One after another, the cities and provincial capitals whose names had adorned the victory communiqués of the French in the fall of 1947—Yen Bay, Thai Nguyen, Tuyen Quang—had to be evacuated. Early in 1948, the position of the French outside the delta was again what it had been a year before. All the French had gained from this gigantic effort was some progress in understanding the peculiar nature of this war. However, only the soldiers, not the generals or politicians, had a premonition that France had lost the Indochina War then and there.[12]

That the generals had learned too little could be seen from their refusal to evacuate the distant and now even more isolated positions the French held on Colonial Route No. 4. Starting at Caobang in the far north of Tongking, this road ran close along the Chinese border in a southeasterly direction toward the Gulf of Tongking. Since the Vietminh now controlled all direct road connections between Hanoi and the Chinese border, supplies had to be brought by ship from Haiphong before they could start their perilous journey on Route 4 to the garrisons at Langson, That Khe, Dong Khe, and Caobang. For a while, the French even clung to Bac Kan at the northern approaches to the Viet Bac, supplying it, at a tremendous cost, via Route 4 and Caobang. Nowhere in the many "battles of the road" did the French lose more lives and more equipment than on Route 4, to which they held on until a successful evacuation was no longer possible.

The strategy of destroying the Vietminh with one great stroke had failed, at least for the time being. This was clear both to the military and the political leaders of the French. Both, therefore, had to adapt their thinking and tactics to the reality of the situation created by this failure. Bollaert intensified his wooing of Bao Dai, but the generals, never too quick to realize that what they had once learned might no longer be valid, were temporarily without any plan at all of how to proceed. Since for them the war was still primarily a military contest, they were far from grasping all the implications of their failure. However, in the spring of 1948, even official optimism could not ignore that Vietminh resistance had fought the French armies to a standstill, and that new methods had to be devised for dealing with an enemy who refused to fight according to tested military procedures. Among the French there were, of course, also people who had learned nothing from

Valluy's debacle and who dreamed only of preparing and throwing an even greater and better-equipped army against the northern bastion of the Vietminh. But even they knew that much time would elapse before another great offensive could be mounted and that in the meantime some other ways of fighting the Vietminh had to be found.

Making a virtue of necessity, French military cerebration produced what was pompously offered as an entirely new strategy to bring about the collapse of Vietminh resistance. The guiding idea of this new strategy, which was simple, indicated that there was really very little choice. Instead of attacking and destroying the main enemy forces in the Viet Bac, the French would now proceed to cut them off from all other Vietminh regions and concentrate on "pacifying" these regions —i.e., bringing them under their full control. Isolated from the rest of the country and deprived of their indispensable supplies of food, raw materials, taxes, and manpower, the Vietminh Government and army leadership would then have only one alternative to surrender: to move out of its stronghold, face the French in open battle, and suffer defeat.

The main drawback of this strategy was that it would take time, and time, General de Gaulle's opinion notwithstanding, was not working in favor of the French. Great efforts were indeed made all during 1948 to reduce areas under Vietminh control vital for supplying the Viet Bac, but all gains were temporary, since to preserve them would have meant to use the entire army for static and defensive tasks. The French simply lacked the fantastic number of troops needed to pacify and hold the entire country. To do this in the Tongking Delta alone would have left no mobile forces needed to stop Vietminh attacks on convoys and isolated strong points, and would thus have resulted not in extending but rather in diminishing the areas under French control. The more territory the French tried to occupy, the less effectively they controlled what they already had, and the dimmer grew their prospects of ever building up a mobile striking force with which to try again one day to deal a decisive blow to the Vietminh. An advance, in November, 1948, into Sontay and Vetri, north of Hanoi, although it led to the capture of large Vietminh supply depots and manufacturing sites, merely underlined that in 1948 the offensive power of the French was considerably lower than it had been in 1947.

The year 1949, too, produced no change in the new pattern of the war, nor any significant change in the relative strength of the two sides. It brought the French not one step nearer to their goal. Hundreds of small actions, usually short and brutal, were fought all over the country, imposing on the soldiers of both sides a load of suffering that no living being should be forced to bear. But these engagements only proved that the Expeditionary Corps, after having failed to destroy the army of the Hanoi regime, was also unable to disperse or destroy the local guerrillas and regional units of the Vietminh. While the French, in a few major operations, fought to widen the delta region under their control, the Vietminh continued to infiltrate behind their lines, strengthening their many pockets of resistance, and reducing the number of villages under French military supervision and Bao Dai administration.[13] The guerrillas in the Red River Delta threatened again and again to cut the most important French line of communication in Indochina, the road between Haiphong and Hanoi. On the other hand, the French never succeeded in blocking the roads, paths, and waterways so vital for the Vietminh that connected the rich provinces south of the delta with the Viet Bac. They could no longer even threaten them after their weakness had made it advisable for them to evacuate the strategic city of Hoa Binh southwest of Hanoi. Far from extending their hold on Tongking during this theoretical period of pacification, the feeble French grip on it became even weaker, particularly after they had been forced, in August, 1948, to relinquish Bac Kan, held since paratroops had taken it at the beginning of Valluy's offensive. This removed the last threat to the backdoor of the enemy's training base and headquarters.

In May, 1949, the French Government, disturbed over the lack of progress in the war, sent General Revers, Chief of the General Staff, on an inspection tour to Indochina. In a secret report, he recommended the evacuation of the isolated garrisons along the Chinese border, which, lying in the midst of Vietminh country and being difficult to supply, were a drain on French resources and could probably not withstand a serious attack. General Revers, one of the first prominent Frenchmen to urge the rapid build-up of the Vietnamese Army, also insisted that before another offensive against the Viet Bac could be undertaken, the delta had first to be completely pacified and its defense turned over to the Vietnamese Army. Not only did he recognize that without a strong Vietnamese army to support the French, victory over the Vietminh would be difficult to achieve, but he also knew something about the political conditions that would make such an army effective. In this war, he said, "diplomacy" must have precedence over military considerations.

The report of General Revers can be considered the first one of a long series of investigations by special commissions into the causes of Communist military strength in Vietnam. His recommendations shared the fate of most later ones—being misunderstood or disregarded. In any case, they had no influence on either the military or political conduct of the war. Not only did "diplomacy" fail to create the political conditions for a Vietnamese army willing to fight; even the suggestion to liquidate the obviously untenable positions along Route 4 was not acted upon by those who made military decisions. No satisfactory explanation has as yet been given for the failure to follow this important recommendation. It may have been due to simple negligence, to a cowardly refusal to assume responsibility for an unpopular decision, to a conflict in command authority between High Commissioner Pignon and the generals in charge, but possibly also to justified fear that the Vietminh might turn the evacuation into a military triumph for them, since they, to the consternation of the French, had succeeded in obtaining a copy of General Revers' secret report.[14] Waiting, however, could only change the likelihood of an immediate minor disaster into the certainty of a major catastrophe later.

An indication of the turn military events might take during 1950 came early in the year, when the Vietminh began to move in strength up along the Red River against the important city of Laokay on the Chinese border. This advance led to the first engagement in which Giap used strong units of his regular army. He attacked the French at Laokay with five infantry battalions supported by 81-mm. mortars obtained from the Chinese Communists—the forerunners of vastly greater Chinese aid to come. The French, outnumbered five to one, were defeated after a brief struggle. This was in February, 1950. On May 25, Giap attacked and took the post of Dong Khe on Route 4, some 15 miles south of Caobang, but lost it again to paratroopers dropped by the French only two days later. The rainy season prevented major operations for almost four months, but on September 16, Dong Khe was attacked again and its garrison of 800 overwhelmed by the Vietminh on September 18.

This was the prelude to an all-out Vietminh effort to clear the Sino-Vietnamese border area of all positions still in French hands. The most distant French garrison at Caobang was entirely cut off by the fall of Dong Khe. The French had no choice but to attempt a fighting retreat toward Langson before being encircled by the Vietminh. They started out from Caobang on October 3, with 1,600 regular soldiers, 1,000 partisans, and many civilians who feared for their lives. With a column of 3,500 men, mainly Moroccans who had been stationed further south, at That Me, the French command tried to protect the retreat of their Caobang garrison. Both groups were ambushed and attacked by six Vietminh battalions, forced to abandon their vehicles, and driven into the hills, where they were tracked down, killed, or taken prisoner by the numerically superior Vietminh forces. A battalion of paratroopers sent in to cover the now chaotic retreat was almost entirely wiped out. Langson, in immediate danger of being overrun, was hastily abandoned in the night of October 17–18, with the assistance of two battalions of paratroopers, but the large supplies of arms, ammunition, and vehicles the French had stocked at this important location had to be left behind. "By October 19, this disastrous phase was over. The French had been completely driven out of northern Tongking, from the sea to the Red River, and a huge slice of territory adjacent to China was now completely under Vietminh control." [15] The Expeditionary Corps, in addition to the vast amounts of equipment it had to abandon, lost 6,000 men. The Vietminh, without themselves suffering many casualties, inflicted on the French what was then considered the greatest military debacle in the colonial history of France.[16] It was then that the French, wiser although too late, began, on November 6, to evacuate the town of Hoa Binh, gateway to the hilly and wooded Muong country along the northwestern border of the Red River Delta. This meant not only widening the corridor through which the Vietminh brought men and supplies from the region south of the delta into the Viet Bac; it also brought the Muong minority population, which was not too friendly toward the Hanoi regime, under firm Vietminh control.

The French in charge of Indochinese military policy now began to realize that time was not on their side, that the strategy of slowly reducing the areas of Vietminh predominance and of isolating the Viet Bac had failed, too, and that they had in fact made no progress at all since the beginning of the war. The years from 1948 to 1951 could at best be regarded as a stalemate, and since this stalemate had now been broken by the Vietminh, it was evident that a shift in the relative strength of the two parties in favor of the Vietminh had taken place during these three years. This had resulted in a new kind of war, one engaging larger units in open battle—not in place of, but in addition to the guerrilla war all over the country which was relentlessly pursued in the northern delta, in central Vietnam, and with renewed vigor also in the South. On the fourth anniversary of the outbreak of the war in Hanoi, French morale was understandably low, whereas Vietminh confidence was such that their radio station in the Viet Bac began to predict the early return of Ho Chi Minh to Hanoi.[17]

Indeed, Giap regarded his recent victories not merely as proof that in the North the French could no longer maintain themselves beyond the delta; he felt that his victories were the first waves of a great tide that would sweep the French out of the delta as well.

Although the Vietminh leaders conducted a war that was most unorthodox by any known Western standards, they, too, fought their war according to the book. Their canon—a modified version of the laws of revolutionary warfare laid down by Mao Tse-tung [18]—said that the war would go through three stages, which, however, would not be divided by fixed points in time. Although these stages would overlap, they would be distinctly different. They were described in a style in which propagandistic exhortations were mixed with pedantic theorizing by Truong Chinh (alias Dang Xuan Khu)—not by Giap, whose writings on the subject are of a later date and lack distinction. Truong Chinh was then not only the chief theoretician of Vietnamese Communism, but also a central figure in the Party's organizational life.[19] Secretary General of the Indochinese Communist Party until its dissolution in November, 1946, he became Secretary General of the "Marxist Study Group" that took the place of the Party, and later held the same position in the Lao Dong (Workers) Party, as the Communist Party was called after its revival in February, 1951. Truong Chinh's small book on the nature of the Indochina War, entitled *The Resistance Will Win*, appeared in June, 1947. It expounded the theory that the war would proceed through its three stages in the following manner: In the beginning, the Vietminh will be weak, the enemy strong. The Vietminh will therefore be on the defensive, the enemy on the offensive. In this first phase of the war, the task of the Vietminh will be to preserve its forces, to retire into protected territory, and to be content with harassing the enemy's convoys and bases. In the second phase, called that of the "equilibrium of forces and of active resistance," the enemy can no longer make progress, but the Vietminh is not yet able to regain lost territory. The military task during this period is to engage, tie down, and, if possible, exterminate units of the enemy forces through ever-larger attacks by guerrillas and regional troops, and to sabotage the enemy's economic activities. This second phase will be the longest of the three. It will end when the Vietminh has built up enough strength to open its own general counteroffensive, beginning with a war of maneuver, passing through a war of large movements, into a war of position, and ending with the victory of the Vietminh.[20]

According to the Vietminh, the war so far had proceeded according to the book. The first phase came to an end with Valluy's failure to reach and destroy the Vietminh forces in the Viet Bac. The following three years, up to the defeat of the French on Colonial Route No. 4, were regarded as the second phase. Elated, but also misled by his victories at the end of 1950, Giap made the mistake of believing that this phase was now over too, and that Vietminh strength had become sufficient for a war of movement and large-scale attacks on the French.

Three such attacks were undertaken early in 1951, for which the bulk of Giap's regular army moved for the first time out of the Viet Bac. The first of these offensives which started on January 13, aimed at Hanoi. On a 12-mile-wide front between Vetri and Luc Nam, north of Hanoi, Giap attacked with eighteen of his best battalions, whose logistic support was organized primitively but effectively by an army of 180,000 porters. The battle lasted four days. The firepower of the French mowed down wave after wave of the attackers, but even after their piled-up bodies gave protection to the soldiers thrown later into the battle, the Vietminh Army was unable to break through the main defenses of the French. After losing at least 6,000 of his best troops, Giap returned to the Viet Bac with his battered army.

With a stubbornness that is said to have almost cost him his position, Giap refused to admit that the time for large-scale Vietminh offensives had not yet come. On March 24, 1951, he began his second offensive, moving from Langson in the direction of Dong Trieu. His plan was to cut off the coal region of Moncay and then to overwhelm the port city of Haiphong. This would have forced the French to evacuate Hanoi and probably to give up the entire delta. Only after eight days of fruitless attacks, costly in men whose heroism was completely futile, did Giap recognize that despite his vast numerical superiority he had failed once more. French fire power and ample use of aircraft stopped the Vietminh at a village called Mao Khe, far short of their objective, after inflicting another 3,000 casualties.

Since Giap was a very determined man, but apparently not yet a great general, it took another debacle before he learned his lesson.

With his third offensive, Giap tried to force the French out of the delta by attacking them from the south. The new battle, which became known as the Battle of the Day River, began on May 29, 1951. The Day River runs along the southwestern edge of the delta, from Sontay 20 miles northwest of Hanoi to the Gulf of Tongking. South of it, in the province of Than Hoa, the Vietminh had succeeded in building up an entire division (the 320th) of their regular army—the only one formed, trained, and equipped outside of the Viet Bac. In a movement remarkable for the logistic achievement of the Vietminh Army long before Dien Bien Phu, Giap brought two more of his divisions (the 304th and 308th) all the way down from the heart of the Viet Bac, over a distance of more than 150 miles. The Vietminh had then neither trucks nor other vehicles and had to travel and transport its supplies on foot and by night. Hidden camping places had to be found and prepared every day for 60,000 people, since the 20,000 soldiers needed at least double that number of men and women to carry the reserves of food, ammunition, and other supplies. These porters were locally recruited and exchanged a few times during the long march, which meant that for this offensive, too, the total number employed was more than 100,000. Surprised by this feat, the French would admit no other explanation for it than Vietminh terror, while the Vietminh, with an equally deliberate distortion of truth, ascribed it to popular enthusiasm for their regime.

The Vietminh attacked first at Phu Ly and Ninh Binh on the Day River some 50 miles up from the coast. Giap's strategy was to force the French commander to throw his reserves in the delta into this battle area; Giap then sent his 320th Division, stationed farther south, over the river into the delta. The French held fast at Phu Ly and Ninh Binh without committing many of their mobile reserves. The Vietminh pushed deep into the heart of the Catholic province Phat Diem, attempting to link up with two regiments already operating in the delta and now ordered to prevent the French from bringing any reinforcement to the main battle areas. The Vietminh would then attack the French defenses at Phu Ly and Ninh Binh from the rear. But popular support, so vital for Vietminh military success, was conspicuously lacking in the regions inhabited by Catholics; instead, resistance by the local Catholic militias was strong, which helped the French enormously, since they gained time and protection from guerrilla ambushes over vast regions between the Day River and the southern Red River branches some 80 miles to the northeast. Two other reasons made this Vietminh invasion of the delta another costly failure. The French Navy was able to move enough attacking craft up the Day River to cut Giap's supply lines, and the French, profusely and to great effect, used napalm bombs (jellied petroleum) on a surprised enemy who, for the first time, had left the protection of the jungles to fight in open fields. After being battered and stalled in all his moves for ten days, Giap saw that to continue would merely increase his losses and demoralize his men. It took him a full week to pull his troops back behind the Day River, where he discovered that a third of his army was lost.[21]

Lost was also Giap's hope to eject the French from the delta, since this required offensive strength the Vietminh as yet did not possess. Under the monsoon clouds of the summer of 1951, the war again assumed its previous aspect, that of the long "second phase" of Truong Chinh's theory when an "equilibrium of forces" prevented either party from achieving decisive results. During the fifth year of the war the contestants were back again where they had been before Giap had prematurely embarked upon a war of movement. There was now more action on a larger scale than in 1948 and 1949, and because of a French attempt to exploit Giap's setback, a number of fierce battles were fought at the western edge of the delta. But the over-all picture remained that of the former stalemate: The French were no longer able to make progress, while the Vietminh could not yet win the battles into which they had been tempted to rush by their growing strength.

3

The outcome of the battle for Route 4, which had made Giap overoptimistic, had had an extremely sobering effect on the French. Scapegoats had to be found; the first of these was General Alessandri, who was relieved of his post as commander of the French Army in Tongking. But the Commander in Chief of the Expeditionary Corps, General Carpentier, and the High Commissioner for Indochina, Léon Pignon, were also recalled. The French Government, convinced that conflicts of authority had impeded called-for action at the right time, decided to put all civilian and military power into one hand. It offered both the positions of Commander in Chief and High Commissioner of Indochina to General Jean de Lattre de Tassigny.

De Lattre, together with the Generals Leclerc and Juin, had acquired great fame as a commander and strategist during World War II. But although de Lattre was esteemed as a general, he was a highly controversial man. His excessive reliance on his power of command combined with the "artistic" features of his temperament served to put terror into the hearts of the men subject to his authority. His personality prohibited any kind of collaboration, since the only relationship with anyone he accepted in his post was that of subservience to his authority. Donald Lancaster, who served at the British Legation when de Lattre took over on December 17, 1950, describes the general's "egocentric personality" in revealing though quite unflattering terms. De Lattre, says Lancaster, had a "legendary capacity for volcanic expressions of displeasure," an "overbearing manner," and a "disregard for normal civilities" that was only occasionally mitigated by a "considerable ability to charm." His fantastic megalomania may have appealed to some of his soldiers, who nicknamed him *le roi Jean*, but it was hard to swallow for the people directly under him, if for no other reason than that their "personal convenience was ruthlessly subordinated to his own." In the "frequent excesses of his autocratic temperament," de Lattre committed many "injustices." He constantly humiliated his most loyal collaborators and imposed quite unnecessary hardships on soldiers and officials. The new Commander in Chief

> continued to insist that all local personages, together with important contingents of troops, should be present whenever, on his frequent journeys, he was due to arrive at, or to leave from, an Indochinese airfield. This idiosyncrasy resulted in much waste of time, while his frequent outbursts against those subordinates whose decisions or actions failed to meet with his approval led to increasing reluctance, particularly on the part of his civilian staff, to take any initiative if there was a chance that the person responsible might thereby bring down upon his head an expression of de Lattre's displeasure.[22]

De Lattre's life ended tragically. He died in Paris of cancer on January 11, 1952, after having served in Indochina less than a year. But grief had stricken him down long before he fell victim to a painful and incurable disease. Only a few months after assuming his command he lost his only son in the defense of a position he himself had ordered held at all costs. Bernard de Lattre fell at Binh Dinh on May 30, 1951, the night after Giap started the battle of the Day River. But de Lattre's pride was not to be broken by grief or physical suffering. In the last bitter hours of his struggle with death, the general, on hearing that the government had decided to appoint him Marshal of France, made it clear that he regarded himself as his country's most deserving soldier. "The news is reported to have been greeted by the dying man with the demand for an assurance that he was the only one to be thus honored." [23]

Strange as it may seem to the civilian mind, the army, although they hardly loved de Lattre, admired him. He instantly raised the army's low spirits when he reversed the decision of his predecessor to evacuate French women and children from Hanoi. His faults cast a dark shadow over his character, but they did not impair his talents. As a strategist and commander, he was probably more than merely competent. If his excessive pride, his unlimited self-esteem, and his crude enjoyment of authority were destructive of decent human relations, they were at the same time evidence of an explosive energy and thus capable of creating confidence in an army longing to be taken off the dismal road of defeat. This de Lattre achieved, at least for a short time, since it was his skillful and courageous leadership that defeated Giap's attempts to throw the French out of Hanoi and the delta. When the tide turned once more against the French, de Lattre was already dead. His leadership probably averted a major disaster for the French in 1951, but "his failure to effect any basic change in strategy which would enable the French Union troops to recover their mobility makes it unlikely that the Expeditionary Corps was deprived of final victory by his death." [24]

De Lattre indeed had no lasting military achievements to his credit, notwithstanding his success in stopping Giap's triple attempt to drive the French out of the delta: Since in these battles de Lattre merely preserved existing positions, the defeats he inflicted on the Vietminh were of no positive consequence for the French. De Lattre did try to exploit the rout of the Vietminh on the Day River by reoccupying the strategically important town of Hoa Binh on the Black River, 50 miles southwest of Hanoi. But this action, undertaken because of pressure from France to produce some kind of tangible success, was a great strategic mistake. It led to a long, costly, and quite pointless series of battles lasting three months, and ended with one of those retreats that the French like to celebrate as victories, since they managed to extract their reduced and exhausted contingents from positions that had been considered lost. Hoa Binh, taken by de Lattre on November 14, 1951, was evacuated by his successor, General Raoul Salan, in February, 1952. The Vietminh, in a brutal revenge for their Day River debacle of spring, 1951, first defeated all French efforts to supply Hoa Binh by the Black River, and then made life impossible for the French garrisons and convoys on the road that connected Hoa Binh with Hanoi. On February 24, the last French troops ("elements of the 13th Foreign Legion Half-Brigade—which was to be totally destroyed later at Dien Bien Phu" [25]) returned to the relative safety of the delta, whose extension under de Lattre was undone in one of the greatest Vietminh efforts of the war.[26]

The one action that might have helped the French stop the increase of Vietminh strength de Lattre was unable even to consider: an attempt to interfere with the rising flow of Communist China's aid for the Vietminh by reoccupying the positions along Route 4 lost in October, 1950. There can be no doubt that de Lattre thereby "tacitly admitted that a military victory at this stage was beyond the grasp of the Expeditionary Corps." [27] He recognized that offensive action broad enough to promise success was possible only under three conditions: The delta had to be made safe, the Expeditionary Corps had to be strengthened and relieved of its static and purely defensive duties, and the United States had to help France carry the mounting burden of the war.

The attempt to make the delta safe led to the construction of the so-called de Lattre Line—fortified concrete strong points built in groups of five or six, 1 or 2 miles apart, all around the delta; the desire to have at his disposal a larger mobile force for offensive action impelled de Lattre to urge Bao Dai to speed up the formation of the still embryonic Vietnamese National Army; and in order to mobilize help for the French war effort, de Lattre went to Washington to plead for massive military aid.

In all three respects, de Lattre was only moderately successful. From Washington, which he visited in September, 1951, he wanted aircraft, trucks, tanks, amphibious vehicles, and other equipment, such as automatic weapons and artillery. But the United States was still involved in the Korean War, and although de Lattre obtained a promise of increased aid,[28] the large quantities he desired were as yet not forthcoming.[29]

The construction of a line of fortified posts around the delta had already been recommended by General Revers in his report in May,

1949, but the weak towers that had so far been set up proved less an obstacle to Vietminh penetration than a target for guerrilla attacks. Building a line of strong and continuous fortifications around the entire delta was a tremendous task, but de Lattre embarked upon it without a moment's hesitation, keeping an eye on the work to see that it was done with speed. Within six months, six hundred strong points were erected on a line stretching from the Bay of Along up to Vinh Yen 45 miles north of Hanoi. Six hundred more were completed before the end of 1951, in order to give protection to some 7 million people on the delta's 7,000 square miles. Unfortunately, the de Lattre Line did not serve its purpose too well. General Navarre later disparagingly called it "a sort of Maginot Line." Although the roads between these static defense positions were continuously patrolled by small armored units (troops that were mobile, but only for defensive purposes), infiltration could still not be prevented. It had been particularly heavy, as General Navarre pointed out in his book on the last years of the war, while the French were engaged in their futile effort to hold on to Hoa Binh. The result was that the Vietminh forces operating inside the delta were stronger after completion of the defense line than before. Furthermore, manning 1,200 strong points and patrolling the areas in between required a substantial portion of the troops that were available to de Lattre in the North, leaving him with insufficient forces for offensive action against the Vietminh. These posts were also the object of constant nightly attacks by the Vietminh. Many were captured and destroyed, often by the same people conscripted from the delta villages for the construction of de Lattre's line. Even if the defense of this line had been successful, it would not have meant that the French were making progress in the war against the Vietminh.

It was for these compelling military reasons, and not due to deeper political insight, that de Lattre and later Salan and Navarre kept stressing the need for a Vietnamese national army large enough to free the Expeditionary Corps for offensive action by taking over the task of defending and pacifying the areas not under effective Vietminh control.

In 1952, before the Bao Dai regime had made much progress in building up its own army, a point had been reached when the French disposed of fewer permanently mobile battalions than the Vietminh. The Vietminh

> had over 125,000 full-time, well-trained, regular soldiers of the main force, which were disposed into six divisions (the new 325th Infantry Division had just been formed in An Khe Province of the South Delta Base), at

least six independent regiments, and a few independent battalions, some of which were in the process of expanding into regiments. There were three independent regiments established in the Delta inside the de Lattre Line, and there were two independent battalions actually operating within the limits of Hanoi itself. In addition, the Viet Minh main force was actively supported by over 75,000 regional troops, which although having less mobility, were invaluable for limited operations. In the background were somewhere between 200,000 and 350,000 village militia—no one knew exactly how many.[30]

These French estimates may have been exaggerated, since the French generals always tried to prove to their government the need for reinforcements; but there is no doubt that Giap, by absorbing the better-trained units of his regional fighters, had raised his regular army to 110,000. Chinese aid had enabled him to add a heavy (artillery) division (the 351st) to his five infantry divisions, all of which he had brought up to full strength since his losses early in 1951. The Vietminh fighters were now also better equipped, both with small arms and artillery. Lack of arms, not men, had been holding back the expansion of the regular army. Chinese aid, which became massive after 1952, removed this obstacle to the growth of Vietminh armed strength. During 1952, the Vietminh were said to have received at least 40,000 rifles, 4,000 submachine guns, and much artillery, including some badly needed anti-aircraft guns, from China.[31] Giap, who now again was looking toward the start of a war of movement, could always mobilize several hundred thousand people to serve as porters; he had at his disposal a host of well-organized and disciplined spies and informers (including Vietnamese mistresses of French officers);[32] and for the initial stages of a battle, he had special groups of so-called "death volunteers" (or suicide squads) ready to be sacrificed in the job of forcing a gap in the enemy's defenses. In short, the Vietminh had at least 300,000 men who carried arms and fought, and an equal number of noncombatant auxiliaries (including women) to keep the fighting units supplied and to facilitate their rapid movements. And to these advantages must be added that Giap did not have to waste much of his strength on static duties. The Vietminh had hardly any cities to garrison and defend, no posts or blockhouses to guard and hold, and except for the Viet Bac, which was almost impregnable, few territories so vital for their survival that they could not be temporarily abandoned if defending them proved impossible or too costly.

The French were at a disadvantage against the Vietminh in all respects except in the number of regular troops and heavy equipment, including aircraft and "river tanks" (Dinassauts).[33] French superiority in heavy equipment was even growing, since American aid soon vastly exceeded Chinese aid to the Vietminh. The regular army of the French was always larger than that of their opponents. In 1952, its strength was 190,000 men, which included the air force and navy, manned respectively by 10,000 and 5,000 French nationals. The army itself never counted more than about 50,000 French nationals. The rest were 30,000 French colonial troops (North Africans and Senegalese), 20,000 Foreign Legionnaires, and about 70,000 Indochinese. To these well-trained, unusually well-led, and always well-equipped French forces must be added the troops of the religious-political sects in the South and the Catholic militia in the North. The total number of men fighting under the three sect banners was probably 30,000,[34] but their contribution to the struggle, as that of the Catholic militia, was only of local importance and purely defensive, since they aimed only at keeping the Vietminh out of the territories under their control.

The great disadvantage of the French, loudly lamented by de Lattre in 1951, by Salan in 1952, and by Navarre in 1953, was that with an organized and better-equipped fighting force, almost twice the size of Giap's regular army, fewer troops were available to them for offensive action than to the Vietminh. Navarre estimated that of the total of 190,000 men in the Expeditionary Corps, at least 100,000 were tied down in static defense duties.[35] Lacouture and Devillers claim that of the 500,000 soldiers of which the French disposed after the build-up of the Vietnamese National Army in 1953, no less than 350,000 were engaged in "static duties." The Vietminh battle corps consisted of six divisions; the French had only the equivalent of three, including their eight parachute battalions.[36] The other 350,000 were assigned to defending cities, holding isolated strongpoints, accompanying convoys, patrolling highways, and conducting punitive actions against villages suspected of hiding and feeding the guerrillas, and of informing them about French moves.[37] Alone sealing off and trying to pacify the delta absorbed almost one-third of the Expeditionary Corps, a force obviously still insufficient for the task: When Navarre, in May, 1953, overlooked the northern scene, he discovered that of the 7,000 villages in the delta, the French could boast of fully controlling no more than 2,000.[38]

Beginning with de Lattre, the commanders in chief of the French troops had become the most determined among the promoters of a Vietnamese national army. Because of their insistence, steps were at last being taken which until then had been only talked about in Hanoi, Saigon, and Paris. The policy of merely "yellowing" the Expeditionary Corps, as the recruiting for it among the Indochinese was called, had to be discarded.[39] For obvious political reasons, a Vietnamese national army had to be officered by Vietnamese nationals. But there was also another reason that "yellowing" the Expeditionary Corps no longer sufficed: Not enough French officers were available for an expansion of the French-led forces by a few hundred thousand men. The high casualty rate among their officers was one of the major problems the French had to deal with in this war, in which, by 1950, 800 French officers had already been killed.

It was de Lattre who broke French resistance to a Vietnamese national army, a resistance of which High Commissioner Léon Pignon seems to have been the leader. De Lattre knew that political opposition to sending French conscripts to Indochina could not be overcome in France, and that the reservoir of colonial troops from Africa was as nearly exhausted as was the yearly crop of French officers produced by St. Cyr. He also knew that of the steps necessary to bring a Vietnamese army into existence, the most important one was the training of native officers. It had been sabotaged even by people who wanted Vietnamese troops by the hundreds of thousands; but most French officers in Indochina, used to command whatever native military units existed, were opposed to a native army not totally subject to French control. De Lattre's authority helped to change this attitude. Much too late, and not because of political sagacity, most French military leaders now agreed that a Vietnamese national army should be led by Vietnamese nationals, whose talents as organizers of troops and leaders in battle the Vietminh officers had proven beyond question. A Vietnamese military academy was opened in November, 1950. It was expected to produce 150 officers yearly. Officers of lower grades had been trained before, about 50 per year, but these were not being used to form the cadres of an autonomous national army. They still served only in the "yellow" units of the Expeditionary Corps, which meant that they were not Vietnamese but French soldiers.[40]

At the urging of de Lattre, who knew how to get his way with Bao Dai and the then Prime Minister Tran Van Huu, conscription was introduced in July, 1951, but due chiefly to the lack of trained officers, only a token number of young men was called up. Among the heads of the Bao Dai regime there was also justified fear that conscription would have unfavorable political effects. In order to avoid being called up for the National Army, many young men in the South joined the Cao Dai and Hoa Hao militias. The men who were enlisted during 1951 formed a rather pitiable, small army. They were poorly trained and equipped, but the major deficiency then and for a long time to come was a lack of competent officers: The best elements of the Vietnamese educated middle class had no desire to serve in an army created to fight, still under French over-all direction, for a regime they despised and against people who, even if led by Communists, were still known to be fighting primarily for national independence. For these political reasons, which the colonial French mind failed to grasp, the Vietnamese National Army never became much of a fighting force. It remained indifferently trained, poorly led, and dubiously inspired. At the end of the war, the French had at their disposal a Vietnamese force of 300,000 men, organized in various formations, including local militias, and in various stages of training and availability for combat. But not another square mile of territory had been pacified as a result of its creation, and very few French troops had been relieved of their static duties or become available for offensive action against the Vietminh.[41]

To say, as some Frenchmen have done, that the Vietnamese could not be made into good soldiers was, of course, only one of the many French self-deceptions to prop their belief that their Indochinese policy made sense. The contrary was proved not only by the extraordinary valor and skill of the Vietminh fighters, but also by the French-led Indochinese in the Expeditionary Corps, who usually fought well and whose casualty rate was higher than that of any other French-led group.[42] A Vietnamese national army could have had military value only in fighting for or defending independence. As an instrument of the Bao Dai regime, which was still only a cover for French colonial rule, no kind of training or propaganda could produce inspired officers or men willing to risk their lives. For a long time Bao Dai himself was reluctant to push the build-up of his army. He not only doubted its usefulness, but even thought that it might constitute a liability. "It would be dangerous," he said to one of his advisers, "to expand the Vietnamese Army, because it might defect en masse and go to the Vietminh."[43] In fact, the first units created and used in the South "were a disappointment: a few companies deserted *en bloc*, some refused to move from their home district or go out on patrols, while others showed no offensive spirit at all." [44] Nguyen Van Hinh, son of the "French patriot" Nguyen Van Tam, and himself a French citizen and officer of the French Army, was made general and chief of staff of the Vietnamese Army. He too had something very sobering to say about the army, which was to change the fortunes of the war in favor of the French. It would take seven years, said Hinh, before the National Army would be ready to relieve the Expeditionary Corps of its static duties and take part in offensive operations against the Vietminh.

The truth of this gloomy prediction rested on reasons that General Hinh himself was quite unable to perceive. Given an entirely different political climate—for instance the one that supported the military efforts of the Vietminh—the National Army might have been turned into an efficient and inspired fighting force in less than three years. De Lattre thought that he had failed to regain territory and to start offensive action because he did not have a Vietnamese army. But his successors, Salan and Navarre, had such an army, which in 1953 comprised at least 200,000 men. Nevertheless, they too failed to regain territory and to free the Expeditionary Corps for the task of destroying the Vietminh. They failed not because the army was still too small and inadequately trained, as Navarre thought. He expected that the Expeditionary Corps would be free to undertake major offensive action in the fall of 1955—but he lost the war before this could be put to a test. The reasons were political rather than lack of numbers and training, and for these same reasons Navarre's expectations would have been disappointed in 1955 as well. Salan, who had a political mind of sorts, had learned what was required for victory against the Vietminh after he had held his thankless position for a year. "We shall win," he said, "when all vital forces of the nation, from the peasant in the rice field to the bourgeois in the cities, participate in the fight against the Vietminh." [45] Salan knew that this alone could turn the National Army into the instrument needed to win the war. What he too failed to realize was that both the peasants and most city dwellers would have considered active participation in the struggle against the Vietminh only if the French had granted full independence to the anti-Vietminh state of Vietnam. "The condition for military success," said Lacouture and Devillers, "which was political, was never achieved. It was the creation of a unified Vietnam, independent and truly democratic." [46]

It was the power of the nationalist sentiments that prevented the

French-sponsored Vietnamese National Army from ever becoming an
effective fighting force against the Vietminh. These sentiments, which
determined the people's attitude during the entire war, favored the
Vietminh exclusively, raising the morale of its soldiers far above that
not only of Bao Dai's army, but also of most men serving in the French
Expeditionary Corps. There was a great deal of heroism on the French
side too, particularly among the officers, but neither the Algerians and
Senegalese nor the Indochinese serving in the French Army could be
expected to court certain death in battle, as so many Vietminh soldiers
did in their suicidal missions. In fact, even before the attackers at Dien
Bien Phu were slaughtered by the thousands, the Vietminh command
acted at times as if its entire army consisted of volunteers of death.

4

The "secret weapon" of the Vietnamese Communists—if they possessed anything deserving this name—was their ability to organize,
indoctrinate, discipline, and lead the masses—a Communist, not a spe-
cifically Vietnamese, talent, which has never been, and still is not, part
of any other political movement in Vietnam. A few hundred gifted
men, the sons of both rich and poor, had acquired, and adapted to
Vietnamese conditions, the techniques of mass propaganda and organization developed chiefly by the European labor movement before
World War I, and by the Bolsheviks before and after the Russian
Revolution.

But although these techniques owed much to "Marxist" and "Lenin-
ist" inspiration, Vietminh mass propaganda was not aimed at filling the
people's minds with Communist ideas. The Vietminh, as long as it existed as an instrument of the Communists, concentrated on the aims for
which it had been founded: national liberation and a "progressive,"
"democratic" state. The objection that being Communists the Vietminh leaders thereby merely pursued their ultimate Party aims is politically misleading, for it implies that the nationalism of the Communists
was fraudulent, that they merely "used" nationalism as a means to advance their cause.

Unless one understands this point it is quite impossible to understand
why the Vietminh could become the vehicle through which the Vietnamese Communists achieved their victories. To say that the Commu-

nists "used" nationalism is true only in the sense in which this applies to all nationalists. The point, however, is that for the Vietnamese Communists, nationalism was an integral part of their cause, not something merely adopted to camouflage their real political aims. Their image as the most extreme and uncompromising nationalists did not mean that they were more "deceitful" or more "clever" than their opponents. In fact, the adjective "deceitful" could be applied with much more justification to some of the anti-Communist nationalists who supported Bao Dai and collaborated with the French. The truth is that being Communists did not prevent the Vietminh leaders from also being authentic nationalists, and as such as extreme and determined as any the Vietnamese anticolonial movement has produced. In fact, history put the Vietnamese Communists into a position in which they could become effective only by being nationalists first and Communists second. This was true in more than just the chronological sense imposed on them by obvious strategic considerations, since the ultimate aims of the Communists could become objects of policy only after the triumph of the people's national aspirations. For this reason the national aspirations of the Communists were as genuine as those of any non-Communist who either followed or opposed the Vietminh.

To judge by their programs and actions, the Vietminh Communists became Communists only after their victory as nationalists; but so did many non-Communists who had fought in the ranks of the Vietminh. What made the Communists so successful during the Indochina War was neither their "deceitfulness" nor their "cleverness," but rather the genuineness of their nationalism, which attracted the educated national elite as well as the masses. Only thus could the Communists successfully use their talents and training as organizers, qualities which were as essential for survival and eventual victory over the French as was their complete identification with the nationalist aspirations of the people.[47]

The evidence that the Vietminh leaders were a group of highly talented, energetic, and devoted men can be ignored only at the risk of not grasping the reasons for their success. Their spoken and printed propaganda reached every corner of the country, and to the known methods of indoctrination they added some new ones of their own. They also invented numerous ways of organizing great masses, openly and clandestinely, for military, economic, cultural, and political action, both in their own territories and in French-controlled regions. And with organization they fought widespread hunger and overcame a crippling lack of such industrial products as agricultural tools and basic medicines.

Their tasks in all fields important for survival were gigantic. At the beginning of the war they had practically no means of transportation, no heavy weapons, not a single airplane, and had themselves destroyed most of the roads, railroads, and bridges to prevent the French from moving into their retreats. They even lacked shoes for their soldiers, clothes for their children, soap to wash the one, worn-out garment they owned, and, above all, a diet sufficient and varied enough to sustain them in the tremendous physical efforts the regime asked of soldiers and civilians alike. For the Vietminh to have survived the war economically, and to have in the end won it, must therefore be regarded as a truly extraordinary human achievement.

Apart from the primary concern of preserving the regular army, the chief preoccupation of the Hanoi Government after the outbreak of the war was how to feed its people and how to overcome the innumerable difficulties of supplying the growing number of soldiers needed to fight the French with food and equipment. No outside help could be expected, and in fact none was received during the first four years of the war. The Vietminh had to survive entirely on what could be produced or procured from local resources.

The chief means of mobilizing the country's economic resources were not social or economic reforms but an intensified use of human working capabilities through organization and propaganda. Land rents were lowered to 25 per cent of the crop, but the larger landholdings were not divided up and landlords were not expropriated. The government concentrated on achieving self-sufficiency in basic foods by improving production methods and increasing yield through more intensive work. The policy of introducing new crops, begun in 1945, was continued. Also, fish was made a greater food resource than ever before. Dams and dykes were carefully maintained and new ones were built to gain new irrigated lands. The greatest efforts were extracted from the population through propaganda and direct intervention—by central supervisors and local committees. The people were constantly admonished to work harder in meetings, through posters, and even with songs, theatrical performances, and poems. The rice field was called a battlefield, the hoe and plough weapons, and all working people were urged to rival the soldiers at the fronts. Since the rich food-producing areas were largely French-held, rice was collected by night in the "occupied zones" and carried by teams of porters into the Viet Bac, for instance from the Red River Delta and the south delta zone. Sampans and junks, moving only by night, brought rice from many Mekong regions to the Vietminh-held coast of Central Annam.

But in spite of the never-ending exertions imposed on the people, the aim of the Hanoi regime to harvest and collect sufficient food supplies was never achieved. Although production rose, it could hardly keep pace with the mounting needs, one reason being that more and more people were taken into the army or at least temporarily withdrawn from production jobs to work on road construction or as porters for the army—people who, like the growing army itself, all had to be fed moderately well. Periods of scarcity were common even for the army, and pockets of starvation existed at least until 1952. But by 1952, thanks to their own efforts, the Vietminh began to make progress in feeding the people, as well as see prospects for a general economic improvement in several other fields.

One of the hardest blows for the Hanoi regime after the outbreak of the war was losing access to the country's industrial production. Nor did it have free access to markets abroad where, in exchange for its own exportable goods, it might acquire products essential to its war effort and to maintaining a minimum of industrial production at home: machines on the one hand, and the more sophisticated weapons and military equipment on the other. Radio receivers for field communication and medicines to treat the many wounded and seriously ill were among the most grievously felt shortages throughout the war. Consequently, medical care, including that of wounded or sick prisoners of war, was poor, and together with the food shortage, was one of the reasons that Ho Chi Minh failed to keep his promise of 1946 that "prisoners of war shall be well treated." [48] But the Vietminh managed to avoid catastrophe by using substitutes for unavailable goods or by eventually producing them at home.

Priority in the setting-up of small-scale industries was of course given to the production of arms, and, significantly, to that of paper, since the Vietminh regarded its newspapers and other propaganda material as no less essential for winning the war than guns. Some factory equipment had been moved from Hanoi and other cities into the Viet Bac, but lack of machines limited industrial production largely to goods whose manufacture required no more than the existing handicraft skills and equipment. These, fortunately for the Vietminh, had survived, thanks to the French policy of preventing the industrialization of Vietnam, and of keeping the peasants too poor to buy imported goods. In small establishments, located chiefly in the Viet Bac, textiles, soap, paper, sugar, small metal tools (knives), and simple agricultural implements were produced in growing quantities, in spite of the continuing emphasis on the production of arms. Some articles of prime importance, such as mechanical pumps, were made from the motors of captured automobiles. The French Air Force had difficulties finding and destroying the many production sites, very few of which deserved to be called factories. They were well hidden in dense jungle, and in many cases operated either underground or in caves.[49]

Although the Vietminh had little success in mass-producing small arms, they were "near geniuses"[50] in the fabrication of grenades, mines, bombs, and all sorts of booby-traps, and competent also in refilling empty ammunition shells and in repairing any kind of weapons. They produced small mortars and eventually succeeded in copying many of the newer weapons they captured from the French.

Much of the success the Vietminh had in this field was due to the ingenuity of their technicians and workers, but the extent and continuity of their achievements was primarily the result of meticulous organization.

Organization, coupled with some pressure and a great deal of propaganda, was the key also to another economic achievement, consisting in the mining and the export of phosphorus, tungsten, tin, lead, and other minerals. All mines were nationalized. The transportation of these valuable products to the coast for shipment and sale abroad was a most difficult organizational task. Much of the no less valuable poppy seed for opium from northern Tongking and Laos, pepper from Cambodia, and even rice from the Mekong Delta, was also harvested for export. To obtain foreign currency was the more important as the Ho Chi Minh piaster no longer had any value even in Vietminh-controlled territories. The profit from these sales, many of them on the black market, was used to buy arms, radio sets, medicines, and machines in Hong Kong, Singapore, and the Philippines[51]—goods which came largely from American Army surplus stocks. Both overland and sea transport of these cargoes out of and into Vietminh territory was extremely hazardous and time-consuming, and was possible only because the Vietminh controlled most of the country's 1,200-mile coastline. Overland, which often meant through French-held territory, these imports were carried to their destination—chiefly the northern Vietminh strongholds—on the backs of thousands of porters, whose role for the war economy was as vital as was the logistic support they gave to the Vietminh Army whenever it moved en masse to give battle to the French. (It has been said that the Vietminh victories were "first and foremost logistic victories." [52]) Inside the "free zones," as the Vietminh called the regions they controlled, transportation problems were easier to solve, particularly after the Chinese had begun to deliver trucks. Railroads were kept running in part (for instance several long stretches of the so-called Indochinese Railroad in Central Annam), and many roads and bridges were built or repaired. But in these "free zones," too, small carriages, bicycles, buffaloes, sampans, junks, and human backs remained the chief means of transportation. In convoys of thousands, men traveled by night, dispersing in case of danger, lying still until danger passed, for security was always more important than speed. Nevertheless, the losses suffered in transporting food, equipment, and other cargoes were high.[53]

In spite of these overriding preoccupations, which absorbed the energies and organizational talents of thousands of the best military and political cadres, the Vietminh always had people to spare for work in other important fields. The campaign to eradicate illiteracy was continued all during the war years. Vietminh claims, which are likely to be exaggerated, said that between 1945 and 1949, more than 11 million people learned to read and write.[54] "Learn in order to fight better" and "Study for resistance" were among the slogans used in the campaign.

Combating illiteracy, of course, had a direct political purpose: The people had to be indoctrinated, and propaganda had to be spread into the last village, not only by speakers but also through the more lasting printed word. This is why paper for government propaganda had priority over all other paper needs. But speakers, leaflets, posters, and slogans chalked on walls or vehicles continued to remain more important than newspapers, whose production was limited and whose distribution difficult. The official figures claimed a circulation of 27,000 for the Party organ, *Nham Dan* (*The People*), and 176,000 for the paper of the National Front, *Cuu Quoc* (*National Salvation*).

In the schools, technical training was strongly emphasized, but other branches of higher education were by no means neglected. A Vietminh branch of the University of Hanoi operated classes widely dispersed all over the North. There was training for everything, including physical culture, which even the tired soldiers were often forced to practice. Like all fanatical social reformers, the Vietminh were strong believers in physical fitness. For the Party elite, particularly the younger members, intensive courses in Marxism were conducted with as much zeal as was displayed in the training of officers in military schools at Ha Giang and Bac Kan. Officer training was of course also largely political, and if these men were deficient in military science compared to the French officers, practice in the field and a rich combat experience even before they went to school made them superior leaders, at least in the type of small-scale "revolutionary warfare" [55] that continued to dominate all fighting to the end of the war. In the preparation of ambushes on convoys or patrols, in attacking isolated posts, and in the arts of dispersion, reconcentration, hiding, and camouflage, the Vietminh military leaders developed a degree of perfection that never ceased to astonish the French.

But more important still, these officers and guerrilla leaders, no matter how they perfected their military skills, never forgot that in this war ideas were more important than bullets. This was one reason that the so-called political officers never played as great a role as they at one time did in the Russian Red Army.[56] This double training, which started in 1945, when the Vietminh began to found army units, made it possible for leaders whose groups were isolated to act on their own and yet to conform to higher Vietminh intentions. This was the case during most of 1947, when strict central direction was not yet established.[57] The practice of "self-criticism," which was also introduced in the army, even though not an exercise in democracy, undoubtedly improved a group's morale and sometimes probably also its tactical performance. But open criticism of officers was soon discouraged in the regular army, which developed along the conventional hierarchical forms prevalent in the West. In time, the Vietminh Army also ceased to consist primarily of volunteers. In order to recruit the men needed for its expansion, the Hanoi Government decreed general mobilization on February 21, 1950.[58]

It is this total mobilization of the entire people (which led to organized control of thinking and action) and the integration of military and political life that made the Vietminh leadership such a formidable and invincible opponent for the French and the Vietnamese behind Bao Dai. Children too were indoctrinated and used even for such tasks as the gathering of information about the movements of the French. The entire nation was in one way or another engaged in the war, working and fighting on all economic, political, cultural, and military "fronts." This total integration of all aspects of life with the multiform military steps devised for winning the war is probably the only new political phenomenon since the end of World War II. Be that as it may, it was certainly the key to the victories Communism was able to win in Vietnam.

The extent to which the people were organized for political indoctrination was truly fantastic. The different local and national groups that composed the Lien Viet (National Front) claimed a membership of 8 million, held together by professional, religious, and special political, regional, or racial interests, organized according to age and sex. Even recreation was organized, if such a word can be applied to the austere forms of leisure permitted under the Vietminh. The great variety of these organizations, their separate activities and a safe ritual of "electing" their leaders gave the impression of an autonomous and highly decentralized existence, but control over them was also total, although discernible only to the trained political eye. All leading positions in all organized bodies and on all vital economic, cultural, or military fronts were in the hands either of Communist Party members or their proven allies in the Viet Minh.[59] The Communist Party, which had been officially dissolved on November 11, 1945, but had led a clandestine existence, counted 5,000 members in 1945. During 1946, the Party membership jumped to 210,000, and a year later to 365,000. These 365,000 became the founding members of the Lao Dong Party (Workers Party) when the Communist Party was officially re-formed under this name on March 3, 1951.[60] Never in the modern history of Vietnam, either before or after the Indochina War, had any other Vietnamese political party succeeded in gaining even as much as 10 per cent of such organized strength.

The military branches of the vast mass organization created by the Communists were at the base largely identical with its civilian contingents, as the latter were always mobilized for either direct or semimilitary tasks. The Dan Quan (People's Guards), for instance, might consist of men who were engaged in fighting only at night or on special occasions, but they constituted the reservoir from which permanent guerrilla or regional units were drawn, which in turn might move up into the ranks of the regular army. The Dang Cong (People's Service

Corps) provided the masses indirectly engaged in the war, such as porters and laborers for military projects. Other groups in these formations were active as clandestine agitators or saboteurs in the so-called "occupied regions," which the French, "at the price of a prodigious waste of military means," [61] tried to control. Secret Vietminh cells were operating not only in every important locality but even in the remotest villages in the South (which were the most difficult for the French to control). It is safe to say that the Hanoi Government maintained some kind of acting administration all over French-held Vietnam, and that its agents, partly because of the mounting fear of a Vietminh victory, were able to collect large sums in "taxes" even from the rich. The peasants were as a rule persuaded, sometimes by threats, to make "voluntary contributions" to the war effort. Taxes from them were collected only in goods, chiefly rice, which became in fact the official currency of the Hanoi regime.[62] Even its budget was set up in kilos of rice, and rice was also the form in which officials, generals, and even ministers received their salaries. Needless to say, these men, in contrast to their counterparts of the Bao Dai regime, did not lead a life of luxury and also lacked all opportunity to enrich themselves at the expense of the people.

The Vietminh was always able to recruit men also in the "occupied regions," not only for its organized fighting units, but also for spreading terror in cities by throwing bombs, for organizing strikes and demonstrations, and for acts of sabotage against public works, factories, and plantations. Sometimes the Vietminh used the threat of sabotage or attack only as a means of extracting large sums of money or quantities of needed goods. Chinese and Vietnamese as well as French businessmen, particularly if their merchandise had to be transported between far-flung localities, paid regular tributes to the Vietminh in order to travel unmolested over certain waterways and roads. The Vietminh were infinitely more successful, at almost no cost, in destroying bridges and sabotaging transportation than the Americans in 1965 with their jet planes and bombs, many of which were aimed at the same targets.

An erroneous opinion concerning French understanding of Communist political-military tactics gained currency soon after the outbreak of the Indochina War. This opinion tended to explain the defeat of the French by their alleged ignorance of Vietminh military theory and Vietminh ingenuity in mobilizing the entire people for the war.[63] But the French knew a great deal more in 1952 than the Americans had learned by 1965.[64] They failed militarily for basic political reasons, which they could not overcome even if, instead of using napalm, they had made more extensive use of their own counterguerrillas than they actually did.[65]

Nor was the failure of the French due to massive outside (Chinese) aid to the Vietminh, as was and still is maintained by Western propaganda.[66] The French were losing long before Chinese aid became effective. Even de Lattre, in 1951, seems to have thought that victory was impossible, and that the best he could hope for, with quick and adequate American aid, was to gain the strength needed for obtaining an acceptable political solution of the conflict.[67] Navarre later stated categorically that he understood his task to consist not in winning the war but in creating "the military conditions for an honorable political solution that must be sought at the proper moment." And he added, "I have never promised more, and I have never been asked for more." [68] Since Chinese aid prompted the United States vastly to increase its support of the French, and into speedier delivery of new equipment (including planes), it is safe to say that the Vietminh would have prevented a French victory also without Chinese aid.

The victory of Communism in China, however, had far-reaching political effects, on the national Vietnamese as well as on the international scene. It led to the recognition of the Ho Chi Minh regime by China, the Soviet Union, and the East European Communist states, and it led the West to recognize the Bao Dai regime as the legitimate government of a nominally independent Vietnam.[69]

The effect of this upon the Vietminh regime was a slow and not entirely voluntary transformation in the direction of a so-called "people's democracy," or a more or less openly Communist state. It would be hard to prove that this development had been historically determined from the moment the Vietminh regime was formed. Since French policy between 1947 and 1950 had worked toward ruling out a peaceful settlement (which would have required a compromise between the Vietminh and the forces around Bao Dai), the Hanoi Government, in spite of verbal assurances to the contrary, was now interested chiefly in gaining a military victory. This meant not only that Ho had to depend more and more on Chinese aid, to which there were, he knew, several strings attached; it also had an effect on his internal policy. The Vietminh could now afford to stop wooing Bao Dai and the Vietnamese middle class, which had anyway been as unsuccessful as their attempts to gain recognition as a government of national unity by the West.[70] French policy, said Lacouture and Devillers, left Ho with hardly any other choice.[71] Since he gained nothing by pleasing the West and the pro-Western forces around Bao Dai, he put his regime, hesitatingly but unmistakably, into the camp of the Soviet Union and Communist China.

One of the steps in this direction was the open reappearance of the Communist Party as the Workers Party (Lao Dong), another a change in crucial government and other command positions in favor of Party members and reliable allies. Critical observers had always been convinced that the Hanoi regime would end up as a typical people's democracy, but before 1950 there was more than just a façade covering its tendency toward becoming a Communist state—not because the Communists would ever renounce their ultimate aims, but simply because it was theoretically still possible to mobilize the non-Communist forces inside and outside of the Vietminh for a different solution. Before 1950, the Hanoi Government was not at all keen to undertake drastic social and economic reforms and was always seeking compromises with the classes and groups opposed to such reforms. Proof of this was its opposition to dividing up the land. Its reforms did not make it a socialist, but merely a "progressive" regime, whose black spot, excused by some because of war conditions, was the suspension of the broad civil liberties contained in its constitution. The argument was that anyone could enjoy these liberties, but not against the interests of the nation, which in practice meant that no criticism and, of course, no active opposition to the regime was tolerated. But the "Democratic Republic of Vietnam" (D.R.V.N.) was a rather "modern" state by any standards, with a new "civil code" and a most progressive educational system, and it was a promoter, outside the political arena, of all kinds of "freedoms" formerly unknown in Vietnam. In regard to political freedom, too, the people were hardly at a disadvantage compared with the population under the French-sponsored Bao Dai regime. There was as little "democracy" on the side that claimed to fight for "freedom" as there was in the regions administered by Hanoi.

The most far-reaching change after the Hanoi regime's proclaimed solidarity with the Soviet and Chinese camp and the founding of the Lao Dong Party was a gradual purge of all leaders and officials not sufficiently subservient to the Communists.[72] In this process, the Vietminh was completely merged with the Lien Viet (National Front), since the rise of the Lao Dong Party and its control of the Lien Viet made the Vietminh superfluous as a separate instrument of Communist domination. After February, 1951, the Vietminh, although apparently immortal in all later writings about Vietnam, ceased to exist. The Communists now also considered it compatible with their new course to undertake at last a land reform, but only after much hesitation and long preparations. This reform, which aimed at the "total liquidation of the old feudal regime," was conducted with great legal circumspection. It was announced by Ho Chi Minh in a speech on December 19, 1952 [73] (the seventh anniversary of the outbreak of the war in Hanoi), but it took shape only with the decrees of April 12, 1953, and was given its final form in a law adopted by the rump National Assembly (elected in 1946) on December 4, 1953.[74] The soldiers who fought at Dien Bien Phu, says Jean Chesneaux, knew that if they won the war and returned home, they would own an adequate piece of land, instead of remaining tenants or through indebtedness losing the little piece of land that had been theirs.

Thus, when Giap and Navarre, during 1953, were preparing themselves for the final encounters of the Indochina War, the conflict, without ceasing to be a colonial war, had definitely taken on two new aspects. The existence of the Vietnamese National Army under Bao Dai added to the colonial war the element of an internal civil war; the growing involvement of the Communist powers on the one side and the United States on the other turned the war more and more into an international conflict. This was the beginning of the struggle, widely considered as inevitable, between Communist China and the United States for control of Southeast Asia.

5

The conditions of war caused great misery for the mass of people all over Vietnam, most of all in the constantly contested areas; but life was harder in the regions ruled by the Vietminh than in the territories under firm French control. The latter included most of the cities, into which a great many people from the war-torn countryside fled. The Saigon-Cholon area, which before the war had a population of less than 300,000, grew to a city complex inhabited by almost 2 million. These people lived in extreme poverty—houses for most of them were unavailable—but they enjoyed at least one advantage: They were no longer exposed to the ordeals which the civilian population in most other territories of the country suffered because of the war. There was also less hunger in the French-controlled regions; there were more doctors and medicines; and there were probably fewer demands made for the sort of extreme physical exertion the Vietminh imposed on its own people.

The sufferings of the soldiers, particularly those of the guerrillas, were probably also greater on the side of the Vietminh. However, the efforts required from the soldiers and the hardships they endured on both sides were such that a little more or a little less could hardly make much difference. There are limits to the time a man can languish before he dies of exhaustion, disease, uncared-for wounds, or from tortures inflicted during brutal interrogations,[75] limits that were constantly exceeded in the demands this war made on the soldiers on both sides.

For the people who enjoyed the privileges of wealth or the advantages of an important political and administrative position, both French and Vietnamese, life under the French, however, was entirely different from life under the Vietminh. The leading people on the Vietminh side, including those holding the highest governmental or military posts, led a truly Spartan existence. To be sure, they did not suffer hunger, seldom slept without their mosquito nettings, and as a rule had adequate medical care. But most of them lived under conditions that made life hard even for people in good health. Most of these leaders lacked many simple necessities, and no one had luxuries, except perhaps in a relative sense: on a cold night in the Tongking mountains, some might have kept warm with a blanket, while others without it froze. Not even their worst enemies have accused the Vietminh leaders of corruption, and if none was known to have enriched himself, the reason was not only lack of opportunity: As dictators on their diverse levels, they simply resembled Robespierre rather than Trujillo—a breed of men entirely different from the men on the other side, who had either long collaborated with the French or had risen to social and political prominence since the beginning of the Bao Dai solution.

If the people behind and around Bao Dai lacked some of the faults that revolutionary fanaticism is likely to breed, they unfortunately also lacked most of the virtues their Communist adversaries possessed: a deep devotion to their cause, and the personal disinterestedness through which a man like Ho Chi Minh commands the respect even of his opponents. The models for most Bao Dai ministers and high officials were the many French and Vietnamese war profiteers who led a wildly luxurious or at least a very good life while their countrymen starved and died. For many Frenchmen, profits were higher than ever not only because imports, largely for the war and the army, were so much bigger; they also profited from higher local production. The increased production of distilleries and breweries, to meet the enormous demands of the Expeditionary Corps, was only one such instance. Gains thus made were not reinvested—no war profiteer acted as if he believed that the war could be won; profits were sent home, or, if the profiteer was a rich Vietnamese, deposited abroad. Due to the lack of any democratic controls and to the tradition of buying the collaboration of Vietnamese willing to serve the French, corruption had become too widespread to cause surprise or shock. Bao Dai officials sold high administrative positions offering opportunities for what might be called "second-line corruption" at fantastic prices; [76] the eagerness to grab the larger benefits of power at the very top was greatly enhanced by the cool cynicism with which these officials regarded the war that was supposedly being waged for the "defense of the free world." Since professing this belief did not in the least interfere with the flow of funds into their private pockets, some of the worst grafters and extortionists posed as the most determined defenders of freedom against the threat of a Communist Vietnam. The soldiers of the Vietnamese National Army, in so far as they really believed they were serving a cause, were shamelessly betrayed by these leaders, though no less so than the French officers and men who fought, suffered, and died, supposedly for their country: They too were sacrificed in cold blood for the gains of their speculating and profiteering countrymen in Indochina and at home.

One way for the rich, or the well-placed, to make extra sums of money was to take part in the "traffic of the piaster." The piaster was greatly overvalued in relation to the French franc—17 francs for 1 piaster was more than double the piaster's real value measured in purchasing power (or what was paid for it on the black market). This was one condition for the "traffic." The other was the artificial economic prosperity created by the war and all the spending it required, as well as the chances of making money in high public positions; thus thousands of Frenchmen and Vietnamese were able to increase their

often illegitimate profits by engaging in money transactions that became the greatest financial scandal in the entire history of colonial
Indochina. Anyone wishing to enter into this unholy partnership of
trading piasters who had, say, 10,000 to spare, only needed permission to transfer this sum to France, at the official rate of 17 francs.
Permission was obtained through the right connections from an office
effectively controlled by the Bank of Indochina. "The operation took
place in a dusty and lamentable building in Saigon called the Office of
Exchange, which, rather than the office of the High Commissioner or
of the Army Chief of Staff, was the real center of Indochina." [77] Receiving permission for the transfer meant that the original sum was
doubled. But this was only the beginning of the operation. The 10,000
piasters, after being turned into 170,000 francs, were now used to
acquire piasters at their real value of 7 or 8 francs. This could be done
legally by importing goods into Indochina, or illegally by changing the
francs into dollars and by buying with these dollars the cheap piasters
on the black market. The 10,000 piasters had now become 20,000–
25,000, and if retransferred to France, 250,000–300,000 francs, four
times their actual value. Theoretically, this operation could go on
forever, and in fact went on long enough to produce quite a number of
new French and Vietnamese multimillionaires, at the expense of the
French treasury, which bought piasters for 17 francs that could be sold
only for 7 or 8.[78]

The piaster traffic went on for years, although it was not unknown
that one of its scandalous by-products was aiding the war effort of the
Vietminh. Piasters collected by the Hanoi Government in the form of
taxes or as "voluntary contributions" were sold on the black market
for dollars that came from the speculators on the French side, dollars
the Vietminh desperately needed to purchase arms and equipment it
could not produce at home.

There was, however, in addition to the problem of the "traffic," another, much broader and more directly economic aspect to the question of the piaster-franc exchange rate.[79] The piaster had not been
overvalued when its rate was fixed at 17 francs in December, 1945. But
the devastations of the Indochina War had caused the piaster to fall
more quickly than the franc. True, France had to pay for the war, but
France was not being destroyed. What could the French Government
do when it saw that the sinking value of the piaster was becoming a
drain on its finances? It could not cut off the piaster from the franc

without economically cutting off Indochina from France. This would have meant giving up France's economic control of Indochina. And to maintain this control was precisely why France's unenlightened political leadership after World War II had allowed its powerful colonial party to push the country into war. But France, as long as she hoped to win the war, could not very well devaluate the piaster, since this would have destroyed the modicum of economic stability existing in Indochina. To maintain the rate of 17 francs to the piaster meant maintaining the purchasing power of the Indochinese states, enabling them to buy the goods they needed, which were mainly imported from France. Consumer goods were of course bought almost exclusively by the French, the wealthy Vietnamese, and the members of the Expeditionary Corps. For the latter, the high rate of the piaster also meant that they could save and send some of their earnings home. In order for France to realize all the benefits of her monopolistic economic position in the Indochinese states, she had to make it possible for these customers to buy whatever imports French business was used to selling in Indochina. Prime Minister Nguyen Van Tam was well aware of this particular French interest in maintaining the high rate of the piaster. In a speech in Paris before the Center of Foreign Affairs Studies on November 27, 1952, he said that imports from France had never been as great as in 1952, when they were expected to reach a total of 222 billion francs. And he asked his audience to think what this figure means and what part French exports to Indochina play in the economic stability of France.

These imports, obviously, were possible only because the French Treasury, by maintaining the price of 17 francs to 1 piaster, was giving desperately needed assistance to the Indochinese economy—"to an apparently opulent client who was in reality utterly ruined." [80] Without this assistance, the economy of the so-called Associated States of Indochina would have collapsed. However, the billions of francs earned thus by the importers and exporters of French goods represented only a fraction of the enormous sums which the French taxpayers (soon to be joined by their American co-victims) had to supply for keeping Indochina in the French Union. Businessmen and speculators were the only ones able to exploit this situation. They made their gains at the expense of the French nation. As always, but now more than ever, French privileges in Indochina were profitable for the few and costly for the many.

It came as a terrible economic, political, and psychological shock when France, on May 11, 1953, devaluated the piaster from 17 to 10 francs: a political shock, because this unilateral action was "a flagrant breach of the Pau agreement," [81] making a mockery of the "national sovereignty" of the Indochinese states. It was a psychological shock, because it seemed to imply that France was no longer either able or willing to carry the heavy costs of the Indochina War. Furthermore, since the devaluation of the piaster "took place after French financial and commercial interests had completed the transfer of their capital and activities to other parts of the world," [82] Vietnamese nationalists concluded that the French in Indochinese business, and in particular the Bank of Indochina, no longer believed in a military solution of the conflict.

The economic impact of the devaluation compounded its political and psychological effects. It was cushioned for the members of the Expeditionary Corps,[83] but allowed to hit the indigenous population full force. Almost from one day to the next, all prices, even those for rice and other local products, rose 50 per cent. In a population already living in extreme poverty this was bound to have severe political repercussions, repercussions more disastrous for the French than a serious military defeat.[84] Even people who had believed themselves unaffected by the political maneuvering between the French and the Bao Dai nationalists suddenly realized that independence was not something theoretical, something which concerned only the political elite. The absence of true independence had enabled the French Government to cut the purchasing power of the Vietnamese almost in half. Independence, obviously, had not only a moral and spiritual value, but was also of the greatest practical and material importance. Those whose judgment was keen enough to anticipate the trend of events rightly concluded that France, being unable to uphold the near starvation standard of living of the Indochinese populations, would not be able to continue the war much longer either. And since France had not complied with even her limited promises regarding the sovereignty of the Indochinese states, most people also concluded that independence could become real only after the French were forced to leave. The mood in the country was such that even Prime Minister Nguyen Van Tam felt obliged to speak not as a French but as a Vietnamese patriot. In a radio broadcast on June 8, 1953, he stated: "Our relations with France have recently been burdened. The frailty and inadequacy of the agreements of March, 1949, and of 1950, have become clear. If the principle of our adherence to the French Union is to be upheld, it must be recognized that the constitution established by France in 1946 no longer conforms to the needs of the nations asked to adhere to the Union. It is important that we no longer remain in this Union as tenants of a house built without us." [85]

This statement, born of Tam's desperation with the impossible task of serving both French and Vietnamese national interests, was evidence that the permanent crisis of Bao Dai nationalism had entered its final, climactic phase. There no longer was any hope of producing a fighting spirit against the Vietminh, either in the army or among the civilian population. The number of Vietnamese in the National Army kept increasing, but nothing could be done to lift their morale. Those who joined during 1953 were driven to it largely by the poverty caused by the rising prices. Even before that time, the government, in order to get the necessary officers, had been compelled to conscript university students.[86] A rapid deterioration of the Bao Dai regime on all levels took place, and its one predictable outcome was the fall of the government of Nguyen Van Tam.

In order to forestall this, Tam played a rather bold political game all during 1953. He tried to improve the image of his regime by demanding more actual independence from France and by introducing, largely on paper, a number of basic social and political reforms. This brought him into conflict not only with the French but also with the few groups of Vietnamese on whose support his survival depended: Bao Dai and his conservative counselors, the rich Vietnamese in the cities, and in particular the large landowners, whose privileges Tam threatened—"not out of conviction but for tactical political reasons." [87]

The "era of reforms"—one of the many abortive attempts to gain popular support against Communism—began on November 16, 1952, when Tam proclaimed freedom for trade unions. Although this aroused violent opposition among the conservative elements of the Vietnamese bourgeoisie, it failed to create a following for the regime among the workers. On the contrary, the unions, although largely under "Christian" influence, served only as a vehicle through which the "socialist" tendencies of the masses, and their hostility against the French-installed Bao Dai regime, could be expressed more openly and with legal organizational tools.

On January 25, 1953, the regime held municipal elections, as the first step of a promise already made by Prime Minister Tran Van Huu to give the country an elected assembly. But these elections could be held only in French-controlled territory, which comprised about 25 per cent of the country's surface and 50 per cent of the population. In most French zones only one out of three villages was regarded as sufficiently pacified to be allowed to vote, and in the vital and critical Red River Delta there was not even this proportion. Of the 7,000 delta villages, 687 took part in the elections. Besides, the right to vote was given only to citizens who had registered in the census taken in 1951 for the general mobilization. This meant that no more than 1 million out of a total population of 27 million (or 1 million of the 13 million under French and Bao Dai rule) were qualified to vote. Yet despite all these precautions, candidates who openly criticized the regime gained most of the votes. In Hanoi, an antigovernment list headed by a former associate of Ho Chi Minh, one Nguyen The Truyen, was elected with 60 per cent of the votes, thanks to the open support not only of the Dai Viet, but also of the Catholics and several other anti-Vietminh groups. (The Vietminh had asked the people to boycott the elections.)

The result of the municipal elections killed the project of provincial and national elections.[88] They had been promised for October, 1953, a time when Tam, although still in the fight, already foresaw that the day was not far off when he would be dropped by Bao Dai and the French. Not even the master move of his strategy, a land reform decreed in June, 1953, could avert his downfall.[89] It very likely hastened it, as did his flirtation with "democracy" and his demand for real independence, since landlord opposition to Tam now grew as fast as the disenchantment of the French and the fear of radical reforms in the circles around Bao Dai.

That a policy of reforms did have a chance of creating popular determination to resist the Vietminh was borne out by an experiment conducted by a Catholic Eurasian named Jean Leroy in the province of Ben Tre, 40 miles south of Saigon. After having taken part in the incomplete pacification of Cochinchina under Leclerc, Leroy, now a colonel of the French Army, began successfully to fight the Vietminh with a militia recruited largely among Catholics, though not on a religious basis. It was named Mobile Units for the Defense of the Christian Communities.[90] The French provided Leroy with arms for about 7,000 men, but they were mistaken in their belief that it was either the predominantly Catholic character of his units or Leroy's talents for guerrilla warfare that accounted for his success against the Vietminh. Leroy knew that this war was primarily a political conflict and that success depended on popular support. He obtained it by resolutely siding with the peasants. His was the only province in all of French-controlled Vietnam where the land rents of the tenants were cut in half (on his orders, which were also enforced), and where a provincial assembly thereupon could be safely elected by universal suffrage. Unfortunately, all of this was begun too late and for lack of support remained a transient and local experiment.

The trouble with Tam's reforms on a national scale was, as one French critic put it, "that they existed only in the files of the Vietnamese Government." [91] Opposition against them was too strong, and Tam was not qualified for the task of mobilizing the political forces needed to overcome this opposition. Even those who had once supported him, including Bao Dai, no longer trusted him. While the iron grip of the Lao Dong Party on the Lien Viet made the Hanoi regime stronger and more unified than ever, the Bao Dai regime was nearing a state of complete disintegration. Tam's government included only the most discredited elements of the VNQDD and the Dong Minh Hoi— old *émigrés* who had returned to Vietnam late in 1949, again behind Chinese troops, this time with the remnants of Chiang Kai-shek's army that had fled before the Communist advance into Tongking. (The Vietminh wisely let them pass through into French-held territory.) The now quite senile Vu Hong Khanh became Tam's Minister of Youth. The erstwhile followers of these people remained firmly opposed to Tam's regime. The Dai Viet members whom Tam, under de Lattre, had ousted from their positions in Tongking and Annam, had long been called back by Tam himself. Nguyen Huu Tri was again Governor of Tongking. But of this badly split party, which since 1945 had suffered more than any other from Communist and French persecutions, only insignificant factions were on-and-off supporters of the Bao Dai regime, even though they held official positions. The Southern Dai Viet leader Nguyen Ton Hoan, for instance, turned his back on Bao Dai and became *attentist*.

Lost now as supporters of Tam were also the religious-political sects, not so much because of Tam's vain efforts to integrate their troops into the National Army, for in this, the government could have succeeded only with determined French support, which was not given, since the French knew that this would have driven most Cao Dai and Hoa Hao leaders back into the arms of the Vietminh. It was popular discontent that forced the sect leaders into an increasingly rebellious attitude against the Bao Dai regime. Politically, the two major sects, especially the Hoa Hao, were deeply split. Substantial groups of both the Cao Dai and the Hoa Hao withdrew from the fight against the Vietminh.[92] Trinh Minh The, the Cao Dai Chief of Staff, who, at the head of 2,500 men, went into "dissidence" on June 7, 1951, was only the first of a number of sect leaders whose political dissatisfaction led them to attempt the formation of a "third" political force, between the Vietminh and the French-controlled Bao Dai regime.[93] The more conservative elements of the sects, particularly among the Cao Dai leaders, withdrew their support from Tam for other reasons. They feared that a progressive liberalization of the Bao Dai regime threatened the "feudal" privileges they derived from ruling autocratically over the provinces under their control.

The role played by the Binh Xuyen in the maneuvers that led to the fall of Tam differed from that played by the other two sects. The Binh Xuyen, too, indulged in nationalistic propaganda and cared little about the fate of Tam; but they had learned that it was to their advantage to remain loyal to Bao Dai. Bay Vien, alias Le Van Vien, long the uncontested chief of the Binh Xuyen, was tied to the Chief of State with a bond that was stronger than any other known to have existed among the leading figures of the Bao Dai regime: common financial interests. Le Van Vien was made a general, but more important still, he became owner of Le Grand Monde, "the most fabulous gambling establishment in the Far East." [94] From his headquarters in Cholon, he controlled not only gambling, but also the no less remunerative houses of prostitution. Opium was another source of his income, which he knew would be safe as long as he handed a substantial share of it over to Bao Dai. This was indeed the lowest point to which the ex-Emperor had sunk—a steep descent from the time when as a young man he had enthusiastically attempted reforms that the French promptly thwarted, but a fall also from the recent years of his struggle to gain true independence for his state. The least objectionable of his interests now were big-game hunting, yachting, and automobiles, and his main fear was that he might lose the position that enabled him to indulge his expensive tastes. This is why he began to listen more and more to the most cunning and reactionary of his advisers, Nguyen De,[95] one of the many who no doubt desired independence but were unwilling to share its benefits with the people. Social and political reforms in favor of the people seemed to threaten not only the class privileges of the rich but the monarchy itself. Since Bao Dai had become a disgrace to the monarchy, some conservative leaders, determined to save it, openly advocated that Bao Dai abdicate in favor of his son Bao Long.

The depth of the crisis in the camp of anti-Vietminh nationalism was revealed during two national congresses held in September and October, 1953. The first one, which took place in Cholon on September 5, although not convened in defiance of the law, was intended to be a demonstration of all significant anti-Vietminh factions against the Tam Government, Bao Dai, and the French. "Whatever his party," said Pierre Dabezies, "every Vietnamese was an opponent. It was a fatal error [of Tam's] to permit them to express themselves." [96] Even old collaborators of such prominence as the former Prime Ministers Nguyen Van Xuan and Tran Van Huu joined the swelling ranks of *attentistes*, thereby trying, as did Ngo Dinh Diem, Nguyen Ton Hoan, and Phan Huy Dan, to save their names. But since all of them lacked not only a doctrine but also a program concerned with the most pressing needs of the people, their properly motivated refusal to work with the French became mere inactivity accomplishing nothing. This was true even for highly popular men like Dr. Pham Huu Chuong and the lawyer Vu Van Huyen, who, after having spent six years with the "resistance," believed that a sort of authoritarian socialism was the best antidote to the Vietminh Communism which their experience had taught them to reject. They proved only once again that the Vietnamese anti-Communist intellectuals lacked both political originality and the skill to organize and lead the masses. Sensing the mood of the people, they fell back on their easiest demand, which was that the French should leave—a demand supported even by the Catholic bishop of Phat Diem. "As if without us," some Frenchmen observed sarcastically, "nationalist Vietnam could survive." [97]

The September congress marked the appearance on the Vietnamese political scene of Ngo Dinh Diem's younger brother Ngo Dinh Nhu, who masterminded this phase of the rebellion against Bao Dai, the French, and the government of Nguyen Van Tam. Nhu had achieved some prominence as organizer of a Catholic trade-union movement, modeled on France's Force Ouvrière, the Christian-oriented trade-union movement.[98] With ideas largely borrowed from France, and aided in their articulation by a Dominican Father by name of Parrel,

Nhu embellished his passion for power with the presumption of an original political philosophy. This was the creed of the French "personalist" group organized around the periodical *Esprit*, but deprived of its meager relevance by being transplanted from Europe to Asia. Nhu's only real talent was for political behind-the-scenes manipulation, in whose exercise he consistently disregarded the principles he professed.

Nhu's aim in the late summer of 1953 was the creation of "a national union for independence and peace" in support of a new government to be headed by his brother Diem. For his congress on September 5, Nhu gained not only the support of the Cao Dai and Hoa Hao leadership, but also the active help of the Binh Xuyen leader Le Van Vien, at whose headquarters in Cholon the congress met under Binh Xuyen military protection.[99] However, the mood of the congress, which was violently anti-French and anti-Bao Dai, disregarded the sect leaders' need for cautious tactics. This prompted the sect leaders to send a loyalty message to Bao Dai after the proceedings of the congress had become so tumultuous that Le Van Vien ordered his guards to clear the hall. Some speakers at the congress had demanded not only total independence, radical reforms, and free elections, but even the establishment of a republic. Indeed, ousting Bao Dai was already one of Nhu's aims. His too open pursuit of it before the time was ripe was one of the reasons why Nhu's "movement for independence and peace" failed to mobilize all anti-Vietminh nationalists for united action.[100]

But although a failure for Nhu, the September congress was nevertheless a hard blow for Bao Dai, who saw more clearly than ever before how quickly the coalition on which his regime rested could fall apart. He and his advisers decided to wipe out the impression of disunity and opposition to his regime created by the September congress. This was to be accomplished through another congress, one they claimed would be truly representative of the entire nation. Bao Dai summoned his cousin, Prince Buu Loc, Vietnamese High Commissioner in Paris, to Saigon to organize this Congress. Attended by about 200 delegates, whose selection almost wrecked the entire project,[101] this second congress opened on October 12. Although officially controlled, and denounced by Nhu and some leading *attentists* as a "maneuver," the new congress revealed that even for the mildest of nationalists, any further dependence of the State of Vietnam on France had become politically intolerable. A resolution demanding the withdrawal of Vietnam from the French Union was adopted on October 16.

Under official pressure this was amended a day later to read that Vietnam could not stay in the French Union "in its present form," but this was not much of an improvement in the eyes of the French Government, whose Premier, Joseph Laniel, called the conference proceedings "deplorable." The delegates also requested that the congress be constituted as a provisional assembly until elections could be held. Furthermore, in a move clearly directed against Bao Dai and the Tam Government, the congress requested that a permanent committee of this "assembly" take part in all further negotiations between Vietnam and France.[102]

At the end of 1953, the means for maintaining Franco-Vietnamese cooperation without full independence were obviously exhausted. Premier Tam tried to save his government by insisting on his reforms and by adopting some demands of the October congress. This was too much for the people who, at least secretly, wanted Franco-Vietnamese cooperation to continue—the rich landowners, the war profiteers, and the stanchly monarchist and antidemocratic circles around Bao Dai. The Chief of State was urged to drop Tam, which he did on December 17. Bao Dai then charged Prince Buu Loc with forming a new cabinet. This turned out to be the last Vietnamese government before the end of the war brought, in unexpected forms, "total independence."

6

Since the Indochina War was a conflict in which political strategy determined military effectiveness, the consolidation of Communist control on the one side and the disarray of the nationalist camp on the other were bound to be reflected in the further course of military events. In spite of some dissatisfaction with growing Communist domination of the entire "resistance," the Hanoi regime's military strength increased, whereas the expectations that the French and some Bao Dai followers attached to the formation of a Vietnamese national army never materialized. The political conditions for making this army effective could have been created only if France had granted true independence to a non-Communist Vietnam.

Although the war between October, 1952, and the attack on Dien Bien Phu in March, 1954, was one primarily of large movements and numerous fierce battles, nothing happened that was quite as spectacular as the French defeat on Route 4 in October, 1950, or the failure of Giap's three attacks on the delta early in 1951. The initiative was now clearly on the side of the Hanoi regime. During the last third of the war, the object of the French no longer was to break Vietminh resistance but rather to deal with the enemy's mounting power and aggressiveness. On the French side, the will to fight diminished, not only because one had to be blind to believe in victory: The clearheaded who watched the political evolution in the nationalist camp foresaw that France would lose Vietnam even though she might still win the war. On the Vietminh side, rising hopes based on steady military progress, Chinese aid, and the political ineptitude of their opponents produced the conviction that victory was possible, that a military decision in their favor could be realistically pursued.

Giap started out on what became the last phase of the war in October, 1952. He assembled three divisions east of the Red River between Phu Tho and Yen Bay. The French, not knowing what to expect, prepared themselves to repel another attack on the delta. But Giap, after crossing the Red River by night, turned his back on the delta and moved west and north into the region between the Red and the Black Rivers, the part of Tongking inhabited largely by the Thai, Vietnam's largest ethnic minority. Giap's long-term strategy had two aims, one of which he was sure of achieving. The conquest of northwestern Tongking, also called the Thai country, with its threat of an invasion of Laos, was his first aim, and a further dispersion of French forces for purely defensive operations was his second. The French might decide to thwart Giap's first objective by holding on to their fortified positions in northwestern Tongking in order to block a Vietminh invasion of Laos. They could not be certain that they would succeed, but even if they did, Giap would have achieved his other aim: The French could stop him only if to this end they employed most of the mobile reserve units General Salan was building up for future offensive action. Furthermore, these reserves had to be flown into northwestern Tongking and Laos, and there they could be supplied only by air. This was a task that would engage the French Air Force also in purely defensive operations. As it turned out, Giap achieved both his aims, even if not with one stroke. The French, in spite of using many of their meager reserves, were thrown out of northwestern Tongking. By the end of 1953, a military situation had developed whereby the French efforts to win the battle for Laos were leading up to a French defeat in the Indochina War.

The main French posts in northwestern Tongking were in the Black River Valley, which runs from the delta to the Chinese border, reaching it near the northern frontier of Laos. The French still held Lai Chau up north, and Son La and Na Sam in the lower center of the Thai country. They also had a strong position at Nghia Lo, between the Red and Black Rivers, some 25 miles west of Yen Bay, and another one at Moc Chau, farther south toward the province of Thanh Hoa. Between these main positions there were also a number of smaller ones garrisoned largely by Indochinese troops under French officers.

In the night of October 17, 1952, the Vietminh attacked Nghia Lo. Just a year earlier Giap had failed in his first attempt to throw the French out of Nghia Lo. Now he captured it in one night, taking many prisoners, and forcing the French to evacuate their many smaller posts west of the Red River. Their garrisons fled toward the Black River, closely pursued by the Vietminh, who wiped out most of the paratroops dropped by the French to cover their retreat.

The French hastily reinforced their garrisons at Na Sam and Son La, west of the Black River, mistakenly believing that they could block further Vietminh penetration north and west. But this was not the only measure Salan took against the threat that three Vietminh divisions operating along the Black River constituted to his positions in northwestern Tongking and Laos. He decided to use his entire mobile strength for an attack on the Viet Bac, expecting as the one certain result Giap's withdrawal of his divisions from the Black River Valley for the defense of the Vietminh's main Tongking base. Salan's offensive— Operation Lorraine—began on October 29. The French started out from Trung Ha and Viet Tri, two points at the northern confines of the de Lattre Line. They reached Phu Tho, 15 miles north, only on November 5; on November 9, they dropped paratroops on Phu Doan, another 20 miles farther north. An armored column also reached Phu Doan the same day. The French plan was to penetrate from Phu Doan up the Clear River toward Tuyen Quang in the Viet Bac; by pushing up the Clay River more to the west they hoped to intercept Giap's division Salan confidently expected to be rushing to the defense of the Viet Bac.

Operation Lorraine, into which Salan had thrown 30,000 troops and the best of his heavy equipment, was an even more disastrous failure than Valluy's offensive in the fall of 1947. The French captured some of the supplies the Vietminh had left behind when they moved out of Phu Doan, and one armored unit pushed another 15 miles north along

the Clay River to Phu Yen; but the real objectives of Operation Lorraine were not achieved. The French failed to penetrate the Viet Bac,
and the threat to it did not induce Giap to withdraw his three divisions
from the Black River Valley. He ordered no more than two regiments
of his regular army to support his regional units in their attempt to
fight the French to a standstill. Giap correctly assumed that Operation
Lorraine would collapse of its own weight. One hundred miles from
their main supply bases in the delta, the huge army was soon involved
in logistic problems that the French High Command was unable to
solve. Air transport proved insufficient even for the quantities of fuel
needed, while road and river transport became the more hazardous the
farther the French advanced. Constant attacks on convoys and army
units by dozens of Vietminh groups between the delta and Phu Doan
totally absorbed the fighting energies of the French and ruled out any
further extension of their vulnerable supply lines. Moreover, the Vietminh raised a threat of their own by ordering their 320th Division to
attack the delta from its base in Thanh Hoa. The French recognized
that to advance had become impossible; and merely to hold what they
had gained was not only too costly but also futile. On November 14,
sixteen days after the beginning of Operation Lorraine, Salan ordered
the inevitable withdrawal. It took a full week before the French were
back again behind the de Lattre Line. In fact, the withdrawal proved
more difficult and more costly than the advance. "A perfectly executed
ambush" [103] on November 17 at the deep and narrow valley of Chan
Muong underlined the dangers to which the French would have remained exposed if Salan had insisted on trying to hold on to Phu Doan.
Although Giap had refused to give battle and had engaged no major
units of his army, the French suffered 1,200 casualties. They also lost
their positions at Ba Lay and Moc Chau at the southern end of their
defense line along the Black River Valley. As soon as the French had
wound up Operation Lorraine, Giap took these positions by moving
south with one of the divisions he had kept in the Thai country in spite
of Salan's threat to the Viet Bac. The lesson of these events was clear:
The time for successful offensive operation by the Expeditionary
Corps had evidently not yet come. Operation Lorraine proved that the
largest force ever assembled by the French "could barely poke its nose
outside the De Lattre line." [104]

Elated by the failure of Operation Lorraine and made overconfident
by the quick capture of Nghia Lo, Giap now tried to throw the

French out of their remaining strong points in the Black River Valley. He attacked Na Sam on November 23. The Vietminh leader was apparently uninformed about the size of the reinforcements the French had brought by air into Na Sam. The attack was repulsed, but only after Giap had repeated it on November 30 and December 1 did he learn that Na Sam would become merely another name on the list of his major defeats if he did not desist. It was small consolation for him that his 312th Division, in its movement farther north toward Laos, had, on November 30, taken a rather unimportant and poorly garrisoned place named Dien Bien Phu. Giap now decided to bypass the main French garrisons at Na Sam and Son La and move southwest from the Black River toward Laos. He had no trouble overrunning the weak border posts and entering the Houa Pham Province of northeastern Laos. But the difficulties of supplying his fast-moving troops forced him to give up his plan of taking the provincial capital Sam Neua. He withdrew into Thai country, where his three divisions engaged only in minor skirmishes between December, 1952, and March, 1953. Giap used this period to reorganize his supply service. This was done largely with outside manpower, since the Thai population of northwestern Tongking was still uncooperative. The Vietminh had not yet succeeded in gaining the adherence of these people, and Giap considered it unwise to enlist their services by force. The Vietminh built up a new supply center for the divisions in the Thai country at Moc Chau late in 1952. The Vietminh also took the important political step of setting up an autonomous government for the Thai regions.[105]

Although action during the winter months of 1952–53 remained local, it continued to demonstrate the growing aggressiveness of the Vietminh. The French had to repulse another attack on the Catholic province of Phat Diem in the delta, and only with great efforts did they succeed in averting the loss of An Khe in central Annam, where two Vietminh regiments of the regular army had established themselves in the so-called Vietminh Interzone V, threatening all communication between southern and northern Annam. In the highlands, only a prodigious use of paratroops enabled the French to save the towns of Kontum and Pleiku. French initiative during these months was restricted chiefly to the hopeless task of "cleaning up" the delta.

On April 9, Giap resumed his war of movement from the Thai country into Laos. He marched directly west into Laos, containing the French at Na Sam with only one regiment of his 308th Division. From the north, the 312th Division stationed at Dien Bien Phu descended along the valley of the Nam Ou River toward the Laotian capital Luang Prabang, while Giap's third division, the 316th, aimed at the same objective on a route further south that led from its base at Moc Chau to Luang Prabang via Sam Neua. The French, whose air reconnaissance discovered these movements, again sent reinforcements by air into their positions in Laos and the Thai country. However, as always, the Vietminh moved faster than expected, and on April 13 Sam Neua had to be abandoned by the French, who suffered heavy losses in their flight.

This first Vietminh invasion of Laos, although it led to no great battles, was nevertheless a dramatic event full of serious implications for the French. It proved that the French were unable to prevent the Vietminh from overrunning all of northern Laos. A strong French-officered garrison at Muong Khoua, which the 312th Division, on its way from Dien Bien Phu to Luang Prabang, failed to subdue, was surrounded, totally isolated, and could henceforth be supplied only by air. But it could do nothing to stop the Vietminh advance toward Luang Prabang. By April 30, the royal capital had been invested too, an isolated outpost contained by only half of the 313th Division. The 308th Division, which had arrived earlier near Luang Prabang, continued to move south, apparently aiming at the administrative capital Vientiane. In order to block the direct road to Vientiane, the French gave up a position at Xieng Khouang in favor of one farthest west in the Plaine des Jarres, which they strengthened by flying in five additional battalions from the delta. Both the 308th and 316th Vietminh divisions now turned toward the Plaine des Jarres and had the French surrounded by April 23. The new position, too, now had to be supplied by air from Hanoi, at a distance of about 250 miles. The entire French air transport was thus engaged in maintaining the French outposts in the Thai country and in northern Laos, positions which could do nothing to prevent the Vietminh from roaming freely over these regions. They recruited guides, established cooperation with the small "Free Laotian" (Pathet Lao) guerrillas under the pro-Communist Prince Souphanouvong, and harvested the valuable opium crop before they unexpectedly retired, on May 7, to northern Tongking. Only small forces were left behind to contain the French, and agents to give military and political advice to the Free Laotians. Giap, who had outmaneuvered the French during this entire campaign, had once more achieved his strategic aim, which was to absorb all the reserves of the French and to nullify their efforts to build up offensive strength. The action had also been a great training exercise for the Vietminh in moving and supplying large armies over great distances. But Giap had achieved something else, something he himself did not as yet know: He had frightened the French into believing that the defense of Laos justified an exceptional military effort. It was this belief that led to the fatal French decision to retake Dien Bien Phu and build it up into a fortress capable of blocking any new Vietminh attempt to invade Laos.

The man who was later widely blamed for having taken this decision was General Henri Navarre, whom the French Government of René Mayer, upset by the military situation in Indochina, appointed on May 8, 1953 as successor to General Salan. Navarre, who knew nothing about Indochina, but was considered a brilliant strategist,[106] took his post on May 20. (One day later, the fall of the government that had appointed him created a crisis that lasted thirty-four days. It ended with the formation, on June 28, of the government of Joseph Laniel, which fell, a year later, during the Geneva conference.)

After studying the military situation, Navarre updated some ideas of de Lattre and Salan and submitted them to Paris, where they were unenthusiastically accepted by his military and political superiors.[107] The "Navarre Plan" aimed at a slow build-up of military strength sufficient for large-scale action against the Vietminh, but it did not advocate a merely defensive attitude while this goal was being pursued. On the contrary, Navarre favored vigorous and continuous offensive action, even if the means at his disposal limited the scope of his various operations.

These operations began on July 17 with an attack by three paratroop battalions on Langson. Operation Hirondelle, as this attack was called, could be considered a success, since the paratroopers destroyed large Vietminh stockpiles and returned safely to the delta. Operation Camargue, however, which started on July 28, was a failure. It aimed at clearing Highway 1, between Hue and Quang Tri, of Vietminh regional units that had long made this important road link a "street without joy" for the French.[108] An enormous and heavily armored force assembled for this operation succeeded in surrounding the guerrilla-infested area but failed to capture any of the Vietminh fighters. The action was called off on August 4. Superior force and heavy arms alone

were apparently insufficient against Vietminh ingenuity in escaping
from even well-laid traps. The French press described the operation as
a total success.

Navarre's next important operation, which the French also listed as a
success, was the evacuation on August 8, 1953, of Camp Na Sam. This
meant that the lower center of the Thai country was no longer considered defensible. But the French, although they had to destroy much of
their equipment, managed to save their troops. If Giap had anticipated
this move and massed enough strength, he might very well have turned
this doubtful French success into certain disaster. After the evacuation
of Na Sam, the only French position in northwestern Tongking was
the distant camp at Lai Chau. It was easy to foresee that sooner or later
this position would have to be given up too. This was done [109] two
weeks after the French had retaken Dien Bien Phu in Operation Castor, with three battalions of paratroops on November 20, 1953. The
Vietminh moved instantly into Lai Chau. They wasted no time before
starting a strategic project vital for the action they planned if the
French should really attempt to turn the defense of Laos into a major
clash. This project was the construction of a road from supply depots
at the Chinese border via Lai Chau to Tuam Giao, a new Vietminh
major supply center a bit northeast of Dien Bien Phu.

The fate of all other operations staged by the French during 1953
underlined the inadequacy of their military means as much as their inability to deal with the tactics of the Vietminh. On September 22, a
force of twenty battalions had started action to crush a Vietminh regiment operating inside the delta. As on many other occasions when the
enemy they faced was vastly superior, the Vietminh melted away. The
operation ended on October 20. Since the French knew that the Vietminh would soon return they realized that they had failed once more.
Another operation, also undertaken in September, 1953, aimed at
"cleaning up" the guerrilla-infested villages of the Thai Binh Province.
As in all similar operations, the result, if not actually a military triumph, was at least a political gain for the Vietminh. "When the peasants have their villages burned down and have no place to go, they go
to the Vietminh and enlist as porters or soldiers." [110] Punitive action
against villages suspected of hiding guerrillas had always been conducted in a manner that made it impossible to protect people not engaged in the fighting. For any man under fifty, remaining at home became too dangerous. He risked being regarded as a Vietminh fighter in

disguise and shot, or captured and "questioned" when the French arrived for their "cleaning up" operations. Many decided that the best way to escape this fate was to join the guerrillas before being forcefully recruited by them. Furthermore, the Vietminh made sure that no one who refused to work with them survived in a contested village. Their tactics were to send a few snipers into such a village with orders to kill a few of the advancing French. In these instances, the French usually slaughtered all able-bodied men they found in the village, from which the snipers had, of course, disappeared. The French military "had a record of pillage, violence, assassination, and of the burning of villages and the execution of innocents," wrote one observer, adding rather naïvely that this "had not served the interests of France." [111] Even when the French were not attacked, they arrested the entire male population between the ages of fourteen and sixty as prisoners of war. This accounted for the fact that toward the end of the war, most villages in Tongking were populated only by old men, women, and children. Like all his predecessors, the "brilliant strategist" Navarre, too, failed to come up with ideas for methods of warfare that would have been less harmful to the people, less disastrous to the reputation of the French, and less effective in strengthening the ranks of the Vietminh.[112]

Navarre's last major action during 1953, Operation Monette, was also a failure, since it achieved not even one of its four objectives. These were to drive the 320th Vietminh Division out of its south delta base, to reoccupy Phy Ly on the Day River, to clean out the Vietminh units that had crossed over the Day River into the delta, and to frighten Giap into sending part of his three divisions in the Thai country to the rescue of his 320th Division. Unlike Navarre, who had to rush his reserves into regions threatened by the Vietminh, Giap could confidently leave it to his local units to deal with any new French move. Operation Mouette, which started on October 14, was called off on November 7. The French again spoke of a victory, since they had inflicted about 3,000 casualties on the Vietminh; they also thought, mistakenly, that they had put the 320th Division, a constant threat to the delta, out of action for several months.

After the signing of the Korean Armistice on July 27, 1953, Chinese aid to the Vietminh, comprising trucks, heavy artillery, and anti-aircraft guns, began to be massive. As soon as Giap realized that the French had decided to defend Laos, and to this end would give battle to the Vietminh at Dien Bien Phu, he began to direct this equipment toward Tuam Giao and other nearby supply centers for the siege of Dien Bien Phu. In trucks, but also on the shoulders of a vast army of porters, these supplies were carried over distances of several hundred miles toward the hills surrounding Dien Bien Phu, in preparation for the long siege that led to the most famous battle of the French Indochina War.

X

The End of French Indochina

1

THE MILITARY REVERSES of the French in Indochina after 1950, and their failure to turn Bao Dai into an effective anti-Vietminh force, had repercussions in France which, by the end of 1953, darkly foreshadowed the approach of a major political crisis. Since 1947, government policy and the national mood had changed to a point where trying to find a road toward peace in Indochina was at last becoming the subject of daily debate. General indifference, so depressing to the proponents of a peaceful solution during the early years of the conflict, gave way to growing concern, and the government, in trying to find a basis for negotiations, no longer ruled out talks with representatives of the Hanoi regime.

After seven years of fruitless military and political attempts to defeat Hanoi, the people of France had good reason to question the course chosen by its leaders in Indochina. It was primarily the high cost of this policy in money and lives, and its apparent futility, which continued to make the desire to put an end to the Indochina War stronger with every passing year. According to President Auriol, the casualties (in dead, wounded, missing, and prisoners) of the French Union Forces had reached 90,000 by the fall of 1952, and 1.6 trillion francs had been spent on the reconquest of Indochina since 1945, "twice the amount of American Marshall Plan aid to France." [1] A year and a half later, just before the end of the war, the casualty figure stood at 92,000 dead and 114,000 wounded, mostly Africans, Indochinese regulars, and Foreign Legionnaires. But of the 20,685 Frenchmen

lost, 40 per cent (8,200) were officers and noncoms.[2] Having to keep
an army of 150,000 men permanently in Asia meant that France remained militarily weak in Europe, which explains why even some
French generals began to question the wisdom of a military solution of
the Indochina War.

The cost of the war was not only a burden for the French taxpayer,
but also the main reason that the economic recovery of France after
World War II was so much slower than that of defeated Germany.
This remained true also after the United States had begun to help
France carry the financial burden of the Indochina War. For France,
these expenses constituted more than 10 per cent of the national
budget and 33.5 per cent of her military budget. Even in 1953, when
the United States defrayed close to half the cost of the war (270 billion
francs), the expenses shouldered by the French remained nearly as
high as those of the preceding year. One need not go into the exceedingly complex question of the size of America's direct and indirect aid
to the French war effort in Indochina;[3] however, the widespread belief
that the war was largely paid for by the United States, even if it were
true, in no way contradicts the conclusion drawn after 1952 by a
growing number of French parliamentarians: that France could no
longer carry the crushing burden of the Indochina War. In the eyes of
more and more Frenchmen, the war was "a bottomless abyss, an adventure without a solution, and a sacrifice that had become absurd."[4]
Even people whose patriotism was beyond question began to refer to
the Indochina War as *la sale guerre* (the dirty war), as the Communists had been doing for a long time.

Opposition against the war, which had never been confined to the
Communists, was most vigorously articulated by intellectuals of many
political shades. These were not only the people around Jean-Paul
Sartre's *Temps Modernes*, who, in spite of their glittering political in-
consistency lent themselves to the charge of "fellow traveling." The
war was opposed also by the intellectuals of the left Catholic magazine
Esprit, by the group around the *Témoignage Chrétien*, by Catholic
and Protestant youth and student groups, by such writers of renown as
François Mauriac and Albert Camus, by the weeklies *Observateur* and
Express, and even by the respected conservative daily *Le Monde*. To
what extent these intellectuals were possibly under the influence of
Communist propaganda soon became a secondary question. What mattered was that more and more people began to think that the Commu-

nists were right in their opposition to the Indochina War, since to continue the war was nothing but an attempt "to preserve what was already lost." [5]

Of the political leaders of France, themselves largely intellectuals, very few indulged in the luxury of disregarding the attitude of the writers, journalists, students, professors, and artists who demanded an end to a war in which there were so many "profitable deals on the one side and so much useless heroism on the other." [6] The shrewdest among the political leaders of course knew that the intellectuals had very little direct influence on political decisions, but they also recognized their protests as an expression, perhaps premature and overstated, of a popular mood bound to increase in strength. Since the Socialist Party no longer supported the policies of Marius Moutet, their former Minister for Overseas Affairs, the working class now solidly supported the demand to bring about peace through negotiations with Ho Chi Minh, a demand also being raised with growing insistence by some leaders of the parties of the Center (such as the Radicals and the MRP), which continued to form governments supported by parties of the Right.

A study of the Chamber debates on Indochina from 1947 on shows how the refusal to talk to Ho Chi Minh, based on the expectation of a quick military solution, was slowly being undermined—up to March 9, 1954, when the Assembly, by agreeing to the Geneva conference, finally agreed to negotiations with the Hanoi regime.[7] As early as November, 1950, the voice of the Radical leader Pierre Mendès-France was added to the many demanding negotiations with Hanoi. In two speeches, on October 19 and November 22, Mendès-France tried vainly to shake the Assembly and the nation out of an attitude so obviously rooted in a refusal to shoulder the sacrifices required for winning the war: Either we supply the means necessary for a military victory, said Mendès-France, or we negotiate with Ho Chi Minh. To win the war requires an effort that France can make only if new taxes were introduced, economic expansion slowed down through limitations on new investments, and a general lowering of the living standard. Also, France would have to reconcile herself to the impossibility of conducting an effective policy of national defense in Europe and Africa, and of preventing the rearmament of Germany. If you don't want this, cried Mendès-France, then you have to accept a political solution. This requires the recognition of the independence of Vietnam, free and honest elections without delay under the auspices of a bipartisan or neutral commission, no reprisals, and the evacuation of the French Army within a fixed time. Vietnam could be given the status of a neutral state similar to that of Switzerland,[8] and would conclude agreements with France for economic and cultural cooperation.[9]

Mendès-France was no more successful in shaping French policy toward Indochina than were the intellectuals who wrote, the workers who demonstrated, or the soldiers who dared to raise their voice against the war.[10] It took another three-year harvest of political failure and military defeats before France was ready to listen to such counsel and agree to seek an accord—"naturally with those who fight us." [11,]

Jean Letourneau, a member of the procolonial MRP and Minister of Overseas France since 1949,[12] aptly expressed, midway between the rejection and the acceptance by France of talks with Ho Chi Minh, what his government's position had become early in 1952. "France does not refuse to talk with the Vietminh," he said on February 25, 1952, "but we will not take the first step." He even met a Vietminh delegate in Paris and allowed another contact to be made in January, 1953, at Rangoon; but since the French were not yet ready for serious negotiations, and the Vietminh, hopeful of victory, were no longer inclined to accept anything short of their full political aims, neither encounter produced any result.[13]

Resistance among the leaders of France against negotiations with the Hanoi regime broke down only after it had become evident that Navarre's plans and operations, far from improving the military position of the French, had on the contrary only contributed to worsening it. On December 20, 1953, two Vietminh regiments moved from the neighborhood of Vinh westward along mountain paths across Annam into Laos, where, on December 25, they reached and occupied the town of Thakhet on the Mekong River. This meant that communications between North and South were cut both in Annam and Laos. By turning south toward Seno, where the French had a large airfield, the Vietminh forced Navarre to establish another entrenched camp with troops flown in from the always-threatened delta. Vietminh attacks on Seno, beginning on January 4, 1954, and lasting four days, were repulsed; but on January 24, a French mobile group sent from Hue to intercept these Vietminh forces was ambushed on the way and practically wiped out.

On January 20, Navarre had started his much-advertised and later

much-criticized Operation Atlante. Its object was to drive the Vietminh from the coastal areas of southern Annam, where they had been
roaming about rather freely ever since the beginning of the war. In
this operation, the French for the first time relied heavily on units of
the Vietnamese National Army. A large Franco-Vietnamese force
moved northward from Nha Trang along the coast; initially it met little
resistance, but was slowed down as soon as the Vietminh went into action. No units of the regular Vietminh Army were used to stop Operation Atlante; Giap continued to gather his reserves, both from Tongking and Annam, for the siege of Dien Bien Phu, the site Navarre had
definitely chosen, on December 3, 1953, as the one where he planned to
defeat the Vietminh if they should again attempt to cross over into
Laos. Only local Vietminh troops were used in Operation Atlante. The
French reached the coastal town of Qui Nhon, less than 100 miles to the
north of Nha Trang, only after more than six weeks of rather pointless
efforts: The territory between Nha Trang and Qui Nhon was still in
Vietminh hands when Operation Atlante was called off at the beginning of March.

The loud complaints about the poor performance of the Vietnamese
National Army indicated that the French themselves regarded Operation Atlante as a failure. The troops engaged in it might indeed have
been used to better purpose on the mountain plateau of Annam, where
the Vietminh, in spite of their preoccupation with the siege of Dien
Bien Phu, were strong enough to carry out major offensive actions
against all French positions north of Ban Me Thuot. Kontum had to be
evacuated on February 7, and soon afterwards the Vietminh completely invested Pleiku, making it another French outpost that had to
be supplied by air. Today we know that the struggle for control of the
highlands of South Annam, although still overshadowed by the battle
of Dien Bien Phu, was one of the most gruesome episodes of the entire
Indochina War. Some of the more unfortunate French units were engaged in it until and beyond the day when the armistice was signed in
Geneva on July 21, and in a series of harrowing battles Mobile Group
100, one of the bravest and most seasoned French fighting groups, consisting chiefly of veterans from Korea, was completely wiped out.[14]

Even before Navarre started his Operation Atlante, the Vietminh
had completed the encirclement of Dien Bien Phu.[15] The French
knew that Giap had assembled the equivalent of four full divisions
around Dien Bien Phu, one of which was the 351st Heavy Division,

which the Chinese had supplied with 105-mm. guns. These guns, and sixteen Chinese 37-mm. anti-aircraft guns, were placed, not in groups but singly, in caves dug into the hills east and north of the French position, well concealed by the dense foliage of the woods. In fact, the entire Vietminh Army of 40,000 men was invisible, not only to the besieged garrison but also to the reconnaissance aircraft of the French.

Before the great battle started early in March, the French had concentrated a force of twelve battalions at Dien Bien Phu, well supplied with artillery and heavy mortars. Six fighter bombers stood on the airstrip; ten light tanks had been brought in by air and assembled on the spot for the counterattacks the French contemplated launching as soon as they had beaten back the first Vietminh assaults. In the course of the battle, six more paratroop battalions were flown in from the delta. The French fighting force was less than half the size of the besieging army, but both officers and men considered their equipment, their artillery, and their air support sufficient to repel any Vietminh attempt to storm their strongly fortified positions. The enemy would have to come out of the hills into the open, where the superior firing power of the garrison would make it impossible for him to reach even the outer defenses.[16]

What the French failed to learn from their intelligence reports was that the artillery assembled by the Vietminh in the hills east and north of their position was in fact superior to their own; and what they did not foresee was that the Vietminh gun emplacements were too well camouflaged to be bombed out of existence; that these Vietminh guns would be directed against the airstrip and would soon put it out of operation; that weather conditions (morning fog and afternoon rains) limited the use of aircraft in battle and for supply; and, furthermore, they did not foresee that the porter service of the Vietminh which, along with other equipment, brought up another sixty anti-aircraft guns, was able to supply the besiegers with enough ammunition to sustain almost continuous artillery fire and massive infantry attacks. The French had assumed that the Vietminh would run out of supplies after a maximum of four days of concentrated action.

These mistaken assumptions explain the optimism with which the French looked forward to a battle for Dien Bien Phu, and their hope that Giap would launch his attack soon. They were disappointed, and also rather perplexed, as weeks went by during which there were only minor clashes when their patrols, only a few miles from the center of the main French position, met Vietminh forces. Thus they learned that the ring the enemy had thrown around them was both narrower and tighter than they had assumed. The French had expected the attack as early at the night of January 25–26, but Giap was apparently not yet ready, and decided to use the interval before completing his preparations for the battle of Dien Bien Phu for another invasion of Laos, in order to force the French to withdraw still more of their depleted reserves from the delta.[17] Giap conducted this action with his 316th Division, stationed at Lai Chau, without having to weaken the forces encircling Dien Bien Phu. On their new descent toward Luang Prabang, the Vietminh succeeded in overwhelming the French position at Muong Khoua, which they had failed to take in their first descent upon the Laotian capital. On February 7, units of the 316th Division sighted Luang Prabang, whose defense, as Giap had expected, Navarre strengthened by flying in five battalions. However, on February 23, the Vietminh forces engaged in this operation suddenly turned back and joined Giap's army around Dien Bien Phu. Since the strong French garrison established there to prevent another invasion of Laos had proved no obstacle to Giap's tactical new threat against Luang Prabang, some of the French leaders began to question the wisdom of Navarre's decision to engage his best forces in the defense of an isolated outpost of doubtful strategic importance.

Indeed, while there has never been any question about Giap's readiness to accept battle at Dien Bien Phu, Navarre's decision, which offered his opponent this opportunity, was from the beginning regarded with more than slight misgivings by many French military and civilian leaders in both Indochina and France. Although these misgivings were forcefully expressed by only a few, Navarre's plan, which history proved to be disastrous, was made the subject of a bitter debate by people whose guilt in the matter is well known.[18] So much is certain: The worried military chiefs, and Premier Laniel, although they supported the political decision that Laos should be defended,[19] had warned Navarre to make the safety of the Expeditionary Corps one of his prime considerations; Navarre's decision to give battle at Dien Bien Phu had the support of the new High Commissioner, Maurice Dejean, the diplomat who had replaced Letourneau; inspection tours by prominent political and military leaders all ended in approval, even if lukewarm, of Navarre's decision.[20] Navarre took full responsibility for his choice of battleground; and furthermore, neither the government nor its military advisers in Paris, the National Defense Committee, had ever asked that Navarre's decision be reversed while there was still time to evacuate the dangerously exposed camp. The only man who had consistently opposed the idea of giving battle to the Vietminh at Dien Bien Phu was the French commander in Tongking, General Cogny.[21]

The battle of Dien Bien Phu was begun by the Vietminh on the night of March 13, 1954. Its first phase lasted five days. When this ended, the fate of the French garrison at Dien Bien Phu was sealed. The French lost the three outer strong points on small hills to the north of their main position, which was in the upper center of the long valley. "Position Béatrice" [22] was lost during the first night of the Vietminh attack; "Position Gabrielle" fell two nights later; and "Position Anne-Marie" fell on March 18, after a furious artillery bombardment had demoralized a Thai battalion and caused it to desert.

Giap's first success at Dien Bien Phu, at the positions Béatrice and Gabrielle, was largely the result of unexpectedly strong artillery fire, followed by waves of suicidal infantry attacks. The French estimated that these victories cost the Vietminh 2,500 dead. But when, on March 28, the Vietminh succeeded in subjecting the airstrip to constant and precise bombardments, the French knew that the task of holding Dien Bien Phu had become hopeless.

It was at this point that two developments in the diplomatic field opened up two conflicting prospects for the French for extracting themselves from their predicament. One was the possibility of obtaining a cease-fire before a general military collapse would make the Hanoi Government master of Vietnam. All those in France who were ready, for the sake of peace in Indochina, to negotiate and compromise with the Vietminh, looked forward to the conference that was to meet at Geneva on April 26, a conference to which the United States, the Soviet Union, France, and Great Britain had agreed at a foreign ministers' meeting held at Berlin between January 25 and February 18. The Geneva conference was called to seek a solution to the East-West conflict over Korea, but it was, in fact, and by not quite secret intention, called primarily to find a compromise to end the Indochina War.[23]

Others in France, however, still unable to see that the loss of Indochina was inevitable, desperately searched for new military means to save a situation that was so obviously beyond salvage. Since the means that France possessed, or was willing to supply at this late hour, were either not readily available or insufficient to turn the tide, these people insisted that the United States intervene militarily to save the French garrison at Dien Bien Phu and thus prevent the Vietminh from forcing France out of Indochina.

2

After the 1945 episode of political dilettantism involving Major Patti, General Gallagher, and their colleagues, Washington for almost two years had played no active part, and showed very little interest, in Indochinese affairs. The outbreak of the Indochina War at a time when both Great Britain and the Netherlands were working toward a peaceful settlement of their colonial problems was generally deplored in the United States, but widespread sympathy with the aspirations of the Indochinese peoples did not prompt the Truman Administration to criticize the French policy of colonial reconquest. The almost proverbial "anticolonialism" of the American people remained a platonic sentiment—too weak to overcome the many obstacles against a firm American policy in favor of independence for the three Indochinese states. France was too important an ally in Europe to be officially rebuffed by Washington for her Indochinese policy, and the fear that a compromise with the Hanoi regime might create a Communist Vietnam was even then strong in the United States: Washington felt it could not urge France to seek such a solution. The United States remained officially "neutral." But when the hope for an early return of peace, expressed by Secretary of State Marshall in February, 1947, was killed by developments, Washington was gradually induced to drop its policy of detachment and take an active part in the struggle for Indochina.

It is useless to speculate whether this change would have happened had it been possible to predict the extent to which the United States would one day be involved in Vietnam. The active role henceforth played by Washington in Indochinese affairs was not unanimously applauded, but nobody could foresee where the first modest steps would ultimately lead, and fear of agonizing consequences was therefore not among the considerations that ended U.S. passivity in the Indochina War. The nature of these first steps was determined by the country's traditional ideas that had long found expression in an unrecognized ideological "worldview," and the mounting preoccupations engendered by the Cold War, as the evolving conflict between the West and the

Soviet bloc began to be called. The justifiable fear that a French defeat in Indochina might produce a Communist Vietnam was among
these considerations. That changes in the *status quo* of many countries,
particularly those still under colonial rule, were necessary, was part of
the American worldview; but such changes had to conform to firm
American notions about what kind of society should grow out of theoretically welcome "revolutions."

The men who formulated U.S. policy over the next few years, unaware of this strong ideological inclination, were convinced that they
were faithful to the American ideals of political pragmatism. Was it
not obvious, even before the victory of Communism in China, that the
rise of a new Communist state in Asia would upset the existing balance
of power in the world to the disadvantage of the West? That this must
be prevented was not denied by even the fiercest enemies of French
colonialism. The practical question was how this could be done without actually promoting French colonialism, which some at least knew
to be one of the reasons for Communist strength in Vietnam. Here was
a great but as yet still unrecognized new American dilemma: Would
an active role by the United States in Indochinese affairs help to end
colonialism? Was American aid for the French war effort in Indochina
compatible with the need for the evolution of strong non-Communist
Indochinese states? And could Communism be prevented, particularly
in Vietnam, if this meant helping the French, whose desire to maintain
control over Indochina the United States did not wish to support?

The first attempt, still unofficial, to outline a possible U.S. policy
toward the Franco-Vietnamese conflict was made by former Ambassador to France William Bullitt in an article in *Life* magazine of December 29, 1947, entitled "The Saddest War." Bullitt recognized that
"all decent Annamites want independence," that "not one in a hundred
is a Communist," and that "Ho Chi Minh, the Communist leader of the
Annamite fight for independence, is followed by millions of Annamites
who disagree with his political views because he is the symbol of resistance to France."

From this fundamental fact of Vietnamese political life, Bullitt, although apparently ignorant of recent Indochinese history, might easily
have drawn a few obvious conclusions: that the Vietnamese followed
Ho Chi Minh because the French denied them independence; that the
French were apparently firm in their denial of independence, since
they had decided to reimpose their former rule with military means;

and that the "millions of Annamites" would not follow Ho Chi Minh if a non-Communist leadership were to fight with equal determination for their country's independence against the French. Bullitt, however, had a more idyllic view of the Franco-Vietnamese conflict. "The nub of the problem in Vietnam," he wrote, "is the establishment of cooperation between the French and the Annamite nationalists for the elimination of the Communists." And showing how the political mind can disregard the hardest realities if they contradict the wish for simple, or even merely possible, solutions, he added that this was "not impossible because there is no vital conflict between the real interests of the French and those of the Annamites." Since Bullitt saw no "vital conflict," he believed that the war could be ended (and Communism defeated) "by a series of relatively simple actions." What he proposed was indeed simple: French statements promising eventual independence to Vietnam. And what he assumed was even simpler: that the French would keep these promises, and that the anti-Communist nationalists would have "no difficulty in raising at once adequate Annamite forces to defeat Ho Chi Minh."

What makes these naïve pronouncements memorable is that Bullitt's misconceptions and false hopes were to become the basis of official U.S. policy up to the great crisis at the time of the fatal battle of Dien Bien Phu. The United States not only subscribed to the view that since Communism had to be defeated there must be no negotiations with Ho Chi Minh; it also accepted the French contention that this required a military victory over the Vietminh, and that if France lacked the means to achieve this victory, she had a right to appeal to the "free world" for aid. This meant that military aid would soon be extended for the fight against Vietnamese Communism, as the entire resistance movement against the French was henceforth called; and that this aid was not given to an independent anti-Communist government, which did not exist, but only to the French. It also meant that Washington embraced the Bao Dai solution and accepted "independence within the French Union" as the answer to the problem of Vietnamese nationalism. For Washington, too, the struggle between Vietnamese nationalism and French colonialism was transformed into a local encounter in the world-wide struggle between Communism and the "free world."

However, overt U.S. support, both moral and financial, was still slow in coming and became an irreversible policy only after the victory of Communism in China. After Peking and Moscow extended dip-

lomatic recognition to the Hanoi regime early in 1950, Secretary of
State Dean Acheson said that this "should remove any illusions as to
the 'nationalist' nature of Ho Chi Minh's aims and reveals Ho in his
true colors as the mortal enemy of native independence in Indochina." [24]
After the United States, on February 7, 1950, recognized the three
Indochinese states, the State Department said rather cautiously that this
should promote a "peaceful and democratic evolution" of these "dependent peoples toward self-government and independence," implying
that self-government and independence did not yet exist; but only three
months later, in a statement made after consultations between Acheson
and French Foreign Minister Robert Schuman, the State Department
dropped this caution and startlingly asserted that Vietnam, Cambodia,
and Laos "now enjoy independence within the French Union." The
United States had decided to extend military aid to the French, and
some direct economic aid to the Indochinese states, insisting, however,
that the defense of these states was "primarily the responsibility of
France and the peoples of Indochina." [25] On June 27, 1950, after the
outbreak of the Korean War, President Truman announced that the
United States would accelerate military assistance "to the forces of
France and the Associated States in Indochina," and also dispatch a military mission "to provide close working relations with those forces." [26]
The gates were now open. Every new announcement about aid to Indochina disclosed another increase in the grants for military assistance
to the French. These sums jumped from $119 million given through
the Mutual Security program in summer, 1951, to $815 million for fiscal
year 1954.[27] Economic aid to the Associated States on the other hand
still did not exceed $25 million.

The political counterpart to the steady increase of military aid for
the French was an evolution toward an acceptance, with some reluctance, of the Bao Dai solution, as well as of the claims put forward by
French propaganda that this "solution" produced results in the struggle
against the Vietminh: The French Union was seen as adequate to satisfy Vietnamese nationalism. The Indochina War was no longer regarded as a colonial war but one between Communism and the "free
world" and the independence of the Associated States was said to be
approaching full realization. This, at least, is what Secretary of State
John Foster Dulles stated in July, 1953, six months after General
Eisenhower became President. Dulles went even beyond the claims of
French propaganda by comparing the French Union with the British

Commonwealth, and asserting that it "offers a possibility of free association of wholly independent and sovereign nations." [28]

This almost unqualified endorsement by the United States of France's Indochinese policy, however, did not mean that Washington never expressed hesitation or misgivings about the French conception of independence for the three Indochinese states. The Elysée accords of March, 1949, were greeted without much enthusiasm by the United States. The existing agreements, said Washington on many occasions, should not be the last word but would have to be extended if independence should become real. *The New York Times* reported from Paris on March 10, 1950, that the United States might insist on a greater measure of independence for the Associated States as a condition of military aid to France. More important still, there was a great awareness, voiced by Secretary Acheson on several occasions, of the danger of becoming "obsessed with military considerations. Important as they are, there are other problems that press, and these other problems are not capable of solution through military means." [29] American military aid could not furnish the determination and will to fight, nor win the loyalty of the Indochinese people to their governments. Even the fundamental premise of the French—that behind Vietminh resistance was only the imperialist drive of international Communism—was questioned by Acheson. Behind Vietminh resistance there was also "revulsion against the acceptance of misery as the normal condition of life," and there was opposition to foreign rule. De Lattre's claim during his visit to Washington in September, 1951, that the Indochina War was not a colonial war because Indochina no longer was a colony, and that France was defending something that no longer belonged to her,[30] was received with wide-spread skepticism, which was shared, although politely suppressed, even by the Administration.

But although an informed and articulate minority of Americans— some senators and political writers, even some military men—opposed the policy of aiding France in the Indochina War as long as the Associated States were denied full independence,[31] serious pressure to bring about a change in French policy was never applied. That colonialism should end was an American desire, often expressed but unfulfilled, since Washington shied away from action that might have induced the French to make truly significant concessions to the Indochinese states. This was not only because, as some analysts of American policy in Southeast Asia have suggested, the pressure of events forced the

United States to renounce the promotion of social and political reforms and that Washington, instead of insisting on reforms that might
have inspired the Indochinese populations to fight against Communism
relied more and more on superior military force. Nor was the main
reason for lack of pressure on the French by Washington that the leadership of the United States, in spite of a predilection for verbal en-
dorsements of "revolutions," always avoided political steps likely to
produce drastic social and economic changes. Furthermore, Washington had no real reason to fear that France might be lost as an ally
against Communism in Europe if the United States were to make true
independence for Vietnam a condition for military aid. The failure of
the United States to put real pressure on the French had a deeper and
vastly more consequential reason, one that could not be publicly admitted, since it had not yet become a fully conscious motive of U.S.
foreign policy. The great question facing Washington was: Would
France continue the Indochina War if she lost control of Vietnam,
Cambodia, and Laos, as seemed more and more likely, even if American aid enabled the Expeditionary Corps to defeat the Vietminh? The
answer, unacceptable to the United States, was no. The French, no
matter what they said in justification of their policy, would continue
the war only so long as there was hope that its outcome would not
mean the end of the French "presence" in Indochina. A milder form of
colonial domination was still the aim France pursued through the Indochina War, an aim that Washington had no interest whatsoever in
supporting for its own sake. Washington's interest in Indochina was to
contain Communism, not to preserve a modified form of French rule.
However, for the sake of preventing another Communist victory in
Asia, Washington decided that continued French domination of Indochina was by far the lesser of two evils. Thus the Vietnamese, still
effectively ruled by the French, were promoted to the status of a "free
people" resisting "subversion by armed minorities or by outside pressure." [32] Indeed, all the clichés that ten years later would be used to
justify U.S. policy in Vietnam, were already coined when Washington
decided to extend political and military support to the French halfway
through the Indochina War. This is true even of the famous "domino
theory." Based on ignorance of the fact that Communist strength in
Vietnam was a unique and isolated case, this theory assumed that a refusal to defend French Indochina would necessarily lead to the triumph of Communist aggression all over Southeast Asia. The wish to

contain Communism was infinitely stronger than the desire to see colonialism end, and as early as February, 1950, it produced the most dubious and yet most enduring of all propaganda claims, namely that the war was "fostered from abroad."

This American attitude explains why U.S. participation in the struggle for Indochina generated not a single new idea for advancing a political solution of the conflict, in no way modified the course pursued by the French, and contributed nothing to a better understanding of the political conditions for reducing Communist strength. On the contrary, it soon became evident that U.S. intervention multiplied the obstacles to a political settlement of the war. When, after eight years of useless effort, French determination to continue the struggle gave way to a desire to seek peace, if necessary through negotiations and a compromise with Ho Chi Minh, only the United States of all the countries concerned sought to prevent the calling of a conference toward this end. And at the conference, which came about against U.S. wishes, Washington refused to play an active role.

U.S. lack of interest in preserving French rule, and concentration on saving Vietnam from Communism, were the causes of the Franco-American tension that arose when Paris asked for and Washington consented to furnish military aid. This tension explains why the French accepted U.S. aid without genuine enthusiasm, even with bad grace, although American aid paid for more than half the costs of the Indochina War. In Indochina, the French openly expressed their resentment against the arrival of American diplomatic, economic, and military counselors, who came with the U.S. aid. The French firmly resisted direct American military aid to the governments and armies of the Associated States, and they never considered letting the United States share responsibility for the conduct of the war. Navarre, who could not have undertaken a single one of his campaigns without U.S. aid, always spoke disparagingly of American military assistance. He grudgingly admitted that the United States "has granted us financial and material assistance," but complained that this was given only "after a delay of five years." What he deplored most, however, was that U.S. aid allegedly led to the "intrusion of American influence in our affairs." [33] Why, asked one Vietnamese critic of this French attitude, "is the Indochinese War the whole free world's business only when military assistance is needed? And why does it become exclusively French business when policy-planning is discussed?" [34] Another question was raised in all good faith by many Americans both in Vietnam and at home: Why do the French, who keep telling us that this is no longer a colonial war, accuse us of "anticolonialism" whenever we try to proceed as if France had really put an end to Vietnam's colonial status? [35] To keen observers, these contradictions indicated that on the propaganda front, too, the French position was crumbling.

But only in April, 1954, when the fall of Dien Bien Phu appeared imminent, did Washington and Paris, in a test of their policy of joint action against Vietnamese Communism, begin to realize that behind these frictions was a deep conflict of aims. In a dramatic confrontation immediately before and during the Geneva conference, both the nature and the depth of the Franco-American conflict over Vietnam was suddenly revealed.

3

To overcome the difficulties that stood in the way of a compromise solution of the Indochina War was a task for which contemporary diplomacy, debilitated by the constraints of the Cold War, was not too well equipped. It almost failed in taking the first hurdle to a negotiated settlement—the calling of a conference to discuss the Franco-Vietnamese conflict.

Before this conference was held in Geneva, opposition to a compromise solution of the Indochina conflict came not from Moscow or Peking, nor even from Paris. These capitals, although they did not engage themselves as warmly as London, were nevertheless ready, for their own various reasons, to cooperate in a negotiated settlement of the Indochina War. The French, although still divided, were no longer eager to continue the war; most Frenchmen realized that Indochina would be lost to France even if the United States helped prevent a victory of the Vietminh. The Soviet Union, after the death of Stalin, wanted a relaxation of international tension as one condition for realizing ambitious economic projects at home, and also hoped to kill the European Defense Community, in exchange for promoting a settlement in Indochina acceptable to France. But China, too, then still eager for diplomatic recognition, favored a negotiated settlement of the Indochina War. Her leaders looked upon China's presence at the projected conference as a first step toward recognition and toward inclusion of China in the power club of the "Big Five" being propagated by the Soviet Union.

The active opposition to the project of a conference on Indochina came from Washington—the idea of "compromising with Communism" was abhorrent to the Republican Administration—and from Saigon, where not only Bao Dai but also the stanchly anti-French nationalists rightly feared that in a deal with Ho Chi Minh they would be sold down the river. But there were indications that the Hanoi regime, too, was unhappy about the prospect of a negotiated peace. The Vietminh leaders, who for years had pleaded for such a settlement, were now looking toward total victory.

One reason for the Hanoi regime's lack of enthusiasm for the Geneva conference has long been overlooked: The change of mood among the powers involved that finally made the conference possible came about through a step taken by Ho Chi Minh: the publication, on November 29, 1953, by the Swedish newspaper *Expressen* of Ho's reply to questions submitted to him by the paper's Paris correspondent, Sven Löfgen. Ho greatly surprised the French by stating his willingness to study any proposal for a cease-fire. True, only a little while earlier, on November 12, French Premier Laniel had stated that the "conflict need not necessarily have a military solution"; Ho also knew that pressure on Laniel's government to negotiate with the Vietminh kept growing. Vice Premier Reynaud and Minister of National Defense Pleven took that position in the Cabinet, while Mendès-France and the old Indochina expert Sarraut fought for it in the Assembly and in the press. Others, not opposed to a negotiated settlement, preferred an international conference to direct Franco-Vietminh talks. But for Ho this, too, was proof that the French were tired of the war, and that they indirectly admitted the possibility of a Vietminh victory. Why, then, should he negotiate? For this reason, his readiness to study proposals for a cease-fire, after having kept silent on the subject for several years, created a political sensation.[36]

Two days before Ho's reply was made public, the Kremlin had accepted an old Western proposal for a conference of the Big Four (Great Britain, France, the United States, and the Soviet Union). It opened in Berlin on January 25, 1954. Ostensibly called to seek a solution for the East-West conflict over Germany, this meeting was guided, by rather shrewd British and Soviet diplomacy, into exploring the chances for a settlement of the Indochina War. The Kremlin had become convinced that France was at last ready for peace talks, and probably also willing to pay the price Russia asked for urging the Vietminh to accept less than total victory: refuse to join the European Defense Community, and accept Communist China at the conference table.[37] How strong the desire of the French people for peace had become the Russians could have learned from the storm that arose when, on December 19, 1953, the weekly *Express* revealed how Premier Ramadier had suppressed the peace proposals made by Ho Chi Minh in 1947.

Did Ho, then, in accepting talks for a cease-fire, just when Giap was victorious on all fronts, merely lend himself to a diplomatic maneuver undertaken jointly by Moscow and Peking, whose active interest in a conference attended by China was beyond all doubt? [38] It may or may not be significant that the questions of the Swedish newspaper were submitted to Ho through the intermediary of the Swedish Embassy in Peking; what is certain is that the Vietminh was not happy over the Berlin decision to call a conference that might also try to settle the Indochina conflict. Vietminh broadcasts, far from being enthusiastic, "tended at first to discount the prevalent rumors of impending negotiations, but when these rumors proved to be well-founded, incredulity gave place to anger and dismay." [39] But whether the Vietminh leaders changed their minds under Sino-Soviet pressure or recognized that no compromise could in the end deprive them of a victory that they had long won on the political front, they knew that a decisive defeat of the Expeditionary Corps before the start of negotiations would immensely improve their position at the conference table. Dien Bien Phu offered them the opportunity, and whatever the cost, they decided that it had to be grasped. There is in fact reason to believe that Giap's conduct of the battle of Dien Bien Phu was largely influenced by considerations of political and diplomatic strategy. He intended to produce conclusive evidence that the military position of the French was collapsing on the very day the talks on Indochina were scheduled to begin.

The displeasure of the Hanoi regime over the plan to settle the Indochina War at an international conference was temporary and perhaps only tactical. This was not the case with the strong reaction which the prospect of a deal with the Vietminh aroused in Saigon, among the spokesmen of the Bao Dai regime as well as among most of its anti-Communist and anti-French critics. Their negative reaction was lasting, and it hardened into the decision never to accept a compromise that would recognize the Hanoi regime's authority over any part of Vietnam.

To the many reasons that had driven most of these anti-Vietminh forces into their position of extreme nationalism and open defiance of Bao Dai's continued collaboration with the French was now added their fear of being sold out by France. This fear soon became as strong among the confirmed collaborators as among the swelling numbers of their nationalist critics. The true collaborators, and Bao Dai himself, realized that a compromise solution might well leave them at the mercy of the Vietminh. Were the French about to betray the cause of Vietnamese "freedom" for which the war allegedly was being fought? Now the anti-Vietminh nationalists of all shades became even more openly anti-French, and quite a few of the collaborators acted as if their nationalism were superior to that of the Vietminh. Some, concerned for their political future or even their physical survival, now claimed that they had always sympathized with and secretly supported the "resistance." All of them loudly demanded that Vietnam must at last be given "total independence," and some even demanded that the French must depart and leave the fight against the Vietminh to an American-supported Vietnamese army. Above all, they said, Vietnam had to get a new government, genuinely nationalist and not subject to any French control whatsoever. The formation of such a government was most urgently requested by Ngo Dinh Nhu's Movement for National Unity and Peace. But the request had not aroused any popular enthusiasm, and the movement's support was dwindling.[40] The people knew that at the conference table, too, the fate of Vietnam would remain in the hands of the French and the Vietminh. Yet, to be as nationalistic as the Vietminh was the only weapon left to the desperate and helpless spokesmen of anti-Vietminh nationalism, and even Bao Dai and his counselors decided that the demand for total independence offered the only chance for the survival of their state.

During the eight months that had passed since the "solemn declaration" of July 3, 1953, the French Government had successfully postponed discussions on how this latest promise of independence was to be fulfilled.[41] At last on March 3, 1954, Prime Minister Buu Loc was allowed to go to Paris with a large delegation; he hoped to reach agreements on "total independence" before the Geneva conference opened. But not even the former Emperor himself, who left Vietnam for Paris on April 10, could persuade the French that they must save anti-Viet-

minh nationalism from political extinction by freely granting to Bao
Dai what their military weakness would soon compel them to grant to
Ho Chi Minh: true independence. Since they were already thinking of
partition as the basis of a compromise with the Vietminh, the French
of course knew that one half of Vietnam could not be salvaged. But
they still nourished the hope of maintaining a measure of control over
that part of Vietnam which this solution would deny to the Hanoi regime.

What the French failed to see was that if a non-Communist half of
Vietnam remained under a French-sponsored regime similar to the one
that existed, the population of this "free" Vietnam, in its continued
struggle for independence and social progress, would still remain attached to the Vietminh. There were no signs of social or political
progress in the parts of the country under Bao Dai rule. Shortly before
the Geneva conference, a few measures taken by the government of
Buu Loc showed that since the fall of Premier Tam, the Bao Dai regime had made progress in only two directions: moral decay and political impotence. These had reached such a point that Vietminh propaganda did not have to resort to invention.

In order to intensify the prosecution of the war, a newly formed
war cabinet, on April 12, 1954, issued a decree mobilizing all males between the ages of twenty and twenty-five. But of the 150,000 conscripts this measure was expected to produce, all but 9,000 succeeded
in evading military service by hiding, fleeing into Vietminh territory,
or enlisting in the militias of the sects. A subsequent new attempt to
incorporate the sects into the National Army failed, as had those by
Buu Loc's predecessors Huu and Tam. The government achieved
really close cooperation with only one sect—the Binh Xuyen—but at
the price of subordinating the authority of the state to the interests of
the Binh Xuyen war lords. These men had earlier been given the
profitable business of running the opium dens, the houses of prostitution, and the gambling establishment Grand Monde, as well as control
of every other source of revenue from vice in the Saigon-Cholon area.
Now they were also put in control of the Saigon-Cholon police. A
Binh Xuyen leader, Lai Huu Sang, became its head. Hundreds of policemen were forced to leave the service to make room for members of
the Binh Xuyen, and many more left for fear of Binh Xuyen revenge,
since their job had compelled them to fight the many illegal activities
of these former bandits. "It can occasion no surprise, therefore, that an

appointment which entrusted the responsibility for public security in Saigon-Cholon to an armed group whose fortunes were founded upon the very activities which they would now be required to combat, should have given rise to the rumor that this scandalous appointment had been preceded by a generous cash payment to the Prime Minister." [42] In case of a partition of Vietnam, the Bao Dai regime would evidently have to be removed if its non-Communist half were to have a chance of survival.

4

Although the idea of partition was still violently rejected by all spokesmen for Vietnamese nationalism, it nevertheless began to be recognized as the possible condition of a peace that would not be a total victory for the Vietminh. Partition was the main preoccupation of all anti-Vietminh nationalists untainted by collaboration with the French and uncorrupted by the Bao Dai regime. Although rejected on principle, it was nevertheless their only remaining hope for political survival. For many, however, the despair over the Bao Dai regime's moral and political bankruptcy, and over the country's probable fate after a new Franco-Vietnamese deal, was cushioned by the hopes they had begun to pin on the growing involvement of the United States in Franco-Indochinese affairs. These hopes were based on the expectation that United States opposition would prevent a settlement at Geneva that would hand over all or even parts of Vietnam to exclusive Communist control. There was no shortage of statements from Washington to nourish such hopes. What was even more heartening to these nationalists was the distinctly "anticolonial" tenor of these statements.[43] This was understood to mean that if it ever came to American military intervention to thwart a Communist victory in Indochina, this would come about under only one condition: U.S. insistence on wiping out all traces of French colonial rule.

At the Berlin conference, Secretary John Foster Dulles forcefully expressed U.S. opposition to a settlement that required concessions to "Communism" and opposed the holding of a conference in which Communist China would be allowed to participate. The active and rather subtle diplomacy of Eden and Molotov finally succeeded in getting Washington to participate in the Geneva conference.[44] But the differences between the U.S. position and that of its main allies, Great Britain and France, were by no means settled. They exploded into an open conflict among the leading powers of the West shortly before the Geneva conference; they were not resolved during the conference proceedings, and they remained latent until the second, the "American" Indochina War, reactivated them ten years later.

The first great crisis over conflicting allied aims in Indochina, which the boorish diplomacy of Dulles did nothing to mitigate, reached its climax in spring, 1954. On March 20, General Paul Ely, one of France's highest-ranking military men, arrived in Washington, on a mission decided on by the French Cabinet on March 11—only a few days before the first blows against the garrison at Dien Bien Phu dramatically altered the military situation in Indochina. The original request of the French Government—that the United States should threaten direct military action if the Chinese intervened with their air force in the battle at Dien Bien Phu—had become pointless: After March 18, the French realized that Vietminh strength was sufficient for victory at Dien Bien Phu without direct Chinese intervention. Ely's mission was to make clear to Washington the full plight of the Expeditionary Corps, to press for immediate additional aid in the form of supplies, above all bombers, and auxiliary American personnel to increase the effectiveness of the French Air Force.[45] But Ely was also instructed to leave no doubt about the unwillingness of France to continue the war. No longer was American military assistance requested in order to achieve victory over the Vietminh; its purpose now was merely to keep the Expeditionary Corps in the fight until the Geneva conference had produced a settlement acceptable to France.

Since the Administration, the Congress, and the military leadership in the United States were deeply divided over the course to be adopted in this emergency, the reaction to Ely's rather modest demands and to his surprising pessimism was understandably mixed. The circles opposed to steps that might involve the United States in another Korea-type war in Asia—the vast majority of the Congress and even of the Joint Chiefs of Staff—were relieved. So was President Eisenhower, who gave Ely most emphatic assurances of speedy compliance with his demands for increased aid. But to the parties who had expected that American aid would enable the French eventually to defeat the Vietminh, the decision of France to fight for nothing more than an acceptable compromise came as a shock. Was this not another retreat by the West before Communist aggression in Asia? And had the Republican platform not promised that the United States would never again be a party to treaties sanctioning an extension of Communist rule? Not only did the so-called "China Lobby" and the Republican majority leader, Senator William Knowland, denounce the idea of a compromise solution in Indochina as a fresh betrayal of the cause of freedom. That such a compromise must be avoided, if necessary through direct U.S. military intervention, was also the position of Vice-President Nixon, Secretary Dulles, and the Chairman of the Joint Chiefs of Staff, Admiral Radford.

The plans and actions of these three powerful men, which, in the absence of Presidential leadership, remained uncoordinated from beginning to end, would probably have pushed the United States over the brink if wiser counsels had not prevailed in Paris and London, and to a lesser extent in the U.S. Congress.

The moves that Radford, Dulles, and Nixon made during April, 1954, to stop Communism in Indochina are among the saddest chapters of U.S. diplomacy. The first one to act, entirely on his own, to bring about direct American military intervention was Admiral Radford. He induced Ely, who was ready to leave for Paris on March 25, to stay an additional twenty-four hours, during which Radford persuaded the receptive French general that a massive strike by the U.S. Air Force could still save the French garrison at Dien Bien Phu. Radford assured Ely that Eisenhower would approve such action. The plan, which became known as Operation Vautour (Vulture), envisaged the use of planes stationed in the Philippines and on aircraft carriers in the Far East, which were later ordered to move into the Gulf of Tongking.[46]

Radford's offer was submitted to the French Government by Ely on March 27. On March 29, a "war council" convened by the cabinet decided to send an officer to Hanoi, who, on April 2, informed the government of Navarre's belief that such an airstrike could destroy the Vietminh artillery positions around Dien Bien Phu and probably save the garrison, which otherwise would certainly be lost. Another meeting of the war council on April 4 thereupon decided, not without some misgivings, officially to request the intervention proposed by Admiral Radford.

If there is one particular day when the policy that would govern U.S.–Vietnamese relations for more than a decade was decided, it was April 5, 1954, the day Washington's answer to the French request for intervention was given to Ambassador Dillon in Paris. It was a down-right refusal, which, understandably, came as a surprise and shock to both Ely and the cabinet.[47] What had happened, they asked themselves, to bring about this apparent reversal of U.S. policy?

They learned only much later what had happened: The initiative in shaping policy to ward off the threatened loss of Indochina to Communism had passed from Admiral Radford to Secretary Dulles immediately after Ely's departure; and Dulles had an entirely different concept of the U.S. role at this historical juncture, a concept that could be pursued only with full Congressional support. He did not want a one-strike American intervention to save the French at Dien Bien Phu. He wanted more. Indochina—all of it—had to be saved from Communism. Dulles was not interested in U.S. intervention merely to improve the position of the French for a deal with the Communists at Geneva. He was opposed to any such deal; he did not want a compromise to end the war. He wanted the war to continue until Communism was defeated, and he did not want this war to be conducted under the old banner of the French, which was still tainted with colonialism. The war had to be truly internationalized, and the French, who still regarded it as exclusively their own business had to be replaced by a coalition of Western allies under the leadership of the United States. Or, as one recent critic of Dulles' Indochina policy put it: Dulles opposed the Radford plan "because it was too modest. Instead of aiming at total victory, it envisaged a temporary military result that would enhance the chance of a settlement by concessions. He opposed it because it was a short-term operation, certainly not part of an anti-Communist crusade. He opposed it because it would accomplish nothing against French colonialism." [48]

In a speech at the Overseas Press Club on March 29, Dulles had insisted that aggression must be stopped promptly and that this could be done only through "united action"—the first public announcement of his plan for a coalition of the Western powers and their Asian allies against any further Communist advance.[49] With Eisenhower's consent, Dulles killed Admiral Radford's plan, which neither Congress nor the Joint Chiefs of Staff seemed inclined to endorse.[50] In a meeting of Administration spokesmen and Congressional leaders on April 3, Dulles obtained a decision that all action, even a one-time airstrike, must have allied support. The thesis of Dulles that the United States must not act alone, that it should act only as the leader of a "democratic" and "anticolonial" front, was accepted. The United States would decide what steps should be taken only after consultations had determined to what extent her allies, above all Great Britain, were willing to participate in united action.[51] Congress, Eisenhower told Churchill in an urgent letter, would agree to U.S. intervention only as part of a common allied effort.

There is, however, another side to the story of Dulles' readiness to drop immediate American intervention to save the French garrison at Dien Bien Phu for the sake of his broader aims. He did not believe that the military position of the French was as desperate as described by Ely. He thought that even if Dien Bien Phu fell, the French would still be able to continue the war, particularly if there were prospects that united action would materialize soon.[52] As late as March 22, more than a week after the first French debacle at Dien Bien Phu, Dulles stated that the "Navarre Plan" need not be abandoned since, according to his own military judgment, it still promised victory within a year. Neither had the Secretary of State been sufficiently informed about the Bao Dai regime, nor shown willingness to accept the truth about it nor about the reasons that the Vietnamese National Army remained ineffective. Since most Vietnamese believed a Vietminh victory to be imminent, it was too late to turn the Bao Dai regime and its army into a force capable of stemming the waves of Giap's fighters now rolling over almost the entire country.

One notion only dominated the thinking of Dulles: that no time must be lost in preparing "united action," and that at least the threat of it had to become real before the opening of the Geneva conference. Preventing the conference had been his aim at Berlin; torpedoing it was his ill-concealed intention now.[53] But French and British determination to steer clear of anything that might wreck the conference was precisely the reason why Dulles' project failed. The French Cabinet, fearful that a pact for the obvious purpose of threatening military intervention in Indochina would wipe out all chances for a compromise settlement of the conflict, decided, on April 6, to reject the Dulles proposal.[54] The same decision was taken one day later by the British Cabinet. The French Government, said Premier Laniel in the National Assembly on April 9, intended to keep its hands free for Geneva and to follow up every chance the conference might offer to achieve peace.

There now developed, during the next two weeks, what can only be described as the greatest crisis to date in U.S. relations with Great Britain and France. Dulles went to London on April 11, only to learn that both Churchill and Eden (supported by the opposition Labour Party) were adamant in their refusal to agree to any declaration of allied united action before the chances of a settlement at Geneva had been explored. In a joint statement on April 13, Eden agreed merely to an "examination of the possibilities" for such action ("within the framework of the United Nations Charter"); but Dulles interpreted this as acceptance of the substance of his plan. He invited the ambassadors of nine countries to a conference in Washington on April 20. (The countries were Britain, France, Australia, New Zealand, Thailand, the Philippines, and the three Associated States of Indochina.) British reaction, quick and sharp, taught Dulles that there had been a "misunderstanding" between him and Eden. The British Government ordered its ambassador in Washington to stay away from the meeting.[55]

The subsequent behavior of Dulles supported the view that his anger over the rejection by Paris and London of his project for united action was one of the main reasons that American military intervention during the battle of Dien Bien Phu never materialized. Driven into panic by a report from Navarre that without immediate massive air support Dien Bien Phu would soon fall, the French Government, on April 23 and 24, asked Dulles, who was in Paris on his way to Geneva, whether Washington would not reconsider the refusal of April 5 and authorize Operation Vautour. Dulles, after consultations with his own military advisers (including Radford, who had rushed to Paris), decided that it was now too late to save Dien Bien Phu. He advised the French, rather uncharitably, that if Dien Bien Phu fell, they should "react vigorously" against this and other such "temporary setbacks." [56] But although he said that airstrikes could no longer save Dien Bien Phu, he was nevertheless willing to recommend them, provided the French Government agreed to a statement on united action and succeeded also in obtaining London's consent. Thus everything was now made dependent on Eden and Churchill, who would have to take the blame if U.S. intervention at Dien Bien Phu, for which Washington was allegedly ready, failed to materialize.

The despairing French capitulated. However, there are strong indications that they wanted not allied action but merely the threat of it, hoping that the effect upon the Chinese would improve the bargaining position of France at Geneva.[57] But French efforts to persuade London were of no avail. Eden, supported by Churchill, held fast to his position that the chances for an accord at Geneva, and for a general easing of tension in Asia, must not be thrown away. In the House of Commons, Churchill stated that his government was "not prepared to give any undertakings [*sic*] about United Kingdom military action in advance of the results of Geneva." [58] This meant that the Dulles project, too, after having served to kill the Radford-Ely plan, was dead.

During these tense weeks between the Ely visit to Washington and the opening of the Geneva conference on April 26, the third of the important protagonists of U.S. intervention in Indochina, Vice-President Nixon, had come out openly with proposals that neither Radford nor Dulles were willing to embrace. In Nixon's views of the Indochina War, political reality and historical fact were completely subordinate to the needs of anti-Communist propaganda. In a brazen display of cynicism designed to mislead an uninformed public, Nixon in a speech in December, 1953, said that there would be no Indochina War were it not for the existence of Communist China. However, he was on safe ground, for how many people in the United States knew that the French had already been fighting the Vietminh, and had failed to subdue them, four years before China became Communist? It was Nixon's view, expressed on several occasions during the months of March and April,[59] that if Communism were to be stopped in Asia, the United States must act in Indochina—not only with airstrikes, but "by putting our boys in"; and not only in support of French or allied action, but, if necessary, alone—"regardless of allied support." [60]

To a great extent, Eisenhower's fear of engaging U.S. ground forces in another Asian war caused the policy of Dulles, who insisted that U.S. intervention must have Allied support, to prevail in the end. Nixon's notion that "the United States would have to replace [the French] if necessary to prevent a Communist conquest of Southeast Asia" [61] anticipated the future, but in April, 1954, the time was not yet ripe.

The President himself during most of this critical period both supported and opposed military intervention to save the garrisons at Dien Bien Phu, for whose fate he showed a deep concern. What he said seemed to depend chiefly on whom he had last spoken to. He had both endorsed and helped kill the Radford-Ely plan. He pointed out the danger of intervention [62] but would no doubt have approved of it if Dulles had succeeded in obtaining British support for united action. At a press conference on April 29, he denied that there had ever been an

American proposal to intervene with massive air attacks, but in his book he states that he was "disappointed" when "our efforts for a satisfactory method of allied intervention failed." [63] It seems that for Eisenhower, the Indochina crisis was just one more occasion to indulge in the privilege accorded well-meaning but weak leaders of having no opinion of their own. He liked to promise military intervention to reduce the plight of the French but was glad when strong opposition offered him an excuse for not abiding by his promise.

While the statesmen bickered, the soldiers on both sides in and around Dien Bien Phu fought and died. Vietminh artillery had made the airstrip unusable. The wounded could no longer be evacuated, and supplies had to be parachuted into the camp, whose contracting boundaries made the dropping zones smaller and smaller and increased the amount of supplies that fell into Vietminh hands. In a complex network of trenches dug by night and leading to within a few yards of the French defenses, the enemy closed a circle around the garrison that none of the desperate French counterattacks was able to break. Rain turned the camp into a sea of mud, and the trenches into coffins of mire for thousands of Vietminh soldiers. Dien Bien Phu was hell long before the new general assault in the night of May 1–2 brought the besiegers, at an enormous cost in lives, right to the edge of the main French positions. The final attack was undertaken on the night of May 6, and the garrison overwhelmed on May 7, the day before the Indochina conflict was on the agenda of the Geneva conference.

For the statesmen at Geneva, for the people of France, but above all for the soldiers of the Expeditionary Corps, the fall of Dien Bien Phu was a signal, intended as such by the leaders of the Vietminh, that the French military effort in Indochina was about to collapse.[64]

5

The Geneva conference, which lasted eighty-seven days—from April 26 to July 21, 1954—attacked the problem of Indochina on May 8, twenty-four hours after the French High Command had received the last somber message from its doomed garrison at Dien Bien Phu. The problem of reunifying Korea had been disposed of at Geneva by dropping this intractable subject from the agenda.[65]

Delegates from nine states—France, Great Britain, the United

States, the Soviet Union, the People's Republic of China, Cambodia, Laos, Bao Dai's State of Vietnam, and Ho Chi Minh's Democratic Republic of Vietnam (D.R.V.N.)—sat around the conference table when Britain's Foreign Minister Anthony Eden, one of the two chairmen, opened the first of the many sessions devoted to finding a way to ending the war in Indochina, the true purpose of the conference. Later, the conference was attended also by an observer from India.

The decision that Eden and Soviet Foreign Minister Molotov should alternate as chairmen had been easily reached. Of the five big powers, France for obvious reasons was disqualified, Communist China was unacceptable to the West, and the United States, apart from the objections of the Communist powers, was disinclined to play an active part in a conference that Washington participated in only with the strongest reservations. To underline this, Secretary Dulles appointed Under Secretary of State Bedell Smith head of the American delegation on May 3, and he himself left Geneva on May 5.

The first difficult decision to be made was in what capacity the Vietminh, whose D.R.V.N. had not been recognized by any Western power, should participate at the conference. This problem was linked to the question, still open at the start of the conference on April 26, whether Bao Dai's State of Vietnam would agree to go to Geneva at all. It was Bao Dai's contention that there was only one state and only one legal government of Vietnam—his. To go to a conference attended by the Hanoi regime would mean that he recognized not only the existence of the government headed by Ho Chi Minh but also its right to represent Vietnam at Geneva. But, as usual, pressure from the French changed Bao Dai's mind. On April 30, after receiving a joint message from Bidault, Dulles, and Eden assuring him that the sovereignty of his state would not be violated, Bao Dai agreed to let a delegation of his government participate in the conference. The invitations to the two Vietnamese governments were issued only on May 3. The Vietminh delegation, which had been waiting in Berlin for this summons, arrived the next day. It was headed by Deputy Prime Minister and Minister of Foreign Affairs *ad interim* Pham Van Dong, who had last been seen in the West at the Fontainebleau conference in summer, 1946.[66] The delegation of the State of Vietnam was headed by Foreign Minister Nguyen Quoc Dinh (who, like Bidault, was to be out of office before the conference ended). Dinh demonstrated his government's continued opposition to the conference by residing outside

Geneva and by insisting that his delegation had not come to negotiate
with the Communist powers but merely to consult with his country's
Western allies.[67]

This, however, was only a minor feature in the spectacle of disunity
offered by the Western powers before and during the conference.
From the very beginning, only Great Britain was wholeheartedly trying to make the conference a success. Eden, therefore, was the only
Western statesman who consistently worked for an accommodation of
the widely conflicting views concerning the contents of a possible
agreement. The British Foreign Minister, fully supported by his country, which, unlike France, did not have to pay the price of a compromise, and which did not share the American obsession with the dangers
of Communism in Asia, possessed the freedom of action needed to
match the tactical flexibility of the Communist delegations. Eden could
not count on U.S. help. Dulles not only hoped, but for weeks confidently expected, that the conference would fail. The threat of U.S.
military intervention in case the war continued may at one time have
strengthened the weak bargaining position of the French; but at no
time did there exist that minimum of diplomatic coordination between
Paris and Washington which would have enabled their delegations to
use this threat as a weapon.

Nor were the French, as long as Bidault spoke for them at Geneva,
prepared to face the consequences of their crumbling military position
and assist Eden in his search for a solution acceptable to both sides.
Like Dulles, who derived moral satisfaction from acting as though the
Chinese delegation did not exist, Bidault refused all contact with the
head of the Vietminh delegation. He was the only Western spokesman
who lacked the good sense to refrain from the sort of historical recriminations and propagandistic accusations in which the Communist delegates indulged. Bidault's whole manner betrayed that he was quite cool
toward the proposals for a cease-fire that he himself submitted to the
conference in the name of his government. He was strongly attacked
by critics both of the Left and the Right in the National Assembly.
The Assembly produced a majority of only two votes when, on May
13, it expressed its confidence in the government's handling of the
Geneva negotiations. France was evidently getting ready to accept a
compromise solution in the Indochina conflict by making concessions
to the Vietminh, concessions that less than a year earlier had still been

widely denounced as "appeasement." Vietminh prospects at Geneva improved greatly after May 13, when the National Assembly almost overthrew the Laniel Government for its apparent lack of zeal in seeking a compromise with the Vietminh.

Western disunity and irresolution were even more glaringly displayed by the men who spoke and acted for the United States. During the entire period of the Geneva deliberations, the diplomacy of the Eisenhower Administration was never anything but wildly incoherent. It helped neither Eden's conciliatory stance nor Bidault's belligerence. In regard to Eden's position that a peaceful solution had to be found, Washington gradually moved from open hostility toward discouraging skepticism. But the logical counterpart to this unhelpful position never materialized: Washington, inconsistent in everything it said and did, failed to strengthen the French position by upholding, and making believable, the threat of U.S. intervention in case the Communist bloc insisted on the unacceptable demand of Vietminh control of all of Vietnam. On the contrary, Dulles, under heavy attack after his return to the United States, publicly retreated from his interventionist position. This deprived Bidault of the only effective weapon in his struggle to prevent a compromise that was in fact a victory for the Vietminh. Dulles was still interested only in united action. Not discouraged by growing British irritation with his concept, he stubbornly continued to propagate the need for a Western alliance against the Communist threat to Southeast Asia, insisting that united action would become "imperative" if the Communists did not halt their aggression. A few days later, both Dulles and Eisenhower indirectly admitted that Washington had become reconciled to a compromise settlement of the Indochina War. In a radio conference on May 11, Dulles said that the whole situation would not be hopeless if "certain events" occurred, meaning a compromise solution in Indochina. That same day, President Eisenhower discarded the domino theory, which had been an article of faith as long as Washington had played with the idea of direct military intervention. The domino theory could be "counteracted," he said, "if collective defense came about," [68] or, as Dulles put it: The rest of Asia could be held even if Indochina fell. Had the American people been truly concerned with the manner in which the foreign policy was conducted by Eisenhower and Dulles, it would have been no less upset during these weeks than were Washington's European allies. On April

9, Eisenhower said that "the loss of Indochina will cause the fall of Southeast Asia like a set of dominoes," [69] and less than five weeks later both he and his Secretary of State stated flatly that the retention of Indochina was not essential for the defense of Southeast Asia. When were they right? In April or in May?

Even French statesmen who did not want American military intervention but thought that threatening it strengthened them at Geneva were stunned by this brutal disregard for their tactical needs and by the bad taste Dulles exhibited in justifying his change of front. If the leaders of the United States accepted the necessity of a deal at Geneva, should allied solidarity not have induced them to share the burden of responsibility for an unpopular compromise with the leaders of France? Instead, Dulles, in speeches at Los Angeles and Seattle, warned the French that they must now fulfill their pledge of independence for Indochina.[70] This was no doubt a justified demand, but not one to be raised by the man who only a few weeks earlier had stated at Congressional hearings that the French had "really carried out their declaration of independence [for the Indochinese States]." Veiled references to continued colonialism were now used by Dulles to justify U.S. inaction, after he himself, for more than two years, had justified U.S. aid to the French war effort in Indochina with repeated assurances that the independence of Vietnam, Cambodia, and Laos had become a reality.

But more distress was yet to come, also in U.S.–British relations. Allied disunity reached a really dangerous level when France, under pressure from the United States, agreed, on May 17, to discuss a treaty aiming at united action without the participation of the United Kingdom. The French had gone along with this move in hopes that it would worry the Communist powers and make them reduce their demands. But the only ones who worried were the British. Eden protested angrily when he learned from Swiss newspapers that French-American talks were being held, aimed at the conclusion of the Western alliance for united action, but excluding Great Britain, whose leaders considered it an obstacle to a settlement of the Indochina conflict. It was then that Churchill decided that only his personal intervention in Washington could prevent a further deterioration in U.S.–British relations and secure a minimum of American cooperation in the efforts to bring peace to Vietnam.

6

In contrast to the picture of Allied disunity, the Communist powers at Geneva appeared solidly united. They apparently knew what they wanted, pursued their aims with perfectly coordinated tactics, and concealed the differences that in fact did exist in their ranks.

There were no differences in regard to the purpose of the Geneva conference between the Soviet Union and China. If the Chinese Communists had at one time been tempted to use Vietminh strength for a Communist conquest of the whole of Indochina, they had persuaded themselves, or been persuaded by their Russian friends, that they had to settle for less. Their conduct belied the belligerence of their speeches, for they, like the British, were guided by a desire to end the war, and by the knowledge that this required a willingness to compromise. There was, it had been observed, very little jubilation in the Chinese press after the fall of Dien Bien Phu. And during the entire conference, the Chinese delegation accepted every one of the compromise proposals with which Soviet Foreign Minister Molotov, after the tough bargaining for which he was known, kept the road open toward a final settlement. In fact, the "most constructive proposal" after more than five weeks of fruitless negotiations came from Chou En-lai, who, on June 16, agreed to the withdrawal of all Vietminh troops from Laos and Cambodia, and to drop the stubborn Vietminh request that the phantom governments of the Communist Khmer Issarak and Pathet Lao rebels participate at the conference.[71] Only Chinese pressure could have induced the Vietminh to give up a demand that had been the main obstacle to constructive negotiations. Early in July, while the meetings of the chief delegates were temporarily suspended, Chou En-lai held a conference with Ho Chi Minh somewhere in southern China. There is only one explanation for this meeting: The Chinese felt that Ho Chi Minh had to be persuaded to accept the compromise settlement whose terms were no doubt already fixed in Molotov and Chou En-lai's minds.

The settlement Russia and China were willing to accept, and in the end made possible by a step-by-step retreat from their original position, indeed did not at all meet the expectations with which the Vietminh delegates had come to Geneva. The Vietminh wanted a peace that sanctioned a military victory which they believed to be near total even before the fall of Dien Bien Phu. The Vietminh leaders regarded the cease-fire demanded by the French as only a step toward the withdrawal of the Expeditionary Corps, to be followed by elections within a few months. These elections, which they were certain to win, would wipe out the Bao Dai regime and make the Vietminh master of the whole of Vietnam.

It was not entirely unrealistic for the Vietminh leaders to believe in the possibility of such a peace. French military resistance could be expected to collapse, particularly when there was no more danger that American intervention would revive the will and the ability of the French to continue the fight. The French themselves recognized the hopelessness of their position after the fall of Dien Bien Phu.[72] At least 80,000 guerrilla fighters threatened their depleted forces in the Tongking Delta, toward which the Vietminh troops that had taken Dien Bien Phu advanced rapidly despite French air interception. As early as May 19, the first of these troops reached Moc Chau, some 80 miles west of Hanoi. An attack on Hanoi was expected by most French military experts for the middle of June. The route between Hanoi and Haiphong could not be kept open after 6 P.M., and it remained closed on most days also in the morning hours, during which the mines planted and the barricades erected by the Vietminh were being removed. Late in May, heavy Vietminh attacks throughout the delta coincided with the general Vietminh offensive in the central mountain plateau and with renewed guerrilla activity all over the South. The French were forced to evacuate An Khe, their last stronghold in the highlands, thereby conceding that they could no longer dispute Vietminh control of this vast region. In answer to urgent requests by Navarre, Paris scraped together whatever troops could be made available for Indochina, but of the 30,000 Navarre had said he needed to avert a total collapse of the Expeditionary Corps, only about 9,000 left France between May 1 and the end of June. The Committee for National Defense, in meetings held after the fall of Dien Bien Phu, agreed on the necessity of tactical retreats that were "a cruel refutation of all optimism." [73] On May 18, the Generals Ely, Salan, and Pelissier arrived in Saigon with instructions for Navarre that amounted to no less than the early evacuation of Hanoi and a retreat from the delta to a last bridgehead in the North at the harbor of Haiphong.[74] Everywhere, isolated French posts fell to the Vietminh, who knew that the French no longer had the reserves needed to interfere with their rapid concentrations and determined attacks. Navarre now also had to drop the hopes he had attached for the last two years to the growing strength of the National Army. The French had strengthened it vastly in numbers, but they had been unable to raise its low morale. After the fall of Dien Bien Phu, most of its units were no longer fit for combat, and the number of soldiers who preferred joining the Vietminh to fighting them grew with the mounting evidence of an early French collapse.

The prospects of a Vietminh victory had been not nearly as good in February as they were in May, 1954, yet even then they were sufficiently promising to prompt Hanoi to oppose an international conference designed to seek a compromise solution of the war. The demands raised by Foreign Minister Pham Van Dong at the beginning of the conference confirmed the impression that the Vietminh, more than ever confident of their ability to defeat the French, were not at all interested in a peace at the price of political concessions. There can be no doubt that when they accepted the final compromise, which they did with obvious reluctance,[75] they did so not in deference to the judgment of their allies but because they had no choice. The immense last-ditch effort to throw the French out of Indochina could succeed only with Chinese consent, since it required continued and even increased Chinese aid. Whatever motives the Chinese had for favoring a compromise solution of the Indochina War at that time,[76] the fact that the Vietminh leaders were compelled to accept such a solution proves that they lacked Chinese consent for torpedoing the Geneva conference and for continuing the war.[77] They submitted, and no one at the conference could have guessed from their behavior that the unity of the Communist camp at Geneva was achieved only through Sino-Soviet pressure upon the Vietminh.

7

Another party that was surprised and antagonized by China's willingness to compromise was the United States, as represented by the diplomacy of John Foster Dulles. To be sure, this diplomacy was far from consistent, reflecting not only the existing divisions in the Administration, the Congress, and the military, but also the fact that it pursued contradictory aims: It wanted a settlement without concessions to the Vietminh, and it expected the French to give up control of Indochina yet continue the war.

These contradictions explain both the vacillation of U.S. policy during this crisis and its capricious rationalizations. Washington agreed to the Geneva conference but refused to cooperate in achieving its purpose; China's presence at Geneva was accepted but her delegation was treated as if it were nonexistent; military intervention was promised but withdrawn when Britain and France refused to conclude a pact that would have wrecked the conference before it opened. As long as intervention was contemplated, the position of the French in Indochina was described as desperate. When the idea of an airstrike to save Dien Bien Phu was dropped, it was said that such intervention could not have saved the garrison, and that the French were in a position to continue the war even if Dien Bien Phu fell. Washington even denied that it ever had intended to intervene. Nevertheless, the threat of intervention was repeated firmly enough for French Foreign Minister Bidault to make it the cornerstone of his strategy at Geneva, only to have his concept destroyed when Dulles, on June 8, categorically stated that the Administration did not intend to ask Congress to authorize U.S. intervention in Indochina. In order to explain the need for intervention, it was repeatedly said that defeat in Indochina would lead to the loss of the whole of Southeast Asia, but when the refusal to take action had to be justified, it was suddenly found that Southeast Asia could be defended even if Indochina were lost. To top it all, Dulles continued to describe the search for a compromise at Geneva as "appeasement," although he had secretly become reconciled to a compromise based on partition. Partition, long on everybody's mind, was indeed openly pursued after Pham Van Dong, in a speech on May 25, indicated that it was acceptable to the Vietminh as a temporary solution, enabling the two parties to disengage and regroup their troops in two zones, prior to the final political settlement of unifying the country through elections.[78]

Washington's endorsement of partition was a result of the meetings Churchill and Eden had with Eisenhower and Dulles between June 24 and 29. It was contained in a secret Anglo-American memorandum whose seven points gave a surprisingly accurate outline both of the formal agreements reached at Geneva and of the manner in which U.S. policy would later interpret these agreements.[79] A compromise at Geneva on the basis of partition was acceptable to Dulles under two conditions: The part of Vietnam that was to be denied to the Vietminh (along with Cambodia and Laos) must be allowed to arm itself against internal and external aggression; and the agreement should contain no political clause that would enable the Communists to gain control of the entire country. In other words, the United States must be allowed to arm the non-Communist part of Vietnam, and no elections were to be held as long as a Communist victory in elections seemed a certainty. If this made the division of Vietnam permanent, so much the better, since it was Dulles' view that the non-Communist half of Vietnam, once it had shed all traces of colonialism, should become an American-sponsored bastion against any further Communist advance in Southeast Asia. It was to be protected by a Southeast Asia pact, which Churchill and Eden had agreed to join after the Geneva conference. Dulles was determined to deny U.S. approval to any agreement that failed to meet these conditions. With this decision, which mapped out the future course of U.S. policy in Vietnam, the vacillation that had characterized American diplomacy since the Berlin conference came to an end.

In the meantime, some progress had been made in talks between French and Vietminh officers both in Geneva and in Indochina toward solving the complex technical problems of a cease-fire. But more important was the change of atmosphere brought on by the fall of the Laniel Government on June 12. This removed Bidault, whose tactics had convinced Molotov that the Laniel Government was an obstacle to a compromise solution of the war, from the Geneva scene.[80] Mendès-France, the best-known advocate of direct peace negotiations with the Vietminh, who had for years denounced French policy in Indochina, headed the new French Cabinet. "I am ready," he said on June 17 in presenting his government to the Assembly, "to resign if by July 20 I have not obtained a cease-fire in Indochina."

With an energy and skill that showed him to be greatly superior to most of his parliamentary colleagues, Mendès-France went about his task, which in the eyes of most observers he had made doubly difficult by the penalty he had set for himself if he failed to keep his thirty-day limit. Was he not handing his Communist opponents at Geneva the tools to overthrow him if he refused to accept their conditions for a cease-fire before July 20? But Mendès-France replied that this was a necessary risk. It would disclose whether the Communists were really willing to accept a compromise solution; they must know that his failure could only result in a government bent on continuing the struggle. Mendès-France made clear that he would support such a policy by announcing to the Assembly that his last act before resigning would be a request to send conscripts to Indochina. To show that this was not an empty threat he ordered the French troops stationed in Germany inoculated against yellow fever.[81]

Under Mendès-France, allied strategy in Geneva at last became reasonably coordinated—above all between Paris and London, but to some extent also between France and the United States. He succeeded in persuading Dulles that the United States must not withdraw Under Secretary Bedell Smith as head of the delegation. Once in Geneva, Mendès-France also established direct contact with the heads of the Chinese and Vietminh delegations. And he spent many days and nights sparring with Molotov, from whom he obtained the two most important concessions only a few hours before his deadline: the 17th instead of the 13th parallel as the provisional border between the two Vietnamese zones, and a two-year delay of the projected election for preparing the country's political unification.

8

The only government that, after Washington's acquiescence in the proposed settlement, reacted with shock, dismay, and violent opposition to the proceedings at Geneva was Bao Dai's State of Vietnam. Under allied pressure, Bao Dai had agreed to let his government, then still headed by Buu Loc, participate in the Geneva negotiation. But only if the State of Vietnam had cooperated in seeking a political compromise with the Vietminh could its delegation have avoided being a nuisance to the statemen who held the fate of Vietnam in their hands. The followers of Bao Dai, as well as all other anti-Vietminh nationalists, rightly feared that a compromise solution of the war threatened their political survival. They opposed the Geneva conference, since it signified an apparent willingness on the part of the French to end the war through a deal with the Vietminh. The idea that the French, who had always used them as political pawns in the struggle against the Vietminh, would now sacrifice them as an obstacle to such a deal, caused not only panic and deep resentment among all anti-Vietminh nationalists, but also a determination never to become a party to this political "betrayal."

But how could the Bao Dai regime, a creature of the French, combat this danger if its very existence depended on the willingness and the declining ability of the French to defend its miserable life against the growing power of the Vietminh? This was the moment of truth for Bao Dai and his diminishing clique of supporters. It came as a shock even to those who were not really surprised. Caught in a dilemma for which no belated surge of political wisdom could have found a solution, the reactions of these men merely confirmed that in the world of politics, the prospects of doom rarely improve the capacity for sound judgment. Since lack of intelligence had never been among their real shortcomings, but rather the absence of that high degree of integrity which their historical task required, the spokesmen of the Bao Dai regime, and Bao Dai himself, fully realized the hopelessness of their position. But not one of them had the strength of character and the courage needed for the awesome task that would have been theirs had they faced up to their political dilemma. It is true that it made no difference whether they gave or refused their consent to the compromise that was likely to emerge. Since this was the case, they decided for once to be men of principle and oppose even the slightest concessions to the Vietminh, including the one that offered them the only chance, however slight, of political survival: partition, giving the non-Communist half of Vietnam time to build a viable nationalist regime with enough popular support to resist reunification under Communism. On May 12, Foreign Minister Nguyen Quoc Dinh, the head of Bao Dai's delegation, accordingly submitted to the conference the plan for a settlement designed to save a regime that had been created by the French who now lacked the means for its defense. Dinh's major points were that there was only one Vietnamese state qualified to speak for the country—the state headed by "His Majesty" Bao Dai; that the country had only one army—that of the State of Vietnam, into which the soldiers of the Vietminh should be integrated (under some sort of international control); that elections under U.N. auspices should be held "within the framework and the competence of the State of Vietnam" as soon as the authority of this state was established over the country's entire territory; and that as a result of these elections, a representative government should be formed under Bao Dai.

"This plan of a total irrealism, which implied the unconditional surrender of the adversary just when he had achieved his greatest military success, was given a polite but icy reception." [82] Everybody knew that the state of Bao Dai, if dropped by the French, would collapse overnight under the weight of Vietminh military and political power. Only the American delegation felt compelled to give open support to Nguyen Quoc Dinh's fantastic proposals.

But did the expected partition of Vietnam, even if intended to be only temporary, necessarily mean that anti-Communist nationalism in all its known manifestations no longer had a political future? At least two parties engaged in the struggle over Vietnam, one on the national and the other on the international scene, denied that all was lost, provided certain obstacles were removed. One of these was the United States. In the opinion most optimistically expressed by Dulles, united action by a Western coalition to protect Southeast Asia against Communism could also effectively defend whatever portion of Vietnam a Geneva compromise denied the Vietminh. The other party consisted of the Vietnamese nationalists who had rejected collaboration with the French and whose increasingly active opposition against the Bao Dai regime could be taken as a sign that between the extremes of collaborators and the Vietminh, a "third force" might possibly emerge. Without any need to consult each other, these two parties were in full agreement on the conditions for such a development: A substantial part of Vietnam had to remain outside of Vietminh control; all trace of colonialism had to be removed from Vietnam; Vietnam had to get a government of nationalists untainted by collaboration with the French; and the United States had to take over the double task of making the nationalist regime of a divided Vietnam viable and of enabling it to defend itself against Communist subversion and aggression.

Even before partition had become an avowed objective of the men who fought at Geneva over peace formulas acceptable to all parties, steps had been taken toward at least a partial fulfillment of the conditions for the survival of a mutilated but non-Communist Vietnam. On June 3, representatives of France and the regime of Bao Dai initialed a treaty which at last recognized Vietnam as "a fully independent and sovereign state." [83] Two weeks later, Bao Dai took a decision of the most far-reaching consequence for himself and the future of Vietnam. He accepted the resignation of his cousin Prince Buu Loc; on June 16, he invited the most prominent of the nationalists who had opposed the "Bao Dai experiment," Ngo Dinh Diem, to form a new government for the State of Vietnam. The steps that would most likely have arrested the growth of Vietminh strength had they been taken eight years earlier were now being imposed by circumstance on the French and on Bao Dai: Vietnam, about to realize her full independence, was to receive her first independent government since precolonial times, a government not expected to be subservient to the French.

When this government took office on July 7, Diem's Catholic compatriots in Tongking were in full flight before the Vietminh troops that advanced into the delta's Catholic provinces: The French, in order to regroup their forces along the Hanoi-Haiphong Railway, had begun to evacuate these provinces on July 1.[84] There were other signs indicating that the French were no longer planning to fight, that a compromise had now become almost a certainty, and that it would very likely leave much of Vietnam exclusively under Vietminh control. On July 3, Vietminh and French military representatives (with Vietnamese national army officers as observers) opened armistice discussions at Trung Gia in Vietminh territory north of Hanoi. On July 5, agreement was reached on the exchange of prisoners, which for the wounded and sick began on July 14.[85] Obviously convinced that they could no longer defend the North, the French officers insisted merely on retaining a bridgehead around Haiphong.

This being the case, the decision of the Diem Government to set up a "Committee for the Defense of the North" could hardly have been more than a patriotic gesture, unless Diem really believed the claims of his propaganda that Hanoi could be defended by the National Army even after a French withdrawal.[86]

In the meantime, the Geneva conference had progressed to the point at which a settlement on the basis of partition had become a virtual certainty. The moment had come for the French to inform their Vietnamese protégés of the manner in which the powers assembled at Geneva intended to decide the political fate of Vietnam. Bao Dai was informed early in July, but neglected to forward this knowledge to Saigon. Diem was given the bad news a week later by Donald Heath, the U.S. Ambassador to the State of Vietnam, together with a reassuring message from President Eisenhower.

The news, which reportedly came as a shock to Diem, could hardly have surprised any anti-Communist with a more realistic view of Vietminh military power and political strength. Saigon's new Foreign Minister, Dr. Tran Van Don, whom Diem had charged to represent his government at Geneva, had no illusions about the result the conference would produce.[87] Like his predecessor, he too protested against partition, and in particular against the evacuation of Tongking by the French. The role into which Tran Van Don had been cast at Geneva was not one to win honors, but the dignified manner in which he discharged his task evoked a great deal of respect. When the armistice was finally concluded in the night of July 20–21, Tran Van Don knew that all he could do was denounce it in the name of his government. He did so by calling it "catastrophic and immoral." [88] His demand that his government's reservation be included in the Final Declaration of the conference was brushed aside by Mendès-France and overruled by Eden as chairman.[89]

The Geneva agreements consisted of two parts. The first one was a lengthy document devoted exclusively to the implementation of the cease-fire and the regrouping of the French and Vietminh forces in their respective zones. The cease-fire accord was the only document signed at Geneva, and it was signed only by the military command of the French and the Vietminh. The Vietminh signatory was Vice-Minister for National Defense Ta Quang Buu, who acted on behalf of Giap, the Commander in Chief of the People's Army of Vietnam. The French signatory was General Delteil, acting on behalf of General Ely, who, on June 2, had been named Commander of the French Union Forces as successor of Navarre and High Commissioner for Vietnam. The cease-fire accords also covered the territories of Laos and Cambodia, but the delegates of these countries were not asked to sign them.

The cease-fire agreement provided for Vietnam's provisional division along the 17th parallel, with the French Union forces regrouped south of that line and the Vietminh forces north. For their withdrawal, different dates were set for different regions, but the regroupment in the two zones was to be completed within 300 days.[90] These agreements also stipulated that any civilian who desired to move from one zone into the other should be allowed to do so within a fixed period of time, the cut-off date being May 18, 1955. Both parties pledged to refrain from reprisals against persons or organizations for acts committed during the hostilities and agreed to a ban on the introduction of fresh troops, military personnel, arms, munitions, and military bases. An International Control Commission (ICC) to supervise the execution of the cease-fire was set up; it consisted of representatives of India, Canada, and Poland. The chairman was to be an Indian.[91]

The second document agreed upon at Geneva was the so-called Final Declaration. In a statement consisting of thirteen points, the participants at the conference took notice, in their final meeting on July 21, of the cease-fire concluded and signed by the two belligerents. But this declaration served also another purpose, one vastly more important than the formal endorsement of the stipulations for ending hostilities. It attempted to spell out the existing political differences, in particular the question of how and when the partition of Vietnam as set forth in the cease-fire agreement should come to an end. The document essentially contained the concessions on which the Communist powers had insisted as conditions for agreeing to a cease-fire. The most important of these conditions stated "that the military demarcation line is provisional and should in no way be interpreting a political or territorial boundary." The passage concerned with the projected elections was both a political surprise and a semantic monstrosity. The Vietminh had demanded that these elections be held a few months after hostilities ceased, but Molotov, to the astonishment of the French who had not expected this concession, proposed a waiting period of two years. The Final Declaration spoke of these elections in language that would hardly have revealed their true purpose if this purpose had not been known to all concerned, and if it had not been mentioned in point 14a of the cease-fire agreement. The sentence of the Final Declaration preceding the phrase "general elections shall be held" did not say that their purpose was the political unification of the country. With obscure reasoning that defies logical analysis, it stated that elections shall be held "in order to insure that sufficient progress in the restoration of peace has been made, and that all the necessary conditions obtain for expression of the national will"—which probably meant, at least to the Communists, that elections would produce a government in Saigon ready to express the "national will" by uniting the South with the North. The date for general elections was set for July, 1956, with "consultations to be held on this subject between the competent authorities of the two zones from July 20, 1955 onwards." [92] Since the State of Vietnam was not mentioned in this context, it remained open who these "competent representative authorities" might be—the French, the only non-Communist party that had signed anything at Geneva, or the government south of the 17th parallel, which had vigorously protested against the Geneva agreements? This unsettled question was surpassed only by the even stranger fact that the powers that

concluded the agreement concerning elections expected it to be binding although it remained unsigned.

It is indeed inappropriate to justify American rejection of certain
stipulations of the Geneva agreements by reference to the fact the
United States did not sign any of these agreements. With the exception
of the cease-fire accords signed only by the French and Vietminh
High Commands, nothing at all was signed by anyone at Geneva. A
roll-call vote was taken to confirm acceptance of the agreements by all
participants, and this was followed by a number of statements of delegations who desired to voice reservations or give their own interpreta-
tions of certain points, among them the representative of the United
States, Bedell Smith. His government, he said, was not prepared to join
in a declaration by the conference such as was submitted, but it would
refrain from the threat or use of force to disturb the agreements.
However, the warning addressed to the Communists that Smith added
could be interpreted not only as acquiescence but also as qualified endorsement of the agreement. His government, he said, "would view
any renewal of the aggression in violation of the aforesaid Agreements
with grave concern and as seriously threatening international peace
and security." Concerning the elections, Smith repeated a declaration
by Washington made on June 29, 1954, which said: "In the case of nations now divided against their will, we shall continue to seek to
achieve unity through free elections supervised by the United Nations
to insure that they are conducted fairly." [93] In a statement issued in
Washington the same day, Bedell Smith's reservations were endorsed
by President Eisenhower.

The only unambiguous protest came from the Foreign Minister of
the State of Vietnam. In a cable to Premier Diem dated July 22, Tran
Van Don said: "We fought desperately against partition and for a
neutral zone in the Catholic area of North Vietnam. Absolutely impossible to surmount the hostility of our enemies and the perfidy of false
friends. We express our deepest sorrows in this total failure of our
mission. We respectfully submit our resignation." [94] On July 23,
Diem, in a broadcast from Saigon, raised "a most solemn protest"
against the "iniquity which hands over to the Communists the entire
North of the country and more than four provinces of the Center."
All flags were ordered to be flown at halfmast for three days.

However, more important for the future relations between the State
of Vietnam (which henceforth was generally referred to as South

Vietnam) and the Democratic Republic of Vietnam (or North Vietnam) was a statement delivered by Tran Van Don in the name of his government before the conclusion of the conference. "Vietnam," he declared, "reserves to itself the entire freedom of action to safeguard the sacred right of the Vietnamese people to territorial unity, independence, and freedom." [95]

This was a formal announcement of nonconcurrence with the Geneva agreements on the part of Ngo Dinh Diem's Government of South Vietnam. Although this government was then even in the South one in name only, as early as August 3 it called on the people of the North "to rally to the South in order to continue the struggle for independence and liberty." [96]

Dulles, too, had a postscript to Geneva, delivered at a news conference on July 23. What he said was of infinitely greater significance for the future of Vietnam that Diem's empty threat to rally the South against the North. Dulles acknowledged that the Geneva negotiations "reflected the military developments in Indochina," adding that "the French people did not desire to prolong the war." These "basic facts" led to the settlement which "contains many features which we do not like." But "the important thing" for Dulles was "not to mourn the past but to seize the future opportunity to prevent the loss in northern Vietnam from leading to the extension of Communism throughout Southeast Asia and the Southwest Pacific." In spelling out this "future opportunity," Dulles implied once more that French colonialism had been an obstacle in the fight against the Vietminh. "One lesson is that resistance to Communism needs popular support, and this in turn means that the people should feel that they are defending their own national institutions." Carried away by his view of the "future opportunity," Dulles went so far as to speak of "good aspects" of the Geneva conference, one of which was "that it advances the truly independent status of Cambodia, Laos, and Southern Vietnam." And he added: "The evolution from colonialism to national independence is thus about to be completed in Indochina, and the free governments of this area should from now on be able to enlist the loyalty of their people to maintain their independence as against Communist colonialism." In fact, there is some evidence that Dulles was not at all unhappy over the French defeat in Indochina. "We have a clear base there now without a taint of colonialism," he is reported to have said, adding: "Dien Bien Phu was a blessing in disguise." [97]

There was another reason for Dulles' belief in the "future opportunity" to halt any further Communist advance: The obstacles to "united action" were at last removed. "Prompt steps will be taken in this direction," he announced, having secured both British and French consent to proceed in preparing what on September 8, 1954, became, via the so-called Manila Pact, the Southeast Asia Treaty Organization (SEATO).[98]

The mood in which France received the Geneva agreements, although somber, was one of distinct and open relief. The settlement achieved was unquestionably a political triumph for Mendès-France. There was a general feeling in Paris, shared also in Great Britain, that the French had fared better at Geneva than they had had reason to expect. Still, Geneva was a great blow for the French, and no one knew this better than Mendès-France. With the frankness that is part of his political style, he stated in the Assembly: "I want no one to have any illusions about the contents of the agreements that have just been signed at Geneva. Much of what they say is cruel, since they consecrate cruel facts. It could not have been otherwise." [99] The French Chamber, after much praise but also some harsh criticism of Mendès-France, accepted the Geneva agreements, in three separate votes, by overwhelming majorities.[100]

Praise for the conference outcome came also from the Communist powers, pointing to it as evidence of their love of peace.[101] In spite of Vietminh dissatisfaction, the Communists had every reason to be content: A Communist-led national movement of armed resistance had defeated the armies of one of the oldest and greatest Western colonial powers; France, as Ho Chi Minh had predicted, had lost the Indochina War; and the West was forced to become reconciled to the existence of another Communist state.

9

Whatever shortcomings and seeds of future trouble critics have found in the Geneva agreements, their great historical importance cannot be denied. They ended the longest and most senseless attempt of this century to defeat an anticolonial movement of national liberation by military means—the Indochina War, which destroyed French presence in Southeast Asia and Vietnamese national unity. They ended almost one hundred years of French colonial rule in Indochina and produced the two Vietnams that have become known to the world as the Communist North and the anti-Communist South.

This second result of the Indochina War—the division of Vietnam into two states with hostile regimes—received some sort of international sanction from the powers that concluded the Geneva agreements. But as for the conflict between the Vietminh and their nationalist opponents, the Geneva conference failed to produce a workable solution. As a consequence, the promise of national unity—a mere byproduct of the Geneva cease-fire accords between the French and the Vietminh—remained unfulfilled. Even as the Final Declaration was read and taken exception to by the governments of South Vietnam and the United States, it could have been predicted that the promised elections would never be held. As a consequence, it could also have been foreseen that the peace that came to the country as the only blessing of the Geneva bargain would last no longer than a few anxiety-filled years. The antagonism of the two Vietnam regimes would ultimately prove irreconcilable. Both sides would be hardened in their attitudes by the support promised them by their respective big allies, the Western and Eastern power blocs engaged in the Cold War. Far from considering any compromise solution, the government in Hanoi and its sworn enemies ruling South Vietnam could be expected to continue to move farther apart. Soon both would become convinced that unity was possible only if one side succeeded in destroying the other, and both would start working toward this end. Since under prevailing conditions the regime in the South could not have survived general elections, it was predictable that it would oppose the holding of such elections, while the Communists, deprived of this peaceful means for extending their control over the whole of Vietnam, would again resort to force. When they unleashed their insurrection against the regime of Ngo Dinh Diem, the loss of peace, like the loss of unity before, reminded a troubled world how dangerously imperfect the Geneva settlement had been. Ten years after the Geneva conference, a new armed conflict, truly a second Indochina War, reached dimensions and produced international involvements that posed an even greater threat to world peace than the first Indochina War briefly did in spring, 1954.

Finally, the Geneva settlement, along with its failure to bring unity and lasting peace, also failed to open the road to political freedom in both the North and the South. In the North, as expected, the struggle for economic survival and industrial progress barred any retreat from the hard Communist dictatorship into which the regime of Ho Chi Minh had developed during the last years of the war. In the South, where the civil war reinforced the leaders' innate tendency toward authoritarian rule, the sacrifice of freedom demanded of the people also turned the anti-Communist regime into a ruthless dictatorship, which, however, failed to produce what was supposed to be its *raison d'être*—administrative efficiency and military strength. Ten years after achieving independence, the people of Vietnam still did not have free institutions adapted to their way of life, were still deprived of the national unity essential for rapid economic progress, and, subjected to the brutalities of the new Indochina War, were once more in danger of losing what they had fought for during the entire colonial period: a truly independent national existence.

XI

Independence Without Unity or Freedom

1

I N THE HISTORY of modern Vietnam few dates are as important as June 16, 1954, the day Bao Dai asked Ngo Dinh Diem to form a new government for his state. Since the country, on June 3, had at last become fully sovereign, it was inevitable that the existing government of collaborators be replaced by one more in harmony with Vietnam's new status.

Not everyone concerned regarded the man called upon to form this government as supremely qualified for the task, but it was one which he himself was quite eager to assume.[1] Bao Dai, knowing how strongly Diem disapproved of his political flexibility and indulgent private life, had never liked him. The French, whose policies Diem had opposed, and who, for more than twenty years, had kept him from playing an active role in the life of his country, would hardly have chosen him had they still had the power to impose another puppet. Every Vietnamese leader who had collaborated with the French under Bao Dai distrusted Diem, including the leaders of the sects, who knew that Diem's nationalism would clash with their divisive interests and selfish political aspirations. And the Vietminh, who had often denounced Diem for his "contacts with the Japanese Fascists," now, when victory made their propaganda most effective, pictured him as "the man of the U.S. interventionists."

But if some of the open enmities and secret intrigues against Diem were likely to enhance his reputation as a nationalist whose principles might make him the man of the hour, there was cause for concern about his qualifications as a leader that even his strongest supporters could not dismiss. As a Catholic who assiduously discharged his religious duties, Diem's inner life was very different from that of the majority of the people and the educated elite, who have rather undogmatic religious attitudes.[2] To some extent Diem's Catholicism also gave rise to political misgivings. The Catholic community in Vietnam—a minority of 10 to 15 per cent of the population—had often been outside the mainstream of the nationalist and antiforeign sentiments that inspired the non-Catholic majority, and in particular the mandarins and scholars who articulated these sentiments.

More important, however, was the fact that Diem's temperament, social philosophy, and political comportment seemed to preclude all prospects of his ever becoming a popular hero.[3] His stiff demeanor would have doomed any attempt to stir the masses by word or gesture, had he ever been persuaded of the necessity to make himself admired and loved. However, what he wanted was not love but the respect and obedience he considered his due as head of state. To solicit this by trying to ingratiate himself with the people seemed to him politically unnecessary and personally degrading. As a result, Diem was known only to a small politically active circle; beyond it, his reputation as a spokesman of nationalism was vague. His name did not arouse enthusiasm; at best he evoked mild curiosity and uncertain expectations. After all, Diem had been away from Vietnam for almost four years, and he had played no active part in the nationalist upsurge that led to the disintegration of the Bao Dai regime prior to the conference at Geneva.

Diem had left Vietnam in August, 1950, after having been granted permission by the French to attend the Holy Year celebration in Rome. He traveled in the company of his brother, Bishop Ngo Dinh Thuc, but his route to Rome was far from direct. His first stop was Japan, where he conferred with and paid homage to the old conservative nationalist Prince Cuong De, in exile since 1906. In Tokyo, Diem also met Americans who advised him what contacts he should seek in Washington.[4] September and October, 1950, were spent in the United States. It was then that Diem first became known to the small group of Americans concerned about Vietnam but unfamiliar with the complexities of the military and political conditions in Indochina. Diem's thesis combined attractive simplicity with compelling logic: If colonialism were brought to an end and Vietnam to receive a truly nationalist government, the Vietminh could be quickly defeated.[5] Cardinal Spellman, to whom Diem was introduced by Bishop Thuc, was probably the first American to look toward a Vietnamese government headed by the Catholic Ngo Dinh Diem.

Diem's stay in Rome was brief. He had an audience with the Pope, and then left for Switzerland, Belgium, and France, where he talked with prominent Vietnamese in exile. But since there were no prospects for a change in French policy, Diem returned to the United States early in 1951, this time for a stay that was to last two years. He resided at the Maryknoll seminaries in Lakewood, New Jersey, and Ossining, New York. For a while he was moderately active as a lecturer on Vietnam, mainly at Eastern and Midwestern universities; he also made a number of trips to Washington, where he won much sympathy for his views. Among the people who favored both his cause and his personal aspirations were Senators Mike Mansfield and John F. Kennedy, Representative Walter Judd, and Justice William Douglas.[6] But the occasional pleading of these people for Vietnamese independence did not influence the Truman and Eisenhower Administrations, whose policy, in spite of many verbal reservations, remained one of unconditional aid to the French. Discouraged by external events, Diem concentrated on searching in himself for the strength needed to lead his country through meditation, which was more congenial to his nature and talents than actively organizing support for his cause.

At the urging of Vietnamese Catholic leaders in exile (Nguyen Quang Chuc and Truong Cong Cuu among others), Diem left the United States for Paris in May, 1953. He soon realized that the door to power was still closed to him, and he retired once more, this time to the Belgian Benedictine Monastery of St. André les Bruges. But the month of May, 1954, when the fate of Vietnam was being decided at Dien Bien Phu and Geneva, found Diem back in Paris. As his official biography states: "He felt that the day was coming for him to look after his country's fate." [7] The consultations in which he now engaged were no less important for him and his associates than the talks that had started at Geneva. During these weeks, Diem, who did not know how to deal with the shallow political sophistication of Paris, and who lacked the talent to charm, was guided by his younger and more worldly brother Luyen.

Most important for Diem were his talks with Bao Dai, which also began in May, 1954. It was many weeks before the former Emperor decided that Diem should be asked to form a new government for the

State of Vietnam. Since it was known that neither the French nor Bao Dai had any liking for Diem, this decision came as a surprise to most informed French and Vietnamese political leaders. In fact, it gave rise to the still widely accepted legend that the nomination of Diem was brought about by strong U.S. pressure on Bao Dai and the French, and intervention by Cardinal Spellman via members of the Catholic Mouvement Républicain Populaire. But this story, even if it could be substantiated, does not constitute a convincing explanation for Bao Dai's momentous decision. This is not to say that Dulles and Cardinal Spellman were not in favor of a government headed by Diem; they were, although there are indications that Dulles was not overenthusiastic about Diem. Dulles' silence on the subject underlines that no one of any importance spoke up against Diem, for the Secretary of State was not in the habit of keeping quiet if he met with opposition. The point here is that there was no need for American pressure to bring about the nomination of Diem.[8] The French Government did not oppose it. Premier Laniel, too, was silent on the subject, as was Mendès-France, to whom Bao Dai's decision was a matter of indifference. Who was to be the next prime minister of Vietnam was the least of the new French Premier's many concerns. As one observer remarked: "Since the French were scuttling the ship, they no longer cared who stood at the bridge as it went down." [9] (Active opposition against Diem on the French side existed mainly in Indochina, and even there it was firm only among policy-making members of the Sûreté and die-hard colonialists inside and outside the administration.) Some French leaders in Paris actually encouraged Bao Dai to nominate Diem, among them former High Commissioner Jean Letourneau, and the Right-wing deputy Frédéric-Dupont, who for a few days before the fall of the Laniel Government had served as Minister for the Associated States of Indochina.[10]

There was, furthermore, surprisingly little open opposition against Diem among the normally vocal Vietnamese leaders who had collaborated with the French and who shared a healthy hatred of Diem. Many of them, and perhaps Bao Dai too, were convinced that anyone foolish enough to assume responsibility for governing the truncated and demoralized part of Vietnam likely to emerge from the conference at Geneva was marching to his political doom—a fate they all wished on Ngo Dinh Diem.[11]

The fact, however, is that neither these ill-wishers nor American,

Catholic, or French promotion opened the road to power for Diem. He was carried into office by the tide of events. Bao Dai had enough political sense to realize that the man chosen at this hour had to be of Diem's general political complexion—firmly anti-Communist and also known for his opposition to French rule. A new government, now that Vietnam was to be free of French tutelage, could not possibly have been led by another known French collaborator. Such a government would very likely have met with open rebellion in Saigon, where even former collaborators recognized that their last hope was a supernationalist regime as firmly anti-French as the Vietminh. Furthermore, only such a regime could satisfy the "anticolonialist" demands that had been raised, on and off, by Washington, and which Dulles now called a condition for the survival of any non-Communist government in Indochina. There was no need for Washington to tell Bao Dai that without American support Vietnamese anti-Communism did not have the slightest chance of stemming the Communist tide. Without having to consult each other, Washington and the Vietnamese anti-Communists were also of one mind in firmly rejecting another course, advocated by some former collaborators—i.e., to swim cautiously with the Communist tide in the hope of being carried to safe shores. That is why Bao Dai resisted pressure to reappoint former Prime Minister Tran Van Huu, the first prominent Vietnamese leader to accept the Geneva agreement and to advocate what later became known as the "neutralist" solution.

There are still other explanations why Bao Dai, in appointing Diem, need not have been acting under American pressure, and why Diem, therefore, cannot be regarded as Washington's deliberate choice. Bao Dai, in looking for a man that fitted the political requirements of the hour, realized that Diem was virtually without competition.[12] There was no serious contestant of his stature and political acceptability, either because they respected Diem or were afraid of a task that promised little reward. Diem was the only one who was talked about in Saigon as a possible future prime minister. There his brother Nhu had succeeded, on May 27, in forming another coalition of all active political forces. It was called the Front for National Salvation, and also consisted of the sects, the organized Catholics, the Dai Viet, and a few other nationalist parties.[13] The Front demanded a new regime to fight Communism, and the groups that Diem soon afterward decided to destroy now demanded that he be called upon to head this new regime.

In a lively and virtually unopposed campaign, Ngo Dinh Nhu depicted his older brother as the only man fit for the difficult task of saving Vietnam from Communism.

Washington, it might be argued, never considered supporting any other man. The explanation is simple: Diem was the only Vietnamese leader who had made himself known in the United States.

Diem accepted his appointment on June 19, after inducing a reluctant Bao Dai to entrust him with an ordinance conferring full civilian and military powers on the head of Saigon's new government.[14] Nhu, already then obsessed with shaping his brother's political destiny, immediately dispatched one of his closest collaborators to Paris to prepare Diem for his first confrontation with the country and the people he was to rule. The man chosen for this was the lawyer Tran Chanh Thanh, who had long been associated with the Vietminh and who later became Diem's Minister of Information—one of the many modern politicians who have learned all about Communist methods but lack the vital insight that the adoption of these methods by an anti-Communist regime, far from defeating Communism, only serves to throttle the people's desire for freedom.

Diem left Paris for Saigon on June 24, accompanied by his brother Luyen, by Tran Chanh Thanh, and by Nguyen Van Thoai, a relative of the Ngo family and the only prominent exile willing to join Diem's Cabinet. With others, such as the resistance hero Nguyen Ngoc Bich, Diem had no success. He tried unsuccessfully to win Nguyen Manh Ha, a Catholic who had been Ho Chi Minh's first Minister of Economics but who had parted with the Vietminh in December, 1946. These men, and others too, rejected Diem's concept of government, which clearly aimed at a one-man rule. Nor did they share Diem's illusions about the chances of preventing a Geneva settlement favorable to the Vietminh. Diem apparently believed that the National Army, no longer fighting under the French but for an independent government, would quickly become effective and reduce the gains made by the Vietminh.

Diem's arrival in Saigon, although well prepared by Nhu, caused little excitement and no popular joy. The reception accorded Diem was not the sort given to a returning national hero who had fought for the liberation of his homeland. The masses stayed away; it was clear that the name of the man to be honored sparked no fire in their hearts. The five hundred people gathered at the airport were largely bearded man-

darins, Catholic dignitaries, and government officials. And among the
thousand or so who greeted Diem in town, the absence of young people and the lack of enthusiasm were painfully evident. There was only
one fervent message of welcome, sent by Monsignor Phan Ngoc Chi in
the name of the Tongking Catholic communities about to be abandoned to the Vietminh as a result of the decision of the French High
Command to evacuate the southern delta provinces inhabited largely
by Catholics.

Betraying his monastic outlook on life, but perhaps also an awareness
of the trials that lay ahead for him and his people, Diem walked from
the airplane toward the crowd gathered to receive him without a trace
of a smile. The people who had come to greet him as the country's
new leader experienced a moment of great tension. No one of course
anticipated that Diem had set foot on a road that would lead him, over
brief glories and long stretches of despair, to premature death. But
many had a distinct premonition of impending tragedy, and for those
who had never seen him before, Diem's cold expression blighted the
hopes that the strength of his face must have briefly raised.

2

When Diem stepped off his plane at Saigon on June 26, 1954, the
ordinance with which Bao Dai had conferred all civilian and military
powers on his new Prime Minister made him theoretically the most
powerful man in the State of Vietnam. From this ordinance, Diem no
doubt derived moral justification for the measures with which he intended to implement these powers, but at the time the value of this
document was that of any other piece of paper. Within a few short
weeks, Diem realized that he had no powers at all.[15] Power in the State
of Vietnam was not concentrated in the government. Power in the
State of Vietnam remained fractured, as in the past; portions were held
by a number of fiercely competing factions. The interests of the
groups among whom it was divided were quite compatible with those
of the French, whose domination had rested largely on the ancient
principle of "divide and rule." But these interests, and the absence of a
central authority, conflicted sharply with the political needs of an independent South Vietnam, a state engaged in a struggle for survival
with the powerful Communist North.

What were the conditions under which a program designed to make
South Vietnam invulnerable to Communism could be executed? They
were, above all, a government permitted to rule, a government in control of its police and army, a government whose authority extended
over the country's entire territory, a government unhampered by foreign or regional influences opposed to its national aims. In all these respects, the government of Diem could be said to have been nonexistent
in the summer and early fall of 1954.

In addition to dealing with the chaotic political conditions he inherited from the colonial regime, Diem faced equally discouraging tasks
on several other fronts. The country was in ruins. Most bridges had
been blown up. Canals, roads, railways, telephone and telegraph services had been either destroyed or were in disrepair. Dykes, too, were
destroyed; vast regions of rice land were uncultivated; countless peasants who had fled the countryside found themselves unemployed in the
cities. And Diem's administration, run by an incompetent civil service,
politically hostile and disintegrating, had to provide the human and
material resources for receiving, feeding, and temporarily settling hundreds of thousands of refugees who had fled from the North to the
South, adding enormous burdens to a totally insolvent state and government.

With his aspiration to give the country a unified and strong government, Diem represented the supreme national needs of the hour. But
how could he overcome the obstructions of the many forces and factions hostile or indifferent to his efforts? He was opposed by the army,
which was still under over-all French command and headed by Vietnamese officers appointed by Bao Dai and the French. He was disobeyed
by the police and the secret service, which Bao Dai had sold to the
Binh Xuyen, his closest allies among the sects. Diem's national aims
clashed with the "feudal" power structures of the Hoa Hao and Cao
Dai sects, which with their private armies ruled most of the country
west and south of Saigon. He met the hostility of the French and Chinese circles who controlled much of the Vietnamese economy and
who knew that a strong national regime was bound to limit their
powers. This was true also for the Vietnamese landlords, who feared
that Diem's call for a national "revolution" implied radical projects of
agrarian reform. The old collaborators inside and outside the administration sabotaged Diem's every step to secure control of the existing
government apparatus, and the old "fence-sitters," the *attentists*, now

more numerous than ever among the intellectuals, refused to support Diem out of fear of an early collapse of his regime and a take-over of the South by the Vietminh. This possible take-over was indeed the greatest of all dangers that threatened Diem, and, together with everything else, was the reason that the chances for the survival of Diem's regime were generally regarded as nil.[16]

The Vietminh, whose southern military units were being "regrouped" in the North, did not withdraw their political cadres from the South. Most of these remained behind, and although the immediate overthrow of the Diem regime was not their task, their activities constituted the greatest challenge Diem had to meet. The reason for this was that once again the masses were receptive to Vietminh propaganda. The triumph of the Hanoi regime over the French had made a deep impression on the entire population. That the great patriotic demand—no foreign rule—was at last fulfilled, was not due to French generosity or the efforts of Bao Dai, but was the result of the armed struggle led by the Vietminh. The demand for independence may not always have found a strong echo in the hearts of Vietnam's miserable masses, but the achievement of independence aroused enthusiasm even among the politically indifferent, since it brought also the fulfillment of the strongest popular wish: the end to a long-drawn-out war. After almost fifteen years, peace was at last returning to their ravaged land. And it came because the Vietminh had defeated the French. The Vietminh, to be sure, was Communist-controlled, while the masses were as far from embracing Communist ideas as they had been in 1945. But to denounce the Vietminh as Communist was now as inadequate a way of fighting them as it had been then: If the Vietminh were Communists, then the Communists had to be given credit for having liberated Vietnam from foreign domination.

The people of Vietnam—neither those who had suffered under Vietminh rule nor those who had never experienced Communist methods of government—could not possibly have had any accurate idea about the true nature of Communism. Mass misery in Vietminh-held territory largely resulted from the conditions of war, and since the areas that had fallen back under French and Bao Dai rule were neither freer nor less subject to terror, the people could hardly blame their misery on the Communist leanings of the Vietminh Government. Furthermore, Vietminh propaganda now lured the people who had suffered under a foreign-controlled anti-Communist regime, with the promise of change, and the distressed masses could not conceive of a change for the worse. Except for the well-indoctrinated Catholic minority, which had its special reasons for opposing Communism, the people therefore could not be expected to be openly hostile to the Vietminh, nor to be enthusiastic about the firm anti-Communism of the new regime in the South. They could at best be expected to remain neutral until they saw what this new regime meant to them. This was in fact the attitude which the majority in the South adopted toward the regime of Ngo Dinh Diem, realizing that the country had arrived at a turning point in its history, and ready to measure Diem's actions against their own needs rather than against the claims of Vietminh propaganda.

Here lay the great chance for the survival of a non-Communist Vietnam, the chance to break the hold that the Vietminh had gained over the people, the chance at last to find an answer to the problem which the anti-Communist elite, through several crucial decades of modern history, had failed to provide: how to establish "contact with the broad masses," [17] how to create a regime to which the people could feel close. Through the integrity of his nationalism, Diem had secured for himself the position most vital for reversing the historical trend toward a total victory of Communism in Vietnam. But would the forces opposed to him, which had already contributed so much to the failure of anti-Communism, allow him to take the steps necessary to reverse this trend? More important still: Did Diem realize that this required a break with institutions and mentalities inherited from ancient and colonial Vietnam, institutions and mentalities that stood like a wall between the government and the people? Did he know enough about the longing of the masses for justice, their desire to be treated with respect and to be allowed to enjoy the fruits of their labor? And if so, was he ready to institute drastic reforms, tantamount to social revolution?

There is not much evidence that Diem was equipped for this task. His radicalism had expressed itself in nationalist intransigence, not in specific demands for social and political reform. Many of his supporters thought that the obvious strength of his personality held forth a promise of political growth. Indeed, those who believed that South Vietnam would have to be radically reconstructed if it were to survive could only hope that Diem, in carrying out the various parts of his task, would gain the insight and ability needed to preside over the political and social transformation of his country. Only thus would he be able to fulfill South Vietnam's vocation, which was to prove to the people, both in the South and in the North, that something better than Communism could be built on the ruins of colonialism and war.

But a government that lacked mass support and was opposed by the country's police forces and army was obviously not equipped for the execution of reforms bound to hurt the interests of entrenched social and political groups. It was Diem's plausible contention that his first task was to overcome the paralyzing conditions under which he was expected to govern. In this, not a very broad choice of means stood at his disposal. But was not one of them to gain the support of the masses against his enemies, and was not immediate response to the need for social reforms the main condition for gaining mass support? Diem, some argued, could have mobilized the peasant masses behind him by promptly decreeing such popular reforms as a drastic reduction of land rents (as a first step toward a radical land reform); by proclaiming that all land distribution in Vietminh-held territories would be legalized; and by ordering, for a period of rural recovery, a temporary moratorium on all peasant taxes. The peasants would have welcomed such laws like harbingers from heaven. The big landlords, some two thousand odd, would have opposed these reforms violently, but they could have been compensated for their losses. American aid, already considerable for maintaining the army and for settling the refugees from the North, could have been extended to cover the cost of such reforms, with enormous political benefit to the "free world."

But if Diem did not choose this road out of his political impasse, the reason is not merely that he was, by temperament and social philosophy, a conservative man. The difficulties such an attempt to create mass support would have encountered—difficulties that could have been overcome only at enormous political risk—might have frightened even a truly radical social reformer. Diem could have decreed such reforms, but he could not have made them effective. Not even a cut in land rents could have been enforced, since the government lacked the personnel capable of implementing such a measure at the local level. The provincial, regional, and local chiefs everywhere were appointees of the old, corrupt Saigon governments, and themselves were largely corrupt. These men, who showed the lack of respect for the people characteristic of Vietnamese officialdom, were partners of the landlords in exploiting the peasants and terrorizing them into accepting their inhuman conditions of existence. An order to suspend peasant taxes would have had only one effect: They would still have been collected, but instead of going to Saigon would henceforth have gone into the pockets of the local officials.

Diem knew that all of this had to be changed, but the measure he decided upon—to replace these men with his own appointees—was neither of immediate help nor able to attack the roots of the evil. It would take years to find and train a sufficient number of new officials, and they offered no guarantee of any improvement either for the people or the government, since the trouble was not human fallibility but the evil inherent in the system. The means for replacing this system, however, were not available to Diem, at least not at that time. They were the creation of elected local institutions responsible not only to the government but also to the people. Even if Diem had wanted to take this road, he could not have done so in the summer of 1954. Local elections would have given the Vietminh control of most of the rural communities. The Vietminh was not only popular and in effective political control of large regions, but it alone had people with the requisite organizational skills to exploit whatever opportunities for democratic self-expression the regime opened up.

For the same reason, popular enthusiasm for the regime—even if reforms had been devised to create it—could not have been channeled into organizations and parties freely constituted for the purpose of giving active support to Diem. For this task, too, the regime lacked the necessary trained personnel. True, cadres and movements evolve around issues, and the raising of the right kind of issues is proof of a leader's quality. But the Vietnam of 1954 was still dominated by the issues of the immediate past that had led to the victory of the Vietminh and had produced Communist strength not to be overcome in a few short months. Freely constituted organizations too would have been captured by the Vietminh. Immediately after the Geneva settlement, Communist-inspired "democratic fronts" began to be active throughout the South. A Communist-led "movement for peace," insisting on the "guarantee of democratic liberties" contained in the Final Declaration at Geneva, organized demonstrations in Saigon and several other cities. Communist fronts also published several newspapers. It would have been suicidal for Diem to let this movement develop freely. He had to fight it, but he was able to do so only by suppressing all unauthorized political activities with methods that soon included the arrest of people suspected of conducting such activities clandestinely. The regime's inherent political weakness thus manifested itself in an inability to let democracy work, since democracy in action worked only for the benefit of its enemies. This meant that Diem could not even organize the existing potential of mass support for his regime, which probably was more considerable than most observers suspected.

This lack of organized support, and the growing hostility of all groups and factions opposed to Diem, led to the conviction, soon widely held both in Vietnam and abroad, that Diem, if miraculously he were to survive at all, could accomplish this only by sharing the powers Bao Dai had granted him with his anti-Communist opponents—the pro-French army leadership, the sects, and even the more prominent members of Bao Dai's former governments that had collaborated with the French. Such "willingness to compromise" would have had the open blessing of the French, whose High Commissioner was still a more powerful man in South Vietnam than the country's head of government. But Diem, for all his shortcomings, knew that this course, even though it saved him for the time being, would fatally hurt South Vietnam's chances of survival. His sense of history, although defective in many vital respects, warned him against any retreat from the position of uncompromising nationalism that had earned him his onerous position, and he also knew that uncompromising nationalism had been the chief reason for Vietminh strength. Without this one weapon, all others that he might later try to forge against the threat of Communism to the South would remain ineffective. Diem was not deceived by the "unity" of all anti-Communist forces that this policy was supposed to produce: It would have restricted the basis of the regime to the old coalition of rivaling cliques, excluding forever the people whose desire for reforms was irreconcilable with the interests of these cliques. Such a unity would have been fictitious for yet another reason: The cliques that aspired to it were quite unwilling to subordinate their particular interests to the imperatives for national survival. There are times in the evolution of a new state when all groups and factions, no matter how strongly opposed to each other, have to unite in order to save the country; but there are other times, also times of crisis, when unity can be created only by eliminating the elements incompatible with it.

In South Vietnam after Geneva, a politically unified state and a single administrative authority could be created only by setting the government above the army, still led largely by pro-French generals; by taking away control of the police from a private armed group; and by incorporating all regions under the control of the religious-political sects into the national administration. This meant that the openly dissident army leadership had to be replaced; that the Binh Xuyen, if they refused to give up control of the police, had to be destroyed; and that the Hoa Hao and the Cao Dai would be spared the same fate only if they agreed to incorporate their armed forces into the National Army and to put their local administrations under the authority of Saigon. These were the first conditions for South Vietnam's survival, and no other nationalist leader understood this as well as Diem.

But what were the means by which Diem could eliminate the army leadership and the sects, having decided that they must not be appeased? He held a mandate but no real power. What power there was lay in the hands of his opponents. Besides, Bao Dai, still holding the reins of legitimacy as Chief of State, opposed the manner in which Diem intended to apply his mandate. The hopelessness of Diem's position was rather glaringly underlined when the Binh Xuyen–controlled Saigon police brutally dispersed a demonstration in favor of the government staged by Catholic supporters of Diem. Was it surprising, then, that the fall of Diem was predicted daily in Vietnam and abroad even before his clash with the sects in spring, 1955, almost made it a fact? [18]

Yet this man, whose strength and courage was then commonly described as blind stubbornness, was impervious to all proofs of his political impotence and deaf to all voices of despair. Looking upon himself as a man with a mission, which, unlike a mere task, cannot be abandoned, Diem resolutely took the only road open to him: short-term political maneuvers to divide and neutralize his enemies, and even to buy their temporary tolerance and cooperation—until he possessed enough strength to smash them separately. He made concessions to one side, playing it against another, determined at the opportune moment to cancel what he had granted. By separately dealing with his various opponents, he deepened, and then exploited, the existing conflicts between them, in what can be described only as a ruthless and unscrupulous game of many-sided intrigues. For instance, he secured the support of some army leaders through attractive bribes, such as the promise to promote colonels to generals. But he also bought some leaders of the sects with substantial sums. Ably assisted by his brother Nhu, who regarded the crooked paths of intrigue as the only sure road to power, Diem succeeded with these means. But he succeeded for only two reasons: (1) his enemies, apart from being venal and divided, were also politically bankrupt; and (2) he enjoyed the political, moral, and financial assistance of the United States.

3

The bankruptcy of Diem's opponents and the importance of U.S. support was first revealed in the struggle for control of the army, a struggle that led to a crisis lasting almost three months—starting early in September with public statements against Diem by the Chief of Staff, General Nguyen Van Hinh.[19] Hinh was the son of the old collaborator Nguyen Van Tam; educated in France, he became a French citizen, married a French woman, was appointed by the French to head the Vietnamese Army, and, like most of his colleagues, preferred the French to the Vietnamese way of life. Most people of his class could hardly speak with a Vietnamese peasant, let alone understand his problems and sympathize with his needs. Hinh demanded that the country be given a new government, "strong and popular." He openly admitted that he was preparing a *coup d'état*, boasting that he could overthrow Diem by lifting the telephone.

Accepting this challenge, Diem informed Hinh on September 11, 1954, that he was to take a six-week "study vacation" in France and ordered him to leave the country within twenty-four hours. Hinh showed his defiance of this order by riding through the streets of Saigon in shirt sleeves on a powerful motorcycle.[20] On September 19, Hinh released a statement to the press explaining his stand, together with the text of a cable to Bao Dai asking him to intervene. A statement by Diem on the same day accused Hinh of rebellion.[21] Thereupon Hinh, quite unnecessarily, barricaded himself in his home. A few days later, he stationed army tanks around the Norodom Palace (rebaptized Independence Palace), the old seat of the French High Commissioner, which General Ely had handed over to Diem only on September 7. The police guarding the Palace were under the command of Diem's sworn enemies at the head of the Binh Xuyen. Diem could hardly nourish any illusions about the value of this protection, since it was this same police which, on September 21, had dispersed the Catholics—mostly refugees from the North—who had been called on to demonstrate popular support for Diem.[22] In order to defend himself against his "protectors" of the Saigon police, Diem brought several units of more loyal militias from Annam into Saigon. The Binh Xuyen, together with the Hoa Hao and Cao Dai, had by that time openly come out for General Hinh against Diem. In a joint manifesto issued on September 16, the warlords, gangsters, bordello keepers, and dishonest sect politicians demanded a new government in virtuous language that must have caused great hilarity in the Hall of Mirrors, where the prostitutes of the Binh Xuyen chiefs received their customers. The sects wanted a government ready "to put an end to the regime of corruption which is the cause of the people's misery . . . and to free the country of foreign domination." [23] Their request was carried to Bao Dai by Le Van Vien. On September 20, nine of the fifteen members of Diem's government resigned, apparently convinced, like most local and international prophets, that the Diem regime was doomed, since Hinh had stated that coexistence between this government and the army was no longer possible.[24]

But Diem, who knew that his opponents had no plan and were divided, rightly guessed that most sect leaders rallied to Hinh chiefly in order to raise the price he, Diem, would have to pay for their neutrality or collaboration. He was not dismayed by the resignation of people he would sooner or later have dropped anyway. Their presence in the government was due only to the maneuvers he had been obliged to execute because of the weakness of his position. A number of these men —Pham Huu Chuong, Ho Thong Minh, and Phan Khac Suu—had been members of former Bao Dai governments; by charging Pham Huu Chuong, who fled the country on September 20, with corruption, Diem began to limit his Cabinet to members of his family and close personal friends, the only people whose counsel he was willing to take. Furthermore, the resignation of nine ministers enabled Diem to execute another maneuver: He could now offer ministries to sect leaders ready to sell out. His negotiators, well supplied with American funds, went to work, while Hinh was waiting for Bao Dai's permission to carry out his coup. Under the pretext that the army had to prevent a Communist move to exploit the crisis, Hinh kept the Palace surrounded by his troops, failing, however, to make any impression on Diem, whom Hinh and his Vietnamese and French associates regarded as finished. Le Van Vien, just back from his visit to Bao Dai at Cannes, and again "surrounded by his concubines and worrying about his liver,"[25] had begun to negotiate with the Hoa Hao and Cao Dai leaders to form a government to be headed by himself. But Diem's emissaries had not been idle. While a plan of action against the Palace was already being discussed and agreed upon between representatives of the sects and the army, the Hoa Hao and Cao Dai leaders suddenly informed the Binh Xuyen chief that he was not acceptable to them as head of a new government and that they were also opposed to Hinh and Le Van Vien's demand for the return of Bao Dai to Vietnam. On September 24, forty-eight hours before the projected joint action of the sects against Diem, four Hoa Hao and four Cao Dai leaders joined the government they had plotted to overthrow.[26] "This maneuver, according to rumors in the political circles of Saigon, cost the American taxpayers several million piasters that went into the coffers of the two sects."[27] As a matter of fact, it cost them a lot more, as people both friendly and hostile to the Diem regime have since pointed out.[28] But apparently Diem's gains were worth the price. On September 25, the government could already count upon large units of Cao Dai forces, due to the "rallying" to Diem of the famous Cao Dai dissident Trinh Minh The.

Diem's "uncanny ability to divide his enemies by a series of intricate maneuvers"[29] helped him enormously in his struggle against the army leadership supported by Bao Dai and influential French circles in Vietnam. But these talents would hardly have saved him had the end of September not also seen international developments that proved decisive for Diem's political fortunes. A three-day Franco-American conference held in Washington (September 27–29) produced clear evidence that henceforth it was to be the United States, not France, on whose support the survival of a non-Communist Vietnam depended. France, although remaining economically entrenched in South Vietnam, no longer possessed the means to maintain herself there politically. The course of events before Geneva, in particular the growing dependence of France on U.S. aid for the war in Indochina, had laid the groundwork for this historical shift. Now it was being ratified step by step, with measures agreed upon by Washington, Saigon, and Paris that would gradually remove all positions of French political control from South Vietnam. The demand to liquidate colonialism, raised for years by Diem as spokesman for Vietnamese nationalism, and supported with growing impatience by Washington, would at last be complied with. It was this shift that propelled Diem in his struggle for supreme power. Remnants of colonialism were to be found in the French-controlled leadership of the army, the French-supported armies of the sects, and, more remotely, the French-created "legitimacy" of the Chief of State, Bao Dai. At the end of September, 1954, it became evident that all this had to go. Washington footed the bill in Vietnam, still largely for the French Expeditionary Corps,[30] and, confident that it knew better than Paris how to stop Communism in Asia, Washington was determined to call the tune. France had no choice. She had already agreed early in September to join SEATO. Now the French delegates at Washington agreed,[31] either openly or tacitly, to the steps that would, as General Ely had put it on August 30 in a statement to the Agence France-Press, achieve "total independence." Responsibility for the administration of justice, police, security, public safety, and civil aviation had already been turned over to the Diem Government, at least in theory, on September 11, thus abolishing the mixed tribunals set up by the treaties of March and December, 1949, between the French and Bao Dai. The next step, agreed upon in principle at the Washington conference, was permission for Vietnam to issue her own currency, which meant in fact the liquidation of the Bank of Indochina. January 1, 1955, was the date set for this momentous change. The French further agreed to the cancellation of the Pau agreements, which had given France effective control over the economy, commerce, and finances of Vietnam; to the transfer of the overall command of the National Army to the Vietnamese Government; in principle, to put the U.S. military mission in charge of training the Vietnamese Army; to give the government of Vietnam full control over all aid funds from the United States; and, finally, to withdraw the Expeditionary Corps upon request of the Vietnamese Government.

Subsequent events confirmed that these steps had been agreed upon in the Washington talks in September, but this did not become known until Mendès-France's visit to Washington on November 20, and details were made public in a Chamber debate in Paris a few weeks after his return, in which Mendès-France was accused of having sold out the interests of France by accepting the "American solution" for the future comportment of the West toward Vietnam. But this was far from true, said Guy La Chambre, the Minister for the Associated States, in his defense of the Washington agreements. He claimed that their aim was Franco-American cooperation in Indochina. His defense

rested on one point. The objective of France, he said, had been to ensure her citizens a continuation of the economic advantages obtained in
the agreements with the Bao Dai regime in 1949 and 1950. Vietnam and
the United States, he added, have given firm assurances not to interfere
with French economic and commercial interests.[32]

Guy La Chambre was on fairly safe ground: The United States indeed was not interested in replacing France economically in Indochina.
Washington's policy was motivated by strategic and political and not
by immediate economic considerations. Moreover, French business interests for the time being were not threatened by the Vietnamese. On
December 30, 1954, and again on March 30, 1955, the Diem Government concluded economic agreements fully safeguarding French business interests in South Vietnam. French ownership of the profitable
rubber plantations, for instance, was never disputed. Diem's motives
also were primarily political and military. His chief interest was to create the conditions for successful resistance against Communism. One of
these conditions was that the United States assume the military protection of South Vietnam against Communist aggression, which France
was no longer able to do; another, and this one of immediate significance for Diem, that France relinquish her political hold on Vietnam,
which Diem had always regarded as the chief obstacle in Vietnam's
struggle against Communism.

But if the French, by going along with U.S. policy, really gave up
only something they had already lost, it is undoubtedly true that their
new course meant that they had to sacrifice the pro-French Vietnamese forces. Once military aid no longer went to the French but directly
to the Vietnamese Government, the army became financially dependent on Diem. This also meant that the subsidies given by the French to
the sects for maintaining their own armed forces would sooner or later
be discontinued. And what could Paris do to prevent Diem from de-
posing Bao Dai, the symbol of Vietnamese subordination to France, if
Washington concurred in such a move? A great deal of Franco-American friction and a number of dramatic confrontations could still be expected before the French in Indochina would become resigned to giving up their old positions of control; but in the long run, American,
not French, influence would determine the political fate of South
Vietnam.

That is why Diem, who anticipated this development, was never in
real doubt about the outcome of his duel with General Hinh.[33] He

disregarded Bao Dai's cautious advice, given on October 1, to take Hinh,
Le Van Vien, and Nguyen Van Xuan into his Cabinet. All later appeals
by Hinh to Bao Dai for support against Diem failed to produce any
reaction whatever. Only a few people knew the reason for his caution:
On October 2, General Ely, back from the talks in Washington, told
Bao Dai what had been agreed upon and why France was obliged to go
along with the U.S. policy of support for Diem. Ely probably also
warned Bao Dai against antagonizing the Americans, with whom he
was anything but popular. The French, although still wishing to arbitrate the conflict between Diem and the army, could no longer openly
side with Hinh against Diem, at least not officially. After a stalemate of
more than six weeks, during which Diem consistently refused to talk
about any sort of compromise, Bao Dai finally gave in. On November
13, he called Hinh to France for "consultations"; on November 29, he
issued a decree dismissing him from his post.[34] Bao Dai also remained
deaf to all further demands by his supporters to involve himself personally against Diem and to return to Vietnam with Hinh. During October and November, Washington had let it be known that it would
not stand by idly if Diem were ousted. A report submitted on October
15 to the Senate Foreign Relations Committee by Senator Mansfield
had spoken out sharply against plans to replace Diem. If Diem should
be overthrown, Mansfield said, "the United States should consider an
immediate suspension of all aid to Vietnam and the French Union
forces there, except that of a humanitarian nature." [35] On October 24,
President Eisenhower addressed an encouraging public letter of support to Diem, reaffirming earlier promises of aid and informing Diem
that beginning January 1, 1955, all American aid to Vietnam would be
given directly to his government.[36] This was also the first of the many
occasions when the United States expressed the hope that Diem would
carry out "indispensable reforms." On November 17, General J. Law-
ton Collins, appointed by Eisenhower as special envoy to Saigon, stated
on his arrival there: "I have come to Vietnam to bring every possible
aid to the government of Diem and to his government alone." [37]

Thanks to such unreserved support, Diem survived his first major
test in his struggle to create an effective, independent government for
South Vietnam.[38] At the end of 1954, he was ready for the next encounter, one that almost undid what he had so far achieved: the battle
to oust the sects from the political life of Vietnam.

4

Diem started his long campaign to eliminate the sects with an apparently unpolitical move, directed at the head of the Binh Xuyen in the latter's capacity as businessman. The government refused to renew the license for the gambling establishment Grand Monde, which had expired in January, 1955. Acting like the moralist he was, but confining himself to the Binh Xuyen, Diem indicated what tactics he intended to pursue in his battle with the sects: to set them against each other, to split their ranks, and to defeat them piecemeal. The Hoa Hao "Generalissimo" Tran Van Soai, a member of Diem's Cabinet—extortionist and gambling profiteer—could easily compete with Le Van Vien, but Diem might as well have resigned himself to defeat if he had attacked all three sects simultaneously.[39] Besides, Binh Xuyen control of the Saigon-Cholon police and security service posed a more immediate threat to Diem than the Hoa Hao activities in the more distant regions southwest of the capital. Next to obtaining control of the army, Diem's most important objective at this time was to gain control of the capital's police.

In laying his plans for the destruction of the Binh Xuyen early in 1955, Diem was in a much stronger position than he had been during the preceding fall—thanks to his victory over Hinh, but even more because of the advantages he derived from the execution of the measures in favor of Vietnam's full sovereignty, which American pressure had obliged the French to accept. The economic and financial agreements of December 29 and 30 abolished all formal and statutory dependence of Vietnam on France. An earlier agreement provided for the removal of the Interstate Bank of Issue from the three Associated States, which now created their own national banks for the issuance of their currency. They also set up national Exchange Control Offices.[40] This brought to an end the foreign-controlled activities of the Bank of Indochina, to whose abolition the French had agreed on December 29. No other step was as important in ending French control over the finances, the foreign trade, and the economy of the three Indochinese states. By decree of December 3, a National Bank of Vietnam was established—rather hastily, since it had to be in operation by January 1, 1955, when American aid was to go directly to the Saigon Govern-

ment. On January 12, the government formally took over the administration of the port of Saigon from the French. There can be no doubt
that the sum of these measures, and the many others of this kind that
followed, contributed much to Diem's prestige as a nationalist determined to wipe out all traces of colonialism in Vietnam.

The fact that direct American aid also comprised the aid for the Vietnamese armed forces was decisive for Diem's power struggle; this
meant that from then on, the army was dependent on the government
rather than on the French. It also gave Diem another lever against the
sects, since French subsidies to them would come to an end. They
were in effect discontinued on February 11. An agreement signed on
that day between the French General Agostini and the new Chief of
Staff of the Army Le Van Ty marked another big step toward completing Vietnamese national sovereignty. The French command transferred all responsibility for the Vietnamese armed forces to the Vietnamese Government.[41] Although the largely pro-French and pro-Bao
Dai officers would undoubtedly have preferred that someone else hold
the government's purse strings, Hinh's failure served as a warning
against another attempt to overthrow Diem. Not many of them were
completely loyal to Diem, but now the tendency of most officers was
to move secretly closer to the regime rather than to oppose it openly.
These men knew that the training and organization of the Vietnamese
Army would soon be handed over to American officers, most of
whom, if not actually anti-French, were definitely pro-Diem. Diem
had requested this change on January 21; the French formally complied with his request on February 11.[42] Diem now also had a man
whom he considered reliable at the head of the army: General Le Van
Ty, with whom he had replaced Hinh on December 10, 1954, against
strong French opposition. Le Van Ty was a weak man not held in high
esteem by most of his colleagues, but since he professed stanch loyalty
to Diem, he was at least of great temporary use. Diem's victory over
the army, however, was still incomplete, since he got his man only by
agreeing to the appointment of a pro-French and pro-Bao Dai inspector general of the armed forces: General Nguyen Van Vy, whose
thinking was undoubtedly more in harmony with the sentiments of
most higher officers, who were French-educated, French-appointed,
and, like their former chief, more French than Vietnamese in culture
and habits. The fathers of many of these officers were landowners,
high officials, or wealthy "bourgeois." Most higher officers were from

Cochinchina, and like Hinh were French citizens. This was true not only of Nguyen Van Vy, but also of Tran Van Don and Tran Van Minh ("Big Minh"), two colonels who later were made generals, as a reward for their support of Diem at a moment most crucial for his regime. The Generals Ty and Vy became central figures in the struggle to oust the sects, but a more fateful role in the life of Diem and in the political evolution of South Vietnam was played by the Colonels Don and Minh. Early in 1955, however, they were merely two of the many young officers whom prospects of quick promotion transformed into ostentatious patriots and eventually into supporters of Diem.

All these assets of actual and potential strength enormously facilitated Diem's maneuvers against the sects, whose leaders knew that with the end of the subsidies for their armies their power over the provinces they controlled would soon collapse. Obviously convinced that a virtuous man is justified in combating evil with means he considers immoral if employed by his enemies, Diem set about weakening the sects by systematically exploiting the venality of their leaders. On January 14, he succeeded in luring an important Hoa Hao officer, Colonel Nguyen Van Hue, the Chief of Staff of Generalissimo Tran Van Soai, into his camp. Hue brought with him 3,500 men, who were eventually integrated into the National Army. Another officer who joined Diem a few weeks later, Major Nguyen Day, brought with him 1,500 more Hoa Hao soldiers. After pocketing the reward for betraying Soai, their Commander in Chief, who, incidentally, was still a member of Diem's Government, Day and Hue accused him of being "greedy" and a "traitor to the nation." [43] At the end of January the Cao Dai leader Trinh Minh The, who had already rallied in November, 1954, did so again, perhaps only to give another demonstration of growing government strength. He was rewarded by being promoted to general in the National Army. The mercurial The used the occasion of his second rallying to make a speech calling upon Diem not to let up on his campaign against corruption, which Diem was conducting as a means of destroying his enemies and strengthening his own image as the incorruptible leader.[44] Shortly after this, on February 13, The brought his 5,000-man army into Saigon.[45] His black-uniformed troops staged an impressive parade past members of the government and the diplomatic corps. After Diem had thus secured for his government the one Cao Dai faction that had long represented the nucleus of a "third force" between Communists and collaborators, another shifty Hoa Hao "general," Nguyen Gia Ngo, announced his intention to rally, waiting, however, with the transfer of his troops until he was sure that Diem had definitely gained the upper hand.[46]

While Diem's military potential grew at the expense of the sect armies, conflicts between the Hoa Hao and Cao Dai, as well as further dissension in both sects, continued to erode their ability for united and effective resistance against the strikes they knew Diem was preparing against them. The Binh Xuyen, Diem's first target, was solidly behind its leader and suffered no defection, but their interests were too specific, too local, too opposed to national political goals to qualify them for the leadership of a coalition aspiring to govern the entire country. Old rivalries between the Hoa Hao and Cao Dai were intensified when both tried to extend the boundaries of the regions they controlled by taking over territories formerly held by the Vietminh. Yet these political gangsters, whose panic grew as their powers diminished, knew perfectly well that Diem would destroy them one by one if they failed to unite. They had flashes of insight, but these were the products merely of the fear of losing the power to preserve their sources of income, and therefore were not conducive to rational action. Since the leading personages even within the sects competed hotly in plundering the nation's wealth, fear of having their share of the loot reduced only fed their dissensions. This is why so many sect leaders once Diem decided to buy them were willing to act against their own interest, which lay in common action.

It took the intervention of Bao Dai, who saw a chance of blocking Diem's quest for real power, to bring about some kind of truce among the sects. An emissary he sent to Saigon persuaded the sect leaders of the necessity of a united front against Diem. On March 3, the Binh Xuyen, Cao Dai, and Hoa Hao concluded what they described as a "pact of nonaggression" and a "spiritual union" of the three sects, designed, as Cao Dai General Nguyen Thanh Phuong put it, "to protect the country and to serve the people." On March 4, the leading political shark of this shady coalition, the Cao Dai "pope," Pham Cong Tac, demanded a strong democratic government "composed of honest men." [47] The sect coalition was joined also by several nationalist groups opposed to Diem. Some, like the Dai Viet leader Nguyen Ton Hoan, joined because Diem rejected their demand for participation in his government; [48] others, like the "Democratic Party" leader Phan Quang Dan, generally regarded as pro-American, and the former

Trotskyite Ho Huu Tuong, joined under the mistaken notion that the sects could be used to bring about a true coalition government of all reputable nationalist personalities.[49] What was even more surprising, and no doubt a shock to Diem, was that the newly promoted General Trinh Minh The also joined this front—for a few days only, as if to prove once more his rather insolent independence. He left the sect front and returned to Diem on March 7, probably for another cash payment.[50] Not to be outcrooked in this scramble for power and riches, Bao Dai covered up his secret scheme to unseat Diem by expressing satisfaction with Diem's performance.[51]

Since time was unlikely to work in favor of the sects, they had to act. They had every reason to fear that their unpaid troops would sooner or later defect to the government on their own and thus deprive their leaders of the expected cash rewards for incorporating them into the National Army. On March 21, the United Front of the sects issued an ultimatum to Diem requesting the formation of a national government within five days. The ultimatum was signed by the leaders of the various factions within the sects, obviously in order to persuade Diem that any attempts to deal separately with them would no longer succeed.[52]

Diem, who had no intention of complying with the ultimatum, was nevertheless cautious in its rejection on March 24. He held out vague hopes for an integration of the sect armies into the National Army under conditions acceptable to the leaders. Dissatisfied, and realizing that they were once again being held off by a maneuver, they decided to withdraw their representations from the government. But action to overthrow Diem would have required real solidarity among the leaders, the courage to stake everything on one card, and the conviction that the armed strength of the combined sects was a match for that of Diem—all of which the sect leaders lacked, particularly solidarity. The Binh Xuyen fortified themselves in the police and security-service headquarters and in several other buildings in Saigon and Cholon; the Hoa Hao, which controlled much of the river traffic in the Mekong Delta, began to hold up food supplies for the capital; but the Cao Dai, weakened by The's defection, which now was final, did nothing or rather worse than nothing: Some of their leaders again secretly negotiated the price for their surrender to Diem.

In contrast to the thinly disguised disunity and hesitations of the sect leaders, Diem's singlemindedness in pursuing his aims, and confidence that he would achieve them, steadily increased. All throughout March, while his adversaries prepared themselves for a united action that never came off, Diem took measures, both on the military and political front, that would at the proper moment enable him to take the initiative if civil war became unavoidable. On March 1, he announced that three battalions of militia composed of Nung minority soldiers from Tongking had been brought into Saigon.[53] Two weeks later, the government ordered two battalions of paratroopers, also originally from Tongking, into the capital. Their commander, Colonel Cao Van Tri, was known to be loyal to Diem. Together with the troops of General The and those of the two Hoa Hao defectors Day and Hue, these reinforcements put Diem's military strength in the Saigon-Cholon area far above that of the sects, where actually only the Binh Xuyen army numbering about 5,000 battle-ready men was stationed.

On the diplomatic front, too, Diem had succeeded in fortifying his position vis-à-vis his enemies at home. In a television speech on March 8, Secretary of State Dulles assured Diem of unwavering American support, and on March 9, President Eisenhower sent a letter to Bao Dai that might have been interpreted as a warning to the Chief of State to stop making difficulties for Diem.[54] Also on March 8, the National Army, which had never looked with favor on private armies, and even less on military dissidence, started a campaign against a group of deserters, mostly from the National Guard, who, under the influence of the Dai Viet, tried to organize military resistance against the Diem regime in the province of Quang Tri, near the 17th parallel. The action was conducted with seven battalions equipped with artillery and tanks. Its success not only weakened Dai Viet opposition to Diem but also proved the National Army's conditional willingness and ability to deal with open rebellion against the regime.[55]

Diem disregarded an appeal issued by Bao Dai on March 25 for "unity" with the sects; instead, he decided to rely once more on the lure of the dollar in dealing with them, and on his growing military strength. With "swift moves that left each sect chief wondering whether his sworn ally of yesterday had not sold him out for a substantial sum," [56] Diem dealt the "unity" of the sects another blow. On March 29, he succeeded in buying the Commander in Chief of the Cao Dai army, General Nguyen Thanh Phuong, one of the chief spokesmen of the United Front. At a parade of Cao Dai troops on the grounds of the Presidential Palace on March 31, Phuong proclaimed his loyalty to

Diem—exactly four weeks after he had demanded that the Diem Government be replaced by one of "honest men." [57]

By March 31, however, Diem had already burned all bridges to the sect leaders, both those who had refused another bargain and those he had never wanted to buy but always intended to destroy: the Binh Xuyen. Assured already on March 27 of the Cao Dai commander's defection from the sect front, Diem, on that day, ordered his paratroopers under Colonel Cao Van Tri to occupy the Binh Xuyen–held police headquarters and security-service building on the Boulevard Gallieni (the avenue that connects Cholon with Saigon). The Binh Xuyen retreated from the police headquarters, but refused to evacuate the security-service building. Diem, impatient and convinced that the need for compromise was over, decided to use force. On March 28, he ordered Colonel Tri to attack the security-service building. But before the attack got under way, General Ely intervened. He had earlier warned the sect leaders against the use of force; now he used all his remaining means of pressure, as well as his powers of persuasion, to make Diem retract the order to attack. Diem very reluctantly gave in, but in the night of March 29–30 a clash between government troops and Binh Xuyen soldiers took place near the security-service building. The army suffered six killed and thirty-four wounded, the Binh Xuyen ten killed and twenty wounded. Also killed were ten civilians. The figure of wounded civilians was fifty-eight,[58] underlining that in a civil war the innocent were likely to suffer most.

It was at this point that Diem, in his race to achieve undisputed control over the country, was temporarily checked, and in fact driven to the brink of disaster. Fear of a wider civil war, entirely unfounded according to Diem, provoked General Ely's strong reaction against Diem's attempt to settle his conflict with the sects by force. As long as the French Army was in the country, its Commander in Chief, who felt responsible also for the safety of Vietnam's European population, could hardly remain indifferent if Saigon and perhaps several provincial cities as well were turned into battlefields. Apart from Ely's genuine concern, a great many Frenchmen had other motives in insisting that the government be prevented from moving against the sects. Politically, they sided with Bao Dai and the sects. They did not want Diem to engage in a battle he might win, and therefore for once chose to be against the use of force to settle a political conflict. Since it was Diem who insisted on the use of force, it was against him that the French, for the first time since his appointment, now threw the full weight of their remaining influence in Vietnam.

5

The French in Indochina, but also large sectors of public opinion in France, had never been happy with the decision of the government of Mendès-France to go along with U.S. policy in South Vietnam and the toleration of the regime of Ngo Dinh Diem: Too many interests and sensitivities were hurt by Diem's uncompromising insistence on rapid and total decolonization. He, and the U.S. support he enjoyed, had been attacked by most French newspapers long before the sect crisis approached its climax.[59] Quite a few had been predicting, rather gleefully, Diem's imminent fall for months. Now that the hopes of these Frenchmen for a government more to their liking could be kept alive only if Diem was prevented from eliminating the sects, the campaign against him became more and more violent. Diem was depicted as endangering the survival of South Vietnam by many Frenchmen, no doubt out of a genuine fear of a Communist take-over, which even those who at one time had believed in the possibility of "business as usual" under a Ho Chi Minh Government now knew to be catastrophic to their interests. Having done what they could (by siding with Hinh, Bao Dai, and the sects) to prevent Diem from establishing his authority, these people now denounced the weakness of his government, its lack of support, and its consequent inability to contain Communism. Diem's real talents for power, at least the kind of power these people admired, were either ignored or more likely simply denied, since they did not fit into the picture of him drawn by this propaganda. These talents could not possibly have remained unrecognized after Diem had survived for nine months as head of a government which almost every informed observer considered doomed from the day it was formed. The favored adjectives applied to Diem in this French campaign, which evoked extraordinary international response, were "inept" and "rigid," and much was made of his "inability to compromise," without the least awareness that the compromises that were then asked of him would undoubtedly have led to the disintegration of all governmental authority in the country.

This campaign must be seen as the last attempt of many Frenchmen in Vietnam to turn the tide of absolute anticolonialism, which under Diem was clearly running against any future French political presence in Vietnam. Businessmen concerned for their status and their possessions deeply sympathized with Diem's opponents, who, had they gained power, would have formed a pro-French regime. But other circles— army officers, advisers to the former administrations, and the many members of the various "special services" created during the war years, ranging from economic supervision and currency control to all kinds of open or secret police functions, and sometimes no functions at all—were also actively engaged against Diem on the side of the sects. The people who staffed these services, and a great many military men, were as disinclined to relinquish their frequently remunerative positions as they were to give up the exercise of their powers, either overt or behind the scenes. Since they knew that Diem was the man of Washington and that he could hardly survive without U.S. moral and material support, their privately expressed opinions were violently anti-American, which many nourish to this very day. An authoritative spokesman of these rather selfish fighters for a lost cause was the most important member of General Ely's staff, Assistant High Commissioner Jean Daridan.

Ely himself had accepted the necessity of a complete French withdrawal from Vietnamese political life and had become reconciled to the replacement of French political, economic, and military advisers by Americans, and although he could hardly have been enamored of Diem, refrained from maneuvers to oust him. But at the end of March, 1955, he felt it his duty to stand up against Diem. Like many other Frenchmen in Vietnam as well as in France, Ely would have put up both with Diem's ungracious manner and with his intemperate demands on the French had he been convinced of Diem's ability to master the political chaos of South Vietnam; but he had doubts, and when Diem decided to send his troops against the Binh Xuyen, Ely decided to step in. There was genuine fear in Saigon among French nationals that a wider civil war would lead to the breakdown of all established authority, arouse chauvinistic sentiments, and endanger their property and lives. Ely shared these fears.

It was for these reasons that at the end of March, the last High Commissioner for France and Commander of the Expeditionary Corps, although no friend of the sects, stopped Diem from crushing the Binh Xuyen. Not being a Vietnamese concerned with his country's political regeneration, Ely could hardly see that a united and strong regime demanded the suppression of the corrupt sects, and that this had to be done by force, since they could be appeased only if they were allowed to continue to exercise their divisive and destructive powers. Ely also failed to see that at this turning point in the country's history, a man like Diem was precisely what South Vietnam needed for survival, that in fact some of Diem's shortcomings as a leader possibly made him more fit for the task at hand than if his had been a broader and more generous political mind. Ely felt that he had to arbitrate the conflict between Diem and the sects. Moreover, he wanted to make peace between Diem and the Frenchmen with vested interests in Vietnam. Still another of his concerns was the growing friction between Frenchmen and Americans in Saigon, whose attitudes toward the sects and Diem became more irreconcilable with every passing day.

This Franco-American conflict was of serious concern also to President Eisenhower's special envoy to Saigon, General Collins. However, no clashes between Americans and French occurred on the ambassadorial level, either before or after Collins' arrival in Saigon. His predecessor, Ambassador Donald Heath, had never been fond of Diem, nor had he been convinced of the wisdom of Diem's policies. He followed his instructions from Washington with excessive concern for the sensitivities of the French. But Collins, too, after having performed his task of saving Diem in November, 1954, began to have mixed feelings about this stubborn man with whom it was so difficult to establish contact and who seemed not to know the meaning of an exchange of views. Collins was much closer to Ely, an old "comrade in arms," than to Diem. He had his first disagreement with Diem soon after his arrival over the appointment of a new minister of defense.[60] Although Collins' opinions were anything but firm, and his recommendations consequently vague, he nevertheless came to the conclusion that Diem was a failure, and ended up advising Washington to drop Diem. By mid-April, when it was evident that Diem would sooner or later renew his attack on the Binh Xuyen, Collins became almost emphatic in his opposition to Diem.[61]

If Diem had not already known what Collins thought about his policy toward the sects, he would certainly have learned it after March 29, when Collins unequivocally supported the measures taken by the French to stop the army from attacking the Binh Xuyen. These measures were firm enough to force Diem to retreat. The cease-fire that the French High Command imposed on the government forces became effective during the night of March 29–30.[62] The French Army followed up with a series of steps designed to prevent Diem from pursuing his campaign to expel the Binh Xuyen from Saigon. The Binh Xuyen troops were allowed to fortify their positions in and around Saigon, while the French Army, under the pretext of protecting foreign residents, took up strategically important positions in the capital and designated the main routes and a number of sectors of Saigon off limits for the National Army, including the sectors held by the Binh Xuyen. The French command, which still controlled all supplies for the Vietnamese Army, withheld the ammunition and fuel needed to continue the government operation against the Binh Xuyen. Collins strongly urged Diem not to resume the attack.[63] "Our hands have been tied by the intervention of General Collins," claimed a spokesman of the government on April 7.[64]

In his long struggle to gain, and later to preserve, power, Diem went through several periods of agonizing uncertainty. But not even the weeks before his downfall and death in 1963 could have been filled with more anguish than the month of April, 1955. He no longer had a government, not even as window dressing. All sect ministers had resigned at the end of March. But a harder blow for Diem was that his respected Foreign Minister, Tran Van Don, also deserted him, together with Ho Thong Minh, the Minister of Defense, over whose appointment, which the French had opposed, Diem had had his first disagreement with Collins. The government was replaced by a junta consisting of the three Ngo brothers—Diem, Nhu, and Luyen—and a nephew by marriage, Tran Trung Dung. Even the other relative in the government, Nguyen Van Thoai, the only prominent man to return with Diem from Paris, resigned—spectacularly, announcing his decision while serving as leader of the Vietnamese delegation at the Bandung conference. Many high officials, most of them appointees of the French, hastily left government service—the proverbial rats leaving the sinking ship. They hoped to be rewarded by the government that sooner or later would replace Diem. The countryside remained sect territory or Communist-controlled, even after the evacuation of the Vietminh troops. Diem did not have enough provincial loyal administrators and not enough military forces to deprive the sects and the Communist cadres of the administrative authority they exercised over wide regions.[65] The few units of the army willing to fight for the government were needed in Saigon to protect the government against the

Binh Xuyen; all others, whose leaders were either hostile to Diem or fence-sitting were at best a passive force in the struggle for political control of the country, and even that only as long as it seemed that Diem might survive. A delegation of generals made this clear to Diem, warning him that the army was unwilling to take part in civil-war operations. Diem's attempt to get a few more battalions, considered reliable, transferred from Central Vietnam to Saigon was frustrated by the French. General Ely refused to supply the requisite means of transportation.[66] The French continued to prevent the troops loyal to Diem from circulating freely in Saigon, but did not interfere with the movements of the Binh Xuyen, who still controlled the capital's police force. Growing bolder every day, the Binh Xuyen extended their hold on Saigon-Cholon by occupying more and more strategic positions. On April 19, a confident spokesman of the Binh Xuyen told a French correspondent: "Diem is getting weaker every day. The army does not follow him and all his ministers are abandoning him. Bao Dai is encouraging us to hold out until the liquidation of the Prime Minister. The French are now entirely on our side, and the Americans are changing their attitude. If Diem starts a battle, he will only fall that much sooner, and his own safety will be threatened." [67]

Diem's proven method of splitting the ranks of the sects by buying some of their leaders no longer seemed to work. Pope Pham Cong Tac denounced the rallying of the Cao Dai Commander in Chief, denying that the sect's military forces would follow General Nguyen Thanh Phuong into the government camp. General Nguyen Gia Ngo went back on his promise of February to put the Hoa Hao forces under his command at Diem's disposal. And a new attempt to buy the remaining three Hoa Hao leaders—Tran Van Soai, Lam Thanh Nguyen, and Bacut—was rejected on April 23, in a statement issued by the "United Front of the Nationalist Forces." [68] The sect leaders, it seemed, had at last begun to realize that they could preserve their privileges and feudal powers only if Diem were overthrown.

It was not surprising that during these weeks, so critical for Diem, Bao Dai's interest in his country was revived, plainly for the purpose of helping to overthrow Diem. Bao Dai no longer possessed the power to shape his country's political course, but his attitude was of great significance, since, like a barometer able to register if not to predict, it showed the strength of the storm that was descending on Diem. Although impressed by the difficulties Diem encountered from local forces, Bao

Dai was infinitely more encouraged by the change of attitude toward Diem on the international scene. He knew better than anyone else that Diem could not survive without unqualified American support. His keen political perception told him that Washington had begun to entertain serious doubts about Diem's ability to lead the country out of chaos. Statements in support of Diem from the United States began to sound lukewarm. Bao Dai was well informed about the mood in American Government circles, about the anxious reactions of the press, and the strong reservations about Diem among many Americans in Saigon. He also knew that Collins, who was called to Washington on April 23, far from pleading Diem's cause, advocated what had become the French position, namely that Diem had to be replaced.[69]

That this had become official French policy, both Bao Dai and Diem knew long before it was confirmed by the new Prime Minister, Edgar Faure, who had replaced Mendès-France in February, 1955. In a statement on April 29, Faure said about Ngo Dinh Diem: "It appears that for some time past his government has not been well adapted to discharge the mission with which he has been entrusted."[70] Ely's desire to maintain a "neutral" position between Diem and the sects was now less in harmony with his government's view than the position of his many compatriots in Saigon, who demanded greater direct intervention in favor of the sects. The head of this faction, Assistant High Commissioner Jean Daridan, after resigning his post in protest against Ely's moderate course, rushed to Cannes and Paris to urge upon Bao Dai and the French Government a more aggressive stand against Diem. This faction also conducted a vicious campaign against the few Americans in Saigon who stood firmly by Diem and gave him both military and political advice in his struggles, thereby bringing down on their heads the wrath of the French, General Hinh, Bao Dai, and the sects. Outstanding among the men who were convinced that Diem alone could prevent a collapse of the South were Colonel Edward G. Lansdale of the Central Intelligence Agency and Dr. Wesley Fishel, head of a team of Michigan State University professors at the National Institute of Administration.[71] The Franco-American differences, however, were not about whether South Vietnam should be saved or not; the French, too, wanted to save the country, but they insisted that unless Diem were removed, all would be lost.[72]

Bao Dai was already looking around for a new prime minister when he received a request from Diem to dismiss the head of the security

service, a Binh Xuyen chief whom Bao Dai had appointed early in
1954. Diem's request was refused. Instead, Bao Dai demanded that
Diem cooperate with the sects. Urged on by the French, Bao Dai issued a decree making the pro-French General Nguyen Van Vy head
of the army. The next step was to invite Diem for "consultations," and
when Diem quietly replied that he could not leave the country, Bao
Dai ordered him to come to France. He also asked Diem to take General Ty, Diem's chosen head of the army whom Bao Dai had just replaced by his own man, with him.

Toward the end of April it seemed to most observers that Diem was
about finished, and that only his much deplored "lack of imagination"
prevented him from knowing this himself. Every foreign newspaper he
picked up—French, English, or American—told him that his days were
numbered. The French press was openly hostile, claiming that the fall
of Diem would be a blessing for South Vietnam; the British press,
more aloof, regretted Diem's shortcomings but insisted that they made
his being replaced inevitable; and the American press, although only in
part hostile, was almost unanimously defeatist in regard to Diem's
chances of survival. In America, the voice leading this international
chorus was the influential columnist Joseph Alsop, whose earlier prediction of Diem's doom seemed about to come true.[73] Most American
papers, even those friendly to Diem, were resigned to this sad and
probably disastrous event, since civil war and the fall of Diem would
undoubtedly open the door to Communism. South Vietnam, as another
influential voice stated, was "about to retire behind the iron cur-
tain." [74]

6

Would Diem recognize that his position had become hopeless and permit himself to be replaced? Those who knew the Prime Minister intimately were even then convinced that his successor government
would have to be set up over his dead body. On April 23, when practically everybody expected him to announce his resignation, Diem announced instead that general elections would be held within three or
four months—a first indication that in addition to the use of force and
bribery, Diem would henceforth also employ political demagogy to

maintain himself in power. Everybody knew that conditions in South Vietnam precluded the holding of genuine elections.

Diem decided that the time had come to force a decision, confident that it would be in his favor. After urging Washington to bring pressure on the French to stop protecting the Binh Xuyen, Diem told Ely that no amount of French obstruction would prevent him from asserting the government's authority against the Binh Xuyen "rebels." On April 24, he dismissed the Binh Xuyen chief of the security service, Lai Huu Sang, appointing in his place Colonel Nguyen Ngo Le, a Catholic loyal to the government. On April 26, all members of the security service who failed to report to Colonel Le within the next forty-eight hours were threatened with court-martial. On April 27, the government announced that after the expiration of this time limit, the Binh Xuyen troops would be forbidden to circulate in Saigon-Cholon.

Far from being intimidated, the Binh Xuyen on the contrary became more aggressive. This led to clashes with government troops at several points in town. But it was the army that started the real battle. It began on April 28 around noon, when two truckloads of paratroopers fired at a building on the Boulevard Gallieni occupied by a Binh Xuyen commando. The army quickly moved four battalions of paratroopers and one armored unit against other Binh Xuyen strongholds between Saigon and Cholon, the twin city of Saigon where the Binh Xuyen chief Le Van Vien had his fortified headquarters. At 1:15 P.M., the Binh Xuyen fired four shells into the grounds of the Presidential Palace—an incident later cited by Diem, in an unnecessary qualification of historical truth, as the reason that "peace was lost in Saigon." [75] Since mortars were used in the fighting, a vast agglomeration of primitive huts near the battle area was completely destroyed by fire. The people poured into the narrow streets, running up and down between the flaming huts, bewildered and screaming. After only a few hours of fighting, civilian casualties were running well into the hundreds. An estimated 20,000 people were made homeless.

In the course of the afternoon, General Ely, this time unassisted by his friend Collins, who was still in Washington, tried once more to arrange a cease-fire. But Diem, pointing at the shells fired against the Palace, would have none of it. Ely wisely gave up, and French action, at least official action, was limited to protecting the European population of Saigon. On May 1, Ely ordered four hundred French Army tanks to ride through the streets of Saigon—a final gesture of French power, with which Ely reminded Diem that he could easily have frustrated his plan to oust the Binh Xuyen from Saigon.

On May 1, however, the battle for control of the city was already over. The paratroopers, competently led by Colonel Cao Van Tri, had proved superior to the Binh Xuyen, whose fighting spirit turned out to be surprisingly low.[76] The last beaten units of Le Van Vien, who had fled from his headquarters early on April 29, retired from Cholon before dawn broke on April 30. They and the reserves that Le Van Vien had failed to throw into the battle regrouped outside the city. The Binh Xuyen had apparently counted on the French to save them. During the next few days, they were again defeated outside the city by the army and Cao Dai units under General The, and driven into the marshes of Rung Sat, 10 miles south of Saigon.[77]

Hectic activities, both on the political home front and in the diplomatic arena, filled the few days during which the government forces were throwing the Binh Xuyen out of Saigon. It was just after the fighting broke out on April 28 that Bao Dai called Diem and his chief of staff to France, no doubt with the intention of depriving both of their positions. In fact later that same day he dismissed Diem's head of the army, appointed General Vy in his place, and stripped Diem of the military powers he had granted him in June, 1954. April 29 brought not only Premier Faure's statement calling Diem unfit for his job, but also another gesture of French hostility to Diem and support for Bao Dai: French Government recognition of Bao Dai's appointee, General Vy, as head of the Vietnamese Army.[78] Bao Dai, no doubt urged on by the French, sent General Hinh back to Saigon to help the sects against Diem.

For the French and Bao Dai, the news from Saigon on April 29 was bad, since it seemed that Diem was gaining the upper hand against the Binh Xuyen. Washington, on the other hand, was relieved, and immediately began to recover from its "grave apprehensions"[79] concerning Diem, and to express its displeasure over the attempts to unseat him. On April 29, the same day that Faure denounced Diem, Dulles warned the French Ambassador to Washington, Couve de Murville, against further moves to unseat Diem,[80] and Ambassador Dillon did the same in Paris in an audience with Premier Faure. American support for Diem came most conspicuously alive again in a demand to the French that the Vietnamese Army be supplied with the transportation, gasoline, and ammunition needed to fight the rebellious sects; after all, it was the United States that was paying for these supplies. Encouraged by the American Chargé d'Affaires at Saigon, Randolph Kidder, but even more by the success of his troops against the Binh Xuyen, Diem felt on safe ground in refusing to obey Bao Dai's order of April 29 to come to France. Twenty-four hours later, Diem received a cable from the State Department in Washington assuring him of continued U.S. support.[81]

This assurance, and even more the fact that the Binh Xuyen had been decisively routed, made April 30 a good day for Diem. However, it brought another event of great importance for the future of the Diem regime. Bao Dai's futile attempt to unseat Diem—since he no longer had the power to do so—produced a new chain of events in Saigon, initiated chiefly to deprive the Emperor of all prerogatives of legitimacy he still enjoyed as Chief of State.

In other tenebrous phases of the recent power struggles in South Vietnam, the truth can still be glimpsed through the tightly woven screen of intrigues. This is not true of the chain of events that began in the afternoon of April 30, 1955, when a gathering of some 200 people at the Saigon Town Hall constituted itself as a "General Assembly of democratic and revolutionary forces of the nation." The outcome of these events is known, but what actually happened at several critical stages has yet to be revealed by the surviving actors of this drama, many of whom had motives to which they could not admit at the time. It is not known who was for or against whom or what at any given moment, and who changed his mind freely or under duress. The picture that emerges from the available conflicting reports is that of a weird "kaleidoscope"[82] whose most discernible components were hate, lust for power, greed, cowardice, and treachery.

The apparent and immediate purpose of the Town Hall meeting was to provide evidence of popular support for Diem in his struggle to get rid of the Binh Xuyen, Bao Dai, and the French. Eighteen political "parties," none of them representing more than a handful of people in Saigon, together with the Cao Dai leaders that had gone over to Diem, constituted the "General Assembly." After the symbolic act of tossing Bao Dai's picture out the window, the meeting decided that the former Emperor had to abdicate and that a new government be formed under Ngo Dinh Diem. The task of this new government was to restore order, to obtain the early departure of the French Expeditionary Corps, and to prepare elections for a national assembly. The meeting concluded with the election of a thirty-three–member "Revolutionary Committee" which instantly went to the Palace to submit the demands of the General Assembly to Diem.

Although all of this had been prearranged by the sponsors of this meeting and the government—the scheme was generally thought to have been plotted by Ngo Dinh Nhu [83]—there were indications that Diem was not altogether happy with the way it was going, since some of the men called upon to act at this new stage refused to be manipulated. The strongest men on the Revolutionary Committee were the two Cao Dai leaders who had rallied to Diem—the Generals The and Phuong. Both still commanded the loyalty of a few thousand armed followers, and The had already caused uneasiness at the Palace when he stationed groups of his soldiers in sections of Saigon immediately after the paratroopers attacked the Binh Xuyen on April 28. Because of their positions and of the means at their disposal, both The and Phuong could be expected to use the Revolutionary Committee for aims not necessarily identical with those of Diem. Other members of the Committee were suspect for other reasons—two were former Vietminh political commissars (whose inclusion, however, was defended by Nhu); [84] some were known for their contacts with French left-wing circles, and others for their tendency to enhance their image through expressions of extreme nationalism and demands for radical reforms. [85]

No reliable report exists on the events of the next twenty-four hours—the most crucial period in Diem's struggle to become master of his state—but the following version, although based on conflicting testimony, is probably essentially correct. When the Revolutionary Committee arrived at the Palace at about 6:15 P.M., Diem was in conference with the Generals Ty and Vy, the former said to be for him and the latter known to be against him. But on that evening, they both were to affirm their loyalty to Bao Dai, in whose name Vy was to assume command of the army. Neither of them was a hero, and both were at least twenty-four hours behind the decision of history—Vy with his courage to oppose an already victorious Diem, Ty with his cowardly acceptance of Vy's presumption to lead the army. Before going to the Palace at 6:00 P.M., Vy had in fact issued a statement that he had assumed command of the army on orders of Bao Dai.

The appearance of the Revolutionary Committee accompanied by armed followers of The and Phuong put an end to Diem's "negotiations" with Ty and Vy. An attempt by one Committee member to kill

Vy allegedly was prevented by Diem, who, according to some informants, said that he did not wish to have blood spilled on his Chinese
rug.[86] Another version claims that Vy was saved by Colonel Cao Van
Tri, a fellow paratrooper, who had just defeated the Binh Xuyen. Tri
was said to have called Diem and threatened to storm the Palace if Vy
was not released.[87] What is certain, however, is that foreign correspondents who were called to the Palace at 9:30 P.M. found a trem-
bling Vy, guarded by The and Phuong, ready to read a prepared statement repudiating Bao Dai and supporting the Revolutionary Committee's demands that French interference in Vietnamese affairs must
end.[88] Thereupon Ty and Vy were allowed to leave.

The next morning, after a presumably sleepless night for Ty and
Vy, the two generals held a press conference at military headquarters.
That was the same day, May 1, that General Ely demonstrated the
continued presence of France by sending 400 tanks through the streets
of Saigon. Vy announced that his statement of the previous night had
been made under duress, that Diem was a prisoner of the Revolutionary Committee, and that he and the army, of which 90 per cent was
loyal to him, would take over the country.

But this second attempt at a *coup d'état* by a general loyal to Bao
Dai and supported by the French ended even more disastrously than
Hinh's attempt in the fall of 1954. Diem, too, had obviously not gone to
bed after Vy and Ty left the Palace. Only the outcome of his night maneuvering is known: After the press conference at military headquarters, General Ty left his colleague Vy and immediately went to the
Palace, where he was received with open arms. He brought with him
what was most precious for Diem on this morning: the Colonels Tran
Van Don and Duong Van Minh, both respected officers with a large
following in the army, Minh being the commander of the Saigon-
Cholon garrison. Both were instantly made generals, and Ty was promoted from brigadier to lieutenant general, as a reward for undoing his
betrayal of Diem less than twenty-four hours earlier by now betraying
his colleague Vy. The Diem Government, "after tottering on the brink
of dissolution," [89] once again was saved. Vy, realizing that he had been
outmaneuvered, fled to Dalat on the afternoon of May 1, hoping for at
least temporary protection by Bao Dai's Imperial Guard. His predecessor in defeat, General Hinh, who, sent by Bao Dai, was expected to
arrive in Saigon on the same day, decided instead to land at Phnom
Penh, in Cambodia.

But although Diem's victory over the Binh Xuyen was now nearly complete, he still had not gained that total freedom of action which he considered necessary and the right of a man called upon to save his country. The Revolutionary Committee installed itself in the Palace, with the obvious intention of exercising a direct influence on governmental policy. Quite a few of its members expected to enter the new government they had requested Diem to form. Their radical and demagogic nationalism threatened the image Diem was building of himself as the true and only liberator of his country from colonialism; and their demand for the immediate dismissal of Bao Dai interfered with Diem's own strategy for achieving this end: Bao Dai would have to go, but his fall must be made into a historical event that resounded to the glory of Diem.

In his subtle game to free himself of any dependence on the Revolutionary Committee, Diem was aided by an event that, regardless of whether it shocked or pleased him, must be considered as a stroke of luck for the man who was beginning to be convinced that his government could be strong only if he did not have to share his powers with anyone, be it enemy or friend. The only man on the Revolutionary Committee who might have become a rival for power was General Trinh Minh The. The had been known for years as an ardent nationalist; he had presented himself consistently as a champion of the people and a fighter against corruption; and he was certainly a young man of ambition and of considerable strength. But fate would not let him test his talents in a competition for leadership with Diem. On May 3, while fighting to drive the Binh Xuyen from the outskirts of Saigon, The was killed. His death, which occurred "under mysterious circumstances," [90] gave rise to rumors that he had been murdered, but by whom and for what reason remained a matter of dispute. Circumstantial evidence contradicts one of the theories advanced, namely that he was killed on orders from Diem.[91]

After The's death, Diem had little trouble in demobilizing the forces on which he had called at a critical moment, when he had to demonstrate that by crushing his enemies he was executing the people's will. He gradually pushed the Revolutionary Committee out of the Palace, and in order to prove that he no longer needed this body to substantiate his claim that he was acting in the name of the people, he staged a new and firmly government-controlled show of popular support. This was a National Congress held in Saigon on May 5; it was attended mainly by docile civil servants and hand-picked Diem supporters from all over the country. The resolutions of this Congress, milder than the demands of the Revolutionary Committee, nevertheless made it clear that the regime wanted to get rid of Bao Dai. Among other demands compatible with Diem's intentions, the Congress requested a referendum to decide whether the State of Vietnam should become a constitutional monarchy or a republic. A rival congress called by the Revolutionary Committee on the same day merely proved that men who let themselves become tools seldom possess the skill for independent action, and can, once they are no longer of any use, be exchanged for other pawns. The Committee's only possible source of strength was the Cao Dai troops of the generals who had rallied to Diem, troops who were ultimately bound to be loyal to the man who paid them. In forming his new Cabinet on May 10, composed of trusted followers and half a dozen obscure administration officials, Diem could safely ignore all demands raised by the Revolutionary Committee. When its chairman resigned in protest against Diem's authoritarian policies and left the country, the government accused him of having embezzled the Committee's funds.[92] When Diem, in October, 1955, requested that the Committee be broken up, the remaining members soon afterward voted its dissolution. Neither Diem's enemies nor the people willing to accept him as the country's leader seemed able to compete successfully with this determined man for a share in governmental power.

7

More important, however, than the elimination of inconvenient allies were two other by-products of Diem's victory over the Binh Xuyen. He convinced Washington that in order to save South Vietnam, the United States had to give unwavering support to his regime, and he at last obtained an end to French interference with his policy.

After their failure to overthrow Diem, the French, under some pressure from the United States, reconciled themselves to having to liquidate all remnants of colonialism. As one observer wrote: "In a sense, this was the most critical problem of all, for without the achievement of complete independence [Diem's] long-run prospects were hopeless. If Diem was ever to rival Ho Chi Minh as an authentic champion of the Vietnamese people, he had to end any semblance of French control in the South, as Ho had successfully done in the North." [93]

The steps toward this end were agreed upon in another Franco-American conference, this one taking place in Paris from May 7 to 12. Dulles no longer hesitated in his support for Diem. By defeating the Binh Xuyen and proving his ability to survive, Diem had at last also conquered the steadily growing doubt of his protectors in Washington. Dulles obviously enjoyed the opportunity of taking a firm stand against French colonialist intrigues in favor of Washington's brave and clever protégé at Saigon. He extracted concessions ranging from the recall of Frenchmen who had actively opposed the Diem regime to the early and complete withdrawal of all French troops should Diem make such a request. Diem's dossier listing certain French activities during the Binh Xuyen crisis was quite embarrassing to the French Government. The Vietnamese Army had captured French officers serving as advisers to the Binh Xuyen; the Binh Xuyen radio transmitter was found to have been operating from a French Army camp; a French ambulance was intercepted while transporting arms to Binh Xuyen units during the fighting. And after the main forces of the Binh Xuyen had been defeated, the French set up barricades that effectively delayed the National Army's efforts to wipe out remaining pockets of resistance.[94] The French said that these were not official acts, which was true to the extent that they were certainly not authorized by General Ely; but this excuse only strengthened Diem in his demands that those who had committed these acts must leave Vietnam. Acceptance of this demand was made easy for the French when Dulles agreed that Washington, too, would recall officials whose attitude had caused friction with the French.[95]

As a matter of fact, the only American withdrawn from Saigon was the man who had consistently tried to reduce French-American friction, and who, on several occasions, had sided with General Ely against Diem: Ambassador Collins. He left Vietnam on May 14, no doubt without regrets, for a position with NATO. Washington's restored confidence in Diem was unequivocally expressed when, on May 27, the new Ambassador to Saigon, G. Frederick Reinhardt, stated: "I came here under instructions to carry out United States policy in support of the legal government of Vietnam under Premier Ngo Dinh Diem." [96] French representation in Saigon was also due for a change. On May 20, Ely, worn out by his efforts to carry out an impossible mission, de-

manded to be relieved. He left Saigon on June 20. Diem took this opportunity to insist that France henceforth not be represented by another
high commissioner but by an ambassador acceptable to his government. Paris, still unreconciled to "total independence" for Vietnam,
long resisted this plausible demand.[97]

In August, 1955, the French agreed to abolish the Ministry for the
Associated States of Indochina. Its functions, which the realization of
independence for Vietnam, Cambodia, and Laos had radically altered,
were transferred to the Ministry of Foreign Affairs. By agreement of
August 16, the problem of French citizenship for Vietnamese nationals
was regulated in accordance with Diem's demands. French citizenship
for those who had been naturalized after the Elysée agreement of
March, 1949, was automatically abolished. All others were given six
months in which to choose between French and Vietnamese citizenship. For Diem, this was another means of ridding his administration
and army of all pro-French elements, since a decree ordered that those
who opted for France could no longer hold any official position.
Among the many who instantly chose Vietnamese citizenship were the
Generals Duong Van Minh and Tran Van Don, and the Ambassador to
Washington, Tran Van Chuong.[98]

Almost another year elapsed before the departure of the Expeditionary Corps removed the last vestiges of French "presence" from Vietnam. On May 20, 1955, the French command agreed to retire its troops
from the Saigon-Cholon area. On July 2, 1955, the dependence of the
Vietnamese Army Command on the French High Command at last
came to an end.[99] By that time, the Expeditionary Corps, now concentrated in the vicinity of Cape St. Jacques, had been reduced from
175,000 to 30,000 men. Negotiations conducted at Paris in August,
1955, failed to produce agreement on the early withdrawal of all
French troops. But when Diem repeated his demand in March, 1956,
the French finally honored their promise made at Geneva to comply
with such a request. The last French soldier left South Vietnam on
April 28, 1956; on the same day, the French High Command for Indochina was officially dissolved.

France now desired to normalize her relations with South Vietnam.
On June 3, 1956, a parliamentary mission led by Frédéric-Dupont
came to Saigon with assurances of French friendship for Diem's Vietnam. In spite of continued expressions of resentment against U.S.
policy in Vietnam and of hostility toward Diem in much of the French

press, official France—the procolonial Right included—had apparently become reconciled to Ngo Dinh Diem and to the end of French political influence in Vietnam.

Direct and effective French interference, however, had already ended in May, 1955. This meant that the remaining sect forces, deprived of all French support, either had to submit or fight and risk total defeat. They had learned that submission was merely a road to political limbo, and they therefore decided to stake all on the slight chance that armed resistance might still bring about Diem's fall. Diem dealt with them separately. Since most of the military contingents of the Cao Dai had joined the government with the Generals The and Phuong, the problem of how to end the sect's political autonomy, although a delicate one because of its religious implications, required caution rather than strong military action. On October 5, 1955, General Phuong with some of his former military units went to the Cao Dai headquarters at Tay Ninh. He disarmed the 300-man-strong Papal Guard, arrested the two daughters of Pham Cong Tac, the Pope, on charges of corruption and exploitation of the people, and a few days later announced that he had deposed him. Tac remained at Tay Ninh until February, 1956, when the approach of government troops, allegedly called by the sect's high dignitaries to occupy the "Holy See," prompted him to flee to Cambodia, where he died soon afterward. As was to be expected, Diem eventually rid himself of Phuong also,[100] thus eliminating the military leadership of the Cao Dai as well.

A tougher problem was the liquidation of the Hoa Hao. They had made the mistake of giving only token help to the Binh Xuyen in the fighting between April 28 and 30, for they were interested mainly in defending their own fiefs. Since then they had interfered effectively with the flow of food from the Mekong Delta into Saigon. Before sending the army against them, Diem made one more attempt to buy them. Their four rival chiefs—Generalissimo Tran Van Soai, General Lam Thanh Nguyen, the war lord of Chaudoc, General Nguyen Gia Ngo, and Bacut—were not at all of one mind when, on May 24, they received an offer of 100 million piasters (about $1.2 million at the black-market rate) to rally to Diem. But at a meeting also attended by Bao Dai's emissary, General Nguyen Van Hinh, the offer was rejected, not without misgivings on the part of some.[101] The Hoa Hao leaders declared war on the government, but knowing that they were no match for the National Army in open battle, they abandoned their posts and bases after setting fire to their huts and stores and prepared themselves for guerrilla warfare. The government troops, led by General Duong Van Minh, started their offensive on June 5, at Cantho. Five Hoa Hao battalions surrendered immediately, and on June 18, General Nguyen Gia Ngo once again rallied to the government, this time for good.[102] Generalissimo Soai assembled his troops near the Cambodian border, where he was joined by Bao Dai's deposed chiefs of the National Army, Hinh and Vy. But Duong Van Minh's troops dispersed the Hoa Hao forces and on June 19, all three generals fled to Cambodia.[103] Their colleague Lam Thanh Nguyen decided to surrender. Soai himself made his final (and this time profitless) submission in February, 1956, offering his troops to Diem for the fight against "colonialism," which no longer existed, and against "Communism," which his ruthless exploitation of the people had helped to strengthen during the preceding ten years.[104] Hoa Hao resistance was reduced to guerrilla operations conducted by bands of the fanatical Bacut, but ended when Bacut was trapped and arrested in April, 1956. He was publicly beheaded at Cantho on July 13, 1956.

The end of the Binh Xuyen had already come in October, 1955. After months of leeches and mosquitos in the marshes and tidal waters of Rung Sat, and of growing despair, Le Van Vien's troops, surrounded and weakened by desertions, were attacked by the National Army and wiped out in a campaign that lasted four weeks. The Binh Xuyen soldiers who were not killed were captured or dispersed. Their chief, however, succeeded in escaping to France, where he settled down to enjoy the riches he had amassed while serving the French and Bao Dai. Thus ended the military history of the political-religious sects of Vietnam.

8

October, 1955, was also the month when another rotten relic of Vietnam's past was thrown on the junk heap of history: the monarchy, together with its last, unworthy reprseentative, Bao Dai. His fate was sealed when it became clear that the French, who had brought him back as chief of state, no longer directed the destiny of Vietnam. Bao Dai knew that the Americans, at best willing to tolerate him as an absent and nominal ruler, would never defend him if Diem decided that he must be removed. Early in May, 1955, Dulles had agreed in Paris that Bao Dai could be retained if he stopped interfering with Diem's exercise of power. But American dissatisfaction with the "playboy Emperor" was strongly expressed at this time on two occasions: in Paris, where Dulles refused to see Bao Dai, and in Saigon, at the farewell dinner for Ambassador Collins on May 14. Instead of the customary toast to the chief of state, Collins drank "to the people of Vietnam."

If Diem had not already decided in June, 1954, that he would one day remove Bao Dai, he certainly made up his mind after April, 1955. When the Generals Ty, Minh, and Do, on May 1, 1955 informed Bao Dai that they would follow only a regime chosen "by the will of the people," the astute former Emperor knew even before Diem let it be officially known how he was to be discarded: through a referendum on whether Vietnam should remain a monarchy or become a republic.

Diem lost no time and used every trick in his campaign to get rid of Bao Dai. On May 15, he abolished Bao Dai's Imperial Guard; its 5,000 men became the 11th and 42nd Infantry Regiments of the National Army. Diem's next move was to deprive Bao Dai of his extensive crown lands. On June 15, Diem got the archaic Council of the Royal Family at Hue to decide that Bao Dai should be stripped of all his prerogatives and he himself be elected President. On July 7, the first anniversary of his installation as Prime Minister, Diem announced that a national referendum would be held to decide the future form of government. The date set for it was October 23, 1955.

The one-sided "election campaign" that followed, and the methods employed to assure an almost unanimous vote for Diem were quite outrageous—unnecessarily so, since there could hardly have existed any doubt about the outcome of the referendum.

[The campaign] was conducted with such cynical disregard for decency and democratic principles that even the Viet Minh professed to be shocked. Whereas Bao Dai was given no opportunity to defend himself, the government-controlled press proceeded to overwhelm him with scurrilous abuse, special editions of local newspapers being devoted to giving very biased accounts of his life. The press campaign was supported by broadcasts and by posters and effigies depicting Bao Dai as a gambler, of associating him with a pig's head or in the process of caressing a woman with a sack of piasters on his back. In addition police agents and canvassers went from door to door explaining the unpleasant consequences which failure to vote would be likely to entail.[105]

But that was not all. The depth of indignity was reached with the printed ballots with one half showing Diem surrounded by youthful and modern-looking people against a red background (red being the color of good luck in Vietnam), and Bao Dai in old-fashioned robes (which he never wore), against a green background (green being a color of bad luck). The text under the picture of Diem read: "I depose Bao Dai and recognize Ngo Dinh Diem as Head of State, charged with the commission of setting up a democratic regime." Under Bao Dai's picture it said: "I do not depose Bao Dai and do not regard Ngo Dinh Diem as the Head of the State charged with the commission of setting up a democratic regime." The use of these methods to secure the victory of a good cause boded ill for the future of a regime whose leader liked to advertise his acts as morally inspired.

No one doubted what the outcome of the referendum would be. Bao Dai, on October 22, boasted: "I can even tell you that I know the percentage of favorable votes that Mr. Diem has decided to obtain." [106] But even Bao Dai did not foresee that the votes cast "in some cases exceeded the number of names on the electoral roll." [107] The 450,000 voters in Saigon, for instance, cast 605,000 votes, which the authorities, unable to deny the fact, "explained" by pointing out that people of adjacent communities had voted in Saigon. Everywhere the votes were counted by government officials without any kind of supervision, and favorable results were reported to Saigon even from regions where Bacut's Hoa Hao bands prevented voting. Diem received 98.2 per cent of all votes cast (5,721,735) and Bao Dai 1.1 per cent (63,017), "a margin of victory which . . . recalls elections in Communist states." [108] Or, as another Western observer remarked, "the referendum was not, and was not intended to be, an exercise in democratic procedures"; it was intended to be "a collective demonstration of loyalty to the ruling authority." [109]

Some voices were raised in Saigon against a referendum which was held merely to confirm the existing "system of one-man rule," [110] but Diem could afford to ignore them. The mass of the people had no reason to defend or feel sorry for Bao Dai; the forces of the past around Bao Dai were totally discredited; the army was now overwhelmingly loyal to Diem; the sects were virtually destroyed; France was no longer in a position to act in favor of Bao Dai; and the United States was just beginning to celebrate Diem as a new hero of the "free world."

Because Bao Dai knew all this, he had reacted to Diem's move to replace him too late and like a man tired of fighting a useless battle. He protested against the holding of the referendum on October 15, and asked the governments of France, the United States, Great Britain, India, and even the Soviet Union not to support the Diem regime, indicating that it was an obstacle to the peaceful reunification of Vietnam provided for in the Geneva agreements.[111] On October 18, he made the vain gesture of dismissing Diem. On October 19, he denounced "the police methods" of Diem's "dictatorship" and warned the Vietnamese people, somewhat prophetically, "against a regime that was bound to lead them to ruin, famine, and war," [112] a message which, like his dismissal of Diem, Saigon censorship prevented the Vietnamese people from reading. Old collaborators of the French, among them former Premier Tran Van Huu and the Generals Xuan and Hinh, had tried, in a meeting attended also by several sworn French enemies of Diem, to stir Bao Dai to action. Their plan was to have him set up a new "legitimate" government and install it somewhere in the country.[113] But Bao Dai was wise enough to realize that this would be only another useless gesture. He resigned himself to the loss of his position, settling for the unencumbered enjoyment of life, which was probably all he had ever wanted.

Diem, too, had at last achieved his goal: total fulfillment of his political aspirations. On October 26, 1955, he was proclaimed President of the new Republic of Vietnam. All his life he had been driven by an urgent desire to serve his country, but his wish that there be no one above him had been as strong as his desire to serve. Supreme power was all he had ever asked of life. Having achieved it neither surprised him nor made him humble. He was apparently convinced that his rise to power was simply a case of virtue and merit being justly rewarded.

But what did his victory portend for the future of Vietnam? There can be little doubt that in overcoming the opposition of the French, the army, the sects, and Bao Dai, Diem had warded off the universally expected collapse of the State of Vietnam and the swift extension of Vietminh rule over the entire country. South Vietnam had been given a chance. But Diem had created no more than a basis, and gained nothing more than time, for building a viable state. The more difficult part of his mission still lay ahead of him. Success or failure in building a state that could win the allegiance of the people would decide the fate of South Vietnam when the expected attempt to unify the country under the sign of Communism got under way. Now Diem had to show whether anti-Communist nationalism had at last found a leader who was a match for Ho Chi Minh.

9

When Ho Chi Minh returned to Hanoi in October, 1954, almost eight years had passed since his flight from the capital, eight years spent not as an exile abroad but in the jungles and mountains of the Viet Bac, as the leader of a revolutionary war. These long years of war must have been the hardest of his life, both morally and physically. But they had not broken him, nor had the hold he had gained over his government and a majority of the people before the war been weakened by the trials the country had undergone. In transferring the seat of his government back to Hanoi, Ho Chi Minh faced none of the difficulties of his antagonist in Saigon in gaining the power that would make his government real. There was no one to question Ho Chi Minh's right to supreme leadership and no significant force to oppose his government, which was still in the hands of the men whom the August revolution of 1945 had carried to power. Their control of the army, the police, the administration, and the mass organizations they had created was near total. The sects that threatened Diem's survival did not exist in the North. The Catholic militias that had fought the Vietminh chose to disband and join the exodus to the South; the French, who caused such serious trouble to Diem in Saigon were out of Hanoi before Ho Chi Minh's arrival; and if any other group had attempted to contest his government's return, it would instantly have been crushed by the Vietminh.

The last French troops left Hanoi on October 9. The French flag was lowered for the last time in a ceremony at the Mangin Stadium. It was solemnly handed over to the Commander of the Hanoi citadel, Colonel d'Argence, an old officer with a long record of service in Indochina. He was also given the honor of being the last French soldier to leave Hanoi—on foot over the Doumer Bridge, that first great monument of French colonial aspirations in the Far East. Seventy-two years of French "presence" in Hanoi ended on that day.

Both the transfer of governmental authority to the Vietminh and the replacement of the French garrison by Vietminh troops were effected without friction. The administrative personnel of the State of Vietnam had long since gone to Haiphong, together with the last contingents of the Vietnamese National Army; and so had Diem's Committee for the Defense of the North, whose members made themselves useful ministering to the refugees who waited at Haiphong for the boats to carry them South. Vietminh civil servants had begun to arrive in Hanoi on October 3, and Ha Dong, adjacent to Hanoi, had been handed over to detachments of the 308th Vietminh Division on October 6. These and other troops, most of them back from Dien Bien Phu, were assembled in the suburbs of Hanoi on October 9. They marched into town on October 10, and in an impressive military parade celebrated their victory over the French. The city had been richly decked out with Vietminh flags and banners, and the cadres, their task made easy by the understandable curiosity of the population, saw to it that the army received a warm welcome. But there were no frenetic outbursts of joy. Neither Ho Chi Minh nor any other prominent leader was present to lift the somewhat somber mood of the masses, whose capacity for enthusiasm had apparently been worn thin by nine years of exhortations to struggle, suffer, and die for their country. Peace was welcome to all, but too many citizens of Hanoi had reason to be afraid of the future.

Like the Catholic provinces in the south delta, Hanoi, too, saw a mass exodus of people who feared for their safety under a Vietminh regime that no longer disguised its Communist orientation. These refugees included not only collaborators and war profiteers, but also officials, professors and students, journalists and artists who had professed anti-Communist sentiments, businessmen who had the wisdom to foresee that they would sooner or later lose their possessions, and the many dependents of officers and soldiers of the retiring National Army. But great numbers of the property-owning native middle class —shopkeepers, small merchants, people engaged in businesses too trifling to have been monopolized by the French and some lawyers, doctors, and other professionals who did not want to leave their homes and practices—stayed on. Rather than give up their established sources of income and to abandon most of their possessions, they chose the risks of staying behind, under the common illusion that of the two evils they faced, the more remote one was also the lesser. On October 10, these people, rightly apprehensive that the failure to greet the Vietminh soldiers would mark them as enemies of the regime, watched the well-staged parade, but the fear in their hearts made their expression of welcome understandably feeble.[114]

No festivities were organized to greet the Vietminh leaders as they moved from their Viet Bac hiding places into Hanoi. They traveled unannounced and arrived unseen. The first one to appear publicly was Giap. On October 12, he inspected the Vietminh garrison that had replaced the French at the citadel, and, apparently concerned with matters more vital than public receptions for purposes of propaganda, he went to the Hanoi power station to greet the French engineers who had consented to remain till the end of the year. This had been agreed upon in a meeting between Vietminh delegates and the French technician in charge of municipal works (water, electricity, and transport) on October 2. (Others who agreed tentatively to stay on were some scholars of the French School of Far Eastern Studies and of the Radium and Pasteur Institutes, and a number of professors, with whose cooperation the University of Hanoi was reopened on October 11.)

The next leader to be heard of, although he was not seen by the public, was Ho Chi Minh himself, who, on October 17, greeted the first official visitor to his "liberated" capital, Indian Prime Minister Jawaharlal Nehru, who stopped briefly at Hanoi on his way to Peking. Not until January 1, 1955, did Ho Chi Minh show himself to the people. Facing an estimated crowd of 200,000, he gainsaid all rumors of ill health by watching, for five and a half hours, one of those interminable parades from which the Communists seem to derive a special sense of power. Throughout it all, Ho Chi Minh never stopped waving to the marchers and the applauding crowds.[115] It was the best show the Party organizers had ever staged, but it was also the last one for a long time to come at which the waves of popular enthusiasm rolled so spontaneously toward the assembled dignitaries of the regime.

Hard times lay ahead for the people of North Vietnam. Their yearning for a minimum of economic prosperity and some political freedom was not to be fulfilled with the coming of peace and the realization of independence. Colonialism was dead, but misery and unfreedom continued to be the people's lot. For many long years they would have to endure the pain of hunger and uncared-for disease. And in the political conflicts that these conditions were bound to produce, terror would still remain the government's chief weapon against popular discontent.

Some of the difficulties the country experienced resulted no doubt from eight years of war and from the partition of Vietnam. The North would henceforth be deprived of the vital food reserves of the South. To repair what had been destroyed during the war would have made any government exhort its people to greater effort and sacrifice. There is no doubt that the Communist leaders of North Vietnam had the intelligence to realize and the courage to attack the staggering problems they had inherited. It would be ridiculous to claim that they were not concerned about the material conditions of the people. But their desperate efforts to secure an adequate diet for the people were subordinated to their chief concern—namely, a radical transformation of society according to what both they and their enemies called the "Marxist" blueprint. No matter what unnecessary suffering this would cause, or what brutal terror it would require, North Vietnam had to be turned into a "socialist" state immediately, one in which neither economic difficulties nor social discontent would ever challenge the power of the ruling political group, the Communist Party.

10

If Ho Chi Minh's power, after his return to Hanoi in October, 1954, was as supreme as any revolutionary leader could desire, this did not mean that his regime did not face serious troubles, nor that it would remain unchallenged in the exercise of power. The problems that Ho Chi Minh faced, however, were not of the petty kind that forced Ngo Dinh Diem to devote himself to the negative task of mere survival for a whole year. The troubles that soon began to bedevil the Hanoi regime, far from being caused by lack of strength, were the result of an excess of power, which in October, 1954, was nearly total.

The task of rebuilding the country—the North having suffered more destruction than the South—demanded superhuman sacrifices, particularly in view of its hectic pace and the exhaustion and malnutrition of the people. The railroad from Hanoi to the Chinese border at Langson, for instance, was rebuilt in less than six months—a gigantic task requiring the recruitment of 80,000 workers. Tens of thousands worked with too little food and almost no medical care, repairing dams and roads and rebuilding the many hundreds of blown-up bridges. The conditions under which this so-called "voluntary" work force was made to labor were in many respects as bad as had been those of the "coolies" of the colonial regime. To ask devotion to reconstruction of the people was undoubtedly justified, but the demand for superhuman sacrifices and suffering as a patriotic duty was due to the excessive power and ambition of the leaders.

It was precisely this kind of power, and this kind of ambition, that led the Hanoi regime to regard rapid reconstruction as only a first step toward their real goal—nothing less than an immediate transformation of the country's social structure, of radical changes in a people's way of life. Within the shortest possible time, this economically underdeveloped country whose mainstay was its peasants was to become a modern industrial society. The Vietminh leaders intended to accomplish in a few years a task which in more advanced nations had taken many decades. Treading in the bloody footsteps of the Soviet revolution, the regime turned on the peasants, taking more from them than they could spare, keeping them overtaxed and undernourished. None of the meager imports the country could afford, and little of the foreign aid it soon received, went into alleviating the misery of the masses. Whereas in the "good old days" luxury imports had taken priority over badly needed consumer goods, now industrial equipment took priority over such badly needed goods as medicines and textiles and even food stuffs to supplement the country's own woefully insufficient food production. Since the tenet that industrialization alone attacked the country's poverty at the roots was easily proved, the regime felt fully justified in maintaining the lowest possible living standard for the sake of getting industries as fast as possible. Once again the end justified the means. All misery was supposed to end in the future, which was described as rather too rosy and too near.

Such at least was the promise, no doubt based on firm beliefs; and if this were the whole story, the course chosen by the leaders of North Vietnam, although still open to criticism, could not be wholly condemned. The truth, however, is that other ways of achieving the same goal existed, and there was little sense in trying to industrialize the country rapidly. Factories could have been built at a slower rate, and machines acquired by other means than by maintaining the lowest possible living standard. Industrialization through the people's sweat and privations was not dictated by circumstances; it was imposed upon the people by their leaders' political philosophy, by the wish of these men to realize their concept of society, and, above all, by their concern for power: They wanted quickly to create social conditions on which the monopoly of power they had achieved could rest securely. This meant that old classes had to be abolished and new ones created through the systematic intervention of the state in the country's economy.

Given the two basic assumptions of the Vietminh leadership, namely that "Communism" as a social system could flourish only in an industrial society, and that the only secure basis for the power of the Communist Party was a large, well-organized, and firmly indoctrinated working class, industrialization had to be pursued in such a manner so as not to lead to the development of a class of capitalists or of any other social group potentially hostile to the regime. Industrialization, therefore, could not be left to private initiative or capital, which in the case of Vietnam could only have been foreign. It had to be brought about by the state. Moreover, for the same political reasons, existing classes of property owners had to be destroyed, by force if necessary. This meant that not only capitalists, foreign or native, large or small, but also the remaining class of "rich" peasants and so-called landlords —people who owned more than the usual one-acre lot—had to be abolished.

With a touch of megalomania which was not diminished by their victory over the French, the Vietminh leaders embarked upon their self-imposed task, a truly monstrous task, since even its fragmentary realization required inhuman means. The blueprint called for control of the entire economy by the same men who controlled the state. The existing mines, and the many new ones to be opened, were to be run by the government. Factories, being not only privately owned but even largely in foreign hands, had to be taken over by the state. It was the task of the state to build the many new industries needed to make the country prosperous and economically independent. But this was not all. Small private enterprise too, such as existed in transportation, retail trade, and family-scale handicraft production, had to be nationalized, or made into "cooperatives" as a means of subjecting it to state control.

The extent to which this economic policy was motivated by a desire for absolute political control of the population became apparent in the measures taken in the field of agriculture. Economically, these measures made no sense. They did not lead to the predicted increase in productivity, which, important as it was, was only a secondary Communist aim. The chief purpose of the so-called agrarian reform in

North Vietnam was to subject agricultural production, and the producers, to state control. This was achieved mainly through terror, which produced the first and only serious wave of popular opposition against the Vietminh regime. At the end of 1956, when it seemed that Ngo Dinh Diem had at last cleared his path for positive action, Ho Chi Minh was in deeper trouble with his people than at any time since his accession to power in 1945. And unlike Ngo Dinh Diem's troubles, which were caused by his political enemies, the troubles of Ho Chi Minh were entirely of his own making.

11

The leaders of the Hanoi regime attacked the job of reconstruction with the energy for which they were known, determined to complete it in the shortest possible time. A certain amount of foreign aid was immediately made available to them. The Soviet Union, China, Poland, and Czechoslovakia were the main suppliers of the equipment needed to repair the war damages. But only by recklessly consuming the people's physical energy could the North boast that it made greater progress in reconstruction than the South.

However, the pitiless exploitation of labor could not solve certain problems of reconstruction, one of which was caused by the parting blow delivered to the Vietminh by the retiring Franco-Vietnamese administration. Under the direction of Diem's Committee for the Defense of the North, everything movable of any value, both public and private property, was transported to the docks of Haiphong and shipped to the South. Broadcasting stations, railroad repair shops, and harbor installations were dismantled, post offices, libraries, and laboratories were stripped of equipment, the radium from the X-ray machines in the Hanoi hospitals and the Cancer Institute was removed, and most factories were emptied of machinery, tools, raw materials, and finished products. The French had agreed in Geneva that all public institutions and services were to be handed over to the Hanoi regime in working order, but the anti-Communist Vietnamese authorities, whom the French had not even consulted on this matter, did not feel obliged to honor this agreement. The French Government, however, did honor it, and subsequently paid the Hanoi regime the sum of 265 million francs in reparations.[116] The Vietnamese who went South must surely have felt that the removal of these goods was justified, since they themselves left behind jobs, furniture, houses, and land; but to use these goods to compensate individuals for their losses was neither intended nor ever attempted by the authorities in the South.

The number of those who lost almost everything they owned was enormous. Most of the nearly 900,000 persons who came South must be regarded as genuine political refugees.[117] The dangers to which they would have been exposed if they had remained, or even merely their fear of living under a Communist regime, left them no choice but to leave, abandoning their possessions, whether considerable or small. How great was the number whose losses were considerable can be seen from a breakdown into social categories of the total number of refugees, which according to one official source, was estimated to have totaled 927,000. Of these, 706,000 were peasants who lost all their land, 88,000 fishermen, and 133,000 artisans, small businessmen, government employees, students, and professionals.

Official statistics also say that of the total number of refugees, 794,000 were Catholics. Although statistical confusion seems to make it impossible to determine the exact number of Catholic refugees, which might have been as low as 600,000,[118] there is no doubt that they accounted for more than 60 per cent of the total. The Communists have tried to show that going South was not a personal decision for many of the Catholics, who were said to have left under pressure of the community, which, led by priests, departed as a group. The majority, said the Communists, were induced to leave through anti-Vietminh religious propaganda: The priests were accused of having spread the word that God had gone South, that those who remained North would risk losing their souls, and probably also their lives, since the North would be destroyed by American atomic bombs.[119] If these Communist charges, and the instructions by Hanoi to treat the Catholics with prudence, proved that the regime was embarrassed by the scope of the exodus, there is nevertheless reason to believe that Communist discomfort over this psychological blow to their regime was mixed with relief. The regime was freed of a great many implacable enemies, and close to half a million acres of excellent rice land became available for distribution.

Although these lands were quickly distributed, a loss in rice production could not be avoided. And although the Soviet-bloc countries promptly began to replace much of the equipment that had been "stolen" by the authorities of the South, it was not until a year or two after the end of the war that many public services again began to function normally. But the losses suffered caused no more than temporary inconvenience to the regime, without damaging its reputation or threatening its political supremacy.

As procedures were started and pushed on all fronts to cement Communist control over the economy and the people, there was the problem of how to extend this control over the possessions of the French. For quite a while the regime proceeded with great circumspection against the French-owned companies and their managers and technicians. In 1954, about 150 French-owned industrial and commercial concerns were still operating in the North. Among the larger ones were the coal mines of Hongay and Campha, the Portland Cement Factory and glass works of Haiphong, the cotton mills at Nam Dinh, the French-owned breweries and distilleries at Hanoi, and the ship yards and port services at Haiphong. The water and electricity companies of both cities were also French-owned, as was the Yunnan Railway and all public transportation.

In a letter to the French Government written immediately after the end of the Geneva conference, Foreign Minister Pham Van Dong had given assurances of the unhampered operation of French economic enterprises and cultural institutions, but had been ambiguous about French interests in cases of requisition or expropriation.[120] To an observer unfamiliar with Communist strategy, it must have looked as if the Hanoi regime really intended to respect the established French business interests and that it even would try to attract new French investments. Early in December, 1954, two French businessmen, one of them the director of the Renault automobile works, visited Hanoi to see whether such opportunities really existed.[121] On December 10, an agreement was announced by the government spelling out the rather liberal conditions for continued French economic activity.[122]

The efforts to safeguard private French business interests and to maintain a maximum of economic cooperation between France and the Democratic Republic of Vietnam were assiduously promoted through the political contacts that the French Government established with the Hanoi regime. This was the so-called Sainteny Mission, headed by Jean Sainteny, one of the authors of the Franco-Vietminh agreement of March, 1946. Highly overestimating his own diplomatic skill, Sainteny was apparently convinced that with the end of the war, Franco-

Vietminh cooperation had again become possible. The fact that it had failed in 1946 seems not to have dismayed him. He accepted his new assignment and installed himself in Hanoi on October 8.[123] On October 17, 1954, he conferred with Pham Van Dong, and a day later he had the first of his many meetings with Ho Chi Minh, on whom he presumed to have more influence than any other Frenchman. As with all foreign visitors he agreed to see, Ho Chi Minh was consistently friendly toward Sainteny, but became less conciliatory as time went on. The Hanoi Government wanted to be represented at Paris and resented the refusal of the French Government to accept a delegation similar to the Sainteny mission. France was attacked with growing ill-temper for her adherence to SEATO and for her support of American policy in the South. But more important still, developments soon proved that the Communists had never intended to let the French keep what they had, and certainly would not allow new French investments. Stunned by the difficulties of keeping the existing industries in operation, the regime briefly considered a period of cooperation with French business, but soon dropped these short-term practical considerations in favor of its strict and narrow economic doctrines. It was decided that socialism must be established immediately, and totally independent of the capitalist world.

To some extent this decision was forced upon the regime by the attitude of the French, who, like the Vietminh, also pursued a contradictory policy in regard to future Franco-Vietminh economic cooperation. Not only French policy, more and more subordinate to Washington in regard to both Vietnams, but French business as well made no real effort to persuade the Hanoi leaders that it would be worthwhile for them to forget their economic orthodoxy, at least temporarily. Many French firms had dismantled their factories before the French Army, in accordance with the Geneva agreement, evacuated Haiphong on May 13, 1955. Of course, the French businessmen knew that attempts at cooperation made by their compatriots in Shanghai with the Chinese Communists were doomed; they also feared, not without reason, that any French firm operating in Communist North Vietnam might be exposed to American reprisals. Furthermore, the French rightly suspected that ultimately the Communists would expropriate all existing and all new private investments, foreign as well as native. They were cautious from the beginning and were never in real danger of being trapped.

On the other hand, the Communists did not really try very hard to persuade French business that it would be advantageous and safe to invest in a Communist state. They were unreasonable in their negotiations and petty in their treatment of the French engineers and technicians who had agreed to stay on. Although the country was sadly lacking in trained personnel and could not even have kept public services going without French help, let alone put the mines and factories back in operation, they treated the French technicians like suspected spies or saboteurs. Rather than trust these "servants of capitalism" or admit that without them the country and its economy could not be properly run, the Communist regime risked malfunction and breakdown in its public services and delays in reopening the existing factories and mines. As a result, the French technicians left, and the French companies continued to remove from their plants whatever was worth the cost of transport. The regime, on the other hand, even before it turned to Peking and Moscow for massive economic assistance, moved rapidly toward a policy of outright expropriation. As a matter of fact, all French enterprises were nationalized before the end of 1955, and, with two notable exceptions, all without compensation. The exceptions were the coal mines and public transportation in Hanoi. By agreement of April 8, 1955, the Société des Charbonnages du Tonkin sold its mines to the state for one million tons of coal, to be delivered in fifteen yearly installments.[124] In June, 1955, the Public Transport Company of Hanoi sold out to the government for 300 million francs, to be paid over a period of thirty years. After the hopes of the French to preserve their business interests in the North had died, the Sainteny mission, whose activities turned out to be pointless, gradually died, too.

Even before the last French technicians had left, the regime had begun to replace them with an inadequate number of Chinese and Russian experts, and their arrival marked the beginning of Chinese and Soviet-bloc aid. Nonmilitary aid from China began soon after the government's return to Hanoi and contributed greatly to the regime's rapid progress in the task of reconstruction. The first aid agreement with Peking was concluded in December, 1954.[125] It provided for the delivery of equipment for the repair of roads, railroads, water works, and the postal and telegraph services. Chinese technicians supervised the rebuilding and conversion to the Chinese gauge of the Hanoi-Langson Railroad, whose reopening was celebrated on March 4, 1955, in the presence of international guests of honor. But if the regime's ambitious plans were to be realized, aid on a much vaster scale and over a period of many years was needed. To obtain such aid, Ho Chi Minh left for Peking on June 22, 1955, accompanied by his Ministers of Finance, Industry, Agriculture, Education, and Health. In a joint communiqué of July 7, the two governments announced that Peking would extend Hanoi economic aid in the amount of 800 million yuan (about $200 million).

From Peking, Ho and his party proceeded to Moscow. The Soviet Union announced on July 18 that it would grant Hanoi 400 million rubles (about $100 million) in economic aid. (The amount of military aid North Vietnam received from Peking and Moscow was, of course, never made public.) Russia, too, had already begun to assist the Hanoi regime before the agreement of July, 1955. The Soviets had supplied new mining equipment, which enabled the regime to keep the old coal mines in operation and open a new one at Quang Tri. Of greater importance, however, was a three-cornered deal between the Soviet Union, Burma, and the Hanoi regime at the beginning of 1955, through which North Vietnam received badly needed rice from Burma paid for with Russian industrial equipment. Food had become so scarce that rationing was imposed in all cities. Rice which in normal times had gone North was available in the South—about 250,000 tons yearly. But the Diem regime refused any kind of economic exchange with the North, in the hope that food shortages would lead to serious political troubles for Ho Chi Minh. There is no doubt that without the Burmese rice, the North would have suffered widespread famine in 1955.

Apart from demands for pharmaceutical products and help in organizing medical services, the rice deal involving Burma was the only instance of aid being sought for the direct benefit of the suffering people. All other aid obtained from China and Russia, and later also from other "fraternal countries"—Poland, Czechoslovakia, Hungary, Romania, and East Germany—was directed toward speedy reconstruction and industrialization.

The equipment received comprised not only industrial and mining machinery, but also cranes, buses, microscopes, and office machines. But without foreign technicians—engineers, chemists, physicians, and managerial personnel down to bookkeeping teachers—it would have taken years before the former French enterprises were fully reactivated; the country would probably have suffered a breakdown of most public services, and certainly would not have succeeded in creating new industries, both heavy and light, with such astonishing speed.

Critics have for years rightly dwelled on the shortcomings and failures of the regime's economic policies, above all on the low living standard of the people resulting from these policies.[126] Even after the threat of famine had been averted by relatively good harvests in 1955 and 1956, the diet of the North Vietnamese remained woefully inadequate and for years consumer goods were virtually unavailable to the masses. Such goods were produced in growing quantities, but not for the population, which continued to suffer under a painful lack of basic necessities. The new industries, even those producing consumer goods, such as tea plants and a very modern fish cannery, worked chiefly for export. Exports, in particular coal, cement, tin, phosphates, and other minerals, increased steadily, but the profits from them were used primarily for the purchase of more and more industrial equipment. If a Communist had proposed slowing down the rate of industrial growth and using the earnings from export to acquire consumer goods, he would probably have been denounced as a "counterrevolutionary." True, among the goods received from the "fraternal countries," either as gifts or through barter, were many items that would eventually contribute to a higher living standard. East Germany, for instance, supplied an ocean-fishing fleet, Czechoslovakia some crop-dusting aircraft, and Mongolia 100,000 head of breeding cattle together with experts to teach the Vietnamese how to care for these animals. But the regime refused to import textiles, shoes, or essential household utensils, and it allocated a minimum of its resources to their production at home. For many years the people were in rags, undernourished, forced to walk miles for lack of transportation, and uncared for if sick. The industrial workers, who were considered vital for building and defending the socialist state, were better treated than the peasants, traders, and artisans. But when more goods, better medical care, and even some recreation and entertainment became available, these were largely limited to the privileged minority in governmental and Party positions. For almost everybody else life remained dreary in North Vietnam, and for some, politically persecuted, it was worse than under the colonial regime.

The only thing given the people in truly generous quantities was propaganda. To be sure, there was truth in the promise that the shining new factories would eventually also benefit the people, but since the paeans sung to them in statistics and editorials could neither feed nor cover and cure the suffering bodies of the people, no mass enthusiasm for the regime was generated by this propaganda. Enthusiasm about the progress made in "socialist reconstruction" remained restricted to the ruling elite and the privileged lower echelons of the Party and the administration.

These groups, who had reason to be content, found it easy to show pride in the regime's remarkable achievements in industrialization. They were ecstatic about the vast industrial combine around the steel mills that had been built with fantastic speed in the province of Thai Nguyen, and of the great tool factory at Hanoi, probably still the most modern such plant in Southeast Asia. Proudly they pointed to the two air-conditioned tea plants near Phu Tho, at the Soviet-built phosphate plant at Lam Thao, and at another enterprise, also built by the Soviets, for canning and freezing fish at Haiphong—chiefly for export. The Chinese built ten factories, all before 1960, for plywood, matches, tobacco, porcelain, plastics, and kitchenware. But even these factories worked largely for export, to add to the profit from the growing quantities of cement, coal, phosphate, and other minerals traded abroad for new equipment. And the new factories for which this equipment was needed again produced largely for sale abroad, or to pay for the aid received from the fraternal countries.

Some of North Vietnam's modern factories compare favorably with the most advanced production sites anywhere in the world, as for instance the electro-chemical complex at Viet Tri, which normally produces sugar, but can, during a slack season, switch to the production of antibiotics and industrial alcohol. Another unique plant makes paper from pressed cane. Indeed, even before the Soviet Union in 1960 gave Hanoi a long-term loan for forty-three new industrial plants, North Vietnam was well on the road toward becoming the most industrialized country of Southeast Asia. Along the 10 mile-stretch between Ha Dong and Hanoi, which was virtually a desert in 1954, one factory now stands next to the other.[127]

If these factories survive the second Indochina War, there is no doubt that they will soon help make good the promise of supplying the population with badly needed consumer goods, some of which are already available in modest quantities. Textile production, although still behind the country's needs, has substantially increased and has done much to alter the formerly shabby appearance of the people, for so long a characteristic of Hanoi and other cities. Bicycles, a necessity for all city dwellers, are now manufactured in the country, and although they are said to be of poorer quality than the old French product, they are eagerly bought. The same is true of pharmaceuticals and many household goods. But austerity will remain the lot of the masses for a long time to come—as it is, incidentally, in many other Asian countries, most of which have made less progress in industrialization than North Vietnam.

There is another front on which the Hanoi regime, thanks to its foreign aid, has advanced rapidly: in the training of the personnel needed to run the factories, the public services, and the many new institutions through which the state directs and controls the country's economic life. From the very beginning, Chinese and Soviet aid strongly emphasized this training, particularly of technicians, but also of factory workers requiring special skills. Thousands of students and workers have gone to China and Russia during the last ten years to be trained in factories, technical schools, and universities. Even larger numbers were trained at home by foreign experts. Schools were opened, headed by instructors from Russia, China, and several other countries. Physicians from East Germany and meteorologists from Poland, for instance, directed the training of local professional personnel. Still, for many years, there were not enough Vietnamese and foreign engineers for all power plants, railroad workshops, flood-control systems, mines, and factories. But this problem was also beginning to be solved when the first class of 633 engineers graduated from the Hanoi Polytechnical Institute in December, 1961. But the Hanoi regime is still in need of highly skilled specialists, and many hundreds of young people are still being sent to Chinese and Russian universities. But as in many other respects, North Vietnam, which wishes to grow economically without having to rely on China and Russia, has almost succeeded in making itself independent of this kind of foreign aid.[128] By 1963, the regime could boast not only that the bulk of its industry was run by native technicians, but also of having its own banking and foreign-trade experts, its own (but still not very competent) statisticians, and thousands of new, young doctors, research workers, teachers, and professors.

Less than ten years after the initiation of North Vietnam's ambitious program of industrialization, the country was producing items which are not as yet produced in the South: machine tools, electric motors, office equipment, bicycle tires, and even small ocean craft, forerunners of more ambitious marine construction. The number of workers in heavy industry alone jumped from 20,000 to 40,000 between 1957 and 1960. Urban employment expanded greatly. In 1960, Hanoi had a population of 638,600, Haiphong of 367,300, which means that both cities had doubled in size since the prewar years.

If the regime of Ho Chi Minh had been as successful on other fronts as it was in pushing industrialization,[129] it could easily have claimed to have been more successful in fighting its congenital economic ills than any other underdeveloped country, whether aided by East or West.

12

The impressive achievements of the Hanoi regime in the field of industry once more offer a lesson which Western critics of Communism have difficulty in learning: that the Communists are capable of achieving success under the most adverse conditions, and that they can overcome the grave errors and basic faults of their economic policy by being energetic, persistent, and, above all, ruthless in imposing sacrifices on the people.

But persistence and ruthlessness failed to produce spectacular results in the vast field of small-scale, nonagricultural economic activity, in which the Vietnamese had always played a role under the colonial regime—i.e., in small manufacturing and transportation enterprises, in trade and the marketing of goods on the lower levels, and in traditional handicraft production. Even after 1960, when industrial output had already risen considerably, handicraft shops and artisans still accounted for more than half of all nonagricultural production.

As in all other fields, here, too, Communist motivation was primarily political, aiming at the elimination of a property-owning middle class and at establishing government control over this part of the economy. A variety of means was employed to achieve this end. One was political terror. Known or suspected enemies of the regime belonging to this class, basically anti-Communist, were arrested, imprisoned, or sent to labor camps. Their possessions were confiscated. Many more, chiefly those in retail trade, went out of business because the goods in which they traded were no longer available, while others were ruined through excessive taxation. The government controlled all credit facilities, as well as the supply of most raw materials for artisans and handicraft workers. All imported goods were purchased by government agencies and marketed through government retail outlets. The aim was to abolish, together with the class of traders, all traces of a free market, and to dictate the prices at which the small producer could buy and sell.

However, the fewer consumer goods the government was ready to buy abroad, the greater was its interest in maintaining local production. For this reason, outright expropriation of small enterprises was avoided. Under the slogan "peaceful socialization," the regime turned most of them into joint state and private enterprises. "Capitalists" whose managerial and technical skills were indispensable were kept in their former positions, but were paid off gradually as co-owners, ending up as salaried employees of the state. This group of businessmen, which the Communists called the "national bourgeoisie" and classified as "former exploiters," has ceased to exist. Statistically, it is now submerged in the class of "manual and intellectual workers," whose number was given as 750,000 at the end of 1961.[130]

Small traders and artisans met a different fate. They were designated as "toilers," not as "exploiters," and regarded as a segment of the working class. It was thought that their adherence to the Communist state, which was not taken for granted, nevertheless could be brought about through some alteration in their social status. The aim was to change them from "individual workers" into "collective workers," by making handicraft production "cooperative." Such cooperatives had little effect on the working process and certainly did not result in increased production. But they greatly modified the position of these workers in society, chiefly by ending their freedom to buy and sell and produce what they wanted. They were now under state control, exercised directly through the various types of cooperatives into which the handicraft workers were gently pressed. However, in spite of their new status as collective workers, these people, according to a most authoritative official source, continued to cling to their old habits of private ownership, resisting cooperative production and maintaining "a more or less spontaneous tendency to capitalism." [131]

This complaint was even truer of the small traders, who, in spite of also being classified as "toilers," fared considerably worse than the handicraft workers. The government wanted to reduce their numbers drastically and to force those who remained in business into marketing and purchasing cooperatives. Although many were ruined by heavy taxation and by the state-owned retail stores, thereby adding to the number of urban unemployed, the attempt to transform these people into genuine members of the "working class" failed conspicuously. At most, half joined cooperatives, and only about 5 per cent changed from trade to production.[132] The true extent of the regime's failure to integrate this group into its socialist economy was revealed during the food crises of 1960 and 1962. Strict food rationing in the cities and pressure in the villages for more food deliveries at official prices led to widespread peasant hoarding, to the unauthorized slaughtering of animals, and to clandestine food sales. A government paper reported in August, 1962, that the "free" markets in Hanoi "have attracted as many as 6,000 persons who have given up their old professions for trade." [133]

What was even more distressing for the masters of the North than this "resurgence of capitalism" was its cause, the direct result of the regime's failure to provide enough food for the country's rapidly increasing population. The annual rate of increase is 3.5 per cent, which means that 600,000 or more new mouths to be fed are added each year to the almost 16 million counted in the 1960 census. Since the North had been a food-deficit area long before it became Communist, the task of feeding the people without sizable imports would have been difficult under any conditions. Only 5 million of the country's 40-million acreage are arable, and most of this land is already under intensive cultivation. With great efforts, some rice land, but mostly land for crops other than rice, can be opened up. But rice still accounts for more than 95 per cent of all food production. The real solution of the food problem, therefore, would have to be increased productivity of the existing rice lands through improved production methods and incentives for the peasants to work harder and take better care of their land.

North Vietnam's rice crop was 3.6 million tons in 1955. The regime's target was more than double this amount for 1960—an indication of the leaders' estimate of existing and growing needs: The population increase alone demanded an additional 200,000 tons annually. But instead of the projected 7.6 million tons, the 1960 harvest produced merely 4.1 million. "In other words, in terms of essential rice production, the first North Vietnamese economic plan fell 3.5 million tons, or almost 50 per cent, short of its original target." [134]

The main reason for this spectacular failure was the policy adopted by the regime toward the peasants, the more than four-fifths of the population living in the country's 15,000 villages. This is the story of the land reform in Communist North Vietnam, a story not only of economic failure, but also of unbelievable terror, of disastrous misman-agement on all Party levels, and of a crisis brought on by widespread popular discontent, which the regime was able to overcome only by a combination of brutal force and hasty political retreat.

The land policy of the Vietminh before 1953 had cautiously avoided frightening "rich peasants" or even "landlords" by raising the issue of land distribution. Both production and the war effort might have suf-fered from a radical program of agrarian reform. The only lands con-fiscated were those of "traitors," and the only reforms undertaken con-cerned land-rent reductions and lower interest rates for loans. That this restraint was a tactical one Truong Chinh, the Secretary of the Lao Dong Party, put beyond all doubt in 1950, in a report which quite openly stated the ultimate goal of Communist land policy in North Vietnam: the socialization of agriculture.[135]

The first steps of this radical approach to the land problem, which were decided upon in March, 1953, seemed not at all designed to pro-mote the Party's real goal. They called for a redistribution of all land in favor of landless agricultural laborers and poor peasants, which was, to say the least, a very indirect move toward collectivization. But the Party knew that the road toward "socialized agriculture" would be long, and that a number of political problems would have to be solved before more direct steps toward its goal could be taken. One of these problems was how to abolish not only "landlordism," but also the basi-cally anti-Communist class of the so-called rich peasants; another was to create a mass basis for the regime by gaining the gratitude and sup-port of the landless and the poor peasants, who together formed the great majority of the rural population. They would own the land dis-tributed by the regime. But the Communists foresaw that when all land was divided into more or less equal holdings, most families would still not own enough land. It was then that the peasant would have to be convinced of the necessity to collectivize agriculture.

Most revealing of the political motivation underlying the agrarian reform was the manner in which the actual distribution of land was organized. The rural population was divided into five categories: land-lords, rich peasants, middle peasants, poor peasants, and landless agri-cultural laborers. However, the intention to take from the rich and give to the poor was only half of the scheme. In order to eliminate landlords and rich peasants as a social class, it was not enough to reduce them, through partial expropriation, to the status of middle or poor peasants. Since they were rightly regarded as enemies of Communism, and in particular of collectivized agriculture, they had to be eliminated from village life, if necessary physically. To this end, they were accused of all sorts of crimes, tried, sentenced to prison or forced labor, and the more unfortunate ones to death. The physical removal of as many as possible had another advantage: Those imprisoned or killed were of course totally dispossessed. The greater their numbers, the more land became available for distribution to those whom the Communists wished to win over.

Nothing in the history of Communist persecutions can equal the scheme contrived in North Vietnam to get rid of as many peasants as possible who owned more than 2 or 3 acres of land. As a prelude to the ugly spectacle of publicly trying and punishing these people, a hate-campaign was organized among the poor against the "rich," under the direction of specially trained Party cadres. Trial and punishment were not left to existing qualified courts but to People's Agricultural Reform Tribunals created for this purpose. They consisted of all the poor and landless of a village, and the trials became mass meetings dominated by people whose chances of obtaining land increased with every new conviction. This entailed classifying as many landowners as possible as landlords and rich peasants, and finding as many as possible guilty of crimes against the people and the state. But the trouble was that the North had always had few real landlords, and most of these had long been expropriated as "traitors." More than 60 per cent of all land was in the hands of peasants owning around 1 acre, and the number of "rich peasants" was bound to be small, unless those with 2–3 acres were classified as "rich." There was an embarrassing dearth of landlords. In many regions, therefore, the cadres could deliver the necessary quota of victims to the Agricultural Reform Tribunals only by promoting owners of as little as 2–4 acres to the status of "landlords." And in order to obtain enough sentences, either to prison or forced labor or death, crimes had to be invented and charges leveled, even against people who had always supported the Vietminh. There were of course many landowners who had cruelly exploited and mistreated the poor, but the Party was not interested in justice. Its aim was the eradication of a social class, and to this end it mobilized hate and greed, and the desire for personal vengeance. The entire procedure was designed not only to gain enough land to make distribution worthwhile, but also to make the poor peasants and the landless accomplices of the regime in the crimes committed against the "rich."

The first "wave" of land reform—a dress rehearsal in land distribution through "mass mobilization"—rolled over a few provinces in 1953,[136] but fear that the action might get out of control and harm the war effort made the Vietminh leaders decide to call a halt.[137] In 1955, however, when the war had ended and the regime's political power was unchallenged, land reform through mass mobilization was resumed. In November, 1955, Truong Chinh initiated what he called "the fifth crucial wave of mass mobilization," freely admitting that the purpose of the reform was, as in Communist China, to gain mass support among the poor. On December 13, an official announcement said that over 100,000 persons had taken part in the trials and convictions of landlords in villages near Hanoi. The campaign was conducted "with utmost ferocity" [138] in several more "waves," lasting until the fall of 1956, when it was called off on orders from above, apparently before the murderous momentum of the special cadres had exhausted itself.

Something about the campaign had been causing concern among the leaders in Hanoi for some time. On August 17, 1956, Ho Chi Minh, in a letter to his "Compatriots in the country," admitted "errors" in the execution of the land reform and promised "corrections." On August 24, the Party organ *Nhan Dan* reported that among the people wrongly classified, convicted, and executed were many former Vietminh fighters and even Party members. At the end of October, the head of the campaign, Truong Chinh, was dismissed as Party secretary, and his post taken by Ho Chi Minh himself. The Minister of Agriculture was dismissed also. Party and government suddenly began to indulge in an orgy of self-criticism, and conducted what was officially called a "Campaign of Rectification of Errors," whose purpose had already been spelled out in Ho Chi Minh's letter of August 17. "Those who have been wrongly classified as landlords and rich peasants," he wrote, "will be correctly reclassified. Those members of the Party, the cadres, and the population who have been the subject of erroneous judgment will be re-established in their rights and prerogatives and their honorable character will be recognized." [139] On November 1, the government announced that 12,000 persons would be released from prisons and labor camps. Radio Hanoi explained that all persons unjustly condemned, "whatever their class," would not only be freed but also compensated. Those among the unjustly punished who had held military or administrative posts would regain their civil rights and be reinstated in their former positions.[140] On November 8, the government abolished the People's Agricultural Reform Tribunals.

In a speech delivered at Hanoi on November 28, Vo Nguyen Giap, the hero of Dien Bien Phu, defended the land-reform program but confirmed the "errors" committed and tried to regain the confidence of the many Party members and sympathizers who had been deprived of their possessions, jobs, and freedom, or, as he put it, had been "arrested, condemned, detained, isolated" [141]—he did not mention those killed. It is generally believed that the number killed was between 10,000 and 15,000, and that between 50,000 and 100,000 were deported and imprisoned. Many regained their freedom, though perhaps not their former rights and possessions, but the campaign of Rectification of Errors had its limitations, since, as Ho Chi Minh grimly remarked: "One cannot wake the dead." [142] As a substitute, the government offered decent graves and public funerals for the many whom its eager servants had deprived of their lives. Such public repentance, however, did not diminish the leaders' secret satisfaction over the social changes brought about by their agrarian reform. As Giap proclaimed in his speech defending the reform, all vestiges of "feudalism" had been eradicated, which in reality meant that a large peasant class likely to oppose the regime's plan to collectivize agriculture had ceased to exist.

What the agrarian reform had failed to accomplish was to satisfy the land needs of those for whose benefit it allegedly was undertaken. The total land gained through the reform enabled the regime to give 1.5 million families of landless agricultural laborers and poor peasants slightly more than 1 acre each. (They also received one buffalo for every thirteen families.) Welcome as these gifts were to the poor, they were not bountiful enough to turn them into enthusiastic supporters of the regime.[143]

Far from improving the regime's position among the rural population, the land reform, and above all the injustices and atrocities committed in its execution, produced widespread popular resentment, growing unrest, and eventually open rebellion. The brutalities of the land-reform cadres embittered not only their helpless victims, but also many peasants who were lucky enough to escape prison or execution by owning half an acre less than an unfortunate neighbor. Many sons of so-called landlords had fought for years in the Vietminh armies, and even if they themselves were spared persecution, the fate of their families drove most of them into opposition. Party members who were personally hit spoke up loudly, and in many instances became the most effective leaders of peasant opposition. Apart from the "errors" committed through the land reform, there was discontent also with the high taxes and the increasing pressure for ever bigger food deliveries to the state at prices so low that the peasant could not possibly have bought consumer goods even had they been available.

The regime, long deaf to the voices of dissatisfaction over its agrarian policy, began at last to listen to them in the summer of 1956, suddenly aware of the dangers that threatened if it failed to curb the relentless zeal of the agents charged with reshaping village life. But the warnings it began to issue in August, and the measures it began to take at the end of October, came too late. Open rebellion broke out early in November in the province of Nghe An, the more shocking as the population of this region had long been known to be strongly pro-Vietminh. The first acts of active peasant resistance occurred in only one village, on November 2, but within a few days more clashes between local militia and peasants broke out, spreading over an entire district and taking on the form of a broadening spontaneous insurrection. Hanoi, although quickly reacting with measures that virtually ended the land reform, nevertheless also proceeded immediately to suppress the movement by force. This task, which turned out to be a bloody one, was entrusted to the 325th Division, whose members, long accustomed to fighting only the French, undoubtedly disliked shooting at Vietnamese peasants. Whether or not there was hesitation in their ranks is not known, but the task of suppressing the peasant rebels was in the end accomplished with customary Communist ruthlessness. Western observers claim that about 1,000 peasants were killed or wounded between November 10 and 20, and several thousand arrested and deported.[144]

Smaller outbreaks occurred in other parts of the country, in some instances openly supported by embittered local Party leaders. Putting an end to the entire land reform campaign undoubtedly helped to prevent further outbreaks, but not until late February, 1957, did the regime feel safe enough to withdraw the regular army units from the affected areas and to hand over the task of maintaining order to the local militias.

For Ho Chi Minh, the beloved leader, having to use force against his own people, and predominantly in the province where he was born, must have been a distressing experience. But the many predictions of approaching doom for his regime, made by his enemies at home and abroad after the revolts of November, 1956, failed to come true. The excessive self-criticism in Giap's speech of November 29 should have disabused all peddlers of such vain hopes: Communists openly admit the existence of a crisis only after they have made sure that it no longer constitutes a threat to their power.

But the Communist regime in North Vietnam could afford to admit its own troubles and still look with more confidence than ever before into the future for yet another reason. At the end of 1956, it had become clear to Ho Chi Minh that the hold he had gained over the Vietnamese people would not be threatened by developments in the other half of divided Vietnam. In the South, no progress was being made toward freedom or social justice. No truly progressive regime able to win over the entire Vietnamese people had arisen from the postwar political chaos in Saigon, and Ngo Dinh Diem showed no signs of ever becoming a serious rival to Ho Chi Minh. Anti-Communist nationalism, it seemed, would continue to remain politically ineffective.

XII

Toward the Second Indochina War

1

IN 1956, THE COMMUNIST REGIME of North Vietnam was headed toward a serious political crisis; for the Diem regime in the South, 1956 was the first year that its existence was no longer threatened by rival nationalist forces. More important still, it seemed that even the dangers that threatened the Saigon regime from the Vietminh had been banished. By the end of 1956, Ngo Dinh Diem had convinced both his admirers and his critics of his ability to survive. The non-Communist press throughout the world stressed the troubles Ho Chi Minh was having and ceased to concentrate on Diem's shortcomings and instead began to praise his achievements.

Diem's admirers had already compiled a long list of his achievements before the close of 1956, a list to which new entries kept on being added for several years, only to be gradually erased when disenchantment with Diem began to spread after 1960. Significantly, most of Diem's accomplishments, real and praiseworthy though they may have been, were essentially negative, since all they managed to do was to stave off a threatening danger. This is particularly true of Diem's most unexpected and most impressive achievement: his political survival, which, not without good reason, was generally considered identical with the survival of South Vietnam. A "miracle" had happened, and the man who had performed it quite naturally gained respect and admiration. Seen from the perspective of South Vietnam's pressing need for continued survival, this miracle lacked positive content; all it meant was that there had been no political collapse.[1] Nevertheless, it was a great achievement, since it preserved the potential for building a viable anti-Communist South Vietnam.

Moreover, Diem's negative achievements not only preserved a chance that might easily have been lost, but seemed also to justify the expectation that this chance would be used. To eliminate the sects, oust Bao Dai, obtain the withdrawal of the Expeditionary Corps, and terminate all direct interference by the French required a great deal of positive action. In proving that he was capable of such action, Diem seemed to give South Vietnam one of the most urgent requirements for her survival: an outstanding leader, superior to all his rivals both as politician and nationalist. In both these respects Diem seemed the only anti-Communist leader equipped to dim Ho Chi Minh's shining reputation. Negative as most of Diem's early accomplishments were, they yet revived hopes that had been all but dead, hopes for the future of South Vietnam, which for several years remained firmly welded to the name of Diem.

These hopes, however, were stronger in the West than in Vietnam itself, and strongest in the United States, where they arose sooner and persisted longer than in Vietnam or anywhere else. Indeed, it is not possible to write the history of South Vietnam after 1954 without simultaneously telling the story of American acceptance of, enthusiasm for, and eventual disenchantment with, Ngo Dinh Diem, whose fate ultimately was determined by the evolution of American political thinking during the nine years of his reign.

The story of U.S. policy toward the Diem regime richly illustrates the power of wishful political thinking, the shortcomings of U.S. diplomacy, and the fact that the United States still does not know the most effective methods of fighting Communism. But it is not an entirely negative story. In principle, there was nothing wrong with the decision that South Vietnam should be helped to survive as a non-Communist state—if it turned out that this was what its people wanted. But whether or not this was the wish of the people could not have been fairly determined in 1954. It was generally thought by all competent observers that Ho Chi Minh would have easily won a free election even in the South as long as the choice was between his government and the French-controlled Bao Dai regime. However, there no longer was a Bao Dai regime, and thus, putting an end to colonialism in the South no longer required that the people support the Vietminh. For obvious reasons, elections could hardly have been held immediately after the Geneva conference, and if held, could not have been free. But more important still was the absence of a real choice: The procolonial regime that the people detested was on its way out, but the alternative that the people might have chosen did not yet exist, except as a hope. It could not have been realized within the space of a few months. Elections in 1954, therefore, would have deprived the people of the chance to decide for themselves—now that the end of colonialism opened up the possibility of a choice—whether a non-Communist regime was preferable to the Communist regime established by the Vietminh.

To offer the people this chance was mainly why the American people supported Washington's efforts to keep the anti-Communist, anti-colonial government of Ngo Dinh Diem in power, and to help it build a viable state. There was no doubt among most Americans as to what such an anti-Communist South Vietnam should be like: It should be capable of offering the people the gifts of economic prosperity, social justice, and a gradual realization of the freedoms for which the nation had fought in the long struggle for independence—in other words, a state which poor and rich, workers and peasants, intellectuals and soldiers, young and old would unhesitatingly prefer to the Communist regime in the North, precisely because it was in every respect its opposite. This, as some Vietnamese nationalists put it, was the South's vocation, and only if this vocation was fulfilled would the South be viable, defensible, and worthy of survival. The South had to become what a dishonest propaganda in the West had always said it was: a free Vietnam. There was no "free" Vietnam. It had to be created. This, in spite of those for whom anti-Communism was synonymous with freedom, was the understanding of the American people. They would not have supported their government's policy of aiding South Vietnam after 1954 had they foreseen that the country, ruled by brutal and sterile dictatorships, could survive only if the United States went to war.

What makes this story, which for many years was expected to have a happy ending, so tragic is that not only did the prospects for building a viable South Vietnam, for breaking the hold of the Communists on the people, and for avoiding another dreadful war exist, but they were in fact excellent. Despite the ravages of the war and the problems created for the South's economy through partition of the country and withdrawal of the Expeditionary Corps,[2] the South was economically In better shape than the North. It had assets that could be effectively exploited in the political competition with the North. One of these was the potential for a large food surplus. In contrast to the North, enough rice and other foodstuffs could be grown to be sure that even a poor harvest would not bring shortages, and it seemed quite likely that exports of rice could soon be resumed on a large scale. Vietnam's coal and mineral deposits, cement production, and the larger part of her industry remained in the North. But the South had all of its rubber plantations, which had suffered surprisingly little during the war. As expected, rubber soon became the South's major export.

But much more important, for obvious political reasons, was another advantage the South had over its rival in the North. There was plenty of land available for distribution among peasants who owned none or very little. This meant that the millions of poor, exploited peasants and tenants, who still expected the victory of the Vietminh to put an end to their plight, could be turned into a class of politically satisfied landowners and grateful supporters of a non-Communist regime. This, however, required not only the recultivation and distribution of the almost 1 million acres of rice land that had been abandoned during the war, but above all a radical program of agrarian reform. In the Mekong Delta region, where the vast majority of South Vietnam's peasant population lives, "2.5 per cent of the landlords owned half the cultivated land, and 80 per cent of the land was tilled by tenant farmers." [3] For many years, high land rents, high irrigation fees, uncertainty of tenure, and scandalously high interest rates for small loans had made the landlords hated and had turned tenants and poor peasants into Vietminh supporters. The necessity for agrarian reform had been recognized even by Diem's predecessors, whose governments depended largely on the support of the large landowners, both Vietnamese and French. Diem often stated that he regarded agrarian reform as one of his most urgent tasks. It was indeed quite inconceivable that Diem would reject land distribution, even if he did not consider it an act of social justice: He must have known that the creation of a landowning and reasonably prosperous peasantry was the surest way of immunizing the rural masses against Communist propaganda.

There were other reasons that the regime, after seemingly putting its ability to survive beyond all doubt, was seen as being ready to begin the task of building a better and freer life for its people. By the end of 1956, undeniable achievements, if not really spectacular in any one field, nevertheless permitted the expectation that more substantial progress, economic as well as political, would soon be made. In spite of almost two years of civil disorder and political uncertainty, the post-war danger of economic collapse had been averted. In the eyes of most observers the value of this and other accomplishments was not diminished by the fact that they had been made possible only through massive U.S. assistance. As in the North, the pace of reconstruction depended on the amount of readily available foreign technical and material aid. But without some measure of resolve and administrative ability on the part of the regime, repairing the war damages would certainly have taken longer.[4] In rebuilding bridges, putting the railroads back into operation, and reopening canals—tasks that required no revolutionary zeal and no new ideas—the regime's performance was satisfactory, marred neither by undue waste nor by excessive exploitation of labor.

One achievement for which the Diem regime was enthusiastically praised by its admirers, and which even its critics acknowledged to be sound, was its reception, care for, and resettlement of the refugees from the North. Statistics about the number of refugees whose economic integration was made possible through government-directed resettlement programs are at variance. The highest official claim made was that "a little over 500,000 [of the almost 900,000 refugees] live in resettlement villages; the others (merchants, government employees, military personnel with their families) prefer to live on their own in the cities and the countryside."[5] This phase of the program started late, but by the end of 1957, at least 300,000 refugees were settled in some 300 new villages, most of which were expected to become self-sufficient; however, by the end of 1959, only about 50 had done so.[6]

The solution of the refugee problem was of course made possible only through U.S. financial assistance. During the fiscal years 1954–55 and 1955–56, a substantial portion of the total U.S. aid to Vietnam went into the immediate care for and final settlement of the refugees.[7] But the regime's success in this field was greatly aided by two local assets. One was the availability of land that had been abandoned during the war years and was now waiting to be recultivated;[8] the other, no less important factor, was a human one—the existence of a competent and energetic leadership among the refugees themselves. This leadership, consisting largely of Catholic priests, partly made up for the many shortcomings on both higher and lower administrative levels, as well as for some incredible bureaucratic delays in Washington in the actual flow of funds authorized by Congress.[9] The ability of this local leadership to organize self-help among the refugees was probably the most remarkable feature of the entire resettlement effort.[10]

It was thanks to these two assets that a project such as the one undertaken early in 1956 at Cai San was possible at all. More than 20,000 refugees, assisted by 100 tractors supplied by the United States Operations Mission (USOM, as it was then called), began the clearing of 190,000 acres of rice land that had been uncultivated for eight years. One hundred miles of canals were dug in ninety days. Seeds were purchased, houses built along the canals, and only seven months after the first surveys of the desolate fields, a great new agricultural center had come into existence.[11]

The handling of the refugee problem by the Vietnamese Government and the U.S. aid mission, although generally applauded, has also evoked some criticism.[12] The efforts to achieve final settlement got under way too late, chiefly for bureaucratic reasons. In many instances, too little concern was shown for local inhabitants whose interests were affected by the relocation of the hundreds of thousands of Northerners. Many Southerners resented the special treatment accorded the refugees by the authorities, claiming that the losses they had suffered during the war entitled them to government assistance as well. There was also a widespread feeling that the refugees enjoyed special privileges because most of them were Catholics and were therefore thought to be ardent supporters of President Diem. However, these criticisms cannot detract from the positive aspects of the refugee program. The condition of the refugees demanded special treatment, and no matter what "privileges" they received, their lives, with few exceptions, remained as hard as those of their Southern compatriots among whom they had been resettled. Concerning the government's shortcomings, the final judgment may well remain that of John D. Montgomery, an American observer who was never passionately enthusiastic about the Diem regime: "Faults in administration and planning and problems of internal coordination, some of which had tragic results, were not hard to find. But they were insignificant beside the achievements." [13]

2

The solution of the refugee problem, and in particular the manner in which the Cai San project was executed, showed what a combination of local leadership, natural wealth, and American assistance could do. Therefore, full recognition of what was achieved in this instance inevitably leads to rather negative conclusions about the regime's performance in other fields. The more one reflects, on the basis of the work done for and by the refugees, what might have been done in other areas, the more it becomes evident that in dealing with the country's general economic, social, administrative, and political problems, the Diem regime accomplished nothing else that was particularly outstanding, nothing that adds up to an equally well-grounded success story.

This judgment does not rest on negative statistical evidence. Statistics show a steady if slow progress in many economic, social, and other fields, progress that would probably have secured the country's future if the forces threatening it had not existed at all or had been less powerful. But since Diem's mission, as he himself conceived it, was to save South Vietnam despite the forces bent upon her destruction, it is only fair to measure his performance against the generally recognized prerequisites for the country's survival. These prerequisites were not a balanced budget or a favorable balance of foreign trade, none of which the regime ever came close to gaining. In both these respects, Diem could safely count on years of continued American aid. Nor did these requirements necessarily include the rapid creation of armed forces, such as an efficient regular army and civil guards as well as all kinds of local police forces for maintaining internal order. These were no doubt important: the army in case of an invasion from the North, the police forces, together with the army, in the more likely case of Communist insurrection in the South. But by themselves, neither army and police, nor statistical evidence of economic or cultural achievements, could ever become guarantees of internal peace and continued progress. The prime prerequisite for this, and indeed for the very survival of South Vietnam, was broad popular support for the regime. Without such support, the best-trained and best-equipped army and police would be of doubtful value, particularly against an internal uprising, which widespread popular discontent would support. In fact, in the absence of such discontent, the Communists would not be likely to attempt to win power through civil war.

Survival, therefore, required economic, social, and political achievements designed to win the loyalty of the vast majority of the people, a loyalty strong enough to make them determined to defend the regime against armed rebellion.

It was never easy, and still is not, to measure the extent to which the Diem regime enjoyed popular, even though not enthusiastic, support. There is no doubt that between 1955 and 1957, Diem made some efforts to advance on this promising road. Even some of his implacable critics have admitted that the regime seems to have had some popular support, at least for a brief period,[14] a fact that underlines once more that history offered Diem a real chance.

If the reality and strength of the support Diem received from his people is somewhat uncertain, no doubt exists in regard to the support he enjoyed in the United States, without whose aid he would have had little chance of gaining his people's loyalty. American aid, indispensable for the accomplishment of deeds designed to get the people behind Diem, was quite rightly regarded as vital for the survival of South Vietnam. There were people in the United States, military men and others unable to grasp the nature of the Communist threat, who regarded American aid not as a condition but rather as a substitute for popular support—as did Diem himself, after he realized that his policies had failed to win mass approval or the backing of the educated middle classes. In this view, all that was needed to defeat Communism was a powerful military and police apparatus, and the political "re-education" of the masses through propaganda. But official U.S. policy, and public opinion in favor of Diem, were differently motivated: Diem needed aid because without it he could not win over his people. That he would use American aid to achieve this end was taken for granted.

How mistaken an assumption this was had become obvious by 1960. But up to the end of 1957, the belief that the doors to a better future for the people of South Vietnam were still open was by no means mere wishful thinking. There was a period in the history of Diem's rise and decline when it seemed as if under his guidance, anti-Communist nationalism might yet become a force capable of breaking the attraction of the Vietminh. It is clear that in the end Diem failed because the harvest of his policy was not popular support but deep popular discontent. But why, years after his political inadequacy had become apparent, did he succeed in keeping the firm support of the United States Government? And more puzzling still: Why, for so many years, was he defended by so many well-informed and politically mature Americans who on the whole were deeply concerned with the fate of the Vietnamese people and anxious to advance democracy in Vietnam?

In politics there are no such things as real mysteries. Attitudes that seem mysterious are merely cases whose complexity confounds the general desire for easy answers. The U.S. long-lasting acceptance of the Diem regime as viable and even essentially progressive is such a case, defying simple explanations. A further difficulty is that those who are called upon to do the explaining can do this only by admitting to their own errors of judgment.

For a correct appraisal of Diem's performance in terms of his vital need for popular support, and for an understanding of the enduring faith of his American defenders, it seems useful to divide the nine years of his rule into three periods. The first of these lasted roughly a year, during which Diem succeeded, against all expectations, in maintaining himself in office and in laying the foundations of his nine-year rule. This was the first act of the "miracle." The fact that Diem had overcome tremendous obstacles and secured for himself a position of real power made a deep and lasting impression the world over. Diem's qualifications for positive achievements, however, were still unknown, and no critical observer could as yet be sure that the South was out of danger.

The belief that all was well, and that the miracle had really happened, took firm roots only during the second period of Diem's rule, which in Vietnam itself probably lasted no more than two years. But they were two fruitful years, with beneficial effects for Diem, which in the United States lasted well into 1960. Doubts concerning the solidity of Diem's position disappeared almost completely during the first year of this second period. Although the regime was beginning to display disturbing political tendencies, it was during this period that the strong belief in its capabilities for constructive action was created.

The third period—and it is hard to say when it started—ended with the fall of Diem in November, 1963. In Vietnam, disenchantment was widespread already in 1957. In the United States, many former admirers of Diem began to withdraw their support after 1960. In American Government circles, however, the belief that Diem was a failure began to gain ground only after the beginning of the so-called Buddhist crisis early in 1963.

In retrospect, it is quite easy to see why doubts about the viability of Diem's regime began to disappear after 1955. Programs for solving what were considered military and administrative requirements of survival were energetically pursued during 1955 and 1956. When it came to questions of power, Diem rarely indulged his propensity for delaying decisions.

The crowning achievement of this period, however, was again a "negative" one. It was the regime's survival of the critical time of July, 1956, when the elections to unify the country were supposed to be held. When Diem's refusal to hold these elections failed to produce other than verbal reactions from Hanoi, most Americans concerned with Vietnam reached the comforting conclusion that the last and darkest cloud over the country had been lifted: Not even the Communists could any longer endanger the existence of an anti-Communist South Vietnam.

Now there developed in the West, and particularly in the United States, an attitude toward the Diem regime that only some future science of political psychology may fully explain some day. Diem's triumph in 1955 over his anti-Communist rivals, after months of near disaster, had had a profound effect both on his admirers and on his (more numerous) critics, whose prediction had been that he could not possibly succeed. For the admirers, who were relieved of much anxiety, Diem was henceforth a hero, whose faults, if seen at all, had to be forgiven a man who had secured the survival of a non-Communist Vietnam. For the critics, whose pessimism Diem had confounded, Diem turned into a figure whom it was safer henceforth to treat with circumspection. It is important to remember that, for sound political reasons, most of Diem's early critics did not mind having been wrong. But for years they were extremely careful not to repeat the mistake of castigating this extraordinary man, who had apparently performed the miracle of saving South Vietnam for the free world. Up to 1960, it was, at least in the United States, almost indecent to say anything unfriendly about Diem without simultaneously praising him for his astonishing achievement. Only a few observers, most of them in England and France, doubted the assumption that the Communists had been defeated by Diem, questioned the true value of what he had accomplished, and accused him of damaging the cause of freedom by setting up a dictatorial regime that prevented all open political expression and all participation of the elite. The only "miracle" of Vietnam, some of these critics said, was the amazing success of the regime's international propaganda.[15]

In the United States, the rising enthusiasm for Diem was of course primarily due to the popular conviction that a cause embraced by America must necessarily be good, and to a general unwillingness even to consider that a country for which Americans stood up might in the end be lost to Communism. But much of Diem's success in retaining popularity in the United States must be ascribed to organized propaganda. As early as the end of 1955, a group of mostly selfless and highly motivated citizens founded the American Friends of Vietnam, an organization that enlisted the support of the most diverse representatives of American political life. The spokesmen of the American Friends of Vietnam became Diem's most effective defenders. They were valuable for his regime not only because they volunteered their services, but also because they spoke with the authority of experts (which some of them actually were), and because they were in a better position than any Vietnamese agent to convince the American public and government that Diem's achievements were real, that under him the South would become prosperous and eventually also democratic, and that Diem's critics made the mistake of regarding the minor flaws of his regime as omens of failure.[16]

In this American propaganda, the gap between Diem's claims and his actual performance was filled with the praise of achievements that, necessary and welcome though they were, failed to remove the colonial heritage of social injustice, administrative evils, and political backwardness. What an English critic, David Hotham, listed as achievements in a survey written in 1958, crediting them chiefly to American aid, was described by Diem's admirers as achievements of the regime. "American aid," wrote Hotham, "has financed many excellent and well-conceived programs in Vietnam: the resettlement of refugees, the anti-malaria and anti-trachoma work, the agricultural improvements, the supplying of thousands of buffaloes, the restocking of fish ponds, the reclaiming of wastelands, the research on the high plateau of the interior, the invaluable long-term work on statistics, taxation, and other fields, and the training in administration and the introduction of American ideas carried out by Michigan State University." [17]

This list could easily be extended and made more specific. The entire monetary system was reorganized, as were budgetary affairs and central banking.[18] There was a "dramatic increase in the number of hospitals, dispensaries, maternity clinics, and other health facilities." [19] Progress in the field of education, primary as well as higher, was equally remarkable. The number of students enrolled in universities rose from 2,451 in 1954–55, to 7,496 four years later. During the same period, community "pilot schools" increased from 577 to 5,123, and the number of students in primary schools from 400,865 to 1,110,556.[20] About 2,000 young people studied in universities abroad.[21] The National Institute of Administration, which, in 1954, had at most 25 students, in 1957 trained about 300 officials in its day program and 3,540 in evening courses.[22] Education was one field in which the Diem regime was "a match for its Northern rival," [23] although it lagged behind in the training of technicians, especially engineers. Because of its justified concern with security, the Southern regime concentrated instead on producing security and police officials, and more officers for its regular army.

Three valid observations are to be made about the work in most of these fields, including that of repairing war damages: It was possible only because of American aid; it was not so much the work of the political leadership, but largely that of specialists—technicians, doctors, engineers, and administrators, most of them young and dedicated to their country and for a long time also to Diem; and it could be executed without basic social, economic, or political reforms, let alone revolutionary changes (nor would revolutionary changes have advanced or retarded progress in these fields, which in the North was on the whole similar to that in the South).

To some extent, these three factors applied also to the recovery of the country's agriculture and industry, which up to a point proceeded satisfactorily, under the impetus of American aid and with the dedicated help of American and local technical experts. But the absence of a national leadership that, for the sake of higher goals and better performance, was ready to mobilize the masses, encourage initiative on all administrative levels, and accept ideas of social reform precluded the possibility of truly spectacular economic achievements. Rice production, for instance, which declined from 5.3 million to 2.6 million metric tons between 1938 and 1954, reached 3.4 million in 1956, and 5 million in 1959, not quite the prewar level, which the North, although lacking the South's growth potential, had exceeded. Progress in the production of rubber was greater, already topping prewar levels in 1955: Plantations had suffered little damage and production figures had declined only moderately during the war. The prewar levels were also reached, a few years later, in the production of coffee, a minor crop, and by the fishing industry.[24] Production figures of all other agricultural crops, as well as those of most food-producing industries, rose considerably above the low levels of 1954–55, but remained below prewar levels.

However, since most experts agreed that no miracles could be expected in economic growth, the modesty of the regime's economic achievements was not held against it by any serious critic.[25] On the contrary, it was considered wise to proceed slowly, since there was much evidence from other underdeveloped countries that economic progress, particularly in industrialization, would be sound only if its pace was not unduly forced. Besides, after the end of 1956, almost no one doubted that even at its slow pace, the regime would soon reach and surpass prewar production figures. Very few people foresaw that a new civil war would put a stop to economic growth and eventually make all further progress impossible, and almost no one any longer believed that a Communist-led uprising against Diem could succeed. Both early admirers and former critics of Diem clung to their hard-won conviction that all was at last well, some for two or three years, others for four or five.

This attitude and the apparently sound reasoning behind it were well expressed by an informed American observer, who wrote at the end of 1958: "The first central fact about South Vietnam today is that it is one of the more stable countries of Southeast Asia." It is a country in which "no serious contenders for power threaten the government." Disturbing incidents do occur, but "their significance should not be exaggerated, for their extent is far from shaking the general stability." In 1954, the Communists left behind in the South "an elaborate and experienced underground," but "much of this apparatus has been broken up in the past four years." [26] The author of this, in contrast to the many who extolled Diem and his achievements without restraint,[27] was by no means blind to Diem's shortcomings or to the disconcerting imperfections of his regime. "Yet," he concluded, "the important factor is not so much the present state of affairs as the trend of events and the final goals." These goals were economic viability and political democracy, and the trend was toward their realization. For although "the South has still a long way to go," the "important point is that the nation is still moving forward—and, on balance, in the right direction."

This was the view also of people who had no illusions about the Diem regime and therefore refrained from describing the twilight that hung over South Vietnam as a bright new day. But they hoped that it was dawn, not dusk, carrying with it the promise of peace and freedom, not the threat of unfreedom and war.

3

It seemed that American optimism in regard to the Diem regime was nourished chiefly by the very need for it: Only good news from Saigon could sustain the belief that the miracle of Vietnam was real and not a mirage. This need for good news continually prompted all worried anti-Communist observers to overlook, or at least play down, the shortcomings of Diem that threatened to make his achievements politically worthless.

An early instance of this tendency to overlook Diem's shortcomings was the reluctance of most of his supporters to admit that the regime's approach to the problem of agrarian reform was politically disastrous. When the slightness of Diem's plans was revealed, he was not blamed for the inadequacy of his program, but rather was praised for the careful manner in which he tackled the delicate task of agrarian reform. What he proposed was widely considered as only a beginning. This at least was the hope of those Diem supporters who regarded a radical land reform as the most urgent measure in the struggle against the Vietminh, and therefore regretted that he had acted so late, set his goal so low, and worked toward it with such exasperating slowness.

The land-reform program was inadequate in several respects. It was started too late and was carried out too slowly; it did not go far enough, particularly in regard to land distribution; and its provisions for payment by the peasants who received land created an unnecessary hardship and were a serious political blunder. No measures whatever were taken during 1954. It seemed that Diem felt less urgency about the need for agrarian reform than had his predecessors during the last years of the Bao Dai regime. Only after being prodded for months by American advisers, including Ambassador Collins, did Diem take the first cautious steps early in 1955, aimed at a reduction of land rents, at safeguarding the rights of tenants through tenancy contracts, and at providing land for the resettlement of refugees from the North.[28] As to the much more important problem of land transfers from large owners to tenants, nothing at all was done until October, 1956.[29] Still worse than this delay was the manner in which the government embarked on this crucial task, revealing a complete lack of understanding for the disastrous political consequences that the failure to act forcefully in this field was bound to produce.

All figures, no matter how impressive at first sight, underline the disheartening inadequacy of the land-transfer program. The government boasted that it had made available for transfer 1.725 million acres of cultivated and abandoned land. This, however, was only 20 per cent of the total cultivated rice area. (Only rice land was subject to transfer.) Of these 20 per cent marked for distribution, less than two-thirds (1.062 million acres) had actually "changed hands," according to government statistics, by 1962—six years after the start of the program. But not all these acres that had "changed hands" had gone to the needy peasants. Much of the land acquired from French owners through purchase financed by the French Government was sold to the highest bidder. According to Bernard Fall, the total of the land expropriated from Vietnamese owners or purchased from the French,[30] and therefore available for distribution, was about 1 million hectares (2.47 million acres). Of this total, "only about one-fourth had reached the landless farmer" [31] after seven years of transfer operations. The regime and its defenders in the United States pointed proudly at the figure of 109,438 peasants (mostly tenants) who, as of July, 1961, had benefited from the land-transfer program, neglecting, however, to draw attention to the fact that more than 1 million tenants had received no land at all,[32] or, as another observer puts it, "of an estimated 1 to 1.2 million tenant households existing in 1955, about 10 per cent obtained land under the government's land-transfer program." [33]

The limited scope and the lagging execution, however, were not the only negative aspects of the land-transfer program. Politically no less disastrous were the provisions for payment by the tenants for land that had largely been in their effective possession for years. Wherever the Vietminh had been in control, the land of the large absentee owners was given to the peasants. By and large, Diem's land transfer consisted in nothing but the legalization of these conditions. The only change that Diem's land-distribution program produced for most of its so-called beneficiaries was that they now had to pay for land of which they had long considered themselves the rightful owners. And they had to pay for it in six yearly installments, which was too short a period for most. Titles were provisional. Those who received land were consequently as dissatisfied with Diem's land reform as was the vast majority who remained tenants. Peasant dissatisfaction with the land reform consequently became the main theme of Communist propaganda in the South.

As to land rents and security of tenancy through contracts, Diem's agrarian reform no doubt provided a measure of relief for the more than 1 million remaining tenants, most of whom, prior to the reform, had been completely at the mercy of the landlords. But the lack of impartial enforcement agencies greatly reduced the benefits that the peasants might have derived from these reforms: government officials, even if not corrupt, rarely stood up for the peasants against the landlords. To be sure, cases of rents amounting to 50 per cent of the tenant's crop became rare. Also, the tenants realized the advantages of secure tenancy through contracts for three or five years, and "three-fourths of tenant farmers entered into these contracts by the middle of 1959." [34] Furthermore, the plight of hundreds of thousands of peasants was eased by the National Agrarian Credit Office, which was created in April, 1957, to supply peasants in temporary need of funds with loans previously obtainable only at usurious rates.[35] But the absence of any kind of democratic representation of the peasants meant that the rural masses continued to be victimized by landlords and government officials. The legal rent of 25 per cent of the crop was widely disregarded —tenants considered themselves lucky if their rent was no more than 30 per cent. Even after 1960, when insurrection made the struggle for peasant loyalty the overriding political issue, abusive treatment of peasants remained widespread. Landlords, returning with the army to former guerrilla-held regions, extracted rents far above the legal limit. Since this was possible only with the help or acquiescence of the Saigon-appointed local officials, the peasants more often than not regretted having been returned to government control.[36]

The peasants also resented not getting the ownership of formerly unoccupied land, but instead being settled on it as tenants. This was true even of land which the refugees, largely through their own efforts, had opened for cultivation. "At the Cai San development in southwestern Vietnam, for example, there was so much resistance to tenancy contracts by the 43,000 resettled refugees that the government cut off daily subsistence payments in order to bring the refugees around." [37]

The narrow scope and the fragmentary execution of the agrarian reform, so fateful for the country's political evolution, reveal a great deal
about Diem's political philosophy and the hollowness of his claim that
his was a revolutionary regime. Diem was unable to see that Vietnam's
national revolution could be completed and all remnants of colonialism
wiped out only through radical economic and social reforms. For the
peasant masses, exploitation under a feudal land regime had been the
dominant reality of colonialism. Colonialism, therefore, would not end
for them until landlordism was abolished.

Far from being eliminated by a thorough agrarian reform, the landlords, for decades the associates of the colonial regime, were in fact
the group that, more than any other, succeeded in asserting its interests
under Diem. A maximum of 6,300 persons (most of them absentee
landlords) owned 45 per cent of all rice land in the South. The vast
majority of them were not at all affected by the land-transfer program,
since they owned less than the approximately 300 acres the law permitted them to retain. But even of the 2,500 who owned 40 per cent of the
Southern rice land, only 1,584 had been partly expropriated by late
1962. (Land held by the Roman Catholic Church, estimated at about
370,000 acres, was not subject to transfer.)

The landlords were of course compensated, with 10 per cent of the
price for expropriated land in cash and the rest in twelve-year government bonds at 3 per cent annual interest. They did not consider this
satisfactory, and that is why they sabotaged the entire reform after
they succeeded in severely limiting the scope of the transfer program.
Since they were strongly entrenched in the administration, they were
in a good position for this sabotage. "Lack of serious interested administrators" was given as the cause for the slow progress of the reform by
American advisers. "Government officials, beginning with the Minister
of Agrarian Reform, have divided loyalties, being themselves landholders." Of the Minister of Agrarian Reform it was reported that he had
not "signed leases with his tenants as provided by the land reform
decrees, and he is most certainly not interested in land distribution which
would divest him of much of his property." [38] However, for obvious
political reasons, such prominent landowners as Vice-President
Nguyen Ngoc Tho and the Ambassador to the United States, Tran
Van Chuong, eventually relinquished their holdings above the legally
permitted maximum.

But was landlord opposition alone responsible for Diem's totally inadequate agrarian-reform decrees? Was the power of these few thou-

sand people great enough to make Diem reject the advice of his American counselor Wolf Ladejinsky that the land-transfer program be broadened by reducing the upper limit per holding from 100 to 50 hectares? (In Japan, where the Americans had been in a better position to impose their ideas, landholdings were limited to 10 hectares.)

No doubt, in demanding that the agrarian reform be carried out with respect for private property, Diem could only have had in mind the interests of the rich landlords whose private property would be affected by a land-transfer program. The private property of the million or so tenants, being nonexistent, could not have been the subject of his concern. But it would be a great mistake to believe that Diem's regard for the interest of the landlord was the main reason for the inadequacy of his agrarian reform. Nor could it be said that landlord opposition was too strong for Diem to overcome. If Diem had been convinced that a more radical reform was necessary, respect for the property of the landlord would not have prevented him from pursuing it; and he could have mobilized the forces he needed to break landlord opposition. Moreover, he certainly possessed the moral courage required had he decided that the interests of its small upper class had to be sacrificed to save the country.

Why, then, did Diem fail to carry through what was so clearly the one social change called for if his anticolonial "revolution" was ever to be completed? Why did he neglect a task which even moderate "bourgeois" reformers in the nineteenth century recognized as a necessary condition for the development of democracy?

Diem was a highly complex political man: His modern authoritarian ideas, his almost medieval principles of monarchism, and his professed adherence to some form of democracy, which together made up his politics, resist definition.[39] Yet the answer to the question of why he failed as a social reformer could hardly be more simple: Measured against the needs of his country and the spirit of his time, Diem simply was too much of a conservative to discharge his historical mission.

The banality of this explanation makes it difficult to realize that here lies the key to Diem's failure. Diem was radical only as a nationalist and anti-Communist. His nationalism aimed at removing foreign rule, at reestablishing a genuine Vietnamese regime, not at changing the social structure that colonialism had created in Vietnam. Diem's concept of a "free" Vietnam was not concerned with the social aspirations of the masses, and, as it turned out, was also hostile to the political aspirations of the elite. Once the French were out and the Communists kept at bay, South Vietnam was, as far as Diem was concerned, "free" by definition. His nationalism, therefore, had little social content, and his anti-Communism none at all. Had Diem understood that mass support for his regime was indispensable in his struggle against Communism, he would probably have done away with landlordism completely and turned all tenants into landowners at no cost to them at all. The political gains of such a land reform would have been worth an even higher price. But Diem, the conservative, rejected revolutionary social change as a means of reducing the attraction of Communism, and it was this which gradually led him to rely more and more on antidemocratic measures and naked force.

4

At the end of 1956, Diem's defenders in the West could hardly have foreseen what his agrarian reform would turn out to be: not a mere beginning, as they had hoped, but the sum total of social reforms conceived of as necessary by Diem. And even this sadly inadequate program was not fully carried out during the nine years of the Diem regime.

The truth of this became evident to the people of Vietnam long before Diem's admirers abroad began to suspect it. The Vietnamese cared little about the service Diem had seemingly rendered to the free world by maintaining himself in power. They were concerned rather with what his regime was doing for them. They needed no expert knowledge to measure the immediate value of Diem's various achievements. "Every illiterate peasant can test for himself whether the land reform has been a reality or a sham in his district, and whether the local police and administrative officials are really civil 'servants' or a gang of brutes and grafters out to make the most of their stranglehold upon a hapless population." [40]

While after 1956, disenchantment with Diem at home turned rapidly into enmity toward his regime, his American support continued to grow for some years. Not only did the Americans lack the sad experience of the Vietnamese people, but by and large they remained unaware of the slowly emerging evidence that the social and political aspirations of both the masses and the elite were of steadily diminishing concern to the Diem regime. What continued to matter to most Americans was that Diem fought the West's battle against Communism on a threatened front. He had turned from a hopeless prospect into an apparent success. He had saved the South. He had proved himself the equal of Ho Chi Minh as an anticolonialist and had demonstrated to the people that in order to gain full independence they no longer had to support the Vietminh. This was his truly historical achievement, and for most Americans this alone counted in weighing the question whether the United States was right in supporting Diem. But not only did Diem have to be supported: He richly deserved to be supported, because in performing the "miracle" of saving the South in 1954–55, he had also removed the earlier doubts about his qualifications as an effective anti-Communist leader. No matter what shortcomings the Diem regime revealed in the course of time, as long as it seemed effective in combating Communism, Diem for most Americans remained a hero of the free world.

But Diem also had supporters in the West who were not yet convinced that the South was definitely saved, nor that he had already given sufficient evidence of being the man to complete a task that only people ignorant of recent Vietnamese history considered finished. Communism in the South was only temporarily checked; if it were to be defeated permanently, Diem would have to prove that he was more than a determined anticolonialist. As such he had succeeded merely in creating a chance for the South's survival; this chance now had to be used if survival was to become a permanent historical fact. The number of clearheaded people who knew what this required was considerable even in the United States: The masses as well as the Vietnamese elite had always regarded independence not as an abstraction, but as the presupposition for a better and freer life. Nonfulfillment of the people's concrete social and political aspirations therefore could only lead to growing opposition against the Diem regime. Without social and political reforms designed to gain and consolidate mass support for Diem, or for any other anti-Communist regime, the survival of the South could not be lastingly assured. In the United States, the then Senator John F. Kennedy in June, 1956, expressed concisely what would have to be done if Communism in South Vietnam was to be defeated: "What we must offer [the Vietnamese people] is a revolution—a political, economic, and social revolution far superior to anything the Communists can offer—far more peaceful, far more democratic, and far more locally controlled." [41]

Yet Kennedy, and even people with fewer illusions about Diem, supported his regime long after disturbing news from Vietnam made them fear that the chance for the survival of the South was being wasted. One line of arguments in support of this misguided attitude rested upon the perfectly plausible assumption that profound social and political changes required not only time but also an end of conditions under which the Communists would have benefited from certain reforms, as Diem was constantly pointing out. For years, it was in fact difficult, if not impossible, to prove that Diem would never take the measures of which the most obvious ones were repeatedly being urged on him by the United States Government and by most American advisers in Vietnam. Conditions, it was argued, did not yet permit certain reforms, particularly reforms aimed at greater political freedom. Perhaps Diem was too timid and moving too slowly; perhaps he was not as yet sufficiently aware of the need for certain reforms. But once the time was ripe, it was held, he would take whatever action was required to make the South's survival permanent. Had he not himself repeatedly recognized the necessity of radical social reforms, and proclaimed his intention to build "democratic institutions"? [42] And was the word revolution not "a constant part of the Vietnamese Government's vocabulary"? As early as 1949, Diem had specified that this revolution must also be "a social revolution for the economic independence of the Vietnamese farmer and laborer," [43] and as late as 1960, he accused his anti-Communist critics of "trying to crush the social revolution" [44] which his regime allegedly carried out. At the time, Diem's reputation for integrity made it almost impossible for his American admirers to assume that he might not believe what he said. Some suspected that he did not go along with the generally accepted meaning of the words "democracy" and "revolution," but most of his defenders were inclined to believe that objective conditions, not Diem himself, continued to prevent the realization of his true aims.

Because of this attitude, even critical observers considered it politically more helpful to emphasize the achievements of the Diem regime rather than dwell on its shortcomings. This was true again chiefly of the United States, where the public knew almost nothing about the scandalous manner in which the plebiscite to oust Bao Dai had been conducted. The removal of Bao Dai was no doubt necessary; it was a great step forward in the political evolution of the country. But this aim could also have been accomplished in an honest contest, and silence about the undemocratic and despicable means employed to achieve it was inexcusable. The judgment and the integrity of a man who would employ such means should have been questioned, and the whole procedure should have been openly condemned.

Quite a number of liberal Americans who for years believed that Diem would eventually live up to their expectations turned into fierce opponents of Diem, but many more embraced the argument that remained the basis of U.S. support even after Diem had destroyed all hopes for social and political reforms, to wit, that the United States had no choice but to support him. "Sink or Swim with Ngo Dinh Diem" was the famous phrase with which one keen observer who recognized the fallacy of this position described American policy.[45] The reasoning in support of this doubtful proposition reflected not only widespread ignorance and confusion about the real situation in Vietnam, but also the division of opinion about the means considered most effective in the struggle against Communism. True, some argued, it was idle to continue hoping that the social and political aspirations of the Vietnamese people would be fulfilled under Diem, yet any other regime would also encounter the obstacles that prevented Diem from promoting democracy and social justice. But even if it were true that Diem was denying civil liberties from conviction rather than because of the force of circumstances, the United States would still have to support him. This conclusion rested on the belief that no real alternative to Diem existed. Popular disaffection, it was admitted, seemed to be increasing, but there was no sign of an organized opposition strong enough to replace Diem and to promise the establishment of a more democratic, more effective, and more popular regime. Withdrawal of support from Diem, it was felt, would very likely lead to chaotic conditions favorable to a Communist strike for power. Unless it was decided that there was no hope for South Vietnam, Diem had to be supported. Those who realized that this was a perilous course but thought that it could not be changed eased their conscience by demanding greater pressure on Diem for reforms.

There were of course also those to whom the question of whether or not to continue the support of Diem posed no dilemma at all, people who remained convinced that Diem followed the only course that promised success. Democracy, these people asserted, was impossible under existing conditions, and reforms simply had to wait until the battle against the Communists was won. Diem needed more aid, particularly military aid. All else for the time being was unimportant. Making difficulties for Diem could only be of help to the Communists, against whom only force could prevail. If it was necessary to establish a tough dictatorship in order to deal effectively with the Communist threat, then the United States had to support Diem, even if he were a dictator. Those who held this position were not aware that they were accepting the discredited Communist dictum that the end justifies the means.

An official policy based on this dictum became America's greatest political improbity in regard to Vietnam. Those who claim to fight Communism on behalf of democracy and social justice can subscribe to the notion that the end justifies the means only at the risk of betraying their own cause. In doing so, they show not only a lack of integrity but a lack of political understanding as well: It was precisely this betrayal of democracy, the cause in whose name Communism was fought, which brought about the defeat of Diem by the Communists. To be sure, under certain conditions the naked force of a dictatorial, or even an openly fascist regime, can temporarily contain Communism —all the while adding to its potential strength. In Vietnam, force alone could not secure even such a limited and deceptive success.

The history of the Diem regime, from its unexpected early triumphs to its inglorious end, had a lasting effect on American political thinking, an effect which in turn continued to determine the fate of Vietnam. The real lesson to be learned from it is not that the policy of supporting Diem beyond the first two or three years of his rule was a mistake. Much more important is the realization that the decision to withdraw support from Diem signified no break with this policy. Diem was dropped not because he was a dictator. As long as there was hope that his policies could prevent Communism in South Vietnam, his dictatorship enjoyed full American support. He was dropped because the dictatorship he created proved to be ineffective. There was, and still is, little or no awareness of the fact that this failure in the struggle against Communism was caused not by his personal shortcomings as a dictator but by the reactionary character of his regime.

5

The attempt to fight Communism by building a more democratic and socially more progressive state for South Vietnam would no doubt have meant taking risks and struggling against enormous obstacles.

What condemns Diem is that the attempt was never made, that in spite
of his verbal commitment to some measure of democracy he deliberately chose the opposite path.

The evidence of Diem's intention to fight Communism by building a
dictatorial regime, like his neglect of the most urgent social reforms,
emerged only slowly, and therefore remained unconvincing for some
years. There is no doubt that the strength of the Communists and their
determination to unify the country under Ho Chi Minh justified temporary dictatorial measures against them if democracy was to have a
chance in the South. The activities of the well-organized Communists
had to be curbed as long as their power, rooted in the colonial past,
threatened the new regime, and the consolidation of this new regime
through social reforms and economic progress, would, even under the
most effective leadership, have required several years. Only thus could
the people have been offered the choice between Communism and the
better government that the anti-Communist West expected Diem to
create. But temporary dictatorial measures were justified only if restricted to the containment of Communist subversion, and in order to
be effective at all, such measures had to be accompanied by policies
capable of rallying the vast non-Communist majority of the population
behind the regime. To contain the aggressive and still popular cadres
of the Vietminh, and eventually to break them politically, required
more than Diem's determination to use naked force. Force, sharply restricted and judiciously applied within the context of a broad political
strategy, should have been merely an adjunct of policy. The success of
an anti-Communist strategy in South Vietnam depended on three in-
terrelated factors, all of which would have been available to a modern
and truly revolutionary regime: a doctrine consistent with its proclaimed aims, a large body of trained and devoted cadres, and a
minimum of mass support. All modern political regimes that give evidence of stability, including many of a dictatorial nature, meet these
requirements.

Realizing that this is true also of some efficient dictatorships, and in
particular of the Communist regime of North Vietnam, many Americans came to the conclusion that Diem might have succeeded if he had
been a more efficient rather than an incompetent dictator, if his dictatorship had reached that level of perfection of which Ho Chi Minh
could boast. But the logic of the power struggle between democracy
and Communism in countries where the Communists enjoy popular

support shows this to be a fallacy. This logic precluded Diem's ever becoming a successful anti-Communist dictator; the requirements of political efficiency—an anti-Communist doctrine, devoted cadres, and mass support—could have been fulfilled only through the regime's evolution in the opposite direction in which it was going. A consistent anti-Communist doctrine required the advocacy and pursuit of political freedom, even if conditions demanded that freedom be denied to the Communists. The regime's pseudo-doctrine of "personalism" could never become a workable substitute for a genuine doctrine of political freedom and humanism.[46] There could have been devoted cadres only if the youth, the intellectuals, and all anti-Communist groups had been allowed free participation in the country's political life. And mass support depended on the satisfaction of the people's aspirations through social, economic, and political reforms.

The Diem regime failed because it not only opposed the political aspirations of the Communists, but also because it trampled underfoot the justified aspirations of the entire people. It could have succeeded in suppressing Communism only if it had abstained from suppressing everybody else. Not less but more democracy, a basic condition also of social justice, would have made the Diem regime politically effective against Communism.

Instead, the Diem regime, as Robert Scigliano, its least biased and most effective American critic put it, "transformed itself into a light image of its rival," [47] the meaning of "light" obviously being that the Diem regime lacked the strength to deprive the people of freedom as effectively as the North. It would of course be absurd to say that there was no difference between the regimes of Ngo Dinh Diem and Ho Chi Minh. Their aims were irreconcilable, their ideologies as different as day and night, and their positions in the twentieth-century political world could hardly have been farther apart. What is true, however, is that Diem pursued his intended total negation of Communism with means that were either close copies of, or indeed identical with, those employed by the Communists. Diem's republic, says Scigliano, was "for practical purposes a one-party state," [48] which had "its political re-education camps, its Communist denunciation rallies, its ubiquitous propaganda extolling the leader and damning the enemy, its mass organizations." [49] It also had its controlled elections, its secret police, a constitution almost as superbly written as that of the North whose guarantees of civil liberties and political freedom were just as disregarded. As in the North, opposition against the government was not tolerated, no matter how genuinely anti-Communist its inspiration. Opponents were imprisoned and, as a rule, held without trial. Many were tortured. The elected legislature was a tool in the hands of the government, and the press was gradually reduced to the base function of praising the leader and blindly supporting his actions.

One of the chief means which Diem, like all contemporary dictators, employed to hide the true nature of his regime was government-controlled elections. Four such elections were held after the referendum of October, 1955, which ousted Bao Dai and made Diem President. A Constituent Assembly was elected on March 4, 1956, a National Assembly on August 30, 1959, a Presidential election was held on April 9, 1961, and a last Assembly election on September 27, 1963.[50] Like the referendum of October, 1955, these elections were all poorly disguised exercises in totalitarian techniques. Most of the tricks the Hanoi regime had employed in its first elections in January, 1946, were copied under Diem, with the same brilliant results. As Scigliano puts it, both the North and the South "have permitted elections only to the extent that they could control the results; both have used elections to mobilize mass approval of the regime; and in each, minor parties exist only as fronts for the ruling group." [51]

Since mass approval of the regime was the real purpose of the elections, the government's chief concern was the largest possible voter turnout. This was particularly true for the 1956 election, which the Nationalist opposition spokesmen decided to boycott after the government had rejected their demands for fair election procedures. In order to achieve a massive voter turnout, the regime relied less on its propaganda than on intimidation by local government officials, supported by thousands of civil servants ordered into the countryside, whose chief means of persuasion was the threat that failure to vote would lead to difficulties with the authorities. Electoral procedures made it easy for officials to control not only whether or not, but also how, a person had voted.[52] Where intimidation could not be openly practiced, as for instance in Saigon, the government resorted to other means to assure a satisfactory turnout and the election of its candidates. "Soldiers were given the names of government candidates, transported to polling places, sometimes in uniform and sometimes in civilian clothes, and sent into polls in groups." [53] Fraud was used only as a last resort, but it must have been rather common in view of the surprisingly big turnout of voters in districts known to be under Communist control, such as the An Xuyen Province on the Camau Peninsula, where, in 1959, more than 95 per cent of the people were reported to have voted, and, in 1961, no less than 98 per cent—all of course for government candidates. In the Presidential elections of 1961, when the regime allowed opposition candidates of such a low caliber as to reduce the elections to a farce, "Diem got over 99 per cent of the votes cast in Kien Tuong, another Communist base-area in the Plain of Reeds, and in the highland province of Pleiku the opposition presidential candidates together got 7 votes to his 102,031." [54] In the countryside, the threat that those who refused to vote would be treated as enemies of the regime was indeed as effective as were the various measures to induce and frighten the people into voting for government-supported candidates. In Saigon, the regime's inability to coerce an almost universally hostile population, and the desire to offer the world a democratic façade, ruled out the more blatant measures of intimidation and fraud. As a result, no more than 75 per cent of the registered citizens turned out to vote in the elections in 1961, as against 95 per cent in the rest of the country.

The steps designed to assure that only government supporters would be elected to the Assembly consisted simply in making sure that there were no other candidates. Competition among various candidates was encouraged in most districts, but the alternatives offered were meaningless, since all candidates, whether members of the official government parties or so-called independents, were all firm supporters of the regime. The President's brother, Ngo Dinh Nhu, for instance, who was known as the second most powerful man of the South, ran as an "independent," in both the 1956 and the 1959 elections, as did the other members of his Personalist Labor Party whom he decided to put up for election. The secret ballot constituted no threat to the regime, since the program of all nongovernment candidates was identical with that of the government-supported candidates—approval of the regime's policies and its leader. In the 1959 election, Diem permitted two real but undistinguished opposition candidates to run in Saigon, expecting them to be defeated. When, in spite of official precaution, they won—one of them, Dr. Phan Quang Dan, running against fifteen other candidates, with 63 per cent of all ballots cast—both were deprived of their seats by government-directed court action.[55] Electoral competition elsewhere was a farce, notwithstanding the fact that in the 1959 elections, candidates of the government parties lost 22 out of 105 contests, the explanation being that "some government candidates lost to other government candidates and some lost to independents who were really government-preferred." [56] In this, as in many other respects, the democratic façade put up by the Diem regime was less convincing than the show of popular approval put up by its more efficient totalitarian enemy in the North. The assemblies [57] that resulted from Diem's two parliamentary elections were consequently as much instruments of the government as was the "multiparty" assembly which the Hanoi regime chose to have elected in May, 1960. There the voter turnout was also 97 per cent and like Diem in the province of Kien Tuong, Ho Chi Minh, too, was able to garner 99 per cent of the votes in his district.[58]

The main task of the Assembly elected on March 4, 1956, was the adoption, after a reasonably good simulation of democratic discussion, of a constitution for the Republic of Vietnam. The constitution, "basically an executive-drafted document," [59] was promulgated on October 26, 1956, the first anniversary of the proclamation of the republic, after its unanimous acceptance by the Assembly. (On December 29, 1956, the Assembly approved the appointment of Nguyen Ngoc Tho, Secretary of State for National Economy, as Vice-President, as provided for in the constitution. The constitution also extended the life of the Assembly for another three years.)

As a sample in fundamental law-making, the constitution of the Republic of Vietnam could hardly pass as a pioneering document for countries starting out on the road to democracy. Robert Shaplen found it "to have few safeguards against one-party rule and dictatorship." [60] On paper, it is indeed less democratic than the constitution of 1960, with which the Democratic Republic of (North) Vietnam confirmed itself as a Communist state, proving once again that as political counterfeiters, the Vietnamese Communists are superior to their opponents.[61] Bernard Fall believed that "the South Vietnamese constitution of 1956 was as good a constitutional document as could have been drawn up under the circumstances, and nothing in the text itself prevents the eventual development of reasonably representative government" [62]—a surprisingly charitable interpretation of a document that granted the President excessive legislative powers, the right to rule solely by decree when the Assembly was not in session, and suspension of any law in any part of the country even when the Assembly was in session. By stating that "the President of the Republic may decree a temporary suspension of the rights of freedom of circulation and residence, of speech and the press, of assembly and association, and of the formation of labor unions and strikes, to meet the legitimate demands of public security and order and national defense," [63] Article 98 of the constitution undid, at least for the period of the Assembly's first legislative term, whatever merits the document may have had. Diem continued to rule on this basis also after the powers granted him by Article 98 of the constitution had expired.

What mattered more, however, than this open legalization of the emerging dictatorship, was that Diem, without bothering to invoke all his constitutional prerogatives, was able to act as if the conditional safeguards contained in the constitution were nonexistent. "As time went on, Diem and Nhu came to ignore the Constitution completely and acted by decrees and by personal—and often private—orders to underlings all the way down to the village level." [64]

In subjecting even the country's village administrations to the central government's dictatorial powers, Diem, had he cared to, could have claimed to be standing on safe constitutional grounds: He had seen to it that local government was not mentioned in the constitution. Local government was being reorganized by executive decree while the constitution was still under discussion. Village autonomy was one of the strongest Vietnamese political traditions, dating back to the fifteenth century and sanctioned both by tradition and precolonial law.[65] Respect for it was the main reason that elections to village councils were held even under the Bao Dai regime in 1953. Through decrees issued in June and August, 1956, the Diem Government abolished all elective village and municipal councils, replacing them with appointive officials, thus leaving no doubt that, at least in this one respect, there was less political freedom in Vietnam under Diem than under the ancient mandarinal and even the colonial regime.[66]

The elimination of all surviving remnants of village democracy followed upon an administrative reorganization aimed at bringing local government on all levels under direct government control. South Vietnam was organized into forty-one provinces headed by province chiefs appointed by the President and directly responsible to him. The authority of the province chiefs was considerable, since it extended not only over police and security activities, but in many instances also over the regular armed forces. In their hands was put control of all lower government organs, consisting of the chiefs of the 233 districts into which the 41 provinces were divided (all district chiefs were also appointed by the central government), the country's 2,560 villages, and the approximately 16,000 hamlets. The village councils were appointed by the province chiefs on recommendation of the district chiefs, subject to review by Saigon. (The cities of Dalat, Danang, and Hue, which were administered outside of provincial rule, had mayors, and Saigon a prefect, all appointed by the central government.) After the abolition of government control in the villages, the administrative system of the Republic of Vietnam was more centralized than it had been under the emperors or the French.[67]

6

The evils of this system were not confined to those which excessive centralization and the absence of democracy in local government necessarily produce. They were compounded by the manner in which all administrative personnel was chosen from above, by the absolute dependence of all appointed officials on the central government, and by the officials' unlimited authority over a totally disenfranchised and subjugated population.

In order to see these evils, it is necessary to take a closer look at the methods with which the regime attempted to create what can only be called a substitute for mass support. It has been remarked that for all practical purposes, South Vietnam under Diem was a one-party state. This statement, to be accurate, requires two modifications. One is that Diem, too, like Ho Chi Minh in the North, allowed a number of parties to exist, in order to camouflage the fact of one-party rule. The minor parties in the South—a Social Democratic Party, a Socialist Party, and a Restoration League—served "only as fronts for the ruling group. . . . All three were taken over by the regime and their continued existence [depended] upon its benevolence and subventions." [68] They were no more authentic expressions of existing political currents than were the Democratic and Socialist parties in the North. Both in the North and South, these parties were artificial creations. But there was a difference between the party systems in the North and South which constituted the other, much more far-reaching modification of the fact of one-party rule under Diem: The artificiality of the party system in the South extended also to the official government parties—the National Revolutionary Movement, the National Revolutionary Civil Servants League, and the Personalist Labor Party.

The Personalist Labor Party, headed by the President's brother and Chief Adviser Ngo Dinh Nhu, was widely regarded as the Southern counterpart of the Communist Party in the North. But unlike the Communist Party, about which there was surely never anything artificial, the Personalist Labor Party was not the organizational expression of conscious political aspirations either by the masses or by an avantgarde. Although created for the defense of the Diem Government, the party's aims were not pursued through organization and propaganda. Its chief activity was to spy on enemies of the regime and to discover and denounce defectors. Membership was restricted, consisting almost exclusively of civil servants in key positions. All its activities were conducted amid secrecy. The Personalist Labor Party never held a convention, never took a public stand on any issue, and its governing body never met as a group. The party was run by Nhu alone, and its usefulness for him consisted primarily in providing him with intelligence about whomever he wished—suspect members of the government, administrators, generals, and private citizens. On the other hand, the party's usefulness to its members consisted "in the access they have to Nhu and in the material benefits which flow to them through the party's financial graft and related sources of income." [69] Fear and greed, not political convictions, held the Personalist Labor Party together. Nhu's claim of a membership of 70,000 [70] is fantastic, if for no other reason than the fact that no organizational apparatus permitting a count ever existed. It is significant that after the collapse of the Diem regime, people willing to admit past membership were hard to find.

Politically no less artificial was the National Revolutionary Civil Servants League, although its membership was quite substantial, consisting of practically everybody in government employment. In South Vietnam, government service is the main occupation next to agriculture. Nearly 500,000 persons made their living from the state under the Diem regime, the majority of them in the armed services. The number of persons employed in the civil bureaucracy was about 125,000, a large portion of whom (most of the 25,000 persons working for the Department of the Interior) were police and security agents. [71]

The nature of the League's membership lent itself well to the building of a stable organization whose hierarchy more or less paralleled that of the government. Fear of losing their jobs and the desire for promotion were sufficient motives for all civil servants to join, and upon orders from above to participate in the organization's activities. These consisted in group studies to popularize government policy among the bureaucracy, participation in government-sponsored parades, the lining of streets to cheer important visitors from abroad or traveling members of the government, conducting campaigns to get a high voter turnout in elections, and occasionally in "voluntary" labor on special public-works projects. The League, unlike the Personalist Labor Party, did not run its own candidates in the Assembly elections, but it frequently took a public stand on issues of the day. Its political statements, of course, said nothing the government did not wish to hear. The head of the League was usually a member of the Cabinet.

This was true also for the National Revolutionary Movement (NRM). Although like the League based on the civil service, it succeeded, by official intimidation and other means, in attracting members also outside the government administration. The NRM formed the "majority faction" in the Assembly. In the provinces, it was usually headed by province chiefs, district information chiefs, and village political commissioners—all of them appointed by the government and speaking for the government. President Diem was the party's honorary leader, and members of his "official family," as those people in the government close to him were called, were its acting chairmen.[72] Real control of the powers and resources of the NRM was in the hands of Diem's brothers Nhu and Can. The former directed the party's operations in the south, the latter in the center, with complete disregard for the opinions and wishes of either the official leaders or the membership of the party.

Like the Personalist Labor Party, the National Revolutionary Movement in its organizational practices followed Communist dictatorial methods. But it lacked devoted and well-trained cadres, thus underscoring the regime's lack of popular support. This was true of all government-sponsored parties in the South. They were effective only insofar as they operated as adjuncts of the regime's apparatus of intimidation and suppression; as forces capable of inspiring spontaneous political action they were nonexistent, and they consequently disappeared on the very day the Diem regime perished. Since their "revolutionary" names and rhetoric were constantly given the lie by their actions, they dissipated in a few short years the modest degree of political devotion which Diem's early struggle for a truly anticolonial regime had generated among many young Vietnamese.[73] Toward the end, there was a total absence of any kind of voluntary cooperation, and what spontaneous mass participation in politics South Vietnam knew under Diem was more and more directed against his regime. Only paid agents worked for the cause of South Vietnam as represented by Diem after 1960, and these, together with profiteers from the regime, were all that kept the government parties from collapsing before the regime itself did.

Under such a totalitarian system lacking devoted cadres and facing mass hostility, the process of selecting the agents whom the government needed to guide and control the population could produce only highly questionable results. This would have been the case even without two aggravating circumstances peculiar to South Vietnam: the first a heritage of ancient mandarinal and recent colonial Vietnam; the second, closely connected, the disdainful and ruthless treatment by the President's ruling family of those whom they considered their inferiors, meaning, in fact, everybody else.

The typical mandarin of the precolonial regime, although not living in castelike separation from the people, nevertheless considered himself a being apart from the peasant, above him not only because of function but even more because of education. The mandarins' role as ruthless tax collectors, policemen, and judges earned them the hatred of the people, who were naturally disinclined to respect knowledge and a cultivated mind in the service of exploitation and suppression. The mandarins came to take this as evidence of the common people's boorishness and animality, hardly admitting any human bond between themselves and the peasants. This notion was more conducive to the execution of their harsh duties than respect for the masses, and it marked the mandarins' attitude toward the people. Its corollary was an exalted notion of their own worth.

The colonial regime did not put an end to this deeply rooted attitude, not even among the mandarins who fought the French and appealed to the people for support. Of those who made peace with the French, it might be said that although they lost much of their old power, they tried to compensate for their loss by setting themselves even higher above the common herd. Mandarinal insolence and corruption increased considerably under the colonial regime. Even those privileged enough to receive a higher education in French schools, whether they obtained positions in the administration or entered professions, clung firmly to the traditional conceit of the mandarinal class. Among the leaders of the anticolonial movement, only the Communists insisted on a complete change in the traditional attitude of the elite toward the people.

It underlines the limitations of Diem's national revolution that under him the government and civil service largely perpetuated the tradition of oppression, venality, and intellectual conceit of their mandarinal predecessors. It could hardly have been otherwise under a regime in which the example for conduct toward inferiors set by the ruling family exemplified mandarinal officialdom at its worst. "The Ngos" (Diem's family), said Robert Scigliano, "are proud to the point of arrogance, self-sure to the point of sectarianism, and dubious of the abilities, if not the motives of others to the point of contempt." [74] The very nature of the system, with its lack of popular support and its need to resort to suppression, favored the thousands of would-be Ngos who ruled over provinces, districts, and villages just as the almighty mandarin or colonial official before them. Officials who respected the people and showed concern for their needs were unfit for such a regime and consequently were weeded out. Like all other ideas of reform, those aiming at changes in the administration were also dropped. The attempts to train a new type of administrator, pushed vigorously by concerned Americans, were doomed under a government that perpetuated the social injustices of colonialism and glorified the relations that existed between ruler and ruled in precolonial Vietnam. The passion which animated Diem was as one observer put it, "born of a profound, of an immense nostalgia for the Vietnamese past, of a desperate filial respect for the society of ancient Annam." [75] Diem's "revolutionary" regime consequently had no use for a new kind of administrator, nor had it any use for a new kind of judge. Being essentially of the past, it functioned better without a new judiciary; under Diem, justice, like the state itself, was largely administered on the basis of colonial law.

After the better elements of Diem's administration had either been killed by the Communists, dismissed, or fled the country, the regime's typical local leader was at best paternalistic, at worst corrupt and a bully. But whichever he was, he felt himself vastly superior to the people over whom he ruled. All observers sympathetic to the cause of South Vietnam have been deeply disturbed by this aspect of the Diem regime. It is difficult to argue with the "purely subjective judgment" of Malcolm W. Browne, an experienced and sympathetic observer, when he says "that of the thousands of Vietnamese officials I have known, I can think of none who does not more or less hold the Vietnamese people in contempt." A little earlier, Browne remarked: "It is said that when a man puts on a white collar in Vietnam, he has the right to step all over his neighbors and take whatever he can get. Careers in the civil service too often are merely platforms for a lifetime of extortion." [76] The injustice that such statements do to the minority of devoted civil servants that undoubtedly existed in no way contradicts the truth that the core of Diem's bureaucracy was mandarinal in the worst sense of the word, and that disastrous political consequences flowed from this fact. When insurrection started in the South, the Communists, as Browne and other American newspapermen pointed out, often killed government officials because they knew that "such an act would please the local people," [77] or as David Halberstam put it, "If bad local government was the source of [the people's] unhappiness, the Viet Cong would execute the offending village official while the peasants watched." [78] Again and again, Halberstam returns to this distressing subject. The government, he says "appointed police-state hacks to key positions," and a few pages later, after having looked for excuses for some of the regime's failures, he adds: "What cannot be forgiven is the sad but commonplace case of abuse by district chiefs." [79] In another context, the same author says: "All of this [General] Taylor [on a study mission in Vietnam in October, 1961] and his advisers hoped would end what was perhaps the worst characteristic of the Government: corrupt local officials constantly telling peasants that they had not seen the abuses which were in fact taking place before their eyes." [80]

Not only the newspapermen, Americans and others,[81] but also most American Government officials in Vietnam knew very well that the average Vietnamese officials "looked down upon the common people . . . while at the same time milking them for kickbacks." These were the words used by John Mecklin, the U.S. Public Affairs Officer in Saigon during the last year of the Diem regime, in speaking about the quality of the Diem-appointed local administrators.[82] He was not the only one aware of these conditions. Taylor, reports Mecklin, "exacted a long list of promises from Diem in 1961, mostly relating to urgently needed reforms." In listing what reforms Americans then considered most urgent, Mecklin states: "On the political level, we pressed the government toward such reforms as punishment of dishonest village officials." [83]

But why should it have been necessary to "press" for these reforms

under a government headed by a man who was generally regarded as
the country's most determined foe of corruption?

7

Neither General Taylor nor any other American who proposed reforms realized in 1961 why their demands were never acted upon by
the man who lived on American aid but refused to accept American
advice. If Diem had ever seriously tried to raise the level of performance of his officials, he would soon have found that this was impossible.
Opposed by the intellectuals, despised by the educated middle class, rejected by businessmen, hated by the youth and by all nationalists with
political ambitions, and totally lacking in mass support, the Diem Government had to rely for its survival on an apparatus of coercion. It
needed administrators willing to side with the government against
practically the entire people. Its officials were the ones obliged to apply
directly the means required to maintain the regime—primarily force.
They could not be the servants of the people; they had to be watch-
dogs over them. This function, in the long run, could not be exercised
by decent and honest men. Diem, at the beginning of his rule, attracted
some men devoted to him as well as to the people, but as time went on
such officials became exceedingly rare. True concern for the welfare
of the population was incompatible with the interests of a regime opposed to social reforms and relying on force. Sooner or later men who
sided with the people either resigned or were dismissed, to be replaced
by others ready to serve the government unconditionally. An honest
and public-spirited administration for South Vietnam would have meant
a break with the past, an uprooting of the mandarinal concepts of the
official's role. This, however, could have been brought about only
through social change and the creation of a new state, one capable of
arousing the enthusiasm of the youth and of enlisting the help of all
decent men—in other words, a reformed administration could be had
only through the revolution of which Diem constantly spoke but which
his policies effectively prevented.

That people willing to serve their country were to be found in Vietnam no one could doubt. The Vietminh had been able to enlist them
by the tens of thousands and to extract from them superhuman efforts
and sacrifices in the struggle for independence. Diem, once the true

character of his regime had become apparent, attracted only officials with the lowest possible motivation for public service, men who knew how to look after their own interests—the only ones fit to serve in a corrupt, inefficient, and despised police-state. On the higher levels, these were people eager to join the scramble for wealth and power; on the lower levels, where everyone was poorly paid, they were tempted to fill their pockets at the expense of the local population, whom they knew to be at their mercy under a system devoid of democratic controls.

The only control over the many local tyrants and corruptionists was exercised by still mightier bureaucrats, who in turn depended on the willing tools with whom the Diem Government operated the machinery of its central administration. These people were inherited largely from the colonial administration, and they were well trained in the bureaucratic skills necessary for survival under a dictatorial regime: servility toward the men who wielded supreme power; harsh treatment of inferiors; and total abandonment of all initiative for fear of punishment should they fail to guess the intentions of their almighty masters.[84] The prime requirement for the survival of any official in such a system is loyalty to the regime; talent and merit count little, initiative courts danger, and independence of judgment to the point of questioning the wisdom of a superior invites dismissal.

Indeed, to have asked the Diem regime to punish lazy, corrupt, or brutal officials meant asking it to cease being what it had become, meant insisting on its self-liquidation. Punishment was dealt out to the upright, to men who tended to side with the people against the regime, and who therefore had to be eliminated. If they did not resign—and resigning was also dangerous, since it was an act of protest—they were dismissed.[85] Once the regime had progressed along the road of moral decline, it began to apply truly vicious methods of punishing officials thought to be disloyal. It is known that the Communists, for propaganda reasons, killed those whose integrity and hard work were roadblocks to their incitement of the people against the regime. Incredible as it may seem, it became a practice under Diem to send administrators whom the regime did not trust into regions where it was almost certain that they would have no chance to survive.[86]

But even if the nature of the regime had not prevented it from creating an administration serving both the people and the state, Diem's government, a few years after he had consolidated his power, had itself become the greatest obstacle against any attempt at reforming the country's officialdom. It was a peculiarity of Diem's dictatorship that power was not in the hands of one man acting as the leader of a totalitarian organization, but was exercised by a small clique, which very soon comprised only members of the President's immediate family. What Bernard Fall wrote in 1963 about the Diem Government already held true in 1960: "Of the men who came to power with Diem in 1954–55, not one still holds a Cabinet portfolio." [87] Not that holding a Cabinet portfolio meant having any influence at all. The Cabinet, with an occasional exception kept for window-dressing purposes (such as Vice-President Tho and Secretary of State for Foreign Affairs Mau, neither of whom was allowed to participate in policy decisions), were largely second-rate men whom Diem quite properly treated with his customary contempt for career-seeking intellectuals. People who had at one time or another given the slightest hint of a wish to influence Government policy, even if loyal to Diem, were eliminated, usually by being exiled to meaningless ambassadorships.[88] There no longer was a true government. If the Cabinet met at all, it was only because Diem wanted to tell its members what he had decided and to lecture them for hours on their duties.

The ruling family, too, kept shrinking until it consisted only of four Ngo brothers and Mme. Nhu, the President's sister-in-law. Her father, Tran Van Chuong, was made Ambassador to Washington, where he was kept completely isolated from Vietnamese affairs and deprived of any meaningful function whatever. Also eliminated were Chuong's two brothers, Tran Van Don, Diem's first loyal and competent Minister of Foreign Affairs, and Tran Van Bac. Two younger in-laws, Tran Trung Dung and Nguyen Huu Chau, were forced to resign from the Cabinet. The resignation of Chau, considered the most gifted of all of Diem's collaborators, took place under circumstances indicating that the power of Mme. Nhu had become equal to her husband's or the President's.[89] Even Diem's youngest brother, Luyen, because it was feared that he might become a possible rival for Nhu, was prevented from sharing the family's power by being kept at his post as Ambassador to Great Britain.

The people who, more than Diem himself, determined the manner in which the country was to be run were his younger brothers Nhu and Can, Nhu's wife, and to a lesser degree Diem's older brother Ngo Dinh Thuc, Archbishop of Hue and Dean of the Catholic episcopacy of

Vietnam—four people whom Scigliano called "an extralegal elite which, with Diem, directs the destiny of Vietnam today." [90] Thuc, who held no official post, acted as unofficial adviser to the President, as leader of the Catholic clergy, and occasionally as one of the regime's propagandists abroad. Opponents of the regime said that he not only forced local administrators to make available public funds for Church projects but accused him also of participation in lucrative business transactions, for the good of the Church as well as himself. As to the latter accusation, however, no satisfactory evidence has been produced.[91]

Nor did Ngo Dinh Can hold any official position—he agreed to be known as the government's "Supreme Adviser"—but he was in effect governor of Central Vietnam, issuing orders to all officials appointed by Saigon, usually men he himself had picked. In addition to ruling through the established administration, he built up, with public funds and contributions extracted from businessmen, an extensive private network of police and security agents, many of whom he placed in agencies of the central government. A government contract in Central Vietnam could be had only after payment of a fee to the National Revolutionary Movement. To what extent he personally benefited from the graft he practiced as party leader was hard to determine. Can led a rather simple and secluded life, shunning luxury and practicing graft rather as an instrument of power. But it was he who disposed of the money he made by monopolizing the cinnamon trade, by controlling local shipping, and by selling at enormous profits rice obtained cheaply from the government to alleviate local shortages. Mecklin says that Can "controlled a virtual monopoly of Central Vietnam's economy." [92]

More crucial for the destiny of South Vietnam and the fate of the Diem regime than Can's reckless abuse of power was the role played by Ngo Dinh Nhu. Nhu also exercised his enormous influence without holding any kind of government position. There was no constitutional provision for the position of Adviser to the President held by Nhu. It is true that Nhu let himself be elected to the National Assembly, but he never bothered to attend its sessions. His power, which before the overthrow of the regime was generally thought to be greater than that of the President, derived from his influence upon Diem, from his role as head of the Personalist Labor Party, and from his control of the regime's various secret and police services.

The corruptive effect of the almost absolute power Nhu was able to exercise over the government, the administration, and the people made itself felt in many ways. It destroyed whatever sense of justice he may have possessed and ruined his faculty of judging either himself or others. With Nhu, the brothers' tendency to consider themselves superior to any other Vietnamese grew into a form of conceit that only can be described as monstrous.[93] Nhu ended up feeling that he was superior also to Diem, whom, toward the end of the Ngo reign, he treated as nothing more than his most important pawn.[94] It was Nhu who, with his passion for imitating Communist methods, created the various instruments of governmental control over the population that made the Diem regime hated even by people on whose support it depended: the leaders of the armed forces. The regime's secret services and special information and police forces took their orders from Nhu. Halberstam says that at one time there existed no less than thirteen different secret police organizations. The most important of Nhu's secret services was an organization of informers inside the administration headed by Dr. Tran Kim Tuyen, whose euphemistic title was Director of Political and Social Research Service of the Presidency.[95] Nhu held Communist-type "self-criticism" sessions in the semisecret Personalist Party, and with his uniformed Republican Youth, of which he was "Supreme Leader," he imitated fascist methods of popular control. The regime's so-called Special Forces,[96] and the manner in which Nhu used them in 1963, were reminiscent of the role of the Storm Troopers under the Nazis. On the other hand, the setting up of secret cells in existing organizations and in the administration, the attempt to organize all citizens into small groups whose leaders were made responsible for the members' loyalty, the rallies to denounce Communists, the propaganda techniques, and the perpetual harassment of a tired population with meetings and "spontaneous" demonstrations in favor of the regime and its great leader, all these were borrowed from the Communists. There was not one totalitarian stratagem that Nhu did not employ, always pretending that it was his own latest invention. The only weapons he never thought of using in the struggle against Communism were the weapons of democracy.

If there was anyone in Vietnam able to outdo Nhu's arrogance, suspicion, power drive, lack of truthfulness and humanity, it was his "catastrophic wife Tran Le Xuan (Beautiful Spring), who was best known as Mme. Nhu." [97] The help she gave the failing Diem regime was the help rendered a drowning man by a rock tied to his neck. If there was anything admirable about her, it was the energy and will power she displayed in directing the country's political destiny. In this, she outdid both her husband, Nhu, and President Diem, her brother-in-law. She was official hostess, or First Lady, at the Presidential Palace, a role however, that satisfied only her vanity, not the devastating drive for power that possessed her. The public statements she made, usually without consulting the President, invariably contributed to the decline of the regime's reputation. Like her husband, Mme. Nhu interfered directly with the running of the government and even of the army. "She simply issued orders, often on impulse by telephone, on virtually any subject to virtually anyone she wanted, from ministers and generals down." [98] From the fate that had befallen even so important a man as Mme. Nhu's brother-in-law Nguyen Huu Chau, everyone was aware of the risk of disobeying her orders, and they usually hastened to comply.[99]

With a great show of militant feminism, which, far from strengthening the rights of women, served mainly to increase the power of Vietnam's First Lady, Mme. Nhu created her own private party, the Women's Solidarity Movement, and her own private army, a paramilitary corps of young women used chiefly to ornament the parades through which the government tried to impress the people with its strength.[100] Mme. Nhu's exhibitionistic feminism also played a part in her successful drive to outlaw divorce and the remnants of polygamy that still existed in Vietnam. The so-called Family Code, which she pushed through the National Assembly at the end of 1958, and the Law for the Protection of Morality, which the President signed in May, 1962, tried not only to end divorce and polygamy, but also to impose upon the adult population a code of behavior that clashed with their accepted mores. In almost every one of their proscriptions these laws were both vexatious and ridiculous. "With a stroke of the pen," wrote Malcolm Browne, "Mme. Nhu outlawed divorce, dancing, beauty contests, gambling, fortune-telling, cockfighting, prostitution and a hundred other things dear to the heart of Vietnamese men. Neither her husband nor his brother, the President, dared interfere with these amazing legislative decrees." [101] Harsh penalties were provided for the use of contraceptives and for marital infidelity, "which included being seen in public with a person of another sex." [102] Dancing eventually was forbidden also in private homes, and in order to "promote the war effort," Mme. Nhu, in April, 1963, banned what she considered "sentimental songs."

Among the Vietnamese people generally and the intellectuals in particular, these attempts to legislate not only public but also private morals aroused not so much outrage as cynical allusions to Mme. Nhu's allegedly less than perfect moral comportment and "questionable past." [103] Nhu and his wife became the two most hated people in South Vietnam. There was nothing people did not believe them capable of—spying on their collaborators, arbitrary arrests of suspected enemies, and graft on a huge scale. It was, of course, impossible to produce proof of their corruption, since their control over the administration, the police apparatus, the press, and even the courts was practically absolute. But it was common knowledge that they extracted huge sums from Chinese and Vietnamese businessmen who sought import licenses and contracts for public works, neither of which could be had without Mme. Nhu's consent. The money thus collected was probably used chiefly to finance the parties Nhu and his wife controlled, but in Saigon practically everybody was convinced that a large part of these funds was deposited in private accounts of the Nhus abroad.[104] Abuse of power, nepotism, corruption, contempt for inferiors, and heartless unconcern for the needs of the people were the examples the "Family" set for the ministers, legislators, generals, province chiefs, and village commissioners whom they used as their tools. By agreeing to play their despicable roles, these tools of the Family earned the disdain of their masters as well as of the population. The humiliating treatment Mme. Nhu publicly administered to the members of the Assembly in forcing them to accept her Family and Morality laws [105] permits a guess as to the kind of abuse that was administered in private to persons who had incurred the Family's displeasure.[106] Nor was there any praise or reward for people who managed to remain loyal to the regime,[107] except the rewards of tolerance of their abuse of power and immunity from punishment for graft and brutality to the people; such misdeeds by officials were punished only in persons suspected of waning loyalty.

As these abuses gradually worsened and became common knowledge, it was asked again and again why they were apparently tolerated by the President, whom even many of his enemies regarded as honest, well-intentioned, and unwilling to put up with corruption. It does seem odd that Diem's integrity, a quality simply taken for granted in most important statesmen, was constantly emphasized. Did his admirers perhaps feel they had to do so because the incorruptible Diem presided over a family and regime that were generally believed to be corrupt? Some of Diem's supporters naïvely suggested that he was unaware of the abuses perpetrated under him, particularly by members of his family. If so, then he ought to have known. However, to believe that he did not know is absurd. It would mean not only that Diem was incompetent, irresponsible, and unbelievably stupid, but also that he was merely one of Nhu's many tools—surely none of which was the case. He may not have known everything, but he certainly knew more than he admitted. The people who believed in his integrity therefore expected him sooner or later at least to get rid of the Nhus.

Why he refused to do this, even after he knew that this was what Washington expected, is still widely regarded as an unsolved puzzle. Mecklin describes the Diem-Nhu relationship as "a psychiatric curiosity," [108] which it may well have been. Almost every author who tried to explain this relationship emphasizes Diem's family loyalty, and Fall, in commenting on this loyalty, spoke of "its fierceness." [109] But even if Diem would, as it seemed, rather have sacrificed his right arm than dismiss Nhu, family loyalty is not good enough a reason and would certainly be a statesman's poorest excuse for tolerating corruption. The reason that Diem refused to drop the Nhus was political. Diem knew that his brother's instruments of coercion—his spies, secret services, Special Forces, political parties, as well as his talent for corruption and terror—were indispensable to the regime. To eradicate the regime's evils, in particular its inefficient, graft-ridden, and repressive administration, required more than a break with Nhu. It required a radical change in Diem's own political philosophy, in the dictatorial character of his regime, of which he himself was the foremost exponent.

One should credit Diem with knowing what he was doing when he refused, to his dying day, to be separated from Nhu. But for precisely this reason, Diem must be held responsible for the evils of his regime, including the widespread corruption, which he no doubt despised as a means of personal enrichment but willingly embraced as a means of maintaining himself in power.

8

The treatment that the members of the Ngo family meted out to their political servants, hirelings, and even loyal supporters always betrayed the contempt with which they regarded anyone not of the clan. These people were treated with disrespect, but they were not punished unless suspected of having become disloyal. It was of course quite a different matter in the case of those thought to be opponents of the regime. Contempt for them was augmented by a desire to punish, born of the conviction that such punishment was deserved and was a necessary means of defending the regime.

In justifying the harsh measures taken against its enemies, the regime constantly made reference to the dangers that threatened the republic if opposition to Diem was not stamped out, implying that all criticism was Communist or Communist-inspired, or at least effective aid to the Communists. The regime always denied that there was any significant opposition outside the Vietminh, claiming that the inmates of its concentration camps and prisons were without exception criminals and Communists.[110]

Diem's supporters in the West never criticized him for the brutal and politically crude manner in which he fought not only the Communists but also the people of the regions that had long been controlled by the Vietminh. (The full story of the many crimes committed against these people by Diem's army, administrators, and police has yet to be told.[111]) In protesting against, or more often merely complaining about, the manner in which Diem treated his opponents, his Western supporters had in mind only the non-Communists and anti-Communists, people whose wish to save the South from Communism could not be doubted, but who were convinced that the Diem regime was unable to do so.

The anti-Communist nationalists in the South opposed to the Diem regime were deeply divided among themselves and politically not very impressive. Most of them were intellectuals and professionals; businessmen, although no less discontent, would have courted ruin had they failed to offer a show of loyalty to the regime. Not one of the known opposition spokesmen was a truly popular leader—something which apparently did not exist in post-Geneva Vietnam outside the Vietminh.

Like Diem himself, these men also were largely products of the past. Many had discredited themselves through collaboration with the French, and those who were not compromised revealed the shortcomings that illegal activity is likely to produce in politically ambitious men: a penchant for intrigue and sectarianism, a belief that ordinary people can be manipulated instead of having to be won over in open discussion. Since conditions in which their potential for democratic leadership could develop had been denied them in the past and were denied them under Diem, there was really no chance for them to mature politically. They never tried to organize a popular movement, either openly, risking arrest, or clandestinely: This they left to Diem's pro-Communist opponents. Some of Diem's non-Communist opponents, particularly those who had left for Paris after the defeat of Bao Dai and the sects, were known as "neutralists"; being former collaborators with the French, they were not in a position to compete with Diem for leadership of the nation. The entire nationalist opposition, whether formerly pro-French and later "neutralist" or always firmly anti-Communist, demanded that Diem grant political freedoms, but usually not because of democratic convictions. They needed civil liberties in order to pursue their aims legally, not because they recognized freedom as a necessary condition for creating a genuine mass movement favoring an anti-Communist South Vietnam. Their aim was not necessarily a democratic Vietnam, although in seeking American support they paid lip service to democracy. They were primarily competitors for government positions, for which they fought against Diem and among themselves. Their feebleness as a constructive and significant force capable of leading the country on a new road was quickly demonstrated after the fall of Diem.[112]

It is evident that such an opposition, even if it had succeeded in agreeing on a joint program and on united action, could never have become a threat to the Diem regime. Judging by Diem's ill-concealed contempt for his nationalist opponents, he seemed to have known that these people did not constitute a real threat to his power. He could have let them talk, which was about all they did, and even allowed them to hold meetings and publish papers without endangering his position. Such a concession to democracy would have been fervently applauded by Diem's American supporters. What these same supporters did not realize was that this would have contradicted Diem's basic political philosophy, which was antidemocratic, and that Diem's concept of a ruler precluded public criticism. Furthermore, it became only gradually manifest that power had a morally and intellectually corrupting effect on Diem, who began to think of himself as infallible and of anyone who dared to attack him or his family as an enemy of the state.

Diem's intolerance and authoritarianism, and his profound suspicion of other people's motives, made it impossible for him to ignore even mild expressions of discontent, particularly from the intellectuals, whom he despised *in toto*. Even silence, especially of prominent people, was regarded as a sign of opposition that called for countermeasures, such as having them spied upon by Nhu's agents. Those who imprudently spoke up, even if only at cocktail parties or in a bar, risked arrest and months, sometimes years, of imprisonment, usually without trial. The fate of people involved in secret antigovernment activities was worse. Not only were they kept in jails or concentration camps indefinitely, but they were frequently tortured, and revenge was usually taken on their families by Nhu and Can's henchmen.[113]

Diem's persecution of his non-Communist opponents, which became more and more vindictive as time went on, was of course directed almost exclusively at people regarded as actual or potential leaders. To silence the masses, for instance in Saigon, where everybody voiced his discontent rather freely, would have required the incarceration of at least half the population. Denis Warner thought that in 1962, no more than 300 "genuine liberals" were held in prisons (as compared to 20,000 Vietcong suspects).[114] No one knew the exact number, but since the regime toward the end became "almost paranoic in its touchiness,"[115] the number of anti-Communist prisoners grew rapidly after 1962. Diem's treatment of opponents, or people no longer willing to serve, became harsher as fear and the desire to take revenge on critics pushed aside his earlier more decent and more rational motives for persecuting anti-Communist rivals. Nguyen Thai, the editor of *Viet Nam Press*, and Vu Van Thai, the Director of Budget and Administrator of Foreign Aid, in 1960 and 1961 were still allowed to leave the country and take their families abroad. Dang Duc Khoi, the government's chief information officer, barely succeeded in escaping arrest by fleeing Saigon in August, 1963, "a step ahead of Nhu's secret police."[116] By then, "all outspoken anti-Communist, anti-Diem leaders had left the country or were imprisoned."[117]

In an unusual and quite ephemeral show of unity, a number of prominent anti-Communists critical of the Diem regime gathered in late April 1960, constituted themselves "The Bloc for Liberty and Progress," and mustered the courage on April 26, after a meeting at the Hotel Caravelle, to issue a statement about their grievances and demands. They did not aim at overthrowing the Diem regime. All they wanted was its liberalization (election of a new Assembly, a government responsible to the Assembly) and an end of family domination of the civil service and the army. The signers of the "Caravelle Manifesto" were former leaders of the sects, the Dai Viet, the old Nationalist Party, and dissident Catholic groups. Eleven of the eighteen members of the group were former Cabinet ministers (under Bao Dai and Diem), and four had held other high government positions. Among the signers prominent before Diem, and again after his fall, were Phan Khac, Suu, Phan Huy Quat, Tran Van Don, Tran Van Huong, and Tran Van Tuyen.

Although the demands of the Caravelle group were modest, the language used in their manifesto was surprisingly bold. Diem was told that his regime had brought the people neither a better life nor more freedom. "Continuous arrests fill the jails and prisons to the rafters." The constitution existed on paper only. The National Assembly did only what the government wanted. The elections were "antidemocratic," and all this was "copied from the dictatorial Communist regimes." [118]

No Vietnamese newspaper printed the "Manifesto of the Eighteen," thus confirming another charge of its signers, namely that "public opinion and the press are reduced to silence." The regime often boasted that there was no press censorship in South Vietnam. Its methods for silencing the press were indeed less overt. It abolished freedom of the press by more devious and more callous means, of which Nhu was the inventor: mob action against criticism in the press rather than outright legal restraints. If a paper criticized the government too freely or dared to make uncomplimentary remarks about any member of the Ngo family, hoodlums hired by one of Nhu's secret services staged an outburst of "popular indignation," which invariably ended with the wrecking of the paper's offices and plant. The owner lost not only permission to publish, but also much of his property. He was usually fined and jailed as well. By 1958, all opposition papers had been suppressed and applications for new ones were rejected, if answered at all.

The last opposition paper to go was the weekly *Thoi Luan*. In its issue of March 15, 1958, the paper attacked the rubber-stamp Assembly and rigged elections. *Thoi Luan* was suspended and the publisher, Nghiem Xuan Thien, charged with libel for having "insulted" the government, was sentenced to ten months in prison and ruinously high fines imposed on him.[119]

The Caravelle group ceased to exist after its one vain attempt to publicize the grievances and demands of Diem's anti-Communist critics. But Diem and his brothers neither forgot nor forgave the audacity of these eighteen men. After the attempted coup by a group of paratroopers on November 11, 1960, the regime proceeded to restore its shaken authority through mass arrests of anti-Communists suspected of nurturing the hope that the government would fall. Although only one member of the Caravelle group, Phan Khac Suu, was accused of involvement in the coup, most of the others were also arrested, and some were held in jail without trial until the fall of the regime.

The West paid very little attention to the manner in which Diem dealt with the men who made what might be called the opposition's last effort to steer the regime, through argument and appeal, toward a less authoritarian course. American newspaper readers remained ignorant of the manifesto of the Caravelle group and learned nothing about the later arrest of its members. This was in sharp contrast to the sensational reporting and endless propagandistic exploitation of a strikingly similar affair in the North, the so-called "intellectual revolt" that took place in Hanoi in the fall and winter of 1956–57, obviously an echo of Khrushchev's de-Stalinization and its effects in Poland and Hungary, but even more directly inspired by the short flurry of intellectual criticism in China known as the "Hundred Flowers campaign."[120] A number of periodicals sharply attacked Party control of intellectual and artistic life. In these journals, of which *Nhan Van* (*Humanism*) and *Giai Pham Mua Xuan* (*Beautiful Flowers of the Spring*) were the most outspoken, writers and artists not only expressed their own particular grievances but also attacked government policy, charging, for instance, that corruption flourished among Party members and that the peasantry was being driven into opposition by the regime's harsh and unjust methods of agrarian reform.

Measures against these critics were taken late and were comparatively mild. The papers that disobeyed orders to cease their attacks on the Party were quietly suspended in spring, 1957, but action against the leaders of this liberalization movement was taken only in 1958. Professor Tran Duc Thao, the most brilliant of North Vietnam's intellectuals, had to stand trial before a "popular tribunal" at Hanoi University. He was exiled to a remote region of the country, from which he was allowed to return and given a minor teaching position in 1962.[121]

Like Diem's critics in the South, whose intention was not to destroy but rather to build a viable anti-Communist state, the intellectual rebels in the North were not in principle opposed to the existing regime. Their aim was to obtain reforms, to liberalize and humanize it. Both were punished, and both failed for the same reason: The reforms they demanded were incompatible with the nature of the regimes in both halves of Vietnam. Anti-Communists in the West knew that the totalitarian nature of Ho Chi Minh's rule did not allow open criticism, even by confirmed Communists. What was recognized too late was that in the South, too, public criticism of the regime, even by confirmed anti-Communists, was taboo. Diem never stopped talking about the absence of freedom in the Communist North, again and again citing as proof the silencing of the intellectuals involved in the *Nhan Van* affair— although two years later he not only would not allow the Manifesto of the Eighteen to be printed but had most of its signers jailed without trial. The Diem regime was too weak to suppress the population and the intellectuals as effectively as the regime in the North, but to the extent it was able to apply terror it did so without restraint. Indeed, as David Halberstam put it after a year and a half of close observation, the Diem regime "had all the controls, all the oppressions and the frustrating, grim aspects of the modern totalitarian state—without the dynamism, efficiency and motivation that Communism had brought to the North." [122]

9

The inefficiency and lack of dynamism that characterized Diem's dictatorship soon slowed down governmental action in all fields where progress was vital if South Vietnam's survival was to be assured. The rate at which, during the first two or three hopeful years, war damages were repaired and deteriorated public services rebuilt, could not be maintained by a regime that equated initiative among its officials with insubordination. Not even minor decisions concerning local projects or decisions of a purely technical nature were entrusted to men of local or technical competence. They had to consult Saigon and wait until the government, which in most instances meant Diem himself, found time to study the subject and hand down a decision. Diem was apparently convinced that any decision, no matter how simple, was good only if arrived at by him, and he would delay making it for months or postpone it indefinitely rather than leave it to the local administrators or technical experts directly involved.[123]

The general inertia this produced on all levels of governmental decision-making was one of the reasons for the lack of appreciable economic progress under the Diem regime. This failure was particularly pronounced in the field of industrialization. Compared with the dynamic growth of industry in the North, the South was almost stagnant. For each factory built under Diem—there were less than two dozen—the Communist regime in the North built fifty.[124]

The regime's failure to promote economic progress proves that even as a nationalist and anticolonialist, Diem was not a driving force but rather an obstacle to the revolution for which the people were waiting and the country was ready. The denial of industry had been one of the main features of colonial exploitation, and it had kept Vietnam economically dependent on France. To start the country on the road to industrialization was therefore one of the first tasks of Vietnam's national revolution. Without it, the country's independence remained incomplete. The forced pace of industrialization pursued in the North would certainly not have been advisable, but to leave the colonial structure of the South's economy essentially unchanged was even less desirable.

In speaking of the "economic progress" achieved under the Diem regime, much has been said about the introduction of industrial crops (jute, ramie, and kenaf), the rise in the production of rubber, and about the fact, never fully corroborated, that "food production rose an average of 7 per cent a year and prewar levels were achieved and passed." [125] In view of the 50 per cent increase in population since 1938, attaining prewar food-production levels would at best have been a mediocre accomplishment. Indeed, the modest progress in nonindustrial production made under Diem certainly did not vindicate his policy of neglecting industry in favor of agriculture, a policy that one of Diem's American supporters described as the exploitation of "South Viet Nam's great natural advantages in the agricultural realm—fertile land, climate, labor, and skills—as the primary route to increased living standards, reduction of the trade deficit, and eventual self-suffi-ciency." [126] Industrialization would be "gradual," Diem stated at a luncheon of businessmen in New York on May 14, 1957, and consistent with South Vietnam's needs and capacities, and going into detail he said that the government aimed at producing some textiles, sugar, ce-ment, paper, glass, and plastics, and that this, together with some plants producing goods for daily use, would, for the time being, be the core of the industrialization plan.

What was really planned, and how much of the regime's first five-year plan of 1957 was fulfilled, remained unknown, since the plan was kept secret. By 1962, fewer than a dozen new, mostly small, industrial enterprises had either been put in operation or brought near comple-tion, increasing the industrial labor force by 8,000, a number which in-cluded the workers of the coal mine being developed at Nong Son, and the people employed in the construction of an electrochemical com-bine at An Hoa. Mounting insecurity was usually given as the reason that the first five-year plan was not fulfilled on time,[127] and was prob-ably also the reason for the relative modesty of the second five-year plan (1962–66), which, in another dozen or so new establishments, was to increase the labor force by 12,000 industrial workers. "Inse-curity" no doubt later became a valid explanation for the noncomple-tion of the second five-year plan.[128]

However, more important than guerrilla warfare in slowing down industrial development was the government's own attitude both as regards projected aims and methods used in their realization. Diem, who in this field, too, remained the final arbiter, had little understand-ing of economic problems and could never quite decide whether to promote industrialization through public or private enterprise. The precepts of the regime's personalist philosophy demanded that the imperfections of a system of private enterprise be corrected with a dose of "socialism," the latter narrowly conceived of as public enter-prise under direct government control. Diem insisted that the govern-ment's share in the mixed enterprises favored by his regime be 51 per cent. But the allocation of priorities in the distribution of government funds left only inadequate resources for government-sponsored indus-tries; and private investors were not coming forward to buy the shares Diem allowed them to have. In fact, there would not have been more progress in this field even if Diem had realized that his "gradual" indus-trialization was far from consistent with the country's needs [129] and had made more ambitious plans. One reason for this was the nature of the regime, whose lack of efficiency and dynamism precluded the realization of any plan requiring initiative on all leadership levels and officials trained for more than administrative routine. Another reason was the state of political uncertainty, which prevented any significant mobilization of private capital for industrialization of the South. And finally, the funds needed for a development policy based on public enterprise also were not available. Any sizable industrial project could have been undertaken only with U.S. aid funds. But the United States, unlike the countries supporting industrialization in the North, looked with disfavor upon the use of aid money for industries run as public enterprises.

As to the regime's lack of qualification for pursuing a more ambitious development policy, everyone seems to be in agreement, whether he opposes public enterprise as the best means of achieving economic progress or accepts it as a necessity for underdeveloped countries. "The Vietnamese government," says Scigliano, "has been more of a drag than a stimulus to economic development," [130] and Lloyd D. Musolf says not only that "the South Vietnam government has lagged in applying development policy," but also stresses "the failure of the regime to give full weight to its own announced philosophy of public enterprise." [131] Montgomery cites the fact that during 1955, the loans made by the National Investment Fund, "a government-backed development agency that preceded the Industrial Development Center, were made to private, not public enterprise," [132] as an example of the regime's inconsistent development policy. More significant still was that "the fund's loans were made on considerations other than industrial development policy, and were not all for productive facilities." [133] In 1957, an Industrial Development Center (IDC) was created with American aid. "It was to be a lending agency to new or existing [private] enterprises. At the end of 1959, the government had approved only 27 of the 125 projects submitted to it, of which a number appear to have been loans to pay off previous loans." [134] There, too, it was usually the President himself who spoke the final word, after months of waiting or study or indecision. The exasperating slowness with which his decisions were made seemed to confirm the view held by some that Diem and Nhu were basically hostile to private enterprise.[135] It certainly confirmed that the regime was unfit to proceed dynamically in promoting development, either through private or public enterprise,[136] and that in regard to both, the leaders of South Vietnam betrayed indifference rather than firm views.[137]

As to private enterprise, it can be said that the belated and lukewarm efforts to attract foreign investors failed as conspicuously as did the feeble attempts to mobilize indigenous capital for industrial development. American capital in particular showed no inclination at all to disregard poor prospects of early gain and the risks of losing all in order to support their government's efforts to make South Vietnam prosperous.[138] This cautious American attitude could hardly induce local capitalists to overcome their traditional fear of loss or slow profits. Also, the President's "anti-Chinese" ordinances of August and September, 1956, although justifiable on several grounds,[139] were not likely to improve the climate for mobilizing local capital. They increased the reluctance of prospective Chinese investors without overcoming the aversion of the wealthy Vietnamese to assume an active role in the country's industrial development under prevailing conditions. The landowners who had been given government bonds in compensation for expropriated land made almost no use at all of the opportunity to transform them into industrial shares. As late as September, 1961, the land-reform bonds invested in industry amounted only to 7 million piasters. Since about 1,600 landowners had received bonds in the total amount of approximately 750 million piasters, the portion actually invested in industrial enterprises was less than 1 per cent of the total.[140]

Should all of this not have been an incentive as well as a justification for Diem to pursue more vigorously a development policy based on public enterprise? And if the United States opposed the use of aid funds for financing public enterprise, should Diem not have fought for his views, as he did—usually with success [141]—whenever he and Washington were in disagreement? It is more than likely that here, too, Diem would have been successful,[142] but his belief in the need for industrialization was obviously not strong enough to make him insist upon using aid funds to finance public enterprises. In fact, Diem and Washington were always in basic agreement on the main purpose of American aid—its use as a means of securing the country's survival, by directing the bulk of all aid toward building up the regime's military strength, and in the clashes over secondary issues, Washington, not Diem, usually demanded, albeit in vain, that a greater share of the available funds be devoted to social and economic projects. If 78 per cent of the total U.S. aid was absorbed by the regime's military establishments, and no more than 1.25 per cent spent on industrial development and mining, this was because both the United States and Diem thought of maintaining security and the conditions of survival primarily in military terms, neglecting, despite frequent assurances to the contrary, the social, economic, and political requirements for making security measures effective. It is precisely this joint policy of neglecting economic development that explains why, as Milton C. Taylor put it in 1961, "after six years of large-scale American aid, Vietnam is becoming a permanent mendicant." [143]

American aid to Vietnam has been the subject of much expert investigation, public debate, and Congressional scrutiny. The sums involved are enormous (the total in grants had already reached $1.311 billion by mid-1960) and the question why still more was being asked for, and considered essential for South Vietnam's survival, quite understandably agitated American lawmakers and the public. But the debate rarely dealt with the imbalance between military and economic aid: Congress always favored the former over the latter. It concentrated chiefly on the problem of waste in the program's administration, and, in a more serious vein, on the question how much direct impact aid had on the lives of the people.

As to waste, nobody denied that there was some, but most of the sensational accusations in one of the press campaigns in particular were proved either wrong or highly exaggerated in later Congressional hearings.[144] The program on the whole was well administered, both on the American and Vietnamese sides, and in its actual administration there was little of the friction that occurred on the higher political levels.[145]

The frequent complaint that such massive aid should have resulted in more direct tangible improvements for the people, and that the people should have shown more awareness of (and gratitude for) the benefits they derived from American aid is another matter. This criticism would have been more meaningful and perhaps more effective if it had been directed against the program's general orientation, which was determined by the almost exclusive reliance upon military means for maintaining security. The funds left over after direct and indirect expenditures for military purposes were allocated were entirely insufficient to have a meaningful social and economic impact.[146] Aid for nonmilitary projects, usually referred to as "project aid," added up to no more than 22 per cent of all aid received. Of this 22 per cent, 40 per cent was spent on transportation, mostly on rebuilding the country's highway system. Agriculture, which included expenses for the administration of the land-reform program and the establishment of agricultural credit and cooperatives, received 17 per cent of nonmilitary aid. The same amount was spent for administration, most of which was devoured by police and security services, largely for equipment. This left 7 per cent of nonmilitary aid for health and sanitation, another 7 per cent for education, and as little as 3 per cent for the much-talked-about community-development programs, social welfare, and housing. This 3 per cent was approximately 0.6 per cent of the total aid. The 20-mile stretch of highway from Saigon to Bien Hoa "cost more money than the United States provided for all labor, community development, social welfare, housing, health, and education projects in Vietnam combined during the entire period 1954–1961." [147] As Milton C. Taylor has shown, Vietnam in 1960 received from the United States the equivalent of $13.70 per capita.[148] It is easy to figure out that, directly and indirectly, the sum spent for all the programs of social and community services, including education, amounted to no more than 50 cents per inhabitant for the entire year, and it should cause no surprise that this ridiculously small sum failed to produce a noticeable improvement in the lives of the people.

It might, however, be said that the economy as a whole must have been stimulated enormously by the influx of such vast sums of money. Indeed, whatever modest economic progress the South did make was no doubt due to American aid, and a great many people benefited directly. The hundreds of thousands in the army and the various paramilitary forces reduced unemployment; the great mass of these people, although themselves unproductive, must as consumers have given employment to many others, as both public and private construction did on an even larger scale. The point here is not so much that this was too little, but that it contributed almost nothing to economic development. The *Annual Statistical Bulletin* of USOM published revealing figures about the kind of construction activity carried out between 1957 and 1960.[149] During this period, South Vietnam built 47,000 square meters of cinemas and dancehalls, but only 6,500 square meters of hospitals, and 3,500 square meters of rice mills, compared to 56,000 square meters of churches and pagodas. The figure for school building at first sight looks more impressive—86,000 square meters—but it lagged considerably behind the existing needs [150] and is insignificant if compared with the 425,000 square meters for high-rent villas and apartment buildings.

Nothing was done about city slums, whose growth and desolation, particularly in the Saigon-Cholon area, were hardly ever mentioned by the people who liked to compare the drabness of Hanoi with the glitter of Saigon.

In quoting the above figures, Bernard Fall remarks: "That is the sort of thing—far more than weapons and infiltrators from across the 17th parallel—that makes Communist guerrillas out of peaceable peasants." [151] He might have added: And out of city-dwellers, too.

10

If the enemies of Diem had been made up only of the divided and unorganized anti-Communist nationalists at home and abroad, the regime's lack of economic progress, neglect of urgent reforms, and denial of basic freedoms would hardly have threatened its existence. The world is full of examples of the survival of such regimes. South Vietnam might have been just one more country in which the sullen masses become resigned to their fate and in which clandestine activities of small groups aspiring to overthrow the regime are successfully handled by the police.

Unfortunately for Diem, however, South Vietnam also had a Communist opposition, and this opposition was a well-organized, exceptionally strong movement. The Vietnamese Communists, after 1954, enjoyed greater popular support and were closer to victory than any other Communist movement in the world. Indeed, what might be called the uniqueness of Vietnam and what after 1960 turned the country into the principal battleground between East and West was precisely the strength of Vietnamese Communism—a heritage of the colonial regime and of the misguided French attempt to suppress the Vietnamese national revolution. The fate of the Diem regime therefore depended chiefly on the success or failure of the measures to reduce, and eventually put an end to, the deadly power of the country's native Communist movement.

During the war against the French, the Vietminh in the South, although less strong than in the North, had built up an efficient and almost indestructible network of underground organizations, and also enjoyed broad popular support. After the military units of the Vietminh were withdrawn from the South, as stipulated in the Geneva cease-fire agreement, Vietminh control of the countryside was hardly less effective than before. In part of the country it grew even stronger, since in many regions the French withdrew before Diem's army and administration were ready to establish control. Probably only a fraction of the best-trained cadres and guerrillas were sent North, joined by insignificant numbers of the people that had sympathized with and supported the Vietminh during the war. Vietminh control therefore long remained unchallenged in vast regions of the South, and was near total in such provinces as Quang Ngai, Binh Dinh, in the so-called Zone D, between Saigon and the Cambodian border, in the Plain of Reeds, on the Camau Peninsula, and in numerous other districts, both in the highlands and the Mekong Delta.[152] The fighting was over, the French had left, there no longer was any need to secure Vietminh control by military means. The substantial quantity of arms left behind by the troops who had gone North were buried; Vietminh power, for the time being, was to be based on organization, open and secret, and on the influence the movement had gained over the people. Some Communist cadres in the South found it hard to accept the Party's orders from Hanoi to limit their struggle against the Diem regime to organization and propaganda, but the majority was content to wait and lie low, particularly in regions under government control. Nothing was farther from the minds of the Communists and their close allies than the thought of organizing armed insurrection against the Diem regime. They were convinced that in the South, too, victory was already theirs, even if its consummation had to await the elections of July, 1956, through which the country would be united under Ho Chi Minh.

This was the situation Diem faced in regard to his chief enemy, Communism, during the first two years of his reign. It would seem that any leader of even moderate political intelligence should have been able to determine at the time what strategy would be most likely to defeat the Communist threat to the South. Such a strategy would have had to have two aims, neither of which could have been pursued successfully as long as anti-Communism was tied up with colonialism. One of the objectives should have been to separate from the Communist core of the Vietminh the various forces attached to it only because of their determination to oust the French. Diem, after his assumption of power, was supremely qualified for this task by reason of his anticolonial past and by his struggle to liquidate all remnants of French power. But his mind, blighted by dogmatism and filled with the pathological notion that he alone had been called upon to save the country, was unable to conceive of the measures that might have turned allies of the Communists into friends of his regime: the right to organize, to voice their grievances and demands freely, and eventually also to share in the government. Only the granting of a minimum of political freedom could have induced these people to break away from the Communist-led Vietminh. The loss of these allies would have greatly diminished the ability of the Communist cadres to keep their hold on the masses of the Vietnamese people.

But it would have been even more important for Diem to set his course on the second aim of a sound anti-Communist strategy: depriving the Communist cadres of the true source of their strength—popular support. What this required was known to everybody in Vietnam, including the spokesmen of the regime: the reforms that would have added up to the "social revolution" and the "genuine democracy" about which Diem talked so much but which his actions negated. This is what the people waited for during the first two years of Diem's regime, hoping that their modest expectations would be fulfilled, and ready to change from neutrality to full acceptance of an anti-Communist South Vietnam. And this is what Ho Chi Minh and his Communist cadres in the South feared most. What would have become of their hold over the people if Diem had grasped the simple idea that popular support had to be earned, and that the people, if he improved their lot, would no longer have to depend on the Communists to realize the promised "social revolution"?

The fear of the Communists turned out to be unfounded. Diem's method of fighting Communism was to concentrate on destroying their cadres, if necessary physically, instead of making them politically impotent by depriving them of mass support. He had not learned the lesson of the Indochina War—i.e., that a political movement cannot be destroyed by killing its exponents; he and his chief adviser, Nhu, subscribed to the primitive notion that the only good Communist was a dead one rather than a politically helpless one without popular support. The thought that in the South Vietnam of that time a dead Communist might prove more dangerous than a live one never entered their minds. They never realized that for every Communist killed, especially if he was a popular one who had fought in the resistance, two new ones were likely to spring up. Their almost total reliance on naked force in fighting political ideas was of course a corollary of the denial of politi-

cal freedom and social justice. Instead of the bit of land the peasants
wanted, they were given, in conjunction with a manhunt against Vietminh cadres, an unending series of sermons about the evils of Communism, delivered in compulsory meetings by officials whom the peasants
had every reason to despise.

To persecute former resistance fighters, whether Communist or not,
and moreover to deny them their democratic liberties, was of course a
breach of the Geneva agreement.[153] But Diem's position was that
South Vietnam was neither legally nor morally bound by the agreements, a position which, in view of the unusual character of the
Geneva accords as international treaties, could not really be attacked.
The Hanoi Government certainly had no moral right to complain
about Diem's noncompliance with the provisions concerning reprisals
and democratic liberties, being themselves no less culpable than Saigon.
But aside from any legal or moral considerations, Diem's persecution
of people known to have belonged to the Vietminh was disastrous
politically. It was an almost incomprehensible violation of common
sense, and one of the major contributions to the success of the later
Communist-led insurrection.

The manhunt against the Vietminh began only after the regime's
military and police apparatus was sufficiently developed and firmly under government control. Two major campaigns were made with
massive participation of the army. The first one swept through the
provinces west of Saigon, lasting from June 8, 1956, to October 31,
1956. The second one was much longer—from June 17, 1956, to
December 15, 1957—since the territory covered, east of Saigon, contained a great number of important Vietminh bases which the French
had never succeeded in dislodging,[154] one of the many regions where
the regime had "failed to implant itself on the local level [and] where
the Communists were able to consolidate and to expand their position." [155] It was in these regions that army action also brought back
many landlords eager to collect land rents from peasants who had for
years considered themselves the owners of the land they tilled.

Very little reliable information has come out of Vietnam about the
manner in which these and later campaigns to uproot the Vietminh
were conducted by the army and the political cadres specially trained
for these campaigns. It is of course impossible to accept as true the fantastic claims and accusations of Communist propaganda, which counts
the number of killed and imprisoned in the hundreds of thousands,

speaks of systematic torture, the shelling and burning of "uncooperative" villages, and the arrest of whole families on the strength of denunciations.[156] But there can be no doubt, on the basis of reports by
the few impartial observers who have treated the subject, that innumerable crimes and absolutely senseless acts of suppression against
both real and suspected Communists and sympathizing villagers were
committed.[157] Efficiency took the form of brutality and a total disregard for the difference between determined foes and potential friends.
Most of the real Communists escaped and, in hiding, prepared themselves for the day when conditions for successful insurrection would
be ripe. Those who were caught were usually killed, and judging by
the treatment the South Vietnamese Army later accorded to captured
guerrillas, most likely also were tortured.[158] The American public,
which a little while later was told of the many Diem officials murdered
by the so-called Vietcong, learned nothing at all about these earlier
events, not so much because of Saigon censorship but rather because of
the West's reluctance openly to condemn crimes committed in the
name of anti-Communism.

These military and police actions, which produced more enemies for
the regime than were killed or imprisoned, were accompanied by civic
action, of which only the positive aspects were reported abroad and
cited as evidence of the benefits foreign aid brought to the villagers.
Roads were repaired, bridges rebuilt, and schools and infirmaries
opened, though not nearly enough to take care of existing needs. Medical services were particularly welcome, but since they were rarely
maintained after being introduced in these campaigns, the people were
again disappointed, for now they knew that there were cures for their
diseases but that these were not available to them.[159] However, another aspect of civic action made it even more difficult to be grateful
for these gifts, which the peasants had every right to expect. This was
the so-called psychological campaign designed to remove the poison of
Communism from the people's minds. The means employed in this
many-pronged operation were all copied from the Vietminh, the
whole campaign being, in Scigliano's words, an "experiment in defeating Communism by boisterous Communist methods." [160] These methods included "brainwashing" in "re-education camps," denunciation
rallies similar to those held in the North during the land-reform campaign, nightly meetings with loudspeakers blaring for hours, and,
worst of all, an attempt to establish control over the population

through a system of groups the smallest of which comprised five families. The members of these groups were supposed to watch one another, and the group leader was responsible to the authorities for the good behavior of all the members.[161] The "theoretician" of this program had, appropriately, been trained by the Vietminh. He was Tran Chanh Thanh, for several years Diem's Secretary of State for Information and Youth, and former director of the Vietminh judiciary services. After some trouble of an undisclosed nature with the Communist Party, Tran Chanh Thanh left the Vietminh zone in 1951 to become, in 1955, the intellectual father of the many schemes of "rural pacification" through which Diem and his successor regimes have tried, so far without success, to regain control of the countryside.[162]

The views about the results of these campaigns to eradicate the Vietminh expressed by spokesmen of the regime clearly reflected their declining ability to see either themselves or their enemies realistically. In only ten months, said Tran Chanh Thanh, the government had "entirely destroyed the predominant Communist influence of the previous nine years."[163] He apparently believed that the great majority of Communist cadres had been killed or captured, and that his "psychological action" had turned the masses of former Vietminh sympathizers into admirers of Diem. The evidence, let alone future events, proved these assumptions to be utterly wrong. According to the official figures, 20,000–30,000 former Vietminh cadres were put into concentration camps (most observers believe the number to be considerably higher); but P. J. Honey, whose anti-Communist record was well known, had occasion to visit these camps. He reported that "the majority of the detainees are neither Communist nor pro-Communist."[164] This was probably true also of the many who had been killed, and who, together with their outraged families, might very well have closed their ears to Communist propaganda if the regime had brought them social justice and economic progress instead of unfreedom, misery, and death. The true result of the regime's attempt to destroy the Vietminh, says Bernard Fall, was that "the countryside largely went Communist in 1958–60."[165] The Diem Government itself created the conditions that pushed the population to the brink of open rebellion, and this convinced the Communist leadership that the South could be conquered by force.

Although the Communist leaders, in the South as well as in Hanoi, had persistently worked toward making themselves masters of the entire country, they had not considered force as the primary means for achieving this end. Their tactic was to prepare for the elections provided for by the Geneva agreement, even if they must have had doubts as to when, if ever, these elections would be held. However, from a legal point of view, they had a perfect right to insist upon them, since the Vietminh had agreed to partition as only temporary. They clung to the belief that had they rejected the Geneva compromise and continued the war after the fall of Dien Bien Phu, their armies would have defeated the French and they themselves become masters of the entire country. They never regarded the election provisions of the agreement as anything but a face-saving device for the French and the West, correctly assuming that not only the Chinese and Russians, but also the British and French architects of the Geneva agreement shared this view. The Vietnamese Communists therefore held the refusal of the South to hold elections for the unification of the country to be a violation of the Geneva agreement. Diem, they said, with U.S. support and French connivance,[166] was trying to cheat them out of the total victory they believed they had gained, and which in their eyes the Geneva conference had sanctioned. Had they not agreed to the Geneva settlement, the Communists argued, the South would not exist as a separate state; Diem wanted to enjoy the advantages of the Geneva agreement yet refused to comply with its obligations.

Although the Vietnamese Communists, and also Moscow and Peking, did not go beyond verbal protests against Diem's refusal to hold the 1956 elections, it was a mistaken belief that the Hanoi regime would ever resign itself to permanent partition. This belief arose because only belatedly, and only after having exhausted all diplomatic means of obtaining their aim through elections, did the Communists decide on the use of force to bring about unification—an alternative, however, for which they had been preparing themselves ever since their acceptance of temporary partition at Geneva.

Diem's refusal to hold general elections became official on July 16, 1955. In a statement that ranks among the most preposterous he ever made, Diem not only extolled "free elections" and "true democracy," the realization of which he was working hard to prevent in the South, but also promised the people of the North that "the National Government will bring you independence in freedom." [167] This was Diem's answer to Hanoi's request that he agree to hold the preliminary discussions for the July, 1956, elections (discussions provided for in the Final Declaration at Geneva). All further requests by Hanoi in regard to the elections, as well as to the many proposals for postal, cultural, and economic exchanges between North and South, remained unanswered by Saigon. Diem held to the position that his government, not having signed the Geneva agreements, was not bound by them, and that the North would not live up to the stipulation of free elections.

In view of the curious nature of the Geneva agreement, whose political provisions were not signed by any of the contracting powers, there has so far been no satisfactory answer to the question whether Ho Chi Minh stood on more solid "legal ground" in asking for the elections, or Diem in rejecting them.[168] Legally, this question has always been irrelevant. What mattered was the impact of the policies of the two regimes on the people of Vietnam, and to a lesser degree on world opinion. Diem's argument that the democratic liberties demanded by the Final Declaration as a condition for elections were non-existent in the North no doubt carried considerable weight, but it would have made a greater impression, both at home and abroad, if his government had created these democratic liberties in the South. Indeed, the whole question is not so much a legal as a moral and political one. Diem's moral right to ignore the Geneva agreement was contingent upon his regime's fulfillment of its obligations toward the Vietnamese people, including those who had fought with the Vietminh against the French. And one of these obligations was to provide the people of the South with democratic liberties—a clear example of a morally correct action also being the only road to political success. If the people of the South had preferred a dictatorship to the freedoms in whose name the country was kept divided, this would have been one more reason for them to be ruled by the more efficient and in many respects more progressive North. What the people would probably have decided for, had they been well informed and had they enjoyed the right of self-determination, was a state of peaceful coexistence between North and South.[169]

Few people below the 17th parallel knew that despite the North's progress in industrialization, life under the Hanoi regime was harder than in the South. Saigon constantly spoke of the miserable life under Communism, but few believed this in a country whose daily experience was that the claims of official propaganda contradicted obvious facts. The less confidence people had in the truth of official propaganda, the more they became inclined to listen to Communist propaganda claims that the people in the North led a better life.

But the North's inability to provide this better life was largely why the Hanoi regime could not resign itself to permanent partition and why the Communists were impelled to attempt to win control of the South by force. Food production, although rising, could not keep pace with the population increase, and the policy of forced industrialization prohibited imports that might have relieved the appalling shortage of consumer goods. The hectic pace at which the collectivization of agriculture was pursued beginning early in 1958 increased the regime's difficulties with the peasants.[170] At the end of that year, only 4,722 so-called Work Exchange Teams had been created; a year later, the number of these "collectives" had risen to 28,775; in 1960, it stood at 41,401; by March, 1963, these had been "consolidated" into about 30,000, comprising 87.7 per cent of all rural families.[171] Land was worked collectively but the work was not mechanized, except on the fifty-five state farms covering a total of 200,000 hectares and employing 60,000 workers. (Thirty-three of these large farms were run by the army.) But far from remedying the North's age-old problem of insufficient food production, collectivization of agriculture retarded the achievement of the regime's food production plans. No accurate statistics about food production were ever made available, but Le Duan, to whom Ho Chi Minh relinquished the post of Party secretary in 1961, admitted in September, 1962, that "a period of decline had resulted from the socialization of agriculture." [172]

At that time, the campaign of terror and guerrilla warfare, aimed at getting control of the South and its vast food potential, had been going on for five years. But not until September, 1960, at the Third Congress of the Lao Dong (Communist) Party, did the policy of overthrowing the Diem regime by force and of "liberating" the South receive quasi-formal endorsement. Le Duan, a Southerner, and, as Secretary of the Lao Dong Party, soon to become one of the most powerful men of the regime, directed the Communist efforts to bring a unified military command to the insurrection in the South. He also brought directives for a political platform broad enough to attract all elements ready to overthrow the Diem regime. The aim was to create a "democratic coalition," not necessarily pledged to early unification with the North. These efforts resulted in the formation of the National Front for the

Liberation of the South (usually called National Liberation Front), at a congress held on December 20, 1960, "somewhere in the South." [173] One hundred delegates, representing a dozen or more political parties and religious groups, including some from the old sects, are said to have attended the congress. Both the composition and the program of the new "Front" testified to the proved ability of the Communists to adapt their strategy to the needs of a new situation. In its emergence as a broad yet Communist-dominated political coalition, the National Liberation Front was truly the Vietminh reborn. Non-Communists doubtless formed the majority of its adherents and combatants, but they would all either have to become pro-Communist or drop out long before victory could be achieved, as had been the case with the Vietminh. This similarity, or better near identity, of the Vietminh and the National Liberation Front was underlined by the manner in which the Communists emphasized their own role as that of a minority faction within a broad front of non-Communist groups. They joined the Front as an openly Marxist group, and controlled it as effectively as they had done during the Vietminh era. Their new party for the South, the People's Revolutionary Party, ostensibly independent from the Communist Party in the North, was founded on January 15, 1962. Obviously, the Communists had decided that the tactics they had so successfully pursued ever since the founding of the Vietminh in 1941 were still valid, and that only as the guiding force of a non-Communist "popular front" could they ever achieve their ultimate goal—a Communist regime for the whole of Vietnam.

11

In both East and West, propaganda has given the world a highly distorted version of the beginning of the fighting in South Vietnam that was to lead to the second Indochina War. The Communist story, put together in Hanoi and spread abroad by Peking and Moscow, claims that there was a spontaneous uprising of almost the entire people, and the Communists could not help but join. The fact is that the uprising, as a concerted effort to overthrow the Diem regime and its successor by force, was organized by the Communists, and while it would have made little headway without wide popular support, neither would it have had its amazing success without guidance and assistance from the North.

But the Saigon-Washington version of these events, which has been reduced to the flat assertion that "the Vietnam war is the result of external aggression," [174] strays even farther from historical truth. Neither the strenuous efforts of Saigon nor those of Washington have produced evidence that anti-Diem terror and guerrilla warfare started as a result of the infiltration of combatants and weapons from the North.[175] No significant infiltration occurred before 1960, and very little during the next three years. The Saigon-Washington version, which tries to deny that the war started as a civil war in the South, "omits the embarrassing fact that anti-Diem guerrillas were active long before infiltrated North Vietnamese elements joined the fray." [176] In 1961, years before any large-scale infiltration such as was claimed to have taken place after 1963, "the Communists had in fact extended their influence, in varying degrees, to about 80 per cent of the Vietnamese countryside." [177]

There is another distortion in the version Washington and Saigon persisted in propagating as the truth about the origin of the Vietnamese war. While it is likely that the Communists, deprived of the chance of winning the South through elections, would sooner or later have resorted to terror and guerrilla warfare, the historical fact is that force in the struggle for the South was first used by the Diem regime, not by the Communists. Diem's terror against former Vietminh fighters, against known Communist cadres, and against villages and entire regions suspected of sympathizing with the Vietminh started long before the Communists slowly began their own campaign of terror. The military and police actions of 1956 against the Vietminh were not undertaken in reply to Communist acts of terror, which even by the admission of Saigon propaganda did not begin until 1957.

In contrast to government terror, which resulted even then in the indiscriminate killing and imprisonment not only of real enemies but also of mere suspects and innocent people, Communist terror was selective, and although in many instances also directed against the innocent, it was always guided by clearly defined political considerations. The aim of Communist terror was to paralyze the Diem administration by killing or kidnaping its officials and by interrupting all contact between the administration of the countryside and Saigon. The means of communication and economic resources were destroyed only in regions where the Communists failed to set up their own administration, and Saigon-appointed village officials, if willing to work under Communist control, were left at their posts.

In killing officials, the Communists concentrated largely on the brutal and corrupt, since this was likely to gain them the sympathy of the people. But honest and able administrators of strong anti-Communist convictions were also killed or kidnaped, the latter fate being reserved chiefly for medical officers and teachers, whom the Communists hoped to convert and use in zones "liberated" from Saigon control.

The killing of officials started in 1957. The Saigon Government claimed that during this first year of systematic Communist terror, more than 700 officials were murdered. The number of these murders continued to rise, and was said to have been 2,500 in 1959, and 4,000 in the period from May, 1960, to May, 1961. Bernard Fall believes that by 1963, perhaps as many as 13,000 Saigon officials had been murdered, and some 1,200 teachers kidnaped, of whom some were probably killed.[178] But Fall also reports the amazing cases in which "the very Dan Ve [Civil Defense] guards who are supposed to protect the village officials hand them over to the Viet Cong." [179]

By 1960, the movement that had begun with isolated acts of terror in 1957 had developed into full-fledged insurrection. It enjoyed broad support not only of the Vietnamese peasants in the Mekong Delta and the coastal provinces northeast of Saigon, but also of the ethnic minority tribes in the highlands of central Vietnam, among whom the propagandistic and organizational efforts directed from Hanoi were particularly effective.[180] Insurrection took the form of guerrilla action against villages still under government control; it usually led to the surrender or the wiping-out of the local self-defense units and Civil Guards charged with ousting the guerrillas. Organized, indoctrinated, and led by Communist cadres, the Vietcong, as these guerrillas were henceforth called,[181] soon controlled almost the entire countryside by night and about two-thirds of it in daytime. The Vietcong set up their own administration, imposed their own taxes, conscripted the local youth into military service, provided education and medical care, collected food supplies for their fighting units, dug bomb shelters, built defense works along the regions they controlled, and continuously trained new men for stepped-up military operations.[182] For years, they increased the number of their fighting men (if not their cadres) entirely through local recruiting, and their arms supply more through the capture of arms from government units than through infiltration from the North. "The misery of the people was their ally, and they played on it." [183] From 1960 on, they began to operate in ever-larger groups, and to attack and overrun government outposts held by the army, as well as to ambush and destroy army units sent to relieve outposts under attack. Saigon's chief preoccupation was how to maintain a minimum of security along the main lines of communication.[184] By 1963, the military situation had become catastrophic for the Diem regime, and at least some American military advisers became aware of this in January of that year, when a great offensive staged against a group of guerrillas in the Mekong Delta revealed the inability of the army to match the fighting spirit of the Vietcong and to cope with their military tactics.

The event has gone down in the military history of the Vietnamese war as the battle of the Ap Bac. On January 2, 1963, an army force of 2,500 men, equipped with huge quantities of automatic weapons and armored amphibious personnel carriers, and supported by bombers and helicopters, failed to overrun, destroy, or capture a group of 200 guerrillas, who after inflicting heavy casualties on the army and shooting down five helicopters, succeeded in escaping almost unharmed.[185]

American military and civilian observers in the field had no trouble at all in finding out why the armed forces of the Diem regime failed so conspicuously in fighting the Vietcong guerrillas. It needed no military expert to see that the army had been trained for the wrong kind of war. Organized under American direction on a division basis instead of in small mobile units, and equipped for the task of holding off an invasion from the North, the army was technically unprepared to counter insurgency. When, after 1960, it dawned upon some of the military leaders that guerrillas have to be fought on their own terms, everyone talked about the need for organizing counterinsurgency units, but the little that was done had no effect on the senseless and futile way the war was being conducted.[186]

But the main reason for the failure of the regime's armed forces to contain the Vietcong was political: Political conditions prevented the reforms needed to make the army effective, and still more important, they prevented the armed forces from ever becoming determined about fighting the Vietcong. There is overwhelming evidence that neither men nor officers wished to pursue the war seriously. This came as a surprise only to people who refused to believe that the Diem regime, even before 1960, was hated by the majority of the men expected to fight for it, as well as by the majority of the civilian population. There could be no more authoritative confirmation of the army's unwillingness to fight for Diem than a statement made by Prime Minister Nguyen Cao Ky in February, 1966: "We were dying for a cause, but we saw little evidence that the cause was worth laying down our lives for." [187]

The fact is, however, that the officers were in a much better position to avoid "laying down their lives" than the soldiers. The soldiers in action rarely saw anyone above the rank of captain leading them. "The whole point of being a major or colonel was that you didn't have to go into the field." [188]

The effects of Diem's system of preferring loyalty to ability and initiative were even more disastrous in the army than in the civil service. Almost all senior officers in the army were political appointees "of uncertain character and intelligence." [189] Prominent generals like Duong Van Minh and Tran Van Don, who had saved Diem in 1955, were deprived of their command and replaced by inept officers, "mainly because Diem trusted them not to stage a coup." [190] Only six of the army's eighteen generals commanded troops. Promotion depended of course entirely on Diem's estimate of a man's personal loyalty to him, and to ascertain this, Nhu planted informers in the army.[191] It would have been indeed surprising if the officers' corps had not been demoralized.

But even men loyal to the President, as most senior officers undoubtedly were for a long time, were constantly in danger of falling into disfavor if ability and initiative made them into competent military leaders. Not only was it dangerous to attract notice and become popular with the troops; it was equally unsafe to be energetic in the conduct of the war and to risk losses in order to inflict damage to the Vietcong. Since according to the official view all was more or less well in South Vietnam, reports of great battles and casualties contradicting this view were unwelcome at the Palace, even if they brought defeat to the enemy.[192] Diem's constant interference with military operations and his disapproval of initiative in the field had the ludicrous result that commanders, when confronted with the necessity for immediate action, preferred to postpone action until receiving permission and instructions from the Palace.

Generals and colonels who strove to live up to the Presidential expectations about the conduct of the war were soon the only ones in actual command. The need for avoiding casualties, and the risk of defeat in battle, led them to shun direct contact with the enemy. Instead, they fought the hidden and dispersed guerrillas with artillery and planes, dropping not only bombs but also napalm, often on villages where the presence of Vietcong fighters was merely suspected. This inevitably resulted in the killing of civilians rather than guerrillas, leading most American observers—foreign correspondents as well as military advisers—to the conclusion that the army's conduct of the war produced more Vietcong fighters than it killed.[193] But this method of waging war against the elusive guerrillas produced government "victories," and high casualty figures not in the army but among the Vietcong. However, "many a victory thus was based on the claim of a pilot flying at 150 or 200 mph over a battlefield, often under fire from the ground, that he had counted 50 or 100 [Vietcong] bodies." [194]

One of the most outstanding American military advisers, Colonel John Vann, a professional soldier of strongly conservative political views, summed up his experience in Vietnam in a statement whose truth has unfortunately not been recognized: "This is a political war and it calls for discrimination in killing. The best weapon for killing [a guerrilla] would be a knife . . . (the next best a rifle). The worst is an airplane. The next worse is artillery." [195]

If planes and artillery were not available as substitutes for the only effective way of fighting guerrillas, the cautious generals who needed victories without casualties conducted large operations in areas where there was no enemy, reporting high Vietcong casualty figures, certain that this was what Saigon wanted to hear and to believe. And if, in spite of all precautions, contact with the enemy could not be avoided, operations were conducted so as to enable the enemy to escape.[196]

Given such leadership, even troops more willing to fight than Diem's could scarcely have performed feats of bravery. But the soldiers, almost all sons of peasants who had every reason to detest the regime, had even less motivation than the officers to "lay down their lives." Defections from the army were too numerous to be concealed entirely,[197] and morale was unbelievably low. The troops, because of the inefficiency and corruption of their leaders, were poorly cared for, and often could feed themselves only by stealing from the peasants.[198] Even Diem's political cadres, engaged in converting the peasants into government supporters through psychological means, were seen in villages taken by the army "handing out government leaflets and stealing ducks." [199]

Another aspect of the war was the brutality practiced on real or merely suspected members of the Vietcong, partly in retaliation for brutalities committed by the guerrillas, but largely as a result of the frustrations regular army officers and soldiers suffered in the vain attempt to lay their hands on a ubiquitous enemy who never ceased to harass the weary troops. Chasing a group of guerrillas for days usually ended in frustration—the Vietcong would mix with the people of a village, only to reappear again and stage an ambush when least expected. "If a friend of a unit commander had been killed in the ambush, the temptation would be strong to take it out on the villagers who refused to talk." [200] Torture of prisoners and villagers suspected of sheltering guerrillas was routine, and the shooting of prisoners normal practice,[201] but neither torture nor killing was of any help in defeating the Vietcong.

Nor did the regime come closer to achieving this aim with its measures to prevent Vietcong control of the countryside through the establishment of so-called agrovilles and later of the strategic hamlets. The building of agrovilles—large concentrations of villagers in fortified "peasant towns"—was soon abandoned as impractical, but only after the brutal manner in which the peasants were driven from their native villages had created fresh hatred for the regime.[202]

Of greater consequence for the outcome of the struggle between the Vietcong and the regime was the failure of its attempt to re-establish government control over the countryside by fortifying the existing villages. The military objective of the so-called strategic-hamlet program was to prevent the Vietcong from overrunning villages in open attack and from "infiltrating" them at night. This was to be achieved by surrounding the hamlets with barbed wire, ditches, hedges, and fences of pointed bamboo stakes, and by setting up defense positions at the entrances. The people had to be inside after nightfall, and members of the Civil Defense Corps remained on guard all night. Communist propaganda called the strategic hamlets "concentration camps." [203]

Not only the regime, but its American advisers, too, expected the program, which was started late in 1961, to produce a radical reduction in Vietcong control of the countryside. When this expectation did not materialize, most Americans blamed the failure of the program on its "overextension" and on the unrealistic pace of its execution. The government, in fact, reported that by the end of June, 1965, more than 7,000 of these "rural fortresses" had been built, containing two-thirds of the country's population, and that another 2,398 were under construction.[204] From a military point of view, this was indeed overextension, even if the figures had little relation to reality, for many of these strategic hamlets existed only on paper. Provincial chiefs, in order to curry favor with the program's chief advocate, Ngo Dinh Nhu, tried to outdo each other in fortifying hamlets, knowing well that neither the local Defense Corps, nor the Civil Guards who were to defend them, had sufficient manpower for this task.[205] But the main reason for the program's lack of success was again political, and, like all other failures in the struggle to defeat the Vietcong, this one, too, was rooted in the nature of the regime. For Nhu, the strategic hamlets were largely just another means of trying to wrest control over the population from the Vietcong through police coercion, not through reforms that would have taken care of the people's needs and thus gained popular support for the regime. Promises for improved medical care and better educational services in the strategic hamlets were never kept. "Sometimes all you found representing the government inside these hamlets were the Cong An—the local police officials working for Nhu —usually ill-trained men who were there because they were related to someone in Saigon, who were ignorant and tough, and who abused the population. No wonder the Vietcong looked like Robin Hoods when they began to hit the hamlets." [206] They did so with mounting success, not so much because the regime lacked sufficient military forces, but rather because of their deficient morale and the people's reluctance to defend these hamlets against Vietcong attacks. More often than not the attackers had allies in the hamlets without having to "infiltrate" their agents: They were inside from the beginning of a hamlet's construction, and even if known to the people, were seldom betrayed to the agents of the regime. That is why this last attempt under Diem to regain control of the countryside began to collapse in mid-1963, and why the chief American adviser for the program, Rufus Phillips, warned Washington in September, 1963, that the strategic-hamlet program in the Mekong Delta was in a "rotten state." [207]

This late-hour warning, which seemed to indicate that the war against the Vietcong was being lost, was apparently listened to; but earlier ones to the same effect had been consistently dismissed by the heads of the U.S. Mission in Saigon,[208] by the Pentagon, the State Department, and the White House. Such warnings came almost exclusively from American news correspondents stationed in Saigon.[209] The first ones to speak up were Homer Bigart of *The New York Times*, and François Sully of *Newsweek*. They were attacked not only by U.S. officials, but more furiously by spokesmen of the regime, in particular by Mme. Nhu, who insisted that all criticism of the Diem regime was Communist-inspired. In March, 1962, Mme. Nhu persuaded the President, himself as intolerant as she of any criticism, to expel Bigart and Sully. Sully was actually forced to leave (as was James Robinson of NBC), and Bigart was replaced by David Halberstam—no improvement over Bigart in the eyes of the regime. Nhu, his wife, and the Vietnamese official press began to slander anyone critical of Diem's policies and of the "Family," or anyone who dared to suggest that the war was not being won. Sully was called a Vietcong spy, an opium smuggler, and a participant in sex orgies. Halberstam, Neil Sheehan of the United Press International, and several others were accused of being part of an international Communist-inspired conspiracy to slander the regime. They were shadowed, and some of them were attacked and physically mishandled by Nhu's secret-service agents.[210] Their telephones were tapped, and they were prevented from sending uncensored dispatches out of the country.

The U.S. Mission was anything but forceful in defending these correspondents against abuse and ill-treatment, and almost apologetic in explaining that these men were merely trying to live up to the American concept of a free press.[211] Ambassador Frederick E. Nolting, Jr., and General Paul Harkins in particular were incensed by the American newsmen's attacks on the regime. Both stanchly believed that there was no alternative to Diem, and were therefore on the whole inclined to accept as true the regime's claim that the Vietcong were on the way to defeat.[212] They, as well as their superiors in Washington, spoke repeatedly of the "slanted" or even "irresponsible" press reporting out of Saigon, convinced not only that the correspondents who criticized the regime did harm to U.S.–South Vietnamese relations, but also that they were wrong. Washington's belief in Diem and in his final triumph was apparently unshakable. Secretary of Defense McNamara called Diem "one of the great leaders of our time," and Vice-President Lyndon B. Johnson in 1961 likened Diem to Winston Churchill. As to his chances of winning the war, skeptics were referred to General

Maxwell D. Taylor, who, in 1962, spoke of "a great national movement that was crushing the Vietcong." And Ambassador Nolting went so far as to predict that "the Republic of Vietnam will take its place in history as the country where the tide of Asian Communism was reversed and the myth of Communist invincibility forever shattered." [213]

Grave events that should have been warnings did not shake this stubborn official optimism in regard to the state of the war and the qualifications of Diem as an anti-Communist leader. On November 11, 1960, three paratroop battalions stationed in Saigon—the elite formations of the National Army—staged a coup against the government. It failed not only because its leaders were taken in by the maneuvers with which Diem worked himself out of an ominous predicament, but also because the officers who led the coup never thought of mobilizing the population of Saigon in support of their move, revealing, as did all later military and civilian aspirants for power, that the Vietnamese elite still tried to shape the destiny of their country without permitting the people to play an active role.[214] In February, 1962, two of the air force's top pilots, reflecting the desperate political mood in their ranks, tried to kill the President and the Nhus by bombing the Palace. They destroyed one of its wings, but Diem and his family were unharmed. During the paratroop coup of November, 1960, Diem, before he succeeded in crushing the rebels, had promised to form a coalition government, but like all his other promises of reform, this one too was never kept. Instead, the regime more furiously than ever used terror against opponents, whether pro-Communist or not. This terror had been "legalized" by a law of May 6, 1959, the like of which has been promulgated only by the most brutal dictatorships in our century. "Special military tribunals were convened which could only pass sentences of death or hard labor for life, with no provisions for appeal against their decisions." [215] Anyone opposed to the regime had henceforth only the choice of silent submission, exile, prison, or armed resistance. Official Washington apparently regarded this barbaric and outright fascist law as a necessary weapon in the defense of "freedom."

But it would be a mistake to believe that the U.S. Mission in Saigon, the State Department, the Pentagon, and President Kennedy were unaware of, and undisturbed by, the decline of the Diem regime and its obvious inability to deal effectively with the insurrection. (Even Ambassador Nolting had occasional misgivings.) Washington's concern had evidently become strong by 1961, the year in which President

Kennedy sent three important missions to Vietnam. In April, it was Vice-President Johnson, in May and June, a large commission headed by Professor Eugene Staley of Stanford University, and almost on the heels of the Staley mission another one headed by President Kennedy's chief military adviser, General Maxwell D. Taylor. The Johnson mission produced only public assurances of American support for the Diem regime in language as close to Orwell's Newspeak as that used in Communist propaganda. Ngo Dinh Diem was praised for his "defense of liberties" against "unprovoked aggression" and for his "stand for freedom." Of the reforms Washington considered necessary, next to the "priority" given to military assistance, a joint declaration issued at the close of the Johnson visit on May 13, 1961, said only that "appropriate measures in other fields" would be pursued "vigorously." [216] As a result of the Taylor mission—the only one seriously concerned with the need for administrative, social, and political reforms—U.S. officials began to insist that these "appropriate measures" promised by Diem in return for increased U.S. aid be carried out. The regime's reaction came in a series of articles in the government-controlled press protesting American "imperialist" interference in Vietnamese affairs.[217] None of the many reforms proposed by the Taylor mission was ever acted upon.[218] Only the views of the Staley mission, dealing primarily with military measures and with increased American aid, were taken under immediate consideration. But these also were not carried out in all respects. The training of the regular army for jungle warfare, for instance, still made no significant progress. On the other hand, the Staley mission was largely responsible for the misguided zeal with which the strategic-hamlet program was tackled.

After 1961, American policy more and more was based on military considerations only. U.S. military personnel in Vietnam, which in 1954 numbered 685, increased sharply, and American officers soon began to participate in combat in an advisory capacity. By 1963, their number had jumped to 15,000. The Vietnamese Army was increased from 170,000 to 210,000. Also substantially increased were the Civil Guard and the Self-Defense Corps, and both were abundantly supplied with modern weapons. Fortified "special forces" camps under American command were set up in critical areas, and there was a great deal of "psychological" training of army and civilian cadres charged with persuading the population to support the government against the Vietcong. But the battle of Ap Bac in January, 1963, showed that all this had not improved the effectiveness of the army against the guerrillas, had not changed the behavior of the military toward civilians and prisoners, and had not raised the morale of the troops. The Vietcong, consequently, continued to make gains in the struggle for the minds of the people and for control of the country.

For almost two years after the Taylor mission had diagnosed some of the evils that threatened the survival of a non-Communist South Vietnam, Washington and the U.S. Mission in Saigon either allowed themselves to be deceived about the performances of the Diem regime [219] or excused their continued support of it with the astounding assertion that the United States could not interfere in South Vietnam's internal affairs. The full improbity of this argument was revealed only when it was dropped in 1963, the year that brought conclusive evidence that Diem was losing the war.

During 1963, the American public also began to reconsider the policy of supporting Diem, about which it had hitherto lacked the requisite information. The self-immolating flames that consumed the body of the Buddhist monk Thich Quang Duc on June 11, 1963, produced the light by which to see what South Vietnam had become under Ngo Dinh Diem. Some Americans gained only the limited insight that the war would be lost unless Diem was overthrown. For others, however, the crisis that shook South Vietnam in 1963 marked the beginning of a deep concern with the foreign policy of their country. A great many Americans began to sense that the cause of freedom in Vietnam could not be served by supporting a reactionary, antidemocratic, and morally rotten regime.

12

Until the spring of 1963, the actions of the Diem regime, which were to lead to its fall in the autumn, had caused a steady but slow drift from crisis to crisis; after May, 1963, the evolution of the regime became a mad race toward disaster.[220] The accumulated failures and crimes of oppression finally also drove the non-Communist segments of the population into open rebellion. The fear that even firm anti-Communists might join the National Liberation Front in order to overthrow the regime had one immediate result: It convinced the country's military leaders that Diem had to be overthrown by the army if a non-Communist South Vietnam was to survive.

Now began the last and most turbulent phase in the life of the regime. It started when the President, misled by his own Catholic sectarianism, added yet another cause for popular discontent to the many existing ones by provoking a religious clash between the majority of his people and the government.

At least 70 per cent of the Vietnamese people consider themselves Buddhist; less than 10 per cent are Catholics.[221] The Buddhists had always had some grievances under Diem. They had long complained of the fact that Catholics held a disproportionate number of high official posts. Almost all province chiefs, apart from being military men, were Catholics, and so were a great number of other high officials and generals. Many of them were recent converts to Catholicism. According to the growing list of Buddhist complaints, Catholic villages received a greater share of government aid, and when the government started its unpopular resettlement of villagers from the central coastal area into the highlands, Catholic villages were exempted. In order to avoid being moved, whole villages tried to be converted. The Buddhists furthermore claimed that Catholics, at the intervention of their priests, were often exempted from the conscripted labor for building the strategic hamlets. The Buddhist priests also resented the regime's refusal to abolish an old colonial law that defined Catholicism as a religion but Buddhism merely as an "association."

But open conflict between the regime and Buddhism did not erupt until May, 1963, in a tragic event at Hue, the city that the Vietnamese Buddhists regard as their religious capital.[222] Shortly before the celebration of the 2,587th anniversary of Buddha's birth, the government issued an order forbidding the display of religious flags. This rather senseless order was the more provocative as the Catholics of Hue, just before the order on religious flags was issued, had celebrated the twenty-fifth anniversary of Ngo Dinh Thuc's promotion to bishop with a profuse display of flags. On May 8, the Buddhists of Hue, in a huge demonstration, protested against the flag order and demanded that it be rescinded. Troops were sent against them, and when, using tear gas, they failed to disperse the demonstrators, their callous commander, an appointee of Ngo Dinh Can, ordered them to fire into the crowd from their armored cars. Nine persons were killed, among them three women and two children, the latter decapitated by shells.

The news of this brutality spread rapidly throughout the country and led to the sudden release of much stored-up Buddhist anger, forcefully expressed by the spokesmen of Buddhism, in particular the younger priests. But the older conservative leaders also spoke up. Thich (the Venerable) Tam Chau, the head of the Buddhists in Saigon, formulated a series of demands, one of them being that the officials responsible for the killings at Hue be punished and the families of the victims compensated.[223]

But the government, instead of putting out the fire that, spreading from town to town, threatened to turn into a gigantic conflagration, rejected these demands. Diem insisted, as he had done ever since the news of May 8 had reached Saigon, that the nine dead Buddhists at Hue had been murdered by a plastic bomb planted by the Vietcong.[224]

The Buddhists, being refused satisfaction, got ready to fight. A broad mass movement developed, and it soon became obvious that part of its strength came from political sources: the popular hatred for the regime, for which the Buddhist protest movement offered a welcome outlet, and which the younger Buddhist priests quickly learned to exploit.[225] Buddhist religious zeal was soon coupled with barely disguised political aspirations. When Thich Tam Chau called on the Buddhists to be ready for martyrdom, he could hardly be accused of appealing to anything but religious fervor. But it was different with the organizers of mass demonstrations, such as Thich Tri Quang, a young and exceedingly brilliant monk from Hue, who became the leader of the movement in all its direct and indirect political manifestations.

On May 30, several hundred Buddhist priests demonstrated peacefully before the National Assembly in Saigon. On the same day, one thousand priests and nuns began a protest fast in the pagodas of Hue. Then came June 11, the day when the Buddhists produced the first news from Vietnam that shook the entire world, Christians and Buddhists alike, people concerned with religious freedom even more than those worried about South Vietnam's political fate. This was the day of the dramatic suicide of Thich Quang Duc, the elderly monk who burned himself to death in the center of Saigon by having gasoline poured over his body and setting himself on fire.[226] Between June and November, six more Buddhist monks and one nun offered their lives in this heroic manner to dramatize the plight of the Vietnamese people not only as Buddhists, but also as the exploited and persecuted subjects of an oppressive regime. Political protest was certainly the motive for the suicide of the famous Vietnamese writer Nguyen Tuong Tam.

After a second monk had immolated himself, on August 5 at the coastal city of Phan Thiet, the world was horrified, not only by the event itself but also by Mme. Nhu's cynical and callous dismissal of the suicides as "barbecues," and by her expressed hope that there would be more.[227] Her wish was soon fulfilled. On August 15, another monk burned himself at Hue, followed three days later by a nun at Ninh Hoa. Not wishing to lag behind his wife in callousness, Ngo Dinh Nhu soon afterward stated that "if the Buddhists want to have another barbecue, I will be glad to supply the gasoline." [228]

During early summer, 1963, the Buddhists were still concerned primarily with obtaining redress of their grievances. Although they kept on demonstrating, fasting, kneeling in prayer in the streets, and stirring up their followers by speeches and leaflets, they continued to try to negotiate with Diem. Diem hesitated to suppress the movement by force, but he also refused to make meaningful concessions. The dangers of this policy became apparent when, on August 18, a Buddhist call for a demonstration was answered by 15,000 people, who marched through the streets of Saigon to the Xa Loi Pagoda, headquarters of the movement, to listen to defiant speeches by their leaders that could be heard over loudspeakers many blocks away. Most American officials in Saigon thought that Diem could not fail to see the danger to his regime if he refused to satisfy the Buddhist demands.

Indeed, nowhere did the Buddhist crisis cause as great a shock as in the United States. Guilt over the support of a regime that seemed to practice religious persecution, and the fear that growing public resistance would hardly be of help in winning the war, drastically reduced sympathy for Diem, which so far had blocked his American critics' efforts to show that his regime was failing. Washington strongly urged Diem to settle the Hue affair by accepting the Buddhist demands. In the absence of vacationing Ambassador Nolting, the views of the Kennedy Administration were forcefully presented to Diem by Nolting's deputy, William Trueheart, who, according to Mecklin, "applied direct, relentless, table-hammering pressure on Diem such as the United States had seldom attempted with a sovereign, friendly government." [229] Even the strongest admirers of Diem in the Administration regarded his refusal to make concessions to the Buddhists as an inexplicable blunder, and some, like Averell Harriman and Assistant Secretary of State for Far Eastern Affairs Roger Hilsman, demanded increased pressure on Diem for reforms. In fact, Trueheart made it clear that the United States might publicly dissociate itself from Diem's regime if he failed to reconcile the Buddhists. Washington's surprising firmness was of course largely a response to the shock and indignation of the American public over the growing evidence of religious persecution of a Buddhist nation by a Catholic-dominated regime. The regime's accusation that the Buddhist protests were "Communist-inspired" found few believers. There was of course a danger that the movement might be exploited by the Vietcong, but not a shred of evidence has ever been produced that Communists had infiltrated the Buddhist leadership.[230]

Even the outgoing Ambassador Nolting, after returning from his vacation for a brief final stay in Saigon, urged Diem, in terms more forceful than he had ever used, to adopt a policy of reconciliation with the Buddhists. Nolting believed himself to have been successful. Diem promised him that he would settle the affair. In an interview with Marguerite Higgins of the *New York Herald Tribune*, Diem stated that it was his policy to reconcile the Buddhists.[231] A grateful Nolting, relieved by Diem's promise and also because his thankless assignment in Saigon had come to an end, made a farewell speech at the airport on August 15, saying his last words of praise for Diem on Vietnamese soil.[232]

The manner in which Diem, guided more and more by Nhu and his wife, in his frenzied exercise of power, "settled" the Buddhist affair six days later, must have incensed even his faithful admirer Nolting. During the night of August 21, units of the special forces and armed groups of Nhu's secret police attacked the Buddhists in their pagodas, and with a great deal of vandalism and bloodletting arrested all the priests and nuns they could lay their hands on. Raids on pagodas were also conducted at Hue, Quang Nam, Phan Thiet, Quang Tri, and several other cities. Thousands of priests all over the country were imprisoned that night, and since most of them offered passive resistance, they were dragged from the pagodas and thrown into trucks to be carried off to prison. Many were killed. At the Xa Loi Pagoda in Saigon, "the orgy lasted about two hours";[233] Americans who tried to rush to the scene could hear the screams, the gunfire, and the explosion of grenades from the distance at which they were kept by Nhu's stormtroopers.

"Thus," remarked Mecklin, "was Nolting rewarded for his loyalty [to Diem]." [234]

The attempt to settle the Buddhist affair by trying to suppress the movement with terror was like putting out fire with gasoline. The movement not only grew in strength but became increasingly political. It no longer aimed merely at obtaining redress of grievances. Convinced that Diem had decided to crush their movement, the Buddhist leaders began to think that their goals could be achieved only through the overthrow of the regime. And it was precisely for this reason that the movement continued to gain the support of people impelled not by religious but by political motives.

Even men who for years had supported Diem now turned against him. Immediately after the pagoda raids, Foreign Minister Vu Van Mau resigned his post, denounced the raids in a speech before the Faculty of Law at Saigon University, shaved his head to express his solidarity with the Buddhist movement, and asked for permission to go on a pilgrimage to India. He was arrested when he tried to leave. An even harder blow for Diem was the resignation, on August 23, of the Ambassador to the United States, Tran Van Chuong, father of Mme. Nhu, who stated in Washington, and repeated it in dozens of speeches later on, that there was not a chance in a hundred for victory under Diem. The Ambassador's wife, the mother of Mme. Nhu, resigned from her position as Observer at the United Nations. Saigon propaganda, long used to flat denials of the truth, said that Vu Van Mau was not arrested but only "unavoidably detained," and that Tran Van Chuong had not resigned but had been dismissed. But apart from a handful of U.S. officials, there was now no one left in Saigon who believed anything the government said.[235]

On August 24 and 25, the students of Saigon University began to demonstrate. In spite of ruthless police action against them during which a young girl was killed, they continued to fill the streets calling for the resignation of Diem. Three American newsmen who took pictures of the brutal attacks on the students were arrested.[236] More than 4,000 university students were rounded up during the next few days and thrown into jail. But new demonstrations followed, largely of youngsters of high-school age, of whom hundreds were also arrested. The universities of Saigon and Hue, and all of Saigon's secondary schools, were closed. "It sounds like the students in Korea," remarked the head of *The New York Times* bureau in Hong Kong, Robert Trumbull. "Vietnam may be ripe for it." [237]

These students came mostly from the well-to-do families of Saigon. They were sons and daughters of the highest officials and of officers of the army, many of whom were later to be seen at police stations trying to get their children released. Many were released, only to be rearrested for taking part in subsequent demonstrations.

The reaction of the ruling family to the increasing evidence of popular hostility toward their regime became more and more frantic. When the Voice of America began openly to criticize Diem for his action against the Buddhists, people were arrested for listening to it. Of the thousands in jails, many were brutally beaten by Nhu's police thugs, and some subjected to ugly tortures. [238] Nhu drew up a directive to all civil servants requiring "sincere self-confessions" of their ideas about the Buddhist movement. In a five-hour long talk for the benefit of U.S. officials, he described supporters of the Buddhist movement, such as Prince Sihanouk of Cambodia, as fools, and openly accused Diem of weakness in dealing with the Buddhist leaders. (Cambodia broke off diplomatic relations with Vietnam over the persecution of the Buddhists on August 28.) Mme. Nhu later boasted that it was she who had persuaded Diem to order the pagoda raids. Angry over American expressions of displeasure with the regime, both Nhu and his wife became more and more preposterous in their denunciation of the United States and in their attacks on the Americans in Vietnam. Mme. Nhu called the officers of the U.S. military mission "little soldiers of fortune," [239] and Nhu went so far as to say that "without the Americans we could win the war in two or three years. With the Americans, who knows? Perhaps never." [240] Nhu accused the Voice of America of being the voice of a group of capitalists who, he said, controlled it. [241] He even engaged in a maneuver designed to frighten Washington into continued unconditional support for Diem by threatening to open negotiations with the Hanoi regime. [242] It was not the first time in history that people, observing the convulsions of a dying regime, began to believe that its leaders had gone mad. [243]

There must have been moments when Diem realized that he was doomed if the United States turned against him, and that this was bound to happen if he did not change the course he had adopted with the pagoda raids of August 21. Ever since then, American disenchantment with Diem had been increasing and now found expression not only in sharp press criticism but also in official statements. Symptomatic of the changed tone of the press was a furious attack on the Diem regime by Stanley Karnow in the *Saturday Evening Post*.[244] But more important were the criticisms voiced by President Kennedy, who was said to have been outraged by the attacks on the pagodas. In a press conference shortly after the raids, Kennedy appealed to Diem to show respect for the rights of others, and in a television interview on September 2, he spoke of "repression," deplored that the government had "gotten out of touch with the people," and even said that the chances of winning the war under such a government were "not very good." It seemed that President Kennedy at last was persuaded of what some American newsmen had been saying for two years.

The great sensation of this Kennedy interview, however, was his remark about "changes in policy and perhaps personnel," which could only mean a demand that Diem get rid of the Nhus.

American patience with Diem had obviously reached the point of exhaustion. In their flight from reality, Diem and Nhu behaved as outrageously toward Americans as they did toward their own people. After the raids of August 21, the barbed wire and guards around the Xa Loi Pagoda were extended to enclose, "for reasons of security," the building of the U.S. aid mission. "The bizarre result was that the Americans engaged in giving away more than one million dollars a day to the Vietnamese government were unable to go to work." [245] Only one hour after the start of the raids, the telephones of all U.S. officials and newsmen, both in their homes and in their offices, were disconnected (except a special line from General Harkins' headquarters to the Embassy). The newsmen were prevented from sending uncensored dispatches out of the country. They had to smuggle them out by air hostesses or GI's via Hong Kong, Manila, Singapore, or Bangkok. Some foreign newsmen (their number had swollen to more than sixty by the end of August) were threatened with arrest, and some, like Denis Warner, with assassination.[246]

The new Ambassador, Henry Cabot Lodge, who arrived in Saigon on August 22, the day after the pagoda raids, firmly protested against these outrages, and from the beginning of his mission made it clear that Washington's attitude toward the Diem regime had ceased to be one of uncritical acceptance.[247] Unlike Nolting, Lodge listened to, and largely accepted, the devastating reports of some key American officials about the deteriorating military situation.[248] He insisted on the

removal of John Richardson, the head of the CIA in Vietnam, who, like
General Harkins, was a stanch believer in Diem and clung to the view
that the war was being won. And within forty-eight hours after his arrival, Lodge proved to the State Department that the regime's claims
concerning the role of the army in the pagoda raids were totally false:
Diem had informed the U.S. Mission that his hand had been forced by
the generals, and the Mission, despite the reliable information of the
newsmen to the contrary, had accepted this attempt to put the blame
for the raids on the army.[249] Only a few days later, the Voice of
America broadcast to Vietnam, both in English and Vietnamese, that
the raids had been the work of Nhu and his Special Forces. Indeed,
when the raids took place, most of the generals had already begun to
plot against the regime.

But although a great change had come about in Washington with the
appointment of Lodge, the Administration still shrank from putting
really effective pressure on Diem. A two-man mission consisting of
Joseph Mendenhall of the State Department and General Krulak of the
Pentagon was sent to Saigon early in September. Its conflicting reports
to the National Security Council after a twenty-four hour investigation were of no help at all in bringing about a clear decision. Mendenhall's report was gloomy, General Krulak's was "glowingly optimistic," prompting Kennedy to ask whether the two gentlemen were sure
they had visited the same country.[250] On September 24, a higher-
ranking mission, headed by Secretary of Defense Robert McNamara
and General Maxwell Taylor, arrived in Saigon. Although Arthur
Sylvester, the Pentagon's Assistant Secretary for Public Affairs, only
twenty-four hours after the mission's arrival informed the newsmen
that the war was "getting better rather than worse," McNamara seems
to have returned to Washington with a considerably more skeptical
view.

There was still a ray of hope and regard for the Diem regime in the
U.S. statement released after the McNamara-Taylor mission reported
back to Washington, but the President's actions no longer bore out the
restraint of his words. Washington demanded that the Saigon regime
send the 2,000 men of Nhu's Special Forces, which the regime was
keeping in Saigon for its protection, to fight the Vietcong. Kennedy
gave weight to this demand by ordering that the funds for maintaining
these forces be canceled. Twenty-two Senators had already demanded,
on September 12, that all aid be withheld from Vietnam unless the

"cruel repression" practiced by the regime was ended. On October 16, the Foreign Relations Committee authorized Presidential actions to that effect. A first step, however, had already been taken: The imports that served to feed the regime's treasury had been halted during September.

Although these measures did no immediate material harm to the regime,[251] they had a tremendous psychological effect. It appeared to the Vietnamese that Diem was being dropped by Washington, even if Washington claimed merely to insist that he reform. Thus there was created an atmosphere in which a coup against Diem became possible. Washington's only fear now was that South Vietnam's resistance against the advancing forces of the Vietcong might collapse before the crumbling regime of Diem could be removed by a military coup.

13

It is still too early to attempt an accurate and complete account of the coup that brought about the fall of the Diem regime. What is known at this time has been said by David Halberstam and Robert Shaplen, two writers whose passionate concern with the fate of Vietnam has brought to light all ascertainable facts.[252] However, the story they tell has too many holes and is full of contradictions—like an unfinished jigsaw puzzle from which some pieces are missing and in which many others do not seem to fit.

But although the story is both incomplete and in some respects inaccurate, there can be no doubt about the political significance of the coup and the motives of the men who brought it to pass. The Vietcong and the Buddhists had brought the Diem regime to the brink of military and political disaster, but it was Diem's own army which put an end to his rule. The colonels and generals who organized the coup were anti-Communists motivated not so much by democratic convictions or revolutionary zeal as by their concern over the regime's inability to combat and defeat the Vietcong. Furthermore, the men who overthrew Diem were fully convinced that their project, although never publicly endorsed by any authorized U.S. spokesman, had the blessings of the U.S. Government.

This fact is more important than any other in explaining why the coup came about, since the generals who planned it would never have proceeded without sufficiently firm assurances from the United States. Although no agent of the U.S. Government was actively engaged in the preparation of the coup, Washington's contribution to it was nevertheless "substantial." [253] It became possible only when, after nine years of almost unconditional support for Diem, Washington reached the conclusion that Diem had to be replaced if South Vietnam was to survive.

One curious aspect of this passive yet exceedingly effective promotion of the coup by Washington was that the highest U.S. military officials in Saigon were not only uninvolved but quite unaware that the forceful overthrow of Diem was being prepared by his own army leaders. General Harkins and his top aides did not enjoy the confidence of the Vietnamese generals, and neither Ambassador Lodge nor the many newsmen who knew what was coming thought that Harkins should be informed.

An infinitely more complex and highly confusing picture emerges from a description of the persons and forces engaged in the coup on the Vietnamese side. Not only were there two groups of plotters working toward the same goal all during the summer of 1963, but the government, too, at least in the person of Ngo Dinh Nhu, was preparing a coup, or countercoup, designed to trap and then eliminate its enemies, whether actively working for the fall of Diem or merely looking forward to it.

Ironically, the most ardent among the conspirators against the regime was one of its highest secret-service officials, Dr. Tran Kim Tuyen, the tiny and sinister "physician" at the head of the so-called Political and Social Research Service of the Presidency, and for more than eight years Nhu's most valuable assistant in spying on ministers, officials, and generals. Dr. Tuyen fell out of favor in early 1963, and immediately began to organize a group of young colonels eager to stage a coup. In September, Dr. Tuyen was sent as Consul General to Cairo (his family was not allowed to join him), but by that time his group was sufficiently well organized to manage without his guidance. Headed by Colonel Do Mau, who was in charge of military security, and Colonel Pham Ngoc Thao, then military inspector of the strategic-hamlet program, the group succeeded in enlisting General Tran Thien Khiem of the Joint Chiefs of Staff. Khiem had much to say about troop movements in the entire country, and he had enjoyed Diem's confidence ever since he had come to the President's aid during the paratroopers' coup in November, 1960.

Through General Khiem, contacts were established in early summer, 1963, between the group of plotting colonels and the senior officers who, since May, had been working toward the same goal. This second group was led by the Generals Duong Van Minh, Tran Van Don, and Le Van Kim, all three without command posts and Kim even without a job since his dismissal as head of the Military Academy. The colonels wanted to strike as early as July, but the more cautious generals thought that the time was not yet ripe.

It was through General Tran Van Don that the Americans were kept informed about the preparations for the coup. A high civilian official whose name no one has as yet divulged was the secret contact man between the generals and the U.S. Government, no doubt via the Saigon Embassy. General Don informed this official on October 2 that a coup was definitely being prepared; and it was this same official, according to Shaplen, who told General Duong Van Minh on October 10 that Washington would not stand in the way of a military coup.[254] Indeed, Shaplen is fully convinced that the coup "would not have occurred without prior approval of one man in Washington, President Kennedy." [255]

Two problems had to be solved by the plotting generals before they could risk action. One was presented by Nhu's scheme to foil the threatening coup with his countercoup, which he intended to launch before any plot against the regime could ripen. Nhu's coup was of course intended only as a fake, and was to be quickly put down by loyal army troops, the Special Forces, and the Palace Guard. The Commander of the Special Forces, Colonel Le Quang Tung, and the head of the Palace Guard, Colonel Nguyen Ngoc Khoi, were given the task of rounding up all enemies of the regime after "defeating" Nhu's fake coup. The fate reserved for all officers and civilians suspected of plotting against the regime was death.[256]

The generals now knew that they had to strike before Nhu, whose first act of deception was in fact an order to the Special Forces to leave Saigon on October 30. But the generals and colonels could strike only after they had solved their second major problem. The troops of the Saigon garrison and a division near Saigon were commanded by two officers apparently determined to fight for Diem: General Huynh Van Cao, the unbelievably incompetent Commander of the 4th Army Corps, whose 7th Division was stationed at Mytho, 40 miles from Saigon, and General Ton That Dinh, a "boisterous, eccentric, whiskey-drinking paratrooper" [257] in his mid-thirties, the youngest general in the army, whom Diem trusted implicitly and treated like an adopted son. Dinh—cunning, vain (he never went anywhere without his personal photographer), and ambitious, but not too bright—was the only army general who had prior knowledge of the pagoda raids and had approved of them. Both Cao and Dinh were recent converts to Catholicism and members of Nhu's Personalist "Labor" Party.

There is no need to go into the intrigue that led to the removal of General Cao and his 7th Division as an obstacle to the coup. It constitutes an entirely successful subplot, of which only the results are relevant to the story of the coup: On the day the generals struck, the 7th Division was under the command of a conspirator, and General Cao was under arrest.[258]

In dealing with General Dinh the plotters faced a more tricky problem. Dinh's strength was too great to be overcome in battle, even if his troops' loyalty to the regime was uncertain. He was too cunning to be maneuvered into a position of neutrality, and his ambitions were too great for him to be a mere onlooker in a struggle for power whose outcome might be uncertain. To try openly to win Dinh as an ally was also dangerous, since his loyalty, if gained at all, would be extremely fragile. The generals finally hit upon the simple device of playing on Dinh's vanity. They told him that he was the most important man in Vietnam, and that without him, Diem could hardly remain in power; it was of course a shame that he and some other key generals were being kept out of a government which the army alone sustained; Diem ought to appoint two or three generals to his Cabinet, but above all he ought to make Dinh Minister of the Interior, in recognition of his vital role in buttressing the regime.

When Dinh made these demands, Diem, as expected, rejected them angrily. It was then that the generals told Dinh that Diem would be overthrown, and that if Dinh joined the coup, he would be appointed Minister of the Interior in the new government. The plotters even bribed a fortuneteller to help persuade Dinh that a great political future lay ahead of him.

Although there are indications that Dinh, up to the last moment, remained undecided about which way he should turn, the conspirators' psychological gamble proved superior to that of Diem and Nhu. Nhu, with his contempt for people, never believed that a man of his experience could be outwitted by the generals, of whom he disparagingly said as late as October 28 that they were incapable of staging a coup.[259] His and Diem's self-delusion had become almost limitless, and their reaction to the threat of losing their personal power bordered on the psychotic. They apparently believed that they were winning the war, since reports to the contrary no longer penetrated into the heavily guarded and totally isolated Palace;[260] and they were sure that their own mastery of intrigue was not to be surpassed. They never realized that at this stage of the game intrigue had become merely a secondary, or auxiliary, weapon in the struggle for power, and that the really decisive weapons, which were political, were all in the hands of the plotters: The majority of the people, but also of the men working for the regime in the army as well as in the administration, at the top as well as the bottom, were hoping that Diem would fall.

When the coup finally got under way, two important members of the Ngo family were out of the country. Monsignor Ngo Dinh Thuc had been ordered to Rome by the Vatican. The political statements Thuc had made during the Buddhist crisis had been frowned upon by his superiors in the Catholic Church. Mme. Nhu had left Vietnam on September 9 for a propaganda tour abroad that took her from a meeting of the Interparliamentary Union in Belgrade to Rome, Paris, and the United States. Official Washington ignored her visit and her parents refused to see her; but curiosity, and the wish to show fairness to a person who did not know the meaning of the word, gave Mme. Nhu a hearing such as few nonofficial foreign visitors have ever received in the United States. Politically, however, her tour was a glaring fiasco, and only the personal tragedy that hit her toward the end of her stay tempered the American people's contempt for her with pity.

On Friday, November 1, the day of the coup, Ambassador Lodge accompanied Admiral Felt on a farewell visit to the Palace. This was around 10:30 A.M. Before they left, Diem remarked that they might hear rumors of a coup but that they should pay no attention to them. Diem apparently thought, as he still did on hearing of troop movements into town early in the afternoon, that Nhu's countercoup was getting under way.[261]

Whole units of the armed forces—army, navy, marines, air force, and paratroopers—commanded by officers firmly behind the coup moved into Saigon. The generals, as was their custom every Friday, had invited all important high officers to a luncheon conference, including the commanders of the Special Forces and the Palace Guard, Colonels Tung and Khoi. General Don announced to the assembled officers that a coup was under way. General Minh produced a tape recorder, read a prepared proclamation in which the plotters set forth their aims, and asked each officer who agreed to go along with the coup to make a statement to this effect.[262] Nobody dared to protest. Four unreliable officers had already been arrested, and the pro-Diem commander of the navy had been shot by the escort sent out to bring him to the meeting. Dinh, not fully trusted by the plotters, had been told to remain at his headquarters. Colonel Tung of the Special Forces was forced at gunpoint to order his troops to lay down their arms; later in the afternoon he himself was shot.

The coup was carried out with great precision. The radio station, the post office, the central police headquarters, the Ministries of the Interior and of National Defense were all occupied within one hour. The Palace, defended by the Presidential Guard, was surrounded by troops under the command of Colonel Thao and attacked by tanks and mortars. General Dinh, seeing the direction in which the wind blew, now decided to be so firmly in favor of the coup that he later regarded himself as its chief organizer. Nhu called Dinh's headquarters at 1:30 P.M. to order him to counterattack, but Dinh did not answer the phone; instead he brought additional troops stationed near Saigon into town to support the coup, deploying them at strategic points of the capital.

Soon afterward Diem and Nhu, realizing what was happening, began to call for help over a transmitter at the Palace. They urged their chiefs of provinces, who were all military men, and the corps commanders to come to the rescue of the legitimate government. Not one answered. All division commanders, too, it turned out, had decided to go along with the coup, and so did three of the four corps commanders. (The fourth one, General Cao, had been arrested by the plotters.) Diem also called on the Civil Guards, and Nhu ordered his Republican Youth and his wife's paramilitary Women's Corps to take up arms against the rebels. Nobody stirred. The regime's political bankruptcy was total.

When the generals, early in the afternoon, called on Diem to surrender, Diem invited them for "consultations," as he had so successfully done with the leaders of the paratrooper coup in November, 1960. But this time the rebels were interested only in surrender. At 4 P.M., Diem called Ambassador Lodge, who advised him to give up the fight and offered him asylum. Diem replied that he would try to restore order.[263] He still hoped for help from General Cao's 7th Division at Mytho, some of whose units, however, had already joined the coup.

It was 8 P.M., according to most reports, when Diem and Nhu fled from the Palace; the Palace Guards were not told that the men they were fighting to protect were no longer there. The brothers are said to have left the building through a tunnel. They then went by car to Cholon, where they found refuge in the large house of a rich Chinese. There they learned in the early morning hours that the Palace had fallen and that most of their "loyal" troops had made common cause with the rebels. Shortly before 7 A.M., Diem telephoned General Don that he was willing to surrender, but dissatisfied with the conditions he was offered he refused to say where he was. However, the secret had apparently been betrayed to Colonel Thao, who in the meantime had stormed the Palace.[264] Colonel Thao appeared at the hiding place, but Diem and Nhu managed to escape into a nearby Catholic church. From there, Diem, at about 9 A.M., got to a telephone and once more offered to surrender; speaking to General Khiem, Diem now said where he and Nhu could be found. An armored car was immediately sent to fetch them. With it arrived the commander of the Civil Guards, Colonel Duong Ngoc Lam, whom Diem considered loyal. Lam had in fact joined the coup only at a late hour. But behind Lam, Diem saw General Mai Huu Xuan, an ardent plotter from the very first. Xuan is said to have given the orders for Diem and Nhu's murder, allegedly acting in full agreement with General Duong Van Minh.[265] Diem and Nhu were dead when the armored car got back to Saigon. Their bodies were brought to Xuan's headquarters at 11 A.M. At 4 P.M., they were identified at the St. Paul Hospital at Saigon by a relative, the wife of Tran Trung Dung, a former minister who had long ago broken with Diem.

Thus did the reign of Ngo Dinh Diem come to an end.

14

The fall of Diem was celebrated in Saigon by lively, joyful crowds of younger people who felt that they had helped to bring it about. Symbols of the old regime were instantly removed, and the homes of several prominent ministers were destroyed, as were the offices of the *Times of Vietnam* and of a number of other papers. Dr. Tuyen rushed

back from Cairo, but the generals who set up a ruling junta headed by
Minh, Don, and Dinh, saw in him the chief of Nhu's most important
secret service rather than one of the first plotters, and they threw him
into jail. Also jailed were other prominent figures of the Diem era, but
their number was small. The victors apparently realized that they
themselves had a share of responsibility for the Diem regime, which
most of them had supported long after it had begun its descent into
political crime and military ineptitude. However, the junta saw to it
that Ngo Dinh Can was brought before a court, sentenced to death,
and executed.

Many of the measures taken by the junta immediately after the coup
were warmly acclaimed. Imprisoned anti-Communists, among them
Dr. Dan and Phan Khac Suu, were released. The National Assembly
was dissolved and new elections promised within a year. Also dissolved
were the official government parties—the National Revolutionary
Movement, the Personalist Labor Party, and the Women's Solidarity
Movement—a mere formality, since these organizations had ceased to
exist the moment the coup succeeded. Mme. Nhu's vicious Family
Code and absurd Morality Laws disappeared, together with many of
Diem's arbitrary and unnecessary restrictions on civil liberties, and
eventually also his constitution.

But the hope of some of the younger conspirators that the new
regime would carry out a genuine revolution remained unfulfilled. The
heads of the junta were not inspired by ideals of democracy and social
justice; they were ignorant of economic problems and unaware of the
need for a drastic reform of the entire administration. They showed no
more concern for the plight of the peasant masses than had Diem. The
word land reform was not even mentioned. In all these respects, South
Vietnam remained what it had been under Diem.

Thus, the new regime did not inaugurate an era of political stability.
But above all, it was as unsuccessful as Diem in combating the Vietcong. The military situation, if not actually deteriorating at a faster
rate than before, certainly remained as irreparable as it had been before
the fall of Diem. Perhaps it was too late to improve the prospects of
victory through drastic social and political reforms. The generals
probably no longer enjoyed the chance that history had given South
Vietnam and that Diem had thrown away. But even had they still had
it, they would not have known how to use it. Under their rule, the
danger to the survival of a non-Communist Vietnam grew as rapidly as

it had under Diem. And the death of the one man who, in spite of his tragic shortcomings, was the only outstanding leader in the anti-Communist camp did not arrest the mounting fury of the second Indochina War.

In the United States, about to become still more deeply involved with the fate of Vietnam than it had been under Diem, the news of the successful coup was greeted with relief, although the murder of Diem was generally deplored as brutal and senseless.[266] On a moral level, the question of whether Diem deserved his fate can indeed be answered with an emphatic no. The generals, if they did not act out of political fear or a desire for personal revenge, must have felt justified in pronouncing and executing their irreversible verdict. But no man should have the right to pronounce such a verdict, and the generals, former collaborators of Diem, certainly lacked moral justification.

On the political level, however, the horrible deed must be judged in a different light. To be sure, a truly democratic conscience will condemn the slaying of Diem also on political grounds. But Diem and Nhu themselves did not reject murder as a means of preserving power. Had the coup failed, the plotters would certainly have been executed. Diem and Nhu therefore had forfeited any claim to be spared when defeat turned them from ministers of death into victims.

The political instability that followed upon the overthrow of Diem led some observers to the conclusion that if Diem had remained in office the military situation would not have deteriorated to the point where only U.S. military intervention could contain the Vietcong.[267] But such a view ignores the well-established fact that the Vietcong were as close to victory shortly before the fall of Diem as they were a year later. It is more than likely that with Diem still in power, the survival of an anti-Communist South Vietnam would have required the presence of a large American army already in 1964. Furthermore, the prospects of obtaining a negotiated settlement of the second Indochina War would have been even poorer with Diem still in power than they were after his fall. Diem would never have considered going back on his refusal to recognize the Vietcong as an indigenous and important political force. Like the French during the first Indochina War, who for nearly eight years refused to recognize the Vietminh, Diem expected the Vietcong, who controlled more than two-thirds of the country, to accept unconditional surrender.

In trying to assess responsibility for the tragic American involve-

ment in the second Indochina War, it may be helpful to recall that
Diem repeatedly remarked that the borders of the United States extend
to the 17th parallel. This was the line that divided Diem's antidemocratic state in the South from Ho Chi Minh's Communist state in the
North. It is more than likely that Diem and Nhu, in a desperate attempt to avert defeat at the hands of the Vietcong, might have plunged
the United States into a war with Communist China by sending their
army across this fateful line.

This, it may be said, is mere speculation. But in view of Diem and
Nhu's state of mind, the fear that they might have embarked on such a
course can hardly be called groundless. It is also true that this danger
continued to exist under some of Diem's successors. But if the generals
who staged the Saigon coup of November, 1963, accomplished nothing
but a lessening of the threat which the second Indochina War constitutes to world peace, the people of the entire world have reason to be
grateful to them for having put an end to the Diem regime.

For the Vietnamese people, however, the coup, although greeted as a
deliverance from an evil, soon turned into just another disappointment.
The gates to a better life remained closed to them, and the day when
peace would return to their embattled land was as far away after the
fall of Diem as it had been before.

Notes

VIII. The "Bao Dai Solution"
(pp. 667–734)

1. As quoted by Jean Lacouture and Philippe Devillers, *La fin d'une guerre: Indochine 1954*, p. 17, n. 5.

2. Philippe Devillers, *Histoire du Viet-Nam de 1940 à 1952*, p. 459.

3. *Le Monde*, December 27, 1946.

4. Paul Rivet said in the French Assembly: "A high official who, on his return, came to share his apprehensions with me, told me that at the present time when we occupy only the cities in Indochina—I insist on this fact— there are four times more officials than in 1940" (*Journal Officiel, Assemblée Nationale*, March 10, 1949, p. 1516; as quoted by Ellen Hammer, *The Struggle for Indochina*, p. 229).

5. In a conversation with *colons* in Saigon, Lucien Bodard was told: "If only we had had sense enough to cut off some dozens of heads at the right time, we would still have a French Indochina. Imagine that before 1940 any Frenchman could freely roam the most savage regions without a gun in his pocket. The 'notables' were only too happy to receive him with flowers. Alas! The 'Frenchmen from France' we got here in 1945 provoked the catastrophe by thinking they could flatter Ho Chi Minh." To the colonial society, the time of the protectorate seemed like paradise, wrote Bodard. "What did we not do for the *nhaques*, the peasants! We took them out of their misery, gave them schools, roads, hospitals, and, above all, brought them justice and security." Why then, Bodard asked, did these "happy people" yearn for independence? Not feeling in the slightest ashamed of their colonialism, he wrote, the *colons* became indignant at his question: "Ah, if only the newcomers had listened to us who knew the Annamites so well, who loved them and were loved by them. But the d'Argenlieus and consorts accused us of being exploiters of the Annamite people; it is only fair that they were not proven right." Bodard asked whether the old Indochina had not in fact been dead for a long time, whether it had had substance, since it needed only a crack to bring the whole structure crashing down. "We

would have saved Indochina in spite of events, without the illusions of the new chiefs nominated in Paris," was the answer (*La guerre d'Indochine, L'enlisement*, pp. 54–55).

6. See Lacouture and Devillers, *op. cit.*, p. 15.

7. Two illusions are apt to give a misleading picture of the French political scene in the years between 1945 and 1954. One is that the French Communists and/or Socialists actively sympathized with the Vietnamese cause against the colonial imperialism of the Center and the Right; the other is that the MRP was in sympathy with the Left on Vietnam. The true policies of the French Left are discussed elsewhere (see Chapter VII, n. 26, and n. 9, below). As for the MRP, which was said to be without the vested interests in Vietnam that, for example, the Radical Socialists had built there under the Third Republic (beginning with Doumer as their strongest exponent), the MRP, once in power, quickly acquired interests of its own in Vietnam, although less of an economic than of a political nature. To be sure, a small group of the MRP joined with other political-religious groups in protesting French policies in Indochina, yet this was but an insignificant faction, with no influence on the over-all policies of the MRP. As Miss Hammer wrote: "Contrary to expectations, the MRP did not support its coreligionists in the empire, but acquired a vested interest in the somewhat doctrinaire and certainly inelastic policies, which allowed concessions to the Vietnamese only reluctantly and when forced to do so, of Georges Bidault, Paul Coste-Floret, and Jean Letourneau." Clearly speaking of the MRP, Miss Hammer states the reasons: "There was thus no public opinion to force the Indochinese problem from the obscurity of the political limbo to which the three major parties by common consent had consigned it; and, in practice, French government policy toward Viet Nam was left to be formulated and implemented by a surprisingly small group of men in key positions—professional administrators, men with large economic interests in Indochina, and politicians dreaming of power and empire—who were able to have their own way because of the peculiar nature of the French political scene" (*op. cit.*, p. 299).

8. This is almost the main point of criticism expressed by Devillers, who states: "It became impossible . . . to formulate policy. It seemed preferable to gain time, to defer a thorough examination of the problem to some future date" (*op. cit.*, p. 369). General Henri Navarre, who wrote a book about his command in Indochina, and who described the Indochina War as "seven years of incoherence," commented: "We never had continuity in the pursued political line. More exactly, we never had a political line at all" (*Agonie de l'Indochine, 1953–1954* [Paris, 1956], pp. 34, 43). Wrote Paul Isoart: "France offered the Vietnamese nationalists the sad spectacle of divisiveness and of a feeble leader state incapable of determining its own orientation"; and: "More than a national objective, the Indochina policy became a weapon for internal strife." And he concluded: "In fact, there was no valid policy, no well-defined leading principle. A complex affair was handled on a day-to-day basis, serving as a backdrop to gainful traffic by some

and futile heroism by others" (*Le phénomène national vietnamien*, pp. 378, 381, 384). J. J. Servan-Schreiber, the well-known editor of the weekly *L'Express*, wrote in *Le Monde* on April 30, 1953, that the blame could be laid on the "natural tendency of the military proconsulate to perpetuate itself" and on "certain French political groups who have found in the war the principal source of their revenues . . . through exchange operations, supplies to the expeditionary corps and war damages" (as quoted by Hammer, *op. cit.*, p. 300). And Arthur Laurent, who wrote a damaging exposé on the activities of the Bank of Indochina during the war, commented: "Since the beginning of the Indochina war, not one single government of all those who succeeded each other was able to define the cause and the aim of this rotten and corrupt war that bled the French and Vietnamese people" (*La Banque de l'Indochine et la piastre* [Paris, 1954], p. 19).

9. See Chapter VII, n. 26. Bernard Fall wrote: "The varying positions taken by the French Communist Party towards the war in Indo-China have provided a striking example of the difficulties and contradictions which a party encounters when it tries to conciliate its local political objectives with the over-all grand design of the Soviet Union" ("Tribulations of a Party Line: The French Communists and Indo-China," in *Foreign Affairs*, April, 1955, p. 499). Fall makes it quite clear that the French CP sought to retain Vietnam within the French Union because of "Communist hopes of being able to get control of France and her overseas possession in one swift sweep." This was true in the early postwar years, and Jacques Duclos, "the Number 2 man of the PCF after Thorez," stated in 1947, "we are for the presence of France in the Far East, contrary to what is asserted by the newspaper *Le Monde*. We have understood only too well that our departure from the Far East would result in the arrival of certain other elements of a not-too-democratic character." Fall quotes this statement by Duclos in his article but does not make clear that these "certain other elements" were undoubtedly the United States, and that France feared being displaced by the American presence in Vietnam as much as being displaced by the Vietminh. Nevertheless, the French Party thereafter was to oppose the Indochina War on the grounds that it was an "imperialist" war. The Cold War had begun, and, as Fall stated, "in less than three years the party line of the PCF had gone full circle, from all-out support of a French Union in its narrowest colonial interpretation to outright sabotage of French governmental actions aimed at maintaining the integrity of the French Union, even in the diluted version of a loose association with the Indo-China states."

10. Blum, speaking in the French Assembly on December 23, 1946, said: "The old colonial system, which was founded on conquest and maintained by constraint, and which tended toward the exploitation of conquered lands and peoples, is finished today. . . . The award given the colonizing people is therefore to have wakened in the colonized people sentiments of gratitude and affection, to have created the penetration and solidarity of thought, culture, and interests which permit one and the other to freely unite together" (as quoted by Hammer, *op. cit.*, p. 191).

11. After the November elections in 1946, the Communist Party emerged with increased strength. Together with the Socialists, who had suffered a slight setback at the polls (as had the MRP), the leftist parties held no less than 46 per cent of votes, enough to forecast a domination of the government. Under the circumstances, the Bidault Government, which had assumed power at the end of June because the MRP, Bidault's party, held the balance in the coalition with the leftist wing, was in no position to carry on until January, when the Constitution of the Fourth Republic was slated to go into effect. On November 28, the Bidault Cabinet resigned, remaining in a caretaker position until a new premier and cabinet were agreed upon by all parties. The Communists immediately put up their own candidate, Maurice Thorez, but although he was supported by part of the Socialists (e.g., Léon Blum, Guy Mollet, and Felix Gouin) he was rejected by the Assembly on December 4. In the ensuing stalemate, in which the Communists refused to participate in an MRP government, Bidault's renewed bid for power was defeated, but Bidault remained at his post until December 12, when Blum was called upon to resolve the impasse between the Communists and the MRP. He formed his government on December 16. But, as Ellen Hammer puts it, Blum's government was only a "stop-gap regime appointed to serve out the few remaining days of the Provisional Government until the constitution of the Fourth Republic would go into effect" (*op. cit.*, p. 186). In January, 1947, a coalition cabinet under Paul Ramadier, also a Socialist, came into power. Interestingly enough, the Socialist Marius Moutet remained Minister for Overseas Affairs throughout these various cabinet changes, serving under the MRP as well as under the Socialists.

12. Miss Hammer commented: "And certainly there is good reason to regard the professedly anticolonialist Socialists and Communists as seriously culpable in regard to Indochina ever since 1945" (*ibid.*, p. 297). The Socialists, she continues, were no less opportunistic in practice than the Communists. She accuses the Socialist Party of being more interested in "retaining nominal political power as a member of the governing coalition, which it did not leave until February, than in any program of principle or of action." And finally she states: "If the Socialists never found it easy to reconcile the war with their Marxist anticolonialism, they found it even less easy to translate their anticolonialism into effective practice" (*ibid.*, p. 298). If it was indeed as Jacques Raphael-Leygues, a Radical Socialist, was to state in October, 1952, namely that "since 1946 the war in Indochina has been a series of lost opportunities" (*ibid.*, p. 297), the blame for losing these opportunities can certainly be placed on the Socialists as a party and on Marius Moutet as the man most intimately in charge of Vietnamese affairs in Paris.

13. In March, 1949, the Socialist Oreste Rosenfeld was to express his criticism as follows: "If we truly want to determine who was responsible, I do not hesitate to say that the great responsibility falls on the government of 1946 which let its High Commissioner formulate a policy contrary to government policy. You know very well that the High Commissioner, M. Georges Thierry d'Argenlieu, appointed by General de Gaulle, had exorbitant powers in Indochina. He was not even under the authority of the Min-

ister of Overseas France, but directly under the President of the Council (the Premier, Georges Bidault) and so of the government. . . . The great responsibility of the government of M. Georges Bidault and M. Maurice Thorez was not to have its authority used to prevent Admiral d'Argenlieu from following a policy contrary to that of the French Government" (*Journal Officiel, Assemblée de l'Union Française*, March 9, 1949, pp. 337–38; quoted by Hammer, *op. cit.*, p. 189). Another critic was Dr. Léon Boutbien, who as member of the Executive Committee of the Socialist Party had accompanied Moutet on his first trip to Vietnam. As Miss Hammer describes it, Boutbien "brought back . . . a report totally at variance with that of the Minister of Overseas France. . . . He told newspapermen that the French as well as the Vietnamese were to blame for the fighting. He was bitterly critical of Admiral d'Argenlieu, and he dated the beginning of hostilities, as the Vietnamese did, not from December 19 but from November 20 and the Haiphong affair." Miss Hammer adds that Boutbien based "his report on unofficial talks he had had with Vietnamese nationalists; not only, it seemed, had the Viet Minh government contacted the Moutet Mission, but Boutbien had actually met some of its representatives. It was Moutet, apparently, not the Vietnamese, who did not wish to negotiate" (*ibid.*, p. 194).

14. *Journal Officiel, Assemblée Nationale*, March 18, 1947; as quoted by Hammer, *ibid.*, p. 199.

15. See n. 13, above. Miss Hammer also writes that Dr. Boutbien published a series of articles in *Franc-Tireur* in January elaborating "his conclusions with enough impartiality to enable Ho Chi Minh later to recommend the series as showing 'the real cause of the present conflict'" (*op. cit.*, p. 194).

16. Quoting from Andrien Dansette, *Leclerc*, p. 216, Ellen Hammer writes: " 'They want to use you,' General de Gaulle warned Leclerc. 'You don't know politics. They will make you take the responsibility for abandoning Indochina. They will make you an instrument of capitulation' " (*op. cit.*, p. 195). Miss Hammer also states that Leclerc told Ramadier his conditions for acceptance would have been "full civil and military power for himself and an army of 100,000 men, 90,000 of them Europeans; eventual negotiations with the Viet Minh; and independence for the Vietnamese within the French Union with safeguards for French interests and military bases." (There is some conflict between this and Lacouture and Devillers' statement that in January, 1947, Leclerc had announced he would need 500,000 men for a rapid liquidation of the "insurrection" [*op. cit.*, p. 25].)

17. Leclerc explained: "It is a question of coming to terms with an awakening xenophobic nationalism, of channelling it in order to safeguard, at least in part, the rights of France" (quoted by Hammer, *op. cit.*, p. 193). Summarizing the situation on April 30, 1946, Leclerc declared in his report: "Negotiations and agreements are necessary. At this stage it is not a question of imposing oneself by force on masses who desire evolution and change. Otherwise no relaxation of our military effort will be possible for a long time" (quoted by J. R. Tournoux, *Secrets d'état* [Paris, 1960], p. 453).

18. Fall writes that contrary to the belief that the idea to use Bao Dai

originated with d'Argenlieu, it was at first attributed to William C. Bullitt, wartime American Ambassador to the de Gaulle Government, but that "there is now some evidence that French General Le Bris, who commanded Central Viet-Nam in 1945–46, had been impressed with the affection and loyalty the absent ruler still commanded there and had recommended the 'Bao-Dai solution' to his government as early as December, 1946 (*The Two Viet-Nams*, p. 209). For Bullitt's advocacy of Bao Dai, see n. 76, below.

19. In a paper included in an international symposium on nationalism in Southeast Asia ("Vietnamese Nationalism and French Policies," in William L. Holland [ed.], *Asian Nationalism and the West*, p. 212), Philippe Devillers wrote: "Why Bao Dai? Because in these circles, where some of the high officials from the period of the protectorate were now the counsellors most listened to and most influential, it was believed that Bao Dai would prove a partner who would make few demands, and that—to judge from experience still recent—*it would be easy to manage him* [italics added]. To persuade him to return to the political arena, perhaps even to the throne, did not appear too difficult; and once this was accomplished it would not be too difficult either to make him appear at the same time as the symbol of national tradition, hence in a position to rally the rural masses, and also the symbol of Franco-Vietnamese friendship." According also to Devillers, Léon Pignon, d'Argenlieu's political adviser, stated: "Our objective is clearly determined—to transport onto the Annamite interior level our quarrel with the Vietminh party and ourselves to be engaged as little as possible in the campaigns and reprisals which must be the doing of the autochthonous adversaries of that party" (*Histoire du Viet-Nam*, p. 364).

20. This famous remark, which Leclerc made in Saigon to Colonel Repiton-Preneuf, his Chief of the Deuxième Bureau, in January, 1947, at the end of the mission on which he had been sent over d'Argenlieu's protests simultaneously with Moutet, has been quoted by almost everyone who has written about Vietnam because of its prophetic truth. Quoting it, Lacouture and Devillers (*op. cit.*, p. 20) precede it with the statement: "The only means of avoiding that Communism become definitively identified with patriotism, as it has been for fifteen years, was to resolve the national problem." Repiton-Preneuf quotes Leclerc as having told him during the same conversation that "as long as a strongly armed resistance exists, the solutions we are attempting will only be fragmentary. Moreover, the teams which come to power with us will, as soon as they gain some vigor, not remain indifferent to the issue. If at all possible, our role must not be to side with one camp but to be arbiter to all [camps]" (in a study written in 1947 and quoted by Tournoux, *op. cit.*, p. 457).

21. On December 21, 1946, Ho Chi Minh addressed this proclamation to his people: "The clique of French colonialists pursues its design once more to subjugate the Fatherland. The hour is grave. Rise and unite! Differences of ideology, race, and religion no longer matter. Fight with all means at your disposal. Fight with your arms, your shovels, your axes, your sticks. Save the independence and unity of your country. Victory shall be ours.

Long live Vietnam, independent and indivisible. Long live Democracy!"
(Devillers, *Histoire du Viet-Nam*, p. 357, n. 6.)

22. Lacouture and Devillers, *op. cit.*, p. 21.

23. The quoted phrases are from Donald Lancaster, *The Emancipation of French Indochina*, p. 182.

24. The overseas deputies (Africans, etc.) also abstained. The vote was 400 to 0. In a speech in the Chamber made on January 27, 1950, Thorez (who had been Vice-Premier in March, 1947) revealed that an agreement had been reached between the tripartite members of government concerning Bollaert's instructions. These instructions specified that the French armed forces were not in Vietnam for conquest or reconquest but to guarantee the security of the garrisons and lines of communications; and that the new High Commissioner "was to realize the integration of the Indochinese States into the French Union in accordance with the Constitution of October 27, 1946—this Constitution of the French Union on which, let it be said in passing, no Indochina State had been consulted—and to seek out men from the Vietnamese side who would accept to deal with France on this basis. No group was a priori excluded from this search" (Devillers, *Histoire du Viet-Nam*, p. 370, and n. 17.) Jean Chesneaux writes that the Minister for Overseas France, Jean Letourneau, acknowledged the accuracy of the statements made by Thorez in 1950 during the same debate (*Contribution à l'histoire de la nation vietnamienne*, p. 267).

25. Characteristic of the position behind Bollaert's May statement in *Le Monde* was his observation: "We have, in Indochina, rights and legitimate interests. We have sowed much, and we are not ashamed to say that we don't want to be deprived of the harvest" (quoted by Chesneaux, *ibid.*, p. 291).

26. The three main conditions of the French demands relayed by Paul Mus were "return of prisoners and hostages taken, delivery of a large part of the arms and ammunitions, free entry of French troops to all territories under Vietminh occupation," wrote Devillers (in Holland [ed.], *op. cit.*, pp. 210–11). For the fourth condition relative to non-Vietnamese aid to the Vietminh with military advice, see Chapter VII, n. 78. Ho Chi Minh's famous reply (also quoted by Chesneaux, *op. cit.*, p. 267) was: "There is no place in the French Union for cowards. I would be one were I to accept," Mus reported on his mission in his book *Viet-Nam: Sociologie d'une guerre*, pp. 315–16, and in an article entitled "Ma mission auprès du Viet Minh," which appeared in *L'Observateur d'Aujourd'hui*, December 24 and 31, 1953. He ascribed the impossible terms he had to transmit to Ho Chi Minh to the military and political optimism of the French Government.

27. These reinforcements did not arrive when expected, due to the outbreak in May of a rebellion in Madagascar, which forced the French to divert troops destined for Indochina to their new theater of colonial warfare. Some believe that this was the reason why the 1947 fall offensive to crush the Vietminh did not succeed.

28. Quoted in *Le Figaro*, May 14, 1947, and *Combat* of the same date; as

cited by Devillers, *Histoire du Viet-Nam*, p. 394, n. 1, and Hammer, *op. cit.*, p. 207.

29. See Service Français d'Information, *Notes documentaires et études*, No. 752, July 5, 1947; interview of Bao Dai with the journal *L'Union Française*.

30. The name of the nationalist was Ho Dac Lien. Bao Dai would probably have strengthened his position vis-à-vis the French and the Vietminh if he had accepted this proposal, if only to show that both the French and the Vietminh aims were incompatible with a truly free Vietnam. Bao Dai's envoy, Tran Van Tuyen, made reference to this contact in his interview in the *Journal de Saigon*, August 24, 1947 (see *Notes documentaires*, No. 752, July 5, 1947)

31. Bollaert knew that August 15 was the day on which the transfer of British sovereignty to India was to take place.

32. In reply to a public statement by Bollaert in July, saying that neither victors nor vanquished would emerge from this conflict, the Vietminh had answered eagerly: "If this clear view of the situation guides French policy, a peaceful solution can certainly be found" (quoted by Hammer, *op. cit.*, p. 212). For further peace offers, see Chapter VII, n. 73. The text of the peace offer made by Ho Chi Minh on October 27, 1948, can be found in Allen B. Cole (ed.), *Conflict in Indo-China and International Repercussions: A Documentary History, 1945–1955*, pp. 69–70.

33. The circumstances under which the term "independence" was changed to "liberty" by the French Cabinet (presided over for the occasion by no less a person than President Vincent Auriol) assume the proportions of a tragicomic farce in Tournoux's description (*op. cit.*, pp. 8–9). The MRP, he wrote, objected to the word "independence" because it would pave the way for the dissolution of the French Union. Others added that it would affect the French position in Tunisia and Morocco. Bollaert, who had been permitted to attend the meeting, declared himself solely responsible for the French position in Indochina. "If I cannot pronounce the word 'independence,'" Tournoux quoted him, "it would be better to suppress the speech than to block out the word." What to do? An ingenious idea took shape under the gilded ceiling. Would not repercussions of the word "independence" throughout the French Union be avoided if it were not said in French? How so? Very simple. Say it in Vietnamese. Only the natives will understand it. As for the translation, "independence" and "liberty" were the same in Vietnamese—*Doc Lap!* The Committee drew a sigh of relief. An astonishing compromise *à la française!* In his speech, Bollaert shouted: *"Doc lap trong khoi Lien Hiep Phap."* (Freedom within the French Union. This at least is what Bollaert thought he was saying; however, he was misinformed. "Independence" and "freedom" are not the same word in Vietnamese. The Vietnamese word for freedom is *Tu Do.*) In Paris, Ramadier and Moutet stressed the importance of the speech. In Vietnam, the colonials insisted that "nothing had changed." (For excerpts from Bollaert's Ha Dong speech, see Cole [ed.], *op. cit.*, pp. 62–66.)

34. After the 1954 armistice, Ho Chi Minh and Giap told General de

Beaufort (later special chief of staff to de Gaulle), then president of the French delegation to the International Control Commission, that they sat pressed against each other in a hole covered with branches while the French patrols passed and repassed several yards away from them, beating the bushes and tapping the ground (as told by Tournoux, *op. cit.*, p. 11).

35. Quoted by Chesneaux, *op. cit.*, p. 261.

36. See *The New York Times,* February 8, 1947.

37. Harold Isaacs was probably the best-known advocate of the Vietnamese cause in the United States at the time. See in particular his book *No Peace for Asia.*

38. Giap was nominated Commander in Chief of the National Army instead. Pham Van Dong reappeared in the public eye in August, 1949, when the Viet radio announced first his appointment to the Vice-Presidency, and later in the month his nomination to the Presidency of the Superior Council for National Defense. In the new government in 1947, three were Communists (instead of the former six), four Democrats, four Socialists, two Nationalists, three Catholics, one Buddhist, eight Independents, and two former mandarins. Ta Quang Buu had been a Boy Scout leader under the French regime; the Catholic Minister of Veterans and Invalids was Vu Dinh Tung, a surgeon; Phan Anh, who held the post of National Economy, a lawyer by profession, had been Minister of Youth in the Japanese-backed regime of Tran Trong Kim in 1945, and then gone over to the Vietminh; Hoang Minh Giam had been a teacher; Le Van Hien, Minister of Finance, a Communist, had been a minor employee in the Commerce Ministry; Nguyen Van Tao, Minister of Labor, was a veteran of the Cochinchinese workers' movement; Hoang Tich Tri, Minister of Public Health, a Socialist, was formerly with the Pasteur Institute and the author of important works on paludism. Other important members of Ho Chi Minh's government were: Phan Tu Nghia, an intellectual "returnee" from France, who had been a member of the Socialist SFIO in Hanoi in 1936 and the founder, in 1945, of the Socialist Vietnamese Party, of which he was Secretary General; the intellectual Duong Duc Hien, formerly a student leader, then Secretary of the Democratic Party since 1944; Chu Van Tan, a brigadier general, former Tho chief, who was Minister of War in the Provisional Government of 1945, and now became President of the Military Committee for Viet Bac, responsible for affairs dealing with the minorities; the Reverend Pham Ba Truc, Vice-President of the Permanent Assembly Commission; the Reverend Vu Xuan Ky; the Buddhist Le Dinh Tham; the Independents and Moderates Bo Xuan Luat, formerly Dong Minh Hoi member, Nguyen Van Huyen, ethnographer, Minister of National Education, To Ngoc Van, Director of the Fine Arts School in the Free Zone, formerly a high official of the French fine-arts administration.

39. When interviewed on the reconfirmation of Bao Dai (Vinh Thuy) as Supreme Counselor, Ho Chi Minh stated: "Many members of the government as well as myself, all friends of Counselor Vinh Thuy, are anxious to see him again and hope that he will return soon to take up the affairs of

state. But Counsellor Vinh Thuy cannot now leave Hong Kong. We are far separated from him in space but not in thought. The government and the people of Vietnam have full confidence in the faithfulness of Counsellor Vinh Thuy, who continues to work for the national government of which he has never ceased being a part while residing in a foreign country" (Devillers, *Histoire du Viet-Nam*, p. 402).

40. For the English text of Bollaert's speech of September 10, 1947, see Cole (ed.), *op. cit.*, pp. 62–66.

41. The best known of these nationalists were Nguyen Tuong Tam, Vu Hong Khanh, and Nguyen Hai Thanh, members of the VNQDD and the Dong Minh Hoi respectively, who at the time resided in China, and Nguyen Van Sam in Saigon, as well as Le Van Hoach. Also declaring for Bao Dai were Truong Dinh Tri, a former member of the Vietminh Government and a member of VNQDD, and Tran Van Ly, who represented Ngo Dinh Diem's Catholic grouping in Annam. In October, 1947, Nguyen Van Sam and Truong Dinh Tri were assassinated by the Communists. Twenty-four delegates went to see Bao Dai on September 9 in Hong Kong, "not without our services having managed to slide in among them some safe personalities such as Nguyen Van Tam," wrote Pierre Dabezies (*Forces politiques au Viet-Nam*, p. 170), and thus Nguyen Van Sam, Tran Van Tuyen, Tran Quang Vinh, Tran Van Ly, Truong Dinh Tri, and the journalist Nguyen Phan Long were to assist Bao Dai who was in the company of the *émigrés* from China, Nguyen Hai Thanh, Nguyen Tuong Tam, Nguyen Tuong Long, Phan Huy Dan, and Dinh Xuan Quang, the latter two, wrote Dabezies, the personal counselors of the ex-Emperor.

42. "It was well known at that time that in the Maquis many guerrilla groups were almost wholly composed of young people whose convictions were free from any taint of communism, and who fought under the Vietminh banner only because at that time it was the only organized movement that did fight for national independence" (Devillers, in Holland [ed.], *op. cit.*, p. 210).

43. For the attitude of the Cao Dai toward the French, see Chapter VII, n. 50; for the attitude of the Hoa Hao, see *ibid.*, n. 51. Lancaster commented: "Moreover the habit which the Cao Dai and Hoa Hao militia forces were developing of deserting the French-controlled zone, under energetic and unscrupulous guerrilla leaders, together with the intrigues and pretensions of nationalist personalities who professed allegiance to Bao Dai but refused to support Xuan's Government, threatened, in the absence of an agreed political programme and an arbitrator, to reveal the incapacity of the nationalists to dispute Viet Minh claims to leadership" (*op. cit.*, p. 192). Although Lancaster speaks of a period somewhat later than that discussed in the text, the tendencies already existed in 1947. The sects were unwilling to be deprived of their military power. "At the end of 1948 the Hoa Hao leaders, Nguyen Gia Ngo, Lam Thanh Nguyen, and Le Quang Vinh, together with their armed followers, had deserted the French-controlled zone, and in February 1949 the Cao Dai military commander, Nguyen Van Thanh, fol-

lowing the rejection of a proposal to create a neutral zone around Tay
Ninh, instructed the Cao Dai militia forces to oppose any attempts by the
French or by the Viet Minh to occupy their defence posts" (*ibid.*, p. 192, n.
29). For the story of Trinh Minh The, the Cao Dai Chief of Staff, see Chapter IX, n. 93. For further details on the sects, see Chapter V, nn. 45, 46, 47,
48, 49.

44. "There can be no doubt as to the fact," wrote Bernard Fall, "that the
Catholic Church of Indochina stood in the forefront of Vietnamese nationalism during its early days, and in so doing received the wholehearted support of the French Catholic Church. There is also no doubt that the Catholic Church of Vietnam merely expressed the deep feelings of its members"
(*The Viet-Minh Regime*, p. 62). While the "wholehearted support of the
French Catholic Church" is debatable, there is no doubt that the Vietnamese
Catholics were not only caught up by the wave of nationalism that swept
over the country in August, 1945, but also sought to counteract the old ac-
cusation that the Catholic missionaries had always played a large role in
French colonial imperialism. On August 25, 1945, the very day of her hus-
band's abdication, Bao Dai's wife, the ex-Empress Nam Phuong, wrote a letter to friends abroad in which she appealed for support against the French.
On September 23, the four Vietnamese bishops, with Monsignor Tong, the
Apostolic Vicar of Hanoi, as their spokesman, addressed an appeal to Pope
Piux XII, in which they asked the Holy See to support Vietnam's struggle
for independence. With this appeal, which bypassed the Apostolic Delegate,
a Frenchman, wrote Jean-R. Clementin in an article in 1954, the Vietnamese
bishops agreed to be the spokesmen for the revolutionary government of
Ho Chi Minh ("Les institutions catholiques au Vietnam," *Les Temps
Modernes*, June, 1954, p. 2263). A similar appeal went to England and the
United States several weeks later, asking for intervention. Until 1949, relations between Ho's government and the bishoprics in the North were cor-
dial. "The government did not intervene with the administration of the
quasi-feudal bishoprices of Phat-Diem and Pui-Chu," wrote Fall. "A Catholic, Vu Dinh Tung, became Minister of Veterans Affairs . . . and little or
no interference was felt by the missionaries and nuns who were still free to
go about their ecclesiastical duties" (*The Viet-Minh Regime*, p. 63). After
Bao Dai's departure for Hong Kong in March, 1946, Monsignor Le Huu
Tu, the Apostolic Vicar of Phat Diem, was made Supreme Adviser to the
Ho Government, wrote Lancaster (*op. cit.*, p. 196), but since the Communists began to interfere in the administration of the communities, militia
forces were formed in Phat Diem and Bui Chu under the white and yellow
flag of Vatican City, and "were able for three years to keep the Viet Minh
at bay and to maintain a precarious neutrality. It was only toward the end
of 1949, following a Viet Minh attack on the area, that the Apostolic Vicars
of Phat Diem and Bui Chu abandoned their pretensions to neutrality and
proffered their allegiance to Bao Dai" (*ibid.*, p. 197). Although Ellen Hammer reports that Bishop Le Huu Tu allowed French troops to move into the
area on condition that no white troops would appear in his diocese, and that

accordingly in October, 1949, "only Vietnamese parachutists were dropped" on Phat Diem and Bui Chu (*op. cit.*, p. 276), Dabezies states that the paratroopers were dropped against the wishes of the bishops of Phat Diem and Bui Chu, "whose nationalist intransigence remained as strong as ever" (*op. cit.*, p. 181). Dabezies further states that even though the bishops recognized Bao Dai's authority, they continued to show their hostility toward the French and to declare their solidarity with the non-Communist resistance (*ibid.*, p. 182). The Most Reverend Peter Ngo Dinh Thuc, the brother of Ngo Dinh Diem, was to remark in an article that "Bao Dai followed the example of Ho Chi Minh and appointed the Bishops as *his* representatives in the area. An odd situation, surely" ("Viet-Nam Through Vietnamese Eyes," in *World-Mission*, February, 1951, p. 70; quoted by Hammer, *op. cit.*, p. 267, n. 51). According to Fall, when the Vietminh attacked Phat Diem in autumn, 1951, and French paratroops and ground forces "saved the bishop in the nick of time from being captured . . . war began now in earnest between the Viet-Minh and the Catholics, now ranged in their majority on the side of the Franco-Nationalists" (*The Viet-Minh Regime*, p. 63). For a Catholic comment, calling for a greater role of the Vietnamese Church in social justice for the Vietnamese population, see E. Jacques-Houssa, "Situation du catholicisme au Viet-Nam," in *La Revue Nouvelle*, December 15, 1946.

45. Dabezies, *op. cit.*, p. 171. Dabezies also gives a harsh description of the inability of these nationalists to serve a common purpose. No sooner had the Bay of Along agreement been signed, he wrote, when "the nationalists went back to their intrigues. It must be said in their defense that the negotiations dragged out interminably and that the best minds ended up by having reasons for doubting our sincerity regarding independence as well as unity. The adversaries of the Bao Dai experiment were triumphant, the lukewarm ones hesitated to engage themselves any further, and the most convinced arranged their activities in such a manner as to take into consideration the future or, in any case, their interests. With the National Vietnamese Assembly, Doctor Le Van Hoach renewed his attacks on General Xuan. At his instigation, the movement held a new congress at Hue in July, where the support given until then to the Central Government was again placed in doubt. Since the Northern section was supporting the General, the vote was moved up at the last minute so as to avoid their presence. Other meetings took place here and there, too often marked by the secret intervention of Hoach and his accomplices Nguyen Ton Hoan and Nguyen The Truyen, who seemed to be wanting to play 'with their own cards.' After numerous intrigues and subtle maneuvers, a last congress of the RNVN gathered at Hanoi in December. But the disagreements were such from that moment on that the delegation from Central Vietnam only arrived the day when that from Cochinchina left. From then on, despite the speeches and resolutions, the split had taken place: Each local section reclaimed the right to independent action, and union was never referred to again" (*ibid.*, p. 175). See also list of political parties and movements, 1947, Appendix VII.

46. "With its armored cars, its air force, its paratroops, its overwhelming superiority of equipment, the French command for a long time believed itself capable of imposing a solution. In September, 1947, General Valluy still thought that he could eliminate all 'organized resistance' within three months" (Lacouture and Devillers, *op. cit.*, p. 23).

47. See *Notes documentaires et études*, No. 752, October 30, 1947. (Tran Van Tuyen, having survived twenty years of political changes, became Vice-Premier of the Saigon Government in February, 1965.)

48. Lacouture & Devillers, *op. cit.*, p. 19.

49. *Ibid.*, p. 21.

50. See *Le Monde*, May 15, 1948.

51. So referred to by Paul Rivet in *Débats Assemblée Nationale, Journal Officiel*, March 11, 1949, p. 1516 (as quoted by Isoart, *op. cit.*, p. 379, n. 166).

52. *Bulletin d'Information de la France d'Outre-Mer*, January 15, 1948.

53. The French had also failed in their attempt to enlist the aid of the Church in their fight with the Vietminh. Early in 1948, Bollaert went to Rome, reportedly to enlist the influence of the Vatican among Vietnamese Catholics, wrote Hammer, citing an article that appeared in *The New York Times*, January 18, 1948. "The Church, it seemed, was unwilling to take a firm stand against the Viet Minh as long as most Vietnamese Catholics as well as the native clergy favored the resistance," she added (*op. cit.*, p. 217). See note 44, above, for the attitude of the Vietnamese Catholic Church and its faithful in the early years of Vietnamese nationalism, and for the slow evolution of its stand.

54. Caput, who had already been in constant touch with the Vietminh in 1945, and who had assumed the role, although unofficial, of mediator between the Vietnamese and the French (see Chapter VI, n. 87) had also assisted in the negotiations leading up to the March agreement of 1946. That he seems to have been used in spring, 1948, by Paris and Bollaert in a scheme in which he was an innocent participant, he himself realized when in a letter, dated September 18, 1948, he wrote: "I am more and more convinced that I was asked to go to Hong Kong only in order to facilitate his [Bollaert's] *rapprochement* with Bao Dai and hasten the conclusion of the accords of June 5 [1948]" (Hammer, *op. cit.*, p. 220). When Bollaert called for Caput on March 27, a deadlock had been arrived at with Bao Dai. Caput seems to have gone to Hong Kong in April, 1948, "in good faith," as Miss Hammer puts it. At that time, Miss Hammer says, he wrote that "there was not a plane which did not bring to or take back from Hong Kong French and Vietnamese emissaries. But I was certainly the first who undertook this famous 'pilgrimage' while being firmly hostile to negotiations with Bao Dai" (*ibid.*, p. 220). That the French had calculated their psychological pressure well on Bao Dai with this move became clear when, soon thereafter, Bollaert and the ex-Emperor resumed negotiations.

55. See text, p. 695, and n. 30, above, for Bao Dai's rejection of a coalition with the Vietminh in July, 1947. Later that same year in Paris, Bao Dai's

wife proposed to her husband's cousin, Prince Buu Hoi, who lived in France and who had been a delegate of the Ho Government at the Fontainebleau conference, that he rally nationalist support for the ex-Emperor. Buu Hoi posed the condition that Bao Dai join his action with the Vietminh, and since this was unacceptable to Bao Dai, the proposal to Buu Hoi was dropped. Early in 1948, the Vietminh again proposed, in a letter signed by Pham Khac Hoe, former secretary to Bao Dai and secretary at the Fontainebleau conference, that Bao Dai engage in joint action with it, a letter which was delivered by Buu Hoi. But again Bao Dai energetically ruled out contacts with the Hanoi Government (to the satisfaction of the French) and refused to speak for it, or include members of the Vietminh in a government of his own (see Hammer, *op. cit.*, pp. 216, 217).

56. "On April 12, Doctor Phan Huy Dan had brought a letter to Bollaert in which Bao Dai made the straightforward statement that the protocol had been judged totally insufficient by the chiefs of the political and religious groups and that, consequently, 'a new base of understanding more conducive to rallying the Vietnamese people would have to be studied.' Moreover, Bao Dai confirmed, this protocol had only been a basis for discussion, and as a private individual he had only bound himself" (Devillers, *Histoire du Viet-Nam*, p. 429).

57. The list of the Xuan Government members is an impressive one and includes also a few good names. But most of the ministers never served and many soon left the government. Before long Xuan was unable to fill all his Cabinet posts. (For a list of members, see Devillers, *ibid.*, p. 430, n. 1.)

58. Through an official spokesman, the ex-Emperor declared: "1. Bao Dai looks upon the present government as a step in the negotiations between Vietnam and France. 2. Bao Dai will not return to Vietnam until he has received from France formal assurances that the legitimate aspirations of the people of Vietnam will be recognized—that is to say, true unity and real independence in the bosom of the French Union, and admission of Vietnam as a state freely associated with the French Union and accepted in it on a basis of equality as regards both rights and obligations. 3. Although the new Central Government does not owe its existence to the Emperor, close contacts will be maintained, and a solid community of purpose will exist between the Government and Bao Dai" (Devillers, in Holland (ed.), *op. cit.*, pp. 229–30).

59. The Bay of Along agreement of June 5, 1948, stated "1. France solemnly recognizes the independence of Vietnam, whose right it is to bring about freely its unity. Vietnam, on its part, proclaims its adhesion to the French Union as a state associated with France. The independence of Vietnam has no limits other than those emanating from its membership in the French Union. 2. Vietnam undertakes to respect French national rights and interests, to assure in its Constitution respect for democratic principles, and to utilize preferably French counselors and technicians for its needs in its internal and economic organization. 3. After the constitution of a Provisional Government, the representatives of Vietnam will agree with the rep-

resentatives of the French Republic on various special arrangements in the cultural, diplomatic, military, economic, financial, and technical spheres" (quoted from Cole [ed.], *op. cit.*, p. 72, as published in *Journal Officiel*, March 14, 1953, p. 2409; for the original French text, see Devillers, *Histoire du Viet-Nam*, pp. 431–32). In his contribution to *Asian Nationalism and the West*, Devillers comments: "Just what had happened? Though the Central Government was able to take office, it could not govern. The general services were not transferred to it. Certain regional services and certain revenues were passed on to the governors of the Kys, but these remained much more under the tutelage of the French Commissioners of the Republic than they came under that of the Central Government of Vietnam. Although this government had been promised the income from the government monopolies, actually it did not enjoy a single actual source of financial revenue. It lived on advances from the Indo-Chinese Treasury. From fear of desertions, practically nothing had been done to give the Central Government any armed forces of its own. It did not even have control over its police force. That was the way in which France chose to interpret the 'Bao Dai solution'; that was how, from the start, it compromised its chances and jeopardized its practical and concrete basis" (pp. 235–36).

60. Ellen Hammer's comment on the Bay of Along agreement was: "It was an unusual document: for the first time the word 'independence' appeared in a Franco-Vietnamese accord; and the French had at last accepted the idea that Cochin China was a part of Viet Nam. But the Ha Long Bay Agreement (with a secret protocol attached) was nothing more than the accord which Bao Dai had signed and regretted at Ha Long Bay the previous December. The independence it recognized was hedged with qualifications and the unity to which it referred had yet to be translated from principle to practice; also, the accord was signed with a government which did not control the country" (*op. cit.*, p. 225).

61. Devillers, in Holland (ed.), *op. cit.*, p. 230. Speaking of the "mental climate" in which the agreement had been signed, Devillers mentions on the French side emotions varying from outright resistance ("France has sold her sacred rights!") to the hope "for an end to the long uncertainty," whereas on the Vietnamese side Bao Dai's stock went up because he "had succeeded where the Vietminh had failed" and the word "independence" had at last been spoken; in Vietminh circles, adds Devillers, "this turn of events produced a certain amount of confusion." In short, "one thing all Vietnamese had in common: nobody took the Declaration lightly" (*ibid.*, pp. 231–32).

62. *Ibid.*, p. 236.

63. *Ibid.*

64. Viet Nam News Agency, June 7, 1948.

65. Such old-time colonialists as Bazé, Beziat, Lachevrotière, and Bonvicini were the spokesmen for the campaign that depicted Xuan as a dangerous nationalist and Bollaert as a traitor to the interests of France. This group pleaded for a return to the pre-World War II status, for Cochinchina

as a French colony represented by a deputy to the metropolitan Assembly, for a protectorate over Annam and Tongking under a powerless monarch, in short, for a regime against which, Devillers said, the entire Vietnamese people had risen. The old-time colonialists were upheld to a certain degree by the French Government itself, when Coste-Floret, on June 8, stated in the National Assembly that in fact nothing had changed. "The signed agreement . . . does not mean an immediate return to peace, but it does mark an important step toward the pacification of the country," he declared. "The elements of order can henceforth unite around a national government responsive to Vietnam's aspirations and guaranteeing the rights of France and of the French Union." As to Cochinchina, he said, the agreement had not automatically recognized its union with Annam and Tongking; and as to the status of the three Vietnamese "kys" fixed by the treaties signed with the court of Annam, that too had not changed. Consequently the colonialists refused to recognize the authority of Xuan's Government and through their spokesman Bazé declared that they would resist "as long as the population had not expressed its wish to be united with the rest of Vietnam by means of a referendum ratified by the French Assembly" (see Devillers, *Histoire du Viet-Nam*, pp. 432, 435, 436; see also Devillers, in Holland [ed.], *op. cit.*, p. 231).

66. Isoart, *op. cit.*, p. 379.

67. "In the south particularly, Governor Tran Van Huu openly flouted the authority of the central government. Cochin China remained a juridical monstrosity; it was at one and the same time a French colony, an autonomous republic, and one of the three divisions of the country ruled by the central government" (Hammer, *op. cit.*, p. 229).

68. From a mimeographed manuscript by Dr. Phan Quang Dan entitled *The War in Indochina* (1954; p. 27). Dr. Dan later became a victim of Diem's persecution of political opponents. A French parliamentary commission on an annual visit to Indochina discovered that the state of Vietnam had no budget (Lancaster, *op. cit.*, p. 249).

69. "Aware that their tenure of office was short-lived, some ministers were not above exploiting their position to their own personal profit; and the impotence of the government was aggravated by the widespread corruption among its members" (Hammer, *op. cit.*, p. 230).

70. Lacouture and Devillers, *op. cit.*, p. 21.

71. Reported by *Le Populaire*, March 10, 1949, and quoted by Hammer, *op. cit.*, pp. 231–32. A similar analysis by *Combat* in a series of articles published on May 19, 20, 22, 1948, is quoted by Lancaster, *op. cit.*, p. 194.

72. Quoted by Lacouture and Devillers, *op. cit.*, p. 20, n. 11. They add that the Right-wing deputy M. Frédéric-Dupont wrote, although later: "In an insurrection, time always works for the insurgents" (*Mission de la France en Asie* [Paris, 1956], p. 197).

73. The appointment of an old colonial official was said to have resulted from the inability of the coalition parties to agree on a political personality. (See Pierre Célerier, *Menaces sur le Viet-Nam* [Saigon, 1950], pp. 239–40.)

"Pignon, who was a member of the Colonial Service," wrote Lancaster, "had first been posted to Indochina in 1932. During the war he had rallied to the Free French Forces and was Secretary of the Brazzaville Conference. In September, 1945, he returned to Tongking, and after serving on the staff of Sainteny and d'Argenlieu he had been appointed French Commissioner in Cambodia, whence he had been transferred early in 1948 to the Political Section of the Ministry of French Overseas Territories (*The Times*, 21 October, 1948)" (*op. cit.*, p. 191, n. 26).

74. "Today it can be seen that neither M. Bollaert nor those circles which had been in favor of the 'Bao Dai solution' had expected so astute a play on the part of the former ruler and his counsellors" (Devillers, in Holland (ed.), *op. cit.*, p. 227).

75. *Ibid.*, p. 236.

76. "In December 1947, *Life* magazine carried an article by Bullitt detailing the merits of a policy directed at winning the majority of the Vietnamese nationalist movement away from Ho Chi Minh and the Communists to Bao Dai ('The Saddest War,' *Life*, December 29, 1947). Bullitt's prestige was great in France and his words were invested by Frenchmen with a semiofficial character; his support for Bao Dai was interpreted by a number of people, particularly among the French Left, to mean American support for Bao Dai and it contributed to the conviction, widely held among Frenchmen, that the United States had taken an initiative in launching the Bao Dai policy" (Hammer, *op. cit.*, p. 216, n. 21).

77. Devillers, in Holland (ed.), *op. cit.*, p. 236.

78. The Assembly and the High Council of the French Union were the two new advisory bodies provided for in the constitution of 1946. The Assembly was to bring together delegates from all French overseas territories as well as from metropolitan France. The High Council was to assemble representatives of the Associated States and of France and to assist in the general direction of the French Union. "Under the French constitution, however, Associated Statehood was far removed from independence; in this respect comparisons between the British Commonwealth of Nations and the French Union, so often made by foreigners, were highly misleading. The provisions on the empire in the constitution of 1946 were drawn up according to the traditions of French imperial practice; within the newly named French Union the constituent parts of the empire were accorded varying degrees of subordination to metropolitan France" (Hammer, *op. cit.*, p. 234). Commented Isoart on the Associated Statehood: "It was neither a federated nor a confederated state; it was a half-sovereign state" (*op. cit.*, p. 377). And Lancaster stated, considerably more acidly: "The existence of these advisory and consultative bodies, which in spite of their high-sounding names were without any authority and served for the most part to provide agreeable sinecures for French Union personages, who welcomed an occasion to visit Paris without expense to themselves, was a subject of ironic comment among the Vietnamese, who pointed out the manifest inability of the National Assembly to provide anything more substantial than a façade

for the generous conception of the French Union foreshadowed in the first Constituent Assembly of 1946, as 'France enriched, ennobled and expanded' which will 'tomorrow possess a hundred million citizens and free men'" (*op. cit.*, p. 215). For literature on the French Union, see H. Culmann, *L'Union française* (Paris, 1950); Nguyen Quoc Dinh, "La question du statut de l'état associé d'après la constitution," *Revue juridique et politique de l'union française*, V, 1951; Pierre Lampue, "Le territoire associé et l'état associé suivant la constitution," *Chronique*, 1951; M. H. Fabre, "L'union française," in *Le fédéralisme* (Paris, 1956); Lampue, "Nature juridique de l'union française," in *Revue juridique*, January–March, 1953; and "La citoyenneté de l'union française," *ibid.*, 1950; R. de Lacharrière, "La fonction du haut conseil de l'union française," *ibid.*, III, 1949; F. Luchaire, *Le haut conseil de l'union française* (Penant, 1950); Lampue, "Les attributions de l'assemblée de l'union française,' in *Évolution du droit public* (Paris, 1956). (All the above works are cited by Isoart, *op. cit.*, pp. 376–77, nn. 160–65.)

79. For the English text of the Elysée agreement, see Cole (ed.), *op. cit.*, pp. 72–79. During all of 1949, the agreement remained a piece of paper whose implementation depended on the adoption of specific conventions that were not signed until December 30, 1949. Even these conventions did not improve the situation. For instance, the March agreement provided for mixed jurisdiction (Franco-Vietnamese) in cases of nationals who belonged to the French Union but were not Vietnamese; the convention of December 30 specified that this mixed commission in the courts of appeal would have a French majority in all cases dealing with interests of the French state or a French citizen. Furthermore, in all such cases French, not Vietnamese legislation was to be applied. In an appendix to the judicial convention of December 30, 1949, it was set forth that legislative Vietnamese measures could not be applied to French nationals in Vietnam except if there was complete agreement between French and Vietnamese authorities and if the text of such measures was published by the French High Commissioner of Indochina. This in fact gave the French a veto over all Vietnamese legislation and executive measures applying to French nationals in Vietnam. Article 12 of the convention, dealing with policy and security, stated that French police were permitted to arrest Vietnamese nationals on Vietnamese territory. Also, no Vietnamese could obtain a passport or move about in Vietnam or leave Vietnam without authorization not only of the Vietnamese but also of the French police. No Vietnamese, not even the Vietnamese state, could make purchases abroad or obtain foreign exchange except to the degree authorized by the French-controlled Office of Exchange. Furthermore, the purchasing power of the piaster depended entirely on French control, as was shown on May 9, 1953, when the piaster was suddenly devaluated by French Government decree without advance notification of, or consultation with, the Vietnamese Government.

80. *Le Monde*, March 9, 1949.

81. Hammer, *op. cit.*, p. 241. In a footnote, Miss Hammer adds: "The offi-

cial French report that 80 per cent of the qualified Vietnamese electorate outside Saigon-Cholon voted was highly misleading in view of the fact that the qualified electorate in the provinces was limited to 185 people, as contrasted to 4,899 in Saigon-Cholon." Fall writes that out of an adult population of 3 million, the total number who voted was 1,700 (*The Two Viet-Nams*, p. 214).

82. General Aumeran of the Parti Républicain Liberal, *Journal Officiel, Assemblée Nationale*, May 22, 1949, p. 2767; quoted by Hammer, *op. cit.*, p. 241, n. 27. General Aumeran was a Right-wing critic of the Elysée agreement in the National Assembly.

83. That a large number of Vietnamese preferred unity to separatism in Cochinchina became clear in the quarrel that developed over the so-called Article 3, put forward by the French members of the Assembly, which provided "that the effective and legal attachment of Cochin China be . . . null and void in case of a change in the status of Viet Nam within the French Union." The French who hoped to achieve a separate status for Cochinchina, and a direct relationship with France, were resisted by twenty-three of the forty-eight Vietnamese members who insisted that the article not be included. It needed the direct intervention by General Xuan to have Vietnamese unity approved (with fifty-five present, six opposed, and two abstaining), the disputed article included. At the same time, Miss Hammer (from whose account this is drawn) writes, the Assembly formally reminded Bao Dai of a letter he had written to Tran Van Huu, President of the South Vietnam Government, on March 16, promising to reserve for South Vietnam a special status within Vietnam, taking into account "its present situation and its most sincere desire to conserve in the South its old habits of life by a large administrative decentralization" (*op. cit.*, p. 242). High Commissioner Pignon said at the closing session that "the only loser is Ho Chi Minh," but General Xuan held out the possibility of Ho Chi Minh's participation in the new regime, which, he was quoted as saying by *Le Monde* of May 3, 1949, would depend "on the proof that the head of the Vietminh can give as to the purity of his nationalist sentiments."

84. Bao Dai's return to Saigon on June 13 was almost completely boycotted by the population. Quoting Lucien Bodard, who was present, Fall writes: "There were many flags fluttering colorfully in the breeze; there were policemen, and there were bowing civil servants. From the people, there came not a living soul. It was a fantastic reception" (*The Two Viet-Nams*, p. 215).

85. The lapse of over a year between the Elysée accord of March 8, 1949, and the eventual opening of the Pau conference on June 27, 1950 (which had actually been planned for January, 1950) was noticed only by few, but that the ensuing five months of negotiations at the conference table produced little real change was noticed by many in Vietnam. To be sure, in March, even before the conference opened, Jean Letourneau, who had become Minister for French Overseas Territories, had said: "What the agreements of March 8, 1949, have created can be understood by merely reading

them properly—sovereignty and independent status within the French Union. Let me add that in none of the three Indochinese states are there any positions of power which remain in the hands of the French authorities." And during the conference he reiterated that "there was no question of France reassuming on the federal level the powers that it had recognized as belonging to the Associated States." But he also told the three Associate States—Vietnam, Cambodia, and Laos—that "each of the three states [must] strengthen itself by supporting interstate bodies which can operate in liaison with the French Government." The specter of the Indochinese Federation erected by Paul Doumer loomed large at the conference table, and the three states, which had been unwilling partners in this federation, regarded each other with suspicion, with Cambodia and Laos pressuring the French for support of their claims for parity of representation in the envisioned joint economic and financial committees, especially since an "examination of the French residuary estate that was to be divided among the Associate heirs revealed that all the nascent industries, and almost all of Indochina's economic equipment were in Vietnam" (Lancaster, *op. cit.*, p. 210). Not unwillingly assuming the role of mediator among the states, France was able to inject her presence into every important phase of the economic and financial lives of the states by naming French personnel to participate and sit in on every committee formed. Therewith the French were also able to defend the interests of private French business groups "which made no secret of their desire to ensure the inclusion in the agreement of formal guarantees to protect French commercial interests" (*ibid.*, p. 211). Finally, the French could successfully exploit a weakness produced by their own colonial rule in the three states: the lack of trained native administrators; it necessitated the filling of important positions with Frenchmen instead. When a consultative commission to direct navigation on the Mekong was agreed on, the Vietnamese protested "the presence of Frenchmen on the commission as a survival of the old federal structure." But they protested in vain because the French could point out that "100 per cent of the military fleet using the Mekong was French, as was 80 per cent of the commercial shipping" (Hammer, *op. cit.*, p. 278). When a similar agreement was worked out for the port of Saigon, granting France, Cambodia, and Laos free and equal rights there, the French were in effect "left in control of navigation and the police" (*ibid.*). Not even the postal, telephone, and telegraph agreements, which were speedily reached because the systems were simply being turned over to the respective states, remained free of French influence; the French were to be members of the committee which was to rule on operational questions whenever the Union was concerned. Although officially each state was sovereign in the question of immigration, here too important limitations were imposed because the French Government "was given free access to Indochinese immigration files; and the French High Commissioner received the right to propose the expulsion of any foreigner whose presence he regarded as harmful to the security of French troops" (*ibid.*, p. 279). After protracted negotiations agreement to form a customs union was reached and committees were scheduled to be set up ultimately to oversee customs and foreign trade—naturally, with the French as members. The French retained a virtual veto right in all important matters whenever they wished to modify or halt measures undertaken by any of the Associated States. Yet even so, the conclusion of the conference raised an immediate outcry in France that French interests had been fatally injured. Wrote Paul Bernard, the eminent French economist: "By accepting the eventual restriction of trade within the French Union, by losing all effective authority over the issuance of money, by renouncing control over foreign trade, by permitting a system of controlled prices for exports and imports, we have given the Associated States all the power they need if they wish to assure the ruin of our enterprises and compel their withdrawal without in any way molesting our compatriots" ("Bilan de la Conférence de Pau," *Documents de France Outre-Mer*, Supplement to No. 256, p. 3; quoted by Hammer, *op. cit.*, p. 280). Bernard need not have feared for his compatriots. In spite of a formally proclaimed political independence for the three states, the Pau agreements kept the direction of the Union's economy in French hands, preventing the states from making any significant changes within their own countries without French approval. This meant not only a continuation of the *status quo*, but it meant in fact its perpetuation. And shortly thereafter even those advantages which had accrued to the three states from the Pau conference were to be yielded up again. Hammer wrote: "Specific conventions were drafted to implement the Pau agreements and French officials demonstrated an inclination to withdraw in practice the concessions they had made in principle. For example, when the Vietnamese had accepted the existence of interstate committees, it had been with the understanding that these would in no way replace the old federal structure but would be simply advisory, with the power to make recommendations to the four states but without the power to enforce them. French officials seemed desirous of changing this interpretation, making obligatory on each of the Associated States the decisions of the various economic committees in which Frenchmen, Cambodians, Laotians, and Vietnamese were all represented. Furthermore, Vietnamese foreign trade remained completely under French control; and even American economic aid to Viet Nam was channeled through this French monopoly" (*ibid.*, p. 280). Consequently, wrote Isoart, "the restrictions thus imposed on the exercise of the internal and external competence of Vietnam made the nationalists judge that their country had no democratic status in the French Union, that pyramidical institution in which only France ruled at the summit" (quoted from André Blanchet, "L'état actuel des relations franco-vietnamiennes," in *Le Monde*, November 23, 1950, by Isoart, *op. cit.*, p. 386). For excerpts in English of the Pau agreements which, in Fall's words, "filled a 258-page, 7-by-10-inch volume," giving Vietnam and France with their legalistic bent "a golden opportunity to debate endlessly over phrases and paragraphs without really going anywhere" (*The Two Viet-Nams*, p. 216), see Cole (ed.), *op. cit.*, pp. 110–16. For specific literature on the Pau conference, see references cited by Isoart, *op. cit.*, p. 386, nn. 189, 190, and 191.

86. Prince Sihanouk left the capital of Cambodia in protest against this

measure. I am told that Bao Dai was advised to protest by leaving the country and going possibly to New Delhi, but it was probably "his natural propensity to inaction," if not his "taste for big-game hunting" (Lancaster, *op. cit.*, p. 197), that prevented this move.

87. For instance, the "directeur de cabinet," or chief secretary, both of Tran Van Huu and later Nguyen Van Tam, was a Frenchman, writes Ellen Hammer (*op. cit.*, p. 284). The one under Tam was moreover a member of the Sûreté, the French police. Even in 1954, Miss Hammer says, most official government documents were still written in French, "because of the presence of numerous French officials in the administrative services" (*ibid.*, p. 282, n. 57a). The story of the French grip on power in Saigon has been told often and well, by French patriots (such as Isoart and Devillers), and Vietnamese writers (such as Le Thanh Khoi), as well as by foreign observers. The best and most extensive treatment of it is found in Miss Hammer's book. She weaves a fascinating tapestry of the intrigues with which the French vied with the Vietnamese for the retention of power. The occupancy of Norodom Palace, the seat of government, was a particularly sore spot with the Vietnamese, to whom, Miss Hammer writes, "the symbol of continuing French control over the entire Bao Dai administration was the consistent refusal of French officials to hand over to the Vietnamese Government Norodom Palace in Saigon, the traditional seat of the French Governor General" (*ibid.*, p. 282).

88. As reported in *The New York Times*, October 20, 1950. Huu's lack of integrity becomes apparent if one recalls that in December of that same year, after the Pau conference, he said: "I solemnly proclaim that our independence is now complete" (*Chronique d'Outre-Mer*, January, 1951).

89. Printed in *L'Express*, May 23, 1953. The members of this mission were Frank Arnal (Socialist), Louis Christaens (Independent), Paul Devinat (Radical Socialist), and André-François Mercier (MRP) (see Hammer, *op. cit.*, p. 283, n. 58).

90. Dr. Phan Quang Dan, *The War in Indochina* (mimeographed; 1954), p. 25. (For the expressions "bastard solution" and "shabby independence," see Lacouture and Devillers, *op. cit.*, pp. 21, 23, where they speak of *"indépendance de pacotille,"* ascribing its coinage to the nationalists grouped around Ngo Dinh Diem, and they accuse Paris and its representatives of these bastard solutions "which could lead to nothing.")

91. From an analysis in the French paper *Combat*, May 19, 20, 22, 1948 (quoted by Lancaster, *op. cit.*, p. 194).

92. Dabezies. *op. cit.*, p. 78.

93. Hammer, *op. cit.*, p. 246.

94. *Ibid.*, p. 245.

95. Ngo went first to Japan, where he saw Prince Cuong De shortly before the latter's death. During the winter of 1949, Hammer narrates, Cuong De had appealed from his exile in Japan to the free world to assist Vietnam in achieving independence from the "French colonialists" and the "Vietminh Communists"; he made his appeal in the name of his party, the Phuc

Quoc, and addressed it particularly to the United Nations and the United States. Ever since the beginning of the Franco-Vietnamese war, Cuong De had taken an independent nationalist stand. In a letter to the Vietnamese press he appealed to Ho Chi Minh to step down in favor of leaders who would be acceptable to the West, acknowledging, however, Ho's patriotism. He turned down an invitation sent him by Bao Dai through the French Embassy in Tokyo to return home, because he did not wish to support what he considered a French-controlled government. Ngo, who sympathized with Cuong De but did not publicly criticize the Vietminh at that time, went to the United States. Hammer also writes that other Vietnamese of varying political complex went to France; they ranged from Hoang Xuan Han, Minister of National Education in the Tran Trong Kim Cabinet and a member of the Vietminh delegation at the Dalat conference, to Nguyen Manh Ha, Minister of National Economy in the first Ho Chi Minh Government and a delegate to the Fontainebleau conference (*op. cit.*, pp. 247, 275, 286). Speaking of Ngo's attitude prior to his departure from Vietnam, Dabezies describes him as moved by hostility toward France, and by a desire to obtain control in some form or other, to keep a connection with the nationalist resistance. "Ngo Dinh Diem, it is true, refused to evolve, and for years contented himself with a proud and sterile opposition, joining therein the numerous republican and *attentist* groups which, since 1948, agitated a little all over" (*op. cit.*, p. 178).

96. The ranks of the *attentists* were in fact so much strengthened that the government of Tran Van Huu was obliged in 1950 to establish the right to draft intellectuals and technicians in order to fill higher positions of administration in some services that gradually were being turned over by the French.

97. Tran Van Huu, an agricultural engineer by training, had served in the Department of Agriculture under the French from 1915 to 1929, when he joined the staff of the Indochinese Land Bank (a subsidiary of the Bank of Indochina) as an agricultural inspector. He is said to have employed somewhat harsh methods of foreclosure when working in the mortgage section, which resulted in the ruin of many Cochinchinese families and, it was said, in his personal enrichment. Huu was considered competent and shrewd, with a capacity for political maneuvering and for administering his fortune. He was also known to be vain, susceptible to flattery, and capable of holding a grudge. (This information is taken from Lancaster, *op. cit.*, p. 432, biographical notes.) Both under Huu and Tam, French control was all-pervasive, down to the provincial and regional levels, which were still generally supervised by Frenchmen, according to Miss Hammer. Although self-supporting to a certain degree from revenues derived from customs duties and the old monopolies of opium, alcohol, and salt, the administration "remained dependent on French economic, as it was on French military, support" (Hammer, *op. cit.*, p. 282).

98. See Lancaster, *op. cit.*, p. 250, and n. 16. When Ngo Dinh Diem became Bao Dai's Prime Minister in 1954, he initiated a move to arrest Phan

Van Giao, presumably for illegal financial transactions. Warned in time, Giao hurriedly left for France and lived in Cannes until his death on November 13, 1965. In a description of the corruption then rife in Saigon, particularly among government members, Lucien Bodard tells of an official reception at which two Vietnamese women, talking in French, commiserated with each other over their poverty. Astonished, one of them remarked: "But your husband is provincial chief. That is at least worth 100,000 piasters per month in profits." The other complained: "But none of the money stays with us. To be nominated, my husband had to promise he would pay a million piasters in twelve monthly installments. That takes all we get. Only in another year will the money be ours." Bodard added, speaking of the nationalists: "Their only ideal is to maintain an equilibrium between the French and the Vietminh, and above all to make lots of piasters at 17 francs" (*op. cit.*, pp. 180, 182).

99. See Chapter IV, n. 129, for further details on Tam's earlier exploits for the French. The son of a small shopkeeper at Tay Ninh, Tam, "by dint of energy, determination, and industry," had obtained his diploma at Hanoi University in law and administration. After the Japanese coup of March, 1945, he was arrested and tortured, and later that year two of his sons were murdered by the Vietminh during the ensuing uprising. When released by the Japanese, he aided Leclerc in the pacification of Cochinchina and was subsequently appointed administrator of Tan An Province, "being the first Vietnamese since the French conquest to occupy such a post" (Lancaster, *op. cit.*, pp. 430–31, biographical notes). Under Huu, Tam had been head of the political police, "in which capacity he fought the terror of the Viet Minh with terror of his own" (Hammer, *op. cit.*, p. 281).

100. "Torture had been employed by the French in their efforts to combat the Viet Minh, particularly when information was urgently required from recalcitrant prisoners. The methods were reported to include the administration of electric shocks by means of wires attached to terminal parts of the body, more energetic methods, such as that of the 'aeroplane,' which entailed hoisting the victim to the ceiling by the thumbs previously attached behind the back, being occasionally employed. The creation of a Vietnamese Security Service enabled the French to abandon the use of such methods to the Vietnamese, who incurred the resultant odium" (Lancaster, *op. cit.*, p. 20).

101. *Paris-Match*, July 12–19, 1952; as cited by Hammer, *op. cit.*, p. 282.

102. On this everyone agrees. Wells C. Klein and Marjorie Weiner, in George McTurnan Kahin (ed.), *Governments and Politics in Southeast Asia*, p. 335), write: "The 'Bao Dai solution' failed in its intent. In the French design Bao Dai was supposed to draw nationalist support away from the Viet Minh but he was of no use to the French unless he accepted less than did Ho Chi Minh. But to compete with the already established Viet Minh and to rally nationalist forces to his government, Bao Dai had to offer as much if not more than Ho, and this the French would not allow. Bao Dai was caught between the French and the Viet Minh and could not represent

an effective alternative until the French quit Vietnam and left real power in Vietnamese hands. This they refused to do." Summing up the situation in *The Lost Revolution* (New York, 1965), Robert Shaplen states: "The French had won their battle with the Emperor—at least for the moment—but they were now losing the war against the Vietminh, and the Bao Dai government they had managed so painfully to create would prove no defense" (p. 63).

103. Nguyen Ton Hoan, in a mimeographed outline of the history of the Dai Viet, written in 1964, says (p. 6) that his party was advised strongly to enter the Long Government by a member of the first American Legation in Djakarta (Indonesia). Dabezies, using rather strong language, calls the Dai Viet "ultranationalist, totalitarian, anti-Communist, and xenophobic" (*op. cit.*, p. 140).

104. Dabezies, *ibid.*, p. 185.

105. *Ibid.*, p. 187.

IX. *Political Failure and Military Decline*
(pp. 735–96)

1. The literature on the Indochina War is vast and keeps growing, but no comprehensive and systematic study has yet appeared. Edgar O'Ballance, *The Indo-China War, 1945–1954: A Study in Guerrilla Warfare* (London, 1964), is a good outline. Other books are either memoirs of generals and other participants or accounts restricted to short periods and particular events, such as major battles. Among the latter, Jules Roy, *The Battle of Dien Bien Phu* (New York, 1965 [originally published in Paris in 1963 under the title *La Bataille de Dien Bien Phu*]), and B. B. Fall, *Street Without Joy: Insurgency in Indochina* (Harrisburg, Pa., 1961), are of great value for an understanding of the nature of this war as a military phenomenon. (For further literature on Dien Bien Phu, see Chapter X, n. 18.) The wealth of literature on the subject is reflected in the bibliography of the French edition of Jules Roy's book. Bibliographies are also to be found in Fall's *Street Without Joy*, O'Ballance's *Indo-China War*, and George K. Tanham, *Communist Revolutionary Warfare: The Vietminh in Indochina*. Other books on the Indochina War, French policy in Vietnam, and conditions in both the Democratic Republic and the State of Vietnam, chosen by me at random from the many written on the subject are: Bernhard Newman's superficial, embarrassingly uncritical, pro-French *Report on Indochina* (New York, 1954); Hoang Van Co, *Un peuple qui renaît: Le Vietnam devant les problèmes de l'indépendance* (Paris, 1950; chiefly pro-Bao Dai and pro-French propaganda); Yvonne Pagniez, *Naissance d'une nation: Choses vues au Viet Nam* (Geneva and Paris, 1954), a pro-French study of conditions and expectations in Bao Dai's Vietnam; also Yvonne Pagniez's *Le Viet Minh et la guerre psychologique* (Paris, 1955), even more propagandistic, and politically slanted toward praise of the Vietminh; Léo Figuères, *Je reviens de*

Viet-Nam libre (Paris, 1950); a rather serious study of the life of a Vietminh soldier by Ngo Van Chieu, *Journal d'un combattant Viet-Minh* (Paris, 1955); Werner Stage, *Hong Chi, Vom Legionär zum Vietnamoi* (Berlin, 1955), the story of a member of the Foreign Legion who went over to the Vietminh (straight Communist propaganda, but containing some telling episodes of what the war was like; at least half a dozen books of this type have been published in East Germany); another German book, with a more detailed, idealized description of life in the so-called "free zones," and of conditions for the civilians under the Vietminh, is Fritz Jenzen's *Erlebtes Vietnam* (Berlin, 1955); also, Günter Halle, *Légion Étrangère: Tatsachenbericht nach Erlebnissen und Dokumenten von Rückkehrern aus Viet Nam* (Berlin, 1952). Other books used as references are mentioned in these notes, and a few of these should be mentioned here: Joseph Laniel, *Le drame indochinois: De Dien-Bien-Phu au pari de Génève* (Paris, 1957); Henri Navarre, *Agonie de l'Indochine (1953-1954)*; Jacques Dinfreville, *L'opération Indochine* (Paris, 1953); Paul Mus, *Vietnam: Sociologie d'une guerre;* General de Crevecoeur, *Raccourci de la campagne d'Indochine (depuis 1945 à 1950)* (Paris, 1952; mimeographed); Henry Ainley, *In Order To Die* (London, 1955); Peter Paret, *French Revolutionary Warfare from Indochina to Algeria* (New York, 1964); Claude Goëldhieux, *Quinze mois prisonnier chez les Viets* (Paris, 1953; prisoner-of-war experiences); George Armstrong Kelly, *Lost Soldiers: The French Army and Empire in Crisis, 1947-1962* (Cambridge, Mass., 1965), Part II: "Indochina," pp. 31-107.

2. These were designated as the 304th, 308th, 312th, 316th, and 320th divisions. With the exception of the 320th, which had been built up at a safe Vietminh base south of the Red River Delta, they were all stationed in the Viet Bac (see O'Ballance, *op. cit.*, p. 112).

3. "The French forces were hardly ever able to make a move without the Viet Minh knowing about it, usually in advance" (O'Ballance, *ibid.*, p. 82).

4. Other raw materials and minerals were important not only for certain industries set up in the Viet Bac and other protected areas, but also to sell and obtain foreign currency for arms purchases. (The Vietminh were always trying to harvest poppies and market the opium won.)

5. Lucien Bodard's *La guerre d'Indochine: L'enlisement* (p. 73) contains a map of Tongking showing the extent of Vietminh control.

6. Even this coastal strip, vital for French communications and the defense of these important cities, was not fully controlled. This was the region of the "Street Without Joy," on Highway 1, where the Vietminh held "a string of fortified villages along a line of sand dunes and salt marshes stretching from Hue to Quang-Tri" (Fall, *op. cit.*, p. 141).

7. Paul Isoart, quoting from a report in *Le Monde*, September 30, 1953, wrote: "Action was always brief and brutal, meticulously prepared. The men grouped together a few hours before the attack, thereafter to disperse. Against this extraordinarily fluid tactic, our tanks, our planes, our artillery were more or less powerless" (*Le phénomène national vietnamien*, p. 401). A vivid account of such an ambush of a convoy in the South is given in a

French novel on Indochina by Jean Hougron entitled *Le soleil au ventre* (Paris, 1952).

8. "Having the freedom of the countryside, the Viet Minh Security Service collected taxes, especially heavy from suspected sympathizers of the French, eliminated local opposition and recruited men" (O'Ballance, *op. cit.*, p. 83). Describing the atrocities practiced by the Vietminh in revenge on villages loyal to the French, Bodard writes: "The Viets freely push the French toward excesses, knowing that they are superior to them in cruelty, being more efficacious and cleverer. For them, the war of tortures is, in the final analysis, a technique that allows them to take hold of and impose themselves on the populations" (*op. cit.*, pp. 80–81).

9. The term "sieve" was first used in this context by Bernard Fall in *Street Without Joy* (p. 177), in which (p. 335) there also are two maps illustrating the degree of French vs. Vietminh control of the delta, one according to the "official view," the other showing "the real situation." There is a lengthy and vivid description of the "war of the posts" in Bodard, *op. cit.*, pp. 81–94. But by far the best picture of the kind of war this was, of the difficulties encountered by the French, and of the suffering endured by soldiers and civilians on both sides, can be found in a large volume of photographs entitled *Guerre morte*, with text and captions by J. P. Dannaud, published in Paris in 1954 as a supplement to the journal *Indochine Sud-Est Asiatique*. Some of the captions are as moving as the photographs themselves. The whole book is divided into the five major aspects of the war: the struggle for the roads, for the posts, in the jungles, in the delta, climaxing in the open battles. I know of no other book that describes the horrors of the Indochina War so graphically.

10. One of the first public indications that the French had gained some real understanding of the sources of Vietminh strength was shown in an article by the General of the Far Eastern Air Force L. M. Chassin entitled "Guerre en Indochine," in *Revue de Défense Nationale*, July, 1953. General Chassin cites among other factors the Vietminh's "extraordinary endurance and frugality," its ability to imbue the populace with a spirit of resistance and loyalty ("when the Vietminh army takes the offensive, it does not leave an enemy in its rear," Chassin writes on p. 14), and its "incredible mobility." Chassin, speaking of the need for political reforms in order to raise the morale of the population under French control, calls for a Vietnamese "efficient and honest administration," "necessary social reforms"(!), and moral values with which to create enthusiasm.

11. For the most telling illustrations in word and picture of this kind of war without a pause ever, see *Guerre morte*, particularly the chapters "La Route" and "La Brousse." Of the jungle (*la brousse*), Dannaud writes: "One may well hurl oneself into the jungle to escape the enemy in the bracken, but one does not get far there. Wounded, exhausted, a man watches the vultures draw in large circles close to him, and reads in their flight the announcement of his death." And his comment on the roads: "Little by little, one becomes accustomed to the daily ritual of opening the road,

one recites automatically the morning prayer which gives as one of the ten commandments, 'In the Morning, the Road Shall Be Opened; in the Evening, the Road Shall Again Close.' And then, one day, drily, nervously, the ambush bursts out over the patrol that is doing the opening, or over the convoy."

12. It is curious how little attention most writers pay to this early lesson of the Indochina War. Most of them mention Valluy's offensive only briefly. An exception is Bodard, who realizes the catastrophic consequences of this fiasco. He vividly describes it on a few pages containing an interesting account by a participant (*op. cit.*, pp. 70–77), and he tells what disastrous consequences the French suffered from their refusal to give up positions on Route 4 (Caobang, That Ke, and Langson). "The reports of the Deuxième Bureau [Intelligence] describe the dangers of the situation well enough," he writes, "and presage what is going to happen. But the military in the high chiefs of staff, informed as they are, knowing as they are, cannot bring themselves to believe what they are told. The faculty of the Command's 'incredulity' is in itself incredible."

13. This process of *"pourrissement"* in the delta continued at an ever-increasing rate as the war went on. At the end of 1953, the Vietminh was said to have had 80,000 fighting men in the delta. In 1952, the Vietminh controlled over 600 of the 2,700 villages in the four major delta provinces; in July, 1953, they controlled more than half—1,486. (Cf. Jean Chesneaux, *Contributions à l'histoire de la nation vietnamienne*, p. 305.) This process of strengthening its hold over the delta was described in eloquent terms by General Chassin in his article (see n. 10, above). "It must be understood," he wrote, "that the Vietminh have an administrative organization that covers the entire territory of Vietnam. Although clandestine in the zones 'controlled' by us, it is no less powerful and often obeyed. It is able to raise taxes and recruit troops even in the interior of these zones. The regular Vietminh troops move from one base to another, leave the Tongking Delta or re-enter it, and make sure of their relief troops, with us being unable to oppose them efficiently. Even convoys with French and Vietnamese prisoners could pass from the south to the north of the delta, crossing it in the full center of the controlled zone, going by night from pro-Vietminh village to pro-Vietminh village. To be sure, our mobile groups continually carry out 'clean-up' operations. Sometimes they succeed in apprehending regular Viets and cause them losses. But most often the latter penetrate the military cordons at night, a difficult thing to do in the ricefields, and reappear in back of our troops. If they know themselves surrounded in a village, they hide their arms and turn into peaceful peasants. The terror that they inspire in the notables prevents their being denounced by them. After we leave—for we cannot occupy the thousands of villages in the delta, and evidently we do not want to destroy them—they take up their arms and resume their guerrilla actions. Thus there is no 'front' in Indochina, and operations there often take on a heterodox aspect that surprises the uninformed Westerner" (*op. cit.*, pp. 7–8).

14. "The Revers Report," O'Ballance said, "was confidential and was made for the private information of the French Government, and something of a scandal blew up when the Viet Minh radio station, which functioned in the Viet Bac, broadcast extracts from it. . . . This showed clearly the extent to which the Viet Minh were successful in obtaining information. . . . For the French on the other hand, information about the Viet Minh was scarce and unreliable" (*op. cit.*, p. 94). Revers recommended that the frontier garrisons along the Chinese border, especially at Caobang and Dong Khe, be withdrawn, and that a solid line of resistance be established south of the mountain region where the roads from the China border led into the delta; Langson and Moncay were only to be given cursory protection. He felt that thus the lines of maneuvering would be shortened and that the enemy, who would be forced to extend his lines of communication, could be hit that much more easily by the air force. But most important, Revers felt that an effective control over the entire Tongking Delta would have to be obtained; pacification of that region would permit the Bao Dai regime to install its administration and by rallying the population would cut off the Vietminh from vital rice supplies. Pacification, he recommended, in the Tongking Delta ought to be undertaken by the Vietnamese Army, therewith freeing French troops for the defense of Tongking, an area, incidentally, that Revers considered the bastion of French military action (see Philippe Devillers, *Histoire du Vietnam de 1940 à 1952*, pp. 448–49; Donald Lancaster, *The Emancipation of French Indochina*, pp. 407–10). Equally important, perhaps, was Revers' criticism of the caliber of men working on the French side. "If Ho Chi Minh has been able to hold off French intervention for so long," he wrote, "it is because the Viet Minh leader has surrounded himself with a group of men of incontestable worth" (quoted by Ellen Hammer, *The Struggle for Indochina*, p. 246). The effect of the Revers report on the Vietminh was to strengthen the "Chinese wing," which was also the extremist wing, Devillers commented (p. 450), because it showed the French afraid of Chinese intervention. The spokesmen for the "Chinese wing" were Dang Xuan Khu (alias Truong Chinh), Hoang Quoc Viet, Ho Tung Mau, and Tran Huy Lieu. The "something of a scandal," as O'Ballance with British understatement describes the "affair of the generals" that followed the Vietminh broadcast of the Revers report, was to evolve into a full-fledged scandal in which French generals were as much involved as French financial interests and "the machinations of the Vietnamese Deputy Prime Minister, General Xuan." A Vietnamese, Hoang Van Co, an agent for Xuan, had been found to hold copies of the report, received, he claimed, from Roger Peyre, "a Frenchman of dubious commercial antecedents who claimed that he had received it from General Mast, a former Resident-General in Tunisia who was a candidate at that time for Pignon's post." The investigation of the intrigue by the French Government brought on a series of incidents "that served mainly to discredit the regime." Peyre was allowed to escape to Brazil, evidence believed to incriminate certain deputies and newspaper editors disappeared, and related documents were

destroyed by a fire within the precincts of the Ministry of Interior. Lancaster, from whose account the above is quoted, adds: "All revealed the official determination to conceal the identity of the persons implicated in this affair. Moreover, evidence produced . . . revealed a propensity on the part of senior generals to indulge in political intrigues in order to promote their career, and also a state of rivalry, perhaps more properly described as a state of feud, between the intelligence services attached to the Ministries of Interior and National Defence respectively; while at the same time damaging, and in some cases reckless, accusations were levelled against civil and military officials who were alleged to be involved in illicit currency deals, and against politicians who were accused of having accepted bribes." The inquiry, Lancaster concluded, "served to show the interplay of politics and finance, and the readiness of a section of the community to traduce the Expeditionary Corps" (*op. cit.*, pp. 408-10).

15. O'Ballance, *op. cit.*, p. 116. Lancaster recalls an interesting historical fact with regard to that area. He writes that "the dispossessed Mac princes were able to maintain themselves with Chinese support in that inaccessible area from 1652 to 1677, in spite of repeated attempts by the rulers of Tongking to evict them" (*op. cit.*, p. 217, n. 45). It may be recalled here that Revers had recommended withdrawal from the Caobang ridge in his report. When it finally took place, "out of some 10,000 troops disposed along that ridge, the losses were calculated to be 6,000 men, 13 guns, 125 mortars, 950 machine-guns, 1,200 sub-carbines, and over 8,000 rifles. In addition some 450 trucks were either lost or left behind. The majority of the 6,000 soldiers were taken prisoner, and to look after them Viet Minh POW camps were installed along the Chinese frontier zone. They were very primitive, lacking amenities and medical supplies and attention" (O'Ballance, *op. cit.*, p. 118). In a footnote, O'Ballance adds: "The Viet Minh already had up to about 2,000 French prisoners, who had been accumulated since 1945, held mainly as hostages. As the Viet Minh headquarters had moved, these POWs had been moved with it, too. Until this moment there were no POW camps as such." (Photographs of such POW's in *Guerre morte* look like pictures of survivors of Dachau or Japanese prison camps.) In *The Two Viet-Nams*, Bernard Fall mentions that the commanding officer at Caobang had been instructed to blow up his heavy equipment and his motor transport before leaving the garrison to meet up with a Moroccan task force at Dong Khe, but that the Caobang force began "its eighty-five-mile trek southward, *but with its artillery and trucks.* Its commander, not recognizing the extent of the threat hanging over his head, had decided—against orders—to save his equipment along with his men. He was to lose both in short order, and engulf the whole border line in his own catastrophe" (p. 110). With the courtesy shown by one military man toward another, General Navarre in his book calls the Caobang disaster "unfortunate fights to which the name of Caobang remained attached," and in a footnote praises General Alessandri for having had the courage formally to state that he opposed the retreat (*op. cit.*, p. 19). Alessandri, who was then commander of the Tongking

forces was consequently recalled. See also *France-Indochine*, Nos. 69 and 70, November and December, 1950, continuing a series of articles entitled "La situation militaire en Indochine" dealing with the Caobang disaster.

16. Commented Fall in *Street Without Joy* (p. 30): "When the smoke cleared, the French had suffered their greatest colonial defeat since Montcalm had died at Quebec. . . . Their abandoned stocks alone sufficed for the equipment of a whole additional Viet-Minh division." And Lancaster, quoting from Chassin's article, writes: "The only consolation that the French can be said to have derived from their defeat was due to their air force, which raided Caobang on the night of 24–25 October and surprised the Viet Minh imprudently celebrating the 'liberation of the frontier area.' The raid abruptly terminated these festivities, and two battalions of Chinese Communist troops who had been invited to the fete retired in confusion, together with their casualties, to Chinese territory" (*op. cit.*, p. 219).

17. Some authors (e.g., Lancaster, *op. cit.*, p. 219) say the Vietminh radio spoke of a return by the Vietminh Government for the anniversary of the outbreak of the war (December 19); others (e.g., Denis Warner, *The Last Confucian*, p. 44) tell that the Vietminh's slogan was they would celebrate Tete, the Vietnamese New Year, in Hanoi. Tete usually falls in the middle of February.

18. As early as in 1928, Mao Tse-tung began his military writings with *Struggle in the Chin Kan Shan Mountains*. In 1936, he wrote *Strategy of the Revolutionary War in China* (published for the first time in 1950). In 1937, just after completing the famous Long March, he wrote *Guerrilla Warfare*, and in 1938 a treatise called *Strategic Problems of the Anti-Japanese War*. His most widely known books in the Western world are *Strategic Problems of China's Revolutionary War* (published in Peking in 1954) and *On the Protracted War* (1960). Mao set down four basic conditions for the struggle with an enemy: (1) a semicolonial country of great size and of uneven political and economic development; (2) the presence of a powerful enemy; (3) a revolutionary army that started out by being weak as well as small; (4) a revolutionary leadership that could rely on popular acceptance of its ideas, at least in the sense of an agrarian revolution. The three stages in which the enemy was to be defeated, Mao described as (1) an initial military inferiority of the revolutionary forces, in which they had to be on the strategic defensive. During this stage, the Communists had to trade territory, industries, and population, if necessary, for the preservation of their weak military forces, and furthermore had to reckon with the possibility of a temporarily increased military weakness. The enemy, however, would also grow weaker because of lengthening logistic lines, harassment by guerrillas, weakening morale, and increasing unfriendliness of the population; (2) in this stage, the enemy would cease his advance and concentrate on holding and consolidating his gains. Guerrilla activities would remain the chief form of warfare during this phase, allowing the regular revolutionary forces to be trained and equipped for the final stage of the war; (3) the final stage would be the counteroffensive. During this phase, Mao anticipated the revolution-

ary forces to gain the tactical numerical superiority, but the timing of the counteroffensive would depend on the international as well as the internal situation (see Tanham, *op. cit.*, pp. 10, 11). According to O'Ballance (*op. cit.*, pp. 41 ff.), Giap was guided by Mao's 1928 writing for the first stage of the Vietminh war, because "it gave advice on raising guerrilla forces from scratch and discussed the problems and difficulties involved." The second stage of the Vietminh war, O'Ballance continues, was guided by Mao's 1937 work, in which the Chinese leader asserted that "during progress guerrillas gradually develop into orthodox forces that operate in conjunction with units of the regular army" (*ibid.*, p. 90). Mao's four golden rules, by which Giap abided, O'Ballance wrote, were (1) when the enemy advances —we retreat; (2) when the enemy halts—we harass; (3) when the enemy avoids battle—we attack; (4) when the enemy retreats—we follow (*ibid.*, p. 147). It is erroneously assumed, however, that Giap formulated the Vietminh adaptation of Mao's military doctrine. As Fall wrote, "it was Truong Chinh who . . . first formulated a Vietnamese adaptation of Mao's *On Protracted War*. . . . Giap's own *La guerre de libération et l'armée populaire* (1952) is only a restatement of Mao's principles in a simplified form and a resumé of VPA operations from 1945 until 1950. Giap's brochure *L'armée populaire de libération du Viet-Nam dans la lutte pour l'indépendance nationale, la démocratie et la paix* (November, 1951) merely emphasized the importance of the 'war of movement' during the second phase" (*The Two Viet-Nams*, pp. 112–13). Fall judges that "Giap's own best contribution to the art of revolutionary war was probably his estimate of the political-psychological shortcomings of a democratic system when faced with an inconclusive military operation," in proof of which he quotes Giap's prediction: "The enemy will pass slowly from the offensive to the defensive. The blitzkrieg will transform itself into a war of long duration. Thus, the enemy will be caught in a dilemma: He has to drag out the war in order to win it and does not possess, on the other hand, the psychological and political means to fight a long-drawn-out war." In his foreword profile of "the very tiny, sentimental college professor of the 1930's, the self-taught guerrilla leader of the early 1940's, and the brilliant strategist of the 1950's," to Vo Nguyen Giap's *People's War, People's Army* (New York, 1962), Fall lauds Giap, "who defined the role of the Vietnam People's Army as being 'the instrument of the Party and the revolutionary state for the accomplishment, in armed form, of the tasks of the revolution'" (p. xi). Fall says in *The Viet-Minh Regime* that Giap's impatience with the slowness of the timetable indicated in Mao's writings caused him to commit a costly error in 1950: Fall tells, in Giap's own words (based on a captured document—a study of Giap before Commissars of the 98th Infantry Regiment, in October, 1950), that "in 1949 the situation looked propitious (for the third phase—the counteroffensive), and the preparatory mission for the General Counter Offensive was set ahead of time with the view of a shortening of the second phase." Fall adds: "Giap dearly paid for his mistake . . . but the grim lesson was learned, and thus far the Republican forces have returned to step 2 of Mao's war doctrine, with conspicuous success" (p. 82 and n. 34). E. L. Katzenbach, Jr., in "Time, Space, and Will: The Politico-Military Views of Mao Tse-tung" (in Lt. Col. T. N. Greene [ed.], *The Guerrilla—And How to Fight Him* [New York, 1962], p. 20), argues that the Vietminh fought according to Mao, despite claims that they had improved on his doctrines. Malvin Gustov, in a thesis submitted to the East Asia Institute, Columbia University (New York, 1965), goes so far as to say that in Truong Chinh's writings, "Mao's strategic insights were influential to the point of plagiarism." A recent study of guerrilla warfare is Robert Taber, *The War of the Flea* (New York, 1965), particularly Chapters V and VI, which deal with Indochina. Other books on the subject are Gabriel Bonnet, *Les guerres insurrectionelles et révolutionnaires* (Paris, 1958), and Pierre Rolland, *Contre-Guérilla* (Paris, 1956).

19. A French translation of Truong Chinh's book appeared in Hanoi, 1962, under the title *La résistance vaincra;* the English translation is to be found in Truong Chinh's *Primer for Revolt: The Communist Takeover in Viet-Nam* (New York, 1963; a facsimile of the 1956 Hanoi English edition), to which Bernard Fall wrote the introduction and notes. Truong Chinh (alias Dang Xuan Khu), and not Vo Nguyen Giap, Fall asserts, wrote what Tanham called "the fullest expression of Vietminh doctrine" (*The Two Viet-Nams*, p. 112; Tanham, *op. cit.*, p. 15). Le Thanh Khoi says of Chinh's book that "one must know this work which has since inspired every action of the Democratic Republic" (*Le Viet-Nam: Histoire et civilisation*, p. 484). Truong Chinh, generally regarded as "pro-Chinese," is called an "extremist" by Pierre Dabezies (*Forces politiques au Viet-Nam*, p. 110). It was that extremist wing of the Vietminh, Dabezies contends, which demanded of Ho Chi Minh a total collaboration with Peking, entailing the role of a satellite to China, a fate the Vietnamese escaped only because of the immense prestige of their chief. The same opinion was expressed in an article by Jean Lacouture, press attaché of General Leclerc in 1946, in *The New York Times Magazine*, March 28, 1965. "In the past," wrote Lacouture, "he [Ho Chi Minh] dominated his colleagues, all of whom were his faithful pupils. . . . Nowadays the system has become more collective at the expense of Ho's supremacy. He is too deeply committed to the Soviets to be accepted as the sole arbiter of a party in which the pro-Chinese wing has gained much influence since 1960. . . . Men like Truong Chinh, the best-known theorist in the ruling Lao Dong party, and Le Duan, the party's First Secretary, share power on the same level as President Ho and are perhaps more efficient. Truong Chinh is pro-Chinese. . . . General Giap, chief of the general staff and Defense Minister, is strongly pro-Russian, like his master, Ho. In addition, Giap has a personal hatred of Truong Chinh. The majority of young officers reputedly favor Peking, whose help has been more important in the past five years than Moscow's." Truong Chinh was perhaps best known for his land-reform measures. Wrote O'Ballance: "In 1951, when Truong Chinh was appointed secretary-general of the Viet Minh Party, he had launched a vicious land expropriation campaign that

alienated many whom the Viet Minh needed to support their programme."
And in a footnote O'Ballance added: "Truong Chinh was the son of a
landlord, and it is reputed that he authorized the execution of his parents
who had been condemned to death by a land tribunal" (*op. cit.*, p. 205 and
n. 1).

20. Speaking of the third phase, the general counteroffensive, Truong
Chinh wrote: "There are two factors determining our strategy of general
counter-offensive. First, the strength of our army and people, and second,
the weakening of the enemy and the extreme demoralisation of his troops. It
may happen that our material forces are still not superior to those of the
enemy. Granted that our material forces are even relatively weaker than the
enemy's, still, as a result of the special conditions in Indochina, France, in
the French colonies and the world over, and the tendency to disintegration
in the enemy's morale, we can switch over to the stage of general counteroffensive. . . . As a result of the long war the enemy troops become weary
and discouraged. . . . The French economy and finances are exhausted
. . . the French people do not want the war in Viet Nam to go on any
longer. The movement against the war . . . grows stronger and more
fierce. . . . World opinion severely condemns France, which is isolated
diplomatically. The world movement for peace and democracy scores great
successes. . . . Such factors would have considerable influence on our
liberation struggle, and create many favourable conditions for us in launching the general counter-offensive" (*op. cit.*, pp. 152–53). Summarizing
Truong Chinh's views on the strong points the Vietnamese had versus the
French, Le Thanh Khoi wrote: "Our strong points—which are equally the
enemy's weak points—are: a high ideal (the fight for independence), the national union, a high spirit of sacrifice and heroism in the army and among
the people, a war on our own soil which provides the three advantages of
being accustomed to the climate, knowing the terrain, having the support of
the population. Our weak points—which are equally the strong points of the
enemy—are: the inferiority in modern weapons, the lack of trained troops,
the low level of organisation (notably in the military, political and techno-
logical fields), the weakness of international propaganda. Our strong points
are principally political—they are fundamental. Our weak points are
military—they are secondary and will shrink in time" (*op. cit.*, pp. 484–85).

21. For a fuller description of these three battles, see O'Ballance, *op. cit.*,
Chapter VI, pp. 120–39 ("Viet Minh Defeats of 1951"). Also, *France-
Indochine*, Nos. 73 and 75, March and May, 1951 ("La situation militaire en
Indochine"), as well as No. 76, June, 1951 ("La bataille du riz au Tonkin").
Also, cf. Navarre, *op. cit.*, p. 21, for his view. A later description is con-
tained in Fall, *Street Without Joy*, pp. 32–44. In *The Two Viet-Nams*,
Fall says the reason that Giap was not fired for his mistakes in making
these attacks in 1951 was twofold. Probably, he writes, it "took all Ho's
prestige to keep Giap in the saddle; or, more probably, Giap was retained
because the erroneous decision to launch the offensive had been made collectively by the whole senior Party hierarchy. The VPA retreated in full to
Phase Two of Mao's precepts" (p. 117).

22. Lancaster, *op. cit.*, pp. 221–23. Perhaps the French counterpart to George Patton, the colorful American World War II general, de Lattre also fired the area commander of Hanoi "five minutes after landing there because the honor guard was not turned out the way he felt it should be" (Fall, *The Two Viet-Nams*, p. 115). Dabezies analyzed de Lattre's attitude thus: "For him, to govern meant above all to command" (*op. cit.*, p. 184). One of the general's first acts, wrote O'Ballance, was "to cancel the shipping ordered to evacuate French families, as he was of the opinion that the French would hold on to Indo-China better if they were there with them rather than thousands of miles away in France" (*op. cit.*, p. 120). O'Ballance also says that there was some surprise in France at de Lattre's accepting the job "which was really a step down in status, as he had been the Commander-in-Chief of the Land Forces in Europe," but that "Giap was pleased by the appointment of such an illustrious soldier . . . regarding it both as a compliment to himself and his army" (*ibid.*, pp. 120–21).

23. Lancaster, *op. cit.*, p. 242. In 1955, an Englishman published a rather overly enthusiastic biography of de Lattre (Sir Guy Salisbury-Jones, *So Full a Glory* [New York]). One of the most recent French books on the Indochina War (Pierre Darcourt, *De Lattre au Viet-Nam: Une année des victoires* [Paris, 1965]) is highly laudatory of de Lattre.

24. Lancaster, *op. cit.*, p. 243. Lancaster's summation of de Lattre's achievements in Vietnam is that "his contribution in the military field was not decisive." O'Ballance is even blunter on the subject. "In Indo-China General de Lattre had narrowly missed wrecking his reputation as a great general. . . . He had not changed the over-all strategy of the war, nor had he regained control over any Viet Minh–held territory. Had he lived, he would have been hard put to have retained his laurels over the Hoa Binh battle, and his reputation might have gone the way of those of Generals Le Clerc and Carpentier" (*op. cit.*, pp. 167–68).

25. Fall, *Street Without Joy*, p. 57. Fall gives a very detailed and graphic description of the "meat-grinder" action in the many fierce battles that ultimately led the French to abandon their attempt to hold Hoa Binh (pp. 44–57, and maps). "The French had stabbed with all their might—and had encountered empty space" wrote Fall (p. 46), and describing an encounter of French tanks with Vietminh "human clusters," he tells how the heavy treads of the tanks were "crushing heads, limbs, and chests by the dozens as they slowly moved like chained elephants in the little open space left in the post. But soon they, too, were submerged by the seemingly never-ending human wave, with scores of hands clawing at their turret hatches trying to pry them open; stuffing incendiary hand grenades into their cannon, firing tommygun bursts into their driving slits; finally destroying them with pointblank bazooka bursts which lit up their hulls with the sizzling of white-hot metal. The sweetish smell of searing flesh rose in the air. All the five tank crews died to the last man, roasted alive in their vehicles" (p. 50). Explaining the strategic importance of Hoa Binh, O'Ballance wrote that it was a "staging point on the Viet Minh north-south supply route . . . it was [also] the centre of the Muoung tribe, which was loyal to France. Muoung

tribesmen were fighting with the French against the Viet Minh, and many Muoungs and their families had been forced to take refuge within the Delta. From a strategical point of view, if successful, the operation would enlarge the area of the Red River Delta, now hedged in almost completely by the De Lattre Line" (*op. cit.*, p. 159). O'Ballance describes the mass evacuation from Hoa Binh on February 22, 1952, when "the garrison, all its vehicles and stores, and hundreds of Muoungs . . . moved out, abandoning the town." Over 20,000 French troops were involved in the two-day fighting retreat along the 25-mile road, O'Ballance says, with the Vietminh laying ambush after ambush (p. 166). General Navarre's criticism of this particular action was from a strategic point of view. "Unfortunately," he wrote, "the battle of Hoa Binh kept our mobile forces for too long a time away from the Delta, permitting the enemy to infiltrate it massively and to entrench himself there. This was the beginning of the great *pourrissement*" (*op. cit.*, p. 23).

26. O'Ballance claims that the supply service of the Vietminh had out-done itself. "Porters had been conscripted on a gigantic scale, and at one time it was estimated that between 150,000 and 160,000 men and women were carrying loads for Viet Minh troops. . . . Practically the whole of the Viet Minh–controlled area around Hoa Binh was converted into a vast labour camp" (*op. cit.*, p. 167). Using almost the same phraseology, Lancaster speaks of between 150,000 and 200,000 porters used in the "human supply trains" at the disposal at Hoa Binh (*op. cit.*, p. 246). In *The Viet Minh Regime*, Bernard Fall speaks of the masses of porters and untrained laborers as the "primitive means multiplied by a huge number of individuals [by which] the Viet-Minh actually succeeds in winning its battles, which are first and foremost logistical victories," and he calls "the hordes of porters who are attached to each operational unit" the "logistical backbone of the Repub-lican forces." Fall writes that "a simple calculation shows that in order merely to feed a Viet-Minh division on a forced march for 15 days, the same division—for 12,000 combatants—would have to be trailed by about 50,000 porters" (pp. 76–77).

27. Lancaster, *op. cit.*, p. 242.

28. See *Le Monde*, September 25, 1951.

29. Lancaster writes that de Lattre "counted on his powers of persuasion" to obtain the desired military aid. But his success was mainly a personal one, inasmuch as he succeeded in arousing "interest in his cause and sympathy for his person" (*op. cit.*, p. 232).

30. O'Ballance, *op. cit.*, p. 195. He speaks of five Vietminh infantry divi-sions brought up to strength, and of an artillery division (the 351st Heavy Division) in which existing artillery battalions, with 75-mm. and 57-mm. field and anti-aircraft guns, were grouped together. This latter division consisted of three regiments, two artillery and one engineers (*ibid.*, p. 155.). By mid-summer, 1952, the individual strengths of the three elements of the Vietminh forces probably included 110,000 regular troops, and 60,000 to 75,000 regional (or part-time) troops. The active village militia totaled over

120,000 (*ibid.*, pp. 171–72). O'Ballance also quotes Navarre's estimate "that the Viet Minh had over 125,000 full-time, well-trained regular soldiers . . . disposed into 6 divisions . . . at least 6 independent regiments, and a few independent battalions, some of which were in the process of expanding into regiments" (*ibid.*, p. 195). Lancaster writes that in May, 1953, the strength of the Vietminh forces was estimated at approximately 125,000 regular, 75,000 regional, and 150,000 guerrilla troops (*op. cit.*, p. 265, n. 46). See also Ngo Van Chieu, *Journal d'un combattant Viet Minh* (Paris, 1955), pp. 117–24, for further details on Vietminh regular army regional forces, guerrillas, and militia, and an article by Bernard Fall in *The New York Times Magazine*, May 2, 1965. As for figures on French Army strength at various periods, O'Ballance writes that in the summer of 1952, the strength of the Expeditionary Force was given as 51,000 French, 18,000 Legionnaires, 25,000 North Africans, 56,000 Indochinese, and 42,000 other native auxiliaries (*op. cit.*, p. 174); by May, 1953, this strength had increased to 54,000 French, 20,000 Legionnaires, 30,000 North African troops, 70,000 locally enlisted Vietnamese, 10,000 air force, and 5,000 navy (*ibid.*, p. 195). General Navarre writes that in spring, 1953, the Expeditionary Corps had 175,000 regular troops, including 54,000 French, 30,000 North African, 18,000 African, 20,000 Legionnaires, and 53,000 locally raised troops, with an additional 55,000 auxiliary troops (*op. cit.*, p. 46, n. 3); there was also a naval contingent of 5,000 and an air force contingent of 10,000. As for the Vietnamese Army, Navarre states, there were 150,000 regular and 50,000 auxiliary troops. (Earlier in his book [p. 26, n. 2], Navarre complains that the French Government had imposed a reduction of 16,000 from 190,000 to 174,000) on the Expeditionary Corps after de Lattre. Le Than Khoi speaks of a Vietnamese Army of over 120,000 at the end of 1952, and of 251,000 in the Expeditionary Corps and 310,000 in the Indochinese armies in 1954 (*op. cit.*, pp. 479, 483, n. 130). Generally speaking, the figures I cite here and in the text may differ from figures in other books the reader may consult. This is only partly due to the fact that the counts were made at different times; the accuracy of all the figures published by either side is not necessarily beyond all doubt.

31. See O'Ballance, *op. cit.*, pp. 169–70. Chinese aid to the Vietminh consisted for the most part of arms of American manufacture captured either from the Kuomintang armies or from American forces in Korea, writes Lancaster (*op. cit.*, p. 255, n. 32). It was estimated that this aid averaged some 3,000 tons per month alone for the three-month period between January and end of March, 1953. The Vietminh also received enough artillery and small arms to re-equip completely the infantry divisions of the main force with modern weapons and to equip partly the 351st Heavy Division, says O'Ballance (*op. cit.*, p. 171). Other weapons consisted of mortars and field and anti-aircraft guns. Peking authorized the opening of training camps for Vietminh officers in Chinese territory, according to Isoart (*op. cit.*, p. 396), and provided high officers as military advisers, among them General Lo Kuei-po. Hoang Van Chi (*op. cit.*, p. 63) says that Lo Kuei-po was soon

followed by a flood of Chinese experts, but they had no perceptible impact on Vietminh political and military conduct (see Allan B. Cole [ed.], *Conflict in Indo-China and International Repercussions: A Documentary History, 1945–1955*, pp. 125, 130, giving the text of a handbook for Chinese political workers going to Vietnam, December, 1952). A few Molotov trucks also appeared, the first to be seen by the French in Operation Lorraine, and guns from the Skoda works in Czechoslovakia. Toward the end at Dien Bien Phu, the Vietminh was said to have had about 1,000 trucks. On Chinese aid, see also Robert Guillain, *La fin des illusions* (Paris, 1954); and Harold C. Hinto, *China's Relations with Burma and Vietnam* (New York, 1958).

32. Lucien Bodard gives most graphic descriptions of Vietminh intelligence at work. "The Frenchman must be constantly on his guard," he writes. "The Viet know everything about him. . . . There are eyes everywhere to watch him, ears to listen. . . . The naked youngster astride the buffalo in the neighboring river, the so-very-dignified old man fishing in the arroyo, the village notable with the bun who offers welcoming flowers—they are all spies! If a Frenchman leaves on patrol, the old fisherman has only to lift his rod in a certain manner to indicate thereby the road he took" (*La guerre d'Indochine: L'enlisement*, p. 83). Bodard tells how a French post commander will try to ensure the loyalty of his Vietnamese men by having them execute Vietminh, in the hope that this will earn them the hatred of the enemy as well as aligning them with his, the French cause. But often these men will have received instructions from the Vietminh to gain the French commander's confidence by implicit obedience in this and every manner. "When this is done, they notify the chief of the *chidoi*, and arrange with him the timing of the action. They will choose a night in which one of them is on guard duty. They will invariably indicate the hour and minute around three in the morning, for it is then that the chief of the post, overcome by fatigue, will have fallen asleep. He will not wake up again" (*ibid.*, p. 88). Bodard also tells of Vietnamese mistresses of French officers who spied on the posts for the Vietminh and betrayed French positions (*ibid.*, p. 89). And there are the stories of the peasants who, seemingly harmless, got the French accustomed to seeing them inside the post on market days and who one day pulled out guns and machine guns from their fruit and vegetable baskets and killed everyone in sight (*ibid.*, pp. 90–91). Bodard tells endless stories about the poisonings, desertions, and betrayals to which the French were subjected in the course of the war.

33. About the latter and especially their effectiveness, Fall writes in *Street Without Joy* that they played an important role in the defense of Mao-Khe and a decisive role in holding the Day River line, saving the key position of Yen Cu Ha. They were also "to render invaluable services to the hard-pressed defenders of the Hoa-Binh pocket" (pp. 41, 46, 51). Fall adds that after 1957, "the valuable *Dinassaut* were largely disbanded since the French had invented them and there was no equivalent in American manuals, and were soon followed into oblivion by the cammando forces" (p. 334).

34. Exact figures on the military strength of the sects are unavailable, for the leaders of the three sects refused to furnish the French precise information. O'Ballance indicates that in 1947, the Hoa Hao's armed force of some 2,000 men (which strength increased "without French protest") was controlled by Tran Van Soai, who "undertook to keep the ferry over the Bassac River, between Can Tho and Cai Von, open to enable the considerable volume of rice to be transported across from the south" (*op. cit.*, p. 84). In 1953, O'Ballance writes, the Binh Xuyen, under General Le Van Vien, had a known strength of over 8,000 men—Vien's private army—with "most of the money to pay them coming from French sources" (*ibid.*, p. 195). Of the Cao Dai, Denis Warner writes that they "controlled an army of some 25,000 men" (*op. cit.*, p. 77).

35. Twenty battalions alone were used to seal off the delta, according to Navarre (*op. cit.*, p. 22). For a critical view of French defensive strategy, see Major Lamar McFadden Prosser in *The Army Combat Forces Journal*, V, June, 1955.

36. See Jean Lacouture and Philippe Devillers, *La fin d'une guerre: Indochine 1954*, p. 36.

37. The search in villages for guerrillas was a particularly frustrating and time-consuming preoccupation of the French, leading often, out of anger over failure to find the hide-outs known to exist, to the punishment of innocents and the arrest of all males. About the various ingenious ways of subterranean and subaqueous hide-outs, see Fall, *Street Without Joy*, pp. 110, 111 (with a drawing of a hide-out). About French search methods in villages, see Doctor Phan Quang Dan, *The War in Indochina. A Comparative Study of the Vietminh and the French Union Forces* (mimeographed; 1954), p. 21. On French attacks on villages suspected of harboring guerrillas, see John Mecklin, *Mission in Torment: An Intimate Account of the U.S. Role in Vietnam* (New York, 1965), p. 9, where he writes that the French "tried to use tanks and planes and artillery against an invisible enemy—like attacking mosquitos with a sledge hammer. In frustrated fury they repeatedly wiped out whole villages with shells and napalm on mere suspicion of concealed Vietminh troops, adding to the people's hatred."

38. O'Ballance, *op. cit.*, p. 194.

39. Wrote Lacouture and Devillers (*op. cit.*, p. 25): "From the very first, the policy of 'yellowing' of the units followed. This method would not have been sterile had it opened up the way to an authentic Vietnamese army and led to a division of duties that would progressively have placed the fight against the guerrillas under a Vietnamese command, with the Expeditionary Corps reserving to itself the mission of seeking out and facing the regular Vietminh Army. This never happened, and until 1953, the Vietnamese units were considered as auxiliaries of the French forces, enjoying practically no autonomy whatever. Furthermore, their organization posed enormous problems and forced us to weaken more and more the metropolitan troops, as well as those from North Africa and Black Africa, and to institute from one end to the other of the French Union a veritable chain of officers and noncommissioned officers."

40. Frenchmen whose memory reached back to the year 1913 may have wondered whether France should not have listened to the advice of General Pennequin, who insisted even then on the need for a Vietnamese national army (see Chapter III, n. 52).

41. Early in 1952, when General Salan succeeded de Lattre as Commander in Chief, the Vietnamese National Army consisted of between 100,000 and 150,000 men. The number given varies in every source, since some count all men enlisted while others exclude units not fully trained and armed.

42. According to O'Ballance, the number of soldiers and officers of the Expeditionary Corps killed during 1952 was 1,860 French, 4,049 Foreign Legionnaires, and 7,730 Vietnamese (*op. cit.*, p. 197).

43. Quoted by Doctor Phan Quang Dan (*op. cit.*, p. 26). Doctor Dan also speaks of "important" desertions that had taken place during the war. In September, 1951, he tells, when general mobilization was decreed, "military trucks were sent to the French-controlled villages to pick up all male adults between eighteen and thirty years of age and transport them into military camps. One week later over half managed to get out and go home." In December of the same year, "300 officer candidates in Nam Dinh, in northern Vietnam, went over to the Vietminh." And in 1953, 500 officer candidates were "kidnaped" by a company of Vietminh "without any fighting." When attacked by smaller Communist forces, "Vietnamese units surrendered en masse"; others defected "on a large scale. . . . As a result 38 military posts fell into Vietminh hands" (*ibid.*, p. 42). Ellen Hammer calls the Bao Dai army "not entirely reliable" (*op. cit.*, p. 287), and O'Ballance speaks of its "falling apart," and gives as the reason that "it had little faith in itself or the success of its declared mission. The men, who had little heart to fight openly and sincerely on the French side, became sulky and uncooperative" (*op. cit.*, p. 243). The French were to voice their disappointment when the Vietnamese Army "made a poor showing" in Operation Atlante, which General Navarre launched in January, 1954. "The comparative failure of the operation," writes O'Ballance, was blamed by them on the "poor quality and disappointing performance" of the Nationalist Army (*ibid.*, pp. 208, 209).

44. O'Ballance, *op. cit.*, p. 175. There was a shortage of Indochinese officers, O'Ballance also writes; because the educated and middle classes were disenchanted with the French regime, they furnished only few officers, and those who did join showed their contempt for the peasants they were supposed to lead. The officers of the militia, who had joined the army with their men, were unable to obtain formal commissions because of their lack of education. Lancaster says that the "mobilization decrees were causing discontent and unrest" resulting in draft dodging and an enrollment in the militia forces of the political-religious sects (*ibid.*, p. 233).

45. Statement given to *Paris-Presse-l'Intransigeant*, January 20, 1953 (quoted by Hammer, *op. cit.*, p. 289).

46. Lacouture and Devillers, *op. cit.*, p. 23.

47. Some of the phoniest nationalists (such as Nguyen Van Tam and a

few Hoa Hao and Cao Dai leaders) were competent organizers; some of the most determined nationalists (Ngo Dinh Diem) lacked both the talent and inclination for organizing the masses. Only the Communists and some of their Vietminh allies combined both qualifications. One effective means by which the Communists appealed to the nationalist feelings of the masses was by giving all campaigns the names of ancient or modern national heroes, such as Tran Hung Dao (who was said to have defeated the Mongols in their thirteenth-century invasion), Le Hong Phong I (after the first Secretary General of the Indochinese Communist Party, who died in a French jail in 1942), Le Loi (the Vietnamese king who defeated the Chinese invaders in the fifteenth century), etc.

48. Hammer, *op. cit.*, p. 192. Hougron (*op. cit.*) describes this and the lack of trained medical personnel. Le Thanh Khoi (*op. cit.*, p. 490) claims that a Dr. Dang Van Ngu invented "a sort of penicillin," but does not say anything about its curative value. On Vietminh prisoners, see also Fall, *Street Without Joy*, Chapter XI, entitled "Death March," pp. 290–305.

49. Hougron (*op. cit.*) also describes the working and subsequent abandonment of such an underground factory operating in the jungles of the South.

50. Isoart (*op. cit.*, p. 393). All who have written on the Indochina War discuss the economic organization and arms production of the Vietminh at least in passing (see *ibid.*, pp. 393–95; Khoi, *op. cit.*, especially p. 490; O'Ballance, *op. cit.*, pp. 82–83). A particularly interesting exposition is given by Chesneaux (*op. cit.*, pp. 277–83, also p. 303, nn. 1 and 2). A still more detailed description and analysis of Vietminh industry and the organization and results of its war production, can be found in Fall, *The Viet Minh Regime*, Part V ("Economic Problems," p. 86, and the map on p. 87, and "War Industry," pp. 88–89). The guidelines of Vietminh economic policy were first defined by Phan Anh in July, 1948, when he stated: "Through our economic policies we envisage becoming self-sufficient and intensifying our production to satisfy all our needs. To realize this policy of intensive production efficiently, we must solve the problem of the utilization of the products at our disposal. We shall encourage and direct exchange, develop interior and exterior commerce. At the same time we shall establish an integral blockade against the enemy economy and sabotage the basis itself of his economic strength. In short, our aim is to arrive at economic independence in our sector and thereafter to establish a national independent economy. . . . Our national economy is an economy 'for the people and with the people,' which only aims at the happiness of the people" (quoted by Chesneaux, *op. cit.*, p. 278).

51. See Chapter VII, n. 61.

52. Fall, *The Viet Minh Regime*, p. 76. Fall also quotes from a magazine article published by the French Information Services in Indochina, in which its author, Claude Guiges, speaks of the tour de force achieved by Vo Nguyen Giap "without cement-mixers or bulldozers; without steamrollers and with hastily-trained technicians . . . in spite of the systematic bomb-

ings. . . . This efficiency is essentially imputable to the veritable mysticism of 'the road at any price' which has been instilled in both the troops and the population" (*ibid.*, p. 76; quoting from "Logistique Vietminh," *Indochine-Sudest Asiatique* [Saigon], March, 1953). Contrary to conditions in the South Vietnamese Army (see n. 44, above), the Vietminh, by the very manner in which a man could rise from the recruitment ranks in his village to the "inner sanctum" of the Chu-luc (regular army), managed to raise what a high French officer quoted by Fall (*ibid.*, p. 75) praised highly by saying "the Viet-Minh infantry may be rated as one of the best in the world" (see also *ibid.*, pp. 76, 77).

53. According to Le Thanh Khoi, losses ran as high as 50 per cent (*op. cit.*, p. 490).

54. See Isoart, *op. cit.*, p. 392. This figure does not agree with Le Thanh Khoi, who says that between 1945 and 1953, illiteracy was reduced from 80 per cent to 30 per cent (*op. cit.*, p. 491), which, based on a population estimate of 14 million, would indicate that close to 10 million had become literate, more than 1 million fewer than claimed. Isoart points out, however, that the circulation of newspapers remained limited (*op. cit.*, p. 392). Lancaster gives a rather obvious reason for "these admirable and rather feverish efforts" at education, namely that "a literate people would more readily absorb Communist propaganda, a calculation based on the knowledge that the printed and written word were regarded almost with veneration by the rural population who believed that such an extravagant medium of communication must enshrine unquestioned truth" (*op. cit.*, p. 420, and n. 5).

55. "Modern warfare" instead of revolutionary warfare for "guerrilla warfare" is the term Roger Trinquier prefers in his book *Modern Warfare* (New York, 1964). On "doctrine of army," see Fall, *The Viet-Minh Regime*, pp. 79–83. In addition to the books mentioned here and in n. 18, above, Peter Paret (*op. cit.*) contributes additional material to the subject.

56. Hougron, in his novel *Le Soleil au Ventre*, gives an interesting account of the relationship between the military commander and the political officer. See also Fall's *Viet-Minh Regime*, p. 74, on the subject of "commissars." Lancaster, in his disquisition on commissars (*op. cit.*, pp. 424–25), writes: "The commissar's duties were . . . not merely confined to the maintenance of morale, as he shared with the military commander the responsibility for the conduct of operations and was expected to give proof, on all occasions, of a devotion to duty and of moral qualities superior to those of any other officer in the unit."

57. Administratively speaking, the constitution had divided the country into three parts: the North, Tongking (Bac Bo); the Center, Annam (Trung Bo); and the South, Cochinchina (Nam Bo). In March, 1948, Ho Chi Minh's government established six 'interzones" (Lien Khu), each under the authority of a committee composed of military and political members, both local as well as men nominated by Vietminh headquarters in the Viet Bac. Further down were "interprovinces" (Lien Tinh), and "intervillages" (Lien

Xa), administered in a similar fashion. The interzones (actually "integrated zones") were: (1) Northwest Tongking; (2) Northeast Tongking (with the Red River as the dividing line between the two Tongking zones); (3) Red River Delta; (4) North Annam (north of Hue); (5) South Annam (south of Hue); (6) Cochinchina (see O'Ballance, *op. cit.*, pp. 88–89). Militarily, Vietnam was to be divided into four types of zones: (1) the free zone; (2) guerrilla bases; (3) guerrilla zones; (4) occupied zones (see Chesneaux, *op. cit.*, p. 275, where he discusses the prevalence of these zones between 1946 and 1954). The free zone included the Viet Bac, the North Annamese deltas (Thanh Hoa, Nghe An, Ha Tinh), the coast south of Hue (Tourane) to Cape Varella (Quang Nam, Quang Ngai, Binh Dinh), the Plain of Reeds, and the Point of Camau. The guerrilla zone was ruled by the French during the day and the Vietminh at night. Operations went on in the Red River Delta and the Mekong Delta, at Hue, and Nha Trang. The guerrilla zone blended into guerrilla bases, and it was constantly contested by both sides. The occupied zone was, most importantly, Saigon-Cholon and suburbs, the lower Mekong, Hue, Hanoi, Nam Dinh (a center of industry), Haiphong (with its harbor), Hongay (for its mines), and the rubber region in the South (see Chesneaux, *ibid.*, pp. 274–77). It must be pointed out here that the reader looking at other maps will not find agreement among the various authors on the extent to which the zones were effectively Vietminh- or French-controlled, quite obviously because the situation was much too fluid for a purely static presentation. Lancaster (*op. cit.*, p. 419) indicates that prior to March, 1948, the Vietminh, for military purposes, had at first divided the country into fourteen zones. He also dwells on the difficulties encountered in communication between the Viet Bac, where radio was the chief means of contact, travel from North to South being hazardous and too time-consuming. North Vietnamese distrust of Southern "individualism" stemmed from "the extraordinary difficulties encountered in maintaining contact," he wrote. While South Annam and Cochinchina thus maintained an almost semi-autonomous status, they also "had to provide for their own needs in food and war material and also to assist the war effort in the North." At the beginning of 1949, Lancaster tells, Pham Ngoc Thach (who had played a part in the Communist seizure of power in Saigon) and Pham Van Dong (who had led the Vietminh delegation at the Fontainebleau conference) were sent by Ho Chi Minh to the South "to impress upon the authorities in those areas the need for stricter conformity with official policies." Nevertheless, the South "continued to fall short of the austere standards set by the formal and reserved Tongkingese." (For further details on organization and administration in the Vietminh zone, see *ibid.*, Appendix II, pp. 418–28.)

58. Fall (*The Viet Minh Regime*, p. 75) says general mobilization of both men and women over eighteen was decreed on November 4, 1949. See n. 52, above, for manner of recruitment. While the Chu-luc, the "main force" of the regular troops, was comparatively well fed, Fall writes, the "war laborers," i.e., "the men and women detailed to constitute the logistical support

for the units," underwent "nothing but a never-ending martyrdom." Quoting from a broadcast made on September 22, 1953, by the Voice of North
Vietnam, Fall writes: "Fifty per cent of the workers of the war services of
Van Chan are women . . . following step by step the People's Troops during the offensives, those workers had to climb many mountains and cross
thick forests for months at a time. Often they covered 50 kilometers (31
miles) in one single night with heavy burdens on their shoulders. . . .
When it rained they covered the rice and ammunition which they transported with their own waterproof coats, in spite of the cold. Very often
they collected the rice grains that had fallen along the way and added them
to their ration . . . offering it to the troops."

59. Isoart compares this dual control in all leading positions to something
like a double-entry bookkeeping system. "The system not only permitted a
quick discovery of errors but also their localization and correction without
loss of time," he quotes from an article entitled "La Stratégie révolutionnaire du Viet-Minh," which appeared in *Le Monde*, August 3, 1954. The
very fact that ministers, generals, political army commissars, high officials,
and heads-of-state associations were Communists provided "the Vietminh
Government and High Command with an immense body of controllers and
informers whose absolute devotion was guaranteed by fanaticism, interest,
and fear," he adds, quoting from *Le Monde* of August 4, 1954. And citing
from "Guerre révolutionnaire et pacification," by J. Hogard, in *Revue
militaire d'information,* No. 280, he sums up: "None could escape this
tightly woven net. It was not unusual to see a son denounce his father, or a
wife her husband, charging them with informing a detachment of the
[French] forces of an order, or killing a pig for private consumption. They
could not do otherwise. Since denouncing was obligatory, they would have
become accomplices had they kept silent. Hence the denunciation was inevitable. By telling the local representatives of the Party or the security police that the guilty ones had escaped the vigilance of those responsible for
the homes, the self-defense, or the economy of the village, they were in
effect making sure that the nerves of a member of their family, perhaps
even their own, would not fail during the meetings of self-criticism held by
the male and female youths, the workers, the farm laborers, the mothers of
the family" (*op. cit.*, pp. 390–91, and nn. 199, 201, 202).

60. Observed Lancaster: "The avoidance of the use of the word 'Communist' was probably inspired by a desire to confuse non-Communist
observers as to the real complexion of the new party." Furthermore, it definitely was the party "with the mostest—the most patriotic, the most ardent,
the most revolutionary workers, peasants, and intellectual workers," as it described itself in the manifesto issued after the National Congress of February 11–19, 1951, at which it was drafted, and at which Truong Chinh
assured the delegates that its policy was based on "Marxist-Leninist theory,
democratic centralism, criticism, and auto-criticism," which "would perpetuate the glorious historic career of the progressive revolutionary parties"
(*op. cit.*, p. 227). For the English translation of the platform and manifesto of

the Lao Dong Party, see Cole (ed.), *op. cit.*, pp. 96–110. Since the Lao
Dong was intended to be the "superparty," the merger of the Viet Minh
League with the "all-embracing and somewhat amorphous Lien Viet bloc"
was designed to incorporate those who had been denied admission in the
Lao Dong, and was resolved at the congress held on March 3, at which "under the firm direction of Ton Duc Thang, a veteran Communist agitator
who was elected president of the Central Committee, the delegates decided
. . . to create a Lien Viet Front with a political platform which would
embody Truong Chinh's directives" (Lancaster, *op. cit.*, pp. 228, 229). The
conference of the United Fronts of Vietnam, Laos, and Cambodia, which
was held later in March, was of strategic importance. There, an agreement
was reached with the so-called representatives from Laos and Cambodia
that, in Lancaster's words, "would justify the continued use of neighbouring
territory for the transit of military supplies and for attacks on French
Union garrisons" (*ibid.*, p. 230). For an extensive treatment of the Lao
Dong Party, see Fall, *The Viet-Minh Regime*, pp. 34–42. (On p. 34, Fall
discusses the "end of the Viet-Minh," concluding on p. 35 with the observation: "For all practical purposes then, the Viet-Minh, like the ICP [Indochi-
nese Communist Party], had disappeared. However, the name of 'Viet-
Minh,' hated, feared, or admired, was to become part and parcel of the
myths of the D.R.V.N.")

61. Isoart, *op. cit.*, p. 392.

62. As stated earlier in the text, the Ho piaster had no value at all. But
prices, measured in rice, rose constantly between January, 1951, and December, 1952, to a total of 260 per cent (Isoart, *op. cit.*, p. 393). In his endeavor
to defend the D.R.V.N.'s economic policies, Chesneaux puts the same figures rather optimistically within the context of a two-year period, stating
that while prices in 1951 rose 160 per cent, they rose "only" 100 per cent in
1952 (*op. cit.*, p. 281). At the same time, taxes, fixed in 1951, which were to
be paid in agricultural products, amounted to 5 per cent on a minimum determined at 61 kilos, to which a local tax of 20 per cent was added. This tax
payment in rice, says Chesneaux (*ibid.*, p. 281, n. 1), served in particular to
feed the army, since it took the taxes of one hundred persons to feed two
soldiers.

63. An example of this type of error, notable for its lack of understanding
and political acumen, is William J. Lederer and Eugene Burdick's *The Ugly
American* (New York, 1958). For a critique of this novel, see Buttinger,
Fact and Fiction on Foreign Aid (New York, 1963; first published in
Dissent, Summer, 1959).

64. This is best demonstrated by General Chassin's previously quoted
article, "Guerre en Indochine." His analysis of the Vietminh methods, for
example, is both accurate and politically informed. Chassin begins by saying
that with the Vietminh, political action always precedes military action, the
establishment of temporary or occasional "bases" constituting the first and
most important consideration. A "base," Chassin expounds, is built in zones
not directly controlled by a military post the moment a Vietminh propa-

gandist arriving at a village is not driven out or denounced to the authorities. This propagandist is a civilian, who knows how to appeal to sentiments of nationalism and social justice in telling language, who presents the Vietminh struggle as a crusade of liberation against the imperialist white robbers. Soon two or more agitators join him in indoctrinating the village, particularly the youth. After propaganda has done its work, some military instructors are sent in who organize a self-defense militia in such a manner that the regular Vietminh troops will be able to install themselves there and find an already prepared defense. Military practice is undertaken with wooden rifles and fake grenades. The manufacture of arms begins. Hideouts are dug and tunnels, through which the entire village can be evacuated in case of attack. All this takes place in the dark and in silence, without the knowledge of anyone on the outside, especially not the Franco-Vietnamese emissaries. Such operations often take place within a few miles of a French-held fortified post. Then begins the recruitment of regular troops, and the "base" is ready for operations, to be undertaken either by guerrillas or regular troops. Usually the Vietminh, to instill the new fighters with self-confidence, undertakes only a limited action, whose most important aim is to prove that the new recruits are capable of winning against the French. A sudden attack, with Viet troops secretly posted, with the population won over so that it will not inform the French, and the French posts fall. And even if the posts are reoccupied, damage has already been inflicted. The regular Viet has proved his valor. From now on those who would collaborate with the French are considered traitors and are mercilessly punished. Thus, Chassin points out, there exists a surface war in Vietnam which is almost incomprehensible in Europe (pp. 5–8). In an article entitled "L'armée viet-minh," which appeared in *Le Monde,* November 11, 1952, Jean Lacouture made similar observations, showing that the French were not ignorant of the strength and advantages their enemies possessed (see Isoart, *op. cit.,* pp. 392–93 and n. 203). On indoctrination of prisoners and psychological warfare, see also Fall, *The Viet Minh Regime,* pp. 48–50.

65. On this comparatively little-known aspect of the Indochina War, see Fall, *Street Without Joy,* particularly the section "The Commando Groups," pp. 262–74. See also Paret, *op. cit.,* and Trinquier, *op. cit.* Countless articles on the tactics and the strategy of revolutionary warfare appeared in French magazines, e.g., the *Revue de Défense Nationale* and *Revue d'Information Militaire,* as early as 1948; see, for example, the article by Pierre Célerier, "Sur la guérilla," which appeared in March, 1948, in *Revue de Défense Nationale;* others were written as late as 1958, such as the one by J. Hogard, "Tactique et Stratégie de la Guerre Révolutionnaire," in *Revue d'Information Militaire,* June, 1958. Mention should also be made here of the study by M. Megret, "La guerre psychologique," which appeared in a special issue of the *Revue d'Information Militaire,* February–March, 1957; J. Martin-Blazquez, *Guerre civile totale* (Paris, 1958); Gallais, Hogard, Lehning, Collin, and Menard, *Contribution à une étude sur la guerre insurrectionnelle* (Paris, 1955; the authors were French officers).

66. An extraordinary example of the playing on national ignorance was given by former Vice-President Nixon in a speech made in November, 1953, in which he stated that there would be no Indochina War if there were no Communist China.

67. See Lacouture and Devillers, *op. cit.*, p. 44.

68. Navarre, *op. cit.*, p. 72.

69. On January 14, 1950, Ho Chi Minh formally invited all countries to establish diplomatic relations with his government, the only representative government of a unified Vietnam. Following his invitation to Communist China on January 15 to establish diplomatic relations and exchange ambassadors, Chou En-lai replied in the name of his government on January 18, recognizing the D.R.V.N. The Soviet Union recognized Hanoi on January 30. Only then was notice taken of the fact that the French Assembly had not ratified the agreements of March, 1949, which supposedly made Vietnam independent. In the absence of such ratification, the United States and Great Britain were unable to extend recognition to the State of Vietnam under the Bao Dai regime. After the French Assembly ratified the March treaties at the end of January, the United States and Great Britain recognized the State of Vietnam on February 7, but with a difference in emphasis: The United States implied in its message that the Bao Dai regime was not as yet considered completely independent but merely on the road to full independence, a point that had also been stressed on February 3 by U.S. roving Ambassador Philip Jessup on his visit to Vietnam. He expressed a desire that the Bao Dai Government soon obtain greater and more complete independence. Great Britain contented itself with a recognition of the "Associate State within the French Union." (Incidentally, the American and British recognition also extended to Cambodia and Laos, with the same subtle difference in emphasis—the United States speaking of "independent states within the French Union," and Great Britain of "associate states.") For the text of the recognition statement by the United States, see Cole (ed.), *op. cit.*, p. 117; for the text of the British recognition, see *ibid.*, p. 120; the exchange of messages between the D.R.V.N. and Communist China is reproduced in *ibid.*, p. 121, and of the D.R.V.N. and the U.S.S.R. on p. 122.

70. Until the beginning of 1950, when the lines were clearly drawn between the Communist bloc behind Ho Chi Minh's D.R.V.N. and Bao Dai's State of Vietnam, the Vietnamese Communists had some success in impressing their image as a government of national union on international public opinion. *The New York Times* wrote on February 26, 1949, that Ho's government was a coalition of nationalists of all tendencies. And the *Herald Tribune* commented on October 21, 1949, that Ho's government was a coalition government of nationalist parties, and that there could be no doubt that a nucleus of Communists existed within the organization. But, the paper said, it was clear that at least 80 per cent of the leaders were not Communists. The same opinions were voiced by the *Frankfurter Rundschau* on January 26, 1950, and the *Scotsman* on February 2, 1950. That this seeming consensus meant little in the final analysis became clear after February, 1950.

71. Lacouture and Devillers, *op. cit.*, p. 31. In his earlier book, Devillers wrote that the d'Argenlieu-Pignon-Valluy trio had imposed on the Vietminh "the test of arms," and the Coste-Floret-Pignon-Torel team had "turned Bao Dai into a war machine" (*op. cit.*, pp. 471–72). As pointed out in n. 19, above, there is a theory, substantiated largely by speculation, that during this period, and from then on, the "pro-Chinese" wing of the Lao Dong Party eclipsed Ho Chi Minh and his moderate associates. To recapitulate: Hoang Quoc Viet (Union Chief), Tran Huy Lieu, and Dang Xuan Khu (better known as Truong Chinh, Secretary General of the Lao Dong Party) were regarded as pro-Chinese. The moderates were said to be Ho Chi Minh, Pham Van Dong, and some former non-Communist nationalists in the Vietminh, for example the Socialist Hoang Minh Giam, Phan Anh, Trinh Van Binh. The highly respected Van Anh had been a member of the Kim Government but joined the Vietminh, as did other members of the Kim Government, such as Doctor Pham Ngoc Thach and Ta Quang Buu. Isoart seems also to have accepted this theory that the pro-Chinese, especially Hoang Quoc Viet, Tran Huy Lieu, and Truong Chinh ("*homme de l'appareil, doctrinaire de talent formé à Moscou*"), were the masters of the country after 1950 (*op. cit.*, p. 396). What basically handed the Vietminh their trump card in its struggle for supremacy was what Lacouture and Devillers described as "the refusal of France to satisfy the Vietnamese national aspirations," which, the authors state, "prevented the nationalists from dissociating themselves from the Communists in a struggle in which the patriotic imperatives outranked all others" (*op. cit.*, p. 19).

72. See n. 59, above. On the take-over by Lao Dong Party cadres of all important positions, see also Joseph Starobin, *Eyewitness in Indochina* (New York, 1954), p. 82. Starobin had visited Vietminh territory. On the effect of increased Communist control over other nationalists, see Nguyen Duy Thanh, *My Four Years with the Viet Minh* (Bombay, 1950). See also Hoang Van Chi, *From Colonialism to Communism*, pp. 109–12, for a description of the purges after 1950.

73. In this speech, Ho Chi Minh admitted, at least by implication, that the peasants lived "more than ever in misery." Said Ho Chi Minh: "More than 90 per cent of our army, of our regional popular forces, our militia, and our guerrillas are peasants. Our peasants have made the largest contribution to the resistance and accepted the greatest sacrifices, and meanwhile they are still among the poorest of our people because they lack land" (Isoart, *op. cit.*, p. 394).

74. This law was promulgated on December 19, 1953. Following up the call for "land to the tiller," which had seen the classification of landholders and agricultural workers under the law of April, 1953 (April 20, according to Fall, *The Viet Minh Regime*, and Cole (ed.), *op. cit.*, and April 12, according to Chesneaux, Khoi, and Isoart) into four categories—(1) the feudal landowners; (2) the rich farmers; (3) the middle-class peasants; and (4) the poor peasants—the December law called for further reductions in the size of legal land holdings, for an additional reduction in interest rates, and the

retroactive wiping-out of debts incurred with certain large lenders-landholders; it also expropriated all French landholdings, and the holdings of *Viet Gian* (traitors), while continuing to promise land to Vietnamese serving in the Nationalist Army if they defected and came over. In itself a summation and tightening-up of earlier land-reform decrees initiated in 1949, the April law had already aimed at lowering interest rates and reducing indebtedness. But while it had been implemented through a local administrative apparatus, the December law nominally called for implementation by means of a "mass mobilization," which meant through peasant unions and agricultural committees, to operate on interprovincial, provincial, as well as village levels. Concomitant with the land-reform program went a tax-reform program, "the aim of which was to impoverish the whole population and to reduce all Vietnamese society to the level of its lowest members" (Hoang Van Chi, *op. cit.*, p. 72). Fall's comment on the Vietminh land program was: "The Democratic Government could not possibly succeed in achieving a large-scale implementation of its own agrarian policy" (*The Two Viet-Nams*, p. 113). For further details, see Fall, *ibid.*, pp. 100–111; Isoart, *op. cit.*, pp. 394–95; Chesneaux, *op. cit.*, pp. 300–302; Khoi, *op. cit.*, p. 491. On the methods used to enforce these land reforms, see Hoang Van Chi, *op. cit.*, Part V, pp. 163–240. For the English texts of the I.D.R. Vietnam Population Classification Decree of 1953, and the Agrarian Reform Law of December, 1953, see Cole (ed.), *op. cit.*, pp. 130–56. The most informative report on the Vietminh land-reform decrees and laws of 1953, and on the reason for their slow execution, can be found in an article by J. Price Gittinger, "Communist Land Policy in North Viet Nam," in *Far Eastern Survey*, August, 1959, pp. 115–16. Gittinger, who administered the economic and technical project in support of the Vietnamese agrarian-reform program from September, 1955, to December, 1959, points out that while "the Communists have made no secret that their land tenure policy goal for North Viet Nam is complete collectivization of agriculture," they were faced by peasant resistance because "the North Vietnamese peasant, who responded to promises of land transfer and individual ownership, is showing himself very reluctant to give up his land and his control over his holding" (*ibid.*, pp. 123, 125). For the earlier position by the Vietminh against land reform see Chapter VI, note 22. In his book *North of the 17th Parallel* (Hanoi, 1957), Wilfred Burchett, a well-known Australian Communist journalist, speaks about the land reform test at Hung Son, where "land distribution methods were being tested . . . preparatory to being applied in another sixty parishes in Thai Nguyen province." In this "dress rehearsal" for the real thing, "rent reduction [in Thai Nguyen province] was being enforced as a sort of softening up for the more radical process of land distribution" (pp. 118, 119).

75. See Bodard, *op. cit.*, pp. 284–96, the chapter entitled "L'Interrogatoire et la technique de la torture"; cf. also Ainley, *op. cit.*, pp. 29–37, 42, 46.

76. See Chapter VIII, n. 98, for Bodard's account of corruption in high places. Even the Prime Minister himself, Nguyen Van Tam, showed "some

coarseness of moral fibre," as Lancaster puts it, "by allowing one of his daughters to accept wedding presents of inappropriate magnificence from the Chinese community in Cholon, and by the licence that he gave his mistress to exploit his official position in order to clinch profitable business deals" (*op. cit.*, p. 283).

77. Bodard, *op. cit.*, p. 172. More revealing even than Bodard's first book is his *La guerre d'Indochine: L'humiliation* (Paris, 1965), which is one long indictment of the corruption under Bao Dai among both the Vietnamese and the French, and how their profiteering and plundering of the treasury helped to prolong a war that was such a gainful affair for so many.

78. A great deal, much of it confusing, has been written about the piaster traffic. Two most revealing though highly controversial books are Jacques Despuech, *Le trafic de piastres* (Paris, 1953), containing photocopied documents, and Arthur Laurent, *La Banque de l'Indochine et la piastre* (Paris, 1954), also with photocopied documents. Despuech's book *Missions inutiles à Saigon* (Paris, 1955), his memoirs as an employee in the Office of Exchange and agent for the Deuxième Bureau, also touches on this. See also Bodard, *La guerre d'Indochine: L'enlisement*, pp. 172–73, who comments that without the traffic in piasters "there would no longer have been any business, policy of pacification, or even war—or, at least, everything would have been different, profoundly changed." For a comparison with earlier speculations in piasters (during the late 1890's), see Chesneaux, *op. cit.*, p. 146. Miss Hammer states that "nominally the inflation-ridden Indochinese economy, its foreign exchange and its foreign trade, was strictly controlled, but in practice the lack of public morality on the part of a number of Frenchmen and Vietnamese who exploited this period of national tragedy to their own profit led to widespread corruption and speculation" (*op. cit.*, p. 272). Further on, Miss Hammer says: "the piastre traffic which was known to fill not only the pockets of speculators but also the military arsenal of the Viet Minh, whose agents bought up on the black market dollars which they used for buying arms and supplies. In 1949–1950 a scandal connected with the piastre traffic had been the occasion of the notorious 'affair of the generals' which had attracted wide publicity and public denunciation of the traffic; but nothing had been done to end it" (*ibid.*, p. 300). Lancaster reports that a parliamentary mission visiting Indochina in 1953 returned with findings to the effect that "after eight years of laissez-aller and anarchy, the presence of a resident Cabinet Minister in Indochina has not led to the suppression of the daily scandals concerning the transfers of piastres, the settlement of war-damage claims, and the allocations of contracts which feature in the daily tittle-tattle of Saigon" (*op. cit.*, pp. 268–69; from reports in the weekly newspaper *Express*, and in *L'Humanité* of May 22, 1953); elsewhere, Lancaster mentions that the rate of exchange was originally intended as an inducement to volunteers for military service in Vietnam. "But in fact it was French financial and commercial interests which derived the chief benefit from a decree appropriately promulgated on Christmas Day" (*ibid.*, p. 412; see also pp. 413–15).

79. My attention to this aspect, much neglected by most authors, was drawn by Mr. Tran Van Chuong, former Ambassador of the Republic of Vietnam to the United States (from 1955 to 1963), who resigned in protest against the Ngo Dinh Diem policies several months before the latter's fall.

80. As described by Tran Van Chuong in an unpublished manuscript on this period of the Indochina conflict.

81. Lancaster, *op. cit.*, p. 270. The devaluation of May 9, Lancaster adds, "resulted in a rise in the cost of living and a fall in national revenue, of which a large percentage had been appropriated for the purposes of national defence."

82. Lancaster, *ibid.*, p. 270, and also pp. 413–14, where he adds: "The success achieved by the Bank of Indochina in this respect [transfer of their financial resources] is revealed by a statement made by the Chairman at a general meeting of shareholders in June, 1953, in which he claimed that although banking activities in Indochina continued to provide more than half the total profits, the Bank's holdings in Indochina represented, at that date, less than 17 per cent of its total investments. This is all the more extraordinary when it is recalled that before 1945 the bulk of the Bank's capital was invested in Indochina, where it had succeeded in building up a vast latifundium embracing every aspect of the Protectorate's financial, commercial, and industrial life."

83. "The devaluation also aroused the resentment of the Expeditionary Corps," wrote Lancaster, "whose rates of pay were adversely affected, and although an attempt was made to mitigate the resultant hardship by the retention of a proportion of service pay, which was reimbursed at the more favourable rate of exchange at the end of a tour of duty, this arrangement, which was a common practice in French prisons, caused additional irritation, while the extra returns now required were to lead in some cases to the withdrawal of n.c.o.'s from front-line positions to deal with this administrative chore" (*ibid.*, p. 270; quoting from Navarre, *op. cit.*, p. 101).

84. See Chapter VIII, note 86, for the reaction by King Sihanouk of Cambodia. Khoi says that Sihanouk, impatient with French shilly-shallying over the granting of true independence to Cambodia, left Phnom Penh and went to Angkor, wherefrom he called on the population to "resist" (*op. cit.*, p. 481). Actually, this action was the culmination of Sihanouk's campaign for independence, which had led him to declare in an interview with a *New York Times* correspondent that French failure to satisfy Indochinese nationalism might within the next few months lead to the people's joining forces with the Vietminh. The interview was printed on April 19, 1953, and had an enormous effect in Indochina. The French tried to treat it as a deplorable indiscretion, but they were forced to begin negotiations in earnest when Sihanouk fled to Bangkok on June 13, 1953, and refused to return unless his people's aspirations for national independence were realized. He also issued a proclamation, addressed to his French friends, in which he stated that he was forced by the attitude of France to take the leadership in the movement for the independence of Cambodia. He returned a week later,

only to assemble in the "autonomous" district of Battambang Siemriep all the forces at his disposal, a total of 20,000 men, thereby showing his determination to wrest independence from the French but also to indicate his willingness to fight against the Communists if independence were granted and the Communists were to attack.

85. The revised constitution, as adopted in October, 1946, made defense and diplomacy matters exclusively handled by France for the French Union. This conflicted with the agreement of March 6, 1946, and withdrawal from the French Union became one of the loudest battle cries of the nationalists in the Bao Dai camp during 1953.

86. See nn. 43 and 44, above. Lancaster mentions that of the 700 Vietnamese officers commissioned, only 80 were field officers, of whom 4 held the rank of colonel, and that during 1952, 50 Vietnamese officers were sent to France to attend courses at the Staff College and at naval, air, and communication training centers. A training school for air force personnel was opened in 1952 at Nha Trang, and a naval training school was established there in 1953 (*op. cit.*, p. 248, nn. 5, 6, and 7). But the fact that the Vietnamese now agreed to enter the army in large numbers did not produce a reliable Vietnamese army, just as their acceptance of offices in the administration did not produce a devoted class of civil servants. Rather, their joining was the result of the increasing impoverishment of the middle and lower classes, most of whom were ruined after eight years of war and forced to accept any means of subsistence available to them.

87. Dabezies, *op. cit.*, p. 190.

88. In an appendix to the Revers report, the secretary of the French Christian trade-union federation, Force Ouvrière, had written: "If the Indochinese were to express their opinion in a free vote, Ho Chi Minh, without pressure on his part, would get 95 per cent of the votes, and Bao Dai not even the total of the remaining 5 per cent" (Chesneaux, *op. cit.*, p. 293).

89. The main points of Tam's land-reform plan of June 9, 1953, were an agricultural credit fund, established on August 12; the transfer of the riceland to farmers who occupied and tilled land abandoned by its owners for three years; a limitation on permissible ownership of land to 36 hectares in the North, 45 in the Center, and 100 in the South; the distribution of concessions to veterans and heads of large families; finally, land rent fixed at 15 per cent of the crop. For the English text of Tam's land reform, see Cole (ed.), *op. cit.*, pp. 166–68.

90. The then Apostolic Vicar of Vinh Long, Monsignor Ngo Dinh Thuc, a brother of Ngo Dinh Diem, forbade Leroy to call his troops "Catholic Militia" (Lancaster, *op. cit.*, p. 429; see also p. 252 for further comment on Leroy). Ellen Hammer makes the point that a number of Catholics continued to live in the Vietminh areas, generally abstaining from political activity, while others were tacitly encouraged by their bishops to organize local "self-defense" militias against the Vietminh with arms supplied by the French. Such was the case with Leroy's organization (*op. cit.*, p. 285).

Dabezies says that Leroy undoubtedly acted somewhat paternalistically, but that his activities nonetheless had deep repercussions in the countryside (*op. cit.*, p. 91).

91. J. R. Tournoux, *Secrets d'état*, p. 22. Dabezies is less positive in his opinion, saying that it will never be known whether the Tam Government was on the right path, "because, in fact, these reforms, apart from being too timid, and because of the war still too undecided, had no time to bear fruit" (*op. cit.*, p. 190). Among Tam's other reforms were a labor code and the institution of a National Consultative Council, which (like the various councils of today) never became active.

92. See Chapter VIII, note 43. After his return from exile in August, 1946, Pham Cong Tac, the "Ho Phap" (Caodaist Pope), proclaimed that the presence of France was necessary in Indochina and that Caodaism had full confidence in France's ability to restore order and public safety. The Ho Phap's declaration caused General Nguyen Van Thanh and his captains Trinh Minh The and Duong Van Dang to abandon the Vietminh and to return with their troops to Tay Ninh. After a Vietminh attack on the Holy Seat, the Ho Phap in January, 1947, ratified the agreements with the French that Tran Quang Vinh, his commander in chief, had initiated. For two years— from January, 1947, to December, 1948—the Caodaists sided with the French against the Vietminh. But the Ho Phap's ambition to play a leading political role soon brought him into conflict not only with the Hoa Hao, to whom he proposed a pact, but with the French as well. He proposed the creation of a neutral zone to the French, under Caodaist control, which was "to serve as refuge for repentant nationalists." The French refused the scheme. Consequently, the Ho Phap proclaimed strict neutrality for the sect and informed the French of his intention to dissolve the Caodaist units in the Nationalist Army and to return their weapons to the French High Command. It was in February, 1949, that Nguyen Van Thanh issued a secret order to repel every attack or attempt, regardless by whom, on Caodaist posts and to halt all offensive action against the Vietminh. At the same time contact was established with the Vietminh to obtain a promise of neutrality. But when the Vietminh profited from the Caodaist inaction to inflict serious losses on them, Thanh, on June 24, 1949, issued orders to renew the fight against the Vietminh. At the same time, the Ho Phap renewed his vow of allegiance to Bao Dai, and Tran Quang Vinh became a member of the Xuan Government. The Franco-Caodaist collaboration was marred by only a few incidents in 1950. In 1951, Tran Quang Vinh left for France and was replaced by Nguyen Van Thanh, who nominated Trinh Minh The as his chief of staff, only to have The declare himself dissident (see n. 93, below). This was followed by inner dissension in the Caodaist camp, with the result that in March, 1953, Tran Quang Vinh reassumed power and re-established collaboration with the French (see A. M. Savani, *Visages et images du Sud Viet-Nam*, pp. 79–84). Although the Caodaist Doctor Le Van Hoach became Minister of Health in the Tam Government, and later replaced Phan Van Giao as Council Vice-President, this did not prevent the Ho Phap from

turning against Nguyen Van Tam and becoming "his worst enemy" (Dabezies, *op. cit.*, p. 187). The relations of the Hoa Hao with the Bao Dai Government and the French were equally equivocal. In 1947, the sect had a program both anti-Communist and anti-French. In March, the Hoa Hao military chief, Tran Van Soai, allied himself with the French and signed a pact with them on May 18, but intrigues did not cease. Thus, at the end of 1948, the sect split into four distinct groups, and Bacut (his real name was Le Quang Vinh), the *enfant terrible* of the Hoa Hao, the counterpart to the Caodaist Trinh Minh The (see Chapter VII, n. 51), became a dissident. In 1949, there were internecine fights among the Hoa Hao groups, and in the following year Nguyen Gia Ngo, the spiritual leader of the Hoa Hao, established contact with the Bao Dai Government to regroup the sect in a close alliance with the authorities. On February 25, 1950, Ngo declared his submission to Bao Dai, and a protocol signed in April established peace among the factions. On August 25, Bacut also rallied to the French. By 1952, the sect had finally achieved a certain "internal equilibrium," which benefited the collaboration with the French. The latter were to show their appreciation by promoting Tran Van Soai to the rank of general on January 1, 1953 (see Savani, *op. cit.*, pp. 91–96). Nguyen Van Tam was also to offer a ministerial post to the Hoa Hao, but they "disputed the vacant seat so violently" among themselves, writes Dabezies, that Tam "tired of their intrigues and soon gave up trying to obtain their cooperation" (*op. cit.*, p. 187).

93. See Chapter VII, n. 51, on various Caodaist military figures. As for Trinh Minh The, he had been the last to rally to the French in 1946, Dabezies wrote, doing so only upon a direct order from the Ho Phap. In 1948, in a gesture of defiance aimed at the "compromises" for which he reproached the Caodaist command, The had gone into dissidence with his faithful Hac Y (Blackshirts), only to return upon a promise by his friends that they would change their position. After that, Dabezies tells, The became the leader of the Viet Nam Phuc Quoc Hoi, the Caodaist political branch in charge of opposition to the regime, where he continued to demonstrate extremist tendencies and signs of independence. His desertion in 1951 (with only 1,000 men according to Dabezies and Savani, not 2,500 as Lancaster maintains) was the beginning of a violent campaign against the Vietnamese regime and against the French, followed by terrorist acts "for the sake of publicity" and a relatively unsuccessful attempt to form a National Resistance Front (Mat Tran Quoc Gia Khang Chine), in which he sought to enlist anti-Communists as well as anti-French elements. Wrote Dabezies: "Contrary to what one might have believed, it was not the question of a simple revolt but of a maneuver that had been undertaken in full agreement with the Pope himself, and which was meant to serve as a means of blackmail to obtain for the sect the advantages it was seeking" (*op. cit.*, pp. 185–86). Lancaster tells that The had been a ferryman on one of the rivers in the South, whose rapid rise had awakened in him "confused ambitions which transcended the vulgar considerations of self-interest that

prompted the actions of his feudal peers." Trinh Minh The's "hatred of graft and self-indulgence, capacity for ruthless action, and periodic hysterical outbursts contributed to the alarm and admiration with which he was regarded" (*op. cit.*, p. 233). Lancaster feels that "the creation of a nationalist maquis was welcomed in these circles [of the Saigon bourgeoisie] on the grounds that it might provide a refuge from French-inspired attempts to dragoon them into active participation in the war against the Viet Minh." When the French sought to cut The off from support by the Ho Phap, he "reacted by instigating terrorist outrages in Saigon" (*ibid.*, p. 234). Lancaster speaks of plastic charges placed in vehicles that were blown up by time-bombs in public parking lots, and of similar bombs attached to bicycles that were left to explode in the court of the Vietnamese security headquarters. Lancaster adds in a note: "The employment of this modern explosive and the ingenuity displayed in its use gave rise to inevitable rumours that The had acquired his 'know-how' from agents of the American Central Intelligence Bureau who, in their desire to promote a third force, had provided the Cao Dai Colonel with some technical assistance in addition to moral support" (*ibid.*, p. 234, n. 26). This accusation became the central point of Graham Greene's *Quiet American* (London, 1955). Greene wrote his book not only to denounce an alleged American policy of interference in the Indochina War, an allegation that is a complete fabrication and contrary to established facts, but he also conceived the American as a ridiculous figure in his attempt to promote such a policy. A much more factual and truthful picture of the Vietnamese political situation and the American role at the time is given by Robert Shaplen in his novel *A Forest of Tigers* (New York, 1956).

94. Hammer, *op. cit.*, p. 285. He also acquired the Nouveautés Catinat, Saigon's largest department store, twenty houses, about a hundred shops, a fleet of river boats, and operated Asia's biggest brothel, known as the Hall of Mirrors. His opium factory, a stone's throw from his headquarters, catered to the dens his police force theoretically put out of business (see Denis Warner, *op. cit.*, p. 77). For a fascinating description of Le Van Vien's financial and political wheelings-dealings, cf. Bodard, *La guerre d'Indochine: L'humiliation*, pp. 93–126.

95. Nguyen De, of whom Lancaster wrote that he had been "generally credited in Saigon with a remarkable capacity for intrigue," had served as Bao Dai's private secretary in 1932. A protégé of the French, he was forced to resign from the Imperial service during the Emperor's early attempts to assert himself against the French. Thereafter he "devoted his considerable talents to promoting the interests of a Vietnamese commercial firm which successfully invaded the exclusively French preserve of export and import trade," Lancaster states. (Others, such as Georges Chaffard, *Indochine: Dix ans d'indépendance* [Paris, 1964], p. 23, state that De, after having been dismissed by the French because of his nationalism, represented an Anglo-American firm at Hanoi. For a while De collaborated with the Vietminh and attended the Fontainebleau conference in an official advisory capacity to

the Vietminh delegation. But soon thereafter he reverted his loyalty to Bao Dai, and in 1950 was reappointed to his former post of Imperial Secretary. Lancaster described De as possessing a "considerable intellectual affinity" with Bao Dai and as having known how to render himself indispensable to the Emperor. Ellen Hammer states that his intrigues were generally believed to have led to the dismissal of Tran Van Huu as Prime Minister, in favor of Tam. When Tam was also compelled to resign, "rumours which originated in Dalat indicated that Nguyen De himself was a candidate for the premiership" (Lancaster, *op. cit.*, pp. 250, 283, n. 42, and p. 430; also Hammer, *op. cit.*, p. 286).

96. Dabezies, *op. cit.*, p. 193.

97. *Ibid.*, p. 196.

98. The Vietnamese Federation of Christian Workers which in July, 1953 had a membership of 45,000, was affiliated with the International Federation of Christian Workers (see *Annuaire des États Associés, 1953*, p. 105; cited by Lancaster, *op. cit.*, p. 276, n. 19).

99. On September 5, the movement was endorsed by such prominent leaders as Pham Cong Tac, the Cao Dai Pope, the Hoa Hao "Generalissimo" Tran Van Soai, To Lien, Superior of Vietnamese Buddhists, the Dai Viet leader Nguyen Ton Hoan, and Nhu's and Diem's brother, Monsignor Ngo Dinh Thuc, the Apostolic Vicar of Vinh Long. The Cao Dai and Hoa Hao were then especially bitter, since Nguyen Van Tam had begun to send National Army units in sect territories (see Lancaster, *op. cit.*, pp. 276–77; Dabezies, *op. cit.*, pp. 198–99).

100. Commented Dabezies: "The Caodaists, Hoa Hao, and Binh Xuyen realized that they had allowed themselves to be manipulated. . . . Also, even among the enemies of the regime agreement was not perfect. . . . For this reason, the new movement in the end was to prove destructive rather than constructive and fell apart when Ngo Dinh Diem assumed power" (*op. cit.*, p. 199).

101. Of the total projected 200 delegates, 140 belonged to the "Big Five" political parties or groups, namely the Dai Viet, Caodaists, Hoa Hao, Binh Xuyen, and Catholics. Eighty representatives were chosen from Cochinchina, 75 from Tongking, and only 40 from the Center. In addition to 29 municipal counselors and 50 communal counselors, they included 8 representatives of professional associations, 25 representatives of political groups (Dai Viet, VNQDD, Dong Minh Hoi), 6 representatives of the commercial community, 3 of the press, 3 of cultural associations, 9 Binh Xuyen, 17 Cao Dai, 15 Hoa Hao, 15 Roman Catholics, 5 Buddhists, and 5 representatives of the ethnic minorities. (Those members lised for their professional affiliations also belonged to one or the other of the Big Five, hence the total account of 140.) Buu Loc replaced last-minute absentees with his friends, among them Doctor Pham Huu Chuong, a Northern extremist who was to prove the guiding spirit of the virulent anti-French speeches made. The first order of business was the creation of a presidium of nine, with Tran Trong Kim (who had been Prime Minister in the Bao Dai Government during the Japa-

nese occupation) as president and Tran Van An (the old-time, pro-French Dong Minh Hoi politician) as secretary general. Three subcommittees were to study the problems involved in the upcoming negotiations with the French for independence, to present a report on the eventual participation of Vietnam in the French Union, and to recommend a slate of delegates who would participate in these negotiations. The Congress was quickly to become inflamed by Doctor Chuong and his friends, and "under the influence of a group of energetic Tongkingese who were acquainted with Vietminh propaganda methods," was to throw "discretion to the winds" and unanimously to approve, "under the stress of intense feeling, a motion in favour of the 'total independence' of Vietnam" (Lancaster, *op. cit.*, p. 278). With Tran Trong Kim in the president's chair, the congress was to state that "the French Union as constructed under the French Constitution of 1946 was contrary to the principle of national sovereignty" (see Isoart, *op. cit.*, p. 388), and even after the language of the resolution was modified the motion still stipulated that no treaties should result from the forthcoming negotiations without the approval of the National Assembly, and that no "discussions, propositions, or decisions concerning Viet-Nam should take place, or be taken in international conferences, without the agreement of the national government" (as reported in the Press and Information Service of the High Command of Vietnam, *Bulletin*, November 1, 1953, pp. 12–13, and quoted by Lancaster *op. cit.*, p. 278, n. 25; see also Dabezies, *op. cit.*, pp. 200–202).

102. For the complete text in English of the congress resolution of October 17, see Cole (ed.), *op. cit.*, pp. 168–70; see also *ibid.*, p. 170, for Bao Dai's message of thanks to the delegates, in which he gracefully bowed to demands he could not reject. Before returning to Paris, Buu Loc handed Bao Dai this request, which was signed by delegates of the sects, Dai Viet, the bishops of Bac Ninh, Hanoi, and Phat Diem (cf. Dabezies, *op. cit.*, p. 202). As always, the sect leaders were ready to desert all others if Bao Dai would be willing to uphold their privileges.

103. O'Ballance, *op. cit.*, p. 184. The reader interested in further details on Operation Lorraine is referred to O'Ballance (pp. 179–84), and for even more details, in particular about the Chan Muong ambush, to Fall, *Street Without Joy*, pp. 58–103, and maps.

104. O'Ballance, *op. cit.*, p. 184.

105. See Chapter V, notes 69 and 71, on ethnic minorities in Tongking and their political leanings. Vietminh policy toward these minorities was a break with the traditional Vietnamese attitude of superiority and governmental neglect. Its propaganda was therefore also more effective than the belated French effort at gaining support among these people. Chesneaux cites the famous eight Vietminh orders on policy for minorities as: (1) protection of life and property of the people; (2) guarantee to everyone that he will freely be able to continue his activities; (3) distribution to poor peasants of the goods of traitors and *colons;* (4) protection of churches, schools, and hospitals; (5) rewards to auxiliaries of the popular army; (6) main-

tenance of security and order; (7) appeal to the peasants to organize themselves; (8) protection of the life and goods of foreign residents (*op. cit.*, p. 285, n. 1).

106. Navarre was serving as Chief of Staff to Marshal Juin, Commander in Chief of the Land Forces of Western Europe, when he was appointed to Indochina. During World War II, Navarre had headed the German section of Military Intelligence and after the French surrender had gone to Algiers with General Weygand, where he was in charge of military intelligence and counterespionage in French North Africa. Recalled to France in 1942, he joined the Resistance and took over the coordination of military espionage throughout the country. After the Allied landings he emerged from hiding and assumed command of an armored regiment of the French First Army, to take part in the occupation of Germany (see Lancaster, *op. cit.*, p. 263, n. 39). Lancaster describes Navarre as an officer "who was virtually unknown to the rank and file of the French army, while his somewhat colourless personality and natural reserve seemed unlikely to appeal either to the imagination or to the affections of the hard-bitten members of an Expeditionary Corps engaged in a desperate struggle in a distant and confused theatre of war." Lacouture and Devillers mention that Navarre was fifty-five years old when he was given his Indochina assignment and that he was considered one of the most brilliant strategists of the French Army (*op. cit.*, p. 37). Warner, speaking of Navarre's appointment, said: "Since the opium-smoking Salan and General de Linares, his Tongking commander, were scarcely on speaking terms, any change at this time seemed a change for the better" (*op. cit.*, p. 57).

107. Navarre also submitted his ideas to Washington, where he sought increased military aid, and where the military at least were very critical of French military performance in Indochina, but where the political leadership, particularly Secretary of State Dulles, welcomed and believed in the Navarre plan. The lack of enthusiasm shown Navarre in his own country was largely due to his request for reinforcements from France before December 1, 1953. He was granted eight battalions on July 28, also some naval aid, more planes (to come from the United States), and additional ground personnel. In describing the French Government's reaction to Navarre's proposal, which the general personally submitted to the various committees, Joseph Laniel wrote that Navarre was informed of the government's intention to engage in negotiations leading to a cease-fire as soon as the signing of the armistice in Korea would have rendered conditions favorable to such an attempt (*op. cit.*, p. 17).

108. Fall, who took the title of his *Street Without Joy* from *la rue sans joie*, the name the French soldiers had given that stretch of Road 1, gives a very detailed account of Operation Camargue (Camargue being the swampy coastal plain west of Marseilles, Fall explains) on pp. 141–70, and points out the reasons for its failure. Telling of the Vietnamese Government administrators who went into the so-called pacified villages around the street without joy, Fall describes a conversation held by two French officers

which accurately reflects the difficulties the nationalists as well as the French encountered. " 'Funny,' said Major Derrieu from the 6th Spahis, watching some of the new administrators in the village of Dong-Que, 'they just never seem to succeed in striking the right note with the population. Either they come in and try to apologize for the mess we've just made with our planes and tanks; or they swagger and threaten the farmers as if they were enemy nationals which—let's face it—they are in many cases.' 'That may be so,' said young Lieutenant Dujardin, standing on the shady side of his M-24, 'but I wouldn't care to be in his shoes tonight, when we pull out. He's going to stay right here in the house which the Commie commander still occupied yesterday, all by himself with the other four guys of his administrative team, with the nearest post three hundred yards away. Hell, I'll bet he won't even sleep here but sleep in the post anyway.' 'He probably will, and he'll immediately lose face with the population and become useless.' 'And if he doesn't, he'll probably be dead by tomorrow, and just as useless. In any case, there goes the whole psychological effect of the operation and we can start the whole thing all over again three months from now. What a hopeless mess' " (*ibid.*, p. 167).

109. Evacuation of Lai Chau was a blow to the French-Indochinese guerrillas operating in the northern Thai country. The GCMA—Groupement de Commandos Mixtes Aeroportes—as these commando groups were initially called (they were given the official designation of GMI—Groupement Mixte d'Intervention—in December, 1953), had been in operation since late 1951, but had "languished for lack of official, high-level enthusiasm" (O'Ballance, *op. cit.*, p. 201). Navarre had decided to give them some support, and in 1953 there were about 15,000 GCMA operating behind Giap's lines. "If General Navarre had stepped up this antiguerrilla movement," O'Ballance wrote, "his position might have been considerably improved" (*ibid.*, p. 202). He also observed: "The French commanders persistently ignored and neglected the one form of counteractivity that might have made all the difference. This was antiguerrilla warfare, which, even when practised on an extremely timid and limited scale, had caused Giap endless trouble and anxiety. At one time, for example, he had as many as ten of his regular battalions deployed to deal with French antiguerrilla activities in the Thai districts. If this effort had been increased tenfold . . . every single one of Giap's regular main force would have been fully occupied in coping with this counteractivity. . . . But regular senior French officers regarded antiguerrilla warfare activities disdainfully and could not bring themselves to enthuse or wholeheartedly support them. The one wide chink in the Viet Minh armour was not pierced" (*ibid.*, pp. 252–53). Fall, with whom O'Ballance agrees on the serious problem the antiguerrillas presented for Giap, tells that General de Gaulle rejected a junior officer's attempt to speak to him about revolutionary warfare, as guerrilla warfare was then known, with the "pithy" remark: "I know of two types of warfare: mobile warfare and positional warfare. I have never heard of revolutionary warfare" (*Street Without Joy*, p. 352). Fall also writes that by April, 1954, at least ten Vietminh

regular battalions were engaged in hunting down commando groups behind their own lines, i.e., doing exactly the same thing the French had been forced to do for so many years—guarding depots and communication lines (*ibid.*, p. 269), and that during the battle for Dien Bien Phu, the GCMA "interdicted the most direct route between Lai-Chau and Dien Bien Phu throughout the duration of the siege" (*ibid.*, p. 271). Critics of antiguerrilla activities in Vietnam pointed out, however, that the GCMA never fully succeeded in cutting Vietminh communications and supply lines. The anti-guerrillas were virtually sacrificed with the cease-fire of July, 1954. Although "frantic efforts were made by the French to broadcast messages to all the groups operating behind Communist lines . . . for many, the broadcasts came too late, or the T'ai or Meo could not reconcile themselves to leave their families exposed to the Communist reprisals which now were sure to come. And the Frenchmen who were with them and who could not possibly make their way back across hundreds of miles of enemy territory, stayed with them, to fight with the tribesmen to the end" (*ibid.*, pp. 272–73). Fall added: "One by one, as the last commandos ran out of ammunition, as the last still operating radio sets fell silent, the remnants of the G.C.M.A. died in the hills of North Viet-Nam. There was no 'U-2' affair, no fuss: France did not claim the men, and the Communists were content to settle the matter by themselves." The last radio message picked up from somewhere in North Vietnam nearly two years after the fighting had officially stopped, said: "You sons-of-bitches, help us! Help us! Parachute us at least some ammunition, so that we can die fighting instead of being slaughtered like animals" (*ibid.*, p. 273). On the destruction by the Vietminh of the Thai partisans, see also Lancaster, *op. cit.*, p. 359, n. 3.

110. Phan Quang Dan, *op. cit.*, p. 25.

111. Eugène Thomas, French Socialist leader, in *Le Populaire*, April 6–7, 1947. Wrote Denis Warner: "Napalm and artillery became French prophylactics. They used them 'just in case.' Through the mountains and plains of Indo-China villages became funeral pyres. . . . Vast mopping-up campaigns killed hundreds of men, women, and children. . . . They smashed down the villages that lay in their path. . . . When there was resistance the planes came in with bombs and napalm" (*op. cit.*, pp. 46, 51). Napalm, Warner went on to explain, "is a fireball, a furnace that scatters its sticky and lethal fire over a wide area before mercifully blanketing itself in a cloud of black smoke. One does not expect to find friends in villages that have been hit by it. The French found no friends here" (*ibid.*, p. 52). As early as 1946, a young Frenchman had written letters to his parents giving similar impressions. He was Henri Martin, a French sailor who, upon his return to France, distributed antiwar pamphlets among troops embarking for battle duty in Vietnam. He was subsequently arrested, tried, and sentenced to five years imprisonment in 1950, after being accused of Communist sympathies and propaganda. In one of his letters, dated May 18, 1946, he wrote: "In Indochina, the French Army acts the same way as the *boches* did at home. I am completely disgusted by this. Why do our planes machine-gun defense-

less fishermen every day? Why do our soldiers rob, burn, and kill? To civilize?" (See *L'affaire Henri Martin*, with a commentary by Jean Paul Sartre, and contributions by various writers, published in 1953 by Librairie Gallimard, Paris.) See also René Riesen, *Jungle Mission* (New York, 1957), and Colonel Jean Leroy, *Un Homme dans la rizière* (Paris, 1955), Preface by Graham Greene.

112. Lancaster describes an incident that took place in Dalat, where the "overwrought" deputy chief of the French security service "had shot out of hand, notwithstanding that Bao Dai himself was then in residence, fourteen men and six women whom he had seized at random, in reprisal for the murder of the French police commissioner by suspected Viet Minh agents" (*op. cit.*, pp. 234–35).

X. The End of French Indochina
(pp. 797–844)

1. Quoted by Ellen Hammer, *The Struggle for Indochina*, p. 297, from *Chroniques d'Outre-Mer*, December 18, 1952. Bernard Fall (*The Two Viet-Nams*, p. 223) also says that the cost was "twice as much as America had pumped into the French economy during this period, and ten times the value of all French investments in Indochina." Le Thanh Khoi (*Le Viet-Nam: Histoire et civilisation*, p. 483, n. 130) gives the cost to France as 3 trillion francs, of which 2.385 came from the French budget and the rest from American aid. Paul Isoart, *Le phénomène national vietnamien*, p. 382, speaks of a total of 1.28 trillion by January 1, 1953. (For additional figures, contradictory because of further considerations, see n. 3, below.)

2. See Isoart, *op. cit.*, p. 382. Isoart also mentions that each year, half the graduating class of St. Cyr died in Indochina. Of the 92,000 Expeditionary Corps members killed, he says, 1,900 were officers and 6,300 noncoms. Edgar O'Ballance, whose figures agree with those indicated for 1945 to July, 1954, in the U.S. Information Service's fact-finding pamphlet *France: Facts and Figures* issued in March, 1955, compares the total enlistment in the Corps, which, he writes, averaged about 150,000 men, with the high rate of casualties, of which the "killed and missing amounted to 29,685 Frenchmen, 11,620 legionnaires, 15,229 North Africans and 26,686 locally enlisted Indochinese. The estimates for wounded are about three times these figures" (*The Indo-China War 1945–1954: A Study in Guerrilla Warfare*, p. 249).

3. A few figures should be quoted here, however, if for no other reason than to demonstrate the complexity of the various forms of U.S. aid. For example, Donald Lancaster (*The Emancipation of French Indochina*, pp. 416–17) cites *The New York Times* of November 3, 1950, to indicate that not only was military and economic aid extended to the French as a means of settling the French deficit of payments with the dollar area, but that military aid was initially intended to be restricted to "items that were either not manufactured or else were not readily available in France." Lancaster illus-

trates the scale of these payments by quoting from *Le Monde*, June 2, 1950, for the announcement that "American dollar aid to the French forces in Indochina would amount, for the fiscal year ending June 1951, to the comparatively modest sum of 23.5 million." Five months later, the United States decided to contribute $300–$400 million to the French war effort, "representing a two-year programme of aid to French and French Union Forces." This allocation, reported in *The New York Times* of November 25, 1950, which, in June, 1952, had been estimated as representing 33 per cent of the total French expenditure, was "further increased during the latter half of the year [1952] to cover some 40 per cent of the total cost of the war, amounting for 1952 to 569 milliard [billion] francs." In 1953, Laniel announced additional dollar grants and supplies that were to raise the American contribution to 70 per cent of the war cost. And shortly before the Geneva conference, Lancaster concludes, "the American Government undertook to underwrite the entire cost of the war, allocating $1,175 million for that purpose." Allan B. Cole (ed.), *Conflict in Indo-China and International Repercussions: A Documentary History* (p. 260), gives a detailed breakdown of the various forms of technical and military aid programs, as well as economic aid extended directly to the State of Vietnam (the comparatively paltry sum of $96 million for the four-year period 1950–54), and for this four-year period comes up with a total of over $4 billion for the struggle in Indochina alone. (During the same period, France received other aid and loans totaling almost $10 billion.) As sources for his information, Cole cites in part the U.S. Information bulletin mentioned in the preceding note, as well as Philippe Devillers, *Histoire du Viet-Nam de 1940 à 1952*, p. 472, n. 13; Devillers gives his own sources of information. These figures are in sharp contrast with those given by Bernard B. Fall in *Street Without Joy: Insurgency in Indochina* (p. 308 n.), in which he speaks of "actual U.S. expenditures in Indochina" as an "approximate total of $954 million by July, 1954." During the 1946–54 period, Fall adds, "the French had spent close to $11 billion of their own funds for the prosecution of the war." I wish to emphasize once again that most sources give conflicting figures about the cost of the Indochina War, as well as about the size of the American contribution, but Fall alone says that the United States by 1954 had contributed less than $1 billion to the French effort. Fall overlooks all sorts of aid; e.g., $500 million alone of ECA and Mutual Security aid from April, 1948, to June, 1953, were officially reported as expended in Indochina. The latest American estimate of French-American expenditures in Indochina is given by Anthony T. Bouscaren, *The Last of the Mandarins: Diem of Vietnam* (Pittsburgh, Pa., 1965), p. 32, who says that the French spent $7 billion and "more than $4 billion in American aid." (On U.S. aid to the French for the Indochina War, see also "Indochina Salvage Job," in *Business Week*, February 26, 1955.)

4. Jean Lacouture and Philippe Devillers, *La fin d'une guerre: Indochine 1954*, p. 42. A French public-opinion survey conducted by the periodical *Sondage* showed that of the persons questioned, 65 per cent favored an end

to the war, 19 per cent were for outright withdrawal, 46 per cent for negotiations to end the war ("La guerre d'Indochine," *Sondage*, Nos. 3 and 5,
1953).

5. Isoart, *op. cit.*, p. 383.

6. *Ibid.*, p. 384.

7. Major debates on Indochina were held in March, 1947, and 1949; November, 1950; December, 1951; October, 1953; and March, 1954. See the
respective issues of *Journal Officiel, Débats Parlementaires, Assemblée
Nationale*. English extracts from some of these debates may be found in
Cole (ed.), *op. cit.*, pp. 66–68 (for 1949), pp. 92–94 (for 1951), and pp.
137–38 (for 1953). As opposition to the war gained in France, the majorities in the Chamber in favor of continuing the war grew smaller. For example, in October, 1950, they stood at 349 to 218; in October, 1953, at 315 to
257; in May, 1954, at 289 to 287; and in June, 1954, the forces in favor no
longer commanded a majority—the vote was 293 to 306.

8. Ho Chi Minh had expressed a similar idea to an American journalist,
Sol Sanders, in December, 1949.

9. See Lacouture and Devillers, *op. cit.*, p. 30, n. 3; also *Débats Parlementaires, Assemblée Nationale*, 1950, pp. 7002–7003. "You will never succeed
in organizing the national defenses in Europe if you continue to send all
your cadres to the East," Mendès-France insisted, "to sacrifice every year,
without any result, the equivalent of the number of officers leaving St. Cyr
in a year and to spend annually 500 billion francs, representing an additional
500 billion of monetary inflation, which will bring in its train want, rising
prices, and further social unrest which will not fail to be exploited by Communist propaganda. . . . By an incredible paradox, we have accorded priority to Asia at the very time when, in opposition to MacArthur's policy, in
opposition to the policy of the old, isolationist Americans, the 'Europeans'
from Churchill to Pleven last year, are upholding the thesis of the priority
of Europe in the United States" (quoted by Lancaster, *op. cit.*, p. 240, from
L'année politique, 1951, p. 401). Commented Victor Bator: "He [Mendès-
France] proffered two alternative solutions of the Indochina crisis, both
equally unpleasant. The first would be, to undertake an all-out fight with no
quarter given and with maximum effort expended. . . . The other solution
would be a political settlement granting complete independence to Indochina, with recognition of Ho Chi Minh as its head" (*Viet-Nam: A Diplomatic Tragedy* [Dobbs Ferry, N.Y., 1965], p. 11).

10. Of the latter occurrences, the "Henri Martin Affair" was the most
famous (see Chapter IX, 111.)

11. Lacouture and Devillers, *op. cit.*, p. 30.

12. Letourneau became Minister of the Associated States of Indochina in
July, 1950. He was also made High Commissioner of Indochina on April 1,
1952, as successor to de Lattre. He continued in both positions until April
22, 1953, when the government headed by René Mayer appointed another
MRP member, Joannes Dupraz, as Letourneau's deputy in Paris. In Indochina, Letourneau was replaced by Maurice Dejean, a diplomat.

13. The Vietminh delegate whom Letourneau met was Nguyen Van Chi, official representative of the Vietminh at Paris. The meeting at Rangoon was between Raphael-Leyques, a young Radical deputy and Buu Hoi, a member of the royal family with contacts to the Vietminh, who talked to the Vietminh representative at Rangoon. This meeting was also authorized by Foreign Minister Pinay.

14. The terrible fate of Mobile Group 100 makes one of the most impressive chapters in Bernard Fall's *Street Without Joy* (Chapter IX, "End of a Task Force," pp. 182–246).

15. Dien Bien Phu was a large village in the middle of a prosperous opium-growing district. Set in a flat, heart-shaped, paddy-field basin, measuring about 12 miles in length (north to south) and about 8 miles across, it was fringed by low but rather steep, heavily wooded hills. Although flat, this basin, or small plain, did contain a few scattered small hillocks and tiny hamlets as well as a small river that flowed past Dien Bien Phu north to south. Dien Bien Phu had little strategic significance in itself, but it was only 10 miles from the Laos border and at the junction of three routes: the northern route to China, the northeastern route to Tuam Giao, and the southern route to Laos (as described by O'Ballance, *op. cit.*, p. 213).

16. Overoptimism about their chances of victory had been a constant feature of French reporting, and this optimism had been shared by U.S. official spokesmen up to the fall of Dien Bien Phu. One of the last to indulge in this was the then head of the Foreign Aid Administration, Harold Stassen, who, after a visit to Indochina, stated on March 5, 1954: "I returned from the Far East with the strong conviction that the forces of freedom are growing stronger and that the Communist position is weakening" (as reported in *The New York Times*, March 6, 1954). Stassen added this was true both in a political and military sense. As late as February 9, 1954, Secretary of Defense Charles Wilson said that the French could still win the war.

17. It is believed, writes O'Ballance (*op. cit.*, p. 209), that an attack on Dien Bien Phu was planned for the night of January 25–26, when General Navarre was preoccupied with Operation Atlante, and when units of the mobile reserve had been wastefully dispersed, but it is thought that it was postponed on the advice of a Sino-Soviet military mission that was at the time in northern Tongking inspecting Vietminh positions and forces. This mission seems to have been of the opinion that the Vietminh main force would not be able successfully to assault the Dien Bien Phu entrenched camp unless it had considerably greater numbers of more powerful artillery pieces. Lancaster corroborates O'Ballance's assertion by quoting from Navarre's book (O'Ballance, *op. cit.*, p. 210 n.; Lancaster, *op. cit.*, p. 288, n. 50).

18. The leading participants in this debate were General Navarre himself, in his book *Agonie de l'Indochine (1953–1954)*; Joseph Laniel (Premier until June, 1954) in his book *Le drame indochinois: De Dien Bien Phu au pari de Génève*; General Georges Catroux, *Deux actes du drame indochinois—Hanoi: Juin 1940; Dien Bien Phu: Mars–Mai 1954* (Catroux wrote the

report of an inquiry into the Dien Bien Phu decision, which was highly critical of Navarre. Navarre replied in speeches and newspaper articles). Other books are: Lacouture and Devillers, *op. cit.;* General Paul Ely, *L'Indochine dans la tourmente* (Paris, 1964). A brief discussion of responsibility for Dien Bien Phu is given in Fall's *Street Without Joy,* Chapter XII, "Why Dien Bien Phu?" On the events leading up to the battle, and the battle itself, the chief work so far is Jules Roy, *The Battle of Dien Bien Phu.* For another criticism of Navarre's decision to defend Dien Bien Phu, see Lancaster, *op. cit.,* pp. 284–85, n. 43, in which he writes that Navarre was to claim that the establishment of a base at Dien Bien Phu, which had been recommended by his predecessor Salan and by General Cogny, the General Commanding in North Vietnam, was essential to the defense of North Laos. Lancaster adds: "But in spite of Navarre's insistence on the imperious necessity that had led him to decide to defend this remote and inaccessible plateau, insufficient consideration appears to have been given to the fact that the 187 miles separating Dien Bien Phu from Hanoi would put the camp outside the range of most of the available fighter aircraft and place an undue strain on the transport planes which would be required to supply the garrison. Moreover the inability of the garrison to operate outside the defence perimeter and thereby to impede the passage of Viet Minh troops and supplies—an inability which had been demonstrated at Hoa Binh, and again at Na Sam—was to immobolize most of the crack French units during the impending Vietminh offensive." For additional literature on Dien Bien Phu, see Camille Rougeron, "Premières reflexions sur Dien Bien Phu," which appeared in *Revue de Défense Nationale,* July, 1954; Jean Renald, *L'enfer de Dien Bien Phu* (Paris, 1955); Erwan Bergot, *2ème classe à Dien Bien Phu* (Paris, 1964); Vo Nguyen Giap, *Dien Bien Phu* (Hanoi, 1964 edition) (Giap's book discusses the military situation in the summer of 1953, the Navarre plan, the winter, 1953, and spring, 1954, strategic planning and campaigns, and the battle of Dien Bien Phu itself, of course); Fall, *Viet-Nam Witness 1953–66* (New York, 1966).

19. The reason for this decision became most urgent when Laos signed a mutual-defense treaty with France on October 28, 1953, thereby confirming its membership in the French Union. "Since France hoped to sign similar treaties with the neighboring states of Viet-Nam and Cambodia, the French felt that an abandonment of northern Laos would adversely influence such negotiations. Navarre felt in addition that to let the Viet-Minh arrive 'in force on the Mekong would be equivalent to opening to it the door to central and southern Indochina'" (Fall, *Street Without Joy,* p. 309). Lacouture and Devillers mention that Navarre considered himself under the moral obligation to defend Laos when Giap suddenly set his 316th Division and other troops into movement toward northern Laos. Operation Castor, the airborne landing at Dien Bien Phu, was to prevent a further Vietminh advance (*op. cit.,* p. 44).

20. Among the people who inspected Dien Bien Phu were War Minister Pleven, General Ely, and the chief of the U.S. Military Advisory Group,

General John O'Daniel. Dien Bien Phu "apparently had been found a sound position" (Fall, *Street Without Joy*, p. 312). Pleven's inspection tour to Vietnam (his first trip to Southeast Asia) is vividly described by Lacouture and Devillers (*op. cit.*, pp. 59–70). Pleven arrived in Saigon on February 9. In a conference with the military chiefs held the same day, he was told that the importance of the Vietminh troops which were ringing Dien Bien Phu was as yet unknown, but that the enemy seemed to shy away from attacking a position in which the French appeared to be solidly entrenched. Dien Bien Phu, Navarre added, had until then retarded the invasion of Laos which otherwise might have taken place two months earlier. General Fay, Chief of Staff of the Air Force (who at the time was also on an inspection tour, together with General Blanc, Chief of Staff of the Army, and the Secretary of War, M. de Chevigné) raised the question whether Dien Bien Phu did not present the risk of being unusable after three weeks of rain. "This weakness," replied General Navarre, "has never been pointed out to me" (*ibid.*, p. 61). On February 19, Pleven went to Dien Bien Phu with Chevigné and Ely. "He found the garrison of the entrenched camp in a state of extraordinary confidence. Everyone, from Colonel de Castries down to the last gunner, wished for a Vietminh attack and seemed to fear only one thing—that the enemy might refuse to do so. The optimism, the certainty of the ability to 'break the Viet battle strength,' struck all the visitors; however, the view of the surrounding hills that dominated the position led them to somber reflections" (*ibid.*). On his return to Paris, Pleven, reporting on the garrison's impatient wait for the attack, remarked: "As for me, I do not wish for it." Evacuation of Dien Bien Phu, Lacouture and Devillers add at this point, had long since become impossible (*ibid.*, p. 63, n. 2). Lancaster writes that General Ely upon his return to France submitted a report in which he described Dien Bien Phu as an "extremely strong position, which could only be attacked by a very powerful force." Moreover, Lancaster reports, even in the event of such an attack, "Ely considered that the advantage would probably lie with the defenders" (*op. cit.*, p. 294).

21. "In Hanoi, General Cogny privately told newspapermen that the battle was a crime against humanity," wrote Denis Warner (*The Last Confucian*, p. 62). What he had wanted, according to Warner was "a diversionary attack into the Viet Minh main supply route or a breakout by the garrison before it was too late. Navarre did not agree" (*ibid.*, p. 63).

22. "These strong-points, which had been named after ladies of whose company the garrison were deprived," wrote Lancaster (*op. cit.*, p. 294), were Anne-Marie, 2 miles to the northwest, Gabrielle and Béatrice, 2 and 1.5 miles, respectively, to the northwest of the main position near the village and airstrip, where the French had a number of connected separate strong points (Huguette, Dominique, Claudine, Lili, Junon, and Eliane). Isolated 4 miles to the south, near the end of the 12-mile-long valley was position Isabelle.

23. According to Lancaster, it was the intention of Molotov to "offer the good offices of his government to arrange an armistice in Indochina in ex-

change for a French undertaking to abandon EDC [European Defense Community]" (*op. cit.*, p. 290). Therefore, when the foreign ministers of the four powers met in Berlin on January 25, 1954, "the Soviet desire to sabotage, and the American intention to defend EDC" assured the French delegation, headed by Bidault, a flattering reception. When it became evident that no agreement on European issues could be reached with the U.S.S.R., the subject of a conference dealing with Korea and Indochina was given priority. On February 18, it was finally proposed that the conference on the Far East be held at Geneva in April. Lancaster further reports (*ibid.*, p. 292) that American support was reluctantly given, and on his return to Washington, Dulles declared in a broadcast that he would not agree to meet the Chinese Communists at the Geneva conference "unless it was expressly agreed and put in writing that no United States recognition would be involved." For further details on the Berlin negotiations, see Anthony Eden, *Full Circle*, which sets forth the British point of view vis-à-vis the American; and Lacouture and Devillers, *op. cit.*, pp. 52–58.

24. Department of State *Bulletin*, XXII, No. 554 (February 13, 1950), 244.

25. *Ibid.*, No. 571 (June 12, 1950), 977–78. The first military aid delivery was made on June 20, 1950.

26. *Ibid.*, XXIII, No. 574 (July 3, 1950), 5.

27. The four-hundredth American ship unloaded its cargo in Saigon in January, 1954. It is a mistake, however, to assume that the Vietnamese nationalists were happy about the military aid France was receiving from the United States. On the contrary. In their eyes the war remained what it had always been: a fight for national liberation. Even the stoutest anti-Communists were therefore opposed to what was obviously a strengthening of the French position. But it came as a surprise to many Americans when a violent anti-American demonstration broke out in Saigon on March 19, 1950, during a visit by U.S. warships. The French tried to present the demonstration as Vietminh-inspired, but a number of well-known anti-Communist Vietnamese were arrested for participating; this resulted in a statement by many politically moderate Vietnamese protesting these arrests and demanding independence for Vietnam along the lines of India. Subsequently, when the representative of the ECA (Economic Cooperation Administration) in Saigon expressed dissatisfaction in January, 1951, with the way in which American economic aid was being administered by the Vietnamese regime, the Vietnamese countered with the argument that what appeared to be incompetence on the part of the Vietnamese officials was nothing but the result of the refusal of the elite to collaborate with the French by serving in the Bao Dai regime.

28. Department of State *Bulletin*, XXIX, No. 735 (July 27, 1953), 100. This comparison with the British Commonwealth was, of course, preposterous, as Dulles himself must have known. At a press conference on July 14, Dulles had also stated that the "solemn declaration" of the French Government of July 3 was an "unequivocal offer of full independence and sovereignty to the states of Indochina." John Mecklin had this comment:

"American policy during that period was little more than a blank-check support for the French" (*Mission in Torment*, p. 8).

29. Department of State *Bulletin*, No. 551 (January 23, 1950), 111–18; text of a speech given by Dean Acheson before the National Press Club on January 12, 1950.

30. Isoart, *op. cit.*, p. 396. De Lattre went so far as to say: "We have given our shirts, and now we are giving our skin." Which was true as far as the fighting men were concerned, but which was a hollow boast in view of the many Frenchmen who profited from the war and for this reason alone insisted that it continue.

31. As early as April, 1950, Walter Lippmann, the elder statesman of American political commentators, wrote in the *New York Herald Tribune:* "Everyone knows that the great majority of the Indochinese are furiously opposed to the continuation of French control and will only unite behind a government when they are confident that Indochina has received the same independence as India, the Philippines, Indonesia, Pakistan and Ceylon. If we do not want to compromise our reputation in Asia, we cannot support this colonial war." On May 20 of the same year, the *Herald Tribune* reprinted an article from the *St. Louis Post-Dispatch* also speaking out against American support of European colonialism in East Asia, predicting that such a policy was doomed to failure. Somewhat later, Philip Talbot, correspondent of the *Chicago Daily News*, wrote: "There is only one way out; the French must do what Great Britain has done—fully and freely renounce a position which can only be held temporarily with excessive forces and which, in the end, cannot be held at all." After a trip to Southeast Asia, the then Senator from Massachusetts, John F. Kennedy, gave one of the best analyses of the Indochinese situation in a speech before the U.S. Senate on June 30, 1953. As Doctor Phan Quang Dan summarizes it in his unpublished manuscript, *The War in Indochina,* Kennedy said that "genuine independence as we understand it is lacking in Indochina," and "local government is circumscribed in its functions, that the government of Vietnam, the state which is of the greatest importance in this area, lacks popular support, that the degree of military, civil, political and economic control maintained by the French goes well beyond what is necessary to fight a war" (pp. 44, 45). General Van Fleet, in an article in *Reader's Digest* of February, 1954, wrote: "Indochina is tottering, in spite of American aid of billions of dollars which seems to have been largely squandered in costly air drops. I can tell Paris, and even Washington, that this war never will be won with French troops—or American." Van Fleet felt that only Vietnamese troops had a chance of winning because they would be "men who are sure they are fighting for their own freedom, and not for faraway France." Doctor Dan also gives excerpts from the *Christian Science Monitor*, which, in an editorial on July 29, 1953, stated: "What can the United States do besides sending more arms to the French? It can recognize that unless American aid is used to promote Indochinese independence rather than to defend French prerogatives, it might as well be stopped tomorrow." *The New York Times* took the same stand. In

an editorial dated February 19, 1954, the paper wrote that French policy ought to give "the Vietnamese the maximum reason for feeling that they are fighting for the liberty of their own country." Another highly respected American to give a critical appraisal of French conduct in Vietnam was Justice William O. Douglas, who stated opinions similar to those voiced above in an interview printed in *Reader's Digest* of April, 1953, and in his book, *North of Malaya* (New York, 1953), in a chapter on Indochina.

32. Dean Acheson, in a speech before the Commonwealth Club in San Francisco, March, 1950.

33. Navarre, *op. cit.*, pp. 27-28. Speaking of his excellent personal relationship with General O'Daniel, head of the American military mission in Saigon, Navarre wrote: "Abusing the right of investigation his control functions over the use of the credits and material delivered by the United States gave him, he [O'Daniel] sought to impose his views in all fields including the operational—a consequence of a blunder in our diplomacy. American pressure soon took on a delaying character, the more displeasing as it coincided with our military difficulties. After the fall of Dien Bien Phu, it became evident that the United States, through the intermediation of General O'Daniel, was determined to make its concepts win out in direct ratio to the rise in aid which we were forced to ask for. If we did not react, our position would more and more become that of mere 'mercenaries.' I felt called upon to inform Paris that more and more I had the impression that the true boss in Indochina was the one of the American mission and that I, for one, was unwilling to give in to it. In reply I was advised to remain on 'personally' good footing with him" (*ibid.*, pp. 137-38).

34. Phan Quang Dan, *The War in Indochina*, p. 34.

35. Several Americans, among them Robert Blum and Edmund Gullion in Vietnam, and Milton Sacks in the State Department in Washington, were unable to hold their positions in the face of French criticism of their expressions of sympathy with anti-Communist Vietnamese nationalism. The stanchly pro-French attitude of U.S. Ambassador Donald Heath never conflicted with Washington policy, and he rather than Graham Greene's "Quiet American" exemplified traditional U.S. policy toward the French and the Indochinese nationalists.

36. Comparing Ho's reply with a bomb-shell, Lacouture and Devillers give these excerpts from the Vietminh leader's declaration: "If the French Government, after having absorbed the lessons of these war years, desires to conclude an armistice and resolve the question of Vietnam by negotiations, the people and the government of the Democratic Republic of Vietnam (R.D.V.N.) are ready to examine the French proposals. . . . The basis for an armistice is that the French Government really respects Vietnam's independence. . . . The negotiation of an armistice concerns essentially the government of France and that of Vietnam" (*op. cit.*, p. 45, n. 24).

37. See n. 23, above. It is also more than likely that the Russians knew of Pleven's and Laniel's desire to extend peace feelers to Ho Chi Minh. Defense Minister Pleven, acting in official agreement with Premier Laniel, asked the

Socialist Deputy Alain Savary to undertake such a mission. But the still intransigent Foreign Minister Bidault opposed this move, telling Savary at the beginning of March, after a delay of three months, that "Ho Chi Minh is about to capitulate; we are going to beat him." By the time Laniel and Pleven prevailed upon Bidault to change his mind, the beginning of the end had already begun at Dien Bien Phu and Savary's voyage came to an end in Moscow in April (cf. Lacouture and Devillers, *op. cit.*, p. 47, n. 2). In December, 1953, at about the time that Pleven pressed for Savary's mission, Laniel, at the suggestion of Pleven and informing only the President of France, sent Rear Admiral Cabanier on a secret mission to Saigon to inquire of Navarre whether he did not think the time opportune for cease-fire negotiations with the Vietminh. According to Laniel, "General Navarre answered in the negative, assuring with the same optimism that the situation would be better still in spring and that it would be more advisable to wait until then" (*op. cit.*, p. 41)

38. "Chinese Communist support for this Soviet proposal was probably obtained before Ho Chi Minh's replies to the *Expressen* questionnaire had been forwarded in November of the previous year through the channel of the Viet Minh diplomatic mission in Peking. Evidence is available that this support was based on recognition that further intervention in the internal affairs of neighbouring countries should be postponed until the Communist regime in China had been consolidated (speech by Chen Yun, *NCNA*, March 5, 1954). Moreover, the Peking Government must have been aware that the increase in American aid to French Union forces in Indochina threatened to involve China in hostilities on behalf of the Viet Minh in a distant area where her forces would be handicapped by dependence on extended and inadequate lines of communication" (Lancaster, *op. cit.*, pp. 290–91, n. 1).

39. Lancaster, *ibid.*, p. 293. Lancaster believes that Communist discipline and a realization of their dependence on Chinese aid for victory brought the Vietminh leaders in line with Moscow and Peking.

40. The movement's support was actually restricted to sect factions and Dai Viet splinter groups. Nhu had with him the Cao Dai General Nguyen Thanh Phuong and the Southern Dai Viet leader Nguyen Ton Hoan—people whom he eliminated from political influence as soon as he achieved power under the Diem regime.

41. On July 3, 1953, soon after assuming power, Joseph Laniel stated: "France deems it necessary to perfect the independence and sovereignty of the Associated States of Indochina in . . . transferring to them the powers she had held in the very interest of those States in view of perilous circumstances of the state of war. The French Government invites the three States to settle with it the questions each of them wishes to discuss in the economic, financial, judicial, military, and political fields." And François Mitterand (a Radical) commented: "We have granted Viet-Nam 'full independence' eighteen times since 1949. Isn't it about time we did it just once, but for good?" (Quoted from Fall, *The Two Viet-Nams*, p. 221.)

42. Lancaster, *op. cit.*, p. 307. Lancaster, in a footnote, adds: "Although the decision to appoint Lai Huu Sang appears to have been made by Prince Buu Loc, Bao Dai approved the Prime Minister's action. His approval may have been based on the calculation that Binh Xuyen control of security in Saigon-Cholon would present certain advantages since the Binh Xuyen 'General', Le Van Vien, who possessed a capacity for friendship and a code of loyalty commonly found among those who prey upon society, was personally attached to Bao Dai. He could be relied upon, therefore, during the critical months ahead, to combat subversive activities. But whatever motive may have prompted Bao Dai's approval, insufficient consideration was given to the inference that would be drawn abroad from an appointment which appeared to offer conclusive proof of the moral bankruptcy of the regime" (*ibid.*, n. 45). Denis Warner asserts that the Binh Xuyen "bought the police concessions in Saigon for forty million piasters" (*op. cit.*, p. 76). In the American press, the Binh Xuyen take-over of the police was reported in the C. L. Sulzberger dispatch of March 14, 1955, in *The New York Times*. The caustic comment of Marjorie Weiner and Wells C. Klein was that the Binh Xuyen "has had the singular opportunity of both operating and policing the rackets of Saigon-Cholon" (in George McTurnan Kahin [ed.], *Government and Politics in Southeast Asia*, p. 399, n. 61).

43. Victor Bator speaks of Eisenhower and Dulles' "anticolonialistic" tenets (*op. cit.*, p. 25) and quotes from Eden to the effect that "Dulles had declared his conviction that American policy in the Middle East as well as in Asia had been badly handicapped by a tendency to support British and French 'colonial' views" (*ibid.*, p. 99; Anthony Eden, *Full Circle*, p. 150). Bator also quotes Sherman Adams' memoirs for existing reliable testimony that, on April 4, 1954, "at a Sunday night meeting in the upstairs study at the White House Eisenhower had agreed with Dulles and Radford on a plan to send American forces to Indochina under certain strict conditions," to which Bator adds parenthetically "that is, coalition with British and French participation, independence to the three Indochinese States" (*op. cit.*, p. 104; Sherman Adams, *First Hand Report* [New York, 1961], p. 122). In the chapter entitled "Dilemma over Indo-China" of his book *Eisenhower: The Inside Story* (New York, 1956), Robert J. Donovan says that in the proposal for united action submitted in early April, 1954, to Churchill, the President specified as one of the conditions for U.S. participation that "France must go beyond her previous efforts in granting unequivocal independence to Vietnam, Laos and Cambodia so that American entry into Indo-China would not have the taint of colonialism" (p. 265).

44. According to Lacouture and Devillers, the formula was found by Anthony Eden. "The English project no longer made the distinction between Big and Small, those who did the inviting and who were invited. It simply listed the interested powers 'almost in alphabetical order' . . . but it maintained the idea of 'favorable perspectives' which was the subordination of the Indochinese conference to the Korean conference. . . . The U.S.S.R. accepted that the conference did not constitute recognition of Peking. The

Western powers, on their side, accepted the problem of restitution of peace in Indochina to be 'equally' examined at the conference which opened on April 26 at Geneva on Korea" (*op. cit.,* p. 58). For a lucid and concise treatment of the Berlin conference, see *ibid.,* pp. 53–58. At this juncture I would like to join Victor Bator, Bernard Fall, and Robert Scigliano in praising Lacouture and Devillers for the important contribution of their *La fin d'une guerre* to the history of contemporary diplomacy. Jean Lacouture, then Editor-in-Chief of the Foreign Department of *Le Monde,* and Philippe Devillers, Professor at the Collège Libre des Sciences Sociales, are highly qualified for what Scigliano, in *South Vietnam: Nation Under Stress* (Boston, 1963), calls "the most detailed account of the closing phase of the Indochina war," and what Bator (*op. cit.,* p. 40) calls an "exceedingly precise, specific, and exhaustive narration."

45. There was a great lack of qualified personnel for the maintenance and operation of the planes already received from the United States. On January 16, 1954, the French Government therefore decided to request 400 specialists —mechanics, etc.—from Washington for the maintenance of the B-26's and C-47's already in Indochina, and ground-maintenance crews for the C-119's and B-26's expected to arrive from the United States. On January 30, Washington announced that it would send 200 mechanics at once, as well as a crew of bombardiers for the requested B-26's. The other planes would be sent when France had the needed personnel (see Lacouture and Devillers, *op. cit.,* p. 51, who mention in this context that "for political reasons, the [French] government failed to request American pilots. Saigon received instructions that under no circumstances were American crews to be used on missions 'concerned with the overflight of operational zones or dissident zones' ").

46. The aircraft carriers were ordered into the Gulf of Tongking on April 19; they were the "Boxer" and the "Philippine Sea," both equipped with atomic weapons—to be used, at least so some U.S. officials believed, in case of open Chinese intervention in Indochina (see John Robinson Beal, *John Foster Dulles* [New York, 1957], p. 207; also, James Shepley, "How Dulles Arrested War," *Life,* January 16, 1956; and Fletcher Knebel, "We Nearly Went to War Three Times Last Year," *Look,* February 8, 1955). About the Ely mission to Washington, cf. Paul Ely, *L'Indochine dans la tourmente,* pp. 59–81; Lacouture and Devillers, *op. cit.,* pp. 73–77; also Laniel, *op. cit.,* pp. 83–84. On Operation Vulture, see also Laniel, *ibid.,* p. 88.

47. At the same time, Dulles called in Henri Bonnet, to expound to the French Ambassador his theory of united action. "In the opinion of the Secretary of State," wrote Lacouture and Devillers, "peace in Indochina, in view of the existing situation, could be negotiated only at the expense of France. Parleys could only lead to an arrangement that more or less dissimulated defeat. To change this situation, it was imperative that the Communists be persuaded that they did not have the slightest chance of gaining total victory despite their actual successes. To this end, a coalition capable

of halting the progress of Communism in Southeast Asia by common and concerted action had to be created without delay" (*op. cit.*, p. 79).

48. Bator, *op. cit.*, p. 45. All of Chapter 3 of Bator's book is devoted to proving this thesis.

49. James Reston, in *The New York Times*, March 31, 1954, disclosed that "according to the official view, while the United States guaranteed Korea against aggression, Southeast Asia was to hold much more importance for the Free World." The text of Dulles' speech is contained in State Department *Bulletin*, XXX, No. 772 (April 12, 1954).

50. Opposition by the military to Operation Vautour or any other American involvement of manpower, especially of ground forces, was most emphatically stated by General Ridgway, the then Army Chief of Staff. For his well-reasoned statements, see "What Ridgway Told Ike—War in Indo-China Would Be Tougher than Korea," in *U.S. News & World Report*, June 25, 1954, pp. 30–33; also, General Matthew B. Ridgway and H. H. Martin, *Soldier: Memoirs of Matthew B. Ridgway* (New York, 1956), pp. 274–78. The following passage from this book proves that Ridgway was adamant in his opposition to entering the Indochina conflict: "We could have fought in Indochina. We could have won, if we had been willing to pay the tremendous cost in men and money that such intervention would have required—a cost that in my opinion would have eventually been as great as, or greater than, that we paid in Korea. In Korea, we had learned that air and naval power alone cannot win a war and that inadequate ground forces cannot win one either. It was incredible to me that we had forgotten that bitter lesson so soon—that we were on the verge of making the same tragic error." This has been quoted recently in the American press in connection with the controversy started by General James M. Gavin (USA, Ret.) with his letter in the February, 1966, issue of *Harper's*, on strategy alternatives for the American forces in Vietnam. According to *The New York Times* of January 17, 1966, "General Gavin recalled that he was the Army's chief of plans and operations in the nineteen-fifties when the United States was considering entering the war against the Vietminh forces of Ho Chi Minh." The *Times* then quotes Gavin: "We were talking about the possibility of sending eight divisions plus 35 engineer battalions and other auxiliary units into the Hanoi delta." And it goes on to say: "He [Gavin] indicated a planned initial commitment of 200,000 men, compared with 190,000 now in Vietnam."

51. Wrote Victor Bator: "This consultation with Congress wiped the slate clean. On April 3, the Radford-Ely project lost the support of President Eisenhower. From that day the reins were again in the hands of Dulles. The direction was from then on not towards the Navarre plan, nor to aid to the British-French project which would pursue settlement and peace through success at Geneva. Whatever interim diplomatic measures might be employed, the ultimate goal of the Dulles diplomacy would be the realization of his victory policy. Thus the answer to the French request based on the Radford-Ely plan had to be NO. Dulles wanted intervention but of a

different kind, a farsighted, comprehensive, long-range operation" (*op. cit.*, p. 50). Bernard Fall describes Congressional reaction and opposition to intervention in *The Two Viet-Nams* (pp. 227–28) along party lines. Although Republican Senator Everett Dirksen, along with Vice-President Nixon, and Senators Knowland and Jenner, did not, in Dirksen's words, "share the anxiety and concern some feel about the danger of sending American troops to Indochina, other than technicians," Fall writes, Senator Alexander Wiley "probably summed up the feelings of the majority of his Republican colleagues when he said: 'Mr. Speaker, if war comes under this Administration, it could well be the end of the Republican Party.'" Then Senator Edwin C. Johnson "summed up the view of most of his party by saying that he was 'against sending American GI's into the mud and muck of Indochina on a blood-letting spree to perpetuate colonialism and white man's exploitation in Asia'" (Fall, *ibid.*, p. 475, n. 5, quoting from the *Congressional Record*, April 6 and 14, 1954, pp. 4402–977, *passim*).

52. Dulles still said so on April 24, while in Paris; but so, that same day, did Navarre (see Lacouture and Devillers, *op. cit.*, p. 88 and n. 4).

53. Navarre, incidentally, also opposed negotiations at that time (see n. 37, above).

54. Ely fully supported the government's view that the Dulles proposal was a threat to China that endangered the chances for a negotiated settlement (see Ely, *op. cit.*, p. 86).

55. The "misunderstanding," the term used by Eisenhower to gloss over strained U.S.–British relations, killed the nine-country meeting. No such misunderstanding by Dulles was actually possible, says Victor Bator, in view of the communiqué issued by the French Government following Dulles' meeting with them after his London visit. The communiqué stated that "no effort should be spared to make the Geneva Conference a success . . . the joint proposed defense arrangement would not follow the pattern of NATO and, in any case, would be profoundly conditioned by the *outcome of the conference* [i.e., the Geneva conference!]" (*op. cit.*, p. 62; quoted from the *Times* of London, April 15, 1954; see also *ibid.*, p. 240, n. 15). Bator goes on to say that it was too late to cancel the meeting altogether, "as it had already been publicized. Thus, Dulles had to convert it into an inconsequential briefing of the Ambassadors on the coming negotiations at Geneva. The fiasco of the 'diplomacy by *fait accompli*' was one of the best-preserved secrets of Washington. No newspaper or commentator reported the original purpose for which the meeting had been arranged" (*ibid.*, p. 63; see also Eden, *op. cit.*, pp. 110–16).

56. It is almost impossible to obtain a true picture of the events during the two weeks prior to May 8, 1954, the day on which the Geneva conference (which opened on April 26) began its discussions on Indochina. Not only does the chronology of the various reports differ—when was what said and done by whom, in response to whom—but it also differs in emphasis. For example, Lacouture and Devillers stress the French efforts to obtain U.S. military intervention for Dien Bien Phu as the main reason for Dulles' ut-

terances, as well as Bedell Smith's and Eisenhower's, whereas Lancaster, Bator, and Eden himself brush off French pleas and the ensuing exchange of notes and opinions; they concentrate on the American-British disagreement resulting from the suggestion of such intervention and present the divergent military assessment on the French position after the fall of Dien Bien Phu without injecting that of the main protagonist in the fight, namely the French. It is not clear, therefore, whether Radford, in his advisory capacity, stuck to his opinion that the eventual fall of Dien Bien Phu would not vitally affect the French strategic situation in Indochina, as Lacouture and Devillers report, or whether he changed his mind in discussions with the British and subsequently stated, as Eden reports, that a French defeat at Dien Bien Phu "would promptly be followed by the collapse of all French resistance throughout Indo-China." Furthermore, it is impossible to ascertain whether the French exaggerated their weakened military situation in Vietnam when addressing their appeals to Dulles, or whether they minimized it—for reasons of their own—when conferring with Eden. Lacouture and Devillers report in great detail on Bidault and Laniel's appeals for reconsideration of Operation Vulture, and Laniel himself, in his book, speaks of such appeals for military aid; the other writers mentioned stress Dulles' desire for intervention as the moving force for all negotiations prior to May 8. There is the question of a letter by Dulles to Bidault, of which Eden speaks but of which, according to Lacouture and Devillers, no trace can be found in the French official archives. There is the question of whether it was Bedell Smith who, on instructions of President Eisenhower, informed the French Ambassador in Washington of the conditions under which an airstrike by U.S. planes at Dien Bien Phu could take place, or whether it was Dulles himself. Lacouture and Devillers state that Bidault's second appeal, which resulted in Washington's renewed demand for British and Congressional approval before going any further, did not reach Dulles until the morning of April 25, but was handled by Eisenhower through Bedell Smith; the others speak only of Dulles' renewed effort to obtain a basic agreement to multilateral action. And, finally, there is Radford's trip to see Churchill as Eisenhower's personal envoy, of which Eden makes no mention, even though Radford was in London at the same time Eden was that Sunday (April 25); Lacouture and Devillers report on Radford's arrival and return, without giving details of what transpired (see Lacouture and Devillers, *op. cit.*, pp. 88–93; Lancaster, *op. cit.*, pp. 313–14; Fall, *The Two Viet-Nams*, 229, 230; Bator, *op. cit.*, pp. 67–73; Robert J. Donovan, *Eisenhower: The Inside Story* [New York, 1956], 265–67). For the exchange of letters between Dulles and Bidault (not the letter mentioned by Eden but earlier letters), see J. R. Tournoux, *Secrets d'état*, pp. 462, 463; also pp. 53–57; on this entire episode, see also Chalmers M. Roberts, "The Day We Didn't Go to War," in *The Reporter*, September 14, 1954; and John Robinson Beal, *op. cit.*, p. 207.

57. See Lacouture and Devillers (*op. cit.*, p. 99), who say that the threat of allied action, which "had to be real to be effective," was advocated most

strongly in the divided Laniel Cabinet by Bidault. Raymond Aron wrote on April 26 in *Figaro:* "How could the American threat be effective if we stated that under no circumstances would we allow it to be executed? We must do everything possible to avoid an extension of the conflict, but we must take the risk of such an extension in order to obtain an honorable peace" (quoted from Lacouture and Devillers, *ibid.*). The conviction that Dien Bien Phu could not be saved at this hour even with a massive airstrike was widespread, and strongly argued by Robert Guillain, a French correspondent in Vietnam, in *Le Monde*, April 29, 1954.

58. *Parliamentary Debates, House of Commons*, DXXVI, April 27, 1954, pp. 1455–56. The attempt to blame Britain was intended to give Dulles and the Eisenhower Administration "a convenient avenue of escape from the cul-de-sac of military intervention they themselves had constructed," said Fall (*The Two Viet-Nams*, p. 229), and was pointed out in the previously cited *Life* article by James Shepley, which Dulles two years later corroborated as substantially correct. On June 10, 1954, Dulles himself said in a speech held in Seattle that intervention failed because "some of the parties held back." One who dismissed this attempt by the Secretary of State to blame all on Great Britain was James Reston, who wrote in *The New York Times* of June 13, 1954, that "this picture, omitting any reference to Congressional or White House opposition to using force in Asia . . . is one of the most misleading oversimplifications ever uttered by an American Secretary of State, but it allocates blame and furnishes an alibi." Donovan (*op. cit.*, p. 267) said: "Public opinion had never been prepared for accepting intervention. . . . Yet if by chance agreement had somehow been reached with our allies on the President's terms and Congress had approved, the United States would presumably have been at war again on the mainland of Asia less than a year after the truce in Korea."

59. For excerpts from Nixon's December, 1953, speech, see Cole (ed.), *op. cit.*, pp. 171–72; also for remarks attributed to Nixon on April 16, 1954, as reported in *The New York Times*, April 17, 1954, see, *ibid.*, pp. 173–75. In these press statements, Nixon is said to have announced that "it is hoped the United States will not have to send troops there, but if this Government cannot avoid it, the Administration must face up to the situation and dispatch forces." He also said: "Communist intransigence in Korea perhaps will teach the French and the British the futility of negotiation and bring them over to the plan of 'united action' proposed by Secretary of State Dulles." See also Bator, *op. cit.*, pp. 40–41, who concludes from Nixon's statements that his policy was "the old policy of the Radford-Ely agreement," rather than the Dulles "united action" thesis. And in a footnote on p. 42, Bator writes that "Vice-President Nixon in a private communication confirmed that though Dulles favored military intervention, he was forced to abandon the plan because Britain and other allies disagreed. On the other hand, Nixon himself advocated military action regardless of allied support. According to him, he expressed in his speech of April 16 the policy that he personally championed. Therefore, in his opinion, his statement was not the

result of a misunderstanding." The misunderstanding Bator refers to here
was the uproar Nixon's speech of April 16 produced, an uproar that grew
still greater after the Vice-President reiterated his thinking in a speech made
on April 20 in Cincinnati, in which he stated: "The aim of the United States
is to hold Indochina without war involving the United States, *if we can*"
(italics added).

60. *The New York Times,* April 20, 1954. Wrote Bator: "Nixon was
damned in Congress for 'whooping it up for war'" (*op. cit.,* p. 41). Already
in November, 1953, Nixon had stated: "It is impossible to lay down arms
until victory is completely won" (*The New York Times,* November 5,
1953).

61. *The New York Times,* April 20, 1954.

62. *Ibid.,* April 30, 1954.

63. Dwight D. Eisenhower, *The White House Years: Mandate for
Change* (New York, 1963), p. 351. On January 13, 1960, after Eden's
memoirs appeared, Eisenhower told a press conference that "there was
never any plan developed to put into execution in Indochina." As Fall puts
it, the President explained Dulles' statement to the contrary by saying that
Dulles had been "a very forceful man. He could very well talk about possibilities that might by then be considered as proposals, when they were not
meant as that at all" (*The Two Viet-Nams,* p. 230).

64. French losses at Dien Bien Phu amounted to 16,000 men, of whom
1,500 were killed, 3,000–4,000 wounded, and 10,000 taken prisoners or reported missing—a total of six infantry battalions, seven paratroop battalions,
two artillery outfits, one armored truck unit, etc. (Lacouture and Devillers,
op. cit., p. 136).

65. The list of those who have written about the Geneva conference is
seemingly endless, since every major work on international affairs after 1954
deals with this event. Yet only one book, Jean Lacouture and Philippe Devillers' *La fin d'une guerre,* gives what can be considered an exhaustive history of the conference and of the events leading up to it. In particular,
Chapter VIII, "Rendez-vous au bord d'un lac," which describes the arrival
of the chief delegates at Geneva, is an extraordinarily lucid and fascinating
political essay.

66. Lacouture and Devillers give a vivid description of the change in
Dong's appearance after eight years in the lime caves of the Viet Bac. The
face ravaged, as much by deprivation and passion as possibly by illness;
burning eyes sunk into their sockets; only the fleshy mouth seemingly
alive; and the voice, brusque, bitter, often broken, a reflection of the face
(*op. cit.,* pp. 114–15). The other members of the delegation, Lacouture and
Devillers write, were the jovial Phan Anh, Hoang Van Hoan, Ambassador
to Peking, Ta Quang Buu and Ha Van Lau of the military commission,
Tran Cong Tuong, Vice-Minister of Justice, "the only one to remain reserved" (*ibid.,* pp. 115–16).

67. Nguyen Quoc Dinh and Nguyen Dac Khe, the key figures of the
Vietnamese Nationalist delegation, had been seen once before—that time as

members of the Vietminh delegation at Fontainebleau, where they acted as legal advisers.

68. See *The New York Times*, May 12, 1954. Victor Bator commented on Eisenhower's domino theory: "Their [Dulles and Eisenhower's] dogmatic domino theory obscured from them the possibility that the fall of one piece, one bastion, one country does not necessarily mean destruction of all others if the others have the time to strengthen their own, independent base. They did not foresee the spectacular recovery of Western Europe and Japan, the new vigor of the Philippines, or the self-assertion of the European satellites. They shut their eyes to the sources of conflict between Russia and China, and China and India, with its balance of terror. It is certainly surprising that Eisenhower as late as 1963, at a time when these earthshaking changes were clearly ascertainable, printed in his *Mandate For Change* the dogmas and obsessions which directed his thinking in 1954" (*op. cit.*, p. 59).

69. *The New York Times*, April 10, 1954.

70. See excerpts of the statement made by Dulles at a news conference, July 23, 1954, in Cole (ed.), *op. cit.*, pp. 176–77, in which he repeated this theme.

71. See Lacouture and Devillers, *op. cit.*, pp. 217–18. The remarkable aspect of Chou's proposal regarding the withdrawal of Vietminh troops from Laos and Cambodia was his agreeing to have them considered "foreign," as the French troops were. Regarding the nonseating of the Khmer Issarak and Pathet Lao rebels, it is said that it was Krishna Menon, sent by Nehru to Geneva as India's observer, who played an active role as mediator and persuaded Chou to have the Communist delegations drop this demand.

72. Navarre felt obliged to remain optimistic. He believed that the Vietminh had suffered too many losses to resume an offensive operation before September. But even he agreed that only part of the delta could be held, and that the French had to "adjust" their positions in Central Annam. General Cogny shared Navarre's opinion (Lacouture and Devillers, *op. cit.*, p. 157). For details of Navarre's projected regroupment in case the Geneva conference failed, see his memoirs, *op. cit.*, pp. 263 ff.

73. Lacouture and Devillers, *op. cit.*, p. 162.

74. See *ibid.*, pp. 162 ff.; also Laniel, *op. cit.*, pp. 106–7. Ely thought the delta south of the Hanoi-Haiphong axis should be given up in ten to fifteen days. At the meeting of the National Defense Committee, held upon his return on May 25, Ely went so far as to suggest that Hanoi be given up in two to three weeks. Salan was even more pessimistic. Navarre, however, did not consider withdrawal to be such an imminent necessity (see n. 72, above), and in the compromise reached with Ely over the proposed regroupment, he kept in mind the two prime considerations which had induced Laniel and Reynaud to send the three generals to Vietnam in the first place: (1) to save the Expeditionary Corps; and (2) to avoid at all costs a repetition of Dien Bien Phu, particularly at Hanoi, which would be certain to cause the immediate downfall of the government.

75. Communist solidarity prevented strong public expressions of dis-

pleasure by the Vietminh with the tactics of Molotov and Chou En-lai. Yet such expressions were to be heard. Tillman Durdin wrote in a report to *The New York Times* (July 25, 1954): "A number of members of the Vietminh delegation have openly declared Chinese and Molotov pressure forced them to accept less than they rightfully should have obtained." That the Vietminh acceded only reluctantly to Soviet and Chinese pressure has become a generally accepted belief, voiced most recently by Seymour Topping in *The New York Times* of February 4, 1966. Writing about Hanoi's peace terms, Topping states that Molotov persuaded the Vietminh to accept division and withdrawal from the South because Moscow feared the eruption of a general conflict in Asia. The Chinese Communists, then under the influence of Moscow, Topping adds, went along with Molotov, but with some reluctance. Topping also writes that members of the Vietminh delegation at Geneva stated privately that they could have won a more advantageous settlement if the Russians and the Chinese Communists had been willing to hold out longer.

76. Various reasons have been advanced for the Chinese position. One was fear that the war would broaden through U.S. intervention if no solution were found at Geneva. The Chinese, it was said, were in no position to repeat their Korean effort in Indochina. Also, they needed peace to proceed with their grandiose projects of economic reconstruction, the basis of all future military and diplomatic strength. For this they needed Soviet technical and economic aid, which was another reason for going along with Russia's wish to end the war and to obtain France's promise to stay out of the European Defense Community—a prime objective of Soviet diplomacy. Another Chinese motive may have been to use their first appearance as a great power at an international conference for wiping out the image of aggressor created by their intervention in Korea, and to open the road toward wider international recognition. It has also been observed that the Chinese grew more conciliatory whenever the United States showed opposition to a compromise solution at Geneva, which, whatever form it took, would mean some kind of concession to the Communist bloc.

77. As the Communist writer Nguyen Kien puts it, the Vietnamese leaders gave proof of political wisdom by accepting inevitable compromises. Kien quotes Ho Chi Minh's speech at the July 15, 1954, session of the Central Committee of the Workers Party in support of this. On that occasion, Ho Chi Minh pointed with pride to the strong position in which the Vietminh found itself diplomatically at Geneva, but he added: "We must never forget that this strength and this weakness [of the French] are all relative, not absolute. We must not succumb to subjectivism and to underestimating the enemy. Our victories have awakened the Americans. After the battle of Dien Bien Phu, they changed their plans of intervention to prolong the Indochina War, to internationalize it, to sabotage the Geneva conference, to seek by all means to supplant the French, to take over Vietnam, Cambodia, Laos, to make these three peoples their slaves, and increase international tension. . . . Up to now we have concentrated our forces to annihilate those of

the French imperialist aggressors. Now the French have entered into negotiations with us while the American imperialists are becoming our chief and most direct enemies. . . . Our efforts must now be concentrated against the Americans." Further on, Ho Chi Minh is heard to say: "It is not easy to obtain peace. It is a long, hard, and complicated fight, and it has its difficulties and its favorable aspects. . . . The following errors might be made: deviation to the Left or the Right. Some people, elated by our continuous victories, might wish to fight at any price, to fight to the end. . . . They see the French without seeing the Americans, they wax enthusiastic over the military action and underestimate the diplomatic action. . . . They pose excessive conditions, unacceptable to the adversary" (*Le Sud-Vietnam depuis Dien-Bien-Phu* [Paris, 1963], pp. 27–29).

78. Lacouture and Devillers recount that Pham Van Dong spoke in a private session on May 25, and it was at once realized that what he had to say in his brusque, dramatic manner was important, so important in fact that two of the French delegation hastily scribbled some notes without waiting for the official text to be handed out. The few phrases they jotted down regarding the demarcation of the zones in which the cease-fire was to take place were that the adjustment should take place in such a manner as to take into account the economic and sociopolitical factors of each part, leaving it as a body that would have the same administrative control and economic activities throughout. The line of demarcation should follow the geographic outline of the country as much as possible, in order to avoid difficulties in the transportation and communication systems of the respective zones (*op. cit.*, p. 188).

79. The seven points were: (1) To preserve the integrity and independence of Laos and Cambodia by ensuring the withdrawal of the Vietminh forces from the two countries; (2) To preserve at least the southern half of Vietnam and if possible also an enclave in the Tongking Delta, with the line of demarcation not to run south of Dong Hoi (north of the 17th parallel); (3) Not to impose either on Cambodia or on Laos or on the part of Vietnam that was preserved any restrictions on their ability to maintain stable non-Communist governments—notably on their right to dispose over sufficiently strong forces for their internal security, to import arms, and to ask for foreign advisers; (4) No political clause of any kind that might lead to the loss of the free zones at the profit of the Communists; (5) Not to rule out the possibility of an ultimate unification of Vietnam by peaceful means; (6) To allow the transfer, under humane and peaceful conditions and under international control, of all those who wish to go from one zone of Vietnam to the other; (7) To establish an effective system of international control (Lacouture and Devillers, *op. cit.*, pp. 244–45). The comment of the authors in a footnote was: "This astonishing text, which anticipated the agreements of July 20, was kept in most surprising secrecy—no better proof of the existence of a common Western doctrine was to be found."

80. Bidault, speaking before Molotov on June 8, summarized the progress which he believed the conference had made in the past weeks. He sounded

reasonable enough, but Molotov bluntly accused the head of the French delegation of double-dealing, of speaking out for peaceful solutions while hoping for the failure of the conference, and of wanting the Indochina War to
continue. Attacking the United States through Bidault, Molotov derided
him as "a partner who had wanted to create fear and had not succeeded, a
spokesman too full of ulterior motives, truly too slow to grasp the offers
. . . made by the Vietminh delegation." The general reaction to Molotov's
attack was what an editorial in the *Geneva Journal* described as "Molotov
wanted to show the French Assembly that Bidault is not the man with
whom Moscow and her partners can negotiate." Bidault at once returned to
Paris, and in the Assembly countered with an attack on Molotov, yet he
offered to yield his place to someone whom the government might think
better equipped to negotiate. Mendès-France added his accusations to those
of the Soviet Foreign Minister. He spoke of the "devilish game of poker"
Bidault had played with the Americans by having asked for their airplanes
to intervene, and he wound up with a demand that everything possible be
done to help obtain an honorable peace. General Koenig and Jacques Sous-
telle, who spoke after him, supported his position. In the Paris press meanwhile the cry went up for a "change of climate" in the French delegation,
which Raymond Aron in the *Figaro* criticized as suffering from "diplomatic
somnambulism"; that same day the *New York Herald Tribune*, well known
and widely read in Paris, reported that a Vietminh offensive in the Tongking Delta was in the making, ready to begin on June 20. Bidault had meanwhile returned to Geneva, but during the night session of June 9, the Laniel
Government fell, being voted out of power 322 against 263 (Lacouture and
Devillers, *op. cit.*, pp. 203–7).

81. Mendès-France may have stood on even firmer ground than his own
determination. According to some sources, a secret agreement existed between Mendès-France and Molotov that would have Russia force the Vietminh to agree to terms acceptable to the French in return for a promise that
France would reject the European Defense Community. This note of a secret agreement is sounded by Lancaster, who writes that some suspicion existed that "Mendès-France, in his patent desire to score a personal triumph,
had been tempted to come to a tacit understanding with the Soviet representative by which, in return for Molotov's assistance in securing an armistice in Indochina on acceptable terms, he had given some undertaking in regard to France's proposed participation in EDC, a *quid pro quo* which
Bidault had stoutly rejected." As documentation, Lancaster cites Jean Wetz
in *Le Monde* of July 13, 1954, and Jacques Fauvet in *Le Monde* of July 23;
also the *Manchester Guardian* of July 23, 1954 (*op. cit.*, p. 336 and n. 63.)
No one knows whether there really was such an understanding. Lancaster
feels that Mendès-France maneuvered to have the EDC rejected by the National Assembly, "ignominiously," on a mere technicality.

82. Lacouture and Devillers, *op. cit.*, p. 147. Partition was rejected by
Dinh in any form—"direct or indirect, definitive or provisional, *de facto* or
de jure" (*ibid.*, p. 146).

83. This treaty gave to Vietnam "all prerogatives of sovereignty within its border, as well as abroad, and abrogated all previous treaties to the contrary" (Fall, "The Cease-Fire in Indochina: An Appraisal" *Far Eastern Survey*, September, 1954, p. 136). The treaty was actually to be signed only after agreements had been reached on future military, economic and cultural relations between France and Vietnam. But these open issues were later decided *ad hoc* and the treaty of June 3 was never formally signed.

84. This was Operation Auvergne. Lancaster notes (*op. cit.*, p. 330) that the Apostolic Vicar of Phat Diem, Monsignor Le Huu Tu, escaped by sea, leaving his militia and his parishioners behind. His colleague, Pham Ngoc Chi, whose vicariate, Bui Chu, was not threatened until a few days later, left at the head of his priests and large numbers of the population.

85. The meeting took place under humiliating circumstances for the French. As Denis Warner describes it, "the Viet Minh had taken steps to insure that the French should not forget the realities of the military situation." "Souvenir of the victory of Dien Bien Phu—May 7, 1954" was painted on the sides of three jeeps and two weapons-carriers; French parachutes captured at Dien Bien Phu decorated the walls of the teahouse adjacent to the conference hut; and Vietminh soldiers lit their cigarettes with lighters taken from French soldiers. Even though Warner narrates that the Vietminh General Van Tien Dung and the French Colonel Marcel Lennuyeux shook hands upon meeting, and that there was a general feeling of cordiality, it must have been a bitter moment for the French when General Dung in his opening speech in Vietnamese let loose a propagandistic harangue in which he spoke of "eight years of patriotic war" and "promised that the High Command of the Popular Army of Vietnam would make every effort to bring about a rapid cease-fire and armistice, and the re-establishment of peace in Indo-China." Colonel Lennuyeux's reply contained the promise of "studying a concrete plan about 'how to remedy certain unhappy problems born of war'" (Warner, *op. cit.*, p. 74). Agreement was also reached on improvement of conditions in prison camps. The President of the French Red Cross estimated in October, 1954, that 65 per cent of the inmates of Vietminh prison camps, where they were kept on a starvation diet, had died in captivity (see Lancaster, *op. cit.*, p. 331). In a footnote, Lancaster adds that "in September Ely announced in Saigon that while 9,886 prisoners had been released, those missing or those who had died in captivity included 4,995 French, 5,349 Foreign Legionnaires, 2,074 Algerians, 2,907 Moroccans, 63 Tunisians, and 1,041 Equatorial Africans, while some 23,000 Vietnamese had disappeared. These figures were subsequently amended in a joint statement by the Ministries of National Defence and for the Associate States, in which it was stated that 14,905 prisoners had been released, including 2,118 Vietnamese, while 2,840 metropolitan French remained unaccounted for (*Le Monde*, 21–22 November 1954)."

86. Diem and Nhu, who had gone to Hanoi on June 30, must have been aware that the city was lost. But Robert Shaplen, writing in *The New Yorker* (September 22, 1962, p. 118), quoted Diem as believing that a na-

tionalist government could have defeated the "exhausted" Vietminh. Georges Chaffard (*Indochine: Dix ans d'indépendance*, p. 35) claims that Diem had been so upset by the withdrawal of the French from the south delta provinces that he considered resigning his mission, and that Nhu, Thuc, and the "representatives of the United States" had to dissuade him. The Committee for the Defense of the North died quietly, after having been of some use in organizing the evacuation of refugees from the North. Denis Warner (*op. cit.*, p. 74) states that the comment made to him by the Chief Secretary of this Committee after the Geneva agreement was: "It is finish, my friend, finish, finish, finish!"

87. According to Lacouture and Devillers (*op. cit.*, pp. 256–57) Tran Van Don reacted with greater calm than did Diem. Diem showed "almost stupefaction" upon being told the news by U.S. Ambassador Donald Heath. He had not been aware that the military situation had deteriorated to such a degree, and he protested that not only had he, a Catholic and nationalist, had to suffer the blow to his prestige of the evacuation of the Northern dioceses, but even more, that now partition was to be imposed upon him. "Bewildered, Mr. Diem assured the American diplomat that he could not associate himself with such a policy." As for Tran Van Don, the authors describe him as having been quite aware of the feeble means at his disposal, once Washington had adopted the Mendès-France–Eden program; "up to the last hours of the conference, he cleverly contented himself with basically not mortgaging the future, and while doing so, to show great dignity."

88. See *Le Monde*, July 20, 1954.

89. Tran Van Don protested also against the "hasty conclusion" of the armistice, and against the attitude of the French, whose High Command in Indochina had not sought a preliminary agreement with the State of Vietnam about concluding an armistice and about fixing the date for elections.

90. The French Union forces were to withdraw from Hanoi within 80 days, from Hoi Duong within 100; the final evacuation from Haiphong was to be completed within 300 days. The Vietminh forces in the South and in Central Vietnam had a similar timetable; according to Isoart (*op. cit.*, p. 402) they had 80 days in which to withdraw from the forest region of northern Cochinchina, 100 days to evacuate the Plain of Reeds, 200 days to leave the Point of Camau, and 300 days to move out of the central provinces of Quang Ngai and Binh Dinh. "These arrangements," wrote Lancaster (*op. cit.*, p. 339), "were completed by an undertaking that the two parties to the agreement would refrain from reprisals or discrimination against persons or organizations on account of their activities during the hostilities, and that the democratic liberties of such persons would be guaranteed. Instructions were also to be issued to local authorities to permit and help civilians residing in a district controlled by one party who wished to go and live in the zone assigned to the other party, to do so, this authorization being restricted, however, to the period of 300 days which had been assigned for the completion of troop movements. Both parties likewise undertook not to in-

troduce into Vietnam troop reinforcements, arms, munitions, or other war material, and to refrain from establishing new military bases, the maintenance of military bases under the control of a foreign state and the contracting of military alliances also being expressly precluded."

91. "These Commissions were to set up fixed and mobile inspection teams, composed of an equal number of officers from each of the three participating states. The teams were to operate throughout Indochina at ports and airfields, in regions bordering land and sea frontiers and, with the exception of Cambodia, at the demarcation lines between regrouping and demilitarized zones. Their duties included the prevention of the entry of troop reinforcements and war material, with the exception of troops relieving units of the Expeditionary Corps up to battalion strength which had completed their overseas service" (Lancaster, *op. cit.*, p. 341). The English text of the Cease-Fire Agreement and the Final Declaration has recently been made available by *Viet Report*, August–September, 1965; and in Marvin E. Gettleman (ed.), *Viet-Nam: History, Documents, and Opinions on a Major World Crisis* (New York, 1965), pp. 137–54. Gettleman also carries a postscript (pp. 154–60) on the final meeting of the Geneva conference on July 21, 1954 (from *Further Documents Relating to the Discussion of Indochina at the Geneva Conference* [Miscellaneous Command Paper 9239, No. 20, 1954, London, Parliamentary Sessional Papers, XXXI, 1953–54, pp. 5–9]); see also Cole (ed.), *op. cit.*, pp. 161–64, containing a summary of both the Cease-Fire Agreement and the Final Declaration.

92. Article 7 of the Final Declaration, which deals with the question of elections, reads as follows: "The Conference declares that, so far as Viet Nam is concerned, the settlement of political problems, effected on the basis of respect for the principles of independence, unity and territorial integrity, shall permit the Vietnamese people to enjoy the fundamental freedoms, guaranteed by democratic institutions established as a result of free general elections by secret ballot. In order to ensure that sufficient progress in the restoration of peace has been made, and that all the necessary conditions obtain for free expression of the national will, general elections shall be held in July 1956, under the supervision of an international commission composed of representatives of the Member States of the International Supervisory Commission, referred to in the agreement on the cessation of hostilities. Consultations will be held on this subject between the competent representative authorities of the two zones from July 20, 1955, onwards" (see Robert J. MacAllister, *The Great Gamble: United States Policy Toward South Vietnam* [unpublished dissertation; Chicago, 1958], p. 69; quoting from *Further Documents Relating to the Discussion of Indochina*).

93. For the full text of the statement made by Bedell Smith, see Cole (ed.), *op. cit.*, pp. 175–76.

94. Fall, "The Cease-Fire in Indochina," in *op. cit.*

95. Quoted by Ton That Thien, "The Geneva Agreements and Peace Prospects in Vietnam," *India Quarterly*, October–December, 1956, p. 378.

96. See *Le Monde*, August 4, 1954.

97. These remarks are reported by Emmet John Hughes in his *The Ordeal of Power* (New York, 1964), p. 182, as having been made to him.

98. For the full text of Dulles' statement of July 23, see State Department *Bulletin*, XXXI, No. 788 (August 2, 1954), pp. 163–64. Also reproduced in Cole (ed.), *op. cit.*, pp. 176–77. The text of the Manila Pact is given in *ibid.*, pp. 177–80.

99. Lacouture and Devillers, *op. cit.*, p. 286.

100. To the astonishment of Mendès-France himself, wrote Lacouture and Devillers, the attacks on the Geneva agreement in the Assembly were rare. Even Jean Letourneau, "who four years back had stood for the opposite policy," concluded his speech with the remark: "With my knowledge of Indochinese affairs, I do not presume the right to criticize the formula you have obtained." The harshest critics were Raymond Dronne, who had served under General Leclerc, and the *colons* Repiton and Crepin—as well as Georges Bidault, "who attempted unsuccessfully to demonstrate that the Geneva texts imposed neutralization on the three Associate Indochina States, to the detriment of their interests and in violation of Article 62 of the Constitution." But in an interview given Philippe Devillers on July 24, 1959, Bidault wondered aloud whether he himself could have obtained better results, and when the votes were taken, the first (vote no. 2,569) showed 569 for and 9 against ratification of the agreement; the second (vote no. 2,570) showed 86 against 455, and the third (vote no. 2,571) showed 471 for to 14 against (*op. cit.*, p. 287, and nn. 4 and 5).

101. Identical statements appeared in *Pravda* and *Izvestia*, July 23, 1954. The Communists were of course counting on the election to complete their victory. Thus wrote *Pravda*: "The Geneva Conference decision on holding free elections in Vietnam in July, 1956 . . . adopted as a result of the persistent efforts by the democratic states, signifies the defeat of those aggressive forces which were striving for the dismemberment of Vietnam in order to make Southern Vietnam a springboard of the proposed new aggressive block in Southeast Asia" (quoted by MacAllister, *op. cit.*, p. 77).

XI. *Independence Without Unity or Freedom*
(pp. 845–916)

1. For relevant facts about Diem's education and youth, see Bernard Fall, *The Two Viet-Nams*, pp. 235–36; Anthony T. Bouscaren, *The Last of the Mandarins: Diem of Vietnam*, a completely uncritical biographical sketch of Diem; Denis Warner, *The Last Confucian;* and Robert Shaplen, "A Reporter in Viet-Nam," in *The New Yorker*, September 22, 1962.

2. According to Fall, Ngo Dinh Kha instilled his sons, especially Diem, with "a religious fierceness bordering on fanaticism." Fall feels that this is the quality in Diem that must be fully understood if one wishes to understand his view of his role in his country's life. Diem's faith, as Fall puts it, was "made less of the kindness of the apostles than of the ruthless militancy

of the Grand Inquisitor," and he cites an exchange between Diem and a French Catholic visitor who appealed to his and Diem's common interests by stressing their common faith. Diem is supposed to have answered: "You know, I consider myself rather as a Spanish Catholic," i.e., Fall stresses, "a spiritual son of a fiercely aggressive and militant faith rather than of the easygoing and tolerant approach of Gallican Catholicism" (*op. cit.*, pp. 235, 236).

3. For some interesting observations on Diem's character, see John Mecklin, *Mission in Torment;* David Halberstam, *The Making of a Quagmire* (New York, 1965); Robert Shaplen, *The Lost Revolution;* and Nguyen Thai, *Is South Vietnam Viable?* (Manila, 1962).

4. Although snubbed by MacArthur, Diem met the man who was to become one of his closest advisers and defenders in the United States, Professor Wesley Fishel, and who for five years was to reorganize Saigon's School for Administration as head of an advisory group of Michigan State University. Fishel wrote a number of articles on South Vietnam's political and social problems, among them "Political Realities in Vietnam," *Asian Survey*, April, 1961, and "Vietnam's War of Attrition," *The New Leader*, December 7, 1959; he also edited *Problems of Freedom: South Vietnam Since Independence.*

5. According to Shaplen ("A Reporter in Viet-Nam," and *The Lost Revolution*, pp. 112–13) who interviewed him, Diem believed that "if we had been responsible for prosecuting the war, we would have won," because, in his opinion, "the Communists were exhausted" (in 1954); Diem accused the French of having been "defeatist in their evaluations." This is a rather unrealistic view of the true situation. The French would certainly have liked to win; and in 1954 it was too late to turn the tide, which probably could have been done before 1950 had French policies toward the nationalist Vietnamese been different.

6. Justice William O. Douglas wrote warmly about Diem in *North from Malaya*, pp. 180–81.

7. Denis Warner, *op. cit.*, p. 71.

8. Quoting from the French press in his book *Mission de la France en Asie*, Frédéric-Dupont regretted the utterances made by such French newspapers as *Le Monde*, *L'Express*, *L'Observateur*, and *Combat*, all of which published statements directed against the government of South Vietnam along these lines of *Le Monde:* "With Diem, Washington thought to make South Vietnam into a third anti-Communist bastion . . . but it has become apparent that Diem is neither a Syngman Rhee nor a Chiang Kai-shek. . . . A Vietminh victory at the 1956 elections can be forecast with certainty." Georges Chaffard also speaks of American pressure to have Diem nominated. According to him, Bao Dai could not stand Diem, and he would have preferred someone like Tran Van Huu as his Prime Minister, but Bao Dai "had to accept him [Diem] under American pressure, at the moment when the French began to tire of Vietnamese affairs" (*Indochine: Dix ans d'indépendance*, p. 52). But Chaffard went even further in his asser-

tion of American pressure. He states that Diem was "pushed by the Department of State," and that Cardinal Spellman and "the Catholic lobby" campaigned for him (*ibid.*, p. 20). Jean Chesneaux, without sounding derogatory, speaks of Diem having been held in reserve by the United States, to replace such "old clients of the French colonial administration" as Buu Loc and General Hinh (*Contributions à l'histoire de la nation vietnamienne*, p. 306). Nguyen Kien, whose political position is pro-Communist, is much more vociferous. In *Le Sud-Vietnam depuis Dien-Bien-Phu*, he claims that it was Cardinal Spellman who took South Vietnam and Ngo Dinh Diem under his wing. Lacouture and Devillers, in their superb character study of political men and national speculations, speak of Diem as the "American card" and of the almost unconditional American support that was one of his trump cards (*La fin d'une guerre: Indochine 1954*, pp. 227 and 299). As can be seen from the above-quoted opinions, virtually all of them stress Cardinal Spellman's alleged role in Diem's rise to power, and if not the Cardinal's, then the Americans'. As to Cardinal Spellman, I consider this a case of unsubstantiated conjecture.

9. Warner, *op. cit.*, p. 65.

10. Frédéric-Dupont was appointed by Joseph Laniel to replace Marc Jacquet, who had resigned on May 30. As Laniel describes it in his book *Le drame indochinois: De Dien-Bien-Phu au pari de Génève* (pp. 95–99), he dismissed Marc Jacquet because of his alleged collaboration with the newspaper *L'Express*, which supposedly was proved when during a search of the *L'Express* premises a letter was seized indicating Jacquet's association with the newspaper. As told by Lacouture and Devillers (*op. cit.*, p. 165, n. 18), the confidential report made by the "three generals," Ely, Salan, and Pelissier, upon their return from Saigon to the government had been leaked in part to the press; upon his resignation, Jacquet defended himself by pointing out that the documents found during the search at *L'Express* had not been of a confidential nature. Although it was later learned that *L'Express* had obtained its information from General Salan in an interview with one of its reporters, the episode was designated "classified information" by General Koenig, Minister of National Defense in Laniel's successor government.

11. Bernard Fall cautiously remarks that "any of the factors widely adduced—American pressure, French pressure, of Bao Dai's own belief that Diem would be a convenient scapegoat for a hopeless situation—may have played its part in the choice" (*op. cit.*, p. 244).

12. Warner wrote: "As Diem admits candidly, there was no competition" (*op. cit.*, p. 66).

13. Pierre Dabezies commented: "The only one that did not disarm was the Ngo Dinh Nhu faction of the 'Movement for Independence and Peace,' which continued to belabor past responsibilities and clamored for a new government to continue the fight against Communism" (*Forces politiques au Viet-Nam*, p. 205).

14. According to Fall (*op. cit.*, p. 244) it took Bao Dai three days to yield to Diem's demands for full powers. "Fully realizing that he was throwing

his throne away," Fall goes on, "Bao-Dai allegedly made Diem swear a solemn oath of allegiance to him, and several authoritative witnesses affirm that Diem also swore on his knees to Empress Nam-Phuong that he would do everything in his power 'to preserve the throne of Viet-Nam for Crown Prince Bao-Long,' son of Bao-Dai." On this point, Donald Lancaster writes that "Vietnamese aware of Diem's dubious loyalty had attempted to dissuade Bao Dai from making this appointment, but Bao Dai, who had been nurtured on legends extolling the loyalty of senior mandarins to the Emperor, dismissed these warnings on the grounds that those proffering such advice did not belong to the official caste, and were therefore not in a position to question Diem's loyalty" (*The Emancipation of French Indochina*, p. 328, n. 37).

15. This was described most tellingly by Roy Jumper and Marjorie Weiner Normand, who wrote: "Political and military authority in the summer of 1954 was dispersed among the three politico-military sects, the religion-based Cao Dai and Hoa Hao and the secular Binh Xuyen; French military authorities and financial interests; the Vietnamese army; the absent chief of state, who held the reins of legitimacy; and the Premier. Not only was political and economic power fractured, but the Diem regime exercised merely nominal administrative authority over large areas in South Vietnam, where the three sects held territorial fiefs. Village life in many other regions was effectively dominated by the activities of local Communist cadres (*Can Bo*) who remained behind when Viet Minh forces were regrouped and were supposedly withdrawn to the North after the armistice." (From George McTurnan Kahin (ed.), *Government and Politics in Southeast Asia*, pp. 399–400; see also Roy Jumper, "The Communist Challenge to South Vietnam," in *Far Eastern Survey*, November, 1956, pp. 161–68, and "Sects and Communism in South Vietnam," in *Orbis*, Spring, 1956, pp. 85–96.)

16. Diem, although not expected to engage in social radicalism and economic reforms, did not even gain the support of the small Vietnamese business "bourgeoisie," which feared that he would be unable to protect their interests. Dismayed by the prospect of Communism, these people wanted a government considered strong enough to meet the Communist threat by being ready to go along with the army and by agreeing to a continued "presence" of the French Army.

17. Fall, *op. cit.*, p. 205.

18. Or, as one observer later put it: "The odds were considered at least eight to one against Diem and the free world" (Carl T. Rowan, *The Pitiful and the Proud* [New York, 1956], p. 350).

19. The Hinh crisis, according to various sources, was only one in a number of attempts to replace Diem either by persuasion of Bao Dai or by a direct coup. Chaffard, for example, says that Bao Dai would have preferred Tran Van Huu to Diem in the first place; Huu's advocacy of a middle-of-the-road liberalism aimed at reconciliation with the sects and at normalizing relations with Hanoi (*op. cit.*, pp. 52–53). Bao Dai, opposed in his choice of the only former chief of government who had publicly approved the

Geneva agreements, gave in to American pressure and nominated Diem, but
soon a movement got under way to make Buu Hoi head of the government,
who, according to Ellen Hammer, "was prominent not only for intransigent
nationalism but also for the active role he had played in the struggle against
French colonial rule during the Nationalist phase of the Viet Minh war."
Buu Hoi, who resided in Paris, was a relative of the Imperial family and a
professor in the fields of cancer and leprosy research; he was singled out by
important sectors of the population to speak for them, says Miss Hammer
(in an article entitled "The Struggle for Indochina Continues, Geneva to
Bandung," *Pacific Spectator*, Supplement to Summer, 1955, issue, IX, No. 3,
29). Comparing him to Ignace Paderewski, who became President of the
Polish Republic after World War I, and Chaim Weizmann, who became
the first President of Israel, Miss Hammer describes how Buu Hoi returned
to Vietnam on a visit (according to Chaffard after a fifteen-year absence,
and ostensibly on a tour for the French Union), where he was greeted "as a
national hero." In the months following, Miss Hammer adds, "his name was
put forward by the Cao Dai and the Hoa Hao, by labor groups and by
army leaders." Upon his return to Paris, Buu Hoi expounded his program in
an article in *L'Express* (November 6, 1954), in which he called for a "government of national solidarity" that would unite the various sects and political groups in the South, with the idea of promoting political life inside each
sect in order to facilitate their integration into the nation once they had
terminated their feudal role (Hammer, *ibid.*, n. 22). Unable to obtain American support for a change in government heads, Buu Hoi ended up making
his peace with the Diem regime, even though "this liberal intellectual nurtured no illusions about its future, and which, moreover, persecuted the
Buddhism of which Buu Hoi's mother, Mme. Dieu Hue, was a fervent ad-
herent" (Chaffard, *op. cit.*, p. 274). There was also, according to Francis
Corley ("Vietnam Since Geneva," *Thought* [Fordham University Quar-
terly], XXXIII, No. 131 [Winter, 1958–59], 543), an Imperial Court-inspired
plan to supplant Diem's government with one headed by Bao Dai's old
adviser (and enemy of Diem) Nguyen De, "the shadowy figure who has
been close to Bao Dai since his early years in Viet-Nam in 1932," who was
the Emperor's *chef de cabinet*. This, in Corley's words, would have meant
"practically a full return of both the French and the discredited Emperor to
power." Of the Hinh crisis, Robert MacAllister wrote (*The Great Gamble:
United States Policy Toward South Viet Nam from July, 1954, to July,
1956,*" p. 88, that while in Vietnam, he was told by "a knowledgeable observer" of what he calls "this literal 'double cross,'" namely that in fact
Hinh approached Ngo Dinh Diem first with a view to carrying out a coup
against Bao Dai. "When Ngo refused, Hinh plotted against Ngo and sought
the support of Bao Dai." This kind of maneuver, which later became so
characteristic of South Vietnamese army politics, does not seem out of keeping with the character of Hinh, who, though allegedly likable and well-
meaning, and perhaps not unjustified in his belief that a "strong and popular" government was necessary, must have suffered from self-delusion in be-

lieving that he—a Vietnamese Frenchman, a collaborator, and a playboy like many generals—could bring it about. Coming back to Buu Hoi, MacAllister interestingly enough also states that he was told that Mendès-France, during his visit to Washington in November, 1954, proposed Buu Hoi as a replacement for Diem, an assertion first made by Sol Sanders in an article entitled "Crisis in Indochina," *The New Leader*, March 21, 1955, p. 4.

20. Calling Hinh's motorcycle ride a "boyish prank," Lancaster adds that the general had attached a sign to the vehicle announcing his "expulsion" (*op. cit.*, p. 349).

21. It is to be found in *La voie de la juste cause*, a French-language collection of statements and speeches by President Ngo Dinh Diem published in Saigon in 1956, pp. 46–48.

22. On this incident Lancaster (*op. cit.*, p. 352, n. 27) quotes Raymond Cartier as writing in *Paris Match*, October 2–9, 1954, that it was Mme. Nhu who was allegedly responsible for organizing the demonstration. When the detachment of Binh Xuyen–controlled police started to disperse the procession of refugees with machine-gun fire as it proceeded to the Norodom Palace, Mme. Nhu was seen rushing into the melee with a passionate courage reminiscent of the legendary ardor of the Trung sisters.

23. Chaffard, *op. cit.*, pp. 54–55. They also asked for measures to combat illiteracy—a sensible request from a group whose two most powerful leaders, Binh Xuyen "General" Vien and Hoa Hao "Generalissimo" Soai, were illiterate. Lancaster comments that "whereas Soai in an expansive mood would occasionally attempt to sign his name, Vien possessed a working knowledge of arithmetic which enabled him to calculate adroitly the takings at the 'Grande Monde' and at the other establishments from which he derived his ample revenue" (*op. cit.*, p. 349, n. 20).

24. Lancaster says that Diem in a countermove made the old collaborator General Nguyen Van Xuan, supposedly popular with the army, Defense Minister on September 17. If this is true, Xuan held the office for only a few days; he is never mentioned as having been Defense Minister, and if he was actually appointed by Diem, he must have been among the nine who left the Cabinet on September 20.

25. Chaffard *op. cit.*, p. 45.

26. According to Lancaster (*op. cit.*, p. 350), Xuan declined Diem's offer to join his new Cabinet. But Nguyen Thanh Phuong and Tran Van Soai did join (Diem took the post of Defense Minister himself); the other sect leaders joined the National Defense Committee founded by Diem, four each representing the Hoa Hao and Cao Dai. Even if Diem at the time was not yet planning an authoritarian regime, there were overriding political considerations for his not wanting to share power with these circles. Therefore I disagree with Lancaster's explanation of Diem's refusal to add former ministers to his Cabinet—i.e., because of his "innate sectarian prejudice" (*ibid.*, p. 329). Prejudice had nothing to do with Diem's playing the power game by temporarily cooperating with very discredited circles; political expediency would be a more correct attribution.

27. This is what I was told by a great many people in Saigon after gaining their confidence in the course of my first visit to Vietnam from October through December, 1954.

28. "Most sources do not quote figures but agree on the fact of financial 'rewards' for 'rallying' to the government," wrote Roy Jumper and Marjorie Weiner Normand, "Vietnam," in George McTurnan Kahin (ed.), *Government and Politics of Southeast Asia*, p. 400, in what might well be considered a conservative statement. Joseph Alsop reported that Cao Dai General Trinh Minh The, the former proponent of a "third force" between the Bao Dai–French and Vietminh camps, once received 20 million piasters (about $570,000 at the official rate). He "rallied" twice. Trinh Minh The was said to have had contacts with Americans long before the end of the war (see note 93, Chapter IX). MacAllister writes: "It is impossible, of course, to ascertain officially if such financial inducement was offered. However, on the basis of the author's experience in Viet Nam, there is no doubt in his mind that financial inducement was offered and that it was accepted by the sects" (*op. cit.*, p. 89). William Henderson, referring to a later affair, wrote: "A major break [in sect opposition] occurred in March 1955 when the Chief of Staff of the Cao Dai army, General Nguyen Thanh Phuong, was induced by bribery and other means to 'rally' to the national cause with most of his units" ("South Vietnam Finds Itself," *Foreign Affairs*, January, 1957). The most outspoken commentator is Bernard Fall, who probably obtained much concrete information from French and other sources he apparently cannot reveal. He writes that "exceedingly generous amounts of American currency were available to bribe key sect leaders" (*op. cit.*, p. 245). (I myself know but cannot name American intermediaries who carried funds to Vietnamese recipients.) Fall (*ibid.*, p. 246) even gives the exact amounts received by a number of people: Trinh Minh The, $2 million; Nguyen Thanh Phuong, $3 million (plus monthly payments for troops); Tran Van Soai, $3 million; the total is likely to have exceeded $12 million. See also Max Clos, *Le Monde*'s noted Far Eastern correspondent, in *Le Monde*, September 25, 1954, and *Life*, May 13, 1957, on the buying-off of the sects. Also Warner, *op. cit.*, p. 82, who speaks of Trinh Minh The as having been "persuaded with a generous bribe" to remain loyal to Diem.

29. Fall, *op. cit.*, p. 245.

30. The United States agreed to pay another $100 million for the Expeditionary Corps for 1955.

31. They were Minister of the Associate States Guy La Chambre, Minister of Finance Edgar Faure, General Ely, and Ambassador Henri Bonnet.

32. During that debate the opinion was voiced by the reporter for the Financial Commission of the Assembly that French credits for South Vietnam should be withheld because the Diem Government was "a government that had given proof of a total ineptness, that was propped up . . . by America. The presence of a strong government is indispensable in South Vietnam, but this government is not possible without a rally of national union being produced and without an agreement between French and

Americans. Unfortunately, we are far from it. America has committed the gravest errors" (Nguyen Kien, *op. cit.*, pp. 51–53; for the full text of this debate, see *Débats parlementaires*, December 18, 1954).

33. My strongest impression on first meeting Ngo Dinh Diem at the end of October, 1954, was that this was a man who did not in the least doubt the favorable outcome of his struggle with his opponents.

34. Hinh was dismissed on the grounds that he had made "ill-advised statements" (*Bulletin du Haut Commissariat du Viet-Nam en France*, No. 87, December, 1954, p. 2).

35. U.S. Senate Commission on Foreign Relations, *Report by Senator Mike Mansfield on a Study Mission to Vietnam, Cambodia, Laos* (Washington, D.C., October, 1954). Senator Mansfield defended Diem on the grounds that he had "a reputation throughout Vietnam for intense nationalism and equally intense incorruptibility," and he denounced "the incredible campaign of subversion by intrigue" and "the conspiracy of noncooperation and sabotage" that had stood in the way of Diem's forging ahead with his proposed "constructive" program.

36. This was the famous letter that in August, 1965, led to a delicate debate between Eisenhower and President Johnson, who claimed that this letter initiated the policy the United States was now pursuing in Vietnam. Eisenhower replied that he had spoken only of economic aid and that the letter constituted no commitment of a military defense of Vietnam by the United States. In reading the original text of the letter it would seem that, as usual, the truth lies halfway between Johnson and Eisenhower's assertions, since it contains passages that lend themselves to either interpretation. "I am, accordingly, instructing the American ambassador to Vietnam to examine with you in your capacity as chief of government, how an intelligent program of American aid given directly to your Government can serve to assist Vietnam in its present hour of trial, provided that your Government is prepared to give assurances as to the standards of performance it would be able to maintain in the event such aid were supplied. The purpose of this offer is to assist the Government of Vietnam in developing and maintaining a strong, viable state, capable of resisting attempted subversion or aggression through military means."

37. According to *U.S. News and World Report*, March 4, 1955, Collins later explained his then still-unequivocal stand in favor of Diem: "One of the things we said right off the bat was that we would support only one army and only if that army was loyal to the President. I had to make a public statement to that effect and I think it had a certain effect in helping General Hinh make up his mind to leave." (Robert Shaplen reports [*The Lost Revolution*, p. 119] that Hinh today is a high-ranking officer in the French Air Force.)

38. As one observer, whose reluctant admiration for Diem was balanced with highly pertinent criticism, put it somewhat later: "Diem could never have survived without American support. We cannot claim credit for selecting Diem or having pushed him into office, but we have since been his

most ardent and effective champion" (William Henderson, "South Viet Nam Finds Itself," *Foreign Affairs,* January, 1957). For an early survey of this entire period of U.S. policy toward Vietnam, see Miriam S. Farley, *United States Relations with Southeast Asia* (New York, 1955).

39. As Bernard Fall wrote in "The Political-Religious Sects of Viet Nam," *Pacific Affairs,* September, 1955, p. 249: "The Hoa Hao fiefs were first and foremost exceedingly profitable economic enterprises. . . . Soai and his fellow leaders, for example, controlled the bulk of rice purchasing and milling operations in the Bassac area. . . . The crop was sold by the farmers to Soai below market prices and the latter stored it until the end of the season (when prices are high) and then sold it to big enterprises in Saigon at huge profits. The second major source of income . . . was the operation of gambling establishments or collecting protection money from operators of such establishments." To add a bit of levity, MacAllister (*op. cit.,* p. 103) said: "Two of the leading war lords of the Hoa Hao were Tran Van Soai with the nickname Nam-Lua (Five Fires), and Le Quang Vinh, alias Bacut (Third Finger Severed). Any resemblance between religious motivation and their activities was purely coincidental." And Fall in his article on the sects says: "The hapless farmers who were under the rule of the maniacal Bacut fared worse, for the latter was given to fits of incredible cruelty and had no sense of public duty." For an intimate account of wheelings-dealings by the sect leaders, in particular the Binh Xuyen, in Saigon, which reads like a story of the Cosa Nostra in New York (if one were available in such detail), see Lucien Bodard, *La guerre d'Indochine: L'humiliation,* Part One, "Saigon, le moteur de la guerre," pp. 11–194.

40. The piaster remained Vietnam's currency. Cambodia and Laos adopted new monetary units, the riel and kip, respectively.

41. General Le Van Ty, whom Diem had named to succeed Hinh, represented the South Vietnamese Army on February 10, 1955, when he and General Agostini signed the transfer agreement that brought the Vietnamese Army under the control of the Diem Government. Chaffard, incidentally, called Le Van Ty "the man with the diplomatic ailments," since Ty on a number of occasions fell ill in order to avoid having to take part in actions he disliked, as for example in March, when the Hoa Hao forces threatened to reinforce the Binh Xuyen forces in Saigon. Eight years later, Ty again fell conveniently ill at the height of the Buddhist crisis and left for the United States, ostensibly to put himself under medical care (see Chaffard, *op. cit.,* pp. 61, 69, 78).

42. The U.S. Military Advisory Assistance Group (MAAG), headed by General John O'Daniel (Iron Mike) since the beginning of 1954, took over on this day.

43. MacAllister (*op. cit.,* p. 106) says that he has it "on excellent authority" that Hue and Day received financial compensation. Day actually brought his troops, which held the Cantho area, into the government camp only on March 10, at the beginning of the great crisis between Diem and the sects.

44. See Chapter VIII, note 98, for Diem's action against Phan Van Giao, the ex-Governor of Central Vietnam. Lancaster also tells of the arrest of Nguyen Van Tam's mistress, Mme. Le Thi Gioi, who was accused of bribery and misuse of official funds and sentenced to five years in prison. Mme. Gioi is said to have caused a sensation in court "by roundly accusing the active and prominent Mme. Ngo Dinh Nhu of indulging in similar activities on a far more extensive scale" (*op. cit.*, p. 381, n. 10).

45. Lancaster in a footnote to his description of The as "this disquieting young man" writes that "the size of the contingent which The produced for enrolment in the national army caused surprise, but these troops are reported to have included 1,000 ex-Viet Minh who had joined The's force to avoid evacuation to North Vietnam" (*op. cit.*, p. 381, n. 12, quoting from a report by Clos in *Le Monde*, June 3, 1955). One of the reasons given by The for rallying to Diem was Diem's success in fighting Communism. At the time, no one could say whether the Vietminh who had enlisted with The would turn into loyal troops or turn out to be infiltrators.

46. Nguyen Gia Ngo kept his promise to join the government only after the decisive defeat of the Hoa Hao in June, 1955. Another Hoa Hao leader, the mercurial and cruel "patriot" Le Quang Vinh (alias Bacut), who had defected from the main Hoa Hao forces with 3,000 men in August, 1954, never rallied; he chose armed resistance to Diem. An attempt by the National Army to defeat him at the end of 1954 failed, possibly because the plan against him was betrayed to him by Hoa Hao members in Diem's National Defense Committee.

47. Lancaster, *op. cit.*, p. 383.

48. I was one of the people who pleaded the cause of the Dai Viet, but was told by Diem in a long letter that Nguyen Ton Hoan could have entered his government but refused when his request that he be made Minister of Defense was rejected. Hoan's version of the incident differs. He claims that the composition of the Diem Government was agreed upon by various groups and Ngo Dinh Nhu before Diem's arrival. These groups were the ones with whom Nhu had formed his Front of National Salvation in May. The Ngo brothers, Hoan claimed, broke the promises they had given to get broad support for Diem's candidacy. Hoan went into exile to Paris. Leading a segment of the Dai Viet there, he occasionally issued publications and claimed to have an underground network in Vietnam.

49. See Max Clos, *Le Monde*, March 5, 1955.

50. The was accused of this by Bacut, who preferred looting to bribes. (The at this time was alleged to have received the 20 million piasters mentioned earlier, also by Joseph Alsop, in the *New York Herald Tribune*, April 1, 1955, in an article entitled "The Rooted and Rootless.")

51. Lancaster writes that Bao Dai appears to have been taken aback by the violent abuse heaped upon him by C. L. Sulzberger in *The New York Times*, March 14, 1955, in which Sulzberger accused Bao Dai as "happily spending [on the Riviera] the proceeds of his sordid profiteering and enjoying the prestige of diplomatic recognition as head of tormented Vietnam," a

situation which the *Times* correspondent called "appalling," adding that "Bao Dai rests on democracy's conscience about as comfortably as the putrefying albatross tied around the neck of Coleridge's Ancient Mariner." Lancaster says of the former Emperor that "although he expressed his approval of the desire for unity revealed by the setting up of a united front, he also sought to deflect American anger by sending a message to Diem expressing his satisfaction with his services" (*op. cit.*, pp. 383–84, and nn. 23 and 24, the last citing the *New York Herald Tribune* and *Le Populaire* of March 16, 1955, as carrying Bao Dai's message).

52. The ultimatum was signed by the same members of the presidium of the United Front who had issued the communiqué of February 23, 1955, from Cao Dai headquarters: General Nguyen Thanh Phuong, Commander in Chief of Cao Dai, and General Trinh Minh The, both Ministers in the Cabinet, and Pham Cong Tac, the Cao Dai Pope; General Tran Van Soai, Commander in Chief of the Hoa Hao forces, General Le Van Vien, Commander of the Binh Xuyen forces, and Generals Lam Thanh Nguyen and Le Quang Vinh (Bacut) (see B. S. N. Murti, *Vietnam Divided: The Unfinished Struggle* [New York, 1964], p. 133, nn. 8 and 9). Trinh Minh The's name appears on the ultimatum even though his loyalty had just been "obtained." Commented Joseph Alsop in his April 1, 1955, article in the *New York Herald Tribune:* "The price was paid. But Gen. Trinh Minh The is now a conspicuous figure in the anti-Diem 'Presidium' of the sects. And the best excuse he has been able to offer American officials is that he wished to exercise 'a moderating influence,' which has not been visible to date."

53. As reported in *Le Monde*, March 11, 1955. As Lancaster explains: "These Nung battalions had been evacuated from Tongking where they had been responsible for the security of an autonomous zone around Mon Cay which was directly attached to the Crown of Annam. The Nungs are of mixed stock, being descended from Hakkas, who had invaded the territory in the nineteenth century and intermarried with the predominantly Muong population" (*op. cit.*, p. 384, n. 26).

54. *The New York Times*, March 11, 1955. The American press became increasingly hostile to Bao Dai (see n. 51, above).

55. In describing the details of this incident, Murti (*op. cit.*, p. 136) speaks of nine National Army battalions launching a campaign against the rebel stronghold at Balang, in the mountain region near the Laotian border.

56. And Fall added (*The Two Viet-Nams*, pp. 245–46): "By the time the greedy sect leaders found out that they had been outmaneuvered and began to fight back, theirs was a lost cause."

57. No one doubted that Phuong was bought. Fall, whose informants were probably knowledgeable Frenchmen in Saigon, says his price was $3.6 million plus monthly payments for his troops (*ibid.*, p. 246). William Henderson confirms this in his article in *Foreign Affairs* of January, 1957 (p. 287), and MacAllister, in quoting Henderson, adds: "This was confirmed to the author by another knowledgeable observer" (*op. cit.*, p. 109).

58. Clos, in *Le Monde*, March 31, 1955.

59. See in particular a series of articles by Clos in *Le Monde*'s weekly editions of December 9–15, 16–22, and 28, 1954.

60. Ely and Collins wanted Diem to appoint Dr. Phan Huy Quat, who had served, usually for short periods, in several cabinets under Bao Dai, also in the last one under Buu Loc, and who was considered a member or at least a sympathizer of the Dai Viet. (Warner, *op. cit.*, p. 82, is wrong in flatly calling the Dai Viet with its authoritarian concept of democracy "fascist"; also in identifying Dr. Quat as a candidate of the Dai Viet; his ties to that party were always tenuous.) Diem rejected Dr. Quat after receiving, via Nhu, a secret-service report stating that Dr. Quat had taken part in a meeting with sect leaders. Diem appointed his own man, Ho Thong Minh, who soon became disenchanted with Diem and was one of the many who left the government during the crisis in spring, 1955. Phan Huy Quat became one of the many ephemeral leaders to emerge after the fall of Diem in 1963, first as Minister of Foreign Affairs, and later, for a few short months, as head of the civilian government that preceded the assumption of power by the "young Turks" under General Ky.

61. According to Warner (*op. cit.*, p. 79), Collins at this time advised Diem's "abandonment at the earliest possible date."

62. *The New York Times*, April 3, 1955.

63. *Ibid.*, April 7, 1955.

64. *Ibid.*, April 8, 1955.

65. In a series of three articles in the *New York Herald Tribune* on December 20, 22, and 24, 1954 (later published in a somewhat expanded version in *The New Yorker*, June 25, 1955) Joseph Alsop described a secret trip he had made into the Communist-guerrilla-held territory in the southernmost part of South Vietnam and strongly voiced his admiration, "a sort of horrified, helpless admiration" for the Communist achievement—"not of course for the thing itself, but for the courage shown, the incredible difficulties overcome, the sheer brilliance of the political-military feat." Speaking of the structure the Communists had erected there, Alsop wrote: "In short the whole mechanism of state power and regular administration was created out of nothing, in the nearly neolithic little muddy villages among the rice fields and in the very teeth of French military power." One reason why the National Government had less territory under its control after the partition was French policy toward the sects. In an article I wrote for the *New Leader*, June 27, 1955, entitled "Are We Saving South Vietnam?," I stated: "The French had favored the sects whenever a territory evacuated by the Viet Minh was to be occupied. They refused transportation of national army units or used other means of physical prevention until the sect armies had taken over the territory in dispute."

66. Cf. Chaffard, *op. cit.*, p. 73.

67. *Le Monde*, April 20, 1955; as quoted by Ellen Hammer, *The Struggle for Indochina Continues*, p. 37.

68. Lancaster says the Hoa Hao at this occasion "had been baited with an offer of 100 million piasters" (*op. cit.*, p. 387). Since Lancaster probably had

easy access to information from all embassies at Saigon (and their secret services) as well as from the French and Vietnamese, including the sect leaders themselves, he must be regarded as a reliable informant on these dealings, despite his anti-Diem bias.

69. MacAllister writes that Collins joined the French in urging Diem not to attack the Sûreté building, which served as headquarters for the Binh Xuyen; that was on April 6. On April 18, *The New York Times'* C. L. Sulzberger reported that Collins and Ely recommended that Diem be replaced. But before leaving for Washington, Collins assured Diem he still enjoyed full U.S. support, and *The New York Times* reported on April 21 that similar assurances had been given in Washington to Ambassador Tran Van Chuong. However, while Collins still was in Washington, reports reached Saigon that he was recommending that the United States cease its support of Diem. On May 1, the United States officially reiterated its support of the Diem Government. But when Collins arrived in Saigon on May 2 and was asked whether the U.S. Government continued to support the Diem Government, Collins replied, "No comment." MacAllister maintains that he was told by a well-informed observer of the fact "that Collins did actually recommend [while in Washington] that the United States cease backing Ngo," and he comments: "By appearing in Vietnamese eyes to be more concerned with the French than the Vietnamese and by recommending that Ngo be replaced, General Collins hardly provided the moral assistance required" (*op. cit.*, pp. 132–138).

70. *Le Monde*, April 30, 1955. *Combat*, April 21, stated in a report from Saigon that the French had suggested to Washington that Diem be replaced but had been turned down by Dulles. Commenting on Faure's statement, and calling him "ill-informed," Frédéric-Dupont wrote: "It was at this moment that General Hinh, an officer on active duty with the French Army, obtained a French visa to execute a mission in Vietnam that might be construed to be of an insurrectional nature." Frédéric-Dupont goes on to quote from Agence France Presse, which distributed the following text on April 30: "French policy has constantly been guided by the concern to do everything possible in preparation for the elections of July, 1956. . . . The methods employed by the Diem Government have never been approved by the French authorities. . . . Undoubtedly, the mediation efforts of Emperor Bao Dai would have a greater chance of success if the American Government would take a greater interest in them." And Frédéric-Dupont comments: "In a full civil war, the Faure Government thus played the sects against the Diem Government" (*op. cit.*, pp. 217–18).

71. In an account of this period, Homer Bigart wrote in *The New York Times*, August 22, 1963, that Edward G. Lansdale sided with Diem against Collins, and that Allen W. Dulles, the head of the C.I.A., persuaded John Foster Dulles that Lansdale was right. A retired Air Force General, Lansdale, who in August, 1965, was named "special assistant on pacification" to Ambassador Lodge in Saigon, is considered by *The New York Times* "a man of legend for exploits in South Vietnam." He is called "a remarkable

and controversial man" by Robert Shaplen, on whose presentation of Lansdale's background this account is based (*The Lost Revolution*, pp. 101–4 and 111–16). Lansdale, who served as a colonel with the Office of Strategic Services during World War II and afterward, "helped rebuild the Philippine Army intelligence service." When Shaplen first met him in 1951 in Manila, Lansdale, at President Quirino's request, had been assigned to help deal with the problem of the Communist-led Hukbalahaps (called Huks, for short), and was working closely with Magsaysay, then Philippine Secretary of Defense, and himself a former guerrilla leader against the Japanese. At the end of 1952, after the Huks were defeated, Magsaysay, "again with Lansdale's encouragement," became a candidate for the Philippine Presidency, and won it in November, 1953. That year, Lansdale was lent to the French in Vietnam to advise them on matters of "unconventional warfare." In the course of his work he got to know a number of Vietnamese political leaders in the North, among them Dr. Phan Huy Quat. At the request of Magsaysay, Lansdale returned to the Philippines during the first half of 1954, but late in May he received an urgent cable from Dulles instructing him to proceed at once to Saigon. His first task "under the broad secret orders given him by Dulles, was to learn quickly as much as he could about the chaotic situation in Vietnam," and he spent most of June getting to know members of the sects, as well as political and military leaders. Lansdale met Diem the day after Diem's arrival in Saigon. Shaplen quotes Lansdale as having stated after his meeting with Diem: "To me he was a man with a terrible burden to carry and in need of friends, and I tried to be an honest friend of his." According to Shaplen, when General Hinh refused to obey Diem's order to leave the country, and it seemed as if he were mounting a coup instead, Lansdale "took advantage of his old friendship with Magsaysay, who was much admired by Hinh and his staff, to spirit most of Hinh's top officers off to Manila in response to what he told them was 'a special invitation' from Magsaysay." Still according to Shaplen, Lansdale "personally rallied to the support" of Trinh Minh The, with whom he got along well despite their linguistic handicap. "Reports later circulated by the French and their Vietnamese agents that Lansdale bribed The to support Diem have been vehemently denied by Lansdale," Shaplen writes, quoting Lansdale as saying: "The rallied for purely patriotic reasons . . . the most I ever paid him was a cup of coffee or a meal when he visited me, and this was scant repayment for the hospitality he had shown me up in the mountains. All he finally got was a month's pay for his troops when they were integrated with the Vietnamese army." In a *New York Times* news story of August, 1965, Lansdale is said to have been the model for the "Colonel Hillendale" in the novel *The Ugly American*. Now in his mid-sixties, Major General Lansdale is attempting to wrest the allegiance of the Vietnamese population in South Vietnam from the Communists by peaceful means, despite the reported opposition by Secretary of Defense McNamara to his unorthodox form of diplomacy. His name is mentioned in every recent book on events in South Vietnam after the Geneva conference.

See in particular Jean Lacouture, *Vietnam: Between Two Truces* (New York, 1966), and Mecklin, *op. cit.*, p. 85.

72. It is in this context that my own activities in the United States for continued support of Diem must be viewed. The "exposure" of these activities in *Ramparts*, July, 1965, entitled "The Vietnam Lobby," is politically misleading. The facts as reported are on the whole correct, but the basic assumption of the article is absurd, for it attempts to prove that the Vietnam lobby was responsible for U.S. involvement in Vietnam. This involvement had long been decided upon, and no one in Washington at any time ever considered abandoning South Vietnam. This had become quite obvious in the U.S. reaction to the Geneva settlement. The question is whether South Vietnam's survival was helped or hindered by Diem's policies in 1954–55. Whether to support or drop Diem, not whether to defend or abandon South Vietnam, was the issue. I still believe that without Diem, South Vietnam would very likely have been lost to the Communists at that time. A version similar to the *Ramparts* story about my activities at that time in behalf of Diem appeared in the official Soviet journal *International Affairs*, October 5, 1965, in an article entitled "The Invisible State Department," by Vic. Zhukov. A still later version, which greatly expands my sinister role in Vietnamese affairs, emanates from the lunatic fringe of the American Right, in a book by Hilaire du Berrier entitled *Background to Betrayal: The Tragedy of Vietnam* (Belmont, Mass., 1965). According to Mr. du Berrier, I was the head of an international conspiracy that was using Diem to make Vietnam into a socialist country. Du Berrier also reveals another secret, namely that I alone "was responsible for breaking the anti-Communist front in Hungary" (p. 119), a statement that well illustrates the level of information and judgment the author has brought to the subject of Vietnam.

73. In his December, 1954, series in the *New York Herald Tribune*, Joseph Alsop made a facile comparison between the strong underground government left in South Vietnam by the withdrawing Vietminh and the "mere shadow of a shadow" of the government led by Diem. He accused Diem's government of having "hardly attempted to govern," and the U.S. Government of "naïveté" for "giving all-out support to President Ngo Dinh Diem without any very clear idea of what he would do with his power when he achieved it." He further accused Diem of seeking, above all, "personal power over the army," and, although being a devout Christian, of taking his political ideas from the ancient maxim of Confucius: "To put the country in order, the Son of Heaven needs only to have a pure heart and to sit facing south." In Alsop's eyes, Diem's regime at that time was comparable to Chiang Kai-shek's dying regime in China, the situation in Saigon comparable to a "squalid, aimless chaos," over which Diem "honest and virtuous but wholly out of contact with reality, presides with obstinate certainty that all will yet be well." And speaking in April, 1955, of the crisis of the sects, Alsop pronounced Diem "virtually impotent" and said that he would be "still less able to govern in the future." Alsop declared "the Diem experiment has failed." The trouble was, he wrote on April 4, that even long be-

fore the crisis with the sects, "the odds against President Diem putting over his program were somewhere between five and ten to one." In one major respect, however, Alsop was to be proved right in 1965, even though he was wrong in 1955. Speaking in June, 1955, of the possibility of a Communist-staged peasant rising in South Vietnam, he declared that "Premier Diem will be doomed unless he gets massive outside aid." What did not hold true for Diem, nor for the envisioned peasant rising, held true for Diem's successor governments and for the Vietminh efforts to have the Vietcong take over South Vietnam by force: Alsop's predicted massive American aid, "composed, furthermore, of American ground forces," had become necessary.

74. Graham Greene, in an article in *The New Republic*, April 19, 1955, reprinted in the London *Sunday Times* of April 24.

75. See Diem's Speech to the Free World, May 8, 1955 (Vietnam Embassy, Washington, D.C., Press and Information Service, May 13, 1955).

76. On this, Lancaster makes the following pertinent comment: "The exploitation of the gambling concession and of prostitution, the collection of tithes on paddy, rubber, fish, and coal, the exaction of protection money from the owners of bars, shops, and public transport, together with the time-honoured custom of blackmailing the wealthy Chinese community, had proved of such absorbing interest that military training had been neglected" (*op. cit.*, p. 389).

77. Lancaster feels that the defeat of the Binh Xuyen was as much due to their own weakness as to "the readiness of the national army to fight in defence of a Prime Minister whose authority they had decisively rejected in the autumn of the previous year." He ascribes this as much to the dislike felt by the regular units for the Binh Xuyen as to the fact that the troops involved in this operation had not been directly involved in the events culminating in General Hinh's dismissal (*ibid.*, pp. 389, 390). Chaffard writes a more detailed account, but one also more hostile to Diem; according to him, the operation against the Binh Xuyen had been planned and staged under American supervision, under the leadership of Colonel Cao Van Tri, who was directly attached to the Presidency (*op. cit.*, pp. 77–81). Warner, adding a touch of sensationalism to his account, writes that Tran Van Khiem, the brother of Mme. Nhu, announced after the taking of the Binh Xuyen headquarters (in his capacity as press officer to Diem) that human bones and bits of Vietnamese uniform had been found in the cage of the tigress that Le Van Vien had kept together with other wild animals, such as a leopard, a python, and crocodiles. This must be considered a sort of dress rehearsal for the regime's many later fabrications in its own defense (*op. cit.*, p. 85).

78. As reported in *The Times* (London), April 30, 1955.

79. See Henderson, *op. cit.*, p. 289.

80. See *The Christian Science Monitor*, April 30, 1955.

81. This cable was the result of Lansdale's wire to Secretary Dulles, in which he told of the successful routing of the Binh Xuyen by Diem. Prior to the receipt of Lansdale's wire, and as a result of Collins' recommendation

that Diem be dropped, Kenneth Young, of the State Department's Vietnam Task Force, had drafted and sent a telegram to the Embassy in Saigon (over Dulles' signature) proposing to "kick Diem upstairs," i.e., to have him become President of Vietnam, the "symbolic nationalist leader," but to have someone like Dr. Phan Huy Quat become the "functioning general manager," i.e., Premier. After the receipt of Lansdale's wire, which was read in Washington with "total consternation," the Dulles brothers, in consultation with each other, decided that the policy as set forth in the Young cable had become obsolete even before it went into effect; a second cable was sent, on the basis of which "the first one was burned." As Shaplen, the source for the background of this incident, describes it (*The Lost Revolution*, pp. 122–24), "by the time Collins' plane arrived back in Saigon, the whole American policy had again been reversed." Shaplen reports that Collins, angry at first, "pointedly accused Lansdale of inciting a mutiny," but in the end "he was satisfied that the turn of events had justified the switch." Nevertheless, even the positive statements made in Washington at the time the congratulatory cable was sent to Diem, reflected the fact that the support was given without enthusiasm. On April 29, Henry Sydam, Department of State press officer, stated: "The present head of the legal government of Free Vietnam which we are supporting is Diem and we acknowledge Bao Dai as Chief of State" (as reported in *The New York Times*, April 30, 1955). Senators Mansfield and Humphrey, as if aware of the need to strengthen the Executive's lame pronouncement, on April 29 and 30, respectively, came out with strong statements in favor of Diem.

82. The expression was used in this context by Miriam Farley, who tried to give the earliest account of these events in "Vietnamese Kaleidoscope," *Far Eastern Survey*, May, 1955. For the text of the manifesto that resulted from the Saigon Town Hall meeting of April 30, see Allan B. Cole (ed.), *Conflict in Indo-China and International Repercussions: A Documentary History, 1945–1955*, p. 223; the other recommendations of the Committee were, according to Scigliano (*op. cit.*, p. 23, n. 34), "that Diem put down the rebellion, gain full independence for the country, and request the complete withdrawal of the French Expeditionary Corps."

83. Only Chaffard, who saw American machinations behind every move of Diem, ascribes the meeting to the "team of the University of Michigan," meaning the professors of Michigan State's advisory group at the Saigon School of Administration, in particular Professor Wesley Fishel (see Chaffard, *op. cit.*, p. 82).

84. This is what Denis Warner, one of the most reliable and best-informed witnesses of the contemporary Vietnam scene, reports (*op. cit.*, p. 83).

85. In his article "Vietnam Since Geneva," published in *Thought*, XXXIII, No. 131, Winter, 1958–59 (p. 546, n. 55), Francis J. Corley gives the members of the Committee as follows: Nguyen Bao Toan, Hoang Co Thuy, General Nguyen Thanh Phuong, General Trinh Minh The, Nhi Lang, Van Ngoc, Huyn Minh Y, Doan Trung Con, Nguyen Huu Khai, Ho

Han Son. Corley notes that Nhi Lang "was later most courageous in aborting the attempted coup of General Vy." Nguyen Bao Toan "subsequently resigned from the committee in protest against what he considered the government's authoritarian manner." Cf. also, Clos, in *Le Monde*, April 3 and 4, 1956, on the "Assembly" and the composition of the Revolutionary Committee.

86. See Warner, *op. cit.*, p. 84. See also Chaffard, *op. cit.*, pp. 86–89; MacAllister, *op. cit.*, pp. 115–20; and, again probably the most reliable version, Lancaster, *op. cit.*, pp. 391–95.

87. Lancaster, *ibid.*, p. 392.

88. Clos, *Le Monde*, May 3, 1955.

89. Corley, *op. cit.*, p. 545.

90. Hammer, *op. cit.*, p. 38, note 31.

91. Nguyen Kien flatly asserts that The was killed on orders of Diem (*op. cit.*, p. 65); Chaffard argues firmly against this assumption (*op. cit.*, p. 89). Lancaster (*op. cit.*, p. 394) deals gingerly with the argument, citing the facts that The had been "shot from behind and that the wound was powder-blackened gave rise to a belief that he had in fact been assassinated at point-blank range by one of his entourage," and that his "fanaticism, terrorist methods, and ruthless ambition" had made him many enemies. Shaplen writes that Lansdale was with Diem when Nhu brought the news of The's death, and that Lansdale saw tears come into Diem's eyes. "It was the only time I ever saw him give in to his emotions," Shaplen quotes Lansdale as saying (*The Lost Revolution*, pp. 125, 126).

92. Nguyen Bao Toan sought political refuge in Cambodia. As he fled South Vietnam, he saw the Social Democratic Party, whose head he had been, purged and put under pro-Diem control. When later he went to the United States, where he protested against continued support of Diem (see *The New York Times*, March 17, 1956), I also saw him. He struck me as an honest man, and even then I believed that the accusations against him were slander, a tactic used by the regime against anyone who openly opposed it, as was later the case with Vu Van Thai. Toan took up residence in France, together with a number of other self-exiled Vietnamese. Scigliano mentions him and Nguyen Ngoc Bich as "perhaps the two most popular of the Paris oppositionists" (*op. cit.*, pp. 23–24, 79–80, and 82).

93. Henderson, *op. cit.*, p. 289.

94. See Paul Devinat, "Un Renouveau Franco-Vietnamien Est-il Possible?" in *Politique Etrangère*, July–August, 1955(?), p. 433; also, *Washington Post and Times Herald*, May 8, 1955. In his memoirs, General Ely frequently touches on the anti-Diem feelings among his collaborators, civilian and military alike. And in a most puzzling account of General Salan's departure from Vietnam (in October, 1954), Ely mentions that he learned after Salan had left that the latter had given the "go-ahead" signal to certain Vietnamese elements in order to "unleash a movement against Diem after his departure" (*op. cit.*, pp. 296–97). However, Ely insists that Diem's charges that the French command furnished arms and ammunition to the

Binh Xuyen were false, and he issued a formal denial to that effect (*ibid.*, p. 314). This still leaves open the possibility that those French officers who disagreed with Ely's policies disobeyed him and aided the Binh Xuyen on their own.

95. Nothing of the sort happened, and it is doubtful whether Dulles ever intended to abide by this agreement. As far as the French were concerned, they had in mind the firmly pro-Diem, and consequently "anti-French," activities of a number of military and civilian officials working in various capacities (see Chaffard, *op. cit.*, p. 75); their main targets were, of course, Wesley Fishel and Colonel Lansdale. According to Lancaster, Lansdale was known for his "pronounced 'anti-colonialist' views," and it was rumored that his advice to Diem "ran counter to the American Ambassador's encouragement of Ely's efforts to prevent the outbreak of civil war." (Still according to Lancaster, Ely's staff was split into pro-Diem and anti-Diem factions, "while the activities of certain French officers gave rise to a suspicion that the Expeditionary Corps was providing the sects with unofficial support in their opposition to the Prime Minister" [*op. cit.*, pp. 386–87].) Chaffard speaks of Lansdale as a "Lawrence of Indochina" (*op. cit.*, p. 53). Fall comments that "the exact nature and extent of American-French relations in those hectic days of spring 1955 in Saigon has thus far remained, on both sides, clad in official secrecy. What *seems* to have happened is that, for a short while, the 'young colonels' of both nations eluded the restraints imposed by their elders" (*The Two Viet-Nams*, p. 255). The term "young colonels" was also used by Lancaster (*op. cit.*, p. 386, n. 35), who cites Robert Guillain in *Le Monde*, May 18, 1955, as having referred to American advisers in this manner. For the strength of French feeling against these Americans, the testimony of John Mecklin, then correspondent for *Time*, is revealing. In recording his experiences during 1954–55, Mecklin relates: "French despair, mixed with petulant insensate arrogance as the reality of defeat settled upon them. Their vindictive resentment of American support for Diem. 'Children leading children,' sneered a French businessman who had made a fortune selling French textiles to Vietnamese peasants at exorbitant prices fixed by colonial authorities. Threats against American newsmen for reporting the sordid spectacle of French maneuvering against Diem. My hurt dismay when my friend, M. Boyer, proprietor of l'Amiral, my favorite restaurant, refused to serve me" (*op. cit.*, p. 4). Describing his personal experience in Vietnam, MacAllister, who arrived in Saigon in March, 1955, as my replacement in the International Rescue Committee's effort to aid the Northern refugees, wrote that the advice given him by many high American officials was: "Whatever you do, don't antagonize the French." He was also told that articles written by me upon my return to the States (see "Saigon Intrigue: France and Frenchmen," *The New Republic*, February 29, 1955; "An Eyewitness Report on Vietnam," *The Reporter*, January 27, 1955; and "Are We Saving South Vietnam?," *The New Leader*, June 27, 1955) had "antagonized the French." When invited to join the Board of Directors of the newly formed Vietnamese-American Association,

he was told that "Ambassador Collins wanted a French member." To which he added: "There is little doubt in the author's mind that General Collins had strongly advised all Embassy personnel to bend over backwards to avoid antagonizing the French" (*op. cit.*, pp. 133, 134).

96. *The New York Times*, May 30, 1955.

97. In fact, in the face of this demand, for which the stated reason was that it would "remind Vietnam of the burden of the old colonialist's regime," Paris named Henri Hoppenot to become Ely's successor in the capacity of "Ambassador on an extraordinary mission to Southeast Asia charged with the functions of High Commissioner to Vietnam." Diem rejected Hoppenot in such a capacity and insisted that prior to naming its ambassador, Paris should have consulted with the Vietnamese Government whether the envoy was *persona grata*, in accordance with diplomatic practice customary between independent countries. After negotiations conducted by Nguyen Huu Chau for the Diem Administration with the French Government, the French finally agreed to name Hoppenot Ambassador *"en mission extraordinaire"* (although the title "High Commissioner" was bestowed on him by the French residing in Vietnam), and to leave him without the military powers accorded former French representatives; the Vietnamese Government was also accorded the right, hitherto never granted by the French, to declare the French Ambassador *persona non grata* if it so wished and to demand his recall (see Murti, *op. cit.*, pp. 153 ff.; MacAllister, *op. cit.*, pp. 170–74)

98. According to the Saigon newspaper *Tin Dien* of March 14, 1956, a total of 866 persons opted for Vietnamese citizenship between August 16, 1955, and February 15, 1956. This means that the vast majority of Vietnamese holding French citizenship (their number was estimated at about 7,000) preferred to remain French—citizens of the country they were beginning to look toward as a place of exile.

99. Commenting on the withdrawal of the Expeditionary Corps, Chaffard wrote: "For the last time our troops filed through Saigon to the strains of *Le Boudin* and *Marche lorraine* and marched down *rue Catinat* to the port of embarkation. Conscious of the historical moment in which a century of living together was drawing to an end, and never having associated itself with the xenophobic rantings of the manipulated press, the capital's population gave an ovation to the battalions of the Legion, the parachutists in their red berets, the Moroccan infantry. Women wept. French civilians who witnessed this last parade amidst the crowd were the object of demonstrations of sympathy" (*op. cit.*, p. 109). Chaffard adds that Diem sent a message to General Jacquot, the last chief commander, which contained his greetings to the departing Corps in *"termes dignes."*

100. As Lancaster reports, Nguyen Thanh Phuong was arrested in 1957 on a number of charges, including that of being party to the murder of one Ho Han Son, a former member of the Revolutionary Committee and Vietminh political commissar, whose body was found at the bottom of a well near Cao Dai military headquarters (*op. cit.*, p. 397, n. 65). But Phuong

turned up during the Presidential election campaign in 1960, when he was an opposition slate candidate together with one of the odd opponents who ran against Diem. According to Scigliano, Phuong "had led a quiet life since the 1955 turbulence" (*op. cit.*, p. 92). In 1962, when the Diem regime instituted another dragnet of political opponents, Phuong was apparently once more among those arrested (see Warner, *op. cit.*, p. 100).

101. According to Lancaster, Tran Van Soai would probably have been prepared to accept Diem's money offer, but was no longer in a position to do so, due to the decision of the sect's leaders to reject the offer. This decision, Lancaster writes, was endorsed "with particular reluctance" by Soai's wife, Mme. Le Thi Gam, the notorious leader of a group of Hoa Hao amazons, who was known to have tortured her own and her husband's enemies, and "who was fearful of jeopardizing the wealth which she had amassed" (*op. cit.*, p. 395). This was also undoubtedly true of Nguyen Gia Ngo, who had already twice promised to bring his small army (1,000–2,000 men) into the government camp.

102. Nguyen Gia Ngo had a great talent for survival. After serving Diem for many years, he did not go down with his chief, but was among the generals whose conspiracy overthrew Diem on November 1, 1963.

103. Hinh returned to France, where he immediately received a relatively high position in the French Army.

104. See n. 39, above. According to Fall, a French officer assigned to train the sects noted that "the smaller and less well organized sect units' war effort closely resembled banditry . . . military units of the sects were largely concerned with acquiring larger fiefs" ("The Political-Religious Sects of Viet Nam," *op. cit.*, p. 241). For further details on the sects, see Darell Berrigan, "The Ordeal of South Viet Nam," in *The Reporter*, September 20, 1956.

105. Lancaster, *op. cit.*, pp. 397–98.

106. Murti, *op. cit.*, p. 142, n. 21.

107. Lancaster, *op. cit.*, p. 399; quoting *L'Humanité*, October 28, 1955.

108. Scigliano, *op. cit.*, p. 23. Surprisingly enough, Lacouture, in his latest book on Vietnam (*op. cit.*, p. 28), fails to condemn the methods employed in this election.

109. Warner, *op. cit.*, p. 86.

110. Former Premier Nguyen Phan Long and sixty other political personalities protested against the referendum, asking that the "system of one-man rule which has lasted too long should be done away with as quickly as possible and be replaced by a truly democratic regime" (Murti, *op. cit.*, p. 142).

111. *Le Monde*, October 14, 1955.

112. Chaffard, *op. cit.*, p. 101.

113. *Ibid.*, p. 100.

114. Lancaster (*op. cit.*, p. 362) writes that French onlookers, who could recall the popular enthusiasm displayed during the years 1945 and 1946, were surprised at the comparative indifference shown by the crowd. But as seen through the eyes of a Communist reporter, there was not indifference

but "calm and order," and "everyone was waving flags and flowers," in short, "it was a day of tears and cheers" (Wilfred Burchett, *North of the 17th Parallel* [Hanoi, 1957], pp. 89–93).

115. Basing his description of the parade on the eyewitness account of Gérard Tongas (*J'ai vécu dans l'enfer communiste au Nord Vietnam* [Paris, 1960], pp. 74 ff.), Chaffard (*op. cit.,* pp. 127–28) tells of the gigantic portrait of "Uncle Ho" behind the over-60-foot-high reviewing stand from which the North Vietnamese Party leaders and their guests (among them the French sailor Henri Martin, who had been court-martialed but later was released, and Frédéric Joliot-Curie) watched the innumerable military units and civilian organizations file by, waving flowers and flags, carrying bigger-than-life pictures of Marx, Lenin, Stalin, Mao Tse-tung, and other Communist heroes. In addition to Ho Chi Minh, Pham Van Dong, then still only Foreign Minister, and Vo Nguyen Giap also delivered speeches. The enthusiasm of the masses seemed overwhelming, Chaffard writes, and the spectacle was "moving."

116. See Frédéric-Dupont, *op. cit.,* p. 232.

117. This seems a fairly accurate figure, according to the Commissariat Général aux Réfugiés (usually referred to as COMIGAL, which was dissolved December, 1957). In its report entitled *The Exodus of the Northern Vietnamese* (mimeographed; Saigon, December, 1956), the figure given is 887,931. Approximately 120,000 persons in the southward evacuation movement were military and quasi-military personnel, in addition to the over-all figure of 900,000 civilian refugees. A lesser figure for military evacuees has been given by Francis J. Corley in his article "Vietnam Since Geneva," p. 528, where he says that 70,000 refugees were members of the armed forces. In his contribution to a symposium published by the American Friends of Vietnam entitled *America's Stake in Viet Nam* (New York, 1956), Monsignor Joseph J. Harnett estimated that approximately 212,000 persons were dependents of military personnel. For a discussion of these and other figures, see Bui Van Luong, former Director General of the Refugee Commission of the Government of Vietnam, and his exchange of comments with Bernard Fall, in Richard W. Lindholm (ed.), *Viet-Nam, The First Five Years: An International Symposium* (East Lansing, Mich., 1959), pp. 48–62. It seems that the failure to agree on exact figures has many and complex reasons, the main one being that the files of the Refugee Commissariat were destroyed in a fire during the fighting with the Binh Xuyen in spring, 1955. For an exchange of views on the roles played by French and American ships and planes in the evacuation of these refugees, see Luong and Fall, *ibid.,* pp. 48–76. Fall, in his comment on Luong's discussion on the role of friendly nations in the evacuation program, writes: "His [Luong's] remarks with regard to the part played by France in making the movement of the refugees a success is the first such statement published in the English language, and he should be congratulated for his fairness. American newspapers at the time made it appear as if the refugee evacuation operation had been a wholly American 'show.' . . . The French Air Force . . . flew a

round-the-clock airlift, whose difficulties and distances made the famous Berlin airlift . . . look like 'a walk in the sun' " (*ibid.*, p. 55). Luong countered Fall's assertion that the French should be credited with the evacuation of about 750,000 from North Vietnam with the statement that French ships and planes carried half, and not three-fourths, of the refugees, adding that "public opinion viewed this French effort only as the fulfillment of an obligation of France toward Viet-Nam. . . . Confronted with needs which far exceeded provisions, it was forced to declare its inability to assume this burdensome responsibility alone. Therefore, if it had not been for the swift and chivalrous assistance of the United States 7th Fleet, the Free World would have suffered a second Dien Bien Phu. Therefore, it seems natural to the Vietnamese that the American press should have described the refugees' evacuation as a major achievement of the United States government" (*ibid.*, p. 60). Fall retreated somewhat by commenting: "I am grateful to Bui Van Luong for stating the precise figures on refugee migration, which he sets at 747,791 'regular' refugees and 140,712 'irregulars,' and stand corrected in my evaluation of the French evacuation effort at 75 per cent of the refugees. Since no one knows exactly how the irregular refugees came south, the French effort (474,000 according to Luong) represents exactly 66.6 per cent of all regular refugees" (*ibid.*, p. 62). For a fascinating glimpse of the all-around problems the Americans coped with in their naval evacuation effort, see *ibid.*, pp. 63–76, "The Role of the United States Navy, Chronology of Events," by the Commander in Chief, U.S. Pacific Fleet.

118. See Bui Van Luong, in Lindholm (ed.), *op. cit.*, p. 49. See also Francis J. Corley, "Vietnam Since Geneva," pp. 523–31, who cites 676,348 Catholics, 182,817 Buddhists and animists, and 1,041 Protestants, making a total of 860,206. In his report at the conference sponsored by American Friends of Vietnam in New York on October 23–24, 1959, entitled *Social Development and Welfare in the Republic of Vietnam*, Robert J. MacAllister, speaking on the topic "The Refugee in Retrospect," mentioned 60 per cent as being Catholics out of a total of about 800,000. Fall writes that of the 860,000 refugees (this figure, given in *The Two Viet-Nams*, p. 154, differs from his figure of 888,500 in his contribution to *Viet-Nam: The First Five Years*, p. 62), 600,000 were Catholics, 65 per cent of the total Catholic population in the North. Jumper and Normand cite 660,000 Catholic refugees, but state that 800,000 Catholics remained in the North (*op. cit.*, p. 498). Fall makes the point that of the non-Catholic population, 99.5 per cent stayed and that those non-Catholics who left were mostly dependents of the Vietnamese National Army and government officials (*The Two Viet-Nams*, p. 154).

119. In my contribution to *America's Stake in Vietnam*, I posed the question why so many people with strong ties to their native villages left the North, and answered it first by saying that hatred for the Vietminh did not completely account for this historic population shift. Nor did I accept the explanation given by the Communists. Instead I felt that the answer rested

in part in Vietnamese history. Believing that there had been a strong predisposition to leave the overpopulated North, I said: "Vietnamese peasants have gone from the North to the South in search of land, and sometimes also in search of freedom, for at least one thousand years. It is one of the great capabilities of Vietnam that the South has always been able to repair the damage that the body of this nation has suffered again and again in the overcrowded spaces of the North." And I concluded: "The meaning of the refugee movement in the context of our subject, therefore, is a healthy population adjustment within the country as a whole. . . . The South would indeed be capable of taking in another 2 million people from the North if the means for a speedy settlement were at hand, and if the Communists could be forced to open the gates for those who want to leave" (pp. 50, 51). Looking at the problem of overpopulation in the North with an eye also toward Communist intentions, it is not only conceivable but more than likely that part of the Vietminh's objective in conquering the South is its desire to divert the pressure of overpopulation from the Red River Delta to the Mekong Delta. (The Communist allegations, ridiculous though they may sound, were voiced by Giap during the fourth session of the National Assembly in March, 1955.)

120. Pham Van Dong only promised that these interests "would be taken into consideration in such cases of requisition or expropriation" (see Chaffard, *op. cit.*, pp. 115–16, for the text of this letter).

121. One of these men was M. Clerget, director of the Société des Charbonnages du Tonkin; the other was M. Lefaucheux, the director of Renault, who actually proposed to build an assembly plant for the 4-CV Renault at Hanoi (see Chaffard, *ibid.*, p. 122).

122. According to Chaffard (*ibid.*, pp. 121, 122), the French had the choice, under the December 10, 1954, agreement, of maintaining the present status of their enterprises or transforming them into "mixed" companies, with the participation of Vietnamese capital. They would not suffer any discriminatory measures, be given facilities for the purchase of basic machinery and tools, and also be permitted to transfer their earnings to the French monetary zone. They would be free in the choice of location, hiring of personnel, and sale of the manufactured products on the national market. This economic accord was followed on December 15 by a cultural agreement (albeit, only verbal), by which Professor Huard (former Dean of the Hanoi School of Medicine) and Professor Blondel, Chief Physician of the French hospital St. Paul, would lecture at the university. The annual medical exposition, known as the "Bichat conference," which had been sponsored by Professor Besançon, would be held in March, 1955, for the benefit of the Vietnamese physicians. Finally, under an arrangement to be agreed on later, the activities of the Pasteur Institute, the Cancer Institute, the Albert-Sarraut School, and the French Far Eastern School, were to be continued.

123. According to Lancaster, the appointment caused surprise, since after his return to France in 1947, Sainteny had retired from public service with the rank of "Colonial Governor." Lancaster adds that Sainteny's "decision

to accept the post appears to have been due to a belief that his personal acquaintance with the Vietminh leaders, and in particular his past friendship with Ho Chi Minh, would enable him to render useful service" (*op. cit.*, p. 365). Chaffard's description of Sainteny at Hanoi is amusingly malicious. "The man was attractive and had a certain 'style,'" he wrote. "Also ambition, not necessarily a defect. He charmed his collaborators, somewhat like de Lattre, in whose residence at Hanoi he lived but whose stature he did not have. The ostentation he brought to bear on his title of 'Governor' was somewhat ridiculous in post-Geneva North Vietnam, and the ceremonies held in the Maison de France—where a captain continued to function as *aide de camp* to the governor as cover for some naïve, soon uncovered, gathering of intelligence—seemed reminiscent of the colonial period. Actually, after early 1955, Sainteny spent only brief periods in Hanoi, having quickly realized the limitations of his mission and preferring to conduct his business in Paris" (*op. cit.*, p. 121).

124. Chaffard thinks that the company had concluded *"une bonne affaire"* (*op. cit.*, p. 124), even though during four months of negotiations it had argued it owned the land and the subsoil under its coal mines, in addition to the material equipment, which was all the regime would recognize as being French property. The compensation in coal payments to the company was fixed at 5 billion francs. As Chaffard puts it, the company sold the coal to its old customers: Japan, the Philippines, and Hong Kong. Fall called the price obtained "ridiculously inadequate," and reports that the agreement was for ten years only (*The Two Viet-Nams*, p. 192). The fifteen-year period seems to be the correct one, for Lancaster (*op. cit.*, p. 367, n. 13), who also mentions the fifteen-year period, gives *Le Monde*, June 4, 1955, as his source.

125. See *The New York Times*, December 29, 1954. Jumper and Normand (*op. cit.*, p. 507) give an interesting table of Chinese and Soviet aid to Hanoi:

Foreign Aid to North Vietnam (in millions of U.S. dollars)

Year	China Grant	China Credit	U.S.S.R. Grant	U.S.S.R. Credit	Eastern Europe Grant	Eastern Europe Credit	Totals Grant	Totals Credit	Grand Total
1955–57	200	—	100	50	—	—	300	50	350
1958–60	25	75	—	87.5	—	26	25	188.5	213.5
1961–65	—	157.5	5	107.5	—	62.5	5	327.5	332.5
Total	225	232.5	105	245.0		88.5	330	566.0	896.0

The authors observe that evidently Chinese aid consistently surpassed Russian aid, which in some quarters has been interpreted as proof of tacit Soviet recognition that North Vietnam lies within China's sphere of influence. They point out, however, that whereas both countries sent teams of specialists to North Vietnam to help train technicians and workers, by the end of 1961 nearly 3,000 Vietnamese students and trainees were studying in the Soviet Union. (*Ibid.*, pp. 507, 508; from an interview with Nguyen Duy Trinh, chairman of the State Planning Commission [V.N.A. Hanoi radio, November 7, 1962].) See also Nguyen Thai Binh, *Viet-Nam: The Problem and a Solution* (Paris, 1962), pp. 62–64, for further details on Chinese, Soviet, and other "bloc" aid to North Vietnam.

126. Of the numerous works cited in the bibliography, the most comprehensive, politically balanced study available of North Vietnam is Bernard B. Fall, *Le Viet-Minh*. Among the others, the best works on conditions in post-Geneva North Vietnam are: Wilfred Burchett, *North of the 17th Parallel* (Burchett, an Australian Communist journalist, must be regarded as the chief foreign propagandist for Hanoi); Bernard B. Fall, *The Viet-Minh Regime* and *The Two Viet-Nams*; Hoang Van Chi, *From Colonialism to Communism: A Case History of North Vietnam* and *The New Class in North Vietnam* (Saigon, 1958); P. J. Honey (ed.), *North Vietnam Today: Profile of a Communist Satellite* and *Communism in North Vietnam* (Cambridge, Mass., 1963); Roy Jumper and Marjorie Weiner Normand, "North Vietnam," in George McTurnan Kahin (ed.), *op. cit.* An idyllic picture of life in the North can be found in Bruno Frei, *Frühling in Vietnam* (Spring in Vietnam[!] [East Berlin, 1959]).

127. I owe much of this brief description to the information-packed chapter on North Vietnam in Fall, *The Two Viet-Nams*.

128. According to Fall, the North Vietnamese regime's diminishing share of foreign aid, represented in the country's budget in percentages of the total, demonstrated its desire to avoid "a new 'colonialism' (particularly by the ever-present Chinese 'Big Brother')." Fall gives two sets of figures, one dating from 1962, showing "a heavier (and probably more realistic) dependence on foreign aid than had previously been admitted," and figures in parentheses as provided by the D.R.V.N. in 1960. For 1955, he gives 65.3 of the total budget, and in parentheses, 38.6; for 1956, his figure, in parentheses only, is 40.0; for 1957, 60.8, and in parentheses, 36.9; for 1958, 31.3 in parentheses; for 1959, 27.0 in parentheses; for 1960, 21.0, and 17.7 in parentheses; for 1961, 19.9; and for 1965 (est.), 15.0 (*The Two Viet-Nams*, p. 177). There is a wide divergency, however, between the foreign aid figures for North Vietnam given by Fall and those given by Jumper and Normand. Fall quotes from a speech made by Le Thanh Nghi, the D.R.V.N.'s Minister for Heavy Industry, on March 18, 1962, to state that "Communist-bloc grants and loans from 1955 through 1961 totaled more than $1 billion, of which the Soviets supplied $365 million, the Eastern European countries $38 million, and Communist China $662 million. Of this sum, $280 million came from Chinese long-term loans and $47 million from Soviet long-term loans" (*ibid.*, p. 175, and p. 461, n. 5). Communist-bloc aid figures by Jumper and Normand (see n. 125, above) are not nearly as high. Fall also writes that "up to 1961, in terms of strictly economic aid . . . North Viet-Nam had received more than $70 per person, which is about equal to what its southern rival received from the United States." He compares Communist-bloc aid with aid received by South Vietnam from the United States, which, he notes, "according to Agency for International Development figures, South Viet-

Nam had received through June 30, 1961, a total of $1.44 billion in grant aid
and $95 million in loans. Of this, however, only $160 million was allocated to
specific economic aid projects" (*ibid.*, p. 175, and p. 461, n. 4). Scigliano as-
sesses the per-capita dollar contribution in South Vietnam through foreign
aid according to the contribution of that aid, and consequently as much
lower. According to him, "in 1960 Vietnam received from the United States
the equivalent of $13.70 for each inhabitant. . . . Only Laos, with a per cap-
ita assistance of $17, surpassed Vietnam among the countries of South and
Southeast Asia" (*op. cit.*, p. 112). He notes that "since 1954, the United
States has poured another $2 billion of economic aid alone into Vietnam,"
basing his figures on USOM, *Annual Statistical Bulletin, 1961*, which states
(p. 120) that total economic assistance for the period July, 1954, through
June, 1962, is placed at $1.701 billion. Scigliano comments that "it appears
certain, however, that its preliminary estimate of $156.8 million for the last
twelve months of this period has been substantially exceeded as a result of
the intensification in the American aid program during 1962. Indeed, by mid-
1962, newspaper stories were referring to an American expenditure of $1
million per day" (*op. cit.*, pp. 111–12, n. 14). But Scigliano is quick to point
out that "78 per cent of all American aid given to Vietnam between these
two years [1958–1960] went into the military budget," and he further notes
that "the great bulk of American economic aid has supported the Vietnamese military budget largely through funds generated by the commercial
import program, while only about 22 per cent of all aid, whether from imports or provided in other ways, has been used in economic and technical
assistance projects" (*ibid.*, pp. 113, 114). For an early, detailed discussion of
American aid to Vietnam, see John D. Montgomery, *The Politics of Foreign Aid* (New York, 1962), in particular pp. 22–24, and Appendix I, Table 4.

129. The 1965 plan figures in Fall's table of industrial output in selected
sectors in North Vietnam seem inordinately optimistic. (The planned increase in steel production, for example, is anticipated to go from 5,000 tons
in 1962, to 200,000 in 1965, and coal from 2.804 million tons in 1961, to 4.2
million in 1965; *The Two Viet-Nams*, p. 172, Table 6.) Although Fall mentions the relatively small labor force employed in industries and mines
(about 150,000 workers in 1963), he notes that a second steel center is
planned near Yen Bay, in the upper Red River Valley. (The current steel
center at Thai Nguyen was constructed almost on top of the iron-ore deposits, Fall writes, and will receive its fuel from the Quang Yen coal fields
by trains and river barges, with the barges on their return trip bringing steel
to "the excellent Soviet-built machine-tool plant in Hanoi," as well as
clinker to the Haiphong cement plant.) He tells of a phosphate plant that
the Soviets built at Lam Thoa, near Phu Tho, "which began production on
June 25, 1962, with an initial production of 100,000 tons a year and is slated
to reach a yearly production of 500,000 tons at the end of the 1965 plan.
. . . Vast apatite deposits estimated at 1 billion tons" at Laokay, near the
Red River, are providing the wherewithal for this plant. The weakness in
the North Vietnamese economy, Fall notes, is "the shortage of electric

power and the paucity of communications," and he states that "in 1961, the nonindustrialized South produced 273 million KWH's of electricity, while North Viet-Nam produced 276 million. As a consequence, northern cities (including Hanoi) are in a state of 'brown-out,' and the population is exhorted not to use big bulbs and electric fans." Emphasis on road and rail communication with China has contributed to extensive repair in that direction, Fall adds, while such communication toward the 17th parallel seems to have been deliberately held back (*ibid.*, pp. 169–75).

130. See Jumper and Normand, *op. cit.*, p. 466. In a footnote the authors cite Vietnam News Agency, Radio Hanoi, May 5, 1962, as their source and add that the number of workers in heavy industry is said to have increased from over 20,000 in 1957 to more than 40,000 in 1960, with a concomitant increase in the ratio of technicians.

131. Thus was their attitude described by Le Duan, General Secretary of the Party, in his "Political Report of the Central Committee of the Viet Nam Workers' Party," in *Third International Congress*, 1960; as quoted by Jumper and Normand, *op. cit.*, p. 469. See also *ibid.*, p. 470, where the authors again quote Le Duan and an official publication entitled *The Democratic Republic of Viet Nam* in the following résumé: "Although by 1960 a reported 67.8 per cent of the professional, or full-time artisans had joined 'various types of handicraft co-operatives,' the government has been unable to stamp out capitalism 'owing to the state of dispersed individual production.'"

132. Jumper and Normand, *op. cit.*, p. 469, n. 31.

133. See P. J. Honey, "The Democratic Republic of Vietnam in 1962," *China News Analysis*, March 15, 1963, p. 2. In his introduction to *North Vietnam Today*, edited by him, Honey writes: "Oppressed in this manner, the peasants reacted in the only way they could. They hid their produce and kept it for their own use, refusing to sell the allotted quotas to the government, and thus dealt a major blow to the economy. They ceased to devote their former care to the rice fields, for these no longer belonged to them, but to the collectives, and this resulted in a dramatic decline in food production. . . . Consequently, they sought to acquire money by selling some of their produce clandestinely, and from this practice grew the black market in food, which reached its peak during the terrible food shortages of 1961" (p. 11).

134. Fall, *The Two Viet-Nams*, p. 163. On pages 162–68, Fall gives a more detailed discussion of the entire problem and the intricacies of North Vietnamese production statistics, and also of food-production figures other than rice. See also William Kaye, "A Bowl of Rice Divided: The Economy of North Vietnam," in Honey (ed.), *op. cit.* In his contribution to *North Vietnam Today*, entitled "Collectivisation and Rice Production," Hoang Van Chi cites from Gérard Tongas' account of the widespread famine in Tongking during a period for which the statisticians were claiming enormous increases in agricultural production. Tongas (*op. cit.*, p. 225), had this to say about D.R.V. statistics: "Production figures are not merely faked,

and percentages are not merely increased: most of the time both are totally invented—and with what fervor!" Hoang Van Chi's reasoning concerning the slow increase of rice production in North Vietnam is made very plausible in the above-mentioned article.

135. My discussion of land reform in North Vietnam is largely based on "Communist Land Policy in North Viet Nam," by J. Price Gittinger, in *Far Eastern Survey*, XXVII, August, 1959, still by far the best report on the subject by an agricultural economist. It was written while the author was working with the U.S. Operations Mission to Vietnam.

136. "Despite the precautions, mass mobilization showed signs of getting seriously out of control in the late summer of 1953 and it was brought to a halt that September before any substantial transfer of wealth had occurred. The Viet Minh reported the movement had affected 836 villages with a population of 3.5 million but, considering the area reported to have been covered, the actual results appear rather small. People's courts confiscated some 14,000 hectares of rice fields and 2,650 buffaloes from 'reactionaries' and 'cruel notables,' and obliged landlords to repay 12,262 metric tons of paddy representing excess rent collected from 137,000 families. The peasants 'exposed' the 'crimes' of 10,015 landowners who were brought before people's courts. Of these, 135 were condemned to death and about 1,200 imprisoned for 're-education.' Viet Minh broadcasts gave a picture of peasants indulging in open revenge, with full Party approval, and taking booty in paddy, animals and tools. The whole program—even the loss of control—was a foretaste of what was to come on a broader scale in 1955 and 1956" (*ibid.*, p. 116).

137. It was a Communist author who in a vivid description of these proceedings revealed their brutality with a candor uncommon among the literary propagandists of Communism. See Burchett, *op. cit.*, Chapters VII and VIII, pp. 113–49. Another Communist author, Nguyen Kien, says that the agrarian reform was executed radically, "even brutally" (*op. cit.*, p. 175).

138. Fall, *The Two Viet-Nams*, p. 155. Fall's description and analysis of the result of North Vietnam's agrarian reform is to be found on pp. 154–61.

139. *Ibid.*, p. 156.

140. Quoted by Chaffard, *op. cit.*, pp. 141–42.

141. Specifying the "errors" committed, Giap said: "The political party and government line was not fully applied in the rural areas; sometimes it was even countermanded. The cadres . . . seeing the enemy everywhere and acting without discrimination, and sometimes overvaluing the cultivated areas and productive capacity of the land, injured and even acted against certain poor peasants and agricultural workers. . . . In regions with a religious majority, the beliefs of the population were not sufficiently respected. In regions inhabited by ethnic minorities, the habits and customs of the people were violated. . . . All landowners were routinely considered as enemies, even those who had participated in the resistance. . . . During the repression, excessive severity led to a lack of prudence, and illegal means of pressure were applied. . . . Countless innocents were labeled as reaction-

aries and arrested, judged, held in detention, isolated. . . . Our own partisans were struck . . . a large number of valuable members of our organizations." All of which, Giap added, "rendered life difficult and miserable to a certain number of people living in the countryside" (excerpted from Chaffard, *op. cit.*, p. 144).

142. Quoted by Fall, *The Two Viet-Nams*, p. 157. Fall believes that the number executed during the agrarian reform campaign was close to 50,000.

143. According to Gittinger, the average per-capita holding of "landless peasants" was reported to have risen from 199 square meters before the reform to 1,528 square meters (about 0.15 hectare), and that of small peasants from 455 square meters to 1,431 square meters (about 0.14 hectare; *op. cit.*, p. 119). Fall (*The Two Viet-Nams*, p. 159) cites the Russian writer V. Zelentsov, from a September, 1957, article referred to by Jeanne Delattre in the June, 1961, issue of *Economie et Politique*, a French Communist periodical. In her article, entitled "L'économie vietnamienne au debut de son premier quinquennal," Jeanne Delattre gives a table of the average acreages before and after land reform (in hectares):

Social Class	Before	After
Landowner	.65	.10
Rich farmer	.21	.21
Medium farmer	.12	.17
Poor farmer	.05	.14
Laborer	.02	.15

Fall adds that seemingly the "rich farmer" emerged from the reform process even richer, in comparison to all the other classes, and if he was lucky enough to have a family of five over eighteen, he would have received more than 1 hectare of farm land, about the right amount to "make a decent agricultural living." In other words, the 0.5 hectare the poor and landless peasants would have received per family would have been "useless" (Fall, *ibid.*).

144. See Fall, *ibid.*, pp. 156–57; also Chaffard, *op. cit.*, pp. 142–43. Fall points out the coincidence of the Nghe An uprising on the same date on which the Soviet were crushing the Hungarian revolt "at the other end of the Communist bloc," and "under precisely the same conditions." That the Nghe An revolt became known in the Western world was due to the accidental presence of the Canadian members of the International Control Commission when the outbreak took place. Fall also speaks of close to 6,000 farmers having been deported or executed. Chaffard speaks of the possibility of South Vietnamese elements having infiltrated that province and provoked the conflict. But he notes that "sufficiently serious reasons existed no doubt locally to explain this burning anger." (Jumper and Normand, in reporting on this incident, quote VNA, Radio Hanoi, November 25, 1956, as blaming it on a few "saboteurs . . . [who] incited the people to attack the men of the People's Army . . . [and] to oppose and manhandle the administrative personnel and the People's Army personnel" (*op. cit.*, p. 464, n. 10). Git-

tinger reports that "a surprisingly candid picture of the three-day Nghe An uprising emerges from the first descriptions broadcast by Hanoi." Accordingly, peasants "man-handled village cadres and troops stationed in the area," irate peasants organized open demonstrations against land reform "errors" and the treatment of Catholic peasants. When local militia units were sent to quell the demonstration, "28 soldiers were captured, 10 others were wounded, and arms and ammunition confiscated." The peasants set up road blocks, and finally marched toward the district capital, "bearing with them sticks and rudimentary arms." The hastily summoned regular troops were "forced to fight back." By next morning, martial law had been established in the area. Gittinger also quotes Truong Chinh as later admitting that landowners "everywhere" had caused trouble and that there had been a widespread "tendency of . . . peasants toward spontaneous action" (*op. cit.*, p. 119; citing VNA, November 17, 1956, Radio Hanoi, November 20, 1956, and *Nhan Dan*, January 15 and 31, 1957; see also *Land Reform Failures in Communist North Viet Nam*, Saigon, 1957).

XII. *Toward the Second Indochina War*
(pp. 917–1010)

1. Diem, incidentally, was aware of the nature of his early achievement. Robert J. MacAllister writes: "Ngo has often expressed to the author his regret at having to concentrate first on what he called 'negative' tasks" (*The Great Gamble: United States Policy Toward Viet Nam from July, 1954, to July, 1956*, p. 221). Robert Scigliano also called Diem's early victories "essentially negative" (*South Vietnam: Nation Under Stress*, p. 25). But most observers greatly admired these "negative" achievements. Francis J. Corley, S.J., for instance, in an article entitled "Freedom in Indochina," in *Pacific Affairs*, Winter, 1961–62, p. 379, said "that the government survived the prodigious obstacles of July–December 1954 and the military crisis of the spring of 1955 is a magnificent achievement." William Henderson, in a contribution to Richard W. Lindholm (ed.), *Viet-Nam: The First Five Years*, p. 342, also called Diem's survival in the first two years after the Geneva agreement "a political miracle of the first magnitude." I myself, in my contribution to Mr. Lindholm's volume (entitled "The Miracle of Viet-Nam"), called Diem's achievement the major contribution to this miracle (p. 30). However, I must add that Mr. Henderson was not an uncritical admirer of Diem. In the same volume (p. 345), he said: "After four years there has been little moderation of the grim dictatorship which Diem has exerted from the beginning."

2. As Wesley R. Fishel wrote: "The dislocations that resulted from the 1954 partition caused the loss to South Vietnam of the coal, cement, chemicals and other products of the North. In addition, because partition also meant the breakup of the Indochinese Union, the foreign commerce of Laos and Cambodia simultaneously ceased to be plus factors in the Vietnamese

economic picture. Then, during the period 1954–56, the evacuation of the French Expeditionary Corps, a primary source of domestic income and foreign exchange to Vietnamese businessmen, had a sharply depressing effect on the economy. According to official statistics, more than 85,000 wage-earners became unemployed by the French withdrawal. French military expenditures in Vietnam, which in 1954 amounted to approximately $436 million and in 1955, a year after the armistice, $114 million, dropped to insignificance during the next year. With the departure of the French military, thousands of French civilians also left Vietnam, leaving closed business establishments behind them" (*Vietnam, Is Victory Possible?*, Foreign Policy Association Headline Series, No. 163, February, 1964, pp. 29–30). Scigliano, quoting Buu Hoan ("Impact of Military Expenditures on the South Vietnamese Economy," in *Far Eastern Economic Review*, December 25, 1958, p. 839), confirms Fishel's figure by stating that "the departure of French troops, completed in 1956, directly cost 85,000 people their jobs" (*op. cit.*, p. 102). Bernard B. Fall thinks that the scale of damage provoked by the departure of the French troops was even greater. According to him, almost all of the 120,000 Vietnamese who had served in the French armed forces and the 40,000 others who worked in French Army arsenals and workshops throughout the country were thrown out of their jobs. "Nearly 160,000 formerly French-employed Vietnamese were out of work," he stated, "since the 150,000-man postarmistice Vietnamese Army could absorb only a small fraction of the best-skilled specialists" (*The Two Viet-Nams*, p. 291).

3. Fishel, *op. cit.*, p. 32.

4. For data on the work of reconstruction in the South, see Leland Barrows, "United States–Vietnamese Cooperation: The I.C.A. Program since 1955," *Department of State Bulletin*, May 11, 1959, pp. 674–81; U.S. Operations Mission (USOM) reports: "Building Economic Strength," *Annual Report for Fiscal Year 1958, July 1, 1957–June 30, 1958*, and *Annual Report for Fiscal Year 1959, July 1, 1958–June 30, 1959*. Cf. also *Bilan de réalisations gouvernemental 1954–1961*, Saigon, 1961; quoted by Fall, *op. cit.*, p. 294, and Scigliano, *op. cit.*, p. 105, who writes that almost 700 miles of main roads, over a third of the railroad trackage, hundreds of bridges, and a large part of the canal system had suffered destruction or deterioration. "Travel along even main highways was slow and in places nearly impossible," he comments. "By late 1962, the railroad system between Hue . . . and Saigon was in its fourth year of operation and much of the road and canal system had been rehabilitated."

5. See Bui Van Luong, Former General Director of the Refugee Commission of the Government of Vietnam, in Lindholm (ed.), *op. cit.*, p. 52. According to Luong, a total of 319 resettlement villages had been created as of mid-1957. Of these, 288 were for farmers, 26 for fishermen, and 5 for artisans; 207 of these villages were located in the south, 50 in the delta region of central Vietnam, and 62 in the mountain region of central Vietnam. Monsignor Joseph J. Harnett, a leading figure in the Catholic Relief Services, stated that of the approximately 300 resettlement villages "about 267

villages eventually became known as Catholic villages, about 32 as Buddhist villages, and 3 as Protestant villages" ("Refugee Resettlement," in *America's Stake in Vietnam*, p. 43).

6. *Migration Facts and Figures*, No. 20, September–October, 1959. The article states that in 100 other villages aid was gradually being withdrawn, and that the remaining 168 villages still needed substantial help. The story of the care for the influx and resettlement of refugees has been told often and needs no further detailed retelling. The main authors on the subject, apart from the official publications already mentioned, are Monsignor Joseph J. Harnett (see *America's Stake in Vietnam*, and "The Vietnamese Refugee Five Years Later," *Migration News*) and Francis J. Corley, S.J. (see "Vietnam Since Geneva," *Thought*). A very balanced account of both the great achievements and the shortcomings in the execution of the final resettlement is given by Robert J. MacAllister (in an unpublished paper, "The Refugee in Retrospect," read at the American Friends of Vietnam conference in October, 1959). There also exists an unpublished paper on the subject by Alfred L. Cardinaux, entitled "The Refugees of Viet Nam," cited by and in possession of Mr. MacAllister. On U.S. aid, see also "Final Audit Report, Project 30–95–075. Aid to Refugees (Operation Exodus)," reprinted in *Situation in Vietnam*, Hearings Before a Subcommittee of the Senate Committee on Foreign Relations, 86th Cong., 1st sess., July 30, 1959 (Washington, D.C., 1959), cited by John D. Montgomery, *The Politics of Foreign Aid*, p. 85, n. 12, who also speaks of the cost involved: "The American contribution was $55 million in 1955 alone, including $44 million for transportation provided by the U.S. navy. In 1956, another $37 million was contributed for the permanent resettlement of over 300,000 northerners" (*ibid.*, p. 47).

7. Exact figures for aid in the care and resettlement of refugees are hard to come by. See, however, Harnett, Luong, and other sources cited in earlier notes this chapter. In addition, cf. Lindholm, "American Aid and Its Financial Impact," in Lindholm (ed.), *op. cit.*, p. 317, where he says that in the fiscal year 1954–55, U.S. aid amounted to $55.785 million, out of a total of $320.3 million spent on Vietnam aid, and in 1955–56, it amounted to $37 million, out of $196.5 million total aid, or to 10 per cent of the total.

8. For a report on the resettlement of land abandoned during the war, chiefly in the Mekong Delta, see William Henderson, in Fishel (ed.), *Problems of Freedom: South Vietnam Since Independence*. But Vietnam had also much land in the southern and central mainland region that could be opened up for cultivation, and later was—in a new resettlement effort that also included refugees from the North (see *ibid.*, pp. 123–38).

9. See Harnett, in Lindholm (ed.), *op. cit.*, p. 85, who speaks of a "clumsy system," and of administrative procedures that were "strangling the operation."

10. Another factor that deserves mention was the assistance rendered by private refugee organizations, mostly American, and largely religious. The greatest impact was made by the Catholic Relief Services of the National Catholic Welfare Conference (which worked also through the Catholic

Welfare Committee and the Catholic Auxiliary Resettlement Committee), Operation Brotherhood, CARE, Church World Service, the Mennonite Central Committee, the Protestant Evangelical Church of Vietnam, the American Red Cross, the American Women's Club of Saigon, and the International Rescue Committee (a number of whose projects involving refugee intellectuals were taken over by the Asia Foundation in late 1956).

11. See commentary by Alfred L. Cardinaux, former Chief of Division of Refugee Settlement, USOM, Saigon, on Harnett, in Lindholm (ed.), *op. cit.*, pp. 90–91. Cai San lies 125 miles southwest of Saigon, in the region formerly controlled by the Hoa Hao sect war lords Tran Van Soai, Bacut, *et al.* An official publication entitled *Cai-San, The Dramatic Story of Resettlement and Land Reform in the "Rice Bowl" of the Republic of Viet-Nam,* issued by the Secretariat of State for Information, Saigon, indicates that 20,000 former inhabitants who had fled to the cities during the ten years of "civil war" and 50,000 refugees from the North, or a total of 7,500 families and houses, were settled in Cai San; 50,000 additional refugees were also to be settled there at a later time. According to these official statistics (*ibid.,* pp. 23–24), the average family seems to have consisted of at least nine persons, which seems rather a large number. But considering that an average family of five had to make do with ¾ of a hectare in the North, a Cai San family would have been in the category of "rich landlord" by Communist definition. Under the Diem land-reform program, each family signed a contract guaranteeing it tenure for five years with a renewal option. For the first year, no rent was required; from the second year on, the nominal rate rose to the minimum of 15 per cent fixed by law for normal conditions and the maximum of 25 per cent of the value of the annual crop (*ibid.,* p. 17). Cai San not only was, but remained a success after the initial accomplishment in 1956. A report on agrarian reform by the American agricultural expert and adviser to Ngo Dinh Diem, Wolf Ladejinsky, made at an American Friends of Vietnam conference in November, 1959, and published in 1961, states: "The results speak well for the remarkable performance of the settlers, for the Vietnamese administrators who rose to the challenge, and for the American aid which boldly and intelligently provided the financial means for the venture. The promise of only five years ago is now a reality. The settlers received their three-hectare holdings virtually as a gift. They are harvesting good crops, paying their own way, and are refugees no longer. Ordinance 7 succeeded better than was anticipated; not only is the land being rehabilitated, but the refugees have become productive farmers and full members of Vietnam's body-politic" (in Fishel [ed.], *Problems of Freedom,* p. 163). For further details, see "Administrative Planning for the Cai San Resettlement Project," "The Cai San Tractor Loans," "Boundary and Land Questions at Tan Mai Village," and "The Commissar and the Law," in Montgomery, *op. cit.,* and the NIA Case Development Seminar, *Cases in Vietnamese Administration* (Saigon, 1959).

12. See, for instance, the discussion in Lindholm (ed.), *op. cit.,* pp. 45–103, in particular the contribution by Monsignor Harnett (pp. 83–87). Also the friendly criticism by Robert MacAllister in his speech "The

Refugee in Retrospect," given at a conference of the American Friends of Vietnam in October, 1959. Robert Scheer (*How the United States Got Involved in Vietnam* [Santa Barbara, Calif., 1965]) says that the refugees were in effect *not* integrated. I do not agree, but there is some truth to his later comment (made, however, after everything was known, in 1965) about the refugee program: "This was an effective crash program of American aid; it had little to do with the ability of the Diem government to develop the economy as a whole."

13. Montgomery, *op. cit.*, pp. 47–48. A French critic of the Diem regime has said: "One must applaud what has been done for [the refugees] in Cochinchina and in the highlands. True, it can be said that the merit is due to American aid and to the activities developed by the Catholic clergy. Nevertheless, the Diem regime knew how to coordinate these efforts effectively" (Jean Lacouture, *Vietnam: Between Two Truces* [New York, 1966], p. 24).

14. I have not found one serious critic who denies that Diem temporarily enjoyed some measure of popular support.

15. Diem was much criticized in England, but even more so in France, where at least six well-established authorities on Vietnam continued to reveal the most glaring shortcomings, mistakes, and, above all, authoritarian tendencies of his regime. These men were Philippe Devillers, Jean Lacouture, Georges Chaffard, Max Clos, Robert Guillain, and Raymond Cartier. In the United States, the most persistent critic of the Diem regime was Bernard Fall. In England, Diem's sharpest critics were the novelist Graham Greene and the journalist David Hotham, former Far Eastern correspondent for the *Times* of London and *The Economist*. Greene was very hostile to Diem, but seems to have lost interest when his earlier predictions of Diem's imminent downfall (see Chapter XI, n. 74) did not come true. Hotham, on the other hand, developed a keener interest in South Vietnam during the following years of the Diem regime, specializing largely on the uses of U.S. aid, whose good effect he questioned, and displaying a great deal of concrete information and sound political judgment.

16. The author was a co-founder of the American Friends of Vietnam, and for many years one of its leading spokesmen, in his position as Vice-Chairman and Chairman of the Executive Committee, but resigned from the organization in spring, 1965. The AFVN did not conduct straight Vietnamese official propaganda. A great deal of useful information about Vietnam was disseminated by the organization in various publications and at several conferences that attracted wide attention. But the influence of the organization on public opinion has been highly overestimated by its critics.

17. Hotham, in Lindholm (ed.), *op. cit.*, p. 324, discussing American aid. A valid rendition of his opinion, however, demands that this general reservation made by him be added: "It is not the details, but the main lines, of the aid program which are wrong, because they negate the effect of the excellent activities enumerated." See below, particularly n. 22, for comments on the work of the Michigan State University project.

18. See Frank W. Schiff, in Lindholm (ed.), *ibid.*, pp. 259–88.

19. Craig S. Lichtenwalner, M.D., in Fishel (ed.), *op. cit.*, p. 219. This is a detailed review of five years' achievement in the field of public health. According to Scigliano, since 1959, more than 2,500 workers had been engaged in the nationwide spraying of houses in the government's malaria-control program, and more than 6 million people benefited from it. Rudimentary medical stations were established in about 3,300 villages and hamlets, and in district and provincial health centers. Since 1962, medical supplies to the villages have increased greatly (*op. cit.*, p. 106).

20. Edgar N. Pike, "Problems of Education in Vietnam," in Fishel (ed.), *op. cit.*, pp. 75–96. For an earlier survey putting these achievements in perspective, see Elon R. Hildreth, "The Challenge in Education," in Lindholm (ed.), *op. cit.*, pp. 143–61.

21. As Fall comments, "American influence in the field of education and training may well turn out to have been the best American investment in South Viet-Nam's future" (*op. cit.*, p. 313). See *ibid.*, Table 16, p. 314, which gives total school attendance in Vietnam from 1954 to 1962, based on official statistics. In a comparison of education in South Vietnam before and after independence, Scigliano writes that while in 1939 there were only 5,000 high-school students in all of Indochina, a mere 700 students attending the University of Hanoi, and a total of half a million schoolchildren, there were, in 1955, in South Vietnam alone, 2,500 university students and over 400,-000 students in public and private schools below the university level, with approximately 70 per cent of all young people between the ages of five and fifteen getting some schooling (*op. cit.*, pp. 105–6).

22. The National Institute of Administration (NIA) was moved from Dalat to Saigon in July, 1955. A $4 million contract with Michigan State University enabled the government to expand this school, which for five years was in effect directed by several dozen American professors, headed after 1956 by Professor Wesley Fishel. (See Nghiem Dang, Assistant Director of the NIA, in Lindholm [ed.], *op. cit.*, pp. 162–66, and comments by Guy H. Fox, a former member of the Michigan State group to the NIA, on Dang, *ibid.*, pp. 166–72.) About the activities of the NIA, and the role of the Michigan State University Group's assistance in its work, see the sober appraisal by Robert Scigliano and Guy H. Fox, *Technical Assistance in Vietnam* (New York, 1965). A controversy over the MSU's Vietnam project arose after the publication of an article by Stanley K. Sheinbaum, former coordinator of the project, in the April, 1966, issue of the magazine *Ramparts*. In it the author reveals that between 1955 and 1959, the project was used as a cover for the work of a number of CIA agents in Vietnam. For a report on this controversy, see *The New York Times*, April 14 and 15, 1966.

23. Fall, *op. cit.*, p. 313.

24. For exact figures on rubber and rice, see Fall, *ibid.*, Tables 10 and 11, p. 296; Fall's chapter on the economic base of South Vietnam gives the most complete data on the progress (and failures) of the regime in the economic field. Fall also notes that coffee production in 1961 was 4,000 tons compared with 3,500 tons in 1938 (*ibid.*, p. 293). Fishing industry, "in which perhaps

10 per cent of the entire population is involved, has increased its catch from 52,000 metric tons in 1955 to 250,000 in 1962," Scigliano writes (*op. cit.*, p. 107). Most pro-Diem authors (Fishel and others), unlike the highly critical Fall, do not mention prewar production figures. But since the regime had to start out from a low resulting from sixteen years of decline (1938 to 1954), it does not seem unfair to credit any subsequent growth as an achievement.

25. Even people who knew this did not think that the economical performance of the Diem regime could be called poor. The effects of the long war and of the country's partition explained why it would take a long time to achieve rapid economic progress. For the evaluation of the South's overall economic potential after 1954, see the Report of the Economic Survey Mission of the United Nations and Specialized Agencies to the Republic of Vietnam (headed by Professor Carter Goodrich, a well-known economist of Columbia University) entitled *Toward the Economic Development of Vietnam* (New York, 1956). See also the verbatim transcript of the conference on "The Economic Needs of Vietnam," sponsored by the American Friends of Vietnam, and held in New York, March 15, 1957. See further, Buu Hoan, "Economic Consequences of the Geneva Peace," in *Far Eastern Economic Review*, December 11, 1958, and Robert R. Nathan, "The Consequences of Partition," in Fishel (ed.), *op. cit.*, Chapter I. An earlier treatment was given by David C. Cole, "Economic Setting," in Lindholm (ed.), *op. cit.*, and by Lawrence Morrison, "Industrial Development," *ibid.*, as well as various commentaries by John M. Hunter and Richard W. Lindholm. Among the countless publications on economic reports, see U.S. Operations Mission to Vietnam, "Building Economic Strength," *Annual Report for Fiscal Year 1958, July 1, 1957–June 30, 1958*; also, "The Economic Renovation of the Republic of Vietnam," Special Edition published by *Review Horizons* (Saigon, 1956 [?]), a pro-Diem publication; Corley, "Economic Stabilization in Viet-Nam," *Review of Social Economy*, early 1959; also see *Aid to Vietnam* (New York, 1959), a record of an AFVN conference held on April 17, 1959, to examine the effects of U.S. aid program in Vietnam; Louis Andreatta, *Education in Vietnam: A Selected and Annotated Bibliography* (New York, 1961); Corley, "Vietnam Since Geneva," in *Thought*; John T. Dorsey, Jr., "South Vietnam in Perspective," *Far Eastern Survey*, December, 1958; "High Activity in Viet-Nam, Points to Expansion in All Main Sectors," in *Foreign Commerce Weekly*, December 26, 1960; Nguyen Dinh Hoa, "Higher Education in the Republic of Vietnam," in *The Burman* (Rangoon), January 10, 1960; *Investment Conditions in Vietnam* (New York, 1958), a record of a conference held on February 28, 1958, to examine Vietnam's investment policies, opportunities for foreign investment, economic factors and private investment, currency and credit, and U.S. policy toward investment in Vietnam.

26. Dorsey, "South Vietnam in Perspective," *op. cit.* Dorsey also gives a good summary of what was then considered Diem's main achievement. He writes that Diem "not only survived, but during the first four years of his government he was also able (1) to hold universal-suffrage elections de-

throning Bao Dai and establishing a republic; (2) to negotiate the withdrawal of the French troops; (3) to hold further elections to establish a constituent assembly; (4) to overcome the organized military opposition; (5) to shelter and resettle almost a million refugees from the north; (6) to promulgate a constitution prepared by the Assembly which included a reasonably strong infusion of democratic ideas; and (7) to initiate programs of reconstruction, land reform and development, education, public works, and economic planning. These accomplishments would not have been possible without dedicated leadership and political sagacity of unexpected sophistication." I quote Dorsey not because I wish to single him out for special criticism, but rather because he represents the more balanced, more sober judgment of the Diem regime at that time. In fact, I read his article prior to publication and highly approved of it, as I had approved of several others in this general vein, f. i., Corley's "Vietnam Since Geneva."

27. Examples of this attitude are numerous, among them a series of publications by the American Friends of Vietnam, such as *America's Stake in Vietnam;* Ellen Hammer, "Progress Report on Southern Viet Nam," *Pacific Affairs,* September, 1957; Ralph Lee Smith, "South Vietnam: A Success Story," *Foreign Policy Bulletin,* July 1, 1959. Even critical observers like William Henderson ("South Vietnam Finds Itself," *Foreign Affairs,* XXXV, January, 1957) found praise for Diem and hope for the future of his regime. Joseph Alsop completely reversed himself, turning from a vehement critic into an admirer of Diem. Another critic, Robert Guillain, the French correspondent for *Le Monde,* found that Diem was making progress and thought he would probably survive. The list of tributes to Diem seems almost endless and appeared in publications of all shades of opinion, from *Life* to *The Reader's Digest,* from statements by prominent public figures, from the then Senator John F. Kennedy (see *America's Stake in Vietnam,* pp. 8–14, for Kennedy's speech of the same title) to the then Vice-President Lyndon B. Johnson, who called Diem the "Churchill of Asia." At the height of Diem's popularity, those who praised him spoke of "unity on nationalist terms" (Hammer, *op. cit.*) and said that "history may yet adjudge Diem as one of the great figures of the Twentieth Century" (Henderson, *op. cit.,* p. 285). The symposium held by the American Friends of Vietnam in Washington, D.C., on June 1, 1956, brought together almost 250 representatives of government, the armed services, the universities, and civic organizations interested in and concerned with America's stake in Vietnam. All concurred in the general principle stated by Angier Biddle Duke, then Chairman of the AFVN Executive Committee: "The maintenance of a Free Vietnam, and corollary to that a Free Southeast Asia, is deeply involved in the safeguarding of our own freedom" (*America's Stake in Vietnam*). And General John W. O'Daniel, then Chairman of the American Friends of Vietnam, and former Chief of USMAAG in Vietnam from 1954 to 1955, expressed the organization's belief that "the future of Southeast Asia depends largely on the existence of a strong South Vietnamese government" (*ibid.,* p. 7). At the same symposium, Walter S. Robertson, then

Assistant Secretary of State for Far Eastern Affairs, said: "Asia has given us in President Diem another great figure, and the entire free world has become richer for his example of determination and moral fortitude" (*ibid.*, p. 15). All these appraisals were to some extent based on misinformation or lack of information, but mostly on wishful thinking. I feel justified in saying this because it is true of myself as well. For reasons perhaps even more complex and personal, I supported Diem publicly beyond 1958, although with great misgivings after my visit to Vietnam during that summer, and upheld the necessity of supporting Diem in private conversations and correspondence until the end of 1960. It was only then that I became convinced of the futility of my hopes that Diem would accept my personal suggestions for certain changes.

28. An ordinance of January 7, 1955, limited land rents to 25 per cent of the crop; another one, of February 7, 1955, aimed at confirming the rights of tenants, something already attempted, without success, by the Agrarian Code that Bao Dai had signed on June 4, 1953. About American efforts to bring about land reform in Vietnam, which go back to 1951, see Montgomery, *op. cit.*, pp. 121–27.

29. Diem belatedly seemed to open new paths of land reform through an ordinance of October 22, 1956, which limited landholdings to 100 hectares (247 acres), and an additional 30 hectares if the landowner farmed the land himself. (An additional 15 hectares could be retained for "ancestor worship.") Through this ordinance, 700,000 hectares were made available for immediate distribution.

30. Fall writes that while the going price for a hectare of rice land was $200, the French owners received $13 per hectare (*op. cit.*, pp. 311–12). Ladejinsky, who on this matter may be better informed than Fall (who, in turn, quotes *Viet-Nam Press*, English-language air ed., February 26, 1961), states that they received $11 per hectare, against an average price of $60–65 received by Vietnamese landlords in cash and bonds (Fishel [ed.], *op. cit.*, p. 170). The reason for French acceptance of this low price, Ladejinsky writes, was to be found in the agreement between the French and South Vietnamese governments, by which the former allocated $2.9 million for the purchase of all French rice lands; under these terms, payment to French owners was made in francs, deposited in France. The other possibility, available to the French owners, was to receive 10 per cent of the payment in cash and the balance in nontransferable government bonds, bearing a 3 per cent interest rate and amortized over 12 years. The bonds could also be used to pay off debts contracted with the Agricultural Credit Agency or for land and inheritance taxes or, more important to the Vietnamese Government, for subscription to securities of any enterprises created by the state in the framework of a program of national economic development (*ibid.*, pp. 166–68). Interested chiefly in selling the land and in the repatriation of their funds, the French owners chose the terms of their government in late 1959, and by January 31, 1961, had sold 228,858 hectares.

31. Fall, *op. cit.*, p. 312. Fall adds that the mismanagement of the land-

reform program became known only in its barest outlines in 1962 and is "still not openly acknowledged in official circles in Washington" (*ibid.*, p. 311). For this reason it is not surprising to read in Montgomery's book, published before Fall's, that "American advice and pressure" finally "translate[d] policy into one of the most successful agrarian reform programs in the Far East" (*op. cit.*, p. 127). This is not so much an example of misjudgment but of insufficient information and acceptance of claims not fully substantiated, out of fear of seeming too critical and not appreciative enough of the beleaguered regime's efforts and achievements.

32. Here again, figures conflict, as for instance those reported by *Viet-Nam Press* of March 6, 1960, which claimed that by February 1, 1960, 421,338 hectares of rice fields had been expropriated and that 123,295 former tenants had become landowners, and those cited by Fall (*op. cit.*, pp. 308–12), which indicate that the total expropriated land by July, 1961, was even lower than the *Viet-Nam Press* figure of 1960. Fall states that 415,843 hectares had been expropriated by July, 1961, with only 232,451 actually distributed by that time. One reason for this discrepancy is that some sources accept as finally distributed only acreage to which farmers had received title, whereas others take acreage actually worked by tenants who expect to obtain titles sooner or later. No writer has drawn a final balance between what was intended and what was actually achieved, probably because no one knew what was intended and no exact figures of actual achievements were available. Perhaps the best summary, giving figures at the end of 1963, is contained in an unpublished paper by Colonel Charles Bohanan of June 15, 1964, entitled *Summary Estimate of Land Tenure Status in South Vietnam.* It says that of the 435,000 hectares of land purchased by the government from approximately 2,000 landlords, 300,000 hectares were actually distributed to about 121,123 farm families, or approximately 10 per cent of the landless tenants. Of the 210,000 hectares of former French-owned land, none was distributed to the landless. This means that considerably less than half of the 646,000 hectares of land available for distribution was actually given to landless tenants before the reform was suspended. Apart from Fall, sources to be consulted on this are Montgomery, *op. cit.*, pp. 121–28; Scigliano, "Economic and Social Development," *op. cit.*, pp. 101–29; Wolf Ladejinsky, "Agrarian Reform in the Republic of Vietnam," in Fishel (ed.), *Problems of Freedom*, pp. 153–75; David Wurfel, "Agrarian Reform in the Republic of Vietnam," in *Far Eastern Survey*, June, 1957; J. Price Gittinger, "Rent Reduction and Tenure Security in Free Viet-Nam," in *Journal of Farm Economics*, May, 1957, and "Vietnamese Land Transfer Program," in *Land Economics*, May, 1957. Ladejinsky's is probably the most factual although entirely positive account. Mr. Ladejinsky abstained from any kind of criticism of the entire program, probably because his account was written while there was still hope that the land reform program would eventually be fully implemented and perhaps broadened. But Diem and his successor governments have disappointed this hope, although there is evidence that some leaders were aware of the need of a much more drastic program of agrarian

reform. In fact, under the government of General Khanh in mid-1964, an Interministerial Committee on Rural Development was set up under the chairmanship of two Vice-Premiers, the Dai Viet leader Hoan and the Oxford-educated economist Oanh. This Committee came up with the most far-reaching proposals ever made for a meaningful land reform in South Vietnam. The most important of these was a reduction of the retention limit for landholdings from 100 to 10 hectares in the delta, and to 3 hectares in central Vietnam, where land is extremely scarce. Another proposal was to proceed at last with the distribution of former French-owned land. At the insistence of the Minister of Rural Affairs and the Director General of Land Administration, both of whom were big landowners, the Council of Ministers rejected all these proposals. It was only in September, 1965, that the new Premier, Nguyen Cao Ky, promised that a program of distribution of former French-owned land would begin (see *The New York Times*, September 5, 1965). I have seen no report confirming that this promise is being kept.

33. Scigliano, *op. cit.*, p. 123. Writing about the relatively few "impact" programs of immediate benefit to the peasants that would help persuade them to resist Communist subversion, John Mecklin accuses the Vietnamese Government of sabotaging whatever efforts in that direction were made by the United States, and he adds: "American experts helped prepare a sweeping land-reform program, for example, but only about 15 per cent of it was ever implemented" (*Mission in Torment: An Intimate Account of the U.S. Role in Vietnam*, pp. 11–12). The insignificant effect of land transfers is described for one particular Vietnamese village by James B. Hendry, "Land Tenure in South Vietnam," in *Economic Development and Cultural Change*, October, 1960. And for a late confirmation, as late as January 24, 1966, there is a report by Richard Critchfield in the *Washington Star*, which underlines the shocking limitations of Diem's land reform. "In Long An," said Critchfield, "one of Vietnam's most fertile provinces, more than 85 per cent of the peasant population are tenants. This landownership pattern may help explain why, despite a tremendous cost in lives and material, the war in Long An is no closer to being won than it was several years ago. . . . [Yet] the rice-rich heartland of the Saigon region and the upper Mekong Delta, linked together by Long An, remains the price for which the war is being fought. Here, in less than 14 provinces, live almost two-thirds of the 15 million South Vietnamese. . . . American military and civilian advisers agree there are many more Viet Cong than a year ago. Most important in Long An, however, government and the mass of peasantry still seem to be on the opposing sides. . . . Land is of such paramount importance here that the Viet Cong allow only the landless or very poor farmers to command guerrilla units or qualify as party members. The provincial government's social order is the exact reverse. Most of the military officers, civil servants and community leaders come from the landowning gentry. The same is true in Saigon where only one of the 10 generals now sharing power has any rapport with the masses. He is Central Vietnam's erratic Maj. Gen. Nguyen

Chanh Thi, who also is the only one of peasant origin. . . . In the delta, out of 1.2 million farms, only 260,000 are owner-operated. . . . Some 3,000 rich Saigon families still are the big landowners."

34. Scigliano, *op. cit.*, p. 104.

35. See Tran Ngoc Lien, "The Growth of Agricultural Credit and Co-operatives," in Fishel (ed.), *op. cit.*, pp. 177–91. Tran Ngoc Lien was then Commissioner General for Cooperatives and Agricultural Credit of the Republic of Vietnam.

36. See Chapter IV, n. 38, for the *Wall Street Journal*'s assertion of the unchanged condition of the peasantry in recent years. David Halberstam has this comment: "Suspecting that the Government would take their land back, the peasants would simply not inform on the Vietcong, and often they and their families were active agents" (*The Making of a Quagmire*, p. 114). Mecklin, like Halberstam a newspaperman before he became Public Affairs Officer of the American Embassy in Saigon, wrote in a similar vein: "Even this [disregard of the peasants by civil servants] was capped in at least one area where we found tax collectors attached to military units. The idea was that this was a convenient way to collect back taxes for absentee landlords in hamlets where government authority had totally collapsed, often several years earlier. For the peasant in such hamlets, 'liberation' from the Viet Cong meant a demand at gunpoint for payment of taxes that he probably did not know he owed" (*op. cit.*, p. 86).

37. Scigliano, *op. cit.*, p. 123.

38. Quoted by Montgomery, *op. cit.*, p. 126, from a manuscript by J. Price Gittinger, entitled "Agrarian Reform Status Report." Describing American efforts at land reform resisted by the Diem regime, Montgomery noted: "Yet the Vietnamese government, not wishing to disturb the strong landowning classes, resisted the proposed transfers of land and the sharper rent controls" (*ibid.*, p. 124). In retrospect, a mimeographed paper prepared by Vietnam's Secretariat of State for Land Property and Land Reform in July, 1959 (for the upcoming conference of the American Friends of Vietnam) seems clearly an attempt to whitewash the inadequacy of the government's land-reform program.

39. Diem lacked the talent for political theorizing and was too serious a man to engage in the charlatan political philosophy of his brother Nhu. Only once, in an article written before he came to power, did he put his ideas on paper, giving his concepts of society and state, and the relationship between government and people. Entitled "Democratic Development in Vietnam," it appeared in the *Free China Review* (Taipeh), June, 1955, pp. 25–36, with an editor's note stating that it was written in French, before Diem became President. Large portions of it were published in English by Diem's long-time press chief and later opponent, Nguyen Thai, in his book *Is South Vietnam Viable?* (pp. 96–101), published in 1962 in Manila. Thai, in 1961, was unable to find a publisher in the United States.

40. Fall, *op. cit.*, p. 205. "In his very first, and never published, report on South Viet-Nam," Fall writes (*ibid.*, p. 463, n. 1), "Wolf Ladejinsky—until

1962 President Diem's chief agricultural adviser—was extremely critical of the overbearing attitude of Vietnamese officialdom and soldiery. There was no evidence that his recommendations were acted upon, and in 1962 he resigned from his post."

41. From a speech delivered at a conference of the American Friends of Vietnam held in Washington, D.C., on June 1, 1956 (see n. 27, above). Significantly, Kennedy, as ill-informed then as most other serious observers, and still as hopeful about the regime as most supporters of Diem, also said: "We must assist the *inspiring growth* of Vietnamese democracy and economy" (italics added). Kennedy listed what then were considered the various achievements, taking for granted (typically) that all was a mere beginning, that social and economic reforms and democratic progress were around the corner. Almost ten years later, Vice President Hubert H. Humphrey, in a speech at the airport on his arrival in Saigon, on February 10, 1966, expressed the hope for "the realization of a true social revolution, the promotion of a genuine democracy, the war on hunger and disease and the search for a lasting peace"—none of which had obviously been accomplished in the intervening years, neither during nor after Diem's reign. And there is no reason to believe that it would be done now. Humphrey also stated as an additional U.S. aim (in nonmilitary objectives) exactly as it had been stated for more than ten years: "To build a society based on the principles of political freedom, self-determination, social justice, and economic development" (as reported from Saigon by Thomas Wicker, *The New York Times,* February 11, 1966).

42. Diem spoke of this need in his message to the June 1, 1956, Washington, D.C., conference of the American Friends of Vietnam, and more emphatically in his speech at a dinner given in his honor by the American Friends of Vietnam and the International Rescue Committee on May 13, 1957. In an address before the Indian Council of World Affairs in New Delhi on November 5, 1957, Diem stated: "Our Constitution affirms that the sole legitimate end and object of the State is to protect the fundamental rights of the human person to existence and to the free development of his intellectual, moral, and spiritual life." In a statement made at a press conference in Manila on March 22, 1958, he reiterated: "The Vietnamese people are doing their utmost to attain democracy, which is essentially a permanent effort to find the right political means for assuring to all citizens the right of free development and of maximum initiative, responsibility, and spiritual life." (All quotes are taken from a pamphlet entitled *Toward Better Mutual Understanding,* II, issued by the Press Office of the Presidency of the Republic of Vietnam, Saigon, June, 1958.)

43. "A constant part . . ." is Scigliano's own comment; the other phrase is Diem's (Scigliano, *op. cit.,* p. 62).

44. Diem in his "anniversary speech" of July 7, 1960 (as printed in the *Times of Vietnam,* July 7, 1960, p. 1, and as quoted by Scigliano, *op. cit.,* p. 88).

45. It was Homer Bigart, *The New York Times* correspondent in Saigon,

who coined the slogan "Sink or swim with Diem" as applicable to U.S. policy at the time. In March, 1962, Bigart and François Sully (*Newsweek*) offended the Diem regime with their reporting and it took a great deal of effort by U.S. Ambassador Nolting to prevent Diem from expelling them. (Sully was later expelled anyhow.) Bigart left Saigon in July, 1962, and was replaced by David Halberstam. For Bigart's views and reporting, and his troubles with the Diem regime as well as the U.S. Embassy, see Mecklin, *op. cit.* Mecklin quotes Bigart's phrase on p. 129 of his book. Halberstam, who shared Bigart's critical attitude, writes of then Vice-President Johnson's reply to a critical question about Diem: "Don't tell me about Diem. He's all we've got out there" (*op. cit.*, p. 69). The events described in the remaining sections of this final chapter of my book have been reported, evaluated, analyzed, and discussed in a great many books, some of them in such a first-rate manner as to make them invaluable historical documentations. For an understanding of the war as waged under Diem, Malcolm W. Browne, *The New Face of War* (New York, 1965) and Halberstam, *op. cit.*, are indispensable. Mecklin, *op. cit.*, is the best source for the conflict between U.S. correspondents and U.S. officials in Saigon (and in Washington). All three are expert reporters on the rapid deterioration of the Diem regime and Washington's disenchantment. This is true also of Denis Warner, *The Last Confucian*, and Robert Shaplen, *The Lost Revolution*. The pro-Diem view was best presented by the late Marguerite Higgins (see n. 267, below). Fall's *Two Viet-Nams* is a candid though biased portrayal of this period. On the war as waged by the U.S. Special Forces, see Robin Moore, *The Green Berets* (New York, 1965). The Communist side is well represented by the writings of Wilfred Burchett, in particular *Vietnam: Inside Story of the Guerilla War* (New York, 1965). Also of interest here are the various writings of Wesley Fishel and the brief discussion in Chapter IX of Tilman Durdin's small book *Southeast Asia* (New York, 1966). Perhaps the most sophisticated political analysis is given by Jean Lacouture, *op. cit.* Of interest are also Wesley Pruden, Jr., *Vietnam: The War* (Silver Spring, Md., 1965); Bernard Newman, *Background to Viet-Nam* (New York, 1965)—although it is a superficial and uncritical sequence to his earlier book, *Report on Indochina*, in dealing with the political realities of Vietnam; Victor Perlo and Kumar Goshal, *Bitter End in Southeast Asia* (New York, 1964), a pro-Communist work. For a still incomplete but rather comprehensive list of articles on Vietnam during the years 1961–63, see the *Checklists*, published (mimeographed) by the American Friends of Vietnam, compiled and annotated by Louis Andreatta. The articles quoted and annotated by Mr. Andreatta are restricted to English-language publications, largely American. See in particular the issues of 1963: Part I, January–June; Part II, July–October; and Part III, October–December, the last covering the coup and the reaction to it. The *Checklist* also contains a selection of letters to the editor of *The New York Times*, dealing with Vietnam. I would like to mention one series of newspaper articles on this period, written by Richard Dudman and published in the *St. Louis Post-Dispatch* of February 3, 4, and 5, 1963, under the title "Asia's Frontiers of Freedom: U.S. Policy—Pluses, Minuses, and Questions." However, the best book on the Diem regime before its disintegration is still Scigliano's *South Vietnam.*

46. I do not think that at this time it is still necessary to discuss Ngo Dinh Nhu's pretensions to political philosophy. Even an admirer of Diem like Anthony T. Bouscaren calls personalism "a vague mish-mash of ideas," with the emphasis not on democracy but on "good" government, "albeit authoritarian" (*The Last of the Mandarins: Diem of Vietnam,* p. 57). Mecklin, although he calls personalism "a legitimate philosophy," says that Ambassador Nolting once told Diem: "You may be surprised to know that most Americans who have ever heard of Personalism think it means the glorification of your own person as chief of state." Mecklin adds that "such Vietnamese as had ever heard about Personalism apparently had a similar attitude. It died a sudden, unlamented death with the end of the Diem regime" (*op. cit.,* p. 37). Shaplen comments that "a number of Americans, including some visiting scholars, spent considerable time trying to understand and explain personalism, but they usually gave up because it seemed such a hodgepodge, and because whatever it was, it was only a theory, while in practice it was what Nhu wanted it to be" (*op. cit.,* p. 131). Those interested in the subject will find a discussion of personalism in Fall, *op. cit.,* pp. 246 ff. The most detailed and least hostile account of it is by John C. Donnell, "Personalism in Vietnam," in Fishel (ed.), *Problems of Freedom,* pp. 29–69, together with a long list of the relevant literature in footnote 41. See also Georges Chaffard, *Indochine: Dix ans d'indépendance,* p. 160, who tells of the protest by Jean-Marie Domenach, editor of *Esprit,* and "spiritual heir of Emmanuel Mounier" (on whose philosophy Nhu based personalism), against the "usurpation and travesty" of the personalist philosophy by the South Vietnamese regime. Nguyen Thai, speaking of the brochures and pamphlets about personalism that were published by the regime, commented: "Most of them are strongly slanted to fit the propaganda line. Reportedly, Mr. Ngodinh Nhu said that none of the writings on 'personalism' really conformed to the doctrine of the regime. But he himself has not produced anything to enlighten other people on this doctrine" (*op. cit.,* p. 128, n. 1).

47. Scigliano, *op. cit.,* p. 91. Or, as Halberstam put it more bluntly: "Eventually South Vietnam became, for all intents and purposes, a Communist-type country without Communism" (*op. cit.,* p. 52).

48. Scigliano, *op. cit.,* p. 88.

49. *Ibid.,* p. 91.

50. "The National Assembly deputies were elected from single-member districts by plurality vote, and the President was elected on the basis of a national plurality vote. With minor exceptions, all Vietnamese citizens over eighteen years of age were eligible to participate in the elections" (*ibid.*). See also Scigliano, "The Electoral Process in South Vietnam: Politics in an Underdeveloped State," *Midwest Journal of Political Science,* IV, No. 2 (May, 1960), and Nguyen Tuyet Mai, "Electioneering: Vietnamese Style," *The Asian Survey,* November, 1962.

51. Scigliano, *South Vietnam*, pp. 99–100. Commenting coldly on the elective processes as practiced by the Diem regime, Nguyen Thai wrote: "For those who tried to find out for themselves in 1959 whether the second legislative elections were intended to raise the representative standard of the National Assembly, it soon became clear that the leaders of the regime did not see representation as an important feature for the legislative body of South Vietnam. The regime leaders in 1959 allowed a little face-lifting in the composition of the deputies, but on the whole, the basic features of the 1956 National Assembly had to be preserved. . . . The organization of the 1959 elections was misleading. . . . The propaganda work for free and fair elections was carried out so effectively that even skeptics who had refused to participate in the 1956 elections submitted their candidacy in 1959. . . . What actually happened on election day and during the preceding weeks shattered the democratic hopes in South Vietnam. Not only were the campaign procedures designed to give the government-approved candidates a definite advantage, but every elementary standard of justice and fairness was violated on election day in order to get the approved candidates elected. . . . The beneficiaries of the 1959 elections were a selected group of opportunists who succeeded via Dr. Tran Kim Tuyen in getting themselves accepted by either Mr. or Mrs. Nhu, the new centers of power closest to the President" (*op. cit.*, pp. 136–37). Discussing Tran Kim Tuyen's role in the elections, Nguyen Thai elaborated: "Most of the names for Southern deputies had to come from Tuyen's files. In view of his previous involvement in security checks before presidential appointments, he had achieved a certain expertise in this art of presenting to the President the right name at the right moment, with the right facts. The result was that the great majority of the so-called government candidates in the 1959 elections were in fact, Tuyen's candidates" (*ibid.*, p. 140). Finally, Thai offers this analysis of the Presidential election in 1961: "What puzzled the supporters of the regime was that Ngo-dinh Diem, incumbent President of the Republic and an internationally known nationalist leader of thirty years' experience, should have degraded himself by making the presidential elections unworthy of his reputation. Whereas in 1959, the mockery of democracy touched other people, this time Diem allowed it to involve him personally. He allowed himself to run against two presidential candidates who were not even considered 'serious' " (*ibid.*, p. 142). The opposition candidates were Nguyen Dinh Quat, "an adventurous type of businessman who had suddenly become very wealthy during the later years of French occupation (reportedly by getting paid for a huge construction contract in North Vietnam which he did not have to execute after the Geneva partition)," and Ho Nhut Tan, "a seventy-year-old practitioner of Chinese medicine who was completely unknown" (*ibid.*, pp. 142–43). Nguyen Dinh Quat's running-mate for Vice President was Nguyen Thanh Phuong, "who had commanded the Cao Dai military forces but who had led a quiet life since the 1955 turbulence." Ho Nhut Tan's running mate was Nguyen The Truyen, "a chemical engineer

in his early 60's who had withdrawn from public activities" in the late 1940's (Scigliano, *South Vietnam*, pp. 92–93).

52. "At the polling station each voter is given as many ballots as there are candidates, each ballot containing the name and symbol of a single candidate; he is required to place one ballot in an envelope for deposit in the election box and he discards the unused ballots in a trash basket" (Scigliano, *South Vietnam*, p. 94). In his article "The Electoral Process in South Vietnam," Scigliano wrote: "Failure to vote could subject a person to difficulties with the authorities. In 1956, a person's identity card was stamped at the polling place; in 1959, his identity card was stamped when he obtained his voting card, and his voting card was stamped at the polls. However unfounded the concern, many Vietnamese thought it important to have their cards in proper order."

53. Scigliano, *South Vietnam*, p. 94.

54. *Ibid.*, p. 97. All voting records for the Assembly elections were topped in the elections of September 27, 1963, in which Nhu won his seat with a 99.99 per cent majority, something neither Hitler nor Stalin nor Ho Chi Minh has ever achieved.

55. Denis Warner (*op. cit.*, Chapter VI, "The Case of Dr. Dan," pp. 87–101), describes Dr. Dan as "an immensely popular figure in the Saigon electorate," but "detested by the administration." Involved in national politics since 1945, while still a medical student at Hanoi University (Dan was born in the province of Nghe An, also Ho Chi Minh's birthplace), Dan twice turned down offers to join the Vietminh Cabinet in 1946, and during 1947 and 1948 served as adviser to Bao Dai. For a brief period he served as Minister of Information in the Provisional Central Government established in 1948 without Bao Dai but with his blessing, and in 1949 he formed his own political group, the Cong Hoa Dang (Republican Party) and also went to the United States to study medicine at Harvard. He returned to Vietnam in September, 1955, and from then until the end of 1960 was the center of much of the open opposition to the regime (according to Scigliano, *South Vietnam*, pp. 82 ff.). Briefly arrested by the regime on the eve of the 1956 elections and accused of "Communist and colonialist activities," he was forced out of his position at the University of Saigon Medical School. Continuing his political activities until the 1959 election and beyond, he associated himself with the attempted *coup d'état* of November, 1960, was arrested, and but for American and other Western intervention would certainly have been tried and condemned to death. Scigliano says that Dan's opposition record was "exceptional." But much as he was admired by other opposition leaders, they also distrusted him and refused to join forces with him. As usual, the United States earned only recriminations from both sides. Dr. Dan complained to Warner, who went to see him at his clinic half an hour after his release by the police during the Assembly session Dan was to have attended as a duly elected member: "The Americans intervene when they want to. Why don't they intervene when moral issues are at stake?

They accept military and economic responsibilities. They must also accept a moral responsibility" (Warner, *op. cit.*, p. 92). Diem, on the other hand, according to Warner, "had broken finally and irrevocably with the Saigon intellectuals during the 1959 elections for the National Assembly," and once he decided, "despite fairly vigorous protests by the American and British embassies," that Dr. Dan was not to be allowed to take his seat in the Assembly, he remained adamant.

56. Scigliano, "The Electoral Process in South Vietnam," *op. cit.*, p. 149. This is the first critical survey of the subject by the author, and is less critical than the chapter "Election in a One-Party State," in *South Vietnam* (pp. 91–100). For a report on the pressure tactics and fraud committed by the regime in the election campaign by a candidate, see Nguyen Tuyet Mai, "Electioneering: Vietnamese Style," *op. cit.* In her article, Mrs. Mai (wife of the then editor of *Viet-Nam Press*, Nguyen Thai, the author of *Is Vietnam Viable?*) tells of the battle between her and the candidate put forth by Mme. Nhu. "Finally," Mrs. Mai writes, "on the day before the elections, a high-ranking official contacted my husband and asked him to advise me to withdraw. 'The President is very angry' was the reason given. . . . If I decided not to withdraw, a summons would be issued . . . accusing me of electoral violations and, if necessary, cancelling the results of the election" (p. 14). The writer goes on to tell of meeting Vu Van Thai in the United States, the former Director General of Budget and Foreign Aid, who had also resigned from the government; Thai told her husband that Diem had complained to him shortly after the 1959 election about her conduct and suggested that she had used funds belonging to the *Viet-Nam Press* to finance her campaign. Although tacitly required to produce a damning report upon making a thorough investigation of the *Viet-Nam Press* finances, Thai's report exonerated her husband from any abuse of his position (pp. 17, 18).

57. Both Nguyen Thai and Robert Scigliano agree that the assemblies were tools of the regime. As Thai describes it, most of the legislation passed by the National Assembly dealt with administrative matters, and contained only two major pieces, namely the Family Law, sponsored by Mme. Nhu, and the Security Law, which provided for a more rapid processing of cases involving sabotage by special military tribunals, and thus more rapid pronouncements of death or life-imprisonment sentences (*op. cit.*, pp. 132–33). In exchange for their acquiescence to the regime's demands, the deputies drew monthly allowances of nearly 30,000 piasters. As Thai puts it: "This is the salary of the highest government officials (between director-general and secretary of state). A soldier earns roughly 1,000 piasters a month" (*ibid.*, p. 144). That the deputies were not held in great respect by the Ngos is made clear in a note by Scigliano, in which he writes that Mme. Nhu was accused of referring to her male colleagues as "very base" and that according to some reports she called the majority leader of the Assembly "a pig" (*South Vietnam*, p. 45, n. 24). Mme. Nhu, incidentally, was one of the forty-four deputies listed as "independents." The overwhelming majority were mem-

bers of the NRM (National Revolutionary Movement) (Thai, *op. cit.*, p. 135, n. 2).

58. The D.R.V.N.'s Vice-Presidency went to Ton Duc Thang, wrote Fall. Truong Chinh became President of the National Assembly; Hoang Van Hoan became Vice-President of the Committee on Current Affairs. Le Duan was not given a government job, although he had won his constituency with 97 per cent of the vote. A new electoral law had given the rural areas 1 deputy per 30,000 votes, with the cities and newly created industrial towns receiving 1 deputy for each 10,000. "Thus, Hanoi, with 4 per cent of the total population of the country, was allotted almost 10 per cent of the electoral seats. Finally, 458 candidates disputed a total of 404 seats. The mandates of 18 deputies from areas south of the 17th parallel were automatically renewed, making a total of 422 members in the new National Assembly" (Fall, *op. cit.*, pp. 146–47). For further details on the May 8, 1960, election in the North, see Roy Jumper and Marjorie Weiner Normand, "Vietnam," in George McTurnan Kahin (ed.), *Governments and Politics of Southeast Asia*, pp. 481–82. According to these authors, the breakdown of the deputies was as follows: 50 workers, 46 peasants, 65 intellectuals, 78 heroes (army fighters or model workers), 2 national bourgeoisie, 5 clergymen, 2 Buddhist superiors, 56 minority (tribal) people, 49 women, 40 youths between the ages of twenty-one and thirty, 20 army men, and 34 Southern deputies.

59. Scigliano, *South Vietnam*, p. 26. The constitution was drafted by an eleven-man committee composed of Vietnamese lawyers and government officials, assisted by an American, Dr. J. A. C. Grant, and a Filipino lawyer, Juan C. Orendain. Although no Frenchman was included in the group, the original draft was in French, since all the Vietnamese lawyers on the committee were French-trained (see Fall, *op. cit.*, p. 259). According to Scigliano, the major work on the draft "was apparently done by a handful of intimate advisers to President Diem, headed by his Secretary of State at the Presidency, Nguyen Huu Chau" (*South Vietnam*, p. 26). The only committee proposal rejected by the Assembly was the lowering of the age qualification for President and Vice-President from forty to thirty-five years, and most of the opposition came from Mme. Nhu. "It appears that Chau hoped, under the terms of the constitution, to be chosen by Diem as Vice-President of the Republic, and Mme. Nhu, who was Chau's sister-in-law, was determined to prevent this possibility" (*ibid.*, p. 27). According to Fall, there was "an attempt at separation of powers along American lines," but there was "a heavy emphasis on a strong executive beyond what would be considered proper 'balance' in American terms" (*op. cit.*, p. 259). For further details, see Fall's chapter entitled "South Viet-Nam's Constitution" (*ibid.*, pp. 259–68, and Appendix II, pp. 427–41, for text of the constitution). The most detailed discussion is given by J. A. C. Grant, its co-drafter ("The Vietnam Constitution of 1956," *American Political Science Review*, LII, June, 1958).

60. Shaplen, *op. cit.*, p. 134.

61. On the new constitution in the North, see Jumper and Normand, *op.*

cit., pp. 475–78; also, P. J. Honey (ed.), *North Vietnam Today: Profile of a Communist Satellite*, p. 14.

62. Fall, *op. cit.*, pp. 141 ff.; see also Appendix I (*ibid.*, pp. 409–26) for text of the North Vietnamese constitution; and his "North Viet-Nam's Constitution and Government," *Pacific Affairs*, XXXIII, No. 3 (September, 1960).

63. Fall, *The Two Viet-Nams*, p. 431.

64. Shaplen, *op. cit.*, p. 134.

65. On village autonomy, see Scigliano, *South Vietnam*, pp. 8, 10, and 32 ff., and nn. 9–11, citing the following specialized discussions: Luther A. Allen and Pham Ngoc An, *A Vietnamese District Chief in Action* (Saigon, 1961); Lam Le Trinh, "Village Councils—Yesterday and Today," *Viet-My* (Saigon), August and September, 1958; Truong Ngoc Giau and Lloyd Woodruff, *My Thuan: Administrative and Financial Aspects of a Village in South Vietnam* (Saigon, 1961). See also Lloyd Woodruff, *The Study of a Vietnamese Rural Community–Administrative Activity* (Saigon, 1960). A generally more positive though also critical view was taken by Gerald Cannon Hickey, an American civilian adviser who wrote a number of very detached studies on administration, especially on the village level, in his *Village in Vietnam* (New Haven and New London, Conn., 1964).

66. Scigliano wrote in 1963: "It is likely that there is less political freedom in Vietnam today than there was under the French" (*South Vietnam*, p. 98). The reason for the abolishment of elective village councils was the danger of having Vietminh members (or majorities) elected. Shaplen quotes Dang Duc Khoi, who became Diem's press officer but eventually turned against him, as saying: "Even if the Vietminh had won some elections, the danger in doing away with the traditional system of village elections was greater. This was something that was part of the Vietnamese way of life, and the concept could have been retained without interfering with Diem's legitimate desire—indeed, his need—for a strong central government. The security problem existed, but it wouldn't have made much difference if the Vietminh had elected some village chiefs—they soon established their own underground governments anyway. Diem's mistake was in paralyzing himself. He should have adopted a more intelligent and persuasive policy and concentrated at the outset on obtaining the support of the people. In that way, he could have properly challenged the Vietminh" (*op. cit.*, p. 134).

67. Scigliano, *South Vietnam*, p. 33. In Scigliano's opinion, Diem's administrative system was surpassed only by the Communist bureaucracy created in North Vietnam (*ibid.*, pp. 33–34).

68. *Ibid.*, pp. 79, 85 ff. "There is from a legal standpoint no opposition party in Vietnam," said Scigliano. "The approval of the Secretary of State for Interior is required for any political party to function, and his disapproval need not be explained and cannot be appealed" (*ibid.*, p. 80). He went on to state: "The artificiality of the government parties can be seen in their role in the National Assembly. In the first place, legislative elections, as

we shall see later, have been carefully manipulated by the government to produce mostly safe deputies, and there has not yet developed any close relationship between the deputies as a whole and their constituencies. Secondly, the bulk of government policy-making is carried out through the executive branch, and whatever comes before the National Assembly is under heavy executive guidance. In general, party labels have no significance in the National Assembly, for there are no real differences among parties. The same thing is true of the two blocs into which the deputies have been organized" (*ibid.*, p. 86). On political parties in South Vietnam, see also Scigliano "Political Parties in South Vietnam Under the Republic," in *Foreign Affairs*, XXXIII, December, 1960.

69. Scigliano, *South Vietnam*, p. 76. The Personalist Labor Party was described by one American observer as "a clandestine, inner-circle political organization called Can Lao Nhan Vi Dang (Personalist Labor Party), commonly known as the Can Lao, which closely followed Communist methods, such as secret cells inside public and private organizations. This was one of several apparatuses in Nhu's intelligence network" (Mecklin, *op. cit.*, p. 43). Wrote Shaplen: "The Can Lao was dominated and run by Nhu's henchmen in Saigon and in the provincial administrations, and while its structure and organization were weak, and it never held any big meetings, the awe it created, and ultimately the sense of fear it imposed, became key factors in the evolving Diem-Nhu dictatorship. The Can Lao's membership was never disclosed—estimates ran from five to fifty thousand—but it was known to include many members of the National Assembly, a completely controlled body chosen in elections in 1956 and again in 1959, as well as individuals, carefully selected by Nhu, who moved anonymously through all the echelons of government, down to the level of villages and hamlets, factories, schools, and small military units, tracking down cases of malfeasance and corruption and disloyalty to the regime. On the recommendation of any of the seven Can Lao bureau chiefs, a suspected person could be arrested and brought to trial. Nhu . . . blandly admitted the party's structure was not unlike that of the Communists, and . . . used the organization slowly to build up his paramilitary control of the countryside, to stifle any opposition, and to inhibit the formation and operation of any independent political parties" (*op. cit.*, pp. 130–31).

70. *The New York Times*, May 22, 1960, p. 4.

71. According to Scigliano, one out of every eight men worked for the government. In 1960, aside from the 25,000 persons or so working for the Department of Interior, 17,700, mostly teachers, were under the Department of National Education; 12,100 were under the Department of Public Works; and 10,100 were under the Department of National Defense. The Department of Agriculture employed a surprisingly small number—2,900; the Department of National Economy, 912; and the Department of Labor, only 382 (*South Vietnam*, pp. 47, 48). See also Dale Rose and Vu Van Hoc, *The Vietnamese Civil Service System* (Saigon, 1961).

72. The two first chairmen were the Secretary of State for Information

(and personal physician to Diem), Bui Kien Tin, and a subsequent Information Secretary, Tran Chanh Thanh. The third chairman, Pham Van Nhu, was also President of the National Assembly, and the next chairman, Truong Vinh Le, later became Assembly President. "None of these persons," Scigliano adds, "has been able to develop strong personal power from his position of party leadership, with the partial exception of Tran Chanh Thanh, and his influence ended with his replacement as party head in 1958, if indeed it did not in part lead to his replacement" (*South Vietnam*, p. 77).

73. Those who had returned from abroad with Diem or soon after him were the most bitterly disappointed after two or three years. They became resigned, or they tried to go abroad in order to make known and attack the evils of the regime. A case in point is that of Nguyen Thai, whose book *Is South Vietnam Viable?* has repeatedly been cited here. Another who had come to Saigon with Diem was Vu Van Thai, who was forced to resign after seven years of devoted service. Dang Duc Khoi, cited in n. 66, above, was yet another. Many more again became fence sitters, went into business, or were forced to flee the country. Some early supporters wound up in jail.

74. Scigliano, *South Vietnam*, p. 60. Mecklin (*op. cit.*, p. 108) speaks of "the Ngo Dinh family's unshakable belief in its own infallibility."

75. Lacouture, *Vietnam entre deux paix* (Paris, 1965), p. 36. In *Vietnam: Between Two Truces*, the English-language version of this book, this particular sentence is rendered merely as: "He had an attachment to the ancient society of Vietnam" (p. 19).

76. Browne, *op. cit.*, p. 196. Remarked Nguyen Thai: "Figures can give only one aspect of the total picture, because though the number of *fonctionnaires* in important positions may be relatively small, their political influence is considerable. . . . Out of a total of 138,000 government employees, there are only 29,000 career civil servants, the rest, 109,000, being non-career. These figures can be misleading in determining the approximate number of the *fonctionnaires* from the French colonial administration, because among the non-career employees many could be former career civil servants under the French and vice-versa" (*op. cit.*, pp. 51, 52). Thai, as well as Scigliano, make a point of the French education and training of these civil service employees (Scigliano, *South Vietnam*, p. 48; Thai, *op. cit.*, p. 52). For a discussion of the characteristics of the *fonctionnaire* spirit and of the gulf between government and people, see Thai, *ibid.*, pp. 53 ff. For a less emotional picture than Thai's, see Roy Jumper, "The Mandarin Bureaucracy and Politics in South Vietnam," *Pacific Affairs*, XXX, March, 1957.

77. Browne, *op. cit.*, p. 196.

78. Halberstam, *op. cit.*, p. 115.

79. *Ibid.*, p. 188.

80. *Ibid.*, p. 68. That Taylor and his advisers knew what was wrong with the Diem regime can be seen from their proposals—i.e., to broaden the base of the government by taking non-Ngo anti-Communists into it; to make the National Assembly more than a rubber stamp; to cease press restrictions, etc. Taylor's emphasis, as can be seen from this, was on the political short-

comings of the regime, which he then rightly recognized as the main obstacle to military effectiveness against the Vietcong. As Halberstam also commented: "Friends of mine who saw the Taylor report consider it a brilliant analysis of the ailments and symptoms of a very sick country" (*ibid.*, p. 68). Taylor had been preceded in 1961 by Professor Eugene Staley, who headed an economic-military mission upon the heels of the then Vice President Johnson's visit to Vietnam. "Surprisingly enough," wrote Fall (*The Two Viet-Nams*, p. 278), "that mission, though essentially of a civilian character, came forth with few recommendations that were not of a military nature, and none that involved the deep-seated political changes that other observers considered necessary. The Staley mission had hardly completed its first reports when another mission, headed by General Maxwell D. Taylor (then in retirement), in turn made its way to Saigon. . . . Since Taylor was a military man, it was expected that his report would deal almost exclusively with the military emergency. The surprising fact was (and it was a serious shock to Saigon's ruling group) that his report was extremely hard-hitting and forthright on the subject of long-overdue political reforms, including greater freedom of speech and more effective decentralization."

81. Special mention should be made here of the Australian journalist Denis Warner, a veteran correspondent in Indochina, whose observations during the French Indochina War were as pertinent as his criticisms of the Diem regime in his many articles, and especially in his book *The Last Confucian*.

82. Mecklin, *op. cit.*, p. 86. Mecklin's book, too much neglected, is absolutely essential for a proper appreciation of the role of the American press in regard to Vietnam and the Diem regime, and the strange tolerance the United States and its higher officials showed for the regime.

83. *Ibid.*, pp. 20, 25.

84. "The Secretary of State for Interior, in a talk he gave in 1962, frankly acknowledged the government's mistake in using colonial-trained personnel in local government. The Viet Minh, he pointed out, eliminated experienced civil servants when they took power in 1945, introducing in their place a new class of cadres. 'These cadres worked and learned at the same time.' He then observed that 'on the contrary, for the last seven years, we continued to use an outmoded group of cadres because they have diplomas and experience,' and further that the government's local administrators 'fight against Communism [in order] to go backward. . . . Some of them have antagonized the people, driving them to the Communist side'" (Scigliano, *South Vietnam*, p. 64; quoting Bui Van Luong, "Strategic Hamlets to Keep the Roots in the Ground," *Times of Vietnam Magazine*, May 20, 1962). Cf. also Nguyen Thai, *op. cit.*, p. 256, on the conflict of technical efficiency versus political loyalty.

85. "The attrition among capable administrators in the Diem government has been high, especially in the younger group. Perhaps the greatest loss to the government was the departure of Vu Van Thai, the General Director of Budget and Foreign Aid, probably the most brilliant of the regime's high-

level administrators. Thai found his reforms countered at the Presidency and in the old-line agencies, and his personal status sapped; he quit the government and Vietnam in mid-1961" (Scigliano, *South Vietnam,* p. 67). In an interview with the *Washington Post,* on November 24, 1961, Vu Van Thai stated: "We are desperate because we have no means of making our ideas known to the people." He was referring to his colleagues who had resigned from all government service, the article said. It also told of others who had handed in their resignations: Vietnam's Ambassador to Laos, the Chargé d'Affaires in Cambodia, the Chargé d'Affaires in Malaya and Consul General in Singapore, the Consul General in Thailand, the *Chef du Cabinet* in the Foreign Office, the Director General of the *Viet-Nam Press* (Nguyen Thai), "and some dozen junior Foreign Service officers." The article ended thus: "One of these officials, who still is in Saigon and must be protected by anonymity, recently wrote to an American friend: 'We had to conclude that our participation in government affairs does not have any sense any longer—apart from a comfortable situation, materially speaking.'" I myself knew a high official in the Foreign Ministry in Saigon who, in 1960, cried for hours on my shoulder out of shame because he could not resign, because he had to take humiliating orders from Nhu, because he was a coward to stay on, but he feared arrest and the misery this would cause his wife and their eight children.

86. One such place, according to Browne, was Dam Doi, where a number of district chiefs were assassinated by the Vietcong. Browne, whose accuracy and integrity as a reporter I greatly admire, says: "Assignment to places like Dam Doi in the past has generally been the result of incurring the displeasure of officials in Saigon, and has happened in many cases as punishment or even personal revenge" (*op. cit.,* p. 104).

87. Fall, *The Two Viet-Nams,* p. 249.

88. "Tran Van Lam, a very popular Southerner who was, as Diem's first delegate to the Southern region of Vietnam, pronounced by one foreign source to be the second most powerful man in the government in 1956, was sent to Australia in 1961 after he had descended by degrees to the posts of President of the National Assembly, leader of the majority bloc of that body, and ordinary deputy. Tran Chanh Thanh, who also enjoyed a period of power . . . found himself sent off to Tunisia in 1960 after his party leadership had already been taken from him and his administrative authority eclipsed. Bui Van Thinh, who, as Secretary of State for Interior, controlled the police and security agencies and the organization of civil servants and in addition was head of the then-strongest government party, was . . . made ambassador to Japan right after the Bao Dai referendum, which he had directed. Lam Le Trinh, who also headed the Interior Department, was linked to a group hostile to certain key members at the Presidency and was sent to Turkey. It is not known what caused the fall of certain other Cabinet-members-become-ambassadors, including Tran Huu The, Nguyen Cong Vien, and Nguyen Duong Don, who traded the departments of Education, Agriculture and, again, Education, for posts in the Philippines, China, and

Italy, respectively" (Scigliano, *South Vietnam*, p. 67). See also Thai, *op. cit.*, pp. 267, 272, and 279, for his comment on the same subject, as it applied to administrators, ministers, and military.

89. Chau, the husband of Mme. Nhu's sister, was a brilliant young administrator and high in the President's esteem. Marital difficulties led him to seek a divorce in the Vietnamese courts, and the scandal this action threatened to bring on the family gained him the enmity of Mme. Nhu. (See n. 59, above, on Chau's being defeated in his attempt to obtain the Vice-Presidency, via a lowering of the age requirement, by Mme. Nhu.) She prevented Chau's divorce case from being taken up by the judiciary until her family bill, which prohibited divorce, was enacted into law. Chau, his position at the Presidency gradually undermined, finally resigned from the government and then fled to France (Scigliano, *South Vietnam*, p. 61).

90. *Ibid.*, p. 60. And, Scigliano added, "The family is in class, regional origin, religion and temperament sharply set off from the population over which it rules." Thai speaks of "invisible" family government (see *op. cit.*, pp. 120 ff.).

91. "Similar charges" of corruption "have been leveled against Monsignor Ngo Dinh Thuc," Fall writes, "who is said to have acquired large real estate and business holdings for both the Church and his family" (*The Two Viet-Nams*, p. 252). Thai, who comments that it has reportedly been said that Thuc should have been the politician and Diem the religious man, writes: "Thuc tries to convey the impression that he is remote from politics and only concerned with religious affairs. But for the realistic Vietnamese, Thuc is the most influential person in the regime because his word and opinion are final in the Ngo family councils" (*op. cit.*, p. 219). "In April of this year," Denis Warner said, "Thuc made a private visit to Australia, and invested heavily in real-estate there" (*The Reporter*, October 10, 1963).

92. Mecklin, *op. cit.*, p. 33. Various other accusations alleged that Can participated in profitable rice sales to the Communist North and in the illicit opium trade from Laos. The latter charge was made frequently and has lately been repeated by the Vietnamese diplomat-novelist Tran Van Dinh (Chargé d'Affaires in Washington in 1963, he left his government's service in 1964) who, in his novel *No Passenger on the River* (New York, 1965), relates an incident in which an army officer returned from a special mission in Laos for the "Supreme Adviser," as Can was called, a mission that obviously had nothing to do with legitimate business. "Of all the Ngo brothers," writes Scigliano, "Can is the only one who did not receive a Westernized education . . . and he is the only one who has never traveled abroad. Indeed, he very seldom leaves his native Hue where, as the next to youngest brother, he assumes the responsibility for looking after his mother. He is also considered the most severe, some would say primitive, member of the family, and he rules his domain with a strict and sometimes brutal hand" (*South Vietnam*, p. 59). In a shrewd analysis of Can's character, Nguyen Thai stresses the two differences between Diem and Can that speak for Can. One is that Can, "ruling in an autocratic way, is *consistently* autocratic and

to his followers he makes it clear what he wants them to do. They are not confused by double talk about democratic ideals and institutions." The other difference is that "Can seems to create for himself a following which sticks to him because the system of rewards and punishments is clearly defined. Those who serve him well get promoted. . . . Brother Diem, on the contrary . . . has this half-way indecisive approach which tends to discourage really loyal and committed followers" (*op. cit.*, p. 214). After the coup that toppled Diem and Nhu, Can was brought to trial and executed.

93. I remember my embarrassment when Nhu, in August, 1958, told me quite seriously that he was the only original thinker in Vietnam, that no one else in the country had political ideas, that he alone could, if he wished, create an opposition, which he was at times tempted to do, but that having to supply the government with ideas kept him too busy. An interesting sketch of Nhu's outward appearance with reflections on his character was drawn by Tran Van Dinh. Nhu's "piercing eyes, his pale complexion, his high cheek bones, his well-aligned dark eyebrows and his straight nose made him look rather handsome in spite of his thin and bluish lips. But there was something frightening in his face, an air of Machiavellian mystery and cynical vanity, wicked intelligence and calculated malice. . . . Dressed in a short-sleeved shirt made of local yellowish silk and black pants, he gave an impression of studied disdain and provocative arrogance rather than modesty. He . . . spoke in a sticky voice which usually was the trade mark of the opium-smoking perverts" (*op. cit.*, pp. 75–76). Shaplen calls Nhu a Rasputin (*op. cit.*, p. 106). Mecklin feels that "the Diem-Nhu relationship was a psychiatric curiosity." It could best be explained "by the 'Siamese twin' theory, that Diem could not survive without Nhu, whom he trusted absolutely" (*op. cit.*, p. 43). Mecklin describes Nhu as "a small man, slight of build even for a Vietnamese. He spoke softly with a permanently fixed smile (earning him the nickname 'Smiley' in the American community). It was a professorial smile, implying generous tolerance for the listener's stupidity" (*ibid.*, p. 46). Halberstam describes Nhu as "a born intriguer," and adds, "he was an arrogant, vain man, sometimes privately a little contemptuous of Diem, whom he considered to be his intellectual inferior. He told one reporter that he considered himself 'the unique spine of the anti-Communist movement' in South Vietnam, and that the program would collapse without him." When Halberstam once "asked a Palace official which of the brothers he considered more influential," the Vietnamese "thought for a minute and then said, 'Nhu, because he can always influence Diem, but Diem can never influence Nhu'" (*op. cit.*, pp. 51, 52).

94. "Nhu . . . frequently criticized his brother to visitors, implying that Diem was something of an unimaginative oaf" (Mecklin, *op. cit.*, p. 43). Thai writes that "to the foreign governments not quite acquainted with the meaning of [Nhu's] official title of 'political adviser to the President' he made it known that he should be treated as nothing less than Diem's *alter ego*." Which, Thai explains in an example, meant that "when Nhu and his wife went to Morocco in June, 1961, the understanding was that they should be

granted the same protocol treatment as the chief of state, or at least something below that rank, but above that of chief of government" (*op. cit.*, p. 196, and n. 1).

95. Originally conceived by Diem on the model of similar mandarinal agencies whose functions consisted in researching and checking official documents coming to or going from the "sovereign," Dr. Tran Kim Tuyen's So Nghien Cuu—The Service for Political and Social Research of the Presidency—grew in importance as Ngo Dinh Nhu's power continued to increase. Because of his dual functions—that of obtaining secret information on individuals and on departments or offices, and that of disseminating or passing on the wishes and demands of Nhu and of Diem—Dr. Tuyen played a pivotal role in the political life of the Diem regime. Since people had no way of knowing whether Tuyen was acting on Nhu's orders or on his own, wrote Nguyen Thai, nobody dared to disobey. People also knew that he could do a lot for a person he wished to help, and "legion are his friends who have gotten the jobs they wanted." In short, nothing was beyond Tuyen's reach as long as he had the implicit support of Ngo Dinh Nhu. In turn, he provided "Ngo Dinh Nhu, and to a certain extent his wife, with the miniature *real* government which guides, directs, supervises and controls the *official* government" appointed by Ngo Dinh Diem (*op. cit.*, pp. 202-9). Dr. Tuyen came from Phat Diem, says Shaplen, "one of the Catholic enclaves up north, and he had been responsible, in 1954, for persuading a considerable number of Catholics to give up their homes and property in the north and move south. Subsequently, Dr. Tuyen had been among those who had tried unsuccessfully to get Diem to maintain some contact with individual northerners, including members of the Hanoi government, in the hope that even a few might eventually be persuaded to defect. When the idea of creating a mild opposition first came up, Dr. Tuyen was aware that he would have to move cautiously, especially since he was operating under Nhu's surveillance. The group that was created was called the Committee on National Union. Tuyen's top assistant was one of the ten members named to it, so that the government could be kept fully informed of what all the Committee members were doing, publicly and privately" (*op. cit.*, p. 158). A slight, small man, Dr. Tuyen allegedly had not completed his medical studies and held the doctoral degree "perhaps as a matter of deference," wrote Thai. Tuyen had also at one time considered entering a seminary to study for the priesthood. At the time he served the Ngos, he was about forty years old and married. As "step by step Madame Nhu and her husband shut Diem off from the rest of Vietnam" (Halberstam, *op. cit.*, p. 56), Dr. Tuyen gauged their influence on the affairs of the country. Accordingly, he "saw the paratrooper coup as the final warning to the Government and at great risk he wrote a long, carefully documented report for Diem, analyzing what had happened and what it portended for the future. Dr. Tuyen traced much of the trouble to Madame Nhu, and he warned that if the Government were to survive, Madame's role and power must be curtailed" (*ibid.*). Shaplen reports that Dr. Tuyen also repeated the warn-

ings he had expressed after the first abortive coup in November, 1960, after the second abortive effort in February, 1962, when the Presidential Palace was bombed. "When Nhu was shown the first letter, he ignored it, but he took offense at the second, and thereafter Dr. Tuyen was out of favor. However, he kept his job until mid-1963, mainly because Nhu thought he could use the doctor to keep tabs on plotters against the regime" (*op. cit.*, p. 197). By then, Dr. Tuyen himself was deeply involved in "seriously plotting against the regime," Shaplen adds. It was Tuyen who organized the planned coup by the "young Turks," Halberstam says, and it was he who had been able "to get together a select number of combat units" for this coup. "But in the middle of the Buddhist crisis Diem suddenly appointed him envoy to the United Arab Republic in order to get him out of the country; the brothers were reportedly loath to arrest the doctor, in the belief that he probably had too much incriminating information on Palace activities" (*op. cit.*, p. 280).

96. The Special Forces were created late in 1960, and Le Quang Tung—a former servant of the Ngo family in Central Vietnam, and a noncom with the French expeditionary troops during the Indochina War—was put in charge. The Special Forces, "which was in effect a private army for Nhu and Diem," was "responsible for, among other things, the final crackdown on the Buddhists in August, 1963." Dressed in their white uniforms, they "used teargas bombs and grenades in storming the Xa Loi and three other pagodas, arresting several hundred Buddhist priests" (Shaplen, *op. cit.*, pp. 189, 190).

97. Mecklin, *op. cit.*, p. 471. He added: "Fate could hardly have chosen a more unfortunate harassment to impose on the chaste, remote Diem and the emotionally chaotic Nhu at a time of their country's agony than this hair-triggered spitfire." There is no need to describe here this Oriental beauty, since she was fully exposed to American television audiences during her visit to the United States in 1963. She certainly blazed forth from the television screen with such fiery, disdainful pride, frequently with arrogance, and with such a twisted, personal logic (Halberstam wrote, for example, that she once told him "with a perfectly straight face that it was absurd to call the family a dictatorship; after all, she said, every member had a free voice at family councils" [*op. cit.*, p. 56]), so strong and strange a will, that the sobriquet "Dragon Lady" seemed patently appropriate (Joseph Alsop once called her a tigress!). Unlike the American career woman, in politics or out, Mme. Nhu created the impression that she achieved her aims by seducing men to her point of view instead of persuading them. As Nguyen Thai wrote: "It seems that Mrs. Nhu has been able to find subtle ways to make her increasing power acceptable to President Diem" (*op. cit.*, p. 180). Mecklin spoke of "the femininity that she exploited so spectacularly," and that she "often resorted to a trace of a pout that calculating women have used since time immemorial" (*op. cit.*, p. 48). Stanley Karnow, in an article in the *Saturday Evening Post*, September 28, 1963, was even more outspoken about Mme. Nhu's extraordinary power over Diem. Ascribing it to the status she had achieved in the family as "one of the few members . . . to have chil-

dren" (two daughters and two sons), Karnow stated: "At the same time, she frightens Diem. Beyond a passing glance at a girl in his youth, he has led a life of celibacy, not only fearing women in general but particularly fearing female tantrums, at which Madame Nhu is expert." And she is quoted by Karnow as stating with that peculiar logic of hers that Diem without his family stands alone. "His followers were all killed by the Communists, and our followers saved him," Karnow has her explain. "The women follow me, my husband has his youth movement, the Catholics take orders from Archbishop Thuc. . . . If there is nepotism, it is the president who profits." In this same article, Karnow states: "Presented with the case of Madame Nhu, an amateur psychiatrist would be tempted to look into her childhood, and she frankly confesses that her youth was miserable." Le Xuan was a middle child, between an older sister "she had to respect, and a younger brother who received more attention." Her father, Tran Van Chuong, Diem's Ambassador to Washington, had been a wealthy landowner, her mother a member of Vietnamese royalty (and Vietnam's observer at the United Nations during her husband's ambassadorship). When Le Xuan, at the age of twenty, married Ngo Dinh Nhu, her senior by thirteen years, she converted from Buddhism to Catholicism and, as Karnow puts it, "really married the Ngo Dinh family." Mecklin writes that the Americans living in Saigon believed "that Nhu worshiped her, and this seemed to be confirmed by witnesses of the few occasions when they were seen together with their children" (*op. cit.*, p. 49). The Vietnamese First Lady, he comments, seemed to have "what appeared to be a fixation against other people having a good time." Her morality laws, the ban on dancing, cockfights, contraceptives, gambling, sentimental songs, and divorce were notorious, and were the first to go when the regime fell.

98. Mecklin, *op. cit.*, p. 51.

99. Perhaps the most brilliant among those who incurred Mme. Nhu's displeasure, and consequently resigned, was Vu Van Thai, the present Vietnamese Ambassador to the United States. Vu Van Thai's father had also been a fierce nationalist. In 1947, he worked with the Communists in the North, and he was executed by them in their drive for total power. Vu Van Thai was an adviser to Ho Chi Minh at the Fontainebleau negotiations with France in 1945, but he broke with Ho over the signing of the *modus vivendi* with the French. For the next decade he tried to unite the splintered nationalist groups behind a common program of national independence and social reform. In 1954, he declined a political appointment by Ngo Dinh Diem and instead accepted the post of heading South Vietnam's Bureau of the Budget and Directorate General of Foreign Aid. He was soon subjected to constant pressure by the Nhus to authorize fiscal expenditures that he did not consider justified. By 1960, the power of the Nhus had increased to such a point that Thai's life was endangered because of his political independence. He submitted his resignation in September, 1960. Nhu ordered his death sentence but was forestalled by Diem. In July, 1961, after his family had left Saigon, Thai himself received Diem's permission to leave the country, and

his exit visa was granted without the knowledge of the Nhus. After arriving in the United States, he was engaged by the United Nations to head its Technical Assistance Board in Togo, and later, as an Inter-Regional Adviser, became one of the U.N.'s chief economic trouble-shooters (see *Vietnam Perspectives*, I, No. 2 (November, 1965), pp. 1, 2.) My own opinion of Thai was set down in a diary I kept during my visit to Vietnam in 1958. There I wrote: "Vu Van Thai—educated, intelligent. He never speaks without a brief moment of reflection. His face is too thin and pale to pass as handsome, but it is clean-cut and noble. He is frank but never rude, firm yet gentle, even if he disagrees strongly with you. He contradicts without much hesitation, but never sounds opinionated. His judgment of people he disapproves of can be harsh, but it is not malicious. He seems to bear no grudges, holds no personal hostilities, and is completely free of petty resentment, even if he has been personally hurt. I have seen no better man in the government of Vietnam."

100. The Women's Solidarity Movement, writes Scigliano, got logistical support from the Department of Civic Action. "Until March, 1962, this organization was nominally under the wing of the Civil Servants League and bears the mark of this early association, for its central, provincial, and district directing committees are composed largely of the wives of government officials on the same levels. Most of the Movement's urban members appear to consider their affiliation a prudent concomitant of their husbands' employment, but some apparently share Mme. Nhu's determined feminism and are interested in participating in charitable and other activities in aid of their sex. Since 1961, young women have had the opportunity of joining Mme. Nhu's women's paramilitary corps, a volunteer group which provides training in gunhandling, first aid, and morality for high school-age and other women" (*South Vietnam*, pp. 173–74).

101. Browne, *op. cit.*, p. 170. Fall said about the prohibition on dancing: "This is, to the best of my knowledge, the only law of that kind in existence anywhere in the world" (*The Two Viet-Nams*, p. 266; for additional details on the various aspects of the "Family Law" of May 29, 1958, and the "Law for the Protection of Morality" of May 24, 1962, see *ibid.*, pp. 265–67).

102. Scigliano, *South Vietnam*, p. 44. In this largely Taoist and Buddhist country, Fall wrote, polygamous marriages to "secondary wives" had hitherto been legal (*The Two Viet-Nams*, p. 265). Nguyen Thai comments that "divorce in Vietnamese society has never been the topic of much controversy in writing and the silence on the matter of the writers concerned with Vietnam's social problems is highly indicative of the fact that the problem was *not* of critical importance to Vietnamese society" (*op. cit.*, p. 133, n. 1).

103. "For many years, Saigon legends have linked Mme. Ngo Dinh Nhu, the once powerful sister-in-law of the late President Ngo Dinh Diem, with various amorous adventures," writes Browne. "One perennial story has to do with Mme. Nhu and a U.S. Army colonel. Another links her in a tragic adventure with one of South Viet Nam's leading young generals, whose

wife is supposed to have shot Mme. Nhu through the arm. . . . I have never seen a shred of documentation for any of these yarns, but Saigon's cocktail circuit intelligentsia accepts differing versions of the Mme. Nhu stories as established fact" (*op. cit.*, p. 145). In his novel, Tran Van Dinh had one character say of the regime: "They are immoral, but they preach morality; they are corrupted and they demand honesty from the people," and of another, whose interview with Nhu was interrupted by Mme. Nhu's entrance, he said: "Minh looked at the floor, smiled discreetly, as he knew only too well her questionable past, her family and her numerous love affairs" (*op. cit.*, pp. 141, 77).

104. Mecklin states: "The Nhus had an elegant house in Dalat, and they were supposed to have secreted a fortune in Swiss banks, though this was never proved" (*op. cit.*, p. 33). And Fall wrote: "Much has been made in the Western press of the fact that such corruption, in the case of Diem's relatives, could not be 'proved,' as if their indictment or clearance by a grand jury would solve the *psychological* problem of the popular belief that they do take undue advantage of their official position. In any case, two incidents shed some indirect light on the problem: When Le Thi Gioi, the mistress of ex-Premier Nguyen Van Tam, was put on trial for corruption in February, 1955 (i.e., at a time when the regime was far from consolidated), she 'caused a sensation in court by roundly accusing . . . Mme. Ngo Dinh Nhu of indulging in similar activities on a far more extensive scale.' By 1957, rumors about such practices had become so widespread and precise that on August 24 both Nhu and his wife took advertisements in several Saigon newspapers to deny those charges explicitly. Needless to say, this official denial fed rather than quenched the rumors" (*The Two Viet-Nams*, p. 252). Chaffard (*op. cit.*, p. 153) says the reason the bourgeoisie did not like the regime was the police interferences in business—which was the "interference" practiced by Nhu's secret services for kickbacks. In an article by Huynh Sang Thong in *The Nation* of February 18, 1961, entitled "The Greatest Little Man in Asia," he said: "Not the smallest irony about the South Vietnamese government is the fact, that, under a woman-hating president, it has invested a woman with unprecedented power: Mrs. Ngo-dinh Nhu, Diem's sister-in-law and First Lady of the Land. Together with her husband, who is Diem's chief political adviser and strategist, she maintains a stranglehold on the economy and is believed to be at the heart of most major corruption in the country." Communist propaganda played heavily on these rumors and allegations. For an "exposé" type of story on the corruption practiced by the Ngo family, see Wilfred Burchett, *The Furtive War: The United States in Vietnam and Laos* (New York, 1963), pp. 77–94. (Mr. Burchett's well-known Communist sympathies are part and parcel of his reporting.)

105. See Scigliano, *South Vietnam*, pp. 44–45. A number of the deputies demanded that Mme. Nhu apologize for "unseemly remarks," Scigliano reports.

106. The official mentioned in n. 85, above, told me that after writing a

report he thought he had been ordered to write, he received a phone call from Nhu telling him to mind his own business. "Wait until you are told what to do," Nhu said, ignoring the fact that the official had been told by his superior, the Foreign Minister, to write this report. This official, incidentally, had earlier aroused Can's anger, and had been dismissed from his high administrative position in Hue.

107. There is a very interesting chapter on this, entitled "Inconsistent Approach to Rewards and Punishments for Political Loyalty," in Thai's book, citing instances proving this inconsistency (*op. cit.,* pp. 266 ff.).

108. Mecklin, *op. cit.,* p. 43.

109. Fall, *The Two Viet-Nams,* p. 241. "Family loyalty is a common Chinese and Vietnamese trait," Fall wrote. "In the case of Diem it extends even to relatives by marriage . . . and its fierceness brooks no criticism, however slight. This explains why many attempts (particularly by American political experts) to wean Diem away from members of his entourage who are political liabilities have consistently failed in the past and are likely to continue to fail in the future." See also Denis Warner, "Vietnam: A Dynasty in Disorder," *The Reporter,* September 12, 1963.

110. That is what Diem said at his press conference in New York on May 13, 1957, when I acted as his translator. On the very same day, Diem rejected my plea to release the well-known anti-Communist Huu Tuong from the Poulo Condore concentration camp, where he had been interned for almost two years.

111. Communist claims of countless massacres of civilians in the sweep by the South Vietnamese Army into Vietminh-controlled areas cannot be taken as evidence, nor can the reports of Wilfred Burchett, which, though they cannot be dismissed altogether, are certainly also Communist propaganda. The ICC reports in this respect are inconclusive, chiefly because the Diem regime prevented the ICC teams from pursuing their investigation. On this subject, see this chapter, section 10. It is neither possible nor worthwhile to list the many books and pamphlets put out by the Communists on the struggle in the South. The number of publications by the Foreign Languages Publishing House in Hanoi on this subject thus far, both in English and French, probably must be counted in the hundreds. Their titles are usually variations of the phrase "We Will Win."

112. I have had contacts with leaders of the opposition to Diem from 1954 on, and maintained such contacts even with some elements of the sects. Many among them were well-intentioned men and women, most were serious, many merely emotional. Not one, however, struck me as possessing the leadership caliber required to save Vietnam. Some were weak, others blinded by hatred, many driven solely by ambition. Their literary output was largely hysterical propaganda, unreliable in its information and exaggerated in its anti-Diem charges. This is true of Dr. Pham Huy Co, Tran Van Tung, and even of Nguyen Ton Hoan, the Dai Viet leader. Their papers in Paris, such as *L'Epée du Vietnam,* the book by Nguyen Thai Binh (*Viet-Nam: The Problem and a Solution,* published by the Viet-Nam Democratic

Party in Paris in 1962), the *White Paper on Ngo Dinh Diem's Regime* (published by the Free Democratic Party of Vietnam, Paris, 1961), which was merely a collection of newspaper articles, were unimpressive and unimportant. This holds true also of the opposition group Pour le Vietnam, headed by a former close associate of Diem, Ho Thong Minh, the man whom he appointed as Minister of Defense in November, 1954, against General Ely's and Ambassador Collins' advice.

113. Corroboration of the opposition's claim that prisoners were tortured came when anti-Communists were released from jails and concentration camps after Diem's fall. For one particularly shocking story, see Browne, *op. cit.*, pp. 115–17. Burchett quotes an Assembly deputy who once spoke out on conditions in prisons (*op. cit.*, p. 48). The American public was not given this revealing news, perhaps because correspondents concentrated on the overt evils of the regime, and also because a report on political prisoners would surely have meant expulsion from the country.

114. Warner, *The Last Confucian*, p. 100.

115. Halberstam, *op. cit.*, p. 66.

116. *Ibid.*, p. 70.

117. *Ibid.*, p. 195.

118. For the text of the Caravelle manifesto, see Fall, *The Two Viet-Nams*, Appendix III (pp. 432–37). The people Fall lists as signers of the manifesto are particularly impressive because of the frequency of the attribute "former" following their professional status. Most everyone was a former minister or governor or prefect or secretary of state—a sorry commentary on the state of affairs.

119. Wrote Scigliano: "Mob action is always viewed by the government as spontaneous action by some patriotic segment of the population, and in all cases the police arrive too late to prevent damage" (*South Vietnam*, p. 175). Scigliano also quotes the case of the priest-editor of *Duong Song*, whose paper was closed and he himself given an eighteen-month jail sentence for editorially praying to God in March, 1957, "to keep the President in good health and clearsighted so that the confidence of the early beginnings [could] be *regained*." In the case of *Thoi Luan*, the regime had some cause for resentment. As Scigliano describes it, "the government had tolerated a series of critical reviews of its policies anonymously written under the dedication 'Letter to My Deputy,' but the March 2 Letter went too far. This was a long, blistering attack on the constitutional foundations, policies, and leadership of the regime, said to be distinguished from Communist and Fascist rule only by the absence of ideology and organization" (*ibid.*, p. 176). In view of these and all other known facts about the Diem regime (known at least to "experts") it is rather surprising that Dr. Fishel should have written that "the accusations of authoritarianism lack solid substance" (*Problems of Freedom*, p. 25). But not much less surprising is my own defense of the regime, at least in private conversations through 1960, and my earlier denials of widespread corruption, as expressed in "Fact and Fiction on Foreign Aid," *Dissent*, Summer, 1959. I believed most of what I was told

by the leaders of the regime, whom I regarded as honest, and by defenders who I thought knew a great deal more than I and whose judgment I respected. The main reason for this tolerance, of course, was the desperate hope that Diem would at the right moment initiate the reforms we kept urging on him. There was also the fear that open attacks on Diem might hasten a Communist victory and such attacks therefore were harmful. This fear was held not only by U.S. officials not fully aware of the political and military decline of the Diem regime, but was shared by many unofficial and well-informed observers. It was emphatically expressed in a letter to me of October 9, 1961, by Wolf Ladejinsky. He wrote: "The unfortunate thing is that there is, at this juncture, no time, really, for major political changes, save the separation from the Nhus. Since the President will never accept the latter, we might as well lay stress on the military preparedness in the faint hope that with a measure of stabilization the pressures for political changes might mount and lead to something worthwhile. You will not misunderstand me, knowing as you do, that I have stressed the need for political changes even during the happier days of years back. That is why mine is not a case of shifting positions for no substantial reason. It is quite possible that all the military shoring up is no longer of any avail; if this is the case, our best hope is a military anti-Communist take-over under a non-Diem leadership. But it is not for us to say it while Diem is still in power. The Communists would make altogether too much capital of it. And so I come back again to your last paragraph and all it states and implies. I will only add that while I am just as entitled to righteous indignation vis-à-vis the regime as any other fellow on the Executive Committee of the Friends [American Friends of Vietnam], we must temper it with the thought that Vietnam does face the danger of a Communist take-over. The ranks will have to be closed, even though we cannot publicly endorse [Diem's] personal regime. We cannot now condemn it publicly either; after all, the malady is as old as the regime and I am of the opinion that we have not done nearly enough of condemning when the going was much better and yet the danger of the shape of things to come was quite apparent to us." Mr. Ladejinsky and I had already felt rather desperate over our inability to "reach" Diem with sound advice some time before. During my visit to Vietnam in the summer of 1958, we discussed this problem frequently, and found ourselves in agreement on the applicability of a character description by Lionel Trilling to Diem. Trilling's description is of Jane Austen's heroine Emma. I quote it here (only changing the personal pronouns from feminine to masculine): "His fault is the classic one of *hubris*, excessive pride, and it yields the classic result of blindness, of an inability to interpret experiences to the end of perceiving reality, and we are aware of each false step, each wrong conclusion that he will make. Our hand goes out to hold him back and set him straight, but it cannot reach him" ("Emma," *Encounter*, June, 1957, p. 54).

120. "Neighboring China," wrote Fall, "to rouse its own intellectuals from the torpor the regime itself had induced, announced the inauguration of a more relaxed policy toward diversified intellectual and artistic en-

deavors, which became known as the 'hundred flowers' policy. On May 25, 1956, Lu Ting-yi, chief of the Propaganda Section of the Central Committee of the Chinese Communist Party, made a speech in Peking before a select assembly of Chinese scientists and artists on the theme of two lines of poetry attributed to Mao: 'Let a hundred flowers bloom/ Let a hundred schools contend.' According to Lu's comments, the new policy 'permits free criticism and allows free reply to the critics' " (*The Two Viet-Nams*, p. 188).

121. Phan Khoi, the soul of this entire movement, was considered the "grand old man" of Vietnamese letters. He died a few days before he was to go on trial for "deviationism." Khoi had been the editor of *Nhan Van* and *Giai Pham*. "None of the 'sacred cows' of the regime escaped criticism," wrote Fall, "and the situation became even worse after the abortive peasant rebellion of November, 1956: The Viet-Nam People's Army was accused of being anti-intellectual; the Russian experts of being overbearing and of driving around in big cars; the Party of antagonizing the peasantry and allowing corruption to flourish among its members. The Party reacted with its usual heavyhandedness—without waiting for the change of line in Peking which came much later. . . . *Nhan-Van* was forbidden to publish on December 15, 1956, after five issues—on the very day that the D.R.V.N. published a new law guaranteeing freedom of the press" (*ibid.*, p. 189). For further details on the so-called *Nhan Van* affair, see *ibid.*, pp. 188–90, Jumper and Normand, *op. cit.*, pp. 471–72, and Chaffard, *op. cit.*, pp. 145–47. Other discussions of the *Nhan Van* affair are in Hoang Van Chi, *The New Class in North Vietnam* (Saigon, 1958), and in Honey, "Revolt of the Intellectuals in North Vietnam," *World Today*, XIII, June, 1957, pp. 250–60; see also n. 122, below.

122. Halberstam, *op. cit.*, p. 52. Among the many attacks on the lack of freedom in the North was the book published by the Vietnamese chapter of the Asian Peoples' Anti-Communist League: Hoa Mai (ed.), *The Nhan-Van Affair* (Saigon, n.d.). A better brief report and analysis of the *Nhan Van* affair, and about the position and attitude of the intellectuals in the North is Nhu Phong's "Intellectuals, Writers, and Artists," in Honey (ed.), *op. cit.*

123. Diem even decided on who should be allowed to study abroad, who should be granted a passport, or whose wife should be allowed to accompany her husband on an official mission abroad. It took Diem two years to decide on a project for a hotel that Pan-American Airways planned to build in Saigon: He had to choose its location, but since his pettiness and obstructionism exasperated the promoters, they finally dropped the project. The President's desk was constantly piled high with papers containing important proposals submitted for decisions he had no time to make.

124. The British journalist James Cameron, in a series of five articles on North Vietnam published in *The New York Times*, December 7–11, 1965, said (in the third article) that the number of factories in the North (which, according to him, numbered 40 in 1955) was 1,200 in 1965.

125. *A Threat to Peace: North Viet-Nam's Effort to Conquer South Viet-Nam* (Washington, D.C., 1961), p. 6.

126. Lloyd D. Musolf, quoted in an article by Gilbert Jonas, "The Industrial Development of Viet Nam," *The Times of Viet Nam Magazine*, June 17, 1961. (See Musolf, "Public Enterprise and Development Perspectives in South Vietnam," *Asian Survey*, III, No. 8 [August, 1963], p. 359.)

127. For the validity of the assertion that insecure conditions interfered with economic progress in the South before 1961, see Musolf, who says, "It is arguable whether guerrilla warfare has been the controlling factor [in confining the scope of industrialization through public enterprise]" (*ibid.*, p. 366). See also James B. Henry, "Economic Development Under Conditions of Guerrilla Warfare: The Case of Vietnam," *Asian Survey*, II, No. 4 (June, 1962).

128. For further details on industrialization, see Musolf, *op. cit.*, pp. 358 ff.; Fall, *The Two Viet-Nams*, pp. 298–301 (giving a list of plants); and "Investing in Vietnam," published by the Diem regime and distributed on the occasion of the Conference on Investment Conditions in the Republic of Vietnam, held under the auspices of American Friends of Vietnam in New York on February 28, 1958.

129. As to these needs, there was one that certainly was not taken care of: the need to create jobs. According to the outstanding and outspoken economist Nguyen Huu Hanh, "merely to avoid urban pauperization, 400,-000–500,000 jobs would have to be created each year" ("Après cinq années de 'Privilèges d'investissement,'" in *Journal d'Extrême-Orient*, June 23, 1962; as quoted by Fall, *The Two Viet-Nams*, p. 301). Hanh states that fewer than 100,000 jobs were opening up yearly before 1962. For more data on unemployment, see Fall, *ibid.*, p. 308, where he quotes Roger Hilsman ("Internal War: The New Communist Tactic," in Lt. Colonel T. N. Greene [ed.], *The Guerrilla—And How to Fight Him* [New York, 1962], p. 31) as stating that farmers were driven into the urban areas, "there to form the hard core of the unemployed slum dwellers . . . [and] recruits for the city mobs that Communists and demagogues have been turning out . . . for the past fifteen years." Scigliano commented that "unemployment has, since 1961, become even more acute" (*South Vietnam*, p. 117).

130. Scigliano, *ibid.*, p. 129.

131. Musolf, *op. cit.*, pp. 366 and 370. This failure, Musolf thinks, was more responsible for the lack of progress than "the lack of enthusiasm for public enterprise displayed by American aid administrators." Musolf expresses the view that "to a large extent, indications of the likely course that public enterprise was to take were plain before guerilla warfare began to become a major problem around 1960."

132. See Musolf, *ibid.*, p. 368.

133. Montgomery, *op. cit.*, p. 93. For a further discussion and criticism of the policy of the National Investment Fund, see Robert H. Slusser, "Early Steps Toward an Industrial Development Bank," in Lindholm (ed.) *op. cit.*, pp. 245–54, especially pp. 252–53.

134. Scigliano, *South Vietnam,* p. 119. Scigliano refers to the extensive study of the Industrial Development Center by M. N. Trued, "South Vietnam's Industrial Development Center," in *Pacific Affairs,* XXXIII, No. 3 (September, 1960), pp. 250–68. Says Trued: "The I.D.C. has not become . . . the leading organization for promoting industrial progress in Viet-Nam, nor has it evolved a program for assisting a broad range of industrial enterprises."

135. Fall seems to hold this view, at least in regard to foreign private investment (see *The Two Viet-Nams,* p. 302). For a systematic and sharp criticism of the regime's alleged reliance on public enterprise and a planned economy, see Milton C. Taylor, "South Viet-Nam: Lavish Aid, Limited Progress," *Pacific Affairs,* XXXIV, Fall, 1961, pp. 242–56. The subject is also treated by Frank C. Child, *Essays on Economic Growth, Capital Formation, and Public Policy in Viet-Nam* (mimeo.; Saigon, 1961).

136. This brings to mind a discussion by letter between myself and Wolf Ladejinsky during Mr. Ladejinsky's tenure as economic adviser to President Diem. I mentioned a book I had read whose main thesis I found applicable to Diem. The book was *The Strategy of Economic Development,* by Albert O. Hirschman, Irving Fisher Research Professor of Economics at Yale University. I summarized its main thesis for Mr. Ladejinsky's information (he had not yet read it then) as follows: The difficulties or "prerequisites" of economic development in underdeveloped countries are overemphasized, and this is true also for the so-called need for "balanced growth." How can a backward and stagnant country ever reach the perfect conditions supposedly required for economic development? Development has actually taken place without these "prerequisites"; development depends not so much on finding optimal combinations for given resources and factors of production but rather on "enlisting for development purposes resources and abilities that are hidden, scattered or badly utilized." The greatest obstacle to development was failure to take the required number of decisions needed at the required speed. Hirschman sees the problems of development as being rooted there where all problems of human action lie—namely in the mind. He interprets the shortages of specific factors or "prerequisites" of development (natural resources, capital, technical know-how) as manifestations of a basic deficiency which he calls the inability to organize the whole process. This leads him to reduce all factors of backwardness and stagnation to one main cause: paucity of decision-making.

137. An attempt was made once to bring some theoretical clarity to the government's vague personalist notions about development policy and to spell out pragmatically a middle course between public and private enterprise, recognizing the necessity of both. See Vu Van Thai, "Our Concept of Development," a speech delivered at a conference of the American Friends of Vietnam of October 23–24, 1959, at the Roosevelt Hotel, New York City, and reprinted in *Vital Speeches* (New York, 1961). For a warm appreciation of Vu Van Thai's positive role as Director of Budget and Administrator of Foreign Aid, see Musolf, *op. cit.,* p. 365, where he states: "In the

precedent-ridden, legal-minded Vietnamese administrative system, the creative, innovative bureaucrat has been a rarity." Thai was such a rarity.

138. Even "anti-American" authors have conceded that American capital showed little interest in an "economic exploitation" of Vietnam. Investments at home or in developed foreign countries (such as Western Europe and Canada) were considered safer and more profitable, especially since nationalization always loomed large as a threat on the horizon of an underdeveloped country's government policies. For these reasons, the various attempts to persuade prospective investors to take an interest in Vietnam, such as for example those made by the American Friends of Vietnam and by the public-relations firm Harold Oram, Inc. (which for several years represented the South Vietnamese Government in this country) were unproductive. So were direct efforts by the Saigon Government (see Gilbert Jonas [ed.], *Investment Conditions in the Republic of Vietnam*). An investment law was proclaimed only in 1963 (see *The Times of Viet Nam Magazine*, March 24, 1963).

139. The anti-Chinese ordinances, expressions of nationalism rather than of rational economic measures, were issued in August and September, 1956. Ordinance No. 48, of August 21, 1956, made all Chinese born in Vietnam Vietnamese citizens, and Ordinance No. 53, of September 6, 1956, excluded all foreign nationals from eleven professions known to be largely in Chinese hands. For my own defense of these government measures, see Buttinger, "The Ethnic Minorities in the Republic of Vietnam," in Fishel (ed.), *Problems of Freedom*, pp. 99–123.

140. See Musolf, *op. cit.*, pp. 370–71.

141. There were many instances of conflict between Diem and American aid administrators and political advisers. See, for example, the quarrel over the Civil Guards, as related by Montgomery, *op. cit.*, pp. 64–70, where he writes, "the President's determination, coupled with the absence of any possible American sanctions (short of self-defeating termination of the program), gave Ngo Dinh Diem basically what he wanted. But during the interim of wrangling, the Civil Guard was unable to perform its mission effectively." Discussing the doubtful value of the military civic-action teams, Montgomery wrote further on (*ibid.*, pp. 70–72, "Civic Action and the Bureaucracy") that the U.S. proposal for Community action was defeated (in 1957). The province chiefs obtained control of civic action; it survived thereafter only as a semimilitary operation rather than an essentially political community service. This is only one of the many examples of diverting funds from civilian and direct political to military purposes.

142. Public statements by John B. Hollister, Director of the International Cooperation Administration (ICA) from 1955 to 1957 voiced strong opposition against the policy of promoting industrialization through public enterprise, but Musolf thinks that "American aid policy can scarcely be said to have formed a significant policy barrier to public enterprise" (*op. cit.*, p. 368).

143. See Milton C. Taylor, *op. cit.*

144. These were the Scripps-Howard articles on the Vietnam program, by Albert Colegrove. Montgomery refers to them and also discusses them at great length (*op. cit.*, pp. 44, 185, 224–35). In Appendix III (*ibid.*, pp. 304–13) he reports further on this matter, comparing the claims made by Colegrove with the facts given in official sources. It seems evident that the sweeping accusations of this sensational series were based largely on incomplete and incorrect information.

145. As said before, this was largely the merit of the Vietnamese administration of foreign aid under Vu Van Thai, but also of the USOM staff, then headed by Leland Barrows and Arthur Z. Gardiner.

146. James B. Hendry wrote a brief but very enlightening article on the subject entitled "American Aid in Vietnam," *Pacific Affairs*, XXXIII, No. 4 (December, 1960), explaining why it was difficult for the Vietnamese peasant to realize that he was a beneficiary of American aid. Hendry also gives a succinct description of the method of aid transfer (commodity import). On the method of aid transfer, Scigliano wrote: "The United States has injected over 80 per cent of its economic aid to Vietnam into an import-subsidization program, which works as follows: the United States government pays for foreign commodities for Vietnamese importers, using either dollars or other foreign currencies. The importers pay for these goods in Vietnamese piasters which are deposited in a 'counterpart fund.' . . . The counterpart fund is drawn upon to pay for programs, services, and other expenses of the Vietnamese government which are agreed upon by the Vietnamese and American governments" (*South Vietnam*, p. 112).

147. Scigliano, *ibid.*, p. 115. All the figures given here are taken from Scigliano's analysis of the aid program (*ibid.*, pp. 112–15). It should be added here that South Vietnam received aid also from other countries, especially France, and reparations payments from Japan. France helped in the rehabilitation of the railway system, in the development of the Nong Son coal mine, in agrarian reform (by subsidizing the purchase of lands owned by French nationals), and provided aid for a number of other programs as well. The Japanese reparations involved several projects, the most important of which was the construction of the Da Nhim hydroelectric plant (*ibid.*, p. 111).

148. Taylor, *op. cit.*, p. 244.

149. *Annual Statistical Bulletin*, No. 4, 1961, p. 105.

150. Even in this area, accessible to direct improvement, there was, despite the vaunted progress in education, a dearth of means to take care of the existing needs. "Saigon's public schools are so inadequate that every year they are obliged to turn away more pupils than they accept. Vietnam, in its peculiar type of austerity, devotes less than 3 per cent of its budget to education as compared with neighboring Cambodia's 22 per cent for the same item" (Robert S. Brown, a former USOM official in Vietnam and Cambodia, in a letter to *The New York Times*, June 20, 1962).

151. Fall, *The Two Viet-Nams*, p. 315.

152. For a description of the completeness and effectiveness of this control, see the articles by Joseph Alsop cited in Chapter XI, n. 73.

153. Article 13c of the Agreement on the Cessation of Hostilities in Viet-Nam states: "Each party undertakes to refrain from any reprisals or discrimination against persons or organizations on account of their activities during the hostilities and to guarantee their democratic liberties" (quoted from *Viet-Report*, August–September, 1965, p. 17).

154. For a brief description of these campaigns, see Chaffard, *op. cit.*, p. 103–5. Chaffard writes that the two main campaigns, which extended over 1956 and 1957, bore the names of two heroes of the national history: Operation Thoai Ngoc Hau, in the western provinces, and Operation Truong Tan Buu, in the east of Cochinchina.

155. See Jumper and Normand, *op. cit.*, p. 402.

156. Wilfred G. Burchett gives the most comprehensive account of the Hanoi and Vietcong version of these persecutions, with lurid details of the torture of young women, in his *The Furtive War*, and also in *Vietnam: Inside Story of the Guerilla War* (New York, 1965).

157. See in particular Lacouture, *Vietnam: Between Two Truces*, pp. 13, 35, where he speaks of Diem's "launching a wave of oppression against those in the Viet Minh camp who had participated in war operations," and of the pitiless "witch hunt" conducted in the South. See also John McDermott, "Profile of Vietnamese History, Part II," in *Viet-Report*, August–September, 1965, who says on p. 8 that "recalcitrant villages were surrounded and softened by artillery action, after which the Civil Guard moved in and disarmed the self-defense forces. Communists and key leaders were likely to be killed outright, although many fled the more settled districts and gained protection in outlying areas, particularly from the mountaineers of the PMS. Mere sympathizers and families of Vietminh personnel were arrested wholesale. Imitating communist techniques, mass meetings were held to 'denounce communists'; in this way many innocent persons were thrown into the regime's rapidly expanding jails. Ignoring the intense family and kinship loyalties found in Vietnamese peasant life, the government forbade those arrested to communicate with their families except through the little postcard with a handful of boxes to be checked." Philippe Devillers gives the following account: "In 1958 the situation grew worse. Round-ups of 'dissidents' became more frequent and more brutal. The enemy (those suspected of Communist activities or of being affiliated to the sects) were difficult to apprehend. The areas where they took refuge—the Rachgia and Hatien regions in the West, and the Bien Hoa–Thu Dau Mot–Tay Ninh region in the East, with their marshes and forests, were not favorable for operations by government forces. Moreover, the way in which many of the operations were carried out very soon set the villagers against the regime. A certain sequence of events became almost classical: denunciation, encirclement of villages, searches and raids, arrests of suspects, plundering, interrogations enlivened sometimes by torture (even of innocent people), deportation, and 'regrouping' of populations suspected of intelligence with the rebels, etc." ("Ngo Dinh Diem and the Struggle for Unification," in *China Quarterly*, No. 9, January–March, 1962, p. 13).

158. I remember my shock when a high American officer tried to impress me with this sort of "efficiency" by assuring me that hardly any real "Commie" had escaped. "There is no fuss if anyone known as a real 'Commie' is caught," I was told. "He is held under water until he stops kicking." Halberstam tells of a friend who had been to see an American general about coordinating some additional "psy-war" (psychological warfare) teams into the Government program. The general looked at Halberstam's friend "coolly and displayed contempt" for "psy-war." "We're here to teach 'em to kill Communists," Halberstam quotes the general as saying (*op. cit.*, p. 60).

159. Some details on "community action" within the minimal means provided for such projects are described by Scigliano, *South Vietnam*, p. 169. "Most of them were young volunteers without previous government experience, and they did what very few other government officials have done: they dressed and lived like the rural people and they adopted a severe code of ethics to go with their austere life." But these "civic-action" programs were sharply curtailed after 1956, and in fact were made an adjunct of military action. See also Montgomery (*op. cit.*, pp. 70–71) who gives the jealousies of the province chiefs and the departments of Health, Information, and Agriculture as the reason for this curtailment, "who felt that Civic Action had intruded into their jurisdictions." For further details, see n. 141, above.

160. Scigliano, *South Vietnam*, p. 168.

161. For a description of such denunciation rallies, see Scigliano, *ibid.*, p. 167, n. 7, where he writes: "In what was reported as the largest Communist denunciation rally to date, tens of thousands of Saigon residents were witnesses to the conversion of 2,000 former Viet Minh cadres in late February, 1956." On "family groups," which Scigliano calls "another device borrowed from the Vietminh," he writes: "Each family group and each agglomeration has its appointed chief who is responsible to local officials for the activities of his group. The family groups perform a number of functions. They furnish free labor for public projects, settle petty disputes, and disseminate information from higher authority. Most of all, however, they function as security cells. It is the responsibility of each family group to control the behavior of its members and to report any irregularities, including the presence of visitors or other strangers, to village or city security officers. In order to facilitate control over personal movements, every house in Vietnam must indicate on an outside plaque the number and sex of all its occupants." (In the North, these "family groups" were euphemistically called "Street and Inhabitant Protection Committees." They were headed by "block chiefs," of which Hanoi had 4,600.)

162. There is little or no difference in the new programs of "rural reconstruction," conceived in February, 1966, at Honolulu, from those pursued under Diem. Charles Mohr, in *The New York Times* of February 11, 1966, reports on Marshal Ky's views, as expressed in his address before President Johnson at the Honolulu Conference, February 6 and 7, 1966: "As the Viet-

namese see [rural] pacification, its core is not merely 'helping the people to a better life,' the aspect on which many American speakers have dwelled. It is rather the destruction of the clandestine Vietcong political structure and the creation of an ironlike system of government political control over the population"—exactly what Diem's dictatorship had tried to do, with the effect of increasing popular hatred and resistance. This does not seem to agree too well with Vice-President Humphrey's demand of February 10, at the Saigon airport, for "the promotion of a genuine democracy." In another report from Saigon, dated February 12, which appeared in the "News of the Week" section of *The New York Times,* February 13, 1966, Charles Mohr continued to analyze, in his customary skeptical fashion, the new rural-pacification program. What is remarkable in this detailed survey of plans is that land reform is not even mentioned by the official in charge. Of the 15,000 villages, 1,900, or 14 per cent, are to be "pacified" in 1966. It is thought, however, that even this limited objective cannot be achieved. For a completely positive appraisal of these efforts, see *Quiet Warriors—Supporting Social Revolution in Viet-Nam,* a richly illustrated brochure published by the U.S. Department of State (Department of State Publication No. 8041, Far Eastern Series 140, released April, 1966, 48 pp.). A more balanced report on the progress made by March, 1966, and on the enormous roadblocks in the path of this program is Robert Shaplen's "Letter from South Vietnam" of March 1, in *The New Yorker,* March 12, 1966. This is probably the best of the many firsthand reports from Vietnam that Mr. Shaplen has written for *The New Yorker* during the last ten years.

163. As quoted by Scigliano, *South Vietnam,* p. 168, who adds his own cautious judgment on the results of the campaign by stating: "It is true that a considerable number of Viet Minh supporters broke with the Communist-controlled movement after Geneva, but it is highly questionable whether the programs of the Department of Information and Youth were an important factor in their decisions. It is much more likely that the agency's ubiquitous, heavy-handed propaganda antagonized more people than it attracted. It is even more clear that the Anti-Communist Denunciation Campaign gave an exaggerated picture of the agency's achievements. . . . The experiment in defeating Communism by boisterous Communist propaganda methods gradually lost impetus, and in 1960 Tran Chanh Thanh was assigned to serve . . . as ambassador to Tunisia, and his department was reduced to non-Cabinet status and then, in 1961, absorbed by the Department of Civic Action." (For other Cabinet members who were sent abroad when no longer in favor, see nn. 85 and 88, above.)

164. Honey, "The Problem of Democracy in Vietnam," in *The World Today,* February 16, 1960, p. 73. Scigliano wrote: "Estimates vary widely as to the number of persons who have been held in these camps, as well as to the number who actually had Communist associations" (*South Vietnam,* pp. 170–71).

165. Fall, *The Two Viet-Nams,* p. 272.

166. It was generally believed by the Communists that the French, who

by treaty were obliged to insist that Diem agree to the elections, withdrew their Expeditionary Corps from the South before the election date in order not to be involved in any trouble growing out of Diem's refusal to hold the elections.

167. In an article in *New America* of March 26, 1966, Ephraim Friend quotes the following passage from a letter by Honey concerning the circumstances of Honey's visit to one of the camps where anti-Diem prisoners were being held: "When Hanoi alleged a massacre of prisoners in a camp at Phu-loi late in 1958 or early in 1959, Diem refused to permit any foreign diplomats or journalists to visit the camp to see for themselves. He simply denied it. I was living in Saigon at the time, so I drove immediately to Phu-loi and found that my friend, the late Col. Pham Ngoc Thao, was serving at an army camp nearby. Using his influence, I managed to enter the camp and to speak to both guards and prisoners. The truth was that the camp commandant had been buying leftover food from the market for the prisoners and pocketing the money thus saved. Food poisoning had broken out and Communist prisoners had terrified the others by alleging they were being poisoned. This began a riot which lasted for some hours and in which a handful of prisoners were killed before order was restored. I published an article setting out the facts exactly as they happened—Diem was very angry about it—but it set the record straight. Of course Hanoi was furious because it had been exploiting Diem's stupidity to allege that over a thousand prisoners had been massacred. I stand by every word I wrote at the time and would point out that I was at Phu-loi and I carried out my own interviews with the people concerned, and in Vietnamese. Hanoi propagandists were not there, had no means of knowing what happened, and exploited the incident for propaganda with their usual technique of the big lie."

168. It was somewhat different with the cease-fire agreement signed by the representatives of the French and Vietminh armies, which was constantly being violated by both parties—apparently as often by the Saigon Government, which did not feel bound by it as by Hanoi. For an examination of the record, see the reports issued by the International Commission for the Supervision and Control in Vietnam (*Interim Reports of the International Commission for Supervision and Control in Vietnam* [London: Great Britain Parliamentary Sessions Papers]). Extracts of these reports are now easily available; see, e.g., Marvin E. Gettleman (ed.), *Vietnam: History, Documents, and Opinions on a Major World Crisis*, pp. 166–90, and B. S. N. Murti, *Vietnam Divided: The Unfinished Struggle*, pp. 159–60. Diem's hostility toward the ICC was made evident in the violent "popular demonstrations" in front of the ICC headquarters in Saigon's Hotel Majestic which began on July 17, 1955. In a statement of August 9, 1955, Diem claimed that his was the only legal state of Vietnam, that his government, which was "serving the cause of true democracy," aimed to make the whole country "totally free from all dictatorship and oppression" (Embassy of Vietnam, Washington, D.C., *Press and Information Service*, I, No. 20 [August 19, 1955]). An example of the fantastic illusions (or propagandistic ex-

cesses) of the Diem regime is furnished by an article in a Saigon paper expressing official views. It says: "In the North, the fall of the illegitimate regime is near. . . . As soon as the people's hatred of the Communist dictatorship is sufficiently mature for it to succeed in overthrowing it, then general elections which are really free will take place in the whole of Vietnam, and will peacefully bring about the reunification of the country. If [Diem] refuses to have recourse to force in order to liberate the North, while yet realizing the dearest aspirations of the people, the supreme head of the Republic of Vietnam does so solely in order to avoid bloodshed and undesirable fratricidal strife" (quoted by Gettleman, *op. cit.*, p. 220, n. 8, from *Viet-Nam Press*, November 9, 1956).

169. The idea of working toward a lessening of the conflict with the North, of creating conditions for a prolonged "coexistence" of the two Vietnams, never occurred to Diem. Bao Dai, before the referendum, must have had the necessity of adopting such a course in mind when he hinted that Diem's policy endangered the peace in Vietnam. He apparently favored some degree of cooperation with the North (see Chaffard, *op. cit.*, p. 101). Lacouture claims that the North was ready to an agreed-upon postponement of the election, but all proposals for talks were rejected by Saigon (*Vietnam: Between Two Truces*, p. 68).

170. In February, 1958, Pham Van Dong announced the end of the agrarian reform (land distribution), whose mistakes and excesses he said had all been rectified; now the next phase, collectivization of land, was to begin. Chaffard noted: "The leading group, at the top, pursued its aims with the same obstinacy but now with greater prudence and realism. At the bottom, among the peasants, enthusiasm was dead" (*op. cit.*, p. 147).

171. Fall, *The Two Viet-Nams*, pp. 160–61. See also Jumper and Normand, *op. cit.*, pp. 501–2. "Collectives" accounted for 99 per cent of all agricultural production after 1961. For a pro-Communist view of collectivization, see Nguyen Kien, *Le Sud-Vietnam depuis Dien-Bien-Phu*, p. 176, who says collectivization was "relatively easy" and claims the yield was raised considerably. "Median yield per hectare rose from 13 quintals of paddy to 20, new land was opened up, while the old ricefields, with a multiplication of hydraulic works, carried two, sometimes three harvests per year."

172. See Fall, *The Two Viet-Nams*, p. 162. The admission was very likely made only because the decline had been arrested. For a discussion of the effects of collectivization on the peasants and on production, see the excellent study by Hoang Van Chi, "Collectivization and Rice Production," in Honey (ed.), *op. cit.* For the most recent details on life in the North, see James Cameron's articles in *The New York Times*, December 7–11, 1965. Rice is still rationed, though basic foods are not "especially scarce." Also rationed, rather liberally, is cloth (5 meters a month—probably per family), and so are soap and meat. There is practically no private civilian traffic. The economy, according to Cameron, "is increasing immensely in the North. But not much seeps through in consumer goods."

173. The story of the founding of the National Liberation Front has been

told by almost everyone who has written about Vietnam since 1960. For the Communist version, see Burchett, *The Furtive War*, pp. 95–113; the official U.S. version is contained in the State Department's *White Book* (1961) and *White Paper* (1965). The *White Paper* is reprinted in Gettleman, *op. cit.*, and reply to it by I. F. Stone, in Marcus G. Raskin and Bernard B. Fall, *The Viet-Nam Reader* (New York, 1965), pp. 155–62. See also Fall, *The Two Viet-Nams*, pp. 355 ff., in which Fall gives a devastating refutation of Walt W. Rostow's interpretation of the nature of the insurrection in the South (pp. 343 ff.), a view which was also voiced by Under Secretary of State George W. Ball in a speech before the Northwestern Alumni Association at Evanston, Illinois, and reprinted in the *Congressional Record* of February 7, 1966. Ball said that at the Third Party Congress of the Lao Dong (the North Vietnamese Communist Party), held in Hanoi in September, 1960, "that congress called for the creation of a front organization to undertake the subversion of South Vietnam. Within two or three months thereafter, the National Liberation Front was established to provide a political façade for the conduct of an active guerrilla war." Ball's comment on the NLF was: "It is purely and simply a fictitious organization created by Hanoi to reinforce a fiction. To recognize it as the representative of the South Vietnamese population would be to give legitimacy to that fiction." Fall's chief point is that anti-Diem guerrillas had long been active before an infiltration from the North began. Devillers expressed a similar opinion on the responsibility for the outbreak of the insurrection in the South in an article entitled "Ngo Dinh Diem and the Struggle for the Unification in Vietnam," in *China Quarterly*, January–March, 1962. So does Lacouture in *Vietnam: Between Two Truces*, in which he calls the guerrilla activities a reply to Diem's "witch-hunt." While Devillers' article was a first attempt at an impartial report and political evaluation of the NLF, Lacouture gives a more complete report and analysis in the chapter entitled "The Birth of the National Liberation Front" (pp. 51 ff.). The program of the NLF is reprinted in Raskin and Fall, *op. cit.*, pp. 216–21; also in Gettleman, *op. cit.*, p. 254. On the NLF, see also Browne, *op. cit.*, Chapter 12, particularly pp. 240–45. Devillers' article was republished in Honey (ed.), *op. cit.* See also the review of the original French edition of Lacouture's book by Joseph Kraft in the *New York Review of Books*, August 5, 1965, entitled "Who Are the Vietcong?" Lacouture says that the reason the NLF sprang into existence is this: "It certainly cannot be claimed that the Hanoi leaders or the leaders of Two Truces, p. 67). Lacouture also gives brief descriptions of the leaders who were concerned only with the defense of the rights of a hard-pressed people. But it must be admitted that the unleashing of the war machine that faced the Ngos from 1962 on had not been the doing of the insurgents. It was the dictatorship in the South that kindled the fire" (*Vietnam: Between Two Truces*, p. 67). Lacouture also gives brief descriptions of the leaders whose names did not become known until April, 1962. The head of the NLF was "Nguyen Huu Tho, a Saigon lawyer who had been interned for five years as president of the Saigon-Cholon Committee of Peace, an organization whose communist sympathies were apparently considered criminal by the Ngo family. In December, 1961, the Viet Cong network succeeded in organizing Tho's escape. Tho, an intellectual of French culture, was a former student at the law school of Aix-en-Provence; he was a politically uncommitted pacifist until 1952, when he openly advocated for negotiations with the Viet Minh" (*ibid.*, p. 56). Lacouture writes that at the first congress of the NLF, in March, 1962, Tho was elected President and Professor Nguyen Van Hieu Secretary-General. In 1964, at the second NLF congress, the Secretariat-General "headed originally by Professor Nguyen Van Hieu, and then by Tran Buu Kiem, president of the Union of Students for Liberation, passed into the hands of Huynh Tan Phat, a Saigon architect who at age forty-seven was already a veteran of the Cochinchinese guerrillas." According to Lacouture, "Hieu was regarded as very favorably inclined toward China. Tran Buu Kiem was relieved of his function . . . allegedly because his wife had been arrested in Saigon and he had therefore become vulnerable to blackmail. Huynh Tan Phat was a man of action who had assumed heavy responsibilities during the first war of Indochina, and who had aroused attention as a vigorous trainer of men in a Saigon prison in 1946" (*ibid.*, p. 171). Regarding Tho's imprisonment and guerrilla-staged escape, the Diem version, accepted by U.S. officials, was that Tho had not been imprisoned, but had fled to Hanoi and from there had come to the South in 1961. As to the question how subservient the NLF was to Hanoi, Lacouture makes the following interesting remarks: "It certainly is striking to hear the Southern revolutionaries defend the principle of their autonomy with regard to the North, even if it should be a tactic aimed at sparing the representatives of Cochinchinese or South Annamite particularism for the time being. But it is even more striking to find an acceptance of the political if not historical reality of a South Vietnam among the Hanoi leaders. . . . It will be objected that South Vietnam is thoroughly infiltrated by pro-communist subversion, and that the Western diplomats would have strange allies there. But even without appealing to communist 'polycentrism,' or entering into the disputes between Hanoi, Peking, Moscow, and the South Vietnamese guerrillas, one probably can say that a recognition of the N.L.F. and its 'progressive leadership' would not entail South Vietnam's entry into the Marxist-Leninist bloc. Political life in Saigon would remain marked by a deep-rooted pluralism that would flower even better in peace than in war" (*ibid.*, pp. 246–47).

174. Secretary of State Dean Rusk at the Senate hearings on Vietnam on February 18, 1966, as reported in *The New York Times*, February 19. In his opening statement, Rusk repeated the essentials of the speech Under Secretary Ball gave before the Economic Club of Detroit, on April 30, 1962. (Secretary Rusk's statement was drafted by Ball.) In his speech, the Under Secretary had said: "The struggle in South Viet-Nam today is not a local civil war. It is a carefully planned and mounted campaign of subversion and insurgency—equipped and directed from Hanoi" (Department of State Publication No. 7388, Far Eastern Series, released June, 1962, p. 7). It is inter-

esting to see the contrast between this official American view and the view of a prominent Vietnamese anti-Communist, Diem's former Minister of Defense, Ho Thong Minh, who, according to Devillers, stated: "This insurrection is justified. In a country where all basic rights of the citizens are abolished, in which the legality of the regime has become an empty word, the will of the people can express itself only through force, through insurrection, through the attempt at taking power. We nationalists know that between the Viet Minh and ourselves a race against time is going on" (Devillers, in his Introduction to Lacouture, *Le Vietnam entre deux paix*, p. 15; the English-language edition of this book does not contain Devillers' introduction).

175. The main publications in defense of the American and Vietnamese governments' stand were: *L'agression communiste contre la républic du Viet-Nam* (Saigon, July, 1964); U.S. Department of State, *A Threat to Peace: North Viet-Nam's Effort to Conquer South Viet-Nam* (Washington, D.C., 1961). The White Paper of February, 1965 (see Gettleman [ed.], *op. cit.*, p. 284; see also criticism of the White Paper by I. F. Stone in *ibid.*, p. 317) is entitled *Aggression from the North*, Department of State Publication No. 7839, Far Eastern Series 130.

176. Fall, *The Two Viet-Nams*, p. 345.

177. Scigliano, "A Country at War," in *Asian Survey*, III, No. 1 (January, 1963), p. 1.

178. See Fall, *The Two Viet-Nams*, pp. 359–61. Fall cites President Kennedy's message of May, 1961, for his figures of officials killed. In an article in *The New York Times* of February 27, 1966, datelined February 26, Neil Sheehan reports from Saigon on selective terrorism: "Communist terrorism in Vietnam is not, as is commonly thought, the slaughter of entire villages. It is instead a very selective terrorism and is perhaps most effective because of this selectivity, which spreads fear without deeply alienating large numbers of peasants through wholesale murders. The Communists usually select some well-known individual in the hamlet—the hamlet chief, a schoolteacher, or a police agent. When the victim is then killed, sometimes after public trial before a so-called peoples court for alleged 'crimes against the people,' his or her death serves to frighten many others into silence or cooperation with the guerrillas. The Vietcong cadre no longer has to kill others in the hamlet, for now the knowledge that he can have them assassinated at will is enough to have his orders observed." But the figures given above conflict with other figures from the same sources, like all Saigon (or Hanoi) statistics. In 1960, Saigon claimed in another report, 1,400 local officials and civilians were killed by Vietcong. (*A Threat to the Peace*, pp. 12–13; see Jumper and Normand, *op. cit.*, p. 493, n. 54).

179. The fact is based on a report of a Vietnamese Army court-martial involving three such cases, and one of sales of grenades and ammunition by soldiers to the Vietcong (*Journal d' Extrême-Orient*, February 12, 1963).

180. Fall makes the point that the minority policy of the Hanoi regime dealt with the promise of "autonomy" for the ethnic minorities in such a

way as to have local officials be in charge of the provinces in question. "Non-Vietnamese mountaineers will be in ostensible control," he writes (*The Two Viet-Nams*, pp. 148–52). On Hanoi's promise of "autonomy" for the ethnic minorities in the South, see Jumper and Normand, *op. cit.*, pp. 500–501. The cadres of the minorities who had gone North after 1954 were probably the first to be returned to the South to organize the anti-Diem rebellion in the highlands (see Fall, *The Two Viet-Nams*, pp. 352–53, and also his reference to Hoa Hao sect remnants joining the Vietcong, pp. 354–55). Fall has this to say about the strength of Communist influence on the tribes in the highlands: "How well the Communists succeeded among the Southern tribesmen became obvious in mid-1961, when full-fledged 2,500-man Communist mountain regiments began to appear in the hill areas. . . . Communist radio propaganda, couched in mountain dialects, had begun as early as 1956; South Vietnamese radio programs addressed to the tribesmen began four years later. And while Saigon still preached the hollow myth of 'equality,' the Communists were preaching the heady idea of autonomy for the mountain zones" ("Who's Who in Viet-Nam," *The New Republic*, October 17, 1964, p. 12).

181. The term, coined by the Saigon regime, means Vietnamese Communist; it is, in this form, not only derogatory, but was chosen mainly because of its implication that everyone who fought the Diem regime was a Communist. The term has been universally adopted. Use of the term, however, does not necessarily mean acceptance of its implication that all guerrilla fighters are Communists.

182. The only non-Communist report from inside Vietcong territory is a series of four articles by the well-known French journalist Georges Chaffard published in the Paris weekly *L'Express* in April, 1965. A much more detailed but less reliable, and most enthusiastic, report is given by the Australian journalist Wilfred Burchett in his two previously mentioned books, *The Furtive War* and *Vietnam: Inside Story of the Guerilla War*. The situation in regard to effective administrative control of the Vietnamese countryside had not changed by 1966, as is shown in a report by Neil Sheehan from Saigon in *The New York Times* of Sunday, February 27, 1966. Under the dateline of February 26, Mr. Sheehan wrote: "The Communist administrative apparatus parallels that of the Saigon Government from the hamlet through the village, district and provincial level and on up to the Vietcong central headquarters for South Vietnam, which ultimately receives its directives from the Politburo in Hanoi. This Communist administrative apparatus voluntarily recruits or conscripts young peasants for Vietcong fighting units and collects taxes both in money and rice. It registers marriages and births, runs crude schools and dispensaries, collects intelligence for the guerrillas and in other ways performs the functions of a rudimentary if, by Vietnamese standards, effective administration."

183. Halberstam, *op. cit.*, p. 112.

184. "It is far easier for a Vietnamese Government official to travel to Washington, Paris, or Léopoldville, than it is for him to stay alive in an

automobile traveling from Saigon to My-Tho or Cape St. Jacques, fifty miles from his office" (Fall, *The Two Viet-Nams*, p. 205).

185. Ap Bac was a northern hamlet in the delta, about 40 miles northwest of Saigon. Its story has been told by Malcolm Browne (*op. cit.*, pp. 14–15); his book is still by far the most important on this type of warfare conducted by the Vietnamese Army. The Ap Bac story has also been told by David Halberstam (*op. cit.*, pp. 147–62), who described it as a military debacle in which "the Americans in Saigon were, in fact, to do everything but learn from it" (p. 147). For the Communist version of Ap Bac, see Burchett, *Inside Story of the Guerilla War*, pp. 84–89. According to him, "the Ap Bac battle was a turning point in the war. It showed the Front forces had 'grown up' and was followed by a series of shattering defeats inflicted on the Saigon troops that led to a serious decline in their morale, and eventually to the overthrow of the Diemist regime. After Ap Bac, American commentators began speculating for the first time whether the war in South Vietnam could ever be won" (p. 88). Also commenting on the effect of the victory on the enemy, Browne wrote: "For the Viet Cong, Ap Bac became the victory cry. The hamlet's name, in gold letters, was affixed to the 514th's battle flags. Communist propaganda posters, professionally printed in four colors bloomed throughout the delta, all glorifying the fighters at Ap Bac" (*op. cit.*, p. 15). For general literature on the war, see n. 45, above, in which contradictions between official statements and newspaper reports on the Vietnamese story are discussed. In my exposition, however, I have relied chiefly on the evidence in the books of Malcolm Browne, David Halberstam, and John Mecklin, because these sources are easily available and also indispensable for a critical appraisal of the Diem regime's catastrophic effect on the conduct of the war. There are of course literally hundreds of newspaper reports and magazine articles that confirm the observations of these authors—e.g., by Neil Sheehan, Homer Bigart, Charles Mohr, Stanley Karnow, Peter Kalischer (of the Columbia Broadcasting System), François Sully (of *Newsweek*), Denis Warner, and others who have written or reported for the American public. (For a listing of various papers, see Mecklin, *op. cit.*, pp. 122–24.) The wealth of journalistic outpouring can be gleaned from the checklists published by the AFVN for 1962 and 1963, compiled by its then Secretary Louis Andreatta and cited in n. 45, above.

186. The mistaken notion about the enemy's likely intention guided American military thinking in Vietnam not only under the first head of the MAAG, Lt. General John O'Daniel, but also under his successors, Lt. General Lionel C. McGarr and General Samuel Williams. When General Paul Harkins, who took over the command of the Thailand-Vietnam zone on February 8, 1962, came to Vietnam, the spell had been broken, yet the change to a type of warfare able to cope with the small groups of elusive guerrillas and to the jungle and swamps was again and again delayed in favor of reliance on heavy equipment and planes. The first U.S. Special Forces instructors arrived in 1960, but only small units of the Vietnamese Army were

trained as "special 'hunt-and-kill' forces," as Scigliano calls them (*South Vietnam*, p. 165), and large units of them were kept under Nhu's authority to protect the Saigon Government.

187. As reported from Saigon by Charles Mohr in *The New York Times*, February 11, 1966. Halberstam wrote: "The army lacked leadership and it lacked the will to fight" (*op. cit.*, p. 65).

188. Halberstam, *ibid.*, p. 165.

189. Mecklin, *op. cit.*, p. 104.

190. *Ibid.*, p. 90; see also *ibid.*, p. 104. Regarding Duong Van Minh and Tran Van Don and their roles, see Halberstam (*op. cit.*, pp. 145–46), who writes that Minh was made military adviser to the President, without command. Don lost command of the First Corps to become an army commander without a military role. "Which meant that as a kind of official greeter he had to go out to the airport and meet visiting Americans." Pham Van Dong, one of the best officers of the army, was made an inspector of the strategic-hamlet program.

191. Wrote Scigliano: "The President has elevated personal loyalty over military ability in the promotion and assignment of officers, has made use of informers within the military services and has shifted officers who appeared to be too popular with their men or too close to the Americans" (*South Vietnam*, p. 185). Halberstam's comment was: "Promotion on the basis of personal loyalty rather than ability, the use of informers, the banishment of men of integrity and initiative, and the domination of all strategy had not made the army more loyal." And speaking of Pham Van Dong in particular, "who was considered by many Americans the outstanding field commander in the country," Halberstam mentions that Diem "did not trust Dong, and many people—including Dong himself—believed that the American recommendation [to make him a general] had hurt his chances" (*op. cit.*, pp. 59, 146).

192. "Diem frequently fired commanders who reported unpleasant news, or took too many casualties" (Mecklin, *op. cit.*, p. 101). This has also been reported by Halberstam, *et al.*

193. The primary objective of the Vietcong was to "capture the support of the people covertly and to blend themselves with the people," wrote Mecklin. "This in turn tended to provoke the government, in its frustration, to turn its guns and bombs on the people, which seldom hurt the V.C. seriously yet always angered the people and turned them increasingly against the government" (*ibid.*, p. 80). Speaking of a personal encounter with an old Vietnamese in a Communist village during a Vietnamese Army patrol, Mecklin said: "Of the long French colonial war the old man expressed only one emotion: his hatred for 'the big birds that spit fire from the sky,' meaning the French napalm attacks which had twice burned out the village—and killed exactly one Vietminh soldier" (*ibid.*, p. 77). Speaking of bombing of villages, more often than not indiscriminate for lack of reliable intelligence, U.S. newsmen have repeatedly voiced their horror at the results. See, f.i., the photographs in Browne's book, in which the sufferings of the civilian popu-

lation are shown in terrifying pictures. Browne's comment was: "This kind of thing, regardless of whatever tactical advantage it may have, is to my mind little short of slaughter." And: "It is not difficult to conceive of a farmer or his wife joining the National Liberation Front merely as an act of revenge after one of these accidental killings" (*op. cit.*, p. *166*). Mecklin wrote: "Commanders were reluctant to attack without artillery and air support, and often did not press home attacks on the assumption that bombs, napalm and shells would do the job for them. . . . Much of the time the victims were civilians caught in the barrages, or burned to death by napalm in their homes." He added: "There was less wanton killing and property destruction than the French had indulged themselves. American airmen and field advisers did their best to prevent this sort of thing. But there was no question that abuses were multiplying, with serious damage to the government's efforts to win popular support. A good many Americans in Saigon felt that the occasional military profit from air and artillery attacks on inhabited areas was more than outweighed by the psychological damage" (*op. cit.*, pp. *91, 92*). As Dinh said in his novel: "People must be out of their minds to think that this war can be won by planes, bombs and tanks" (*op. cit.*, pp. *124–25*).

194. Mecklin stated: "The government figures of Viet Cong casualties . . . became a joke around Saigon" (*op. cit.*, p. *101*).

195. Quoted by Halberstam, *op. cit.*, p. *167*. Vann's devastating report on the conduct of the war was totally ignored in Washington, and his attempt to submit it to the military chiefs at the Pentagon was blocked by General Krulack, in February, 1966, Commander of the U.S. Marines in Vietnam. The story of Vann's vain attempt to get a hearing is told by Halberstam (*ibid.*, pp. *163–78*). Yet Vann's opinions were voiced in 1963 by a symposium on *The Role of Airpower in Counterinsurgency and Unconventional Warfare: The Malayan Emergency*, prepared for U.S. Air Force Project RAND, in which Air Commander P. E. Warcup, CBE, Commander of the RAF at Kuala Lumpur, 1957–59, stated: "It would be no good banging away with bombs, rockets or 20-mm cannons unless you knew exactly what you were doing . . . not destroying life and property that otherwise might be on your side." And Brigadier General Russell W. Volckmann, who commanded the U.S. Armed Forces in North Luzon from 1942 until the liberation, in 1945, when American guerrilla forces were being hunted by the Japanese regulars, stated: "I can't remember ever suffering one casualty in three years from an air strike. . . . As a matter of fact the air strikes put on us helped us more than they did the Japanese. They brought more people to our side because they killed civilians." These opinions were also voiced by Major General Edward G. Lansdale, now Special Assistant to the Ambassador in Saigon, who wrote in *Foreign Affairs*, October, 1964: "When the military opens fire at long range, whether by infantry weapons, artillery or air strikes, on a reported Viet Cong concentration in a hamlet or village full of civilians, the Vietnamese officers who give those orders and the American advisers who let them 'get away with it' are helping defeat the

cause of freedom. The civilian hatred of the military resulting from such actions is a powerful motive for joining the Viet Cong."

196. "Thousands of men were launched in operations aimed at areas free of the enemy. Escape routes were deliberately left in the planning of every operation lest the Vietcong be forced to hold their ground and fight, thus inflicting more casualties on government troops" (Halberstam, *op. cit.*, p. 141). Mecklin wrote: "It was common practice for government forces to break off battle at nightfall, even when they were winning, allowing the V.C. to escape" (*op. cit.*, p. 97).

197. "In 1962–63," wrote Mecklin, "the Diem regime admitted defections from its regular forces at rates sometimes running as high as a thousand per month, occasionally to the Viet Cong, often simply to go home. The true figures probably were higher" (*op. cit.*, p. 95). In an article by Neil Sheehan in *The New York Times* of February 23, 1966, from Saigon, the number of deserters from the South Vietnam armed forces was given as about 96,000 for the year 1965. Actually the figure reported by the South Vietnamese Government was higher, Sheehan wrote, but it supposedly did not take into account that some of the deserters had later re-enlisted. Total desertions for 1965 were put at 113,000 with 47,000 from the regular armed forces, 17,000 from the Regional Forces, and 49,000 from the Popular Forces, or local militia. "The sources could offer no specific reasons for the high rate of Government desertions other than the intensification of the fighting and a general war weariness that has overtaken the country," Sheehan reported, adding that although figures were not available for desertions during 1964, "it was understood that they had been substantially below the 1965 figures."

198. Wrote Halberstam: "Just as the Vietcong resembled the Vietminh in the peasants' eyes, the Government troops too often acted like the soldiers in the same uniforms who had fought during the days of the French: patrolling the hamlets during the day, grabbing village chickens for lunch, and disappearing after 6 P.M., so that just in case some villager was inclined to help the Government, he would have no protection at night when the Vietcong arrived" (*op. cit.*, p. 113). He also stated bitterly: "Too often the troops had stolen chickens or molested the people; in contrast, the well-disciplined guerrillas would work beside the villagers in the field, and they did not steal from them" (*ibid.*, p. 91).

199. Halberstam reports (*ibid.*) how Neil Sheehan observed this when he accompanied a special psychological warfare team on a mission. Browne mentions that the former Minister of Civic Action (the government organization that was supposed to work with the people in order to convert them), Ngo Trong Hieu, was jailed on charges of "gross corruption." He added: "At best, the average civic action agent looks down on the peasants he is expected to convert as inferior beings" (*ibid.*, p. 152). Mecklin, in enumerating reforms demanded by Americans, mentioned among them "urging Vietnamese soldiers not to steal chickens or otherwise molest the peasants" (*op. cit.*, p. 25).

200. Mecklin, *op. cit.*, p. 83.

201. Halberstam, Mecklin, and Browne all report on shooting and torture

of prisoners by the Vietnamese (Halberstam, *op. cit.*, p. 119; Mecklin, *op. cit.*, pp. 92, 130; Browne, *op. cit.*, pp. 116, 162). Robin Moore, in his book *The Green Berets* (New York, 1965), gives an even more extensive report, with a description of torture as routine. Most authors report American reaction to tortures they see applied almost daily as: "Generally they don't like it." Browne, f.i., said about the American advisers that occasionally "they actively interfere with proceedings, sometimes offering a cigarette or a candy bar to the captive. But they cannot interfere too often without provoking the hostility of the officers and men they are supposed to be advising. And, like it or not, they must learn to make distinctions between various degrees of torture" (*op. cit.*, p. 117).

202. The regrouping of peasants was begun quietly around February, 1959, says Scigliano, in areas of the southwest strongly infested with Vietminh. The peasants were regrouped either into one type of center in which Communist suspects were herded together or one that supposedly was to "protect loyal peasants from Communist reprisals." Scigliano remarked: "Security was the only consideration in the regrouping. Peasants were transported from their regular homesteads to a new place where, often far from their rice fields, they were expected to re-establish their lives with only minimal assistance from the government." In July, 1959, the Diem regime revived the program, which had been abandoned in March, with so-called improvements through the creation of "prosperity and density centers." Each agroville "was to be divided into residential, commercial, and governmental quarters, laid out according to a master plan. In the government's view, the agroville's attractions were sure to win peasant support. . . . Most peasants, however, saw the agroville program quite differently, whether they were included in the new settlement or not. They had to prepare the sites, without pay and often providing their own tools. . . . Since the number of people who could be moved into the total number of planned agrovilles did not exceed 500,000, it was obvious that most of those forced to work on the sites would not profit from their labor." He also said that the peasants did not want to abandon their old homesteads with the ancestral tombs, small garden, and fruit and shade trees "for a desolate plot of ground in a strange place." Not only did the peasants have to build their new houses from materials taken from the old ones, the only help they received from the government was the gift of about $5.50 and the offer of an agricultural loan. "The loan was necessary, because the peasant had to pay for the acre and a half of land he had been allotted. Whatever he thought of having neighbors and administrative services close at hand, he did not like the long distance which he generally had to walk to his rice fields." Scigliano reports that "the program came virtually to a halt in early 1961, with about 22 agrovilles actually completed" (*South Vietnam*, pp. 179, 180). See also J. J. Fasloff, "Rural Resettlement in South Vietnam: The Agroville Program," *Pacific Affairs*, XXXV, No. 4 (Winter, 1962–63), pp. 327–40; and Nguyen Khac Nhan, "A Policy of Key Rural Agrovilles," *Asian Culture*, III, Nos. 3–4 (July–December, 1961).

203. Nhu claimed the strategic-hamlet program was one of his many orig-

inal ideas, but the idea had been tried out in several variations against Communist rebellions, particularly by the British in Malaya. Mecklin wrote that "the main force in getting the program started was probably the British Advisory Mission, which arrived in September, 1961, and consisted of a group of old Malaya hands headed brilliantly by Robert G. K. ('Bob') Thompson, who had served in a capacity comparable to minister of defense in Kuala Lumpur" (*op. cit.*, p. 44). Fall writes of Nhu's attempt to "transfer the Malayan experience to Viet-Nam lock, stock, and barrel," while overlooking the differences between the two situations in that in Malaya "the squatters could not provide the CT's with the demographic 'water' that Mao's guerrilla 'fish' needs to survive," adding that "popular grievances were not sufficient to make a Chinese guerrilla look like a 'liberator' to a Malayan peasant" (*The Two Viet-Nams*, pp. 339–41). An official report on, and defense of, the strategic-hamlet program was published in Saigon by the Directorate General of Information in February, 1963, under the title *Vietnam's Strategic Hamlets*. The book contains a map showing the distribution of the hamlets as well as illustrations. The authors claim that "the development of the strategic hamlets brings about a social revolution" (pp. 12–13).

204. See Scigliano, *South Vietnam*, p. 208.

205. "Province chiefs competed with one another over the number of hamlets they could build," wrote Halberstam. "The more hamlets they built, the more they were in favor with Nhu and the more U.S. aid they received; consequently, one problem for the American mission was the tendency of Vietnamese officials to divide a hamlet in half and count it as two, thereby getting twice the aid. Each chief engaged in a mad scramble to build hamlets faster than the next: 'If you stand still long enough down there, they'll throw a piece of barbed wire around you and call you a strategic hamlet,' one American said" (*op. cit.*, p. 186).

206. Quoted by Halberstam (*ibid.*, p. 187) as the opinion of one high Vietnamese official in the Mekong Delta. Warner quoted a general as saying: "We can put ten thousand miles of barbed wire round the hamlets and arm half a million Self-Defense Corps. . . . But until we stop these arbitrary arrests and give a better deal to the peasants we are never going to win this war" (*op. cit.*, pp. 100–101).

207. See Halberstam, *ibid.*, p. 172. Halberstam also reports on the efforts made by Rufus Phillips, a young protégé of Lansdale's, who, by July, 1963, had become convinced that the program was not working; he decided to warn Washington but his warnings were not heeded (*ibid.*, p. 171).

208. The term "U.S. Mission" was applied to the combined services— diplomatic, military, ICA, information, and economic aid (USOM).

209. See nn. 45 and 211, this chapter, on U.S. news coverage vs. diplomatic reports.

210. On July 7, correspondents watching a Buddhist procession were surrounded by Nhu's plainclothes police. Malcolm Browne and Peter Arnett, both of the Associated Press, were beaten up, but rescued by Halberstam.

Police arrested Browne and Arnett and interrogated them for four hours, implying that they had attacked the plainclothes men.

211. The story of the conflict between American correspondents, the American Mission, and the regime forms a major part of Mecklin's *Mission in Torment*. Mecklin gives a fair account of the rights and wrongs of both sides, and he leans toward the opinion that the correspondents were right (as they turned out to have been) and the Mission wrong. He summed up the conflict in the fourth chapter of the book, entitled "Meck the Knife" (pp. 99 ff.), quoting the charge by newsmen who worked in Vietnam in 1962–63 that "the U.S. Mission deliberately lied to them about the war and the Diem regime." Charles Mohr of *Time* (he later resigned to join *The New York Times*), writes Mecklin, complained that "the Mission attempted to portray defeats as victories and otherwise was 'deliberately misleading.'" Stanley Karnow (*Saturday Evening Post*) wrote: "It became part of American policy to camouflage the shortcomings of the Diem oligarchy." Halberstam held: "The U.S. Embassy turned into an adjunct of dictatorship. In trying to protect Diem from criticism, the ambassador became Diem's agent." And Neil Sheehan (United Press International) stated: "A tremendous amount of misinformation [was] put out." An editorial in *The New York Times* on May 21, 1964, said: "The harsh facts of the war in South Vietnam were only brought to public notice through the enterprise of American newspapermen on the spot." Mecklin wrote in the Mission's defense: "Events were to prove that the Mission itself was unaware of how badly the war was going, operating in a world of illusion." In explanation of the Mission's ignorance, he added: "We made the error of basing critical judgments of both the political and military situations on information provided mainly by the Vietnamese Government. This was sometimes prettied up to keep the Americans happy. Mostly it was just plain wrong." Moreover, "the U.S. Mission made little effort to distinguish between information provided by Vietnamese sources and the reports of American advisors in the field." (As can be seen from Halberstam's writings, the warnings of the American advisers went largely unheeded.) Even the Mission's knowledge "of what was going on inside the Vietnamese Government, and among its officials in the provinces, was casual and incomplete." Thus, the U.S. Mission "accepted the judgment . . . of a government that had so desperately lost contact with its own people that its very survival now depended on U.S. aid." However, Mecklin blames Washington as much for the quarrel with the newspapermen as the Mission, because official policy on press relations "attempted on one hand to discourage publicity of any sort about our operations in Vietnam, and on the other to pamper the Diem regime." Placing himself squarely on the side of the reporters, he commented: "This kind of foolishness quickly stirred the wrath of newsmen working in Vietnam, especially when the Viet Cong began killing Americans who were clearly engaged in combat missions. Excessive American secrecy became a news story in itself and was widely reported, with the implication that the U.S. Government was cheating on its own people, trying to fuzz up a policy that

was costing the lives of American servicemen. The main result of the secrecy was considerably more publicity than the U.S. buildup would otherwise have generated. It also provoked indignant editorials and, more importantly, queries from congressmen." The height of Washington insensitivity to the need to keep the American public informed and to assist those who were engaged in gathering the necessary information was State Department Cable No. 1,006 of February 21, 1962, paraphrased in a Congressional Subcommittee report on October 1, 1963, to the effect that news stories criticizing the Diem regime "increase the difficulties of the U.S. job," that newsmen "should be advised that trifling or thoughtless criticism of the Diem government would make it difficult to maintain cooperation" with Diem, and—the most incredible evidence of manipulation of the press in a so-called free society—an order that newsmen "should not be transported on military activities of the type that are likely to result in undesirable stories." Thereafter, both the Diem regime and American officialdom often implied that newsmen were Communist sympathizers for reports unfavorable to the situation. As Mecklin put it, "still worse was the frequent official suggestion that a 'negative' report was somehow un-American." He cites Admiral Felt's reaction when asked a difficult question at a press conference during his visit to Saigon. "Why don't you get on the team?" he snapped at the offending reporter. Mecklin cites numerous other examples of U.S. "insensitivity" and "self-righteous witlessness" of official attitudes. But the result was that "excessive classification infected newsmen with distrust of everything we did and said on the understandable assumption that we probably were not telling the whole truth" (Mecklin was then a member of the U.S. Mission, as Public Affairs officer), while "one of the spectaculars of the American performance in Vietnam was the compulsive official optimism about the state of war." Official optimism reached new heights, with "McNamara, Felt, and Harkins repeatedly" predicting "publicly that the war would be in hand by 1964 or 1965, often coupling their remarks with disdainful references to 'slanted' or 'irresponsible' press reporting from Saigon." One of the few not sucked in by official self-delusion was Senator Mansfield, who visited Saigon in early 1963 "and departed without commenting on the war at all." As Mecklin put it: "Things had reached such comic-opera proportions that the newsmen regarded this as news and reported it widely." (Halberstam also speaks of McNamara's insensitivity to the situation, giving the example that even as late as September, 1963, on a tour of the country, McNamara asked all his questions in the presence of General Harkins, "thus talking only to largely inhibited officers" [*op. cit.*, p. 257].) But attacks on the newsmen continued, partly by deriding their "inexperience" and "youth," partly by having someone like Marguerite Higgins write: "Reporters here would like to see us lose the war to prove they're right." Yet public recognition of the excellence of the newsmen's output was given when the Pulitzer Prize for international reporting was awarded jointly to Malcolm Browne and David Halberstam, the Louis M. Lyons Award for

Conscience and Integrity in Journalism went jointly to Halberstam, Browne, and Sheehan, and the Sigma Delta Chi Award for Foreign Correspondence went to Browne. Mecklin adds that the Overseas Press Club of America gave no fewer than five awards and citations to members of the Saigon press corps: Browne and photographer Horst Faas (Associated Press), Peter Kalischer (CBS), photographer Larry Burrows (*Life*), and Richard Tregaskis for his book *Vietnam Diary* (in part a last-ditch defense of Diem). The beginning of the end—the open feud and ensuing break between the regime and American newspapermen—came with Mme. Nhu's reply to Sully's *Newsweek* report of August 20, 1962, in which he called the war "a losing proposition." Mme. Nhu accused Sully of having been "bought" by the Vietcong and demanded his expulsion, "on behalf of the women who have been tortured by the Communists." Upon Sully's departure in September, 1962, the Saigon press was full of invectives against the other American reporters, and *The New York Times* was accused of having paid $40,000 for an interview with Vietcong leader Nguyen Van Hieu, with Mme. Nhu calling the *Times* part of "an international Communist-inspired conspiracy aimed at slandering Vietnam." U.S. newsmen, the First Lady of Vietnam stated, were "intoxicated by Communism," and Vietnam was not required to observe our "crazy freedoms." Next to be ordered out was James Robinson, of NBC, after telling an interpreter that he considered his interview with Diem "a waste of time," and because, in a broadcast, he used the term "family clique." *Newsweek* replaced Sully with Kenneth Crawford, who found "things were going well," and called Mme. Nhu "the beautiful, strong-willed sister-in-law of the President." With the American Mission watching impotently while the Diem family took its toll of freedom of the press, Nhu told an American visitor that any newsman who deprecated any member of the Ngo family would be expelled. (For further details, see Halberstam, *op. cit.*) Events reached their climax during the Buddhist crisis, in which the U.S. Mission, up to the arrival of Ambassador Lodge, sided with the regime, while the newsmen sided almost 100 per cent with the Buddhists. As it turned out, the newsmen had better information than the Mission and beat official acknowledgment of certain events by prior reporting thereof. How matters currently stand on the attitude of the press in Vietnam is well expressed by Hanson W. Baldwin, in his article "The Information War in Saigon," in *The Reporter*, February 24, 1966. Wrote Mr. Baldwin: "Because press and public have become aware of a tendency to give the best version of the conflict, because of past evasions, distortions, or half-truths in Washington, and particularly because of vivid memories of government public relations in Saigon under Diem and General Paul D. Harkins, a considerable credibility gap remains. A number of important and able correspondents who were bruised by official antagonism and denunciation during the stormy period leading to Diem's overthrow are still reporting the war in Saigon. They have built-in skepticism and mistrust of government announcements and government figures that date back to the days when Secretary McNamara was claiming that we were winning the war at the same time the correspondents were reporting—with far greater accuracy—that we were deep in trouble."

212. Prior to his arrival in Vietnam in May, 1961, Nolting, a foreign-service officer with a doctorate in philosophy, had been a member of the U.S. Mission to NATO in Paris. Before leaving for Vietnam, Nolting was told in Washington that it would be a miracle if South Vietnam lasted another three months. Harkins had been Admiral Felt's deputy at Honolulu before coming to Vietnam in February, 1962, and during World War II had served on General George Patton's staff. "Harkins shared Nolting's determination to keep Diem in power" (see Mecklin, *op. cit.,* pp. 17–18). Nolting's predecessors were G. Frederick Reinhardt, who was in Saigon at a time when these conflicts did not exist and Diem was still generally regarded a success and likely to institute the reforms expected of him, and Elbridge Durbrow, favorably disposed toward Diem but increasingly critical of his refusal to reform. Durbrow gradually became ineffective with Diem, who was affronted by Durbrow's often rather frank criticism.

213. Mecklin, *op. cit.,* p. 117. Mecklin quotes from a ditty circulating throughout the American field messes in Vietnam to the tune of "Twinkle, Twinkle, Little Star": "We are winning; This I know. General Harkins told me so. If you doubt me, Who are you? McNamara says so too."

214. The regime accused the Americans (then not quite openly) of having supported the coup. Later, Mme. Nhu was quite firm about this. In an interview in the *Weekly Tribune* of Geneva, November 1, 1965, she stated that "the United States went to the point of allying itself with the Communists to crush [all leading nationalists]," and "all Vietnam believed that the *putsch* of November 11, 1960, was tacitly supported by Washington." The November, 1960, coup was planned by a small group led by Hoang Co Thuy, a wealthy Saigon lawyer, Lt. Colonel Nguyen Trieu Hong, Thuy's nephew, Lt. Colonel Vuong Van Dong, Hong's brother-in-law, and Colonel Nguyen Chanh Thi, the commander of the paratroopers "who was brought in after the plot had been hatched" (see Scigliano, *South Vietnam,* p. 188). See Nguyen Thai, *op. cit.,* p. 153, on Diem's promises made to the coup leaders, his statement over the radio promising a government change, and his subsequent reneging on these promises.

215. Devillers, "Ngo Dinh Diem and the Struggle for the Reunification in Vietnam," in *China Quarterly,* No. 9, January–March, 1962, p. 14. Gettleman reproduced the text of this amazing law (*op. cit.,* pp. 256–60) from a North Vietnamese source (see p. 256 n.). The death penalty was decreed for "assisting Communists," and life sentences for the "intention" to commit sabotage. It was up to the military tribunal to decide who harbored such intentions. See Lacouture, *Vietnam: Between Two Truces,* pp. 30–31, for excerpts from the military tribunal laws.

216. Department of State *Bulletin,* June 19, 1961, pp. 956–57.

217. See Scigliano, *South Vietnam,* p. 212.

218. To be accurate, one *was* acted upon: An ordinance to establish pro-

vincial councils, as proposed by the Taylor mission, was issued in April, 1962, but again, these councils were not elected but appointed (see Fall, *The Two Viet-Nams*, pp. 273-74).

219. Halberstam makes this bitter comment on American reaction to Diem's refusal to reform: "Having failed to get reforms, our officials said that these reforms were taking place; having failed to improve the demoralized state of the Vietnamese army, the Americans talked about a new enthusiasm in the army; having failed to change the tactics of the military, the Americans talked about bold new tactics which were allegedly driving the Communists back" (*op. cit.*, p. 69). For details on the Taylor and Staley missions, also see Fall, *The Two Viet-Nams*, p. 332; Scigliano, *South Vietnam*, p. 212; Lacouture, *Vietnam: Between Two Truces*, pp. 64-66; and Halberstam, *op. cit.*, pp. 65-66. The joint American-Vietnamese eleven-point declaration of January, 1962, "clearly is the result of a compromise in which the Vietnamese (or their defenders within the Administration) watered down whatever 'bite' there was in the Taylor report," wrote Fall (*The Two Viet-Nams*, pp. 369-70).

220. Observing these events, David Halberstam remarked it "was like watching a government trying to commit suicide" (*op. cit.*, p. 199).

221. A sample survey of Saigon, conducted in 1961, found that 83 per cent of its Vietnamese inhabitants considered themselves Buddhists, 13 per cent considered themselves Catholics, and 3 per cent called themselves "Confucianist." This was long before the onset of the "Buddhist crisis." The higher percentage of Catholics in the cities than the country's average was due to the great number of officials, many of whom became converts out of opportunism (see Scigliano, *South Vietnam*, pp. 53-54).

222. About the specific character of Vietnamese Buddhism and how it differs from other versions in Asia, see Lacouture, *Vietnam: Between Two Truces*, pp. 108 ff.

223. The other demands were: (1) lifting the ban on religious flags; (2) giving Buddhists the same legal standing as Catholics; (3) giving Buddhists full freedom to practice their religion.

224. This preposterous version was effectively destroyed by foreign observers present at the demonstration of May 8, among them the German physician Doctor Erich Wulff, who had been teaching at the University of Hue. Doctor Wulff wrote an article on the Buddhist affair in Hue which appeared in *The New Republic* of August 31, 1963, under the title "The Buddhist Revolt," a report which tries to be fair to Diem in judging the Buddhist crisis. But Diem, who must have known the truth, stuck to this rather stupid lie, and Mme. Nhu later repeated it with as straight a face as possible in her speeches in the United States. Halberstam writes that on May 9 he received a phone call from the Vietnamese Director General of Information, who said that the Vietcong had murdered nine Buddhists in Hue. "I was immediately suspicious," Halberstam adds, "because it was highly unusual for the Government to take the initiative in press matters; when it did, it was usually trying to conceal something rather than enlighten

us" (*op. cit.*, pp. 195, 196). Mecklin writes that a court after the November 1 coup confirmed that the nine were killed by Diemist troops and sentenced the officer in charge to life imprisonment (*op. cit.*, pp. 153, 154).

225. "The young priests represented a new force in Vietnamese politics. Generally in their thirties and early forties, they were men who were clearly affected by living in a nation which had undergone thirty years of political revolution and war. They had grown up in a country in which the mandarin way of doing things had almost always failed, and they had noted the appeal to the population of the Vietminh's dramatic techniques. They were highly skilled in politics, and they had a keen insight about the psychology of their people. Foreigners were always awed at the way the priests could move their people, whether joking with them or inciting them; their mass meetings, in which they encouraged the Buddhist population to participate, resembled the civil rights rallies in Southern Negro churches. They were articulate, brilliant men; the Vietnamese Buddhist movement was clearly one of the few in the country where men of true talent, instead of second-raters, had risen to the top. They could discuss the populace, the war, the family and American foreign policy skillfully and with originality" (Halberstam, *op. cit.*, p. 214).

226. The story is told by Malcolm Browne, an eyewitness to the gruesome scene (*op. cit.*, pp. 175–80). Browne was the only correspondent who had arrived on the scene after being alerted; the other correspondents, after many false reports of alleged coups, etc., had failed to take this one seriously. Browne was also the only one to take pictures of the scene; they received instant world-wide distribution and reaction and are published in his book.

227. "All that the Buddhists have done for the country is to barbecue a monk," Mme. Nhu is quoted by Mecklin as having said to an American TV reporter (*op. cit.*, p. 170). She claimed that Thich Quang Duc had been drugged and burned against his will. She later tried to deny having made some of her cynical comments.

228. As reported by Mecklin, *ibid.*, p. 178.

229. *Ibid.*, p. 169.

230. Mecklin says "not a scrap of hard evidence of Communist penetration of the Buddhists turned up during the 1963 crisis" (*ibid.*, p. 160).

231. *Ibid.*, p. 180. Miss Higgins defended Diem in a series of articles in the *New York Herald Tribune*, August 26–30, and September 2, 1963.

232. Nolting, wrote Halberstam, appeared a depressed and lonely man on this day. He knew that the vast majority of the Americans in Saigon disapproved of his continued support of Diem. He spoke on this occasion of the progress in education, agriculture, and commerce under Diem, but also of the "inculcation of democratic principles." (He did not claim that they were being practiced.) On equally wrong footing was his statement that Diem was conducting "a winning war" (see Halberstam, *op. cit.*, pp. 219–20, and Mecklin, *op. cit.*, p. 180). The Diem regime embarrassed Nolting shortly before he left by naming a strategic hamlet after him.

233. Halberstam, *op. cit.*, p. 231.

234. Mecklin, *op. cit.*, p. 181.

235. "The bitter fact was that an overwhelming majority of all Americans in Vietnam disliked the regime, and many hated it," wrote Mecklin, and "as early as November, 1962, resentment of all this had reached a point where an audience of American servicemen at the American theater in Saigon loudly booed when a newsreel of President Diem delivering a speech was thrown on the screen" (*ibid.*, pp. 62, 63). Characteristic of the grim mood of most Americans was their reference to the bombed-out Independence Palace as "the last strategic village." (The government, after the bombing of the Independence Palace in February, 1962, had moved into the so-called Gia Long Palace.) Skepticism and disbelief were not limited to Americans. Nobody else in the world believed anything the Vietnamese Government said, which is probably what prompted the United Nations, at the request of several Buddhist countries, to send a fact-finding mission to South Vietnam. It arrived just one week before the coup, on October 23, 1963. Its report was submitted on December 7, 1963, and published by the U.S. Senate Internal Security Subcommittee in 1964. On the details of Diem's negotiations with the Buddhists, see Charles A. Joiner, "South Vietnam's Buddhist Crisis: Organization for Charity, Dissidence, and Unity," in *Asian Survey*, IV, No. 7 (July, 1964). On the Buddhist crisis, see also Robert Scigliano, "Vietnam: Politics and Religion," in *Asian Survey*, IV, No. 1 (January, 1964), pp. 666–74.

236. They were Larry Burrows and Milton Orshefsky of *Life* magazine, and Burt Glinn of the *Saturday Evening Post*. They were held for three hours and forced to give up their film, but did so only after switching films, so that the photos reached the States after all. The confiscated unexposed rolls of film were destroyed on the spot.

237. Halberstam, *op. cit.*, p. 198.

238. See Mecklin, *op. cit.*, p. 243, Browne, *op. cit.*, p. 115, Lacouture, *Vietnam: Between Two Truces*, p. 98, and Shaplen, *op. cit.*, p. 196, all of whom speak of various means of tortures. It would be nice to be able to say (in 1966) that such methods are no longer used in Vietnam; unfortunately, however, that still seems to be the most popular means of extracting information from suspected Communists.

239. In an interview in Rome on September 25, 1963.

240. Quoted by Mecklin, *op. cit.*, pp. 238–39.

241. On the role of the Voice of America during these critical months, see Mecklin, *ibid.*, p. 164. Word got around that uncensored reports from newsmen in Saigon on the Buddhist crisis could be heard regularly on news programs beamed to Vietnam by the Voice of America, the British Broadcasting Corporation and Radio Australia, Mecklin writes. "By the fall of 1963, as a result of this, VOA was reaching Vietnamese audiences of unprecedented size. . . . VOA practice, under the direction of Edward R. Murrow, was to give . . . access to the same news that was available to Americans, regardless of its good or bad effect on U.S. policy."

242. See Joseph Alsop's report from Saigon, entitled "Ugly Stuff," which appeared in the *New York Herald Tribune* of September 18, 1963, where he tells of Nhu's contacts with the North. Alsop's report was cabled from Hong Kong, to avoid censorship. It was one of a series written during and after his stay in Saigon. Mecklin, Halberstam, and Lacouture render a more skeptical treatment of this sensational affair, which was thought to have been initiated by Nhu to blackmail the Americans. (See also Shaplen, *op. cit.*, p. 196; Halberstam, *op. cit.*, p. 278; Mecklin, *op. cit.*, p. 238; Lacouture, *Vietnam: Between Two Truces*, pp. 82–83.) Lacouture claims that Alsop's article sounded the alarm "with Nhu's surreptitious help. It quoted facts and proposals by Nhu which tended to prove that with the aid of France's Ambassador in Saigon, Lalouette, and his colleague, the delegate-general at Hanoi, de Buzon, actual negotiations had been opened between the government of Ho Chi Minh and that of Ngo Dinh Diem through the intermediary of the Polish representative at the International Control Commission, Manelli." The allegations, writes Lacouture, were denied by all concerned. But, "if a contact was, in fact, established between Hanoi and Saigon at that time, it was by the president of the International Control Commission, Goburdhun, an Indian diplomat, who had visited the Presidents of both the North and the South, and had been surprised to hear the former say: 'After all, Diem is a patriot after his own fashion.' However, Ho talked not to Manelli but to the communist Australian journalist Wilfred Burchett about a possibility of a cease-fire in the South."

243. Mecklin believed that Nhu's mind was cracking and that he was capable of any kind of madness (*op. cit.*, p. 245). He also noted that "there were those who thought the whole family was mad" (*ibid.*, p. 37). Toward the end, he wrote, the whole regime was "in a near psychotic state" (*ibid.*, p. 212). Shaplen speaks of the "seemingly paranoid condition of Nhu," who came more and more to dwell "in a megalomaniac world of his own." And he relates that Nguyen Dinh Thuan, former Secretary of State, told him that it was known that Nhu was smoking opium in the last year and maybe taking heroin, too, and that this helped create his moods of extremism. "You could begin to see madness in his face, a sort of somnambulistic stare, always with that cold smile. . . . It was as if a devil had taken possession of him" (*op. cit.*, p. 189). Shaplen also writes that Nhu's "chief ally in encouraging him" was his wife, "who had developed her own power obsession, and with increasing hysteria threw herself into political matters" (*ibid.*, p. 190). An indication that Mme. Nhu's condition has not improved but rather worsened with her enforced retirement in Europe comes from her interview with the *Geneva Weekly* of November 1, 1965. (The interview was given to Gene Gregory, chief editor of the *Weekly Tribune* of Geneva. Gregory and his wife Ann were the two Americans closest, both personally and through business matters, to Mme. Nhu when they were the publishers of the Nhu-controlled *Times of Vietnam*, an English-language newspaper, in Saigon, which was sacked the day after the coup. At the time, Gene Gregory, like Mme. Nhu, was out of the country, and Ann Gregory was

given "asylum" at the U.S. Embassy.) In the interview, Mme. Nhu, disputing the right of the then (1965) government of South Vietnam to negotiate with North Vietnam, and claiming that only the "legitimate" government has a right to conduct such negotiation, added that this "legitimate" government was—Mme. Nhu! "After all," she stated, "in the absence of the President Ngo Dinh Diem and of my husband, I alone now, as their nearest collaborator and in my own right, represent the majority of the Vietnamese people: the loyal elements of the army, the paramilitary forces, the combatant youth, the republican youth, the labor unions—all founded by my husband and loyal to him—and, last but not least, the women who alone represent already more than half of the population, out of whom I have made one of the best organized forces of the nation—no one can challenge that position, which is mine." Perhaps "the little lady" whom Lacouture describes as "moulded into her silk frock like a dagger in its sheath," has come to believe what Lacouture also reports as often having been said of her, namely "that she was the true man in the family" (*Vietnam: Between Two Truces*, pp. 79, 80).

244. Wrote Karnow in the September 28, 1963, issue of *Saturday Evening Post:* "The Ngo Dinhs resemble a cross between the Borgias and the Bourbons. Narrow and devious, obstinate and imperious, they have functioned in an atmosphere of neurotic and sanctimonious egotism. They have plotted against their rivals, and played their own subordinates off against one another. They preached puritanism but tolerated corruption, extolled democracy yet rigged elections, and jailed at least 30,000 political prisoners in 're-education camps.'" Another revealing article on the regime was written by Denis Warner in *The Reporter* of October 10, 1963, entitled "Agony in Saigon: The Lady and the Cadaver." (Incidentally, Stanley Karnow had been a *Time* correspondent, but had resigned because of *Time*'s positive attitude toward the regime at a period when all signs, in particular the reportings of its own staff in Saigon, should have swayed this opinion.) By then, the American Friends of Vietnam too had published a statement critical of the Diem regime. Thereupon, General John O'Daniel resigned as National Chairman. Some members (e.g., Frank Leeburger and Diane Lockhardt) had resigned earlier in protest against the organization's continued public support of Diem.

245. Mecklin, *op. cit.*, pp. 181–82.

246. Halberstam and Sheehan, after being threatened with arrest and, after also having received assassination threats, moved into Mecklin's house for greater protection (see Halberstam, *op. cit.*, pp. 240, 264, and Mecklin, *op. cit.*, pp. 184, 201, 204).

247. Mme. Nhu said he would be "on probation for a while" (Mecklin, *op. cit.*, p. 190). Lodge was, however, immediately seen as an enemy. The American Mission had given asylum to three Buddhists after the raids in the USOM building. Lodge, soon after his arrival, paid them a visit. Later two Buddhist leaders, one of them the renowned Thich Tri Quang, sought asylum in the Embassy. They were kept there, since the regime refused

them safe conduct. Americans began to refer to the Embassy as "the Buddhist Hilton."

248. William Flippen, an aid official for six years, in a briefing for Lodge described how the U.S. military heads had been "consistently wrong" in their judgments, saying frankly that the war was being lost. Rufus Phillips informed Lodge about the collapse of the strategic-hamlet program. Lodge also listened to the stories and complaints of the newsmen (see Halberstam, *op. cit.*, p. 249).

249. The story about this is told in great detail by Halberstam, *ibid.*, pp. 234–39.

250. Mecklin recounts the visit and investigation of the two without naming them. Halberstam does (*ibid.*, p. 253).

251. The sum for the Special Forces was a mere $250,000 a month, and the impact of the suspension in imports was not felt because the warehouses in Saigon were loaded with goods from whose distribution the government would derive its revenues. U.S. aid by 1963 had reached a total of $3 billion, and stood at $500 million per year.

252. Halberstam tells his story in Chapter XVII of his book (pp. 277–99) and Shaplen in Chapter VI, "The Untold Story of the 1963 Coup" (pp. 188–212).

253. Scigliano, "Epilogue: The Coup d'Etat," *South Vietnam*, p. 222.

254. See Shaplen, *op. cit.*, pp. 203–4. By that time, General Harkins had also become aware of the making of a coup and that it was secretly approved of by the U.S. Government. He is said to have assured General Don that the Americans would not interfere with the coup (Shaplen, *ibid.*, p. 204).

255. *Ibid.*, p. 212.

256. Nhu gave his "weird pseudo-coup" the name Bravo 1, Shaplen writes. "To fool the Americans as well as the plotting generals, Colonel Tung would send some of his units out of Saigon on alleged combat duty. Meanwhile other loyal troops and tank units would secretly take up positions around the city. Then, suddenly, supposedly anti-Diem police units and goon squads would stage a fake revolt in Saigon. Diem and Nhu, at the first sign of action, were to go to Cap St. Jacques . . . where they had a command post with full communications prepared. It would look, they thought, as if they had fled a bona fide uprising. The phony revolutionary government in Saigon would proclaim a fuzzy new program, and some well-known political prisoners would be let out of jail. Other hired gangster squads would then go into action, and there would be a blood bath, during which, it was planned, some Americans as well as some Vietnamese would be killed. Within forty-eight hours, to 'restore order,' Generals Dinh and Cao, using the troops they had stationed around Saigon, would attack the city and take over. This second stage of the coup, to be called Bravo 2, would culminate in Diem and Nhu returning from Cap St. Jacques as vindicated heroes" (*ibid.*, pp. 204, 205). Halberstam's version of the planned fake coup is substantially the same as Shaplen's. He adds that such prominent anti-Diem politicians as former Ambassador Chuong, Mme. Nhu's father, would

be included "without their consent" in the formation of a revolutionary government, to be proclaimed by Colonel Tung's agents. Halberstam also adds that "thereafter the revolutionary government's radio would attack the Americans, declare that it wanted to end the war against the Communists and indicate that it was sympathetic to a neutralist settlement." When the so-called revolt would be crushed by Dinh's loyal troops, the "false coup would scare the Americans," and "would prove to them that the only alternative to the Ngo brothers was neutralism," and that "the Army still supported the family" (*op. cit.*, p. 279).

257. Mecklin, *op. cit.*, p. 183.

258. Both Shaplen and Halberstam tell the story, although they do not agree with each other in all details.

259. Lacouture, *Vietnam: Between Two Truces*, p. 84.

260. An example is given by Halberstam (*op. cit.*, p. 301), who tells the story of a colonel interviewing a district chief after the coup. Colonel Dong asked the district chief how many villages were in his district. The answer was: Twenty-four. How many did he control? The answer: Eight. And how many did he report as being under his control? The answer: Twenty-four.

261. The scene at Tan Son Nhut airport, from where Admiral Felt was leaving after his courtesy call on Diem, was simply that of another VIP departure, wrote Halberstam. But General Tran Van Don, one of the leaders of the coup, who accompanied Felt to the airport, "kept glancing anxiously at his watch." Halberstam, who knew of Don's alleged participation in the coup, mentions that he was tempted to ask more questions at the press conference Admiral Felt was holding at the airport, to prolong it further, and that he told General Don so a week later during an interview. The General "did not seem amused" (*op. cit.*, p. 289). It is worthwhile to report here what might well be called the most outstanding example of "black humor" engaged in by both the Americans and Vietnamese. Wrote Halberstam: "In his press conference Admiral Felt praised the nation's leadership and said that the war effort was going well despite the growing Vietcong fire power—about which there was some concern. Someone asked where the arms were coming from, and after an embarrassed silence Admiral Felt smiled and said that perhaps General Don knew. Tran Van Don said that weapons were indeed a major problem, and then he too laughed and said that he did not know where they were coming from either" (*ibid.*, p. 289). Of course, both Felt and Don as well as all of Saigon knew that the Vietcong weapons mostly were acquired "by courtesy of the United States"— via ambushes of weapons convoys, etc.

262. Shaplen, *op. cit.*, p. 207. Shaplen also says that the high official American contact man "went to the meeting [of the plotters] after alerting the Embassy that the coup was in progress."

263. There has been much speculation about the role of Ambassador Lodge in the preparation of the coup. Most interesting is Morris West's attempt to describe his part in the story of the fall of Diem, and his moral

dilemma, in the boldly conceived and politically quite incisive novel *The Ambassador* (New York, 1965). A rather curious version of the coup is given by Tran Van Dinh in his novel *No Passenger on the River*. Dinh claims that the generals' coup was a countermove against the coup staged and won by the younger colonels, who were arrested, and some of whom were killed. The victory over Diem was thus vitiated, since the regime of the generals was nothing but the old Diem regime without Diem. For another fictional account of the coup and the murder of Diem and Nhu, see Smith Hempstone, *A Tract of Time: A Novel About Vietnam* (Boston, 1965).

264. Some say a Palace Guard betrayed them; others, a relative of the Ngo family.

265. This version, likely but by no means proved, is advanced by Shaplen, *op. cit.*, p. 210. For a different version, see Lacouture, *Vietnam: Between Two Truces*, p. 86.

266. However, in the U.S. press, almost no regret was expressed on the fall of the Diem regime. One rare and significantly obscure exception was an article by General Thomas A. Lane, in the *Syracuse Post*, November 5, 1963, entitled "A Black Day in Our History." Later expressions of disapproval came from Marguerite Higgins, "Saigon Summary," in *America*, January 4, 1964.

267. One of the people who hold this belief is former Ambassador Nolting. See his letter to *The New York Times*, June 19, 1965. The same thesis was upheld by the late Marguerite Higgins (in *Our Vietnam Nightmare* [New York, 1965]), and even less convincingly by Suzanne Labin, in *Vietnam: An Eye Witness Account* (Springfield, Mass., 1964). Then there is Mme. Nhu herself, who, although no longer heard in the United States, has by no means been silent. Her claim is that the war was just about to be won—thanks to Nhu's strategic-hamlet program—when "traitors" supported by American "imperialists" overthrew Diem. The "traitors," however, acted on the assumption that South Vietnam could be saved only if the Diem regime was overthrown.

Appendixes

Selected Bibliography

Index

Appendix I

Important Dates in the History of Vietnam from Its Origins to French Conquest

LEGENDARY PERIOD
2879–258 B.C.

The country, named the Kingdom of Van Lang, is ruled by the legendary Hong Bang Dynasty. Van Lang extends over present-day North and North Central Vietnam.

PREHISTORIC PERIOD
258–111 B.C.

King Thuc Duong Vuong of the legendary Kingdom of Thuc conquers Van Lang and rules it, under the name Kingdom of Au Lac, from 257 to 208 B.C. In 208, Au Lac is conquered by the Chinese General Trieu Da and ruled as part of the South Chinese–Vietnamese Kingdom of Nam Viet. Nam Viet extends from somewhere north of present-day Canton to the vicinity of Hue in Vietnam. Au Lac is divided into the two provinces of Giao Chi and Cuu Chau.

THE PERIOD OF CHINESE DOMINATION
111 B.C.–939 A.D.

The Chinese General Lo Bac Duc, under the Emperor Wouti of the Han Dynasty, conquers the Kingdom of Nam Viet, whose Vietnamese provinces thus become part of the Chinese Empire.

The first Vietnamese uprising against Chinese domination occurs in the year 39. It is led by the sisters Trung Trac and Trung Nhi, national heroines of Vietnam. The Chinese defeat them and reoccupy Vietnam in the year 43.

Another uprising, also led by a woman (Trieu Au), takes place in 248, but it is squashed.

Chinese governors rule strictly. They introduce Chinese culture, techniques, moral philosophy, ritual, script, art, and instruction into Vietnam. During the fourth and fifth centuries, the Chinese conduct several expeditions against the Kingdom of Champa (located in present-day Central Vietnam).

In 544, a Sino-Vietnamese official, Ly Bon, stages a successful rebellion and establishes a short-lived independent Vietnam. The Chinese, in 547, reconquer part of the country, but confusion reigns and several regions remain independent until 602. During this period, Buddhism begins to spread in Vietnam.

Between 602 and 938, several Vietnamese uprisings take place and are

1193

defeated. But in battles during 938 and 939, the Chinese are decisively beaten under Ngo Quyen. The Ngo Dynasty is established and Chinese domination is brought to an end.

THE PERIOD OF INDEPENDENCE
939–1883

After the death of Ngo Quyen, in 944, the country falls into a period of feudal anarchy. Twelve provincial warlords fight each other for power. They are defeated by Dinh Bo Linh, who proclaims himself Emperor in 968. He calls his kingdom Dai Co Viet, and establishes the Dinh Dynasty.

The Dinh Dynasty is followed in 980 by the early Le Dynasty (980–1009), which further unifies the country and, in expeditions against Champa, extends its border southward. A Chinese invasion is defeated in 981. The earlier Le introduces the first national currency in 983.

The Ly Dynasty replaces the early Le in 1010 and remains in possession of the throne until 1214. Buddhism flourishes in Vietnam under the Ly. The wars against Champa continue. The name of the country is now Dai Viet. Its capital is Thanh Long (Hanoi), established in 1010. In 1069, expeditions against Champa lead to the annexation of the present-day provinces Quang Binh and Quang Tri. The year 1070 sees the construction of the Temple of Literature at Hanoi and the creation of a National College. A Literary Assembly is created in 1075. Chinese invasions are defeated in 1075 and 1077. In 1108, the first dyke is constructed in Vietnam. The government of Vietnam becomes highly centralized under the Ly; a very advanced system of taxation is developed, and a national army, based on universal military service, is created. The Ly also build "royal" roads, and in 1075, the first literary competition of scholars for high office is held. The Chinese mandarinate takes firm root. Under the Ly Dynasty three Khmer (Cambodian) invasions—in 1128, 1133, and 1138—are repelled.

THE TRAN DYNASTY
1225–1400

The country is further unified and organized. The main events in the history of the Tran dynasty are the two Mongol invasions under Kublai Khan in 1284–85 and 1287. Both are defeated by the Vietnamese under General Tran Huong Dao—now the great national hero of both North and South Vietnam. (An earlier Mongol attempt to enter Vietnam was defeated in 1257.) The Tran establish a National Institute of Advanced Studies and a Military College in 1253. In 1272, the first historical document, the "Annals of the Great Viet" (Dai Viet Su Ky), is drawn up.

A usurper, Ho Quy Ly, overthrows the declining Tran Dynasty in 1400. Ho Quy Ly creates a public-health service and issues the first banknotes, introduces an agrarian reform, and modernizes education. He takes two more provinces (present-day Quang Nam and Quang Ngai) from Champa and moves the capital from Hanoi to Thanh Hoa. Ho is defeated by a Chinese invasion in 1407.

INTERLUDE OF CHINESE RULE
1407–1427

The powerful Chinese Ming Dynasty succeeds in holding on to Vietnam for twenty years, during which it vainly attempts to transform the Vietnamese into Chinese. The result is an upsurge of nationalism, which, after a long "war of liberation," leads to the defeat of the Chinese armies. The Vietnamese are led by another great national hero, Le Loi, who, in 1428, establishes a new dynasty.

THE LATER LE DYNASTY
1428–1789

Le Loi, under the name Le Thai To, rules again from Hanoi, and the country again is named Dai Viet. He is followed by Le Thanh Ton (1460–97), considered the greatest Vietnamese emperor. Under Le Thanh Ton, Vietnam's tax system is modernized, dikes are constructed, and mandarins appointed to supervise them. Geographical, historical, and literary works are promoted, and a very modern legal code is promulgated. In 1470, Le Thanh Ton virtually destroys the power of Champa and extends his kingdom southward through the annexation of the present-day province of Binh Dinh. Fifteenth-century Vietnam may well have been the most advanced state of Southeast Asia.

VIETNAM DIVIDED INTO NORTH AND SOUTH
1527–1786

From 1500 on, the later Le Dynasty rapidly declines. Power is first taken by the usurper Mac Dang Dung in 1527. The Macs, in 1592, are defeated by Trinh Tung, head of a powerful feudal family, who puts a Le descendant back on the throne as a puppet and henceforth rules the northern half of Vietnam. The rule of the Trinh is not recognized by the governor of the southern provinces, Nguyen Hoang. The Nguyen family, which began to rule in 1687 from Hue, establishes a Southern Vietnamese Kingdom, which rapidly spreads southward at the expense of declining Cambodia. In 1627, the Trinh lead a first expedition against the South, starting a war that rages nearly fifty years. They fail, as they do in all other attempts to conquer the South, up to the last one in 1672. After that, the Trinh and Nguyen conclude a truce that is to last 100 years. The Nguyen continue to expand southward. Champa ceases to exist. Saigon and lower Cochinchina down to the Mekong River are annexed by 1698, the rest of Cochinchina by 1757.

THE FIRST EUROPEANS IN VIETNAM

From 1540 on, the Portuguese begin to trade with Vietnam at the port of Faifo, south of Danang. The Dutch do not appear until about 100 years later, setting up a trading center in the North, at Pho Hien. Portuguese and Dutch trade with Vietnam is fairly brisk as long as the North and South are at war, but languishes later. Trade is also bad for the British, who establish their first trading center in 1672, and for the French, who arrive in 1680. Only the Portuguese hold on to their trading port after 1700.

European Catholic missionary activity fares somewhat better in Vietnam than trade. The Cochinchinese Mission is founded in 1615, the Tongking Mission in 1627, the latter by the French Jesuit Alexander of Rhodes, who completes work begun by Italian and Portuguese missionaries on the Romanization of the Vietnamese script. But 1630 brings the first proscription of Christianity. Periods of toleration interrupt persecution of Catholic missionaries up to the nineteenth century, when persecution (after 1825) becomes severe and is used as a pretext by France for invading Vietnam.

CIVIL WAR AND REUNIFICATION
1775–1801

Three brothers, named the Tayson, after their native village, stage a revolt in 1773 that soon turns into a genuine revolution. They take Qui Nhon in 1775. The Trinh at Hanoi exploit the civil war in the South by taking Hue. The Nguyen court flees to Saigon. Saigon falls to the Tayson in October, 1777, but is retaken by the young survivor of the ruling family, Nguyen Anh, in November, 1777. The Tayson proclaim one of their brothers, Nguyen Van Nhac, Emperor at Qui Nhon. They recapture Saigon in 1782. Nguyen Anh, defeated, flees to Siam in 1785. He signs a treaty of mutual assistance with France in 1787, negotiated by the famous French missionary Pigneau de Béhaine, Bishop of Adran. The Tayson capture Hue and Hanoi in 1786 and become masters of Vietnam. With French assistance, organized from the French possession in India by the Bishop of Adran, Nguyen Anh returns to Southern Cochinchina in 1788. The youngest Tayson brother, Nguyen Van Hue, is proclaimed Emperor of Vietnam, but Nguyen Anh recaptures Saigon, and, from the South, with French help, organizes the country's reconquest for the Nguyen Dynasty. The Tayson Emperor Hue, in 1789, defeats a Chinese invasion. He dies in 1792. Another ten years of war between South and North follow. Nguyen Anh takes Qui Nhon in 1799, only to lose it again. But he captures Hue in 1801, and proclaims himself Emperor under the name of Gia Long.

THE NGUYEN DYNASTY AND THE CONQUEST OF VIETNAM BY FRANCE
1802–1883

Gia Long completes his victory by seizing Qui Nhon in March and Hanoi in July, 1802. He rules until 1820. He defeats Cambodia in 1813, tolerates, but does not favor, Christianity, and allows trade with France. Under his successors—Minh Mang (1810–41), Thieu Tri (1841–47), and Tu Duc (1847–83)—Vietnam turns more and more against the missionaries and breaks off all relations with the West. Christianity is forbidden in 1825, and the last Frenchmen at the court of Hue are expelled by Minh Mang. Cambodia is annexed in 1834, but given up again in 1841. Since French demands to end persecution of the missionaries are being ignored, the French bomb Tourane in 1847. They storm and take the city in 1858 and capture Saigon in 1859. The towns of Bienhoa and Baria are taken in 1861, and Vinh Long in 1862. By treaty of June 5, 1862, Vietnam cedes three eastern provinces of Cochinchina to France. The French annex the three western provinces in 1867, and, after capturing Hanoi in 1883, establish their rule over the whole of Vietnam by imposing protectorates on Tongking and Annam.

(This chronology is based on Le Thanh Khoi, *Le Viet-Nam: Histoire et civilisation;* Thai Van Kiem, *Viet-Nam: Past and Present;* and Joseph Buttinger, *The Smaller Dragon.*)

Appendix II

A Brief Survey of the Conquest of Indochina

1

COCHINCHINA

Inevitable as the conquest of Cochinchina was in the 1860's, it might not have begun when it did, in February, 1859, had Rigault de Genouilly, the commander of the French forces, been a more devout man. He made his decision to sail south in Tourane, Vietnam's main harbor near Hue, which he occupied in September, 1858. Tourane had already seen French military action in April, 1847. Two warships, commanded by Captain Lapierre, had been dispatched there to demand of the court at Hue the free exercise of the Catholic faith in Vietnam as well as the release of Bishop Lefébvre, who was presumed to be in prison. As it happened, Monsignor Lefébvre had already been released and sent to Singapore four weeks earlier, but Lapierre, whose messages to Hue remained unanswered, was unaware of this. A seemingly threatening approach by Vietnamese ships caused Lapierre, after two weeks of waiting, to order their shelling and the bombardment of Tourane's fortress. The sum of Lapierre's accomplishments was the killing of a large number of Vietnamese and the sinking of five ships; this done, he left. In 1857, the Montigny Mission appeared before Tourane, threatening punitive action if religious persecution of the French missionaries did not stop. The Montigny Mission was one of the first diplomatic missions to the court of Hue, in 1856, headed by the former French consul at Shanghai. Genouilly had captained one of the two warships under Lapierre in 1847. In 1858, he was Vice-Admiral, and his orders were unequivocal: He was to establish himself solidly in Tourane, without any further attempt at negotiations. It was left to his discretion to establish a protectorate over Cochinchina, if that was possible without too heavy sacrifices. But communications with Hue proved impossible. The rains, which in the center of Vietnam start in October, destroyed all chances of proceeding to the capital by land, and for the voyage by water Genouilly lacked the shallow-draft boats needed to go upriver. He realized that he would be prevented from reaching Hue until April, the end of the rainy season. Monsignor Pellerin, his so-called expert on Vietnam, suggested that in the interim Genouilly invade the north. Pellerin's argument was that the Christians were more numerous in Tongking than in any other part of Vietnam, and that they would surely rise against their government as soon as the French approached the Red River Delta. But Genouilly refused to accede to Pellerin's urgings. He could not subordinate important strategic considerations, he said, to "more or less problematical religious interest." Instead, he decided to conquer Saigon, which, he wrote to Paris later, "is destined to become the center of an immense commerce as soon as the port is opened for Europeans." Leaving only a small garrison in Tourane, he sailed south. By February 17, 1859, Saigon was in French hands. But his troops, both in Saigon and in Tourane, were being decimated by tropical and infectious diseases, and reinforcements were not forthcoming; Napoleon III had declared war on Austria in May, 1859. Stymied in his efforts either to defeat the Vietnamese militarily or to make them accept his demands, he finally asked to be relieved of his command. His successor, Admiral Page, was, however, equally unable to reinforce his position. Since meanwhile France and England had jointly declared war on China, all troops and supplies were evacuated from Tourane in February, 1860, and sent to China. Only an isolated garrison, commanded by one Captain Jaureguiberry, was left behind in Saigon. This garrison managed not only to hold out, but even to keep the port open for ships from Europe. In October, when peace with China was at last restored, Admiral Charner was ordered from China to Vietnam with his forces. By the end of June, 1861, Charner had occupied the main points of the three provinces around Saigon: Bienhoa, Gia Dinh, and Dinh Tuong (Mytho). They were the richest part of Cochinchina and stretched from the ocean to the Cambodian border. Charner's successor, Admiral Bonard, even penetrated the province of Vinh Long, beyond Mytho, in the southern part of Cochinchina. It was then that Tu Duc and his mandarins, anxious to have their hands free to deal with an uprising in Tongking, sued for peace. The treaty, signed in Saigon on June 6, 1862, by Bonard for France and by Phan Than Gian for the court of Hue, left France in possession of the three northern provinces and of the long-coveted island of Poulo Condore. Vinh Long was returned to the suzerainty of Hue. The struggle, however, was by no means over, and in May, 1863, Admiral de la Grandière was handed the task of making the south of Cochinchina secure for France. This required another four years of diplomatic and military efforts. Tu Duc had sent a mission to Paris to negotiate a revision of the Saigon treaty, and despite the vociferous protests of the admirals, this was granted and a new treaty actually signed in Hue in July, 1864. But before the year was out, the advocates of further French expansion in Vietnam, led by Genouilly, won out; the new treaty was brushed aside, and de la Grandière was permitted to proceed in the solidification of his position.

The second phase of Cochinchina's conquest took place in 1867, when de la Grandière secretly prepared his southern expansion in Saigon. He was aided and abetted in Paris by de Genouilly, who in January of that year had become Minister of Marine and Colonies. On June 17, 1867, de la Grandière launched his invasion. One week later he could report to Paris that he had annexed the southern provinces Vinh Long, Soc Trang, and Chau Doc, and that all of Cochinchina had become French.

The mission that Tu Duc sent to Paris to negotiate the restoration of the three western provinces was headed by the same man whom he had sent to Saigon in 1862 to conclude the treaty that ceded these provinces to France—Phan Than Gian, Tu Duc's ablest diplomat, an old and distinguished savant who had already served as counselor and minister to Tu Duc's father and grandfather. Escorted by Rieunier, a naval officer, Phan Than Gian left Hue in June, 1863, with an entourage of almost seventy persons, ostensibly to present Napoleon III with greetings and gifts from the Vietnamese Emperor, but in truth to arrange for the repurchase terms of the ceded provinces. Phan Than Gian was accorded a friendly reception. Not only was his case supported by views then current in France that the Asian mentality did not lend itself to the import of Western civilization, but the French budget was suffering from a considerable deficit, and the prospect of filling the treasury with the proffered indemnity opened the old mandarin the door not only to the Minister for Foreign Affairs, but to Napoleon III himself, who received him in audience in November, 1863. Under the terms of the proposed new treaty, France was to relinquish the three occupied provinces as well as cease all further attempts to colonize Cochinchina; instead she was to accept commercial settlements and points of occupation around Saigon, Mytho, and at Cape Saint Jacques. In return, all of Cochinchina was to be declared a French protectorate, its meaning undefined, and France was to be paid a permanent yearly tribute. Happy in the knowledge that he had served his master well, Phan Than Gian returned to Hue in March, 1864. The task of concluding the revised treaty with the Vietnamese Emperor fell to Gabriel Aubaret, a naval captain with long service in the Far East and also a past interpreter and political adviser to Admiral Bonard; Aubaret was among those who did not believe in the feasibility of French expansion in Vietnam. But Aubaret, who came to Hue from his post as Consul in Bangkok, was to encounter unexpected difficulties. The Vietnamese Emperor wanted to renege on several agreed-upon points of the new treaty. In particular, he asked for revisions of those dealing with freedom of French movement in Vietnam, freedom of religious activities, the planned amnesty for converted Vietnamese, and, above all, for a substitution of the permanent tribute with a fixed tribute payable for forty years. After more than a month of negotiations, Aubaret, on July 15, 1864, finally signed the new treaty, in which he made concession to Tu Duc's wishes regarding the terms of payment, but only conditionally, reserving to the French Government the right either to accept or reject the new text. The conclusion of Aubaret's mission was reported to the Minister of War by the man who had accompanied him to Hue, Charles Duval, the most mysterious figure in French colonial history and a violent opponent of any concessions to Vietnam. Charles Duval had once before injected himself into French-Vietnamese politics. Duval, a simple sergeant, came to Cochinchina in January, 1862; he developed an immediate and intense interest in the country, studying the language with Monsignor Gauthier, who had been in Vietnam since 1835. In 1863, Duval obtained a copy of the Saigon Treaty and sent it to the Minister of War, who seemed to have hired him as a secret observer and reporter. With that copy, Duval transmitted a memorandum saying that in his opinion Tu Duc had no intention of ratifying the treaty signed by Phan Than Gian in his name, but that he could be forced to do so were he to encounter increased warfare by the rebels in Tongking. Toward that end, Duval offered to go to Tongking himself and head up the troops of the pretender of the Le Dynasty, then at war with Hue. He did go, in a completely unofficial capacity, and was so successful in his military exploits for the rebels that Tu Duc, unable to engage the French as well as his northern opponent, ratified the treaty in April, 1863. Thereupon Duval considered his mission completed and left Tongking. When, upon his return to Saigon, he learned of Phan Than Gian's voyage to Paris, he immediately went there himself, in order to counteract the old mandarin's efforts. In his report on the treaty signed by Aubaret, Duval made several recommendations, in case "the mistake was made of ratifying the treaty." He suggested that strong French forces remain in Cochinchina for all future eventualities. He further suggested that if the pretender of the Le Dynasty were defeated by Tu Duc, another be found immediately, which would not be difficult since in Tongking "every province contains at least one pretender," and the North be thus kept in a permanent state of unrest to divert Tu Duc's attention. "Once we are solidly established," he wrote, "we can re-establish order and extend the protectorate over the entire kingdom." Finally, he shrewdly speculated on the advantages of Vietnam's predicted inability to pay the promised indemnity *in toto*. "The Annamites are poor. Their government does not have the resources and will never be able to pay us 80 million francs over forty years. So much the better. We shall get what we can, and then their lack of funds will soon enough become apparent and the annuity will not be paid, at least not entirely. We can let the debt grow, and one fine day we can demand total repayment. By then we will have investigated their mines of gold, silver, iron, copper, tin, and coal, and can accept all the concessions regarding the indemnity. Accordingly, this debt will prove a valuable weapon to us." Duval proved to have aligned himself with the victorious faction. Even while Aubaret was in Hue, the opposition pursued an active campaign in Paris; the Catholic press, the navy, the chambers of commerce, and various business groups, upheld by such individual politicians as de la Grandière, his officers, Francis Garnier, Rieunier, and the Maritime Minister, François de Chasseloup-Laubat, succeeded in obtaining a reversal of policy. An order to suspend negotiations immediately was sent to Aubaret on June 8, 1864. But while it reached him too late, some time after he had already left Hue, the lobbying against the treaty continued, culminating on November 4, 1864, in a long report in which the Maritime Minister expounded the reasons for an adherence to the original treaty of 1862. Early in January, 1865, de la Grandière was advised of the government's final decision, and the court of Hue was warned not to go against the original treaty. Two years later, seeking a pretext to annex the three provinces that lay beyond the three he already held, de la Grandière accused Phan Than Gian, who had been made Viceroy, of sheltering anti-French rebels and presented him with an ultimatum. The old man of peace preferred surrender to a struggle he considered hopeless. Exacting from his sons a promise never to collaborate with the French, he sent a last sorrowful message of leave-taking to Tu Duc and committed suicide (see Georges Taboulet, *La geste française en Indochine*, pp. 488 ff.).

2

CAMBODIA

The enfeebled successor to the vanished empire of the ancient Khmer, Cambodia had long suffered from the encroachments of its two powerful neighbors, Siam (now Thailand) to the north, and Vietnam to the east and south. By the middle of the nineteenth century, the power struggle between the two rivals for the rich rice lands of the Mekong Delta had reached an impasse. In 1847, Ang Duong ascended the Cambodian throne by mutual agreement between Vietnam and Siam, and his coronation was witnessed by representatives of both "protector" neighbors. But soon thereafter, the balance threatened to swing in Siam's favor. Ang Duong's heir presumptive and oldest son, Norodom, had been educated in Bangkok, and had taken refuge there with the crown jewels in 1859, after his father's death, when his right to the succession was successfully contested by his younger brother Sivotha. Ready to take advantage of Vietnam's deep involvement in its military resistance against the French, the Siamese sought to use the opportunity to complete their political stranglehold over Cambodia. Under their protection, Norodom in 1862 returned to Oudong, the old Khmer capital, where he was to receive the sacred crown and sword of the Khmer kings (retained in Bangkok) from the hands of the Siamese, after signing a treaty that would have made Cambodia a province of Siam. A Siamese mandarin who accompanied him was already exercising the functions of a *de facto* protector at the court of the as yet uncrowned king. It was at this point that Monsignor Miche, the Bishop of Cambodia, asked Admiral de la Grandière that France intervene. De la Grandière, realizing that the water routes of the Mekong River would be irrevocably closed to France if Siam were to exert absolute control over Cambodia, lost no time in acceding to the bishop's request. In May, 1863, he sent Doudart de Lagrée, a likable and persuasive young naval lieutenant, to establish secret contacts with Norodom, at which France spoke in the name of Vietnam. De Lagrée had apparently no trouble in winning the confidence of the young ruler, who seemed as anxious as the French to be rid of Siamese suzerainty. Hence de la Grandière himself went to Oudong in July, fully aware that he was acting without prior consent of Paris, that he was risking a French-Siamese conflict, and that Siam was in the British sphere of influence. On August 11, 1863, he signed a treaty with Norodom declaring Cambodia a French protectorate. But, conveniently for both parties, the treaty remained secret, for a long time even to de Lagrée, until December, when it was finally ratified in Paris by Napoleon III. It was under this French protection that Norodom was crowned in June, 1864: The royal insignia had been returned by Siam under a French threat of force and were given to the young ruler for his coronation by the representative of France; the representative of Siam was not allowed to attend. Although Siam continued a steady pressure throughout 1863, culminating in December in a secret treaty that negated many provisions of Cambodia's treaty with France, French influence remained dominant. Renewed Siamese efforts in 1864 at winning Norodom back were foiled by de la Grandière, who reprimanded the Cambodian King and caused him to go to Saigon to render his apologies. French-Siamese relations remained tense, despite continuous negotiations, until July, 1867, when Siam agreed at last to French protection over Cambodia in a treaty that France in return cede the rich provinces of Battambang and Angkor, the latter world-famous for its Khmer ruins. These remained Siamese possessions until 1907, when, according to André Masson, "French diplomacy restored them to Cambodia."

3

Tongking and Annam

The treaty of 1883, which made Annam and Tongking protectorates of France, signified the end of a long psychosis of defeat suffered by France as the aftermath of the Franco-Prussian War of 1870–71 and the fall of the Second Empire. In 1873, obsessed with the "nightmare of Bismarck," the young and timid French Third Republic had refused to press its advantage when Francis Garnier, sent north by Admiral Dupré at the request of Hue to deal with the "Dupuis affair," undertook in a short time the *de facto* conquest of Tongking. Garnier had met Dupuis at the time when he and his group discovered the navigability of the Red River (a claim disputed by Dupuis, who insisted he had already discovered it years before). Garnier, in full sympathy with Dupuis, stormed the citadel of Hanoi and, with a handful of men, occupied the surrounding provinces. When Garnier was killed in action outside Hanoi on December 21, 1873, Dupré, at the insistence of Paris, ordered the withdrawal of his troops from Tongking. The incident, however, served to frighten Tu Duc into abandoning his dilatory tactics regarding a revision of the treaty of 1862. On March 15, 1874, a new treaty formally ceded to France the "western" provinces of lower Cochinchina, already occupied by de la Grandière in 1867. For eight years thereafter, France was to remain indifferent to further expansion in Vietnam. Tu Duc took advantage of the prevailing mood in France during that period by negating much of the treaty through passive or indirect resistance, denying in effect freedom of religion and of commerce, and even making it impossible for the French to reach southern China via the Red River. Dupuis was to note with bitterness at that time that, although he had been able to go to Yunnan when the Red River was officially closed to foreigners, it was absolutely impossible for him to make the same trip now that the Red River was legally declared open. In further defiance of the treaty, Tu Duc paid tribute to China and called on her rather than on France for military aid against the Chinese bandits that roamed the north, thus indirectly also requesting China's aid against the periodic insurrections against his government. In 1878, encouraged by what he considered a soft French policy, Tu Duc went so far as to negotiate the return of Cochinchina directly with Paris. But thereafter, Franco-Vietnamese relations were to enter a new phase; France's period of "restrained occupation" had ended. In early 1882, Paris authorized Le Myre de Vilers to send a military detachment to Tongking. De Vilers appointed Captain Henri Rivière as its commander. Although cautioned by de Vilers against any rash acts that might antagonize Hue, Rivière, confronted by a military preparation of hostilities on the part of the northern mandarins, quickly made up his mind to act. On April 25, 1882, he stormed the citadel of Hanoi. (The statement on p. 376 of my earlier book on Vietnam, *The Smaller Dragon*, that Rivière reached Hanoi on April 3, 1883, is a typographical error.) But for the next year, Rivière was held to relative inaction by de Vilers, who was afraid of military disaster and international complications. Yet, by pushing ahead on his own, against constant warnings from Saigon, Rivière was in fact more in step with his country and government than with his cautious superior. When de Vilers was succeeded by Governor Thomson, Rivière finally received permission to act. After receiving reinforcements in February, 1883, he immediately proceeded to occupy Hongay and Nam Dinh. There is no telling whether his military exploits might or might not have been crowned by ultimate success. On May 19, 1883, his luck ran out, and he fell in a skirmish with the Chinese bandits, much like Garnier before him, and almost on the same spot. His death, however, produced the opposite effect of Garnier's. The Chamber of Deputies voted the credits necessary for the imposition of a French protectorate over Tongking. In August of the same year, a strong French expeditionary corps penetrated the Red River Valley, while in a simultaneous move the French fleet bombarded Hue. The court, deprived of its stubborn Emperor (for Tu Duc had died earlier in July), quickly submitted to a superior enemy. On August 25, 1883, the Treaty of Protectorate was signed. Thus the independence of Vietnam came to an end, and the twelve years of slaughter, which history has labeled the pacification of Tongking, began.

4

Laos

It may well be said that France conquered Laos as early as 1887, for it was in that year that a Frenchman, an official in Luang Prabang, a small principality in upper Laos, gained the respect and affection of the Laotian population by risking his own life to save their king. It may also be said, according to Virginia Thompson, that the actual conquest of Laos by France in 1893 was triggered by the suicide of another French official in Luang Prabang, "worn out by his struggles with the Siamese." French interest in Laos had remained dormant during the 1860's and 1870's. At most, there had been a wary realization that Thailand, thwarted in Cambodia by France in its aim to establish Thai hegemony on the Indochinese Peninsula, had concentrated its expansionary drive on Laos, encouraged as it was by tacit British consent and by the struggle between its rivals Vietnam and France. But in 1885, when the Thai used another invasion of upper Laos by the Ho (Chinese bandits come down from Yunnan) as a pretext for a military expedition to Luang Prabang, France became disquieted. A complete Thai take-over of that part of Laos constituted a definite threat, since it would drive a wedge between Tongking and Annam at a point where Vietnam was at its narrowest, a strip no wider than 30 miles. It was decided to send an observer to Luang Prabang, and the choice for that post, which carried the modest title of vice-consul, fell on Auguste Pavie, a short, soft-spoken telegraph operator with a consuming interest in Cambodian and Laotian culture, who had come to the attention of the then Governor of Indochina, Le Myre de Vilers, because of the extensive explorations of the Mekong regions begun by Pavie in 1875. Pavie used his position further to endear himself to the Laotians, whose confidence he gained by his gentleness, his sense of justice, and his many visits to their villages and homes. In February, 1887, Pavie had just returned from one of his excursions into the countryside when the Ho threatened to attack Luang Prabang. The Thai military stationed there fled at the approach of the bandits, leaving the King and his capital helpless and unprotected. Pavie stayed, at least long enough to lead the old King to safety. When the unresisting city fell, a large part of the population was massacred. But the survivors and those who managed to escape remembered Pavie's courage with gratitude, and the King placed himself and his kingdom under the protection of France. During the next two years, Pavie, accompanied by French and native assistants, undertook his famous "Pavie Mission," which was to result not only in the definition of the boundary lines between Thailand and Laos along the Mekong, but also in charts, maps, and findings that were to lead to the first general map of that part of Indochina. Pavie's scientific venture, described by him in his aptly titled book *À la conquête des cœurs* (Paris, 1947), led to the Franco-Thai agreement of 1889, drawn up to halt Thailand's eastward drive. Although bitterly mistrusted by the Thai, he continued his explorations of the contested areas for another two years. In 1892, he was sent to Bangkok, to carry on diplomatic negotiations as Consul General. His successor in Luang Prabang protested in vain against such constant breaches of the 1889 agreement as the wholesale deportations of entire Laotian villages. Pavie, in a fit of depression, took his own life. As Miss Thompson put it: "His death shocked the Chamber of Deputies into voting unanimously for action." Military action in Laos was followed shortly by a naval demonstration before Bangkok. On July 19, 1893, Pavie had transmitted a French ultimatum to the Thai Government. The Thai held out, counting on British support. Not having received an answer, Pavie left Bangkok on July 25, and the French fleet blockaded Thailand. For a while, Anglo-French relations remained tense. But when the British yielded, the Thai had no choice but to accept France's ultimatum. On October 3, 1893, Le Myre de Vilers, acting as Ambassador Extraordinary, signed a treaty in Bangkok by which Thailand renounced all claims to the Laotian territories east of the Mekong. The official acquisition of Laos by France dates from that day. The conquest of Laos, however, was only completed and made permanent after China, too, had recognized France's new acquisition in a convention signed in June, 1895. England also finally concluded a convention with France in January, 1896, in which the two powers agreed on their respective zones of influence in Indochina. (Cf. Auguste Pavie, *À la conquête des cœurs;* André Masson, *Histoire de l'Indochine;* Virginia Thompson, *French Indochine;* Joseph Buttinger, *The Smaller Dragon.*)

Appendix III

The Admiral-Governors, Governors General, and High Commissioners of Indochina from 1859 to 1955

1

Chronological List of the Military and Civil Commanders in Cochinchina, Annam, and Tongking from 1859 to Doumer's administration in 1897

COCHINCHINA

February, 1859
to November, 1859

CHARLES RIGAULT DE GENOUILLY: Vice Admiral; Commander in Chief. Born April, 1807; died May, 1873. Navy career man. Made Captain in 1841, Rear Admiral in 1854. In 1857, he was given the command of the naval division of the expedition to China and Cochinchina; occupied Canton jointly with the British. Vice Admiral in 1858; occupied Tourane on September 1 of that same year. In concert with a Spanish force, his fleet sailed upriver to Saigon in February, 1859, and took Saigon on the seventeenth. Returned to Tourane in the middle of April, he relinquished his command there in October and returned to France. Became Senator in 1860; Admiral in 1864. In 1867, he succeeded Chasseloup-Laubat as Minister of the Navy. At the outbreak of the revolution on September 4, 1870, he goes to Spain where he remained until his death. "There is really no important action but at Saigon, and therefore this is the only action possible." (From a letter to the Minister of the Navy from Tourane, January 29, 1859.)

November, 1859
to April, 1860

THEOGENE-FRANÇOIS PAGE: Rear Admiral; Commander in Chief. Born March, 1807; died February, 1867. Navy career man; participated in Genouilly's Indochina expedition, was handed the command by Genouilly. He opened Saigon to Western commerce. Displeasing Paris with his independence, he was replaced by Charner. Under Charner's command, he participated in the campaign in Mytho and Bienhoa. Vice Admiral in 1861. Returned to France in 1862. Prefect; titular member of the Admiralty's Council; President of Naval Works. "I have proven

—clear as the day—that France can be assured of a splendid, fairytale-like kingdom, which could give it, without cost, millions annually." (From a letter to the Marquis de la Grange from Hong Kong, March 29, 1860.)

April, 1860
to February, 1861
JOSEPH-HYACINTHE D'ARIES: Captain; Superior Commander. Born January, 1813; died December, 1878. Graduate of Naval Academy, 1829. When Page was summoned to China, he handed d'Aries the command of the forces stationed in Saigon. Throughout his entire command, he fought off constant attacks by Vietnamese forces and kept his communications open to the sea. Rear Admiral in 1872; retired in 1876. It was d'Aries who handed the citadel of Vinh Long over to Phan Than Gian, according to the agreement reached in the treaty of June, 1862.

February, 1861
to December, 1861
LEONARD-VICTOR-JOSEPH CHARNER: Vice Admiral; Commander in Chief. Born February, 1797; died February, 1869. Navy career man. In obedience to the instructions of Chasseloup-Laubat, which called for a consolidation of the French position around Saigon, Charner fought a major battle against the entrenched Vietnamese at Chi Hoa. In conquering Mytho, he therewith controlled the flow of rice from the western provinces. Returned to France, he became Senator in 1862 and Admiral in 1864.
"The resistance of the enemy was fierce." (From Charner's battle report, sent February 27, 1861, from Chi Hoa.)

November, 1861
to May, 1863
LOUIS-ADOLPHE BONARD: Rear Admiral; Commander in Chief; first Governor of Cochinchina. Born March, 1805; died March, 1867. Navy career man. Captured in Algiers in 1830, after shipwreck. In Tahiti during the insurrection of 1849; Governor of Guyana in 1853. Arrived in Cochinchina November 29, 1861; conquered Bienhoa and Vinh Long on June 5, 1862, he signed the preliminary peace treaty with Tu Duc's representatives which gave the provinces of Gia Dinh, Dinh Tuong, and Bien Hoa to France. He set up a military hospital in Saigon. Familiar with the type of protectorate as exercised by the French in Algiers, he sought to leave the administration of the French-occupied Vietnamese territories in indigenous hands, supervising it only by inspectors for native affairs. The continuing unrest, however, and the flight of the mandarins together with the disappearance of the official records, forced him into a direct administration. Nevertheless, remaining respectful of Vietnamese customs and ideas, he wished to make peace with the people. On April 2, 1863, he went to Hue, together with the Spanish plenipotentiary, to bring the ratified peace treaty to Tu Duc. He returned to Saigon the twenty-fifth and left for France the thirtieth, taking with him the treaty signed by Tu Duc. Nominated Maritime Prefect in 1867.
"I would be much happier," he wrote to Chasseloup-Laubat in April, 1862, "to lay at the Emperor's feet the good news of a pacified and

organized country on the way to prosperity than the news of another citadel taken or destroyed."

May, 1863
to April, 1868

PIERRE-PAUL-MARIE DE LA GRANDIÈRE: Rear Admiral; Commander in Chief; Governor. Born June, 1807; died August, 1876. Navy career man; saw sea action against the Russians in 1854–55; commanded sea forces off the Syrian coast 1860–62. Called to Cochinchina to relieve Bonard, who had planned on returning to his post but was prevented by ill health from doing so, de la Grandière became the conqueror of all of Cochinchina and the prime mover in extending French influence over Cambodia. Founder of the *Courrier de Saigon*, a monthly magazine. Originator of the scientific exploration of the upper Mekong by Doudart de Lagrée. Returned to France in ill health. During his entire tenure, he retained the confidence of Chasseloup-Laubat because of his "wise, cold, and practical mind"; during a period in which it seemed that France might be willing to abandon her acquisitions in Cochinchina, he never wavered in his belief that it would be detrimental to France to give up what he had obtained for her.
"I am attached to Cochinchina as to a child of which I took care during an illness and which gave me much concern. . . . Yes, we shall maintain this glory, despite of and against our detractors. Yes, we will guide this colony, slowly perhaps, but with the assurance of its brilliant future. And we shall make ourselves loved and respected by our neighbors, by our Annamite subjects, and, what is the most difficult of all, even by our French merchants." (From a letter written January 24, 1865, to Captain Mauduit-Duplessis, a friend and relative.)

April, 1868
to December, 1869

MARIE-GUSTAVE-HECTOR OHIER: Rear Admiral; Interim Governor. Born August, 1814; died November, 1870. Navy career man; Lieutenant under Rigault de Genouilly at Sebastopol; Captain of one of the first battleships. Relieved de la Grandière who, like his predecessor, intended to return to his post after regaining his health. Was unsuccessful in his effort to obtain from Hue a treaty that would have acknowledged *de jure* the possession of the three western provinces by France. Tried to reorganize Vietnamese institutions within the framework of Western parliamentarism. His own health gravely impaired, he returned to France before the arrival of his successor.

January, 1870
to April, 1871

COUNT ALPHONSE CORNULIER-LUCINIÈRE: Rear Admiral; Interim Governor. Born April, 1811; died 1886; Navy career man. Saw numerous actions from Africa to Sumatra to the Crimea. Unable to prevail with Tu Duc, he is upheld, however, by Napoleon III, who informs the Vietnamese Emperor that Cornulier-Lucinière speaks in his name. Upon receiving the news of the Franco-German War on August 5, 1870, he declared a state of emergency and prepared defenses against a possible attack by Prussian ships. In ill health, he asked to be relieved of his command in

December, 1870. After a long convalescence in France, he was put into the reserve in 1873; Mayor of Nantes in 1874. In Cochinchina, he advocated a liberalism unusual for his time, as testified to in the following letter addressed to a complainant: "In your letter you complain about the latitude given the natives occasionally to set off firecrackers in public. We occupy this country under a treaty by which we are bound not to offend Buddhist customs. Even if this were not the case, we would have to abide by this duty, if merely for political reasons. The use of firecrackers, dear to that religion, is reserved for some high holidays. It would be impossible to forbid it entirely without committing the gravest offense. Two races of such differing, even opposing, customs, living side by side, tend mutually to embarrass each other. But they must tolerate each other's habits. The natives suffer our horses, our carriages, our police regulations, which contradict theirs. We suffer, from time to time, from their firecrackers. The kind of equality you demand asks all for us and nothing for them." (Written September 16, 1870, to M. H. Semanne.)

April, 1871
to March, 1874
JULES-MARIE DUPRÉ: Rear Admiral; Governor. Born November, 1813; died February, 1881. Navy career man. Under Admiral Cécille, took part in *démarche* at Tourane; Antilles, 1848–51; action in the Crimea; Chief, Bureau of Fleet Operations 1858–61. In 1862, signed a treaty of commerce with king of Madagascar, whom this treaty cost his life. Governor of Réunion Island in 1864; Rear Admiral in 1867; in China during the massacre of Tientsin and during the Franco-German War. Dupré brought about a number of reforms and innovations in Cochinchina, such as obligatory vaccination; a study, undertaken by Lurò, Philastre, and Le Grand de la Liraye, of public schools; a college to train administrators (Collège des Stagiaires); the creation of a civil corps of administrators. His order to Francis Garnier to come to the aid of the trader Dupuis in Tongking resulted in the Philastre treaty of March 15, 1874. Under this treaty, France recognized Hue's suzerainty over Tongking, and Hanoi, Qui Nhon, and Haiphong opened up to foreign commerce. Recalled to France by a displeased government. Vice Admiral and Prefect, 1875; retired, 1878.
"Nothing is more sensitive than a change of customs, religion, and legislation of a people. It is a question of time. New ideas must infiltrate slowly, over successive generations. . . . Such as it is, with all its imperfections, the Annamite legislation, based on the Chinese, is far from being a barbaric and despicable work. . . . To attempt changing it in its totality . . . would mean a revolutionary act that would profoundly trouble the country and push it toward insurrection. . . . My conscience will not let me accept this responsibility." (From a letter written July 21, 1873, to the Minister of the Navy.)

March, 1874
to December, 1874
JULES-FRANÇOIS-ÉMILE KRANTZ: Rear Admiral; Interim Governor. Born December, 1821; died February, 1914. Navy career man. Nominated to his post against his wishes, Krantz concluded a commercial treaty with Hue

in August, complementing the political treaty obtained by Dupré. Navy Minister in 1888-89.

December, 1874
to October, 1877
BARON VICTOR-AUGUST DUPERRÉ: Rear Admiral; Titulary Governor. Born 1825; died 1900. In complete disagreement with the policy of expansion in Tongking, Duperré did nothing to further commercial relations with the north. Instead, he turned his attention on Cambodia, where he sought to institute certain reforms, and on Saigon in particular, where he built the cathedral and helped the creation of the Bank of Indochina.

October, 1877
to July, 1879
COUNT LOUIS-CHARLES LAFONT: Rear Admiral; last military governor. Born April, 1825; died February, 1908. Navy career man. Took part in the conquest of Saigon, 1859; aide-de-camp to Rigault de Genouilly. As Governor, Lafont clashed with Paris over his tax reforms. His efforts to help the small landowners were hampered by the absence of registration records, which permitted the rich landowners to claim a minimum of property under cultivation. He reduced the tax on land property and introduced instead a tax on rice export, the exclusive undertaking of large land-owners. Although the Minister of the Navy Jaureguiberry favored a tax on rice export, he wished it applied only to rice processed by Chinese and carried on foreign ships, exempting French manufacturers and ships from such a tax. When the difference of opinion between Lafont and Jaureguiberry reached a stalemate, Lafont asked to be recalled and Jaureguiberry, eager to replace the military with civil administrators, accepted it quickly.
"I am taking the liberty to point out to you that if, as you inform me, the budget for 1880 must be drawn up in piasters, the revenue of the colony in francs will be drastically reduced. For obviously the piaster must be given a rate that will come closer to the actual value than 5.35 francs, which is the nominal rate today. Moreover, the colony will have to support a loss of 1.5 million–1.8 million francs in the treasury. These are charges which must be supported, and Cochinchina would find herself unable to do so if her resources are reduced." (From a letter written May 3, 1879, to the Minister of the Navy.)

July, 1879
to January, 1883
CHARLES-MARIE LE MYRE DE VILERS: First Civil Governor. Born February, 1833; died in 1918. Began his career in the navy, but left it in 1861 to enter government service as Deputy Commissioner; Commissioner in Algiers in 1869. Re-entered the navy to participate in the 1870 war; Director of Civil and Financial Affairs in Algiers in 1873. During his governorship, Cochinchina was completely pacified and economically on the upswing. As Lafont before him, he tried to protect the small property owners from an undue tax burden by advocating a fairer distribution of taxes. He unsuccessfully recommended a net of railroad lines. He reorganized the Service of Public Works, giving new impetus to maritime commerce by improved coastal and river service. Of the railroads, only

the Saigon-Mytho line was installed, a "toy offered the curiosity of the natives," as one member of the newly created Colonial Council put it (February 8, 1880). He opened a Court of Appeal designed to check the abuses of the population prevalent under the judicial system introduced by the admirals. He also helped set up numerous surveys in Laos and Cambodia, particularly the Pavie mission. Aware of the growing demand since 1880 for intervention in Tongking, he dispatched Captain Rivière in March, 1882, to guard French commercial interests against the increasing incursions by Chinese pirates. While Rivière, toward the end of 1882, waited for de Vilers' orders to continue his temporarily halted conquest because negotiations were going on both with Hue and with China, de Vilers clashed with the Naval Minister Jaureguiberry over questions of policy. Jaureguiberry wished to take over and occupy Tongking by force, whereas de Vilers favored a policy of peaceful infiltration. Deprived of his military command, de Vilers requested to be recalled. However, another version states that he was summarily recalled by the Minister under the pretext that de Vilers had sent home an official sent out by the Minister. Only after de Vilers left for France did Rivière renew his military campaign, during the course of which he was killed. French military action in Tongking, however, resulted in the Harmand negotiations with Hue in August, 1883, and in the preliminary arrangement to declare Tongking a French protectorate. Minister Plenipotentiary and Resident General in Madagascar from 1886–89; Deputy for Cochinchina in Paris from 1889–1902; in charge of mission to Bangkok in 1893, where, as Minister Plenipotentiary, he signed the treaty of October 3 in which Thailand renounced her interests in Laos. He withdrew from political life in 1902.
"We must extend and consolidate our influence in Tongking and Annam politically, peacefully, administratively." (From de Vilers' instructions to Rivière, January, 1882.)

January, 1883
to August, 1885
   CHARLES-ANTOINE-FRANCIS THOMSON: Governor. Born September, 1835; died July, 1898. Worked in the Ministry of Finance from 1864 to 1870. Underprefect and Prefect from 1870 to 1880; named Governor of Cochinchina November 7, 1882, and representative of France to Annam and Cambodia in March, 1883. Undistinguished in his administration of Cochinchina, he forced Cambodia to a new treaty which caused rebellions lasting from 1885 to 1887, and advocated the bombing of Hue, which Courbet carried out. Rivière's chief after de Vilers' departure, he sent troops and arms to resume the conquest. The Patenôtre treaty of May 7, 1885 (the earlier Harmand treaty had not been ratified by Paris) remained the basic point of reference between the French and the Vietnamese until 1945. It was three months after Thomson's arrival in Saigon that the administration of Tongking was taken from the Governor of Cochinchina and handed over to a Civil Commissioner, leaving Thomson in charge of Cochinchina and Cambodia only.

August, 1885
to June, 1886
   CHARLES-AUGUSTE-FRÉDÉRIC BEGIN: Interim Governor. He created a Cambodian regiment and nothing else!

June, 1886
to October, 1887
ANGE FILIPPINI: Governor. Died at his post in Saigon on October 22, 1887. He managed to assuage the Cambodian rebellion by diplomatic means.

November, 1887
to January, 1888
LT. PIQUET: Governor.

January, 1888
to August, 1888
AUGUSTE-EUGÈNE NAVELLE: Interim Governor. Post abolished April 12, 1888. Reinstated May 16, 1889.

Of the governors of Cochinchina since May, 1889, none reached further prominence in Vietnam's history. For the student interested in their listing, however, the names are given in Antoine Brébion, *Dictionnaire de bio-bibliographie générale, ancienne et moderne de l'Indochine française* (Paris, 1935). The source of the letters quoted is Georges Taboulet, *La geste française en Indochine*, Vol. II (Paris, 1956).

ANNAM AND TONGKING

Chronological List of the Chargés d'Affaires and Commanders in Chief from 1875 to 1884

July, 1875
to January, 1877
PIERRE-PAUL RHEINART: Chargé d'Affaires. Born November, 1840; died 1902. Saint-Cyr; military until April, 1864; Inspector for Native Affairs, 1865. In 1869, he undertook an exploration of lower Laos, to study the navigability of the Mekong River and its tributaries. After the Philastre treaty in 1874, he was sent to Hanoi as the French representative. Left his post in Hue because of "constant insults" by the population.

January, 1877
to July, 1879
PAUL-LOUIS-FÉLIX PHILASTRE: Chargé d'Affaires. Born February, 1837; died September, 1902. A graduate of the Naval School, he came to Indochina in 1861; Inspector for Native Affairs at Mytho, January, 1863; Chief for Native Law, June, 1868; promoted to Inspector for Native Affairs in 1873. In December, 1873, he went to Tongking with Tu Duc's representative to investigate the "Dupuis and Garnier" affair. Arriving shortly after Garnier's death, he arranged for the withdrawal of the French from the Hanoi citadel and made the preliminary arrangements for the treaty of 1874. Representative of the Protectorate in Cambodia in 1876. Returning to civil life in France in 1879, he lectured on mathematics from 1882 to 1894. Expert on the Chinese language, he translated the Annamite Code and Commentaries, which earned him the Stanislas Julien prize of 1877.

July, 1879
to October, 1880
PIERRE-PAUL RHEINART (see above): During his second stay in Hue, he again remained in virtual isolation from the court and the Vietnamese.

A mere bystander, he was aware of Tu Duc's negotiations with Bangkok, Spain, and China, which resulted in a commercial treaty with Spain and China's dispatch of troops into Tongking.

October, 1880
to August, 1881
   LOUIS-EUGÈNE DE CHAMPEAUX: Chargé d'Affaires. Born January, 1840; died June, 1889. A graduate of the Naval Academy, he entered the administration of Cochinchina in January, 1866. In 1867, he became an Inspector "Stagiaire," i.e., a graduate of the special school for administrators. In October, 1866, he was sent by de la Grandière to the two sons of Phan Than Gian, who were believed to be on the verge of joining a group of insurgents; they kept him hostage for some time, although they treated him well. In 1880, he became Head of the Conscription Bureau in Saigon, and the same year was sent to Hue. In 1882, Consul at Haiphong; in 1883, he accompanied Dr. Harmand to Hue. After a falling-out with Harmand, he returned to France in 1884, to be sent back to Hue in March, 1885, to replace Lemaire. He returned to France in October, 1885. Nominated Resident Superior in Cambodia in November, 1887, he stayed there until May, 1889. Falling ill, he took home leave and died at his hotel in Marseilles the day after his arrival.

August, 1881
to April, 1883
   PIERRE-PAUL RHEINART (see above): As France decided to move into Tongking, Rheinart demanded of Tu Duc the disarmament of the Hanoi citadel. When the French moved in more troops after Rivière's death and continued their conquest, Rheinart broke off relations with the court and left Hue.

June, 1883
to October, 1883
   DR. FRANÇOIS-JULES HARMAND: General Commissioner. Born October, 1845; died January, 1921. Anthropologist, diplomat, physician. Went to Cochinchina in 1865 as Assistant Doctor in the Navy; returned to Paris in 1868 to complete his studies; took part in the Baltic campaign of 1870; went to Africa in 1871, and from there back to Cochinchina. Sent to Tongking in 1873, together with Francis Garnier, where he made himself Governor of Nam Dinh during the course of Garnier's military exploits; obtained his medical doctorate in 1875; became a member of the archeological commission for Cambodia and traveled through Indochina until 1877 collecting Khmer inscriptions. In 1878, he arranged the Indochinese section of the Paris World's Fair of 1878, which won him the nomination for the Vice-Presidency of the Commercial Society of Geography. Commissioner and Consul in Bangkok in 1882; sent to Hue in 1883 to negotiate the Protectorate. After sharp clashes between him and the military, he was recalled to France. Consul General in Bangkok in 1884; Consul General in Calcutta in 1885; honorary Minister Plenipotentiary in Tokyo in 1894; retired with title of Ambassador. Author of numerous publications. Dr. Harmand was the first Civil Commissioner whose authority was independent of the Governor of Cochinchina.

October, 1883
to February, 1884

AMÉDÉE-ANATOLE-PROSPER COURBET: Rear Admiral; Commander in Chief of Land and Sea Forces. Born June, 1827; died June, 1885. Entered the navy 1849; Commander in Chief of naval forces off Annam in June, 1883; bombarded Hue August 20. On October 25, he won out over Harmand and was given freedom of action and complete command in Tongking. Engaged China and the Vietnamese in military actions until April, 1885. His health undermined, he died in the Pescadores, in sight of the Port of Makung, which he had taken in March.

February, 1884
to September, 1884

CHARLES-THÉODORE MILLOT: General; Commander in Chief of the Expeditionary Corps in Tongking. Born June, 1829; died May, 1889. Saint-Cyr graduate. Sent to Cochinchina in 1861. After taking over the command of the land forces in Tongking from Courbet, he conquered it completely. He had himself represented as Commander in Chief in Tongking at the crowning of Ham Nghi. He attempted to occupy Langson, Thut Ke and Caobang which, in accordance with the Patenôtre treaty, were to be evacuated by the Chinese. His defeat at Bac Le, together with ill-health, made him request his recall to France.

September, 1884
January, 1885
to June, 1885

LOUIS-ALEXANDRE BRIÈRE DE L'ISLE: General; Commander in Chief of the Expeditionary Corps in Tongking. Born June, 1827; died June, 1896. Saint-Cyr graduate. Came to Cochinchina in 1861. In January, 1863, he became Inspector 2nd Class for Native Affairs. Governor in Senegal in 1877; Brigadier General in 1884. When during the course of an offensive against the Chinese in March, 1885, General Négrier became wounded and the battle appeared lost at Langson, de l'Isle wired Paris the news of the retreat from Langson. This news caused the Ferry government to fall.

2

Chronological List of the Residents General and the Residents Superior from 1885 to Doumer's administration. (In June, 1885, the Chargés d'Affaires and Commanders in Chief assumed the title and functions of Resident General.)

June, 1885
to February, 1886

COUNT PHILIPPE-MARIE-HENRI ROUSSEL DE COURCY: General. Born May, 1827; died November, 1887. Saint-Cyr graduate. Took part in the campaigns in the Crimea, China, Italy, Mexico, Gravelotte. Taken prisoner by the Germans at Metz. Observer at the Turco-Russian War. He arrived in Hue to take up his duties, which for two months in 1884 had been held by Lemaire, and since March, 1885, by de Champeaux. The night he arrived the Residence was attacked by Annamite troops. After the abortive attempt to overwhelm the French, the Regent Thuyet fled with Ham Nghi and the Queen Mother. De Courcy handed the task of reorganizing the court to the Second Regent, Nguyen Van Tuong, although Msgr. Puginier and Silvestre warned him against Tuong's duplicity. Tuong, under Courcy's nose, conducted a bloody persecution of the Vietnamese Christians, until an intercepted letter apprised the general of the situation and he banished Tuong to Poulo Condore. A vindictive and self-opinionated man, he dismissed Silvestre from his post as Director of Civil Affairs in Tongking, and withheld all responsibility from de Champeaux and his successor Hector, delegating only some of his military responsibilities to General Prudhomme. When informed of Paul Bert's nomination as Resident General, he left for France without awaiting his successor.

(Beginning with Paul Bert's term, the Residents General came under the jurisdiction of the Minister of Foreign Affairs, rather than the Minister of the Navy and Colonies as heretofore.)

February, 1886
to November, 1886

PAUL BERT: Born October, 1838; died November, 1886. Physician. Professor of Science in Bordeaux and Paris. Entered public life after the 1870 revolution. Prefect; Deputy to Parliament; Minister of Education. Chosen as Resident General because of his enormous prestige. The originator of the policy of pacification in Annam and Tongking, and, in the tradition of de la Grandière, a firm believer in association. Miss Thompson described Bert's tenure as follows: "Bert's achievements were remarkable for so short a tenure of office. His principal reform was a return to the Protectorate ideal in Annam, by governing through the Scholars and the Emperor, whose prestige and power he partially restored. In Tonkin, however, he favored direct administration. He did not break with French policy in this matter, and by transferring the imperial power to a viceroy, the *kinh-luoc* of Tonkin, he completed the administrative break between the two Annamite countries. . . . He was the first organizer of Indochinese education. . . . To this end he founded the Tonkinese Academy. . . . A Council of Tonkinese Notables was another of the republican ideas which Bert introduced into the government. . . . It was part of his program to do away with intermediaries between the government and the people, but he died before this idea was carried out. Like so much of his work, it had to wait years before his successors actively appreciated his wisdom and foresight" (*French Indochina*, pp. 70–71). Placing duty above his own welfare, Bert did not keep to his bed, as ordered by his doctor, after having caught a fever when traveling from Hue to Hanoi with Klobukowski, his brother-in-law and Chief of Cabinet, through torrential rains; instead he traveled to several places to put in a scheduled official appearance. When he broke down en route, and was returned to Hanoi, he continued to attend to his work while under doctor's care; when his condition became critical he exchanged telegrams with Paris in which he discussed the question of his successor. His last message to the Minister was a request for funds to build an electric station on the Red River, which he signed with the words: "Answer quickly. My days are numbered. Thanks." (Cited by Mrs. Klobukowski-Bert, *Indochine française,* October, 1945.)

The Residents General after Paul Bert succeeded each other in rapid order.

November, 1886
to February, 1887
PAULIN VIAL: Interim Resident General. Recommended by Paul Bert as his successor.

February, 1887 to
September, 1887
PIERRE-LOUIS-GEORGES BIHOUARD: Resident General.

September, 1887
to November, 1887
BERGER: Interim Resident General.

November, 1887
PIERRE-LOUIS-GEORGES BIHOUARD: Resident General.

November, 1887
to July, 1888
BERGER: Interim Resident General.

November, 1887
to May, 1888
PIERRE-LOUIS-GEORGES RICHAUD: Resident General. (Apparently never got to his post.)

July, 1888
to September, 1888
PERREAU: Interim Resident General.

September, 1888
to June, 1889
PIERRE-PAUL RHEINART: Resident General.
On May 10, 1889, the position of Resident General for Annam and Tongking was abolished and the positions of Resident Superior for Annam and Resident Superior for Tongking created. From then on the offices of Residents fell under the jurisdiction of the Governor General for Indochina. (In October, 1887, the post of Governor General and a Council were created, administered by the Colonial Minister.)

3

Governors General of Indochina
(1887–1945)

(The Indochinese Union was established by decree on October 17, 1887.)

(For the sake of clarity, names of interim Governors General who substituted for titular Governors General still in office are not given in this list. The given dates of tenure approximate the actual arrivals at and departures from the post. However, interim Governors at times assumed the titular Governor's duties while the latter was officially still in his post. This is disregarded here.)

November, 1887
to March, 1888
JEAN-ANTOINE-ERNEST CONSTANS: Provisional Governor General; lawyer and industrialist; Associate Professor of Law at Toulouse University in 1870; 1875–1901, Deputy from Toulouse; Minister of the Interior in 1880 and 1882; June, 1886–July, 1887, Envoy and Minister Plenipotentiary to China; resigned from his post as Governor General; 1889–92 Minister of the Interior; 1890–1909, Ambassador to Constantinople; died in Paris in 1913.
"His successor, Richaud, violently criticized his administration in Tongking, and it is said that Richaud assembled very compromising documents against Constans, which disappeared at Richaud's death" (Brébion, *op. cit.*, p. 93).

April, 1888
to May, 1889
ÉTIENNE-ANTOINE-GUILLAUME RICHAUD: Interim Governor General until September, then confirmed as Governor General; Inspector for the Navy from 1880 to 1884, when nominated Governor of India; Governor of Réunion Island in 1887; Resident General for Annam and Tongking from November, 1887, to April, 1888. During his administration in Indochina the French were ceded the rights to Hanoi, Haiphong, and Tourane by Emperor Ham Nghi's successor, Dong Khanh. Richaud died during his return trip to France, on-board ship.
"Recalled, following his disagreement with Constans, and because he had made the true situation in Tongking known in France, the deplorable state to which the disastrous administration of that person had brought it. His departure provoked general protests and Indochina's indignation with the proceedings of Constans, then Minister of the Interior" (Brébion, *op. cit.*, p. 325).

May, 1889
to April, 1891
PIQUET: So pale a memory left this Governor General that posterity does not record his given name, a fate generally reserved to some of the interim Governors. He is best known for the closing of gambling houses and for his misrepresentation of the troubled state of affairs in Tongking to the Paris government.
"In order to keep their remunerative positions, many of the civil officials insisted that the country was pacified. Governor Picquet [Miss Thompson's version of Piquet's name] was one of the worst offenders in distorting such facts in his reports to the Metropole—notably in suppressing news of the ambush at Cho-Bo [January, 1891], which had been partly due to his negligence" (Virginia Thompson, *French Indochina*, p. 73).

April, 1891
to June, 1891
BIDEAU: Interim Governor General.

June, 1891
to December, 1894

JEAN-MARIE-ANTOINE DE LANESSAN: Born January, 1843; died 1919. A physician, he served in the Navy; explorer; Professor at the Faculty of Science, Paris. Came to Cochinchina in 1868; stayed at Bienhoa. In 1873, he received a bronze medal for his doctoral thesis; in 1880, the government sent him on a study mission of the French colonies, which took him again to Cochinchina in 1886. During his administration, he attempted to restore the direct administration of Vietnam to the mandarins; in his struggle with the Cochinchinese *colons* he fell ill and went to Japan from March to October, 1894. (Chevassieu took his place during that period as Interim Governor.) Shortly thereafter he was "brutally dismissed" (André Masson, *Histoire de l'Indochine,* p. 97), and recalled, having been officially accused of divulging state secrets; served as Minister of the Marine from 1899 to 1902. In his last years he devoted himself to scientific and economic writings.

"It is not enough that the government formulate a fixed policy. What is also needed is that it choose for the implementation of this policy men who are capable of understanding and determined to follow it—not because they have their instructions but because they find them good" (de Lanessan, *La colonisation française en Indochine,* p. 160).

"The new governor general had too great a knowledge of colonial affairs not to realize, like Paul Bert, that nothing could be achieved in Indochina without the cooperation of the indigenous authorities" (Jean B. Alberti, *L'Indochine d'autrefois et d'aujourd'hui,* p. 365).

December, 1894
to March, 1895

FRANÇOIS RODIER: Interim Governor General.

March, 1895
to December, 1896

PAUL-ARMAND ROUSSEAU: Born August, 1835; died December, 1896. Trained as construction engineer, he served briefly as such in the army from 1870–71 with the rank of colonel. Turned politician at thirty-six, he became a Deputy to the National Assembly and held posts in the Ministry for Public Works and in the Ministry for Maritime Affairs and Colonies. He was appointed Governor General in December, 1894. It was under him that Gallieni and his group undertook their pacification activities in Tongking and successfully dealt with the suppression of Tongking's rebels and pirates. He died in Hanoi of a tropical fever.

"Rousseau proposed and obtained the creation of an *ad hoc* Tribunal, the Criminal Commission, composed of two Residents, one magistrate, and one military officer," which was later to raise Vietnamese resentment of French arbitrary judicial practices (Alberti, *op. cit.,* p. 367).

For writings about Rousseau, see F. de Dartein, *La vie et les travaux d'Armand Rousseau, gouverneur général de l'Indochine* (Paris, 1902); "Armand Rousseau, son administration en Indochine," by X (extracts from the weekly debates), *Courrier d'Haiphong,* May 31, 1902.

December, 1896
to February, 1897

JULIEN FOURES: Interim Governor General.

February, 1897
to March, 1902
PAUL DOUMER: Born March, 1857. Self-educated, he received a degree in the sciences and law. He entered politics through journalism, having been chief editor of the *Tribune de Saint-Quentin*, then cabinet chief to Floquet. In 1888, he was elected Deputy as a Radical; from May, 1895 to April, 1896, was Minister of Finance in the Bourgeois Cabinet. His career was furthered by a tax reform project he sponsored which aroused heated arguments. It was then that he advocated a loan to the Tongking administration to further major public works there. His nomination to Governor General was partly due to the desire of his opponents to re-move him from the political scene in Paris. As Governor General, his main concern was financial reform and public works. He created the famed Far Eastern French School. Upon his return to France, he renewed his domestic political career and was given various high posts, e.g., Chief of Civil Service to General Gallieni in September, 1914; head of a mission to Russia in 1915; Minister of Finance under Briand in 1921 and again in 1925; and President of the Senate in 1927. He became, in 1931, President of the Republic, and was assassinated while in office, on May 6, 1932. "Doumer's greatest contribution was his freeing of the colony from Parisian supervision, by making it economically self-sufficient" (Thompson, *op. cit.*, p. 79).

March, 1902
to October, 1902
BRONT: Interim Governor General.

October, 1902
to February, 1908
JEAN-BAPTISTE-PAUL BEAU: Born in 1857; died in 1926. Lawyer; joined the Ministry for Foreign Affairs in 1883; Third Embassy Secretary in Rome in 1892; 1894–95, Associate Chief of Cabinet, Minister Plenipoten-tiary and Envoy Extraordinary to Peking in 1901, where he signed the final protocol that closed the negotiations after the Boxer Rebellion. During his tenure as Governor General, the provinces of Battambang, Siemriep, and Sisophon were restored to Cambodia, and the railroad from Laokay to Yunnan Fou was constructed. He opened the first Indochinese university. His aim in Indochina was the "moral conquest" of the Vietnamese. He opened up participation in the administration to Vietnamese, even though only in the lowest ranks, organized medical assistance, and abolished certain corporal punishments. After his recall to France, he became Minister Plenipotentiary in Brussels; he was given the title of Honorary Governor General.
"The Governor General [Beau] had to have courage to impose his re-forms, timid as they were, on a colonial milieu still deeply possessed by an irrational fear of the natives" (Paul Isoart, *Le phénomène national Vietnamien*, p. 211).
A two-volume review of Beau's administration entitled *Situation de l'Indochine française* was published in Saigon in 1908.

February, 1908
to September, 1909
GABRIEL C. A. BONHOURE: Interim Governor General.

September, 1908
to February, 1911

ANTONI-WLADISLAS KLOBUKOWSKI: Born 1855; died 1934. Diplomat and lawyer. In government service since 1873, he became Chief of Cabinet to Governor Thomson of Cochinchina in 1880. After Klobukowski's return to France in 1885, Paul Bert, in February, 1886, chose him as Director of his cabinet and as Resident General in Annam and Tongking. In 1887, he married Bert's second daughter; that same year he was nominated Secretary General of the Indochina government. From 1889 to 1894 he was Consul and Consul General in Yokohama, and was transferred to Calcutta in 1896. In 1901, he became Minister Resident in Bangkok, was sent to Lima in 1903, to Cairo in 1906, and to Ethiopia in 1907. In 1908, he was attached to the Ministry of Colonies and nominated Governor General of Indochina. After his tour of duty in Indochina he went to Brussels as Minister Plenipotentiary, where he replaced Paul Beau.
"The reorganization of the General Services and the *Régies* turned those whose interests were at stake against the Governor General, and he was recalled in 1911" (Henri Brunschwig, *La colonisation française*, p. 193). "If his work was more courageous than effective, he was the first to attack seriously the evils which Doumer had allowed to take root in the colony" (Thompson, *op. cit.*, p. 86).
(Cf. Saumont, *L'œuvre de Klobukowski*, Paris, 1910.)

February, 1911
to November, 1911

PAUL LOUIS LUCE: Interim Governor General.

November, 1911
to November, 1913

ALBERT SARRAUT: Born 1872; died 1962. A liberal leader of the Radical Socialists. He was a Deputy from 1902 to 1924, and a Senator from 1924 to 1940. He held numerous cabinet posts between 1906 and 1940, such as Minister of Colonies in 1923, and was twice Premier, in 1933 and again in 1936. In 1937, he headed a Commission of Coordination for North Africa, following the nationalist uprising in Morocco. After the shooting of his brother Maurice in 1943 by Vichy militia, he took over his brother's newspaper, *La Dépêche de Toulouse*. He was deported from France in 1944 and 1945. In 1947, he became first a member, and then, in 1951, President of the Assembly of the French Union; Jean Sainteny was his son-in-law.
"Through his native policy, Sarraut became the successor to Bert, de Lanessan, and Beau, and was the first Governor General to win native devotion. His first governorship remains green in Annamite memory as that of the most popular man France ever sent to the colony" (Thompson, *op. cit.*, p. 88). (Cf. Sarraut, *La mise en valeur des colonies françaises*, and *L'Indochine*, also *Grandeur et servitudes coloniales*.)

January, 1914
to March, 1915

JOOST VAN VOLLENHOVEN: First Interim Governor, then appointed Governor General when a severe illness forced Sarraut to return to France. Van Vollenhoven "was a victim of local press attacks, and felt compelled to return to France to vindicate his patriotism by being killed at the Front" (Thompson, *op. cit.*, p. 89).

March, 1915
to April, 1916
ERNEST-NESTOR ROUME: It was he who before his departure from Indochina deposed the young king, Duy Tam, who had tried to provoke a rebellion against the French.
"Roume was too ill to undertake the task effectively, and his place was assumed by Charles" (Thompson, *ibid.*, p. 89).

May, 1916
to January, 1917
Eugène-Jean Charles: Interim Governor General.

January, 1917
to May, 1919
Sarraut returns as Governor General.
"Cynics refer to Sarraut's governorship as the era of discourses, and it is true that both he and the Annamites were genuinely moved by his meridional eloquence. Despite certain accomplishments in the labor and educational fields, Sarraut sailed away, and little was ever heard thereafter of those liberal projects, even after he had become Minister of the Colonies. Like the Girondists, he was the first to recoil before the excesses of a nationalism which he had stimulated" (Thompson, *ibid.*, pp. 90–91).
He was Chairman of the Pau Conference in June, 1950, which "when it ended five grueling months later, on November 27, . . . had thoroughly soured the three Indochinese states on each other and on France" (Bernard B. Fall, *The Two Viet-Nams*, p. 217).

May, 1919
to February, 1920
MAURICE-ANTOINE-FRANÇOIS MONGUILLOT: Interim Governor General; he was made Resident Superior in Tongking under the next Governor General, Maurice Long.

February, 1920
to January, 1923
MAURICE LONG: Born March, 1866; died January 15, 1923 while returning to Indochina from France, where he had stayed in 1922 to deal with projects concerning the colony. Lawyer and editor of law journal; Radical Socialist. Long parliamentary career, with specialization in Moroccan affairs; former Minister of Food; particularly interested in financial and economic affairs.

April, 1922
to August, 1923
ROGER-VICTOR-JOSEPH DE BELLEVAL BAUDOUIN: Interim Governor General during Long's absence and after his death until arrival of new Governor General Merlin.

August, 1923
to July, 1925
MARTIAL-HENRI MERLIN: Well-received in Indochina because of his reputation as Governor in French Africa, he was recalled when he turned out

to be highly unpopular in Indochina and because he was unable to solve the financial deficit of the colony.

July, 1925
to November, 1925
M. A. F. MONGUILLOT: Interim Governor General.

November, 1925
to January, 1928
ALEXANDRE VARENNE: Former Vice President in the Chamber of Deputies, he was known for his quick intelligence, and his capacity for work. A Socialist, inexperienced in colonial affairs, he held liberal opinions and possessed financial know-how, which made him succeed where Merlin had failed. With his decree of November 29, 1926, Varenne created the nucleus of a cadre of Vietnamese military officers.
"It was in the field of native policy, however, that Varenne's work was outstanding. Like Sarraut, his sincere desire to ameliorate native conditions won him great popularity" (Thompson, *op. cit.*, p. 93).

January, 1928
to August, 1928
M. A. F. MONGUILLOT: Interim Governor General.

August, 1928
to December, 1928
EUGÈNE-LOUIS-JEAN-RENÉ ROBIN: Interim Governor General.

December, 1928
to January, 1934
PIERRE PASQUIER: Born February, 1877; died in an airplane crash January 15, 1934. A graduate of the Colonial School, and a former collaborator of Sarraut and Varenne, he served as Interim Governor General in 1926, having spent his entire career in Indochina, successively as an administrator in the Civil Service, Director of Cabinet, and Resident Superior in Annam. When Bao Dai returned to Vietnam in 1932 to assume the throne, Pasquier clashed with the young Emperor, who sought to inaugurate reforms not approved by the Governor General.

January, 1934
to June, 1934
GRAFFEUIL: Interim Governor General.

July, 1934
to September, 1936
EUGÈNE-LOUIS-JEAN-RENÉ ROBIN: A functionary of long standing in the colony, Robin took Pasquier's place during the latter's frequent absences. He had been Resident Superior of Tongking.
Robin "saw his task mainly as a matter of 'repressing agitation'" (Fall, *op. cit.*, p. 37).

September, 1936
to January, 1937
SILVESTRE: Interim Governor General.

January, 1937
to August, 1939
JULES BREVIÉ: A former West African administrator.

"In rapid succession, he rammed through an amnesty that reduced the number of political prisoners from 10,000 to 3,000 . . . including most of Viet-Nam's present Communist leadership; he modified the tax base so as to reduce the excessive load on the poorer sections of the population; he greatly simplified acquisition of French citizenship by Vietnamese; and in Cochinchina he authorized political parties and their newspapers to operate openly" (Fall, *ibid.*, p. 38).

August, 1939
to July, 1940
GEORGES CATROUX: Born in 1877. Graduate of Saint-Cyr; served in Morocco and Indochina. A diplomat-soldier, he was sent on missions to the Near East in 1919, 1922, and 1950. After being replaced as Governor General of Indochina by Decoux, he went to London to join de Gaulle's Free French forces and was nominated High Commissioner to the National Liberation Committee and Governor General of Algiers. In 1944, he became Minister for North Africa. From 1945 to 1948, he served as French Ambassador to Moscow. He became a high-ranking officer in the Legion of Honor in 1954, and in 1955 negotiated for the French government the return of Mohammed V to Morocco.
"For the first time since 1880, the supreme responsibilities of Indochina were assumed by a military man" (Philippe Devillers, *Histoire du Vietnam*, p. 72).
See Georges Catroux, *Deux actes du drame indochinois; J'ai vu tomber le rideau de fer* (1945–1948); *Lyautey le Marocain; Dans la bataille de la Méditerranée* (1940–44); *Deux missions en Moyen-Orient* (1919–1922).

July, 1940
to March, 1945
ADMIRAL JEAN DECOUX: Born 1884. Commander in Chief of the French Far Eastern Fleet in 1939. A proud, autocratic man with strong rightist views and a temperament similar to that of "Le Grand Charles," he was unable to make his peace with de Gaulle upon his return to France in October, 1945. After his return he was tried on charges of collaboration with the Vichy government, and in 1949, he was pronounced not guilty.
"Indochina's future is again going to offer practically unlimited possibilities on the day when that country, so prosperous in my time, finally re-establishes peace, raises itself from the ruins, and gets back to work" (Decoux, *A la barre de l'Indochine*, p. 489).

4

High Commissioners and Commissioners General of Indochina
(1945–55)

August, 1945
to March, 1947
ADMIRAL GEORGES THIERRY D'ARGENLIEU: First High Commissioner to Indochina. Born 1889; died in 1964. Graduate of Naval Academy. On active military duty from 1912 through World War I. He entered the Carmelite Order in 1920. In 1932, became Provincial of that order. At the outbreak of World War II, he returned to active duty with the rank of

Lt. Commander. Captured in 1940, he escaped and joined de Gaulle in London. Appointed High Commissioner for the Pacific, Commander in Chief of Free French Naval Forces stationed in Britain, Assistant Chief of Free French General Staff, and, in early 1945, Vice President of the Board of Admiralty and Inspector of Naval Forces. Promoted to Admiral in 1943. After coming back from Indochina, he returned to the religious life, but retained his function as Grand Chancellor of the Order of Liberation until 1958.

"Fiercely loyal to de Gaulle, he shared the latter's love for French grandeur but without his breadth of view. D'Argenlieu's was a world strictly of 'good' and 'evil' and 'evil' was to be eradicated, not compromised with" (Fall, *op. cit.*, p. 72).

March, 1947
to October, 1948
ÉMILE BOLLAERT: High Commissioner, he was a delegate for de Gaulle in occupied France; in 1943, he was arrested by the Germans and deported. A radical Socialist, with no experience in foreign affairs but wide experience in domestic civil service.

"It was clear that Bollaert's actions in Vietnam would be less influenced by local realities than by the idea one would have in Saigon of the respective strength of the different metropolitan parties . . . by the progressive evolution toward the center and right of French politics" (Devillers, *op. cit.*, p. 370).

October, 1948
to December, 1950
LÉON PIGNON: High Commissioner. Former political counselor to d'Argenlieu. Strongly anti-Vietminh.

"Pignon was an old Indochina hand from the Colonial Civil Service, and he brought with him a staff of old-line colonial administrators to whom the idea of a truly independent Vietnam meant total chaos" (Fall, *op. cit.*, p. 213).

December, 1950
to December, 1951
JEAN DE LATTRE DE TASSIGNY: "Le roi Jean," as he was called by his troops because of his grandiose style and manners, assumed full military and civilian powers as High Commissioner and Commander in Chief. His illness forced him to return to France, in December, 1951, where he died the following January.

"De Lattre's failure to effect any basic change in strategy which would enable the French Union troops to recover their mobility makes it unlikely that the Expeditionary Corps was deprived of final victory by his death, but if his contribution in the military field was not decisive, his attempt to rally international support for a war which had hitherto lacked its impresario did meet with considerable success" (Donald Lancaster, *The Emancipation of French Indochina*, p. 243).

December, 1951
to April, 1952
GENERAL RAOUL SALAN: Deputy Commander in Chief of de Lattre, he directed all military operations during de Lattre's absence and after his death. Since no civilian interim High Commissioner was appointed

during this period, Salan remained virtually in charge, except for the supervision by the Paris Minister for the Associated States, with whom rested the authority over all military forces serving in Indochina and the responsibility for Indochina's defense.

April, 1952
to June, 1953
JEAN LETOURNEAU: Carried out the dual functions of High Commissioner and Minister for Associated States, with Salan officially appointed as Commander in Chief.
"Since the death of Marshal de Lattre, who had exercised the dual functions of High Commissioner of France and Commander in Chief, the Minister in charge of relations with the Associated States played at the same time the role of High Commissioner. The Commander in Chief depended on him because of his double function" (Henri Navarre, *Agonie de l'Indochine*, p. 3).

July, 1953
to June, 1954
MAURICE DEJEAN: Resident Commissioner General. (In May, 1953, General Navarre succeeded General Salan as Commander in Chief.)
"The civil functions of the High Commissioner of France passed in part to a Commissioner General of France in Indochina and in part to three High Commissioners of the Republic to Vietnam, Laos, and Cambodia. The former military powers of High Commissioner of France were transferred to the Commissioner General, who, according to the terms of the decree (April 27, 1953, Decree No. 53, 365), was 'responsible to the Government of the Republic for the defense and security of Indochina,' and 'had at his disposal particularly toward this end the aid given the Associated States for the defense of the borders of the French Union and the security in Indochina.' These powers made the civil chief a veritable arbiter over military affairs. They were a carry over of the epoch of the Governors General, during which the army had only to assume the minor tasks of maintaining order" (Navarre, *ibid.*, p. 4).

June, 1954
to June, 1955
GENERAL PAUL ELY: Commissioner General and Commander in Chief. General Salan was his military deputy. (When Salan left in September, 1954, he was succeeded by General Jacquot, who stayed on, after Ely's departure, until all Expeditionary Forces had left Vietnam.)
"Decolonization, the most spectacular manifestation of independence, is no doubt the unavoidable and necessary stage on the road to progress after that of colonization, but it runs the risk of going back several centuries and of letting disorder, misery, and anarchy take the place of legality and internal order" (Ely, *L'Indochine dans la tourmente*, p. 252).

July, 1955
HENRI HOPPENOT: Ambassador to the Republic of Vietnam. (Unacceptable to the Diem regime as Commissioner General, Hoppenot retained the title of Commissioner General for Laos and Cambodia.)

Appendix IV

Excerpts from Phan Boi Chau's Writings

In the foreword to *Tu Phan* (*Self-Appraisal*), the grand old Vietnamese revolutionary spoke candidly of himself as a man and political fighter. "My life's story is one of utter defeat," he stated frankly, "brought about by all too obvious shortcomings." These shortcomings he listed as follows: "(1) I have too much faith in myself; I believe that there is nothing under the sun that cannot be done. I failed in properly appraising my own ability and virtue. (2) I tend to be too honest with people; I believe that everyone in the world can be trusted. This shows my lack of shrewdness and cunning. (3) When judging people and events, I pay attention only to large matters and overlook details. All too often therefore I spoiled important undertakings for trifling reasons. This was due to my negligence and lack of caution." Yet, with the indestructible self-confidence that was his, Chau went on to say: "All things considered, I am not without certain redeeming qualities, however small, from which I derive at least some comfort." These qualities he listed as being: "(1) I have great determination and do not fear danger. I am endowed with that undaunted spirit of which Tan Tu said, 'When he deems his cause just, he will sally forth even if thousands of men oppose him.' In my youth, that undaunted spirit was particularly strong. (2) When I hear someone say something wise and edifying, I remember it for the rest of my life. I always welcome forthright criticism, even rebuke, however severe. (3) Once I have set out to achieve something, I keep my eyes fixed on the goal, intent on winning the ultimate victory; but I never hesitate to change my tactics or strategy if need be."

Chau's first major work was the *History of the Downfall of Vietnam.* The book clearly demonstrates his talent for turning history into propaganda. Opening with a survey of all foreign invasions of Vietnam—from pre-Christian times to the French conquest—Chau concluded that the French were able to defeat the Vietnamese because "neither emperors nor subjects were interested in progress, in developing their minds, or in promoting the talents needed to defend and save the country." He saw it thus: "Had the country reorganized the army in time, and had the people been given more political freedom so that emperors and subjects shared the responsibility for running the country; had they tried to learn from the progress of civilization in the world, and rid themselves of obsolete traditions; had they provided themselves with shelters against the forthcoming storm, disaster might have been avoided." Unfortunately, the opposite was the case. "Vietnam was like a man living in a dream, like a sick man whose body was paralyzed. The emperors were venerated as if they were gods, while the people were looked down upon as if they were trash."

Tracing the lives of the major Vietnamese patriots, the *"lettrés,"* or scholars, who held responsible government positions at the time of conquest—some of whom were killed in battle or were executed by the French, and some of whom committed suicide or were thrown into prison —Chau devoted much space to the tragic story of the great Phan Dinh Phung, the scholar who continued the resistance after the Boy-Emperor Ham Nghi was betrayed to the French and taken prisoner. But it was in the following chapter that Chau cried out against French oppression. "For thirty years Vietnam has now suffered wars, floods, conflagrations, and looting, and the country is almost at the limit of its endurance. How can Vietnam continue to stand the devilish stratagems of the French who flay and skin her people every day? Alas, sooner or later Vietnam will cease to exist as a nation!

"I am going to speak of the cruel tricks of the French, even though those who hear me will think I am exaggerating. . . . But I shall speak only of incidents I was told myself, and I will speak only the truth. Mine shall be no vague guesswork, aimed at slandering the French. If there be untruth in my writing, may Heaven and Earth not spare me from punishment."

Chau's anger was chiefly directed against the "traitors," the collaborators among his countrymen. "In the beginning of their conquest, the French used honeyed words and great rewards to entice the Vietnamese. They offered high government positions and benefits of all sorts to make some of us into their hunting dogs." Those they hired were of low character, Chau wrote, ready to commit numerous crimes against the people. "These dogs hunted hard to please their masters. They were like monsters, devoid of all ethics and sense of justice. They were despised by all Vietnamese, but the French held them in high esteem." Accurately defining a main principle of colonial administration, he wrote: "When a cruel deed had to be done, the French used these men to do it." They murdered and stole, but "after having extorted whatever they could, and squeezing the blood from their countrymen, they had to deliver the stained moneybags to the Resident Superior of the Honorable Protectorate Country."

No people in the world, Chau thought, had a more ingenious way of carrying out "obscurantism" than the French colonialists. He accused them of being afraid that the Vietnamese might develop their talents and culture by contact with Western civilization and therefore deliberately keeping the people ignorant and illiterate. He cited the age-old military examinations, which had been abolished; the literary examinations, which were eventually suspended; the schools set up to train nothing but secretaries and interpreters; the limited curriculum, which did not allow for the training of scholars; the refusal to let students study abroad; the punishment meted out to those who violated this prohibition, the young men themselves as well as their families, who faced confiscation of their property for their defiance.

At the end of his book, Chau spoke of Vietnam's future. Visionary in his faith in Vietnam, the author did not believe the country was fated to lose its spirit. History showed, he reasoned, that the dedication and faith of a single great man can save a nation; therefore there was hope for Vietnam's salvation. "The oppressed people will rise up one day and fight for their independence. And on that day, woe to the French!"

All Chau's other books were written in an equally emotional style, whether he denounced the French, scolded his countrymen for clinging to oldfashioned notions of life, or praised the Japanese for adopting Western technology in their development of industry and trade. His books were poor as history, be it ancient or contemporary, but great as propaganda, and they were avidly read by young and old as long as he was an active political force.

Chau's attitude toward the French after 1925 was described by himself in a booklet entitled *Phap Viet De Hue Chinh Kien Thu* (*Opinions on the Policy of Franco-Annamite Collaboration*). He outlined the gist of it in a long letter, dated October, 1931, which he addressed to Paul Reynaud, French Minister of Colonies, then on an inspection tour to Indochina, and which was handed to Mme. Andrée Viollis, a French journalist who accompanied the Minister during his tour and interviewed Chau, who was under house arrest in Hue.

In this letter Chau was as outspoken as he had been in his earlier writings. "Digging up the bodies of his parents and burning them—that was the punishment inflicted on Phan Dinh Phung; the beheading of a man who committed no other crime than being a distinguished scholar and an excellent teacher—that was the penalty imposed on Tran Quy Cap. In all this there is nothing of the principles of the tricolor. I firmly believe that those who perpetrated these crimes were the worst enemies of France. . . . Actually, the Vietnamese cannot hope for anything better than to have the French as their elder brothers. Conversely, the French could show us no greater generosity than to look upon us as their younger brothers. Alas! The French have never wished to have us as brothers.

"I have never known brothers to keep their brothers in eternal ignorance. I have never seen elder brothers take advantage of their strength to oppress their younger brothers. If the French do not bend down to the Vietnamese as their younger brothers, how can the Vietnamese dare to look up to the French as their older brothers? What are we in the eyes of the French? Nothing but beasts of burden, worthless objects. What are the French in the eyes of the Vietnamese? They can only be enemies. . . . Take these last two years. Have people ever seen elder brothers dropping bombs from their planes on the younger brothers who weep and cry out with suffering? Have people ever seen elder brothers machine-gun their younger brothers who gather in their misery so that their screams of distress may be heard by their elder brothers?"

Chau foresaw the possibility of World War II and the importance of Indochina to France in such an event. Fully aware of Vietnam's position, he offered Franco-Vietnamese collaboration as a solution—one he desired "with all my heart." "What will happen to this Indochina without the Vietnamese? If the French were capable of defending it by themselves, the government could continue its policy of systematic extermination. . . . But things will not turn out that way. When war breaks out, our failure to participate will put the French in a very poor position. They cannot defend their own country against the two eventual enemies—Germany and Italy—and at the same time safeguard their colonial possession against their Asian enemies. Why do the French not envisage this eventuality, why do they not seek our sincere collaboration? If they united the strength of twenty million people, would they not obtain a power very useful to France in troubled times? . . . I admit, the true elite of our people ardently wants independence for Vietnam. But this elite is only a minority and this minority has recognized that our present stage of development and the material forces available to us do not yet justify such a theoretical independence. We would slip from the hands of France only to fall into those of another power, which would create an even unhappier situation. I tell you, Mr. Minister, Franco-Vietnamese collaboration is not only useful to you but also a thing we sincerely want. . . .

"Whatever people say, my conscience tells me that I am a loyal friend of France—of a country that has fought for justice and humanity, a country run not by just a government or just a person. My loyalty is for the noble tricolor, the symbol of liberty, equality, and fraternity. This loyalty compels me to long that these principles be translated into reality. It further compels me to defend them and to protest against those who distort or destroy them. Those who distort or destroy these principles are enemies of France. In protesting against them I show the best proof of my deep loyalty toward France. The day when these high principles, symbolized by the tricolor, will be realized in this Indochinese land, that day I will consider myself a criminal deserving of the worst punishment if I should then persist in my present attitude."

When Andrée Viollis saw Chau in 1931, she found him filled with bitterness toward the French. "They treat us like slaves and often like dogs," he said to her. Although he confirmed to her that he desired his country's independence, "we would have forgotten the word independence, had the French treated us decently." "Tell the French people," he urged, "that the old revolutionary Phan Boi Chau sincerely desires loyal collaboration with France. But tell them to hurry or it will be too late. Too late!" At the end of her interview, which Mme. Viollis reported in her book *Indochine S.O.S.* (Paris, 1949), pp. 134, 136, she made this moving observation: "For a long time Phan Boi Chau continued to expound on this familiar subject in a soft, low voice. I gazed at the tiny house of a touching poverty, the humble, pint-sized garden enclosed by a bamboo hedge, and I thought vaguely of the great patriotic names in our history, the crowns, the columns which were dedicated and erected to them. I thought of the writings about the heroes of the Great War, 'Died in Defense of Our Sacred Soil Against the Invader.' And suddenly I felt ashamed before this old, resigned man. I felt sick."

(For the books and pamphlet from which these excerpts are quoted, see Chapter III, nn. 69 and 78. I wish to express my gratitude to Mr. and Mrs. Truong N. Binh and Mr. Huynh Sanh Thong, who translated these extracts from works by Chau and from recent Vietnamese writings about him.)

Appendix V *

The village lay amidst rice fields near a dense forest that offered a convenient escape. At the first sound, Hong Kop tried to flee. But the French barred the forest; the moon shone on two long, watchful columns. The attacking forces moved forward, through the ricefields, their bayonets gleaming Indian-file above their twin advance. All retreat was cut off. Realizing that he was lost, Hong Kop resigned himself. At his orders his men returned to the village, and the fifth act of the dynastic tragedy opened soberly and disdainfully.

The Emperor seated himself amid his court. The neighboring huts were already burning, set on fire. Without declamations, without tears, he drank the tea that brings release. Smiling. When he died none followed his example, for it does not behoove ordinary men to make themselves the equals of princes. But all waited by the body for the enemy to cut them down. There were fifty-eight men and two children, and they offered no futile resistance, careful not to wear themselves out before their death. The order from Paris was to kill the pirates, and the order was carried out.

They were led outside the village into a ricefield, for the village had turned into one giant blaze. They were not manacled and they knelt voluntarily. Correctly. In two lines. The water covering the ricefield came up to their calves. Some lifted their black mandarin robes a little, to avoid contact with the mud. The executioner arrived, a soldier who looked like the condemned, an Annamite with a glossy topknot and with the air of a girl. He grasped the broad sword that cut heads off so well, and they inclined their heads obligingly. The glow cast by the burning village over the strange scene reddened the wet grass on which grotesque shadows performed a dance. Looking pale, the victorious officers looked into the indifferent, ironic eyes of the condemned. One head fell. Two. Forty. The executioner paused to sharpen his blade. The forty-first rebel watched him curiously. The sharpened sword resumed its task. And it ended with the two children.

After that, the soldiers stuck the heads on a picket fence that the fire had spared. As an example. In the nearby forest a tiger, terrified by the red fire, howled like a dog.

Fierce was there. He had to act swiftly, without the support of remote units, and to attain the necessary strength, half of the navy's artillery had been deployed. Fierce commanded that contingent.

Midnight had been sounded. They camped on the spot, in sections, the sailors nearest to the forest. Since it seemed that there was nothing to be feared, only double guards were posted, and the camp lighted fires, too excited and troubled to sleep. The smell of blood permeated their nostrils

* Claude Farrère, *Les civilisés* (Paris, 1921), pp. 239–41. The events on which this description of a punitive action against a local rebellion is based took place shortly before World War I.

as well as did the smell of the Asian village, a disgusting mixture of pepper, incense, and decay. Suddenly a shot rang out from the forest. There was a commotion. Men ran for their weapons. More shots were heard. A sergeant, his thighbone smashed by a bullet, screamed with pain. A guard, mysteriously strangled, fell without the strangler being seen. A panic might have followed had the officers not thrown themselves forward and had not the men followed their example.

Fierce, his sword held low, was first to penetrate the trees. He felt a savage anger, the anger of a beast disturbed in its rest. Furiously he looked for the enemy. But the enemy had fled. The empty forest was quiet like a cemetery. An arroyo ran through its middle; perhaps sampans had carried the fugitives off; nothing was found but some black huts near the water. No sound came from them. Nevertheless, frustration and an urge for violence made them force down the doors, and the sailors threw themselves inside with shouts and blows.

There were women in the huts, cowering in their homes like animals at bay, helpless females, mute and half dead with terror. They killed them without even noticing that they were women. A murderous rage possessed them all—the little Breton fishermen and the peaceful peasants of France; they killed for the sake of killing. They were possessed of a contagious lust for blood.

Fierce also forced a door and looked ferociously for a living prey. He found her barricaded behind two boards, in a roofless retreat pitilessly lit up by the moon: a young Annamite girl hiding under mats. Finding herself discovered, she jumped to her feet, so terrified that she did not even cry out.

He raised his sword. But this was practically a child, and she was almost naked. He could see her breasts and her thighs. She was pretty and fragile, with eyes that implored as they brimmed over with tears. He held himself back. She threw herself at his feet, hugging his hips and knees, beseeching him with sobs and caresses. He felt her hot and shivering pressure against him, and he trembled from head to feet.

Hesitantly his hands touched her sleek hair, the brown, polished shoulders, her breasts. She pressed him to her with all the strength in her thin hands, drawing him over her, offering herself as ransom for her life. He stumbled. Fell on his prey.

The bruised mats rustled softly, and the worm-eaten board creaked. A cloud passed over the moon. The warm hut was like an alcove . . .

Outside, the shouts of the sailors became faint in the distance. The tiger's whining came closer.

Appendix VI

The Recruiting of a Communist

In March, 1930, Vietnamese Communism and nationalism were to come under the scrutiny of a French newspaperman turned writer. On February 11, the news of the Yen Bay uprising had reached France. Some weeks thereafter, the Indochina Student House was opened in Paris in the presence of Doumergue, the President of France, and Bao Dai, the Emperor of Annam. Cries of: "Free the prisoners of Yen Bay!" interrupted the ceremonies. How could the students who had voiced this protest make common cause with the Yen Bay murderers, the newspaperman wondered? He decided to go to Vietnam to find the answer to his question himself.

Louis Roubaud was to publish the results of his on-the-spot inquiry in a book which he called *Viet-Nam: La tragédie indochinoise* (Paris, 1931). In it he made an honest if vain attempt to reconcile French colonial interests with Vietnamese aspirations. But if he arrived at no other conclusion than the rather disconcerting one that Vietnam would never be given independence by France, he seemed to have been sincere enough in his desire to understand the emotion of Vietnamese nationalism to have been allowed a glimpse at some of the inner workings of Communism in Vietnam. According to him it was inevitable that the two should join forces.

Viet Nam Cong San Dang—Society of Communist Patriots of Annam. The name itself, Roubaud wrote, was a concession by the Communists to nationalist sentiments. To be sure, the Viet Nam Cong San Dang was not the only party operating secretly in Vietnam, but it was the strongest, the most active, the most effective. "Every dissatisfaction is channeled through it. . . . The desire of the young for independence, the social idealism of the Annamite students glories in it. . . . The floods, the epidemics, the famines are exploited by it."

Had the Viet Nam Cong San Dang been involved in the Yen Bay uprising? Roubaud was told it had not. "We do not approve of such tactics," he was told. What tactics did the Communists use? "Protest marches. One, two, three thousand unarmed men, women and children in front, to avoid violence. Passive resistance . . . What will you do against 15 million passive men?"

Pham Binh was the name of the young man, a prospective new Party member in 1926, whom Roubaud wrote about. The party rules had been read to little Pham Binh that day. These, among other things, told him what crimes were punishable by death: (1) Going over to the enemy; (2) Acting without orders, thereby jeopardizing the security of one's comrades; (3) Disobeying orders; (4) Plotting the downfall of the Party; (5) Divulging Party secrets. As those before and after him, he had sworn the oath of allegiance: "I will accept punishment in accordance with the rules." He was assigned three aliases, under any one of which he would receive his instructions. The meeting adjourned. He was to return home.

For several days Pham Binh waited anxiously for a letter whose invisible writing, made visible by a solution of iodine and water, would tell him whether he would be allowed to go to Canton, to study there in the Revolutionary School, or whether he would immediately have to join a workers' cell. At last he received word, though not by letter. A man approached him, using a code. Pham Binh was to be sent to Canton.

What had happened to make Pham Binh, formerly a student at the University of Hanoi, abandon his studies and turn Communist? "When Pham Chu Chinh died," he told Roubaud, "I came to class wearing a white armband, like the rest of the students." Pham Chu Chinh, a "sort of retired revolutionary," had died peacefully in his bed of old age. But throughout Vietnam students had come to class that day wearing mourning for the dead nationalist. Little Pham Binh, together with a hundred-odd other students, had been sent home in reprisal. Not knowing what to do with himself, and blamed by his parents for what both he and they considered a humiliating incident, he had gone for a walk in the country. There he had run into another student who until then had been rather aloof. Now he asked Pham Binh: "What are you going to do?" And: "Would you like to go to Canton?"

Canton! The city every young Vietnamese dreamed about. Canton, the seat of the Grand Committee, the site of the tomb of Pham Hong Tai, a young revolutionary, who, in June, 1924, had thrown a bomb at Governor General Merlin while the latter was dining during a visit to Canton. The bomb killed five Frenchmen, but the Governor escaped unharmed. But even so, Pham Hong Tai had become a hero and his tomb—for he had drowned while fleeing—had become the Mecca for Vietnamese nationalists. Go to Canton? Of course Pham Binh would like to go.

In China, so Pham Binh told Roubaud, he felt free for the first time. Dressed in the uniform of a cadet attending the School of Wampoa, he was taught the use of firearms, attended courses in the arts and sciences, and initiated into Sun Yat-sen's doctrine. He was lectured on revolutionary techniques, instructed in the art of oratory, and taught military strategy. Being trained as a propagandist as well as a leader, he was coming to feel as much at home in a coolie's smock as in the tunic of the intellectual. When his training was finished, he was ready to take up the duties of the Party: "To fulfill its mission as revolutionary guide, the Party must send its adherents into the mills, the mines, the fields, and the factories, to organize the workers in combat units disguised as cooperatives, agricultural societies, and workers' syndicates; it must teach the doctrine, disseminate its program, prepare for strikes and for all other methods of economic and political warfare."

The directive, issued by the Communist Congress on October 1, 1930, in Canton, and quoted by Roubaud, spelled out what Pham Binh and his comrades were to bring home to the people. "French imperialism has stolen our country," it read in part, "our ricefields, our mines, our seas, our rivers, our commerce—in short, all our sources of revenue are in its hands. It beats us down with duties and taxes, relentlessly presses us for loans, and pitilessly steals the fruit of our people's labor."

Having cited the political and economic commandments of the Viet Nam Cong San Dang, Roubaud wrote, almost in spite of himself: "With all their exaggerations and their sometime naïveté, these claims respond to the desires and aspirations of the great mass of peasants and workers of the three Annamite peoples."

Because the French would not accede to Vietnam's legitimate claims, such nationalists as little Pham Binh—who later in his life was to defect from Communism—were to return to their homeland with the purpose of entering "what Dr. Sun called *Min chen*, the life of the people." Little did they know that Dr. Sun's *Min chen* was to transform his own country into one vast, joyless slave-labor camp. Or had they known, they might still have replied: "Better to be oppressed by our own than by foreign masters." And with this answer they might have gone on to pursue their tortuous fate as nationalist Communists.

Appendix VII

Political Parties of Vietnam: 1905-66 *

This appendix does not pretend to furnish a complete list of all parties that have ever existed in Vietnam, for this is impossible to establish. Many parties existed only a few months and had no influence at all on the course of events. At least nine out of ten of those here listed were also ephemeral creations, yet important enough to have been recorded by some chroniclers of recent history. The choice of 1905 for the beginning of this chronicle is not an arbitrary one. Although secret societies with strong political leanings have a long history in Vietnam, nothing resembling a modern political party existed before 1905. The large number of parties, groups, "united fronts," etc., does not testify to the vigor of the nationalist movement, but rather shows the inability of its leaders to agree on aims and tactics, to create united organizations, and to subordinate their personal ambitions and prejudices to the need for unified action. (The Hoa Hao and Cao Dai religious-political sects are not listed here, but the parties created by the sects or by factions of them are. No attempt has been made to analyze the groups that constitute the National Liberation Front, nor their degree of dependence on Hanoi.)

1905: Phan Boi Chau and Prince Cuong De found the Viet Nam Duy Tan Hoi (Association for the Modernization of Vietnam) in Formosa.

1911: After the Chinese Revolution, Phan Boi Chau and Cuong De revive their party in Canton, calling it Viet Nam Quang Phuc Hoi (Association for the Restoration of Vietnam), and name Cuong De President of a provisional government.

1923: French-trained, young intellectuals Bui Quang Chieu, Nguyen Phan Long, and Duong Van Giao form the Constitutionalist Party in the South, which demands reforms of the French administration in Vietnam.

* Sources for this appendix: Pierre Dabezies, *Forces politiques au Viet-Nam;* Philippe Devillers, "The Struggle for Unification of Vietnam," in P. J. Honey (ed.), *North Vietnam Today*, pp. 25-46; Devillers, "Vietnamese Nationalism and French Policies," in William L. Holland (ed.), *Asian Nationalism and the West;* Bernard B. Fall, "The Political-Religious Sects of Vietnam," *Pacific Affairs,* September, 1955; Ellen J. Hammer, *Politics and Parties in Vietnam;* Hoang Van Chi, *From Colonialism to Communism;* Donald Lancaster, *The Emancipation of French Indochina;* Nguyen Kien, *Le Sud Viet-Nam depuis Dien Bien Phu;* Nguyen Thai, *Is South Viet-Nam Viable?;* I. Milton Sacks, "Marxism in Vietnam," in Frank N. Trager (ed.), *Marxism in Southeast Asia,* pp. 102-70 and 315-29; Robert Scigliano, *South Vietnam: Nation Under Stress;* Virginia Thompson and Richard Adloff, *The Left Wing in Southeast Asia.*

1234

Ta Thu Thau, later to become the most outstanding Trotskyist leader, forms an illegal group, Young Annam, in Saigon.

1925: The Phuc Viet (Restoration of Vietnam) is formed in Annam; later it changes its name to Tan Viet Cach Menh Dang (New Vietnam Revolutionary Party). In June, Ho Chi Minh sets up the Viet Nam Cach Menh Thanh Nien Dong Chi Hoi (Vietnam Revolutionary Youth Association) in Canton, and also organizes the League of Oppressed Peoples of Asia, the Comintern Front organization in the Far East.

1926: In September, Pham Quynh, Huynh Thuc Khang, and Le Van Huan formally ask the French for recognition of a reform movement in Tongking and Annam under the name of Viet Nam Tan Bo Dan Hoi (Vietnam People's Progressive Party). Permission is denied. The French crack down on Young Annam (see 1923).

1927: Nguyen Thai Hoc founds the Viet Nam Quoc Dan Dang (National Democratic Party of Vietnam), at first under the name of a library (Nam Dong Thu Xa). The VNQDD (Viet Nam Quoc Dan Dang) derives its name from Kuomintang (Quoc Dan Dang is the Vietnamese pronunciation of Kuomintang, i.e., National Party).
Nguyen An Ninh founds the Nguyen An Ninh Association, secretly known as Cao Vong Thanh Nien Dang (Hope of Youth Party), which dissolves after his arrest in 1929.
By July, when Chiang Kai-shek broke with the Communists, 200 Communist cadres had been formed in China under Ho Chi Minh's supervision and sent back to Vietnam.

1928: In Hanoi, the Socialist Organization, consisting of French members, is founded. In China, the split between Communists and Nationalists leads to the arrest of members of the Revolutionary Youth Association in December (see 1925). Their central office is transferred first to Kwangsi Province, then to Hong Kong.

1929: The New Vietnam Revolutionary Party (see 1925) gives rise to a separate Communist group, the Dong Duong Cong San Lien Doan (Indochina Communist Alliance), which helps found the Indochina Communist Party in August, after dissidents from Tongking and Annam quarrel with the Revolutionary Youth Association at a reunification meeting in Hong Kong and set up their own organization, calling it Dong Duong Cong San Dang (Indochina Communist Party), with a section in South Vietnam. Both the Revolutionary Youth Association and the Indochina Communist Party request Comintern recognition. The initial success of the Indochina Communist Party in winning adherents prompts the Hong Kong leadership of the Revolutionary Youth Association secretly to adopt the name Annam Cong San Dang (Annam Communist Party) in November.

1930: The VNQDD stages an uprising at Yen Bay in February, which leads to severe repressions by the French and the execution of Nguyen Thai Hoc. Surviving party members flee to China, among them Vu Hong Khanh, who sets up an exile VNQDD. In Canton, a splinter group takes the name of Viet Nam Quoc Dan Cach Menh Dang (Nationalist Revolutionary Party) and joins up with Cuong De sympathizers, among them Hoang Nam Hung. In January, the Indochina Communist Party, the Indochina Communist Alliance, and the Annam Communist Party (see 1929) amalgamate into the Viet Nam Cong San Dang (Vietnam

Communist Party). Its central committee transfers from Hong Kong to Haiphong and asks the Comintern for recognition. At the October congress, held in Hong Kong, the unification of the three groups is formalized, adopting the name Dong Duong Cong San Dang (Indochina Communist Party). Its central committee is transferred from Haiphong to Saigon. During that year, the Dong Duong Cong San Dang, although illegal in Vietnam, is reputed to have 2,400 hard-core members, with 6,000 members in illegal red trade unions, and at least 60,000 in peasant unions. Party influence among the peasants is considered even greater.

1931: In April, the Comintern recognizes the Indochina Communist Party as a national section and allocates it a monthly stipend of about $1,250, placing it under the nominal control of the French Communist Party. In May, the first Trotskyist group emerges in the South, calling itself Lien Doan Cong San (Communist League). In August, another Trotskyist group, Ta Doi Lap (Left Opposition), emerges.

1932: In China, the Viet Nam Quoc Dan Cach Menh Dang (see 1930) disintegrates. Some of its members return to Vietnam, others turn Communist, still others enter Chinese military schools. The Socialist Organization of French citizens (see 1928), which during the 1930–32 uprisings had called for action against the insurrectionary Vietnamese nationalists and Communists, splits and disintegrates. By now, three Trotskyist groups have emerged in Vietnam: the Ta Doi Lap (see 1931), the Ta Doi Lap Thang Mui (October Left Opposition), and the Dong Duong Cong San (Indochina Communism). In August, the French arrest thirty-odd of their principal members, and by the end of the year, the underground revolutionary societies of nationalists and Communists are virtually extirpated by the French.

1933: At a meeting held in Nanking, a fusion takes place between the Viet Nam Quoc Dan Cach Menh Dang (see 1930), which had headquarters in Canton, and the VNQDD (see 1930), which worked from Yunnan. The new group is under the leadership of Vu Hong Khanh and Nguyen The Nhiep. It also includes part of the Trung Viet Cach Menh Lien Quan (Revolutionary Military Sino-Annamite League) of Yunnan, and recruits members from among the employees of the Society of the Yunnan Railroad. But its terrorist activities cause Nguyen The Nhiep and Vu Hon Khanh to be arrested by the Chinese. Vu Tien Lu, himself threatened with extradition, replaces them and goes to Nanking, partly to seek the release of the two jailed leaders, partly to escape from the Yunnan authorities. In Nanking, a further fusion takes place between the Kunming and Canton elements of the VNQDD, the two forming the Overseas Bureau of the VNQDD. Meanwhile in Saigon, two more Trotskyist groups emerge: the Nhom Tran Dau (Struggle Group), under Ta Thu Thau (see 1923), and the Nham Thang Muoi (October Group), under Ho Huu Tuong. In the Saigon municipal elections, two Trotskyists, Nguyen Van Tao, a journalist, and Tran Van Thach, a professor, are elected, but the French void their elections.

1934: The Trotskyist October Left Opposition (see 1932) changes its name to International Communist League. The political atmosphere in Vietnam improves with the election in France in June of the Popular Front, and the French Communists' adoption of the united-front policy.

1935: In the May elections in Saigon, the Stalinist Duong Bach Mai and the Trotskyists Nguyen Van Tao, Ta Thu Thau, and Tran Van Thach are elected to the Saigon Municipal Council.

1936: Trotskyists and Stalinists in the South join to create an Indochinese Congress, designed to submit reform demands to the French. They are joined by such moderate nationalists as Bui Quang Chieu and Nguyen Phan Long of the Constitutionalist Party (see 1923), and Dr. Nguyen Van Thinh, of the newly formed Democratic Party, which follows in the footsteps of the old Constitutionalist Party. In Tongking, the underground Communist Party forms a legal Indochinese Democratic Front, led by Vo Nguyen Giap and Pham Van Dong, with the movement spreading to Hue in Annam. Giap is also a member of the newly founded Socialist Federation of North Indochina, which is also joined by Hoang Minh Giam, Phan Anh, and Vu Dinh Hoe; it has some 500 members in Hanoi, Haiphong, Hadong, Langson, Nam Dinh, Hongay, Thanh Hoa, Vinh, and Tourane. A similar, legal Socialist Federation of Cochinchina is formed, with membership in South and Central Annam and Cambodia as well as in Cochinchina. These Federations are sections of the French Socialist Party. In Japanese-occupied Canton, meanwhile, Cuong De forms the Viet Nam Phuc Dong Minh Hoi (League for the National Restoration of Vietnam), Phuc Quoc, for short.

1937: Stalinists and Trotskyists quarrel over interpretation of the French Communist colonial policy line. The Stalinists publish their own newspaper. But again Ta Thu Thau, Nguyen Van Tao, and Duong Bach Mai are elected in Saigon. In June, Ta Thu Thau attacks the Party line of the people's front, and is arrested on orders from Paris.

1939: At the April 30 elections for the Colonial Council in Saigon, Ta Thu Thau, Tran Van Thach, and Phan Van Hum defeat the Stalinists. Duong Bach Mai remains leader of the official Stalinist Communist Party, while Nguyen Van Tao forms his own section. But in September, when the Paris government dissolves the "antiwar" French Communist Party, the French in Indochina do the same with the Indochinese Communists. Some 200 Stalinists and Trotskyists are arrested in Vietnam; the rest are driven underground. At the beginning of November, the central committee in Cochinchina of the Indochina Communist Party holds a plenary session at which the Indochinese Democratic Front (see 1936) is replaced by the United Front of Anti-Imperialist Indochinese Peoples.

1940: The Japanese attack the French at Langson, and Cuong De and his followers cross over into Tongking with them. After the Japanese-French agreement, Cuong De returns to Canton with his aide Hoang Nam Hung, and forms clandestine units of his Phuc Quoc Party (see 1936) in Vietnam, under Japanese protection. In the South, the Phuc Quoc joins up with the Cao Dai (headed by Tran Quang Vinh, after Pham Cong Tac's exile by the French) and becomes a political arm of the sect under the name of Viet Nam Phuc Quoc Hoi (Vietnamese National Restoration League). Another of Cuong De's aides, Nong Quoc Long, a wealthy landowner from the Tongking region, at first continues an armed fight against the French with the troops under his command (the Phuc Quoc Quan), but finally is forced to withdraw to Yunnan, where he forms the Viet Nam Phuc Quoc Dang (Party of National Restoration). In Vietnam, a number of small clandestine movements spring up, such as the Viet Hung (Restoration of Annam), the Cap Tien (Radical Group), and the Quoc Xa (National Socialist). Meanwhile, the Communist Party agitates throughout Vietnam, stages an insurrection in Cochinchina, and is rigorously suppressed by the French. The Communist Party's activities are directed by Ho Chi Minh, who heads the External Bureau of the Indochina Communist Party in Kunming. Late that year, he goes to the Tongking border area as a member of a Chinese Communist mission engaged in training Chinese Nationalist guerrillas in anti-Japanese warfare.

1941: The Viet Hung, Cap Tien, and Quoc Xa (see 1940) merge and form the Dai Viet Quoc Gia Lien Minh, or simply Dai Viet (Party of Great Vietnam). Among its most influential leaders are such former VNQDD leaders as Nguyen Tuong Tam, Nguyen Tuong Long (his brother), and Duong Duc Hien. The Dai Viet leader in the South is Nguyen Ton Hoan. When the French arrest the principal Dai Viet members, Nguyen Tuong Tam and the others flee to China. In China, the VNQDD intensifies its drive for adherents, vying with the Giai Phong Hoi, a Communist-inclined party led by Le Tung Son. Nghiem Ke To, aide to Vu Hong Khanh, obtains important concessions from the Chungking Government for the VNQDD, one of them the training of party members in Chinese military schools. The rivalry for training in Chinese military schools is largely responsible for the VNQDD's long hostility toward the Vietminh. The Vietminh, short for Viet Nam Doc Lap Dong Minh (League for the Independence of Vietnam), was formed May 10–19, at the 8th Congress of the Central Committee of the Indochina Communist Party at Tsingtsi, a Chinese village north of Caobang on the Tongking border. In Japanese-occupied Canton, meanwhile, Tran Phuoc An, who holds the rank of colonel in the Japanese Army, continues the membership drive of the Phuc Quoc Party (led by him) in China and in Vietnam proper.

1942: The Dai Viet (see 1941) in Tongking, under the direction of Truong Tu Anh, a student, undertakes reforms within the party and adopts an ultranationalist, totalitarian, anti-Communist, and xenophobic platform, also turning antimonarchist. It rivals the monarchist Phuc Quoc, which established a branch in the North. French suppression forces both parties underground and causes their leaders to flee. In October, the Chinese call a congress in Liuchow, in an attempt, under the direction of General Siao Wan, aide to Marshal Chiang Fa-kwei, to unify all Vietnamese parties active in China. At this Congress, the DMH, short for Viet Nam Cach Minh Dong Minh Hoi (Vietnam Revolutionary League), is formed under the leadership of Nguyen Hai Than, a Sinicized Vietnamese unable to speak his mother tongue, uniting the Phuc Quoc Dang, the VNQDD, the Giai Phong Hoi (see 1941), several small groups, and the Vietminh. (While Ho Chi Minh is held in a Chinese jail, Pham Van Dong holds the Vietminh leadership in China, and Vo Nguyen Giap, in Tongking.) Principal seats are assigned the Vietnam Revolutionary League at Kunming and Liuchow.

1943: Ho Chi Minh, released from jail, is made head of the Vietnam Revolutionary League in February, after Nguyen Hai Than has proved himself incapable of leadership. Obstructed by the Vietminh, Vu Hong Khan makes an unsuccessful attempt to establish an independent VNQDD branch in Tongking. The Vietminh prove to the Chinese to be the only ones capable of intelligence-gathering within Vietnam.

1944: Ngo Dinh Diem, with the help of Tran Van Ly (like Diem himself a former mandarin and Catholic, and also popular in Thua Thien, the province containing Hue), forms a Japanese-sponsored, anti-French, pro-Cuong De party, the Dai Viet Phuc Hung Hoi, or Phuc Viet (Restoration Party of Great Vietnam). Although monarchist, the program of the Phuc Viet is socialist in its broad outlines. In China, a second congress held at Liuchow in March hands the leadership of the Vietnam Revolutionary League (see 1942, 1943) back to the VNQDD, away from Ho Chi Minh, and establishes a Provisional Republican Government of Vietnam. In Hanoi, Luong Duc Hien, President of the General Students Association, founds the Viet Nam Dan Chu Dang (Democratic Party), assisted by such non-Communist intellectuals as Vi Dinh Hoe, Cu Huy Can, and Do Duc Duc. In an atmosphere of general political unrest, during which the Stalinist Communists in Vietnam continue to attack de Gaulle for his statement of December, 1943, concerning the future status of Indochina, the Trotskyists reconstitute the International Communist League during the latter part of the year, and the Binh Xuyen enter the political arena by having Bay Vien (alias Le Van Vien) join the Phuc Quoc and obtain a post with the Saigon police. The Vietminh not attacking de Gaulle, but merely calling for unity of anti-Fascists in Indochina, form the Vietnam Liberation Army in December.

1945: Following the Japanese coup in March, a few short-lived parties arise in Tongking: the Viet Cach Mang (Revolutionary Party), the Than Nien Ai Quoc Doan (Patriotic Youth), and the Phung Su Gia (League for National Renovation), the last two under the leadership of Vo Van Cam and Nguyen Chu Cuong, respectively. They soon adhere to the Dai Viet (see 1941 and 1942), whose refugee leaders—among others, Tran Van Chuong and Nguyen Huu Tri—return to Vietnam. Also moving close to the Dai Viet are Tran Trong Kim and Ngo Dinh Diem. While the Trotskyist Struggle Group (see 1933) reorganizes during May and June, the Vietminh, in May, officially sets up a "liberated" zone comprising the six provinces of Caobang, Langson, Ha Giang, Bac Kan, Tuyen Quang, and Thai Nguyen. In August, the Vietminh, at a congress held at Tan Trao in Thai Nguyen Province, calls for insurrection, establishes a military committee, and orders the Liberation Army into action. At the same time—in the South—the Cao Dai, Hoa Hao, and minor groups and parties form the Mat Tran Quoc Gia Thong Nhut (United National Front). The Indochina Communist Party founds the Thanh Nien Tien Phong (Advance Guard Youth) under the leadership of Pham Ngoc Thach. Bao Dai abdicates on August 24. On September 7, the Vietminh and the United National Front (which is joined by the Trotskyist Struggle Group) achieve formal unity in a Southern National Bloc Committee headed by Tran Van Giau. The Struggle Group, which assumes the name of Viet Nam Lao Dang Xa Hoi Dang (Vietnam Socialist Workers Party), is represented in the Committee by Phan Van Hum. The other Trotskyist group, the International Communist League (see 1944), does not join the Committee and instead calls separately on the masses to arm themselves against the French. On September 12, Duong Bach Mai, then police chief in Saigon, orders the arrest of the leaders of the International Communist League and shuts its headquarters. Le Van Vien (Bay Vien) of the Binh Xuyen joins the Committee and is placed in command of the Saigon-Cholon troops, which gives him the opportunity to reinforce his own forces. The Viet Nam Dan Chu Dang (see 1944) also rallies to the Vietminh; of the 1.5 million Catholics, with 7 bishops and 1,500 priests, most uphold the Vietminh. On October 23, the Vietminh Government reaches its first accord with the nationalists; on November 19, the second; and on December 25, the third.

1946: While the Chinese still occupy Tongking, the Vietminh and the Nationalist parties form a coalition government in February in the Quoc Hoi (National Assembly) where, in March, seventy Nationalists approve the constitution of the Resistance Government. But with the departure of the Chinese occupation troops, the DMH (see 1942) to all intent and purpose vanishes from the Vietnamese scene, while the Vietminh, with the arrival of the French occupation troops and with French assistance, starts to wipe out VNQDD and DMH influence in the northern provinces. In May, prior to Ho Chi Minh's departure for the Fontainebleau conference, the Vietminh creates the Hoi Lien Hiep Quoc Dan Viet Nam, known by the name of Lien Viet (Popular National Front of Vietnam), and in July, with total victory over the Nationalists, creates its own VNQDD in the North. (In October, only thirty-seven Nationalist opposition members are left in the National Assembly.) Dissident faction leaders of the VNQDD, allying themselves with the Vietminh, are Nguyen Van Xuan and Chu Ba Phuong, and of the DMH, Bo Xuan Luat. Another front group created by the Vietminh in July is the socialist Viet Nam Xa Hoi Dang. Another socialist group in Tongking, the SFIO, joins the Vietminh, while its southern section sides with Bao Dai. Religious movements affiliating themselves, or declaring their sympathy for the Vietminh at that time, are the Cong Giao Cuu Quo (Catholics for the National Welfare), the Lien Doan Cong Giao (League for Vietnamese Catholic Action), the Uy Ban Lien Hiep Ton Giao (Union of Religions), and the Cong Giao Khang Chien Hoi (Association of Catholics for Resistance)—which are either disavowed by the Church or wither away under Communist influence. Among the Buddhists, there are the Youth Section (Phat Tu) of the Bao Ky Phat Giao Hoi (Buddhist Association of the North) and the Phat Giao Cuu Quoc (Buddhist Association for the National Welfare), which becomes part of the Lien Viet. In Annam, the Phat Giao Viet Nam (National Buddhist Union), although sponsored by Bao Dai's mother and some mandarins, expresses its strong anti-French feelings by sympathizing with the Vietminh. In a "grand finale" bid for unity, Ho Chi Minh officially dissolves the Indochina Communist Party in November. Throughout the year, the struggle between the Vietminh and its opponents continues in the South. In July, Nguyen Binh (who has replaced Giau, by directive of the Vietminh) replaces the United National Front (FNU, or Dan Xa) with the United Popular Committee of Vietnam, but in October, the Binh Xuyen chief Bay Vien contacts the French with an offer to aid them against the Vietminh. The Dai Viet turns strongly anti-Communist and pro-American. In central Vietnam, Tran Thanh Dat founds the Quoc Gia Lien Hiep (National Union); in the South, Dr. Pham Ngoc Thach forms the Thanh Nien Tien Phong, an anti-French youth movement. Anti-Communists socialists form the CGT–FO (Confédération Générale des Travailleurs–Force Ouvrière), which works closely with the Vietnamese

Confederation of Christian Workers, under the leadership of Tran Quoc Buu, and also with the Lien Hiep Dan Chung Viet Nam (Union of the Vietnamese People), under the Syndicalist leader Nguyen Dai Thang, whose group is particularly active in Saigon-Cholon. In September, the Hoa Hao leader Huynh Phu So founds the Viet Nam Dan Chu Xa Hoi Dang, or Dan Xa (Social Democratic Party), but, in the hands of a few politicians, it soon becomes a means to exploit inner Hoa Hao tensions. Ngo Dinh Nhu forms the Can Lao Nhan Vi (Personalist Labor Party), which allies itself with the CVTC (Confédération Viet-namienne des Travailleurs Chrétiens), with more than 150,000 members throughout Vietnam.

1947: While the Vietminh remains unchallenged as the party in the North, numerous nationalist movements spring up in the South, with con-comitant movements in the Center which have connections in China. In February, Nguyen Tuong Tam, Vu Hong Khanh, and Nguyen Hai Than, leaders of the VNQDD and Dong Ming Hoi in China, form the Mat Tran Quoc Gia Thuong Quoc (National Union Front) in Nanking. Liaison is established with Nguyen Van Sam, leader of a rival united national front to the old FNU (Dan Xa—see 1946), which com-prises members of the Cao Dai, Hoa Hao, the old Dan Xa, and local sections of the VNQDD and DMH. They support Bao Dai, not as emperor but as spokesman for Vietnam. The Cochinchinese Party, founded by Nguyen Tan Cuong, is replaced by the Cochinchinese Front, headed by Nguyen Van Tam, advocating the establishment of three separate states to be administered by the French. Bao Dai's return to the throne is advocated by the Mat Tran Quoc Gia Lien Hiep (Na-tional Union), founded in the Center under the auspices of the former mandarin Tran Thanh Dat. A short-lived Indochinese Autonomist Party springs up. Dr. Le Van Truong founds the Cochinchinese Popular Move-ment, which links a federalist concept with a socialist program, primarily succeeding only in creating enemies. The Independent Nationalist Party has as its branch a Cochinchinese Autonomist Movement, which advo-cates Cochinchina for the Cochinchinese. A monarchist movement making itself heard in the Center is the Popular Movement of South Annam, founded by Ngo Xuan Tieh, and the Bao Hanh Chanh Dang. While in the South and Center the Nationalists thus play party politics, the Movement for Social and Peasant Action, founded by Nguyen Ba Chin in the North, manages to rally a bare 500 participants in Hanoi. For a brief period it seems, however, as though the nationalists would cease their suicidal splintering: Toward the end of the year, Dr. Le Van Hoach founds the Viet Nam Quoc Gia Tap Doan (Vietnamese National Union), which in the South combines the principal groups of the Dai Viet, VNQDD, Hoa Hao, Cao Dai, and Binh Xuyen; in the Center, it rallies the Quoc Gia Lien Hiep (see 1946), from which it later takes its name. Tran Van Ly and his Catholic group also join, as well as Ngo Dinh Diem (who thus, for the first and last time, joined a party he had not founded, as Pierre Dabezies put it). The Vietnamese National Union manages to rally in Tongking the Dai Viet leaders Dang Huu Chi, Do Quang Giai, Nguyen Huu Tri, as well as the leader of the Buddhist Thoi Su, Nghiem Xuan Thien, the DMH leaders Nguyen Thuc and Nguyen Quy Hung, and the VNQDD's Pham Van Binh. Although some nationalist leaders, such as Le Van Dinh, the representative of the Catholics in the South, and Dang Vu Lac and Le Thang of the Dai Viet in the North, do not join it, the Vietnamese National Union constitutes a brief interlude of unity among Vietnamese nationalists. (The downfall of the party is brought on by the end of 1948 by conflicting interests and results in a split between the three state factions.) The launching of a new party, Tap Doan Dan Chung, in December by Tran Van Ly, foreshadows the disruptive trend. Tran Van Ly's main purpose in forming the new party is to vie for power with Tran Thanh Dat, the leader of the Quoc Gia Lien Hiep, whose very structure reflects the conflicting interests within. While Tran Thanh Dat is the protégé of the Queen Mother, competitors in his party are: the old mandarins Nguyen Khoa Toan and Ha Xuan Te; the Catholics Tran Van Ly and Tran Trong Sanh; and Phan Van Giao, who, according to Dabezies, considered Annam to be his fief.

1948: The Viet Nam Quoc Gia Tap Doan (see 1947) splits into three state factions. In the South, Le Van Hoach competes with General Xuan while being aided by Nguyen Ton Hoan, leader of the southern section of Dai Viet Quoc Dan Dang (see 1941). Hoach and Hoan oppose Xuan and Tran Van Huu, and Ngo Dinh Diem is also said to intrigue against Xuan. While the autonomists continue their activities within the Independent Nationalist Party (see 1947), the Hoa Hao and the Cao Dai engage simultaneously in a struggle for power. In May, Nguyen Binh, the Vietminh leader in the South, attempts to kill the Binh Xuyen leader Bay Vien and to integrate his troops into the Vietminh under the leadership of Duong Van Ha, Bay Vien's rival who sides with the Vietminh. In revenge, Bay Vien rallies to the central government and to the French. Thereafter, the Nationalist Binh Xuyen Armed Forces constitute a solid bloc, until they clash with the Ngo Dinh Diem regime. Meanwhile, in the North, the Quoc Gia Lien Hiep (see 1947) has shrunk to having less than 200 members, and its leader, Nghiem Xuan Thien, finds himself opposed by the Dong Minh leaders Nguyen Thuc and Nguyen Quy Hung, who unsuccessfully attempt to form the Mat Tran Dan Chu Bai Cong (Democratic Anti-Communist Front). In the South, however, the Quoc Gia Lien Hiep continues to play a dominant role within the National Vietnamese Union, which later changes its name from Viet Nam Quoc Gia Tap Doan to Viet Nam Quoc Gia Lien Hiep. Perhaps one of the reasons for the Vietnamese Union's disintegration is its program of unity under Bao Dai, for the Bao Hanh Chanh Dang, a monarchist party (see 1947), also quietly fades away.

1949: In February, the Cao Dai declare their neutrality toward the French, assure Bao Dai of their loyalty, and at the same time make contact with Cao Dai dissidents. The Hoa Hao continue their internecine fight for leadership. The Binh Xuyen, after trying to form an independent nationalist party, the Binh Xuyen Ai Quoc, form a National Front with the Hoa Hao and the Cao Dai, and then form a third Nationalist Force. Nguyen Ton Hoan of the Dai Viet founds a radical youth movement, the Thanh Nien Bao Quoc Doan (Patriotic Youth), which soon extends throughout Vietnam. In June, Tran Van An returns from exile in France and forms the Viet Nam Doc Lap Dan Chung Lien Doan, or Viet Doan (Popular Union for Independence), to replace the moribund

VNQDD. He enlists the Cao Dai, Dai Viet, Thanh Nien Bao Quoc Doan, the Dan Xa faction of the Hoa Hao, the Binh Xuyen, and such political figures as Tran Van Tuyen, Nguyen The Truyen, and Phan Khac Suu. Even General Xuan joins the party, which supports Bao Dai and is more anti-French than anti-Vietminh. The Catholic Bishop Le Huu Tu, who at one point became counselor to the Vietminh government, is ordered to Rome, upon de Lattre's intercession with the Pope, to collaborate with the French, which he does unenthusiastically and passively; even though his diocese in Phat Diem and Bui Chu cooperates with the Bao Dai Government after the French parachute troops, it remains hostile to the French. The Youth for Catholic Action, under Nguyen Manh Ha, remain hostile to Bao Dai's Government and friendly toward the Vietminh. In December, Vu Hong Khanh returns to Vietnam with some 10,000 troops, leaving China before Mao Tse-tung's advance on southern China. Undecided whether to support Bao Dai or not, Vu Hong Khanh is forced by the French in Tongking to submit to Bao Dai's government. From then on, Vu Hong Khanh directs his efforts toward creating an anti-Vietminh army (he is still nominal leader of the moribund VNQDD). (Interestingly enough, the Vietminh did not resist his advance through Tongking but merely evacuated the villages through which his troops passed.) American influence appears on the Vietnamese political horizon. New movements favoring Cuong De, now said to be supported by the Americans, such as the Lien Hoi Giai Phong Quoc Gia Viet Nam (Union for the National Liberation of Vietnam), are formed in Formosa and Tokyo. Such Dai Viet leaders in the North as Le Thang, Dang Van Sung, Nguyen Huu Tri, Vu Quy Mao, Nguyen Dinh Thai, Pham Huy Quat, Nguyen Din Luyen, and Dang Huu Chi, although represented in the Quoc Gia Lien Hiep (see 1948), support Bao Dai, are anti-French and pro-American, and favor contact with certain resistance members. The Phuc Viet party of Ngo Dinh Diem has the same aims. And Dr. Phan Quang Dan founds the Cong Hoa Dang (Republican Party), then goes to the United States to study medicine at Harvard, continuing his political activities from abroad.

1950: Vu Hong Khanh joins with Phan Van Giao, the Cao Dai General Nguyen Van Thanh, Nong Quoc Long, and others, all members of the Committee for the Study of Unification of the National Armed Forces, formed at a military conference at Dalat to create an anti-Vietminh national army. At a nationalist congress in April, the Viet Doan (see 1949) splits into moderate and extremist factions. The moderates, under Tran Van An and Tran Van Tuyen, favor conditional collaboration with the French; a faction of theirs, the Democrats, led by Nguyen Dai Thang, while accepting Bao Dai, calls for a change in the government system. The extremists, led by Phan Khac Suu and Le Van Ngo, are violently anti-French and opposed to Bao Dai's Government. With this split, the movement disintegrates. In the North, the Dai Viet forms a new front to attract Nationalists from the rebel zone, calling it the Phong Trao Quoc Gia Binh Dan (Popular National Party). In November, Pham Cong Tac dissolves the moribund section of the Viet Doan and proposes the Viet Nam Dai Doan Ket (Grand Union). Although the Viet Doan makes its exit, the Viet Nam Dai Doan Ket never gets off the ground. Other flutterings of party formations are the Bao Doan, which attempts to replace the Bao Hanh Chanh Dang (see 1947), and Pham Van Ngoi's anti-Vietminh faction of the socialist SVIO (Section Vietnamienne de l'Internationale Ouvrière—formerly SFIO).

1951: In February, the Communist Party is resurrected under the name Viet Nam Dang Lao Dong, or Lao Dong (Vietnamese Workers' Party), which becomes the official party of North Vietnam. In March, de Lattre exploits the tension between the Dai Viet, who control the administration in the French-held North, and the bishoprics of Phat Diem and Bui Chu, in order to drop Nguyen Huu Tri, known to be anti-French and pro-American (see 1949), as Governor of Tongking. Nguyen Van Tam, strong man of the Bao Dai regime, is charged with eliminating all Dai Viet influence from Tongking's administrative posts of command. As once before (see 1946), the Vietminh, as a result, remains the only strong party in the North. In July, after the assassinations of Thai Lap Thanh, the Governor of Cochinchina, and General Chanson, the Bao Dai regime dissolves the Thanh Nien Bao Quoc Doan (see 1949) in a move aimed at the Dai Viet and the Cao Dai, both implicated in the assassinations. During June, the Cao Dai General Trinh Minh The forms a National Resistance Front, which is violently anti-French, anti-Bao Dai, and anti-Communist, with the aim of forming a nationalist army under Vietnamese leadership. Prince Cuong De dies, and with him his party.

1952: The Bao Doan (see 1950) disappears, despite Bao Dai's support. The Viet Nam Tan Hien Dang (New Constitutional Party of Vietnam) is stillborn. The VNQDD is revived somewhat after the elimination of posts in the French-held North by Pham Van Binh, Governor of Tongking, and the VNQDD Do Dinh Dao is ordered to organize political-military groups to assist in the pacification of recently reconquered regions. The entire VNQDD effort collapses when at the end of the year Nguyen Huu Tri is again made Governor of Tongking. Another supposedly American-sponsored politician appears on the horizon with Dr. Phan Huy Dan, a former monarchist, who, in 1946, was the leader of the Dai Chung (Great Masses) and later was personal adviser to Bao Dai; he forms the Dang Cong Hoa Viet Nam (Vietnamese Republican Party) in Thailand. Phan Huy Dan advocates anticolonialism and anti-Communism, and tries to attract a following in Bangkok.

1953: A French-Vietnamese, Colonel Leroy, Governor of the Province of Ben Tre in the South, attempts to enlist peasant support by forming successively the Liberal Peasant Party, the Progressive Peasant Union, and the Popular Peasant Front. His attempts are futile. (Dabezies comments that "although several hundred parties have so far seen the light in Vietnam, no peasant movement worthy of that name was ever created" [*op. cit.*, p. 90].) The Viet Doan (see 1949) tries to infuse new blood by changing into the Movement of National Union for Independence and Peace. In September, some 50 representatives of all nationalist parties and sects meet at a congress in Cholon and form the Union Movement for Independence and Peace, whose guiding spirit is Ngo Dinh Nhu. The platform of the movement is total independence, limited economic and cultural ties with France, granting of basic liberties, and election of a National Assembly to which the government is to be responsible. Nhu himself unsuccessfully elaborates a doctrine of vast social reforms within a "radical" Republic.

1954: With the announced French withdrawal from Tongking (which took place in Operation Auvergne), Monsignor Le Huu Tu (see 1949) flees to the South, having been officially sentenced to death five times by the Vietminh who are about to move into his diocese vacated by the French. In the South, Ngo Dinh Diem comes to power and arrives in Saigon in June. In October, he founds the Phong Trao Cach Mang Quoc Gia (National Revolutionary Movement). The NRM functions throughout South Vietnam, being government-organized, and in the coming elections wins the majority in the National Assembly. The NRM remains identified with Ngo Dinh Diem, who is its honorary leader.

1955: The early months find both the Diem Government and opposition politicians jockeying for power and position. By March, more than thirty new parties or fronts have appeared, seven of them Catholic, four in the Army, and eight to enlist the youth (e.g. there is a special attempt by the Dai Viet with the formation of Virtuous Youth, and there is a new version of the Thanh Nien Bao Quoc Doan [see 1949, 1951]). The Binh Xuyen launch a National Front, the Trotskyists the Viet Chien, General Xuan founds a Patriotic Front. Yet, the old-time parties remain the most important: the Dan Xa (see 1946), which is the political outlet for the Hoa Hao, and whose head now is Nguyen Bao Toan; the Dang Xa Hoi (see 1945), a former affiliate of the French Socialist movement; and the Phuc Quoc Hoi (see 1940), the political arm of the Cao Dai. In order not to miss any opportunity to saturate the political and social scene with its own groups, the Diem regime, while relying on the NRM (see 1954) to be a "vast political organization grouping in its midst revolutionary forces from all classes of the population," as early as February, sets up the Phong Trao Tranh Thu To Do (Movement to Win and Preserve Freedom), and makes Bui Van Thinh, Secretary of State for the Interior, its leader. Then it effectively establishes control over its own administration by creating the Lien Doan Cong Chuc Cach Mang Quoc Gia (National Revolutionary Civil Servants League); and Ngo Dinh Nhu culminates his ideological and political pursuits in the formation of the Can Lao Nhan Vi Cach Mang Dang (Personalist Labor Revolutionary Party), which aims to appeal to the country's intellectual elite. In addition, government-created, if not -manipulated, "parties" are the Tap Doan Cong Dan (Citizens Assembly), placed under the leadership of Tran Van Lam, the government delegate for the southern region; and the Hoi Dong Nhan Dan Cach Mang (Popular Revolutionary Committee), actually not a party per se but a coalition of the Movement to Win and Preserve Freedom; the Citizens Assembly; and factions of the National Restoration League, Social Democratic Party, and Socialist Party. The Popular Revolutionary Committee achieves much prestige since its chairman is Nguyen Bao Toan, leader of the Social Democratic Party (see above). Furthermore, the Popular Revolutionary Committee with its advocacy of removal of Bao Dai as head of state and his replacement by Diem and a provisional government, its preparation for general elections for a National Assembly, and its backing of the government's fight against the Binh Xuyen, strengthens the government's position in these issues. When these aims have been achieved, in October, the government proceeds to discard its props and to cut down the opposition: It sees to it that the Popular Revolutionary Committee disbands on October 31; it undermines the Movement to Win and Preserve Freedom late in the year by assigning Bui Van Thinh as Ambassador to Turkey; and around the same time forces the Social Democratic Party into reorganization and Nguyen Bao Toan to flee. A sort of resistance is put up by a coalition group created under Dr. Phan Quang Dan (who returns to Vietnam in September—see 1949) which contains as its main components the National Restoration League, the Social Democratic Party, and the Socialist Party. With Diem's victory over the sects, their political parties face disintegration.

1956: The government continues its suppression of political opposition. Such political groups as the Vietnamese People's Party, the Great Vietnam Civil Servants Party, the Dang Dai Viet Quoc Xa (Great Vietnam National Socialist Party), the Dang Dai Viet Duy Dan (Great Vietnam People's Party), the Dai Viet Quoc Dan Dang (Great Vietnam National People's Party) and the VNQDD (see 1927) are subverted from within or effectively muffled by government prohibition of all but the smallest gatherings. In the early part of the year, Dr. Phan Quang Dan is arrested briefly on charges of Communist and colonialist activities, and thereafter loses his position at the Medical School of Saigon University. Ngo Dinh Thuc, then Bishop of Vinh Long, establishes the Trung Tam Huan Luyen Nhan Vi (Training Center in Personalism) in his diocese; the majority of its instructors are Catholic priests. The October promulgation of the Constitution of the Republic of Vietnam finds the uncontested Diem Government at the height of its power.

1957: On February 22, the Communists make an attempt to kill Diem at the Ban Me Thuot fair. In May, Dr. Phan Quang Dan manages to form another opposition coalition group, the Democratic Bloc. Tran Van Lam is ousted from his position as leader of the Citizens Assembly (see 1955).

1958: The Citizens Assembly disappears in a merger with the NRM (see 1954). Dr. Phan Quang Dan withdraws from the coalition Democratic Bloc, which promptly collapses. His application for permission to form his own party, the Free Democratic Party (he is said to have changed from Republican to Democratic labels because of the anticipated change in the U.S. Administration), is ignored by the government.

1959: Several newspapers voicing opposition to government policies, or daring to publish articles by Dr. Phan Quang Dan, are closed down after attacks by organized mobs. The National Restoration League, the Social Democratic Party, and the Socialist Party are reorganized; they are now pro-government, and in this new role, participate in the National Assembly elections with the result that nine deputies from their ranks are elected. In August, Dr. Phan Quang Dan also runs for the National Assembly from Saigon and is elected over the government candidate by a six-to-one margin; government-instituted court action invalidates his election and he is barred from taking his seat. A side effect of the government's manipulation of the elections is the beginning of the decline of Diem's personal popularity.

1960: Early in the year the Civic Action Agency, under NRM auspices, establishes the Thanh Nien Cong Hoa (Republican Youth), whose size and importance grow rapidly as it seeks to mobilize the country in what the government calls an anti-Communist struggle and which the opposition calls the government's "witch-hunt." Late in April, in an unusual and daring show of unity, most of the major opposition leaders, with the exception of Dr. Phan Quang Dan and his group, organize the Khoi Tu Do Tien Bo (Bloc for Liberty and Progress), after issuing a Manifesto of Grievances against the government. The group, known as the Caravelle Group (after the Caravelle Hotel in Saigon, where the public announcement of the manifesto is made), consists of former members of the Hoa Hao, Cao Dai, Great Vietnam Party, Vietnamese People's Party, as well as dissident Catholic leaders; of the eighteen signers of the manifesto, eleven are former cabinet ministers and four had held other high government posts. After the November coup, in which one Bloc member, Phan Khac Suu, is apparently involved, most of the Caravelle Group are arrested, and the Bloc for Liberty and Progress disintegrates. Dr. Dan, who had appointed himself political adviser to the rebels when the coup was launched, is also arrested. Late in the year, a government-created opposition party makes its appearance: the Mat Tran Nhan Dan Chong Cong (Popular Anti-Communist Front, or National Union Front), which has as its reluctant chairman Dr. Pham Huy Quat, former Dai Viet leader (see 1949) and minister in early Bao Dai governments. The budget of the Nha Tong Giam Doc Trung Tam Huan Chinh (Re-education Camps Directorate General) for the year shows it to be more than twice the combined budgets of the Saigon and Hue universities; some 30,000 political prisoners are said to be held in these re-education camps. On December 20, the Mat Tran Dan Toc Giai Phong (National Liberation Front of South Vietnam) officially proclaims its existence, with Nguyen Huu Tho as President and Nguyen Van Hieu as Secretary General, after having been approved in September in Hanoi at the Third National Congress of the Lao Dong Party (see 1951).

1961: In April, Dr. Dong Van Sung, one of the former Dai Viet leaders, forms the Mat Tran Dan Chu Hoa (Front for Democratization). Because of its indecisive program, it does not attract much attention and remains weak and ineffectual. In July, the National Union Front (see 1960), which proves too independent with demands for release of political prisoners and legalization of opposition parties, ceases public activities. In October, Mme. Ngo Dinh Nhu, by resolution of the National Assembly, launches her paramilitary training program for women.

1962: In January, the People's Revolutionary Party (Party of the Working Class) makes its appearance within the framework of the National Liberation Front. It is the Southern section of the Lao Dong Party of the North. An opposition-in-exile establishes itself, primarily in Paris, with such former Dai Viet leaders as Nguyen Ton Hoan, the Social Democratic Party's Nguyen Bao Toan, former Bao Dai Prime Minister Tran Van Huu, and Pham Huy Co representing a segment of the Free Democratic Party (see 1958). Pham Huy Co establishes a National Revolutionary Executive Committee, joined by opposition leaders in France, Cambodia, and Vietnam, and by military officers who fled Vietnam after the abortive coups of November, 1960, and February, 1962.

1963: With the military playing the decisive role in the struggle between the regime and the Buddhists, the Diem regime is overthrown with the coup of November 1. The new junta in power subsequently abolishes the three major political creations of the Ngo family: the NRM, the Labor Revolutionary Personalist Party, and the Women's Solidarity Movement.

1964: In the political chaos that spews forth regime after regime, the Buddhists emerge as the most cohesive political force, with an extremist faction led by Thich Tri Quang and the moderate faction led by Thich Tam Chau. Although difficult to determine which faction is stronger within the Unified Buddhist Church, the mother organization, indications are that the moderates hold wider appeal in Saigon while the extremists have their strength in the northern provinces of the South.

1965: There are still some fragmented thirty-odd political parties in South Vietnam (according to *Life*, February 25, 1966). Pierre Dabezies, in *Forces politiques au Viet-Nam* (p. 97), has attempted to explain why under French rule the anti-Communist nationalists failed to mature politically and to achieve even a minimum of unity of action. "If caught between Communist patronage and ours, between Ho Chi Minh's strict democracy and the even stricter freedom of a state inspired by us, and torn by . . . rivalries, don't sincere patriots have valid reason for hesitation? Where does the truth lie? It is too elusive to permit a single choice, a systematic separation of villains from heroes. So some abstain while others involve themselves haphazardly, because of resentment, of inertia, of self-interest more than out of deep conviction. Often they wind up dodging or rejecting the issue. And even the most convinced do not manage to unite. Each has his own idea of what attitude to take. Each qualifies his participation in the new regime according to his ambition, his intransigence . . . his sympathy or hostility for the resistance, his desire not to seem moderate. . . . Decidedly, on the national level oppositionists multiply, and the concern for independence, instead of being a gauge for unity, only serves to increase distrust." This was written in 1954–55, in the summing up of a situation that seems unchanged some twelve years later, as the following would seem to show:

At the end of 1963, the head of the junta, General Duong Van Minh, in an interview given to Jean Lacouture, stated: "There is not even a party worthy of the name" (see Jean Lacouture, *Vietnam: Between Two Truces*, p. 128).

1966: In February, 1966, the head of the junta, Air Marshal Ky, made the same statement: "There is [in South Vietnam today] not one political party worthy of the name" (as quoted by Charles Mohr in a dispatch from Saigon to *The New York Times*, February 10, 1966).

A final comment: After the fall of the Diem regime, in November, 1963, more than 150 groups applied for permission to form their own parties.

Appendix VIII

Ho Chi Minh

Biographers have not ceased in their attempts to bring a semblance of of order into the chaotic life story of this Vietnamese. Even the date of his birth is uncertain. Jean Sainteny, for example, the first Frenchman to come into official contact with him, in his *Histoire d'une paix manquée: Indochine 1945–1947* (Paris, 1953), seems to rely on French police records and gives 1892 as the year of Ho's birth. The Vietnamese biographer Ho Van Tao (*Le mystérieux Ho-Chi-Minh* [Paris, 1953], p. 5) agrees with Sainteny on the year, but differs with Bernard Fall on the month and day, which, according to Fall was May 19 (Fall says it is a well-established day of rejoicing in the DRVN); Tao gives it as July 15, the day on which the birth of a boy to Nguyen Sinh Huy, Ho's father, was entered in the village register of Kim Lein in the Nghe An Province of Central Vietnam. Another Vietnamese biographer gives 1890 as the year of Ho's birth (Tran Dan Tien, *Glimpses of the Life of Ho Chi Minh*, p. 5); but Tao also notes that *France-Vietnam*, a journal published in Geneva, said in August, 1947, that Ho was born on July 15, 1894. Ho's actual name is also in question. According to *President Ho Chi Minh*, a pamphlet published by Pham Van Dong and the Committee for the Study of the History of the Vietnamese Workers' Party (Hanoi, 1961, p. 35), his name was Nguyen That Thanh, but Fall writes that "many Western Communist sources give his name at birth as Nguyen Ai Quoc, which translates roughly as Nguyen the Patriot'. . . . The late German ex-Communist Ruth Fischer, who knew him in Moscow during the early Comintern days, stated that Ho's . . . name was Nguyen That Thanh (Nguyen Who Will Be Victorious)" (*The Two Viet-Nams*, p. 83). It is generally supposed that Ho assumed the name of Nguyen Ai Quoc in 1914, some say out of respect for traditions, others because he wished to stress his revolutionary leanings. Then there are the numerous aliases Ho adopted during his early development, and it would be futile to attempt to assign dates to these. Ho's first pseudonym, by most accounts, was "Ba," which he assumed when signing on aboard the "Latouche-Treville" as kitchen boy—"so as not to dishonor his family name by so humble an employment," according to Fall (*ibid.*, p. 87). Other known pseudonyms in addition to Nguyen Ai Quoc and Nguyen Tat Thanh (or Nguyen That Thanh) are Tong Van So, Nguyen Van Thanh, Nguyen Sinh Cin, and Ly Thuy. There may well have been fifty more that never became known to the researchers. It is known, however that Ho was not an only child. He had an older sister and brother, both of whom, writes Fall, "seem to have avoided politics and to have stayed in their

native village throughout the period of resistance against the French, till-
ing the family rice fields" (*ibid.*, p. 84). Fall, citing Pham Van Dong,
says they were jailed for a time because of Ho's activities. Ho Van
Tao states that in 1918 they participated in an insurrection in the region
of Vinh and were arrested and condemned to forced labor by the French.
The brother is said to have died in 1950, the sister in 1953. Ho came by
his strong nationalist sentiments as much through his birth place as by his
father. The Nghe An region produced such earlier nationalist revolutionaries as Phan Dinh Phung and Phan Boi Chau, and Nguyen Sinh Huy himself, who had been a minor official under the old imperial regime, had
allegedly been dismissed from service for his implacable animosity toward
the French. According to Communist tradition, Ho's father is said to have
been a poor man, the son of a peasant, but Fall tells that he practiced "Oriental medicine" after his dismissal and became successful in his new profession when he moved to South Vietnam. Ho's education took him to the
Quoc Hoc college in Hue, a school founded "at the initiative of Ngo
Dinh Kha, a high official of the Hue imperial court and father of South
Viet-nam's Ngo Dinh Diem" (Fall, *ibid.*, p. 85). But Ho does not seem to
have finished his studies there. In 1910, he became a teacher in Phan Thiet,
a small fishing village, only to leave again for Saigon in October, 1911,
where he took a three-months' course at a technical school. Perhaps without quite knowing what drove him, Ho went to sea at the age of eighteen,
or nineteen, or twenty, "to see the world." His travels are known to have
taken him to France, Africa, the French colonies, England, and the United
States, but it is impossible to ascertain his precise whereabouts during
those years. According to Pham Van Dong, he returned to Paris at the outbreak of World War I. According to Fall, he was in London at the time.
In London, Ho is known to have worked as a snow shoveler for a school
during the day and as a dishwasher and pastry-cook with Escoffier at the
Carlton Hotel at night. In London he also acquired his first taste for political conspiracy: He joined a secret society (Lao Dong Hai Ngoa, Workers
Overseas), founded, according to Ho Van Tao, by a Vietnamese named
Nam, but according to Fall "largely under Chinese leadership." That society later became the Committee for the Welfare of the Fatherland (Cuu
Quoc Hoi), wrote Tao, and he added: "Without doubt, it was during that
period that Ho Chi Minh's evolution began toward revolutionary socialism
and communism" (p. 8). Still according to Tao, Ho tried to enlist in the
British Army and left for France when he was rejected. It is not clear
whether Ho went to the United States during the war. In 1917 (or 1918),
however, he was in France, earning his living as a photo retoucher and,
some say, as a painter of Oriental scenes. In 1919, already much involved
with other young Vietnamese living in Paris over political questions touching on Vietnam, he issued with them an eight-point petition in pamphlet-
form entitled *Cahiers de revendications du peuple vietnamien* (*List of
Claims of the Vietnamese People*), which they sent to Clemenceau, Lloyd
George, and Wilson at the Versailles Peace Conference. Undaunted by
their failure to respond, he devoted himself from then on with increasing
intensity to the Vietnamese cause—and to Socialist ideas. He became a
voracious reader of Marxist and Communist literature and perfected his
knowledge of languages (Sainteny wrote that Ho spoke perfect French,
English, Russian, and Mandarinal Chinese, in addition to his native tongue

and various Indochinese dialects, and that he also knew German). He furthermore became known among leftist organizations for "his intelligence,
his faith, his sincerity, and his austerity" (Sainteny, p. 165). He began to
contribute articles to *L'Humanité*, and wrote a political satire, *The Bamboo
Dragon*, which gained him an invitation to the French Socialist Party
Congress at Tours in 1920. It was at Tours that Ho sided with those who
voted Communist. "Thus Nguyen Ai Quoc became one of the first members of the French Communist Party and at the same time the first Vietnamese Communist," wrote Pham Van Dong (p. 44). Ruth Fischer's impression of Ho at that time was that it was his "nationalism which impressed us European Communists born and bred in a rather gray kind of
abstract internationalism" (cited by Robert Shaplen, *The Lost Revolution*,
p. 37). Ho learned to debate, to write, and—to organize. In 1921, he
helped to found the League of Colonial Countries and wrote its manifesto.
In 1922, he became editor of the weekly *Le Paria*, a newspaper financed by
the League. In 1923, he went to Moscow to attend the Fourth Comintern
Congress, and again the next year for the Fifth Congress, at which he was
a representative of the French Communist Party and of the colonial countries. In December of that year he went to Canton, where he contacted
such Vietnamese *émigré* nationalists as Phan Boi Chau. Using the alias of
Ly Thuy, he organized the League of Oppressed Peoples and in 1925 the
Association of Revolutionary Annamite Youth (Thanh Nien). (In *The
Last Confucian*, p. 25, Denis Warner gives a slightly different version. According to him, Ho went to Moscow in June, 1923, as a member of the
French Communist Party's delegation to the Peasants' International Congress, and "under the name of Song Man Tcho, he remained in Moscow
for two years as a colonial delegate on the standing committee of the
Peasants' International, learning Russian and studying revolutionary tech-
niques at the newly established University of the Toilers of the East . . .
Early in 1925 he was sent to Canton in South China as an interpreter to
the Russian delegation led by Michael Borodin.") During his stay in China,
Ho wrote *The Revolutionary Path*, an outline of his ideas combining
Marxism with nationalism. When the Kuomintang broke with Communism
in 1927, he left Canton, first for Shanghai, then for Moscow, Brussels,
France, Germany, Switzerland, and Italy. Nothing is known of his activities
during these travels. After a short stay in Berlin he went to Siam, according to some sources at the end of 1927, and according to others in late
1928, where he remained until January, 1930. There he is said to have
adopted many disguises, such as that of a Buddhist monk, a peasant, and a
peddler. Shaplen writes (*op. cit.*, pp. 38, 39) that in Siam he quietly organized thousands of local Annamites and at the same time acted as agent of
the Third International in the Far East, directing the "agitprop" (agitation and propaganda) in Siam, Malaya, and the Dutch East Indies. In February, 1930, Ho went to Hong Kong, where he was instrumental in founding the Vietnamese Communist Party (see Chapter IV, n. 97). The period
from 1933 to 1941 constituted "the most obscure years in Ho Chi Minh's
life," Shaplen notes (*ibid.*, p. 39), adding that during this time Ho was
said "to have married or taken on a regular concubine, by whom he had a
daughter who later worked anonymously for the Vietminh and then disappeared. (The mother died in China during the war.)" Ho himself during
that time was reported in Shanghai, in Siam, in Java, in France, in Portu-

guese East Africa, and in Moscow, "where he attended more party schools" (*ibid.*, p. 40). Whatever twists and turns Ho Chi Minh's political life took thereafter is dealt with in the body of this book. There is no doubt however that it was filled with cunning and violence, inherent in part in the ruthlessness of the Communist doctrine and in part in the cold cruelty of which Asians or, for that matter, all fanatics, are capable. Ho Chi Minh was by no means the gentle and humane "Uncle Ho" Communist propaganda made him out to be; yet neither was he the malevolent spirit of evil which French propaganda painted. He was treacherous toward his enemies but he was loyal to his friends, and a great many of those with whom he embarked on the road to power are still with him today. "I myself from my first contact with Ho Chi Minh had the impression that this ascetic man, whose face revealed simultaneously intelligence, energy, cunning, and sensitivity, was an impressive personality who would not fail to place himself in the foreground of the Asian scene," wrote Sainteny (*op. cit.*, p. 164), and he adds: "His vast culture, his intelligence, his incredible activeness, his asceticism, and his absolute unselfishness gave him incomparable prestige and popularity with the people. It is most regrettable that France should have belittled this man and underestimated his worth and his power" (*ibid.*, p. 166). The tragedy for the Western world is that the man who first called himself Ho Chi Minh (He Who Enlightens) when he appeared on the roster of the new Congress of Unification of all Vietnamese parties at Liuchow on March 25, 1945, was not only a sincere nationalist, but also one of the most capable men the international Communist movement has produced. (For the fullest and most up-to-date biography of Ho Chi Minh, see Bernard B. Fall, *The Two Viet-Nams.* For a terse biography of Ho, in which he is assigned an almost pivotal role in the struggle between Moscow and Peking, see Robert Shaplen's article "The Enigma of Ho Chi Minh," in *The Reporter*, January, 1955, which is still valid today. For biographical panegyrics, see Wilfred Burchett, *North of the 17th Parallel*, pp. 4–26; Tran Dan Tien, *Glimpses of the Life of Ho Chi Minh;* and Manfred Stuhlmann, *Ho-chi-Minh; Ein Leben für Vietnam.* Within the framework of contemporary writing on Southeast Asia and Vietnam, a great many more books and articles are, of course, to be found than are quoted here; no additional pertinent information, however, has come to my attention.)

Appendix IX

Ngo Dinh Diem

Jean Baptiste Ngo Dinh Diem (Burning Jade) was born January 3, 1901, the third of six sons of Ngo Dinh Kha, Minister of Rites and Grand Chamberlain to the Emperor Thanh Thai. Although Diem also had three sisters, little is known about them, but the six brothers made names for themselves. The oldest, Ngo Dinh Khoi, became Governor of Quang Nam Province under the French; he and his son were killed by the Vietminh in 1945 in the village of Co Bi. Ngo Dinh Thuc, the next in age, became archbishop and the most influential prelate in Vietnam. Diem's younger brother, Ngo Dinh Nhu, became his closest adviser and, in Robert Shaplen's words, "ultimately his Rasputin." Ngo Dinh Luyen, the youngest, by training a mechanical engineer, wielded the least influence in the family but served as ambassador to Great Britain. Ngo Dinh Can, the second-youngest, became the "strong man" of Central Vietnam, ruling it from Hue with his police force almost independently of his brother's central government.

The Ngos were an old aristocratic mandarinal family who were among the earliest converts to Catholicism in the seventeenth century. Around 1870, they acquired a degree of martyrdom when an anti-Catholic mob attacked the family home and almost wiped them out altogether. Diem's father survived the massacre because he was abroad, having studied first in China and then in Malaya. Upon his return to Annam, he founded a small private school for children of wealthy families, but he soon entered the Imperial Service at Hue, and by the time Diem was born, Kha already served as adviser to Thanh Thai. Diem's birthplace is in dispute (some say he was born in Dai Phuong, in Quang Binh Province, north of the 17th parallel) but it seems likely that he was born at Hue, as most sources indicate.

When the French deposed Thanh Thai in 1907 on suspicion of plotting against them, Kha retired from court service with a lasting animosity toward the French. His ardent nationalism made him a supporter of Phan Boi Chau, and he passed this on to his sons, in particular to Khoi and Diem, whom he taught that essential reforms had to be brought about by such as them, namely the elite. Whether Kha resigned from his court position, as some state, or whether he was forced out by the French, as Shaplen writes, he withdrew to his modest land holdings, leaving Diem under the tutelage of Nguyen Huu Bai, then Premier at the court of Hue. Diem attended a French Catholic school. He was an excellent student. It is said that he rose at five every morning to study and pray. He continued his schooling at the Lycée Quoc Hoc at Hue, a school founded at the initiative of his father to provide Western education to the Vietnamese elite free from excessive French influence, the same school attended by Ho Chi Minh, Vo Nguyen Giap, and Pham Van Dong. At fifteen, Diem entered a monastery, intending to study for the priesthood. He changed his mind, however, and a year later falsified his age to take the competitive examinations for the equivalent of a high-school diploma. His excellent performance drew the attention of the French and he was offered a scholarship in Paris. He refused, on the pretext that his father was ill, but in truth because he did not wish to place himself under French tutelage. Instead he went to Hanoi, to attend the French-run School for Law and Administration, and graduated at the head of his class in 1921.

As a ninth-class mandarin, Diem was appointed to the Royal Library at Hue. Advised by his "elders," as Shaplen put it, to leave the sheltered library for public affairs, he took an assignment as administrative supervisor of some seventy villages near Hue, and within a few years went further up the mandarinal ladder, being assigned to a region in Central Vietnam embracing some 300 villages. It is said that at no other time of his career did he learn to know the countryside and its people better than during that period, when he went on inspection trips on horseback (as Governor General Paul Doumer had done in his days).

In 1925, he began to become aware of the Communist activities in his region, and until 1929 he sought to combat their influence. In 1929, he arrested the Communist leaders and sent his French superiors a report— which was disregarded, just as had been his earlier recommendations for village improvements. But that same year, at the age of twenty-eight, he was promoted to the post of Governor of Phan Thiet Province, inhabited by mountain tribes and a Cham minority. As Diem told Shaplen in an interview, besides getting to know his charges, he devoted his efforts to fight the revolutionary ideas imported by the Thanh Nien "firebrands" from Canton, Hongkong, and Saigon (see Robert Shaplen, "A Reporter in Vietnam," *The New Yorker*, September 22, 1962).

By 1932, Diem had gained a good reputation both among the French and his own countrymen, and he was asked—Fall says, by Bao Dai; Shaplen, by the French—to head an inquiry into irregularities by Vietnamese officials throughout Annam. In May, 1933, he was nominated Minister of the Interior under Bao Dai, and Fall and Shaplen also differ as to who was responsible for his nomination. Be that as it may, his appointment was short-lived. Frustrated by his inability to initiate the legislative reforms he considered necessary, he resigned from his post in July, after having publicly accused Bao Dai, according to Fall, of being "nothing but an instrument in the hands of the French authorities." He relinquished his titles and decorations (or was stripped of them) and, according to Shaplen, was threatened by the French with arrest and deportation. Actually, he was left to his own devices, and for most of the next ten years lived in Hue with his mother and his brother Ngo Dinh Can, spending his time meeting with anti-French nationalists and corresponding with Phan Boi Chau in Hanoi and Cuong De in Japan. At that time, Diem was known to envision Vietnam's independence along the line of the American Revolution, i.e., national liberation, rather than along the model of the French Revolution, which he considered primarily a class struggle. Although in the 1940's Diem had no specific projects, no organization, and little following, he was kept under French surveillance and his family was implicated by his anti-French stand. Consequently, in 1942, the French forced Ngo Dinh Khoi, who was Governor of Quang Nam Province, to resign.

It appears that when the Japanese occupied Vietnam in 1942, Diem sought to enlist their help in creating a truly free Vietnam. He was unsuccessful and was declared a subversive by the French. When they sought to arrest him in 1944, he fled to Saigon and took refuge with some Japanese friends. In March, 1945, when the Japanese took over the administration from the French, Diem was offered the Prime Ministership of an "independent" government under Bao Dai in Hue. Diem is said to have refused, not so much because he "objected" to the Japanese but "because he still did not feel he would be able to establish a free government" (as Shaplen puts it). Besides, Shaplen adds, "he now saw the handwriting on the wall and did not want to put himself in the position of being declared a collaborator when the war was over." The truth, however, is that Diem was ready to accept the Japanese offer, but the Japanese, on second thought, decided to install a man they considered more manageable—Tran Trong Kim. In September, 1945, when Ho Chi Minh's Government took power, Diem returned to Hue to warn the court and Bao Dai of the Communist danger. He never got there. On the way, at the small fishing village of Tuy Hoa, he was arrested by Vietminh agents who had followed him and taken to a camp in the Tongking mountain region near the Chinese border. There he fell seriously ill and would have died had it not been for the care given him by Tho tribesmen.

In February, 1946, Ho Chi Minh had Diem brought to Hanoi. According to Diem's own version of this confrontation, he accused Ho of having had his brother murdered and walked out on the Vietminh leader. No other source has ever confirmed this version of the encounter.

Once back in Hue, Diem covertly took part in the negotiations to bring Bao Dai back to power in 1949, after having tried in 1947 to form a political party that did not get off the ground. But when Bao Dai offered him the premiership in May, 1949, Diem turned him down, alleging, as Fall writes, that "the Viet-Minh might vent its displeasure upon the hundreds of thousands of Catholics residing in its zone." In reality, Fall states, "Diem thought the concessions made by France were not far-reaching enough for him to commit himself to their implementation." When he learned in the spring of 1950 that the Vietminh had sentenced him to death *in absentia*, he asked for French protection, and, upon being denied it, left Vietnam with French permission, ostensibly to go to Rome for the Holy Year with his brother Thuc. On the way he visited Cuong De in Japan, and eventually the United States.

In January, 1951, Diem returned to the United States from Europe and remained for two years, most of the time staying at the Maryknoll Seminary in Lakewood, New Jersey, but also traveling through the country on lecture tours. During this period, writes Shaplen, he "received three more tentative offers from Bao Dai to return as the head of the Vietnamese government, and the third offer, in the summer of 1953, promised him full political powers. The French, however, would not give in to his demand that the Vietnamese be allowed to conduct the war, and negotiations terminated." When he finally took over the government, on July 7, 1954, the French Indochina war had resulted in Dien Bien Phu and the Geneva conference.

In an assessment of the man who came to lose his life together with his brother Ngo Dinh Nhu in the coup of 1963, General Ely wrote in his memoirs: "Without doubt, the man gave proof of great energy and tenacity as well as much cunning. His reputation for honesty had lent him a certain authority . . . Diem fought resolutely all that which to his thinking hindered him in the exercise of a power he wished to hold complete, along the lines of his tradition as a former mandarin from Hue who was possessed by nostalgia for conservatism" (*L'Indochine dans la Tourmente*, p. 320). Pierre Dabezies speaks of Diem's "ultranationalism," his "intransigence toward us [the French]," and his "notorious animosity toward the former Emperor." And writing of Diem's qualifications, Dabezies remarked: "In fighting against adversity, does the new Prime Minister have at least an ease of manner, a communicative warmth, a full store of sympathy capable of winning over the masses and of realizing miracles? Nothing is further from the truth! Aside from his qualities, he has, on the contrary, serious character defects, largely reinforced by his isolation and his profound conviction that he is always right. Like many timid people, he is given to coldness as much as to rages. He is obstinate, often without flexibility, authoritarian. He has the sadness, the rigidity, and the sectarianism of an ascetic who for years engaged in introspection" (*Forces politiques au Vietnam*, pp. 101–2). Shaplen philosophized: "Some men are destined to be alone all their lives, and Diem, to my mind, was surely one of them. Although he had been an ardent nationalist most of his life, he had spent much of it in spiritual and physical isolation, and this undoubtedly was why he very often found it difficult to establish intimate contact with the people of his country" (*The Lost Revolution*, p. 105).

The following few are among the countless observations on Diem as the leader of his country: "Diem seemed to feel that popular support, and even affection, could be taken for granted. . . . Diem and Nhu talked repeatedly about the people's 'duty' to the government" (John Mecklin, *Mission in Torment*, p. 35). "The concept of executive power subject to popular recall simply goes against the grain of the man, and, in his own eyes, hurts his stature as a predestined leader. . . . In such a *Weltanschauung*, compromise has no place and opposition of any kind must of necessity be subversive and must be suppressed with all the vigor the system is capable of" (Bernard B. Fall, *The Two Viet-Nams*, p. 237). "Diem's membership of the mandarin class, whose haughtiness and greed had been partially responsible for the popular rising in 1945, his adherence to an unpopular religious minority, and his constricted timidity of manner were not designed to appeal either to the robust adventurers who controlled the forces of organized nationalism in South Vietnam or to those members of the middle class who had hitherto refused to participate in nationalist governments" (Donald Lancaster, *The Emancipation of French Indochina*, p. 329). "Not to see who is hostile, not to hear the disgruntled, never to brave a popular demonstration, remaining deaf instead to the clamor of the masses and the complaints of the middle class, shutting himself away in his office with one or two intimate advisers and a handful of faithful followers, from there to command, to rule, to legislate—solely under the guidance of God—is this not the best way to override the opposition, thus almost to suppress it? One hears it not, one sees it not, therefore it does not exist" (Georges Chaffard, *Indochine; Dix ans d'indépendance*, p. 48). *The Last Confucian*, as Denis Warner called his book, referring to Diem, considered himself "The Father of the People." "He knows what is good for the people. Only the father knows, for the people are his total concern. How, then, could he be wrong?" And quoting from Diem's official biography, Warner wrote: "The fundamental fact about Vietnam . . . is that historically our political system has been based not on the concept of the management of the public affairs by the people or their representatives, but rather by an enlightened sovereign and an enlightened government" (pp. 65–73).

Selected Bibliography

Although the following bibliography is long, it must still be called "selected," since it does not list even half the books cited in the notes, and since it contains only a small fraction of the several thousands of items a truly comprehensive bibliography on Vietnam would have to list. (Roy Jumper, in his bibliography on Vietnam, says that the 964 entries he selected were chosen from some 3,500 titles.) Today, bibliographical sources in English on Vietnam are no longer scarce. Several works on Indochina and Vietnam contain excellent selected bibliographies, among them Virginia Thompson, Ellen J. Hammer, Donald Lancaster, Thomas E. Ennis, Robert Scigliano, Jules Roy (in *The Battle of Dien Bien Phu*), and Bernard B. Fall, particularly his "Military Bibliography of Indochina" in *Street without Joy*. A useful selection of seventy-two items on Vietnam is contained in *Southeast Asian History: A Bibliographic Guide*, by Stephen N. Hay and Margaret H. Case (New York: Frederick A. Praeger, 1962). Earlier and larger bibliographies are: *Indochina: A Bibliography of the Land and the People* (The Library of Congress, Reference Department, Washington, D.C., 1950); and *Bibliography of the Peoples and Cultures of Mainland Southeast Asia*, by John F. Embree and Lillian Ota Dotson (New Haven, Conn.: Yale University Press, 1950). More useful for the student, however, because more recent and entirely concerned with Vietnam, is Roy Jumper's *Bibliography on the Political and Administrative History of Vietnam, 1802–1962* (mimeographed and issued in June, 1962, by the Michigan State University Vietnam Advisory Group).

Like any other selection, my own was determined by the themes that dominate the book. Nevertheless, most works of real importance on colonial and contemporary Vietnam will be found, if not here, then among the more than 500 items in the bibliography of *The Smaller Dragon*, of which only a few are repeated here.

On the more recent history, I have included a number of newspaper and magazine articles, chosen because subsequent events have endowed them with unusual historical interest.

Some references are incomplete by American standards, particularly in regard to first names of older French authors. Efforts to ascertain these names have been made but have not always been successful, since in many

1258

cases neither the title page of the book in question nor the most authoritative French bibliographers could supply the missing information.

Aid to Vietnam. New York: American Friends of Vietnam, 1959. A record of a conference held on April 17, 1959, on the effect of U.S. aid to Vietnam.

AJALBERT, JEAN. *Les nuages sur l'Indochine.* Paris: Louis-Michaud, 1912. A continuation, from the author's earlier books, of criticism of French colonial rule in Indochina.

ALBERTI, JEAN B. *L'Indochine d'autrefois et d'aujourd'hui.* Paris: Société d'Éditions Géographiques, Maritimes et Coloniales, 1934. A general survey of the colonial regime, with details of the administration under Governor General Paul-Armand Rousseau.

ALLEN, LUTHER A., and PHAM NGOC AN. *A Vietnamese District Chief in Action.* Saigon: Michigan State University, Vietnam Advisory Group, 1961. Description of the activities and problems of a district chief, with suggestions for reform.

ANH VAN, and JACQUELINE ROUSSEL. *Mouvements nationaux et lutte des classes au Viet-Nam.* Marxisme et Colonie, Publications de la IVe Internationale. Paris: Imprimerie Réaumur, 1947. A Trotskyite account of colonial history and a sharp condemnation of Vietminh policy in 1945 and 1946.

ANLEY, HENRY. *In Order to Die.* London: Burke, 1955. Memoirs, and observations on the Indochina War, by an Englishman who served with the Foreign Legion. Describes the atrocities committed by both sides.

BALDWIN, HANSON W. "A Hell of a Place to Have to Fight In," *Life,* March 31, 1961. Describes the conditions—jungle, marshes, climate, etc. —under which the combatants have to live and fight.

BALL, W. MACMAHON. *Nationalism and Communism in East Asia.* Melbourne: Melbourne University Press, 1952. Important facts on land ownership and on peasant exploitation by landlords.

BARNETT, A. DOAK. *Communist Strategies in Asia: A Comparative Analysis of Governments and Parties.* New York: Frederick A. Praeger, 1963. Part III—" 'Roads to Socialism': Communist Regimes in Power"—contains a chapter by Bernard B. Fall, "A 'Straight Zigzag': The Road to Socialism in North Viet-Nam," pp. 199-227.

BARROWS, LELAND. "American Economic Aid to Vietnam," *Viet My.* Journal of the Vietnamese-American Association (Saigon), No. 1, 1956, pp. 29-40. The director of the U.S. Operations Mission describes and discusses the various aid programs.

BARTHOUET, ARNAUD. *La tragédie franco-indochinoise.* Paris: Delmas, 1948. A study of the Vietnamese nationalist movements against the French going back to the guerrilla resistance after the conquest.

BATOR, VICTOR. *Viet-Nam: A Diplomatic Tragedy.* Dobbs Ferry, N.Y.: Oceana Publications, 1965. A critique of United States policy toward Vietnam offering little-known details, and a keen analysis of the strategy of John Foster Dulles before and during the Geneva conference in 1954.

BAUCHAR, RENÉ (pseudonym of Jean Charbonneau). *Rafales sur l'Indochine.* Paris: Fournier, 1946. First hand observations on the political and military events during World War II.

BERNARD, FERNAND. *L'Indo-Chine, erreurs et dangers: Un programme.* Paris: Bibliothèque-Charpentier, 1901. The book is primarily a polemic against the policies of Governor General Paul Doumer.

————. "La réforme de l'Indo-Chine," *Revue de Paris,* October 1, 1908. Further criticism of colonial policy, in particular, of the public-works program begun by Doumer.

BERNARD, PAUL. *Le problème économique indochinois.* Paris: Nouvelles Éditions Latines, 1934. Next to Robequain's *The Economic Development of French Indo-China* the most important work on the subject. The author sharply criticizes the antidevelopmental character of French economic policy in Indochina from a "liberal" economic viewpoint.

————. *Nouveaux aspects du problème économique indochinois.* Paris: Fernand Sorbot, 1937. A follow-up of the author's earlier book on the same subject.

BERRIER, HILAIRE DU. *Background to Betrayal: The Tragedy of Vietnam.* Boston: Western Islands, 1965. The Vietnamese story from 1954 to 1965 as seen by the "lunatic fringe" of the American extreme right. The story is that of a conspiracy by American "liberals" (Leo Cherne, Angier Biddle Duke, Harold Oram, Wesley Fishel, Lt. General John W. O'Daniel, Joseph Buttinger, and other members of the American Friends of Vietnam) to sell out South Vietnam to the Communists by supporting Ngo Dinh Diem. It seems that anyone who ever wrote in support of Diem was either a member of the conspiracy or was used by its leaders.

BETTS, RAYMOND F. *Assimilation and Association in French Colonial Theory: 1890–1914.* New York and London: Columbia University Press, 1961. A scholarly discussion of French colonial policy, dealing largely with Indochina and based on a study of all important works on the subject. With an extensive bibliography.

BIGART, HOMER. "Vietnam Victory Remote Despite U.S. Aid to Diem," *The New York Times,* July 25, 1962.

BLANCHET, ANDRÉ. *Au pays des ballila jaunes: Relations d'un correspondant de guerre en Indochine.* Saint-Etienne: Editions Dorian, 1947. A diary of events in Vietnam, military and political, from March, 1945, to March, 1946.

BLANCHET, M. T. *La naissance de l'État Associé du Vietnam.* Paris: Genin, 1954. Describes the formation of the Bao Dai State of Vietnam and its institutions, on the basis of official texts.

BODARD, LUCIEN. *La guerre d'Indochine: L'enlisement.* Paris: Gallimard, 1963. A rather sensational account of French and Vietnamese political, financial, and military scandals.

————. *La guerre d'Indochine: L'humiliation.* Paris: Gallimard, 1965. A continuation of the above.

BOEUF, ABEL. *Histoire de la conquête de la Cochinchine, 1858–1861.* Saigon: Nguyen Van Cua, 1927. A brief military and political history covering the first phase of the conquest of Indochina.

BONNAFONT, L. *Trente ans de Tonkin.* Paris: E. Figuière, 1924. Memoirs of a Frenchman in Indochina covering the years from 1889 to 1923.

BONNET, GABRIEL. *Les guerres insurrectionelles et révolutionnaires.* Paris: Payot, 1958. Ideas on psychological warfare largely derived from the experience in Indochina.

BOUSCAREN, ANTHONY T. *The Last of the Mandarins: Diem of Vietnam.* Pittsburgh, Pa.: Duquesne University Press, 1965. A rather superficial account of Diem's life, and an unconvincing defense of his regime.

Breaking Our Chains: Documents on the Vietnamese Revolution of August, 1945. Hanoi: Foreign Languages Publishing House, 1960. Important documents issued by the Indochinese Communist Party.

BRIMMEL, J. H. *Communism in South-East Asia: A Political Analysis.* London and New York: Oxford University Press, 1959. A comprehensive and scholarly study.

BROWNE, MALCOLM W. *The New Face of War.* Indianapolis, Ind., and New York: Bobbs-Merrill, 1965. Browne vividly describes the failure of Diem's army to cope with the fighting techniques of the Vietcong and the decline of the Diem regime. The most important book on the nature of the war before the arrival of American combat troops.

BRUNSCHWIG, HENRI. *La colonisation française.* Paris: Calmann-Lévy, 1949. Chapter V (pp. 123–98) deals with Indochina. Largely a history of Western penetration and of the French conquest. The rest is a sketchy outline and praise of colonial policy up to 1940.

BURCHETT, WILFRED G. *The Furtive War: The United States in Vietnam and Laos.* New York: International Publishers, 1963. The Communist view, ably presented by an Australian journalist.

———. *North of the 17th Parallel.* Hanoi, 1956 (n.p.). An enthusiastic description of the achievement of the Hanoi regime.

———. *Vietnam: Inside Story of the Guerilla War.* New York: International Publishers, 1965. A follow-up on the author's *The Furtive War,* based on firsthand observation in the Vietcong areas.

BUTTINGER, JOSEPH. "Are We Saving South Vietnam?" A supplement to *The New Leader* of June 27, 1955. A report on the struggle of Diem against the sects, a critique of French support of the sects and Bao Dai opposition to Diem, and an analysis of the conflict between U.S. and French policy in Vietnam.

———. "The Ethnic Minorities in the Republic of Vietnam," in WESLEY R. FISHEL (ed.). *Problems of Freedom* (see below), pp. 99–123.

———. "An Eyewitness Report on Vietnam," *The Reporter,* January 27, 1955, pp. 19–20.

———. *Fact and Fiction on Foreign Aid.* Reprinted from *Dissent,* Summer, 1959. This is a critique of the William J. Lederer and Eugene Burdick "novel" *The Ugly American.*

———. "France and Frenchmen: Saigon Intrigue," *The New Republic,* February 28, 1955.

BUTTINGER, JOSEPH. "The Miracle of Vietnam," in RICHARD W. LINDHOLM (ed.). *Viet-Nam: The First Five Years* (see below).

———. *The Smaller Dragon: A Political History of Vietnam*. New York: Frederick A. Praeger, 1958.

BUU HOAN. "Vietnam: Economic Consequences of the Geneva Peace," *Far Eastern Economic Review*, December 11, 1958, pp. 753–57.

CAMERON, JAMES. *Here Is Your Enemy*. New York: Holt, Rinehart & Winston, 1966. A report by the well-known British correspondent of a visit to North Vietnam during the winter of 1965–66.

CATROUX, GEORGES. *Deux actes du drame indochinois*. Paris: Librairie Plon, 1959. Former Governor General Catroux defends his policy in Indochina in 1939–40 and discusses the battle of Dien Bien Phu.

CÉLERIER, PIERRE. *Menaces sur le Viet-Nam*. Saigon: Imprimerie d'Extrême Orient (IDEO), 1950. A valuable examination of the Chinese occupation of northern Vietnam, the outbreak of the Indochina War, and the creation of the Bao Dai regime.

CHAFFARD, GEORGES. *Indochine: Dix ans d'indépendance*. Paris: Calmann-Lévy, 1964. The views of an experienced French reporter who spent much of these ten years in Vietnam, both in the South and in the North. Particularly valuable for its detailed account of Diem's struggle with the sects.

CHAILLEY-BERT, JOSEPH. *La colonisation de l'Indo-Chine: L'expérience anglaise*. Paris: Armand Colin, 1892. One of the many pleas by the son-in-law of Governor General Paul Bert for a more liberal and more pro-native French policy in Indochina. For a list of some of Chailley-Bert's other works, see BETTS, *op. cit.*, bibliography, pp. 208–9.

———. *Paul Bert au Tonkin*. Paris: Charpentier, 1887. Paul Bert's administration favorably reviewed by his son-in-law.

CHALMERS, M. ROBERT. "The Day We Didn't Go To War," *The Reporter*, September 14, 1954. How the danger of a U.S. military intervention to save Dien Bien Phu in the spring of 1954 was averted. Reprinted in MARCUS G. RASKIN and BERNARD B. FALL (eds.). *The Viet-Nam Reader* (see below), pp. 57–66.

CHASSIN, L. M. *Aviation Indochine*. Paris: Amiot Dumont, 1954. Observations by the Commander of the French Air Force in Indochina on the conduct of the war as well as on political problems.

CHESNEAUX, JEAN. *Contribution à l'histoire de la nation vietnamienne*. Paris: Editions Social, 1955. A survey of ancient and modern Vietnamese history by a French Marxist.

CHEZEL, GUY DE. *Parachute en Indochine*. Paris: Sirenes, 1947. A diary dealing with the crucial events of 1945.

CHILD, FRANK C. *Essays on Economic Growth, Capital Formation, and Public Policy*. Saigon: Michigan State University, Vietnam Advisory Group, 1961. A comprehensive study of South Vietnam's economic problems and prospects.

———. "Vietnam: The Eleventh Hour," *The New Republic*, December 4, 1961, pp. 14–16. An early warning of the consequences of Diem's police-state methods with regard to the problem of mobilizing educated people for leadership in public affairs.

CLUTTERBUCK, RICHARD L. *The Long, Long War: Counterinsurgency in Malaya and Vietnam.* New York: Frederick A. Praeger, 1966. The latest but certainly not the last of the many studies on guerrilla warfare.

COLE, ALLAN B. (ed.). *Conflict in Indo-China and International Repercussions: A Documentary History, 1945-1955.* Ithaca, N.Y.: Cornell University Press, 1956. Contains all important documents (most of which are unavailable elsewhere to the English-reading public) on the origin, history, and settlement of the Indochina War, as well as brief, lucid introductions to the major phases of the conflict. With a chronology of events.

CORLEY, FRANCIS J. "Vietnam Since Geneva," *Thought* (Fordham University Quarterly), XXXIII, 1958-59, 515-68. One of the best-informed positive accounts of Diem's achievement before 1958.

COULET, GEORGES. *Les sociétés secrets en terre d'Annam.* Saigon: C. Ardin, 1926. The secret societies of Vietnam, their history and social and psychological characteristics.

CROZIER, BRIAN. "The International Situation in Indochina," *Pacific Affairs*, XXIX, December, 1956, 309-24. Indochina after Geneva, with emphasis on the relations of North Vietnam with the Communist world.

CULTRU, P. *Histoire de la Cochinchine française des origines à 1883.* Paris: Challamel, 1910. One of the earliest and best accounts of the colonial regime and the political and administrative institutions created by the French in Cochinchina.

CUNNINGHAM, ALFRED. *The French in Tonkin and South China.* London: Sampson Low, 1902. A critical survey.

DABEZIES, PIERRE. *Forces politiques au Viet-Nam.* Mimeographed, n.p., n.d. [1957?]. A survey of the national movement in colonial Vietnam (up to 1955). The most comprehensive and politically sound work ever done on this subject.

DANNAUD, J. P. *Guerre morte.* Paris: Georges Lang, 1954. The Indochina War in pictures. A masterpiece of photography as reportorial art.

DARCOURT, PIERRE. *De Lattre au Viet-Nam: Une année de victoire.* Paris: La Table Ronde, 1965. M. Darcourt praises de Lattre's military and political achievements, and depicts him as the father of U.S. military intervention in Vietnam.

DAUFÈS, E. *La garde indigène de l'Indochine de sa création à nos jours.* 2 vols. Avignon: Seguin, 1933-34. A history up to 1932, including chapters on operations by the Indochinese Guard against native rebels.

DECOUX, JEAN. *A la barre de l'Indochine: Histoire de mon gouvernement général, 1940-1945.* Paris: Librairie Plon, 1952. The memoirs of the Admiral–Governor General written in defense of his policy of collaboration with the Japanese.

DEMARIAUX, JEAN-CLAUDE. *Les secrets des Iles Poulo-Condore: Le grand bagne indochinois.* Paris: J. Payronnet, 1956. Life in the huge French concentration camp in Indochina.

The Democratic Republic of Viet Nam. Hanoi: Foreign Languages Publishing House, 1960. An official report, concise and informative, on life in the North after the Geneva conference, with statistics on the regime's social and economic progress.

DEMOCRATIC REPUBLIC OF VIETNAM. *Documents relatifs à l'exécution des accords de Genève concernant le Viet-Nam.* Hanoi: Ministry of Foreign Affairs, 1956. Documented account of the refusal of the Diem government to execute the Geneva agreements.

———. *Vietnam's Fight Against Fascism, 1940–1945.* Paris, 1948 (n.p.). The Communist version of events in Indochina during World War II.

DESCHAMP, HUBERT, and PAUL CHAVET (eds.). *Gallieni, pacificateur.* Paris: Presses Universitaires de France, 1949. Chiefly on the role of Gallieni in putting down armed resistance to colonial rule in Tongking.

DESPUECH, JACQUES. *Le trafic des piastres.* Paris: Editions des Deux Rives, 1953. The author reveals some of the more unsavory scandals in the piaster transactions.

DEVILLERS, PHILIPPE. *Histoire du Viet-Nam de 1940 à 1952.* Paris: Editions du Seuil, 1952. The best account, by an author with firsthand experience, of French policy in Vietnam during and after World War II. Indispensable for an understanding of the causes of Communist strength and the failure of the French in fighting the Vietminh. A book that ought to be translated into English.

———. "Vietnamese Nationalism and French Policies," in WILLIAM L. HOLLAND (ed.). *Asian Nationalism and the West.* New York: Macmillan, 1953. A concentrated version of Devillers' critique of French military and political policy in fighting Vietnamese nationalism.

DIGUET, EDMOND. *Les Annamites: Société, coutumes, religions.* Paris: Challamel, 1906. A study of traditional Vietnamese society.

DINFREVILLE, JACQUES (pseudonym). *L'opération Indochine.* Paris: Editions International, 1953. Deals largely with military questions, with chapters on the Vietminh and the Bao Dai armies, by a senior French officer.

Documents of the Third National Congress of the Viet Nam Workers' Party. 4 vols. Hanoi: Foreign Languages Publishing House, 1960. The proceedings of the important Third Congress of the Party in September, 1960.

DONOGHUE, JOHN D., and VO HONG PHUC. *My Thuan: The Study of a Delta Village in South Vietnam.* Saigon: Michigan State University, Vietnam Advisory Group, 1961. The political, social, and economic life of a typical delta village.

DORGÈLES, ROLAND. *Sur la route mandarine.* Paris, 1929. The observations, mostly critical, of a novelist traveling in Vietnam.

DORSEY, JOHN T., JR. "South Vietnam in Perspective," *Far Eastern Survey,* XXVII, December, 1958, 177–82. A well-informed report on the early years of the Diem regime, typical for the period when even cautious reporters concentrated mainly on the regime's positive aspects.

DOUMER, PAUL. *L'Indo-Chine française: Souvenirs.* Paris: Vuibert et Nony,

1905. Doumer's self-congratulatory report on his achievements as Governor General of Indochina.

DRUMMOND, ROSCOE. "Reports Indicate Viet Nam Winning War Against Reds," *New York Herald Tribune*, June 3, 1963. Typical of the minority of correspondents who remained optimistic during 1963. To quote: "The trend has been so significantly and steadily favorable for so many months that now there is very real confidence that victory is within reach."

DUBRENIL, LÉON. *Paul Bert*. Paris: Felix Alcan, 1935. A biography of Bert and discussion of his plans and achievements as Governor General of Indochina.

DUCOROY, MAURICE. *Ma trahison en Indochine*. Paris: Les Editions Internationales, 1949. A defense of the French administration under Japanese occupation by a former official.

DUMAREST, ANDRÉ. *La formation des classes sociales en pays annamite*. Lyon: Imprimerie Ferréol, 1935. A thorough study of the social structure of colonial Vietnam.

EDEN, SIR ANTHONY. *Full Circle: Memoirs of Sir Anthony Eden*. Boston: Cassel, 1960. Important for the discussion of the Geneva conference.

ELSBREE, WILLARD H. *Japan's Role in Southeast Asian Nationalist Movements: 1940–1955*. Cambridge, Mass.: Harvard University Press, 1953. A survey that also includes Vietnam.

ELY, PAUL. *L'Indochine dans la tourmente*. Paris: Librairie Plon, 1964. The memoirs of the last French Commander in Chief and High Commissioner of Indochina. Important on the role of the French in Vietnam during 1954–55.

EMERSON, RUPERT, et al. *Government and Nationalism in Southeast Asia*. New York: Institute of Pacific Relations, 1942. See in particular Rupert Emerson's Introduction and Part III, Virginia Thompson's "Nationalism and Nationalist Movements in Southeast Asia."

ENNIS, THOMAS E. *French Policy and Developments in Indochina*. Chicago: University of Chicago Press, 1956. A scholarly study of French rule in Indochina with a deep insight into the effect on the educated of Vietnam and the nature of Vietnamese Communism.

FAIRBANK, HENRY G. "The Enigma of Ngo Dinh Diem," *Commonweal*, September 21, 1962. An article in praise of Diem's courage.

FALL, BERNARD B. "The Cease-Fire in Indochina: An Appraisal" (in two parts), *Far Eastern Survey*, September, 1954, pp. 135–39, and October, 1954, pp. 152–55.

———. "The Navarre Plan," *Military Review* (Fort Leavenworth), December, 1956.

———. "North Viet-Nam's Constitution and Government," *Pacific Affairs*, XXXIII, September, 1960, 282–90. A comprehensive report on and discussion of the D.R.V.'s new constitution of 1959.

———. "The Political-Religious Sects of Vietnam," *Pacific Affairs*, XXVIII (September, 1955), 235–53. Probably the best short report on, and discussion of, the origins, the leadership, and the political role of the Cao Dai, Hoa Hao, and Binh Xuyen, and their destructive effect on the political life in South Vietnam.

——. "South Vietnam's Internal Problems," *Pacific Affairs*, XXXI, September, 1958, 241–60. One of Fall's many articles warning against an overoptimistic appraisal of Diem's success in fighting his Communist opponents.

——. *Street Without Joy: Insurgency in Indochina*. Harrisburg, Pa.: Stackpole, 1961. A first-rate contribution to the military history of the Indochina War of 1946–54. The only book in English describing in convincing detail the agonies and frustrations of the French in the struggle against the ubiquitous Vietminh guerrillas.

——. *The Two Viet-Nams: A Political and Military Analysis*. New York: Frederick A. Praeger, 1963. An account and analysis of both South and North Vietnam almost up to the fall of Diem. The book abounds in statistics; it contains a comparison of institutions and achievements of both regimes, and an up-to-date biography of Ho Chi Minh. Highly critical of the Diem regime and of U.S. policy in Vietnam.

——. *The Viet-Minh Regime*. Ithaca, N.Y.: Cornell University Southeast Asia Program and the Institute of Pacific Relations, 1956. The book appeared later in French as *Le Viet Minh: La République Démocratique du Viet-Nam, 1945–1960*. Paris: Armand Colin, 1960. The most comprehensive study of the evolution, military organization, and government of North Vietnam.

——. *Viet-Nam Witness 1953–66*. New York: Frederick A. Praeger, 1966.

FARLEY, MIRIAM S. "Vietnam Kaleidoscope," *Far Eastern Survey*, May, 1955, pp. 77–78. A report on Diem's struggle with the sects.

FARRÈRE, CLAUDE. *Les civilisés*. Paris: Flammarion, 1921. A novel about the corrupting influence of power and wealth in the colonies on the French. For an extract see Appendix V.

FEYSAL, P. DE. *L'endettement agraire en Cochinchine*. Hanoi: IDEO, 1933. A survey showing indebtedness to be heavy, particularly among the peasants.

FIGUÈRES, LÉO. *Je reviens du Viet-Nam libre*. Paris, 1950 (n.p.). A Communist account of life under the Vietminh, also published in Russian, German, and English.

FINKLE, JASON L., and TRAN VAN DINH. *Provincial Government in Vietnam: Study of Vinh Long Province*. Saigon: Michigan State University, Vietnam Advisory Group, and the National Institute of Administration, 1961. Provincial government in the Mekong Delta.

FISHEL, WESLEY R. "Free Vietnam Since Geneva," *Yale Review*, XLIX, 1959, 68–79. A highly positive survey of Diem's achievements during his first four years in office, by one of his earliest and closest American advisers.

——. (ed.). *Problems of Freedom: South Vietnam Since Independence*. Chicago: Free Press of Glencoe, 1961. Contains papers presented at a conference in New York, in October, 1959, organized by the American

Friends of Vietnam. The contributors are Joseph Buttinger, John C. Donnel, John T. Dorsey, Jr., Wesley R. Fishel, William Henderson, James B. Hendry, Wolf Ladejinsky, Craig S. Lichtenwalner, Robert R. Nathan, Edgar N. Pike, Tran Ngoc Lien, and Vu Van Thai. With an introduction by the Hon. Mike Mansfield, United States Senate.

———. "The Role of the Michigan State University Group in Vietnam," *Viet My*, No. 2, 1957, pp. 39–42.

———. *Vietnam: Is Victory Possible?* Headline Series. New York: Foreign Policy Association, February, 1964.

FRÉDÉRIC-DUPONT. *Mission de la France en Asie.* Paris: Editions France-Empire, 1956. The views of a right-wing deputy and Minister of the Associated States of Indochina at the beginning of the Geneva conference. Defends his own and Georges Bidault's role at Geneva and attacks Pierre Mendès-France.

FURNIVALL, JOHN S. *Educational Progress in Southeast Asia.* New York: Institute of Pacific Relations, 1943. Indochina is treated in Chapters 3 and 5.

GALLIENI, JOSEPH. *Gallieni au Tonkin, 1892–1896.* Paris: Editions Berger-Levrault, 1941.

GARROS, GEORGES. *Forceries humaines.* Paris: Delpeuch, 1926. A study of Vietnamese nationalism, highly critical of the conditions created by the colonial regime. The author foresaw insurrection and proposed granting the Indochinese states independence. Contains an essay by Bui Quang Chieu, the leader of the Cochinchinese Constitutionalist Party.

GAUDEL, ANDRÉ. *L'Indochine française en face du Japon.* Paris: Susse, 1947. A survey of the political and military events and of the economic conditions of Indochina between 1939 and 1945.

GAULTIER, MARCEL. *Prisons japonais.* Monte Carlo: Regain, 1950. On the Japanese treatment of French prisoners after the coup of March 9, 1945.

GETTLEMAN, MARVIN E. *Vietnam: History, Documents, and Opinions on a Major World Crisis.* New York: Fawcett World Library, 1965. A collection, with an introduction and comments by Mr. Gettleman, of documents, excerpts from books, articles, public statements, and government declarations ranging in time from precolonial Vietnam to the present discussion on U.S. policy toward Vietnam.

GITTINGER, J. PRICE. "Communist Land Policy in North Viet Nam," *Far Eastern Survey*, XXVII, August, 1959, 113–26. Still the best report on the Communist efforts in the North to create a new pattern of land ownership in preparation for their policy of collectivization of agriculture.

———. *Studies on Land Tenure in Vietnam: Terminal Report.* Saigon: United States Operations Mission to Vietnam, 1959. A report, consisting largely of earlier articles on the land reform in South Vietnam. Contains also text of basic laws concerning land tenure.

GOBRON, GABRIEL. *Histoire et philosophie du caodaism.* Paris: Derby, 1949. A rather confused attempt by a French admirer to explain the Cao Dai religion.

GOELDHIEUX, CLAUDE. *Quinze mois prisonnier chez les Viets.* Paris: Armand Colin, 1960. Life in a Vietminh prison camp.

GOODRICH, CARTER. *Toward the Economic Development of Viet Nam.* New York: United Nations, 1956. Report of the Economic Survey Mission of the United Nations and Specialized Agencies to the Republic of Vietnam.

GOODWIN, RICHARD N. *Triumph or Tragedy: Reflections on Vietnam.* New York: Random House, 1966. These reflections, although informed and sophisticated, lead to rather contradictory conclusions. Goodwin defends the Administration policy of vigorous warfare, yet accepts the opposition demand for a political settlement through negotiations with the Vietcong.

GOSSELIN, CHARLES. *L'empire d'Annam.* Paris: Perrin, 1904. A surprisingly good history of precolonial Vietnam and of the period of conquest by a French officer turned amateur-historian who took part in the conquest and pacification of Indochina.

GOUDAL, JEAN. *Labor Conditions in Indochina.* Geneva: International Labour Office, 1938.

GOUROU, PIERRE. *L'avenir de l'Indochine.* Paris: Centre d'Études de Politique Etrangère, 1947. A survey of the economic problems of Indochina after World War II which emphasizes the need for rapid industrialization.

———. *The Peasants of the Tonkin Delta.* 2 vols. New Haven, Conn.: Human Relations Area File Press, 1955. Originally published in French under the title *Les paysons du delta tonkinois: étude de géographie humaine.* Paris: Editions d'Art et d'Histoire, 1936. The most exhaustive demographic study on the life of the North Vietnamese peasants by a great French scholar.

GOUVERNEMENT GENERAL DE L'INDOCHINE, DIRECTIONS DES AFFAIRES POLITIQUES ET DE SÛRETÉ GÉNÉRALE. *Contribution à l'histoire des mouvements politiques de l'Indochine française.* 5 vols. Hanoi: IDEO, 1930–33. Documents and commentaries by the colonial police authorities on the nationalist movements.

GRAHAM, ANDREW. *Interval in Indochina.* New York: St Martin's Press, 1956. Observations of a former British military attaché in Vietnam.

GRANT, J. A. C. "The Vietnam Constitution of 1956," *American Political Science Review,* LVI (June, 1958), 437–63. An analysis of Diem's constitution by an American who helped frame it.

GRAUWIN, PAUL. *Doctor at Dien Bien Phu.* New York: John Day, 1955. Memoirs, by the chief surgeon of the French garrison, at the battle of Dien Bien Phu and life as a Vietminh prisoner.

———. *Seulement médecin.* Paris: Editions France-Empire, 1956. The Indochina War seen through the eyes of a French medical officer.

GUILLAIN, ROBERT. *La fin des illusions: notes d'Indochine, Février–Juillet 1954.* Paris: Centre d'Études de Politique Étrangère, 1954. One of the best reports on the Indochina War and the battle of Dien Bien Phu by a noted French journalist.

HALBERSTAM, DAVID. *The Making of a Quagmire.* New York: Random

House, 1965. South Vietnam in 1962–63 as seen by the correspondent of *The New York Times*. A devastating critique of the Diem regime, with a detailed description of the events that led to the overthrow of Diem by the army.

HALL, D. G. E. *A History of South-East Asia*. New York: St. Martin's Press, 1955. See the chapters on Vietnam in this standard work on the region.

HALLE, GÜNTHER. *Légion Étrangère*. East Berlin: Volk und Welt, 1952. Typical of the several books by German members of the Foreign Legion who joined the Vietminh after being captured or deserting.

HAMMER, ELLEN J. "Indochina," in LAWRENCE K. ROSINGER, *et al. The State of Asia*. New York: Alfred A. Knopf, 1951. Pp. 221–67. One of the first essays by an American author on the background of the Franco-Vietnamese conflict.

———. *Politics and Parties in Viet Nam*. New Delhi: Indian Council of World Affairs, and Asian Relations Organization, Foreign Policy Reports, 1953. A report on the origin and development of the nationalist parties and the Communist movements against colonialism before, during, and after World War II.

———. "Progress Report on Southern Vietnam," *Pacific Affairs*, September, 1957, pp. 221–35. A positive account by the well-known historian who two years earlier had been highly critical of the Diem regime.

———. *The Struggle for Indochina*. Stanford, Calif.: Stanford University Press, 1954. A pioneering English-language work on the subject, particularly strong and well-documented on French policy toward the Vietminh and the pro–Bao Dai parties between 1945 and 1953.

———. *The Struggle for Indochina Continues*. Stanford, Calif.: Stanford University Press, 1955. A supplement to the earlier book, highly critical of the Diem regime.

HARNETT, JOSEPH J. "The Vietnamese Refugee Five Years Later," *Migration News*, September-October, 1959. A description (by region) of the refugee resettlement in South Vietnam.

HEMPSTONE, SMITH. *A Tract of Time. A Novel About Vietnam*. Boston: Houghton Mifflin, 1966. The tragic failure, because of the political duplicity of the Diem regime, of a well-meaning American adviser among the mountain tribes. A somewhat overdramatized version of the end of Diem.

HENDERSON, WILLIAM. "South Vietnam Finds Itself," *Foreign Affairs*, XXXV (January, 1957), 283–94. A report on the problems that faced Diem during his first two years in office, and a discussion, positive but not uncritical, of Diem's manner of dealing with them.

HENRY, YVES. *L'économie agricole de l'Indochine*. Hanoi: IDEO, 1932. A comprehensive study of Indochinese agriculture.

HERTRICH, JEAN-MICHEL. *Doc-Lap! L'indépendance ou la mort*. Paris: Vigneau, 1946. A Frenchman's dramatic account of the Vietminh revolution of August, 1945.

HEYMARD, JEAN. *Vérité sur l'Indochine*. Paris: Nouvelles Editions Debresse, 1962. The first chapter (pp. 9–79) is a "refutation" of *The Smaller*

Dragon ("Réfutation de l'histoire du Vietnam écri par Joseph Buttinger, sous le titre: *The Smaller Dragon* [*Le petit dragon*]"). After a seventy-two-page refutation of the book, Jean Heymard comes to the surprising conclusion that *The Smaller Dragon*, despite its "tendentious character" and "lack of serenity," is "a remarkable monument to the history of Vietnam. Because of its universality and the perfection of its documentation, it constitutes the most complete historical work on this part of Indochina" (p. 71). The rest of the book is devoted to a series of polemical attacks on U.S. policy in Vietnam.

HICKEY, GERALD C. *The Study of a Vietnamese Rural Community*. Saigon: Michigan State University, Vietnam Advisory Group, 1960. Describes life and administration in a typical delta village.

———. *Village in Vietnam*. New Haven, Conn., and London: Yale University Press, 1964. A broad study, based on the author's earlier work for the Michigan State University Vietnam Advisory Group. The standard text in English on life in a South Vietnamese village.

HOA MAI (ed.). *The "Nhan Van" Affair*. Saigon: Vietnam Chapter, Asian Peoples' Anti-Communist League, 1958. A report on the "intellectual revolt" in the North in 1956, with excerpts from writings by Communist authors in *Nhan Van* and other magazines and newspapers.

HOANG VAN CHI. "Collectivization and Rice Production," *The China Quarterly* (London), No. 9, January-March, 1962, pp. 94–105. Peasant resistance to collectivized agriculture and the drawbacks of collectivization for rice farming are convincingly described.

———. *From Colonialism to Communism: A Case History of North Vietnam*. New York: Frederick A. Praeger, 1964. Deals chiefly with post–World War II Vietnam. Contains much new material about organization and leadership of the Vietminh.

———. (ed.). *The New Class in North Vietnam*. Saigon: Cong Dan, 1958. Articles, stories, and poems published in the D.R.V. selected to show the depth of anti-Communist feeling among the intellectuals in the North.

HO CHI MINH. *Selected Works*. 3 vols. Hanoi: Foreign Languages Publishing House, 1960 and 1961.

HONEY, P. J. *Communism in North Vietnam: Its Role in the Sino-Soviet Dispute*. Cambridge, Mass.: The M.I.T. Press, 1963. A survey and analysis by the well-known authority on Vietnam, lecturer in Vietnamese at the School of Oriental and African Studies of the University of London.

———. (ed.). *North Vietnam Today: Profile of a Communist Satellite*. New York: Frederick A. Praeger, 1962. Contains nine articles previously published in *The China Quarterly*. Introduction and an essay discussing the North Vietnamese leadership by P. J. Honey. Other contributors are Bernard B. Fall, Philippe Devillers, William Kaye, and Hoang Van Chi.

———. "North Vietnam's Party Congress," *The China Quarterly*, No. 4, October–December, 1960, pp. 66–75. A discussion of the Third Party Congress of the Workers' Party held in Hanoi in September, 1960.

————. "The Problem of Democracy in Vietnam," *World Today*, February, 1960, pp. 71–79. A cautious defense of Diem's authoritarian methods of government.

HOTHAM, DAVID. "U.S. Aid to Vietnam—A Balance Sheet," *The Reporter*, September 16, 1957, pp. 30–33. A highly critical report by an English journalist. Hotham's main attack is directed against the "lavish" aid for the army and the neglect of economic aid and industrial development.

HUYNH SANH THONG. "Greatest Little Man in Asia," *The Nation*, February 18, 1961. A sharp attack on the Diem regime and on U.S. support for Diem by a supporter of the Dai Viet Party residing in the United States.

INSTITUTE FRANCO-SUISSE D'ÉTUDES COLONIALES. *France and Viet-Nam: The Franco-Vietnamese Conflict According to Official Documents.* Geneva: Editions du Milieu du Monde, 1947. A compilation attempting to justify the French policy of the reconquest of Indochina.

ISAACS, HAROLD R. *New Cycle in Asia.* New York: Macmillan, 1947. Largely documents on post–World War II developments in Asia, beginning with the Potsdam Declaration of July 26, 1945. Contains important documents concerning Vietnam (pp. 156–75). Notes and introductions by the author.

————. *No Peace for Asia.* New York: Macmillan, 1947. Chapter on Indochina (pp. 134–76) is probably the first comprehensive report on the events of Vietnam in 1945–46 by an American eyewitness. Isaacs then was the Asian correspondent of *Newsweek*. His report still makes exciting reading.

ISOART, PAUL. *Le phénomène national vietnamien: De l'indépendance unitaire à l'indépendance fractionée.* Paris: Librairie Général de Droit et de Jurisprudence, 1961. The last of the great French scholarly works on the history of Vietnam. Isoart's work is up to date, richly documented, and despite the author's lapses into apologies for colonialism, he is objective in his evaluation of French rule in Vietnam. Excessively critical of American policy after 1954.

JACOBY, ERICH H. *Agrarian Unrest in Southeast Asia.* Bombay: Asia Publishing House, 1961. A general survey covering the colonial and postcolonial periods. Chapter VI deals with Indochina.

JOINER, CHARLES A. "South Vietnam's Buddhist Crisis: Organization for Charity, Dissidence, and Unity," *Asian Survey*, IV, No. 7 (July, 1964). A detailed report on the Buddhist crisis of 1963 prior to the fall of Diem.

JUMPER, ROY. "The Communist Challenge to South Vietnam," *Far Eastern Survey*, XXV, November, 1956, 161–68. An early warning of the threat the Communist appeal to the peasants in the South posed to the Diem regime.

————. "Mandarin Bureaucracy and Politics in South Vietnam," *Pacific Affairs*, XXX (March, 1957), 44–58. An analysis of the role played by the Vietnamese mandarins under the colonial regime and of the problems of mandarin mentality for postcolonial Vietnam.

JUMPER, ROY. "Problems of Public Administration in South Vietnam," *Far Eastern Survey*, No. 26, 1957, pp. 183–90. A description of the administration after 1954 and the efforts to modernize it.

——, and NGUYEN THI HUE. *Notes on the Political and Administrative History of Vietnam: 1802–1962.* Saigon: Michigan State University, Vietnam Advisory Group, 1962.

KARNOW, STANLEY. "The Edge of Chaos," *The Saturday Evening Post,* September 28, 1963. The Buddhist crises, the failure of the Diem regime to win popular support, the "family" dictatorship, and its lack of success in fighting Communism. A fierce attack on the destructive role of Mme. Nhu.

KHÉRIAN, GRÉGOIRE. "La querelle de l'industrialization," *Revue indochinoise juridique et économique* (Saigon), IV (1938). See also his other articles on economic problems in 1937–38 issues of the same periodical. Khérian was a firm advocate of industrialization of Indochina.

LACOUTURE, JEAN. "Ho Chi Minh et la tradition révolutionnaire française," in *Cinq hommes et la France.* Paris: Editions du Seuil, 1961. Pp. 11–108.

——. "Inside North Vietnam," *New Republic*, May 21, 1962, pp. 17–20. One of the rare firsthand reports from North Vietnam in English by the foreign correspondent of *Le Monde*, renowned since 1946 as one of the best French reporters in Vietnam.

——. *Vietnam: Between Two Truces.* New York: Random House, 1966. With an Introduction by Joseph Kraft. Largely a collection of articles on both South and North Vietnam. Important for its information on the founding and composition of the National Liberation Front. Highly critical of the Diem regime and its conduct of the war.

——, and PHILIPPE DEVILLERS. *La fin d'une guerre: Indochine 1954.* Paris: Editions du Seuil, 1960. The authors, probably the two best-informed Frenchmen on Vietnam, trace the political and military events of the Indochina War up to the defeat of the French at Dien Bien Phu. The book also contains the best account of the proceedings at the Geneva conference.

LANCASTER, DONALD. *The Emancipation of French Indochina.* London and New York: Oxford University Press, 1961. A well-documented survey of French Indochina from the conquest to the establishment of the two Vietnams by a British diplomat who spent the critical early 1950's in Vietnam.

LANESSAN, JEAN-MARIE-ANTOINE DE. *La colonisation française en Indochine.* Paris: Felix Alcan, 1895. A critical survey of French policy in Indochina by a former Governor General.

——. *L'Indo-Chine française: Etude politique, économique et administrative sur la Cochinchine, le Cambodge, L'Annam et le Tonkin.* Paris: Felix Alcan, 1889.

LANIEL, JOSEPH. *Le drame indochinois: De Dien-Bien-Phu au pari de Genève.* Paris: Librairie Plon, 1957. A defense of his policy by the French Premier who was succeeded during the Geneva conference by Pierre Mendès-France. Largely a reply to the book by General Navarre.

LANOUE, H. "Vietnam: Bases économiques et sociales des sectes," *Cahiers Internationaux*, No. 65, April, 1955, pp. 75–88. A study of the economic and social basis of the Cao Dai and Binh Xuyen sects.

LAURENT, ARTHUR. *La Banque de l'Indochine et la piastre*. Paris, 1954 (n.p). A vehement criticism of the role the Bank of Indochina played in the Vietnamese economy.

LE BOURGEOIS, JACQUES. *Saigon sans la France: Des japonais au Viet-Minh*. Paris: Librairie Plon, 1949. An account chiefly of the trials and humiliations the French of Saigon suffered under the Japanese after the coup of March, 1945. Uncritical of French cooperation with the Japanese prior to the coup.

LE MYRE DE VILERS. *Les institutions civiles de la Cochinchine, 1879–1881: Recueil des principaux documents officiels*. Paris: Emile-Paul, 1908. Mainly a collection of laws, reports, and other official documents by the first civilian head of French Cochinchina.

LE THANH KHOI. *Le Viet-Nam: Histoire et civilisation*. Paris: Editions de Minuit, 1955. A scholarly work on the history of Vietnam from its origin, to 1953 by a pro-Vietminh author.

LEROY, JEAN. *Un homme dans la rizière*. Paris: Editions de Paris, 1955. The memoirs and observations by the Eurasian commander of the largely Catholic militia operating successfully against the Vietminh in the Ben Tre Province, south of Saigon. Colonel Leroy's success was mainly due to the social and political reforms he carried out in the province under his control.

LÉVY, ROGER. *L'Indochine et ses traités*. Paris: Paul Hartmann, 1947. Text of treaties between France and Indochina, and between France and other countries concerning Indochina.

———, GUY LACAM, and ANDREW ROTH. *French Interests and Policies in the Far East*. New York: Institute of Pacific Relations, 1941. A study of French economic and trade policies. It covers also the first months of the Japanese occupation of Indochina.

LEWIS, NORMAN. *A Dragon Apparent*. London: Jonathan Cape, 1951. The lively account of an English traveler in Vietnam, especially notable for its observations on the mountain tribes in the southern and central highlands.

LINDHOLM, RICHARD W. (ed.). *Viet-nam, The First Five Years. An International Symposium*. East Lansing, Mich.: Michigan State University Press, 1959.

LIPPMANN, WALTER. "Troubled Continents," *New York Herald Tribune*, July 24, 1962. An early plea for a joint effort by Washington and Moscow to end the conflict in Vietnam.

LURO, ELIACIN. *Le pays d'Annam*. 2d ed. Paris: Leroux, 1897. A basic study of Vietnamese political and social institutions by one of the outstanding early French officials in Vietnam. Based on the author's lectures at the Collège des Stagiaires (training school for French administrators) at Saigon.

LYAUTEY, LOUIS HUBERT. *Lettres du Tonkin et de Madagascar, 1894–1899*.

Paris: Armand Colin, 1921. The larger portion of this book deals with Lyautey's experiences in fighting guerrillas in Tonkin.

MacAllister, Robert J. "The Great Gamble: United States Policy Toward South Viet Nam from July, 1954, to July, 1956." A dissertation submitted to the Department of Political Science, University of Chicago, 1958 (mimeographed). An extremely conscientious and well-documented survey of two crucial years in U.S.–Vietnamese relations.

Mansfield, Mike. "Reprieve in Vietnam," *Harper's Magazine*, January, 1956. A cautiously optimistic appraisal of Diem's early achievements.

Marchand, Jean. *L'Indochine en guerre*. Paris: Pouzet, 1955. A military history of Indochina from 1870 to 1954.

Martin, Françoise. *Heures tragiques au Tonkin: 9 mars 1945–18 mars 1946*. Paris: Berger-Levrault, 1948. Political commentary by a shocked Frenchwoman on the Japanese coup of March, 1945 and on the rise of the Vietminh.

Masson, André. *Histoire de l'Indochine*. Paris: Presses Universitaires de France, 1950. A short but highly informative history of Indochina in praise of French colonial rule.

———. *Histoire du Vietnam*. Paris: Presses Universitaires de France, 1960. Like the author's earlier history of Indochina, a short and informative book, though rather uncritical of the colonial regime.

Mecklin, John. *Mission in Torment: An Intimate Account of the U.S. Role in Vietnam*. Garden City, N.Y.: Doubleday, 1965. An account of the failure of the Diem regime and the conflict between American correspondents and the U.S. Mission in Saigon over the true situation in Vietnam by a former American official in Vietnam.

Millet, Stanley. "Terror in Vietnam: An American's Ordeal at the Hands of Our 'Friends,'" *Harper's*, September, 1962. An American exchange professor's troubles with the Diem police.

Monet, Paul. *Les jauniers: Histoire vrai*. Paris: Gallimard, 1931. Chiefly on the recruiting and mistreatment of plantation labor.

Monier, René. *La question du monopole de l'alcool au Tonkin et dans le Nord-Annam: contributions à l'histoire financière de l'Indochine*. Paris: Larose, 1913. A comprehensive study by a former French administrator.

Montaigut, Fernand de. *La colonisation française dans l'est de la Cochinchine*. Limoges: Perrette, 1929. A history of the agricultural development under the colonial regime, including the development of the rubber plantations.

Montgomery, John D. *The Politics of Foreign Aid: American Experience in Southeast Asia*. New York: Frederick A. Praeger, 1962. The only comprehensive report, analysis, and criticism of American aid to Southeast Asia, with heavy emphasis on Vietnam.

———, and the NIA Case Development Seminar. *Cases in Vietnamese Administration*. Saigon: Michigan State University, Vietnam Advisory Group, 1959. Twenty case studies.

Mordal, Jacques. *Marine Indochine*. Paris: Amiot Dumont, 1953. Another review of military and political events from 1940 on, with emphasis on naval operations.

MORDANT, GENERAL. *Au service de la France en Indochine: 1941–1945.* Saigon: Imprimerie Française d'Outre-Mer, 1950. The memoirs of the general whom de Gaulle, at the end of 1944, appointed to head the anti-Japanese French "resistance" in Indochina. A defense of his record and a reply to his critics.

MOSCAT, HENRI. "Un échec: 50 ans de colonialisme économique en Indochine," *Les Temps Modernes,* No. 9 (1953), pp. 388–400. A devastating criticism of French economic policies in Indochina.

MURTI, B. S. N. *Vietnam Divided: The Unfinished Struggle.* New York: Asia Publishing House, 1964. The views of an Indian member of the International Control Commission. Critical of both the North and South Vietnamese regimes.

MUS, PAUL. "The Role of the Village in Vietnamese Politics," *Pacific Affairs,* XXII (September, 1949), 265–72.

———. *Viet-Nam: Sociologie d'une guerre.* Paris: Editions du Seuil, 1950. A somewhat rambling yet profound study of Vietnamese life and of nationalism and Communism in Vietnam by a man who obviously admires the Vietnamese and sympathizes with their national aspirations. Like DEVILLERS' *Histoire au Viet-Nam,* this book ought to be published in English, for it would greatly contribute to an understanding of the complex Vietnamese political scene.

———. *Le Vietnam chez lui.* Paris: Centre d'Etudes Politiques Etrangères, 1946. This brochure is extremely enlightening on French-Japanese collaboration and on the background of the Indochina War.

MUSOLF, LLOYD D. "Public Enterprise and Development Perspectives in South Vietnam," *Asian Survey,* III, No. 8 (August, 1963), 357–72. A study of the problem of industrialization of South Vietnam and the conflict of public and private enterprise. In the author's opinion, the regime failed in both respects.

NAVARRE, HENRI. *Agonie de l'Indochine.* Paris: Librairie Plon, 1956. The views of the Commander in Chief of the French Union forces in Indochina during the last year of the Indochina War.

NAVILLE, PIERRE. *La guerre du Viet-Nam.* Paris: Editions de la Revue Internationale, 1949. A collection of articles written during 1947 and 1948 on political, economic, and military subjects by a leftist opponent of French policy in Indochina.

NETON, ALBÉRIC. *L'Indo-Chine et son avenir économique.* Paris: Perrin, 1904. An early plea for a more progressive economic policy in Indochina, with emphasis on the need for industrialization.

NGO VAN CHIEU. *Journal d'un combattant Viet-Minh.* Paris: Editions du Seuil, 1955. Probably the best of all descriptions of combat operations from the Communist side.

NGUYEN AI QUOC (HO CHI MINH). *Le procès de la colonisation française.* Paris, 1926. The famous brochure by Ho Chi Minh on French colonial exploitation and police terror. The writing is mediocre, the accusations exaggerated and poorly documented.

NGUYEN DUY THANH. *My Four Years with the Viet Minh.* Bombay: Democratic Research Service, 1950.

NGUYEN KIEN. *Le Sud Viet-Nam depuis Dien-Bien-Phu.* Paris: François Maspéro, 1963. A Communist account of South Vietnam under Diem.

NGUYEN KIEN GIANG. *Les grandes dates du parti de la classe ouvrière du Viet Nam.* Hanoi: Editions en Langues Etrangères, 1960. Important dates in the history of the Communist movement in Vietnam from 1919 to 1954.

NGUYEN THAI. *Is South Viet-Nam Viable?* Manila: Carmelo and Bauerman, 1962. A devastating critique of the Diem regime by a close collaborator of Diem who for several years headed the government's press service.

NGUYEN TUYET MAI. "Electioneering: Vietnamese Style," *Asian Survey,* II, November, 1962, 11–18. A shocking report by the wife of an official whom Mme. Nhu succeeded in keeping out of the National Assembly.

NGUYEN VAN THAI and NGUYEN VAN MUNG. *A Short History of Viet-Nam.* Saigon: The Times Publishing Co., 1958. A historical survey, from Vietnam's legendary past to 1956. Valuable chiefly for its account of the movements of national resistance to colonial rule.

O'BALLANCE, EDGAR. *The Indo-China War 1945–1954: A Study in Guerrilla Warfare.* London: Faber & Faber, 1964. The only study of the subject in English. An excellent outline and analysis.

PAGNIEZ, YVONNE. *Choses vues au Vietnam: naissance d'une nation.* Paris: La Palatine, 1954. A Swiss journalist reports approvingly on the formation and the activities of the Bao Dai regime.

———. *Français d'Indochine.* Paris: Flammarion, 1953. A Swiss journalist's pro-French comments on the Franco-Vietminh conflict.

PARET, PETER. *French Revolutionary Warfare from Indochina to Algeria: The Analysis of a Political and Military Doctrine.* New York: Frederick A. Praeger, 1964.

———, and JOHN W. SHY. *Guerrillas in the 1960's.* Rev. ed. New York: Frederick A. Praeger, 1962. A short introduction to current theories on guerrilla warfare.

PETER, VICTOR, and KUMAR GOSHAL. *Bitter End in Southeast Asia.* New York: Marzani and Munsell, 1964. A pro-Communist version of recent events in Vietnam.

PERRAULT, GILLES. *Les parachutistes.* Paris: Editions du Seuil, 1961. A study of the role of elite forces in modern warfare.

PHAM QUYNH. *Essais franco-annamites.* Hue: Editions Bui Huy Tin, 1937; and *Nouveaux essais franco-annamites.* Hue: Editions Bui Huy Tin, 1938. A brilliant journalist discusses Franco-Vietnamese relations, aiming at reconciling Vietnamese nationalists and a more liberal colonial regime.

———. *Les paysans tonkinois à travers les parlers populaires.* Hanoi: Imprimerie Tonkinoise, 1930. An attempt to mirror the North Vietnamese peasant in his proverbs.

PHAM VAN DONG and THE COMMITTEE FOR THE STUDY OF THE HISTORY OF

THE VIETNAMESE WORKERS' PARTY. *President Ho Chi Minh.* Hanoi: Foreign Language Publishing House (n.d.). Two articles offering a quasi-
official and highly propagandistic biography of Ho Chi Minh with many
quotations from Ho Chi Minh's writings.

PHAN QUANG DAN. *The War in Indochina: A Comparative Study of the
Vietminh and the French Union Forces* (mimeographed, [n.p.]), 1954.
An anti-Communist's attack on the French and the Bao Dai regime.

POSTEL, RAOUL. *À travers la Cochinchine.* Paris: Challamel, 1887. One of
the earliest surveys by a French official of political and social conditions
of Cochinchina under French rule.

POUVOURVILLE, ALBERT DE. *Les défenses de l'Indochine et la politique d'association.* Paris: Pedone, 1905. An expert on Asia and Indochina expresses
his concern over the dangers that threaten the French position unless a
policy of genuine "association" is adopted. (For a listing of de Pouvourville's many other works on Indochina, see ROY JUMPER. *Bibliography
on the Political and Administrative History of Vietnam: 1802–1962.*)

QUALID, WILLIAM. *Le privilège de la Banque de l'Indochine et la question
des banques coloniales.* Paris: Girard, 1923. On the political and economic
role of the Bank of Indochina.

RASKIN, MARCUS G., and BERNARD B. FALL (eds.). *The Viet-Nam Reader.*
New York: Random House, 1965. Articles and documents on American
foreign policy and the Vietnam crisis.

RÉNALD, JEAN. *L'enfer de Dien Bien Phu.* Paris: Flammarion, 1954. A reporter on the spot describes the military events leading to the end of the
Indochina War.

REPUBLIC OF VIETNAM. *La politique agressive des Viet-Minh communistes
et la guerre subversive communiste au Sud Viet-Nam.* Saigon, 1962.
Documented account of guerrilla activities inside South Vietnam during
1961–62. A follow-up was published in 1964 under the title *Communist
Aggression Against the Republic of Viet-Nam.*

———. *The Problem of Reunification of Vietnam.* Saigon: Ministry of
Information, 1958.

RESTON, JAMES. "General Taylor's Mission to Southeast Asia," *The New
York Times,* October 20, 1961. One of the more perceptive of the many
articles on the Taylor mission to Vietnam.

RIESSEN, RENÉ. *Jungle Mission.* New York: Thomas Y. Crowell, 1957. A
leader of small antiguerrilla units describes jungle warfare in Indochina.

———. *Le silence du ciel.* Paris: Editions de la Pensée Moderne, 1956. The
life of the men in the paratroop commandos in Indochina.

ROBEQUAIN, CHARLES. *The Economic Development of French Indo-China.*
London: Oxford University Press, 1944. The basic book on the French
colonial economy. First published in French in 1939. The English edition
has a supplement by John K. Andrus and Katrine R. C. Greene, "Recent
Developments in Indo-China, 1939–1943."

———. *Le Thanh Hoa: Étude géographique d'une province annamite.* 2
vols. Paris: G. Van Oest, 1929. Geographic study of a North Vietnamese
province.

ROBERTS, STEPHEN H. *History of French Colonial Policy: 1870–1925.* 2 vols. London: P. S. King, 1929. The first comprehensive treatment of French policy in Indochina (Vol. II) in English. Highly critical.

ROLLAND, PIERRE. *Contre-Guérilla.* Paris: Louvois, 1956. An account of counterguerrilla activities by a French captain.

ROSE, DALE L. *The Vietnamese Civil Service System.* Saigon: Michigan State University, Vietnam Advisory Group, 1961. A comprehensive description of the civil-service system.

ROUBAUD, LOUIS. *Viet-Nam: La tragédie indochinoise.* Paris: Valois, 1931. A French journalist reports on the rebellion in 1930 and the subsequent persecution of nationalists, in a book generally harshly critical of the colonial administration.

ROUYER, CHARLES E. *Histoire militaire et politique de l'Annam et du Tonkin depuis 1799.* Paris: Lavauzelle, 1906. Covers the subject up to the end of Vietnamese armed resistance in 1896.

ROY, JULES. *Batailles dans la rizière.* Paris: Gallimard, 1953. Essays discussing the wars of Indochina and Korea by the author of the standard work on the battle of Dien Bien Phu.

———. *The Battle of Dien Bien Phu.* New York: Harper & Row, 1965. With an Introduction by Neil Sheehan. A dramatic and comprehensive account of the fateful battle by a French officer and author of several works on the Indochina War.

SABATTIER, G. *Le destin de l'Indochine: Souvenir et documents, 1941–1951.* Paris: Librairie Plon, 1952. The role of the French military under the Japanese occupation by the general who commanded the French troops in Tongking, offered resistance to the Japanese coup of March, 1945, and led about 2,000 French and Vietnamese soldiers in a fighting retreat into southern China.

SAINTENY, JEAN. *Histoire d'une paix manquée.* Paris: Amiot Dumont, 1953. The memoirs of the leading spokesman of the Free French in Kunming (China) during World War II, and the first French official to return to North Vietnam from China after the Japanese collapse. Important because of the leading role of Sainteny in the negotiations between the French and Ho Chi Minh. Strongly anti-American.

SALISBURY-JONES, SIR GUY. *So Full a Glory.* London: Weidenfeld & Nicolson, 1954. A book in praise of de Lattre.

SANDERS, SOL. "Crisis in Indochina," *The New Leader,* March 21, 1955, pp. 3–5.

SARRAUT, ALBERT. *La mise en valeur des colonies françaises.* Paris: Payot, 1923. The views of a prominent French spokesman of liberal colonial policies who was twice Governor General of Indochina.

SAVANI, A. M. *Visage et images du Sud Viet-Nam.* Saigon: Imprimerie Française d'Outre-Mer, 1955. Particularly valuable because of the author's unusual knowledge of the political-religious sects, and for his description of the political and administrative organization of the French-controlled Bao Dai regime.

SCIGLIANO, ROBERT. "The Electoral Process in South Vietnam. Politics in an Underdeveloped State," *Midwest Journal of Political Science,* IV,

May, 1960, 138–61. Discusses critically the elections held in South Vietnam in 1956 and 1959.

———. "Political Parties in South Vietnam under the Republic," *Pacific Affairs*, XXXIII, June, 1960, 327–46. A report on the nature and role of the legal political parties and their leadership.

———. *South Vietnam: Nation Under Stress.* Boston: Houghton Mifflin, 1963. The best political analysis in English of South Vietnam under Diem. Scigliano acquired his firsthand knowledge during the several years he spent in South Vietnam as an administrative adviser to the government.

SHADBAD, THEODORE. "Economic Developments in North Vietnam," *Pacific Affairs*, XXXI, March, 1958, 36–53. An early critical analysis of the economic achievements of the Hanoi regime, largely based on Russian sources.

SHAH, SIRDAR IKBAL ALI. *Viet Nam.* London: The Octagon Press, 1960. A brief historical introduction followed by a political survey dealing largely with events after World War II.

SHAPLEN, ROBERT. "The Enigma of Ho Chi Minh," *The Reporter*, January 27, 1955. A still valid description of the life and the political role of Ho Chi Minh.

———. *A Forest of Tigers.* New York: Alfred A. Knopf, 1956. A novel about Indochina against the well-drawn background of the conflict between French colonial and Vietnamese national aspirations in the early 1950's.

———. *The Lost Revolution.* New York: Harper & Row, 1965. The comments of a long-time observer on recent Vietnamese history. Important especially for the chapter on the crisis that ended the Diem regime.

———. "A Reporter in Vietnam: The Delta, the Plateau, and the Mountains," *The New Yorker*, August 11, 1962. A report on the state of the war, the strategic-hamlet program, and the Diem regime's need to win the support of the people in order to survive.

———. "A Reporter in Vietnam: Diem," *The New Yorker*, September 22, 1962, pp. 103–31. A first attempt at a biography, based largely on interviews with Diem.

SHARP, LAURISTON. "Paradoxes in the Indochina Dilemma," *The Annals of the American Academy of Political and Social Science*, No. 294, 1954, pp. 89–98. A discussion of the Franco-Vietnamese conflict.

SILVESTRE, JULES. *L'empire d'Annam et le peuple annamite.* Paris: Felix Alcan, 1889. An outstanding early colonial administrator describes Vietnam and the Vietnamese people.

SMUCKLER, RALPH H., et al. *Report on the Police of Vietnam.* Saigon: Michigan State University, Vietnam Advisory Group, 1955. One of the Advisory Group's sober descriptive studies.

STAROBIN, JOSEPH R. *Eyewitness in Indochina.* New York: Cameron and Kahn, 1954. The impressions of an American, then still a Communist, who traveled in Vietminh-held territory.

STUHLMANN, MANFRED. *Ho Chi Minh: Ein Leben für Vietnam.* Berlin:

Dietz Verlag, 1960. A book in praise of Ho Chi Minh as the liberator of the Vietnamese people from colonialism.

SULLY, FRANÇOIS. "Life Under Uncle Ho," *Newsweek*, August 27, 1962. A report based on reports by visitors from neutral nations, by a correspondent expelled by the Diem regime.

TANHAM, GEORGE K. *Communist Revolutionary Warfare: The Vietminh in Indochina*. New York: Frederick A. Praeger, 1961. An analytic report on the organization, tactics, and the political indoctrination of the Vietminh Army, and a discussion of the reasons for its success in fighting the French.

———, with W. ROBERT WARNE, EARL J. YOUNG, and WILLIAM A. NIGHSWONGER. *War Without Guns*. New York: Frederick A. Praeger, 1966. A report on the work of the American civilians in rural Vietnam, written to demonstrate "that United States aid in support of Vietnam has not been solely military."

TAYLOR, MILTON C. "South Vietnam: Lavish Aid, Limited Progress," *Pacific Affairs*, XXXIV, No. 3 (1961), 242–56. Very critical of the entire aid program and the Diem government's economic policy.

THAI VAN KIEM. *Vietnam, Past and Present*. (Published under the auspices of the Vietnamese Department of National Education and the National Commission for UNESCO.) Paris: Commercial Transworld Editions, n.d. [probably 1956]. A richly illustrated survey of Vietnamese history, art, customs, legends, as well as of achievements of the Diem regime.

THOMPSON, VIRGINIA. *French Indochina*. London: Allen & Unwin, 1937. The standard work in English on the French colonial regime in Indochina. A well-balanced account of its achievement and shortcomings.

———, and RICHARD ADLOFF. *The Left Wing in Southeast Asia*. New York: William Sloane Associates, 1950. Chapter II treats Indochina.

TON THAT THIEN. "The Geneva Agreements and Peace Prospects in Vietnam," *India Quarterly*, XII (October-December, 1956), 375–88.

TONGAS, GÉRARD. *J'ai vécu dans l'enfer communiste au Nord Viet-Nam et j'ai choisi la liberté*. Paris: Nouvelles Editions Debresse, 1960. A very biased but lively firsthand report of life under the Vietminh after 1954. The author, a French historian and a former Vietminh sympathizer, became a violent anti-Communist.

TOURNOUX, J. R. *Secrets d'état*. Paris: Librairie Plon, 1960. A rather sensational treatment of subjects the author holds to be "secrets" of French colonial history.

TRAGER, FRANK N. (ed.). *Marxism in Southeast Asia: A Study of Four Countries*. Stanford, Calif.: Stanford University Press, 1959. Contains I. Milton Sacks's study, "Marxism in Vietnam," indispensable for an understanding of Vietnamese Communism. The editor summarizes and discusses the findings of his contributors in a separate essay.

TRAN VAN DINH. *No Passenger on the River: A Novel*. New York: Vantage Press, 1965. A former Vietnamese diplomat gives a fictional account of the failure and collapse of the Diem regime.

TREGASKIS, RICHARD. *Vietnam Diary*. New York: Holt, Rinehart and

Winston, 1963. The lives and experiences of the American combat advisers.

TRINQUIER, ROGER. *Modern Warfare: A French View of Counterinsurgency.* New York: Frederick A. Praeger, 1964. An expert account on the subject, remarkable for its frank defense of the use of torture in fighting guerrillas.

TRUED, M. N. "South Vietnam's Industrial Development Center," *Pacific Affairs,* XXXIII (September, 1960), 250–67.

TRUMBULL, ROBERT. "First Lady of Vietnam," *The New York Times Magazine,* November 8, 1962. A sketch of "the most powerful single female personality to emerge in Asia in recent years."

———. *The Scrutable East: A Correspondent's Report on Southeast Asia.* New York: David McKay, 1964. The views of the long-time Far Eastern correspondent of *The New York Times.* Chapters 13 through 16 treat Vietnam.

TRUONG CHINH. *Primer for Revolt: The Communist Takeover in Viet-Nam.* New York: Frederick A. Praeger, 1963. A facsimile edition of two books by the Vietnamese Communist Party's chief theoretician. The two books are *The August Revolution* (Hanoi, 1958) and *The Resistance Will Win* (Hanoi, 1960). The latter describes the political and military strategy of the Vietminh against the French, based on Mao Tse-tung's writings on guerrilla warfare.

UNITED STATES, DEPARTMENT OF STATE, BUREAU OF PUBLIC AFFAIRS, OFFICE OF PUBLIC SERVICE. *A Threat to Peace: North Vietnam's Effort to Conquer South Vietnam.* Washington, D.C.: Government Printing Office, 1961. Detailed report, with a documentary appendix, of Communist subversive activities in South Vietnam since 1954.

———, OFFICE OF INTELLIGENCE RESEARCH. *Political Alignments of Vietnamese Nationalists,* by I. Milton Sacks. Publications of the U.S. Department of State, No. 3708. Washington, D.C.: Government Printing Office, 1949. Probably the first detailed report by an American on the Vietnamese nationalist movement and leadership.

U.S. SENATE, COMMITTEE ON FOREIGN RELATIONS. *Report on Indochina.* Report by Senator Mike Mansfield. 83rd Cong., 2d sess. Washington, D.C.: Government Printing Office, 1954.

VANLANDE, RENÉ. *L'Indochine sous la menace communiste.* Paris: J. Peyronnet, 1930. The author shows that the threat of Communism necessitates a reform of the colonial administration.

VARET, PIERRE. *Au pays d'Annam: Les dieux qui meurent.* Paris: Eugène Figuière, 1932. A discussion of administrative and social problems, and a report on the revolutionary nationalist activities of 1930 and 1931.

VIAL, PAULIN. *Les premières années de la Cochinchine.* 2 vols. Paris: Challamel, 1874. Another early history of French Cochinchina by a prominent colonial administrator.

Viet Nam and Southeast Asia. Report by Senator Mike Mansfield *et al.* 88th Cong., 1st sess. Washington, D.C.: Government Printing Office, 1963. The report found that at the end of 1962 (after seven years of

Diem), South Vietnam "appears less, not more, stable than it was at the outset."

VIETNAM CULTURAL ASSOCIATION FOR NATIONAL LIBERATION. *Factual Records of the Vietnam August Revolution*. Hanoi, 1946.

VIOLLIS, ANDRÉE (pseudonym of Andrée F. C. Ardenne de Tizac). *Indochine S.O.S.* Paris: Gallimard, 1935. A devastating account of French military, police, and judicial violence against the anticolonial insurrections of the years 1930 and 1931.

VO NGUYEN GIAP. *Dien Bien Phu*. Hanoi: Foreign Languages Publishing House, 1954. The battle of Dien Bien Phu as seen by the commander in chief of the Vietminh Army.

———. *People's War, People's Army: The Viet Công Insurrection Manual for Underdeveloped Countries*. New York: Frederick A. Praeger, 1962. A facsimile edition of Giap's rather undistinguished collection of articles on the subject of guerrilla warfare published under the same title in Hanoi in 1961. With an introduction by Roger Hilsman and a biographical study of Giap by Bernard B. Fall.

WARNER, DENIS. "Vietnam: A Dynasty in Disorder," *The Reporter*, September 12, 1963. An account largely of the Buddhist crisis and Diem's inept handling of it.

———. *The Last Confucian*. New York: Macmillan, 1963. The well-known Australian journalist presents his assessment of South Vietnam after years on the spot. Extremely critical of the Diem regime.

WERTH, LÉON. *Cochinchine*. Paris: Rieder, 1926. Very critical observations by a French socialist on French policy and French behavior in Indochina.

WEST, MORRIS L. *The Ambassador*. New York: William Morrow, 1965. A bold fictional account of U.S. diplomacy in Vietnam and the U.S. role in the fall of Diem.

WOODRUFF, LLOYD W. *Local Administration in Vietnam*. Saigon: Michigan State University, Vietnam Advisory Group, 1961. One of the many valuable reports on the many aspects of Vietnam's administration put out by the Advisory Group. (For several more studies by this and other authors on administrative problems of South Vietnam, see ROBERT SCIGLIANO. *South Vietnam*. Bibliography, pp. 218–219.)

WURFEL, DAVID. "Agrarian Reform in the Republic of Vietnam," *Far Eastern Survey*, XXVI, June, 1957, 81–92. An early, positive account of Diem's land-reform projects and performance.

ZASLOFF, JOSEPH. "Rural Resettlement in South Vietnam: The Agroville Program," *Pacific Affairs*, XXXV, Winter, 1962–63, 327–40. A critical article on the agroville program.

Index

References through page 663 are to Volume I; those from pages 673–1282 are to Volume II. Numbers within parentheses indicate numbers of notes.

Hammer, Ellen (*cont.*)
1015(13–16), 1021–22(44), 1023(53, 54), 1025(60), 1026(69), 1027(76, 78), 1028–29(81), 1030–31(85), 1032–33(87, 95), 1039(14), 1050(43), 1060(78)

Han Dynasty, 1193

Hangchow, 155

Hankow, 363, 596(76)

Hanoi: before World War II, 3, 14, 41, 114, 126, 131, 134, 156, 450(53), 452, 506(42), 518(80), 1194, 1208, 1237, 1239; bridges, 33, 42, 893; Chinese in, 351–56, 357–58, 365, 633(75); exclusion of French from, 338, 342; evacuation of, 431, 830; French in, 64–65, 73, 229, 250, 284–85, 306, 341, 366, 369, 396, 450(53), 468(41), 614(9), 627(59), 648(32), 669, 682, 893–94, 895, 1118–19(123), 1196, 1202, 1211, 1214, 1216; Japanese in, 232, 284–85, 340, 600(83); liberation of, 296–97, 299, 603(94); *lycée*, 91; medical services, 489(109); opera house, 34, 173; press, 65; public transport, 903; railroads to, 28, 32, 445–46(39, 41), 574 (10), 837, 896–97, 903; terrorism, 98, 152, 208, 365, 517(79), 557(104); University of, 47–48, 66, 85, 91, 93, 103, 106, 247, 349, 470(44), 483(98), 484 (102), 632(71), 643(16), 649(34), 769–70, 895, 965, 1034(99), 1118(122), 1130(21), 1141(55); Vietminh at, 311–12, 337–38, 340, 344, 345, 349, 372, 604(97), 606(103), 627(57), 667, 736, 894; Vietnam Hotel at, 207; World War II and after, 275, 293, 314, 318, 334, 353, 430, 431, 432–33, 581(24), 582(25), 626–27(56), 661(80), 688, 698, 718, 723, 728, 732, 742, 746, 747, 752, 756, 767, 830, 908, 964, 972, 1088 (74), 1093(90), 1116(115), 1241

Hanoi Government, 347, 348, 350, 354, 363, 365–66, 368, 374, 386, 394, 397, 398, 400, 416, 419, 425–26, 427, 429, 643(16), 689, 700, 774, 843, 893, 896–916, 1019(38), 1116(115), 1168–70 *passim;* Bao Dai and, 700–701, 825, 1019–20(39), 1024(55); Catholics and, 706, 1021(44); Communist powers and, 722, 773, 807–8, 1057(69), 1119–20 (125); defeat of French, 853; elections, 944, 1143(58); finances, 632–33 (74), 778; French campaign against, 378, 381, 383, 422; French interests and, 901–2, 1118(120–22); in Indochina War, 670, 688, 697, 738, 740,

743, 748, 766, 767, 770, 772, 782, 787, 804, 813, 814, 1041(17), 1052–54 (57, 58); National Liberation Front and, 1169–70(173); negotiations with, 384, 385, 390, 655(55), 658(73), 675–76, 901–2; Ngo Dinh Diem and, 926, 975, 1151(95); Ngo Dinh Nhu and, 998; pro-Chinese wing, 643(17), 1058(71); propaganda, 1167(167); recognition of, 363, 370, 374, 397, 616(15), 670, 671, 673, 700, 773, 807–8, 1057(69); Tran Van Huu and, 1098(19); *see also* Ho Chi Minh; Vietminh; Vietnam, North

Harbors, 34, 96, 188, 348, 570–71(7)

Harkins, Paul, 989, 999, 1000, 1002, 1173 (186), 1180–81(211–13), 1188(254)

Harmand, Dr. François-Jules, 24, 25, 444(34), 1210, 1212, 1213; quoted, 81, 477(74), 540(55)

Harnett, Joseph J., 1116(117), 1269; quoted, 1126–27(5, 9)

Harriman, Averell, 995–96

Harvard University, 1141(55), 1243

Hatien, province of, 336, 443(29), 462 (23), 740–41, 1164(157)

Head tax, 56, 106, 124, 348

Heath, Donald, 837, 874, 1079(35), 1093 (87)

Hector (Resident Superior), 504(38), 1214

Hempstone, Smith, 1269

Henderson, William, 1132(27), 1266, 1269; quoted, 885–86, 1101(28), 1102–3(38), 1105(57), 1125(1)

Hendry, James B., 1163(146), 1267

Henri d'Orléans, Prince, 37, 446; quoted, 31

"Henri Martin affair," 1070–71(111) 1073(10)

Henry, Yves, 1269; quoted, 530(27)

Herbinger, Lt. Colonel, 508(52), 579 (15)

Hertrich, Jean-Michel, 1269; quoted, 584–85(41)

Heymard, Jean, 1269

Hickey, Gerald Cannon, 1144(65), 1270

Hiep Hoa, Emperor, 190, 500(27)

Hiep Hoa, region of, 567(129)

Hieu, 127

Higgins, Marguerite, 996, 1138(45), 1184(231), 1190(266–67); quoted, 1180(211)

Highways: construction, 32, 33, 56, 96, 173, 246, 446(43), 447(48), 767, 1194; destruction, 1126(4); in Indochina

DATE DUE

DEC 4 '69		
MAR 16 '70		
APR 2 '70		
APR 16 '70		
APR 28 '70		
MAR 24 '72		
AP 12'81		
MB 19'81		
MR 28'82		
DE 5'83		
DE 3'84		
DEC 4 '85		
GAYLORD		PRINTED IN U.S.A.